GLOBAL ISSUES
94/95

Tenth Edition

Editor

Robert M. Jackson
California State University, Chico

Robert M. Jackson is a professor of political science and
director of the Center for International Studies at California
State University, Chico. In addition to teaching, he has
published articles on the international political economy,
international relations simulations, and political behavior. His
special research interest is the way northern California is
becoming increasingly linked to the Pacific Basin. His
travels include China, Japan, Hong Kong, Taiwan, Portugal,
Spain, Morocco, Costa Rica, Honduras, Guatemala, Mexico,
Germany, Belgium, the Netherlands, and Czechoslovakia.

A Library of Information from the Public Press

Cover illustration by Mike Eagle

The Dushkin Publishing Group, Inc.
Sluice Dock, Guilford, Connecticut 06437

The Annual Editions Series

Annual Editions is a series of over 60 volumes designed to provide the reader with convenient, low-cost access to a wide range of current, carefully selected articles from some of the most important magazines, newspapers, and journals published today. Annual Editions are updated on an annual basis through a continuous monitoring of over 300 periodical sources. All Annual Editions have a number of features designed to make them particularly useful, including topic guides, annotated tables of contents, unit overviews, and indexes. For the teacher using Annual Editions in the classroom, an Instructor's Resource Guide with test questions is available for each volume.

VOLUMES AVAILABLE

Africa
Aging
American Foreign Policy
American Government
American History, Pre-Civil War
American History, Post-Civil War
Anthropology
Biology
Business Ethics
Canadian Politics
Child Growth and Development
China
Comparative Politics
Computers in Education
Computers in Business
Computers in Society
Criminal Justice
Drugs, Society, and Behavior
Dying, Death, and Bereavement
Early Childhood Education
Economics
Educating Exceptional Children
Education
Educational Psychology
Environment
Geography
Global Issues
Health
Human Development
Human Resources
Human Sexuality
India and South Asia
International Business
Japan and the Pacific Rim

Latin America
Life Management
Macroeconomics
Management
Marketing
Marriage and Family
Mass Media
Microeconomics
Middle East and the Islamic World
Money and Banking
Multicultural Education
Nutrition
Personal Growth and Behavior
Physical Anthropology
Psychology
Public Administration
Race and Ethnic Relations
Russia, Eurasia, and Central/Eastern Europe
Social Problems
Sociology
State and Local Government
Third World
Urban Society
Violence and Terrorism
Western Civilization, Pre-Reformation
Western Civilization, Post-Reformation
Western Europe
World History, Pre-Modern
World History, Modern
World Politics

Library of Congress Cataloging in Publication Data
Main entry under title: Annual Editions: Global Issues. 1994/95.
1. Civilization, Modern—20th century—Periodicals. 2. Social prediction—Periodicals. 3. Social problems—20th century—Periodicals. I. Jackson, Robert, comp. II. Title: Global Issues.
ISBN 1-56134-276-9   909.82′05

Tenth Edition

Printed in the United States of America

Printed on Recycled Paper

Editors/ Advisory Board

To the Reader

In publishing ANNUAL EDITIONS we recognize the enormous role played by the magazines, newspapers, and journals of the *public press* in providing current, first-rate educational information in a broad spectrum of interest areas. Within the articles, the best scientists, practitioners, researchers, and commentators draw issues into new perspective as accepted theories and viewpoints are called into account by new events, recent discoveries change old facts, and fresh debate breaks out over important controversies.

Many of the articles resulting from this enormous editorial effort are appropriate for students, researchers, and professionals seeking accurate, current material to help bridge the gap between principles and theories and the real world. These articles, however, become more useful for study when those of lasting value are carefully *collected, organized, indexed,* and *reproduced* in a *low-cost format*, which provides easy and permanent access when the material is needed. That is the role played by *Annual Editions*. Under the direction of each volume's *Editor*, who is an expert in the subject area, and with the guidance of an *Advisory Board*, we seek each year to provide in each *ANNUAL EDITION* a current, well-balanced, carefully selected collection of the best of the public press for your study and enjoyment. We think you'll find this volume useful, and we hope you'll take a moment to let us know what you think.

As the twentieth century begins to draw to a close, the issues confronting humanity are increasingly complex and diverse. While the mass media may focus on the latest crisis for a few days or weeks, the broad, historical forces that are at work shaping the world of the twenty-first century are seldom given the in-depth treatment that they warrant. Research and analysis of these issues, furthermore, can be found in a wide variety of sources. As a result, the student just beginning to study global issues is often discouraged before he or she is able to sort out the information. In selecting and organizing the materials in this book, we have been mindful of the needs of the beginning student.

Each unit begins with an article providing a broad overview of the area to be explored. The remaining articles examine in more detail some of the issues presented in the introductory article. The unit then concludes with an article (or two) that not only identifies a problem but suggests positive steps that are being taken to improve the situation. The world faces many serious problems, the magnitude of which would discourage even the most stouthearted individual. Though identifying problems is easier than solving them, it is encouraging to know that many of the issues are being successfully addressed.

Perhaps the most striking feature of the study of contemporary global issues is the absence of any single, widely held theory that explains what is taking place. Therefore, we have made a conscious effort to present a wide variety of ideologies and theories. The most important consideration has been to present global issues from an international perspective, rather than from a purely American or Western point of view. By encompassing materials originally published in many different countries and written by authors of various nationalities, the anthology represents the great diversity of opinions that people hold on important global issues. Two writers examining the same phenomenon may reach very different conclusions. It is not a question of who is right and who is wrong. What is important to understand is that people from different vantage points have differing perceptions of issues.

Another major consideration when organizing these materials has been to explore the complex interrelationship of factors that produce issue areas, such as Third World development. Too often discussions of these problems are reduced to arguments of good versus evil or communism versus capitalism. As a result, the interplay of the complex web of causes is overlooked. We have made every effort to select materials that illustrate the interaction of these forces.

Finally, we selected the materials in this book for both their intellectual insights and their readability. Timely and well-written materials should stimulate good classroom lectures and discussions. We hope that students and teachers will enjoy using this book. Readers can have input into the next edition by completing and returning the article rating form in the back of the book.

I would like to thank Ian Nielsen for his encouragement and helpful suggestions in the selection of materials for *Annual Editions: Global Issues 94/95*. It is my continuing goal to encourage the readers of this book to have a greater appreciation of the world in which they live. We hope they will be motivated to further explore the complex issues that the world faces as we approach the twenty-first century.

Robert M. Jackson
Editor

Contents

Unit 1

A Clash of Views

The four articles in this section present distinct views on the present and future state of life on Earth.

Unit 2

Population

The six articles in this section discuss the contributing factors of culture, politics, environmental degradation, disease, and migration on the world's population growth.

The concepts in bold italics are developed in the article. For further expansion please refer to the Topic Guide and the Index.

Unit 3

Natural Resources

Twelve selections divided into four subsections—international dimensions, raw materials, food and hunger, and energy—discuss natural resources and their effects on the world community.

The concepts in bold italics are developed in the article. For further expansion please refer to the Topic Guide and the Index.

The concepts in bold italics are developed in the article. For further expansion please refer to the Topic Guide and the Index.

Unit
4

Development

Eleven articles divided into two subsections present various views on economic and social development in the nonindustrial and industrial nations.

The concepts in bold italics are developed in the article. For further expansion please refer to the Topic Guide and the Index.

Unit 5

Conflict

Seven articles in this section discuss the basis for world conflict and the current state of peace in the international community.

The concepts in bold italics are developed in the article. For further expansion please refer to the Topic Guide and the Index.

Unit 6

Cooperation

Four selections in this section examine patterns of international cooperation and the social structures that support this cooperation.

Unit 7

Values and Visions

Six articles discuss human rights, ethics, values, and new ideas.

The concepts in bold italics are developed in the article. For further expansion please refer to the Topic Guide and the Index.

Topic Guide

This topic guide suggests how the selections in this book relate to topics of traditional concern to students and professionals involved with the study of global issues. It is useful for locating articles that relate to each other for reading and research. The guide is arranged alphabetically according to topic. Articles may, of course, treat topics that do not appear in the topic guide. In turn, entries in the topic guide do not necessarily constitute a comprehensive listing of all the contents of each selection.

TOPIC AREA	TREATED IN:	TOPIC AREA	TREATED IN:
Agriculture, Food, and Hunger	15. Planet in Jeopardy 17. Landscape of Hunger 18. Feeding a Crowded Planet 45. 50 Trends Shaping the World	**Energy: Exploration, Production, Research, and Politics**	11. Greenhouse Effect 15. Planet in Jeopardy 19. Oil: The Strategic Prize 20. Paradise Islands or an Asian Powder Keg? 21. Canada is Ready to Exploit Huge Oil Reserves 22. New Energy Path for the Third World 45. 50 Trends Shaping the World
Communications	3. Economic Time Zones 32. Japan's Non-Revolution 46. Electronic Superhighway 50. Global Village Finally Arrives		
Cultural Customs and Values	2. Jihad vs. McWorld 7. Sixty Million on the Move 8. War on Aliens 9. Hobson's Choice 26. Burden of Womanhood 32. Japan's Non-Revolution 45. 50 Trends Shaping the World 47. World's *Throw-Away* Children 48. Women's Role in Post-Industrial Democracy 49. Post-Communist Nightmare 50. Global Village Finally Arrives	**Environment, Ecology, and Conservation**	1. Preparing for the 21st Century 2. Jihad vs. McWorld 11. Greenhouse Effect 12. Can We Save Our Seas? 13. Sacrificed to the Superpower 14. Green Justice 15. Planet in Jeopardy 16. Facing a Future of Water Scarcity 17. Landscape of Hunger 22. New Energy Path for the Third World 45. 50 Trends Shaping the World
Development: Economic and Social	1. Preparing for the 21st Century 3. Economic Time Zones 4. Global Unemployment 7. Sixty Million on the Move 10. AIDS Pandemic in Africa 18. Feeding a Crowded Planet 22. New Energy Path for the Third World 23. China Sees "Market-Leninism" 25. Africa in the Balance 26. Burden of Womanhood 29. Global Village or Global Pillage? 33. Privatization in the Former Soviet Empire	**The Future**	1. Preparing for the 21st Century 3. Economic Time Zones 5. Megacities 7. Sixty Million on the Move 9. Hobson's Choice 10. AIDS Pandemic in Africa 11. Greenhouse Effect 12. Can We Save Our Seas? 15. Planet in Jeopardy 16. Facing a Future of Water Scarcity 18. Feeding a Crowded Planet 22. New Energy Path for the Third World 25. Africa in the Balance 28. Toward a New World Economic Order 29. Global Village or Global Pillage? 32. Japan's Non-Revolution 34. New Challenges to Global Security 38. Fighting Off Doomsday 40. Dismantling the Arsenals 41. Can the U.N. Stretch to Fit Its Future? 43. What's Next for World Trade? 45. 50 Trends Shaping the World 46. Electronic Superhighway 48. Women's Role in Post-Industrial Democracy
Economics	1. Preparing for the 21st Century 2. Jihad vs. McWorld 3. Economic Time Zones 4. Global Unemployment 5. Megacities 7. Sixty Million on the Move 10. AIDS Pandemic in Africa 13. Sacrificed to the Superpower 14. Green Justice 22. New Energy Path for the Third World 23. China Sees "Market-Leninism" 24. New Tally of World's Economy 25. Africa in the Balance 27. Third-World Debt 28. Toward a New World Economic Order 29. Global Village or Global Pillage? 30. Push Comes to Shove 31. Number One Again 33. Privatization in the Former Soviet Empire 45. 50 Trends Shaping the World 46. Electronic Superhighway		
		Health and Medicine	10. AIDS Pandemic in Africa 13. Sacrificed to the Superpower 45. 50 Trends Shaping the World
		Industrial Economics	1. Preparing for the 21st Century 3. Economic Time Zones 4. Global Unemployment 13. Sacrificed to the Superpower 14. Green Justice 28. Toward a World Economic Order 30. Push Comes to Shove 31. Number One Again 33. Privatization in the Former Soviet Empire 45. 50 Trends Shaping the World

TOPIC AREA	TREATED IN:	TOPIC AREA	TREATED IN:
International Economics, Trade, Aid, and Dependencies	3. Economic Time Zones 7. Sixty Million on the Move 18. Feeding a Crowded Planet 19. Oil: The Strategic Prize 25. Africa in the Balance 27. Third-World Debt 29. Global Village or Global Pillage? 41. Can the U.N. Stretch to Fit Its Future? 43. What's Next for World Trade?	**Population and Demographics (Quality of Life Indicators)**	1. Preparing for the 21st Century 5. Megacities 6. Numbers Game 7. Sixty Million on the Move 8. War on Aliens 9. Hobson's Choice for Indigenous Peoples 10. AIDS Pandemic in Africa 15. Planet in Jeopardy 18. Feeding a Crowded Planet
Military: Warfare and Terrorism	34. New Challenges to Global Security 35. Why Yugoslavia Fell Apart 36. Who'll Stop the Next 'Yugoslavia'? 37. Islam's Violent Improvisers 38. Fighting Off Doomsday 39. Contest over Asia 40. Dismantling the Arsenals 41. Can the U.N. Stretch to Fit Its Future? 42. Can It Really Be Peace?	**Science, Technology, and Research and Development**	3. Economic Time Zones 11. Greenhouse Effect 15. Planet in Jeopardy 21. Canada is Ready to Exploit Huge Oil Reserves 40. Dismantling the Arsenals 45. 50 Trends Shaping the World 46. Electronic Superhighway
Natural Resources	11. Greenhouse Effect 12. Can We Save Our Seas? 15. Planet in Jeopardy 16. Facing a Future of Water Scarcity 19. Oil: The Strategic Prize 20. Paradise Islands or an Asian Powder Keg? 21. Canada is Ready to Exploit Huge Oil Reserves 45. 50 Trends Shaping the World	**Third World**	1. Preparing for the 21st Century 3. Economic Time Zones 5. Megacities 9. Hobson's Choice for Indigenous Peoples 10. AIDS Pandemic in Africa 14. Green Justice 18. Feeding a Crowded Planet 22. New Energy Path for the Third World 25. Africa in the Balance 26. Burden of Womanhood 27. Third-World Debt 29. Global Village or Global Pillage?
Political and Legal Global Issues	2. Jihad vs. McWorld 8. War on Aliens 11. Greenhouse Effect 12. Can We Save Our Seas? 29. Global Village or Global Pillage? 34. New Challenges to Global Security 38. Fighting Off Doomsday 40. Dismantling the Arsenals 41. Can the U.N. Stretch to Fit Its Future? 43. What's Next for World Trade? 44. Hunting for Africa's Wildlife Poachers		

A Clash of Views

Imagine a clear, round, inflated balloon. Now imagine that a person begins to brush yellow paint onto this miniature globe; symbolically, the color yellow represents *people*. In many ways the study of global issues is ultimately the study of people. Today, there are more people occupying Earth than ever before. In addition, the world is in the midst of a period of unprecedented population growth. Not only are there many countries where the majority of people are under age 16, but because of improved health care, there are also more older people alive than ever before. The effect of a growing global population, however, goes beyond sheer numbers, for a growing population has unprecedented impacts on natural resources and social services. Population issues, then, are an appropriate place to begin the study of global issues.

Imagine that our fictional artist dips the brush into a container of blue paint to represent the world of *nature*. The natural world plays an important role in setting the international agenda. Shortages of raw materials, drought and crop failures, and pollution of waterways are just a few examples of how natural resources can have global implications.

Adding blue paint to the balloon also reveals one of the most important concepts found in this book of readings. Although the balloon originally was covered by yellow and blue paint (people and nature as separate conceptual entities), the two combined produce an entirely different color: green. Talking about nature as a separate entity or about people as though they were somehow removed from the forces of the natural world is a serious intellectual error. The people-nature relationship is one of the keys to understanding many of today's most important global issues.

The third color added to the balloon is red. It represents the *meta* component (i.e., those qualities that make human beings more than mere animals). These include new ideas and inventions, culture and values, religion and spirituality, and art and literature. The addition of the red paint immediately changes the color green to brown, again emphasizing the relationship between all three factors.

The fourth and final color added is white. This color represents *social structures*. Factors such as whether a society is urban or rural, industrial or agrarian, planned or decentralized, and consumer-oriented or dedicated to the needs of the state fall into this category. The relationship between this component and the others is extremely important. The impact of political decisions on the environment, for example, is one of the most unique features of the contemporary world. Historically, the forces of nature determined which species survived or perished. Today survival depends on political decisions—or indecisions. Will the whales or bald eagles survive? The answer to this question will depend on governmental activities, not evolutionary forces. Understanding this relationship between social structure and nature (known as "ecopolitics") is important to the study of global issues.

If the painter continues to ply the paintbrush over the miniature globe, a marbling effect will become evident. In some areas, the shading will vary because one element is greater than another. The miniature system appears dynamic. Nothing is static; relationships are continually changing. This leads to a number of theoretical insights: (1) there is no such thing as separate elements, only connections or relationships; (2) changes in one area (such as the weather) will result in changes in all other areas; and (3) complex relationships make it difficult to predict events accurately, so observers are often surprised by unexpected processes and outcomes.

This book is organized along the basic lines of the balloon allegory. The first unit explores a variety of perspectives on the forces that are at work shaping the world of the twenty-first century. Unit 2 focuses on population. Unit 3 examines the environment and related issues (e.g., agriculture and energy). The next three units look at different aspects of the world's social structures. They explore issues of development (for both industrial and nonindustrial societies), conflict, and cooperation. In the final unit, a number of "meta" factors are discussed. However, you should be aware that, just as it was impossible to keep the individual colors from disappearing and blending into new colors on the balloon, it is also impossible to separate these factors into discrete chapters in a book. Any discussion of agriculture, for example, must take into account the impact of a growing population on

soil and water resources, as well as new scientific approaches to food production. Therefore, the organization of this book focuses attention on issue areas; it does not mean to imply that these factors are somehow separate.

With the end of the cold war and the collapse of the Soviet empire, the outlines of a new global agenda are beginning to emerge. Rather than an agenda based on the ideology and interests of the two superpowers, a new set of factors have emerged that interact in an unprecedented fashion. Rapid population growth, environmental decline, and lagging economic performance are all parts of a complex situation to which there is no historic parallel. As we approach the twenty-first century, there are signs abounding that a new era is being entered. As Abraham Lincoln said, "As our case is new, so we must think anew." Compounding this situation, however, are a whole series of old problems such as ethnic and religious rivalries.

The authors in this first section provide a variety of perspectives on the trends that they believe are the most important to understanding the historic changes at work on the international stage. This discussion is then pursued in greater detail in the following sections.

It is important for the reader to note that although the authors look at the same world, they often come to different conclusions. This raises an important issue of values and beliefs, for it can be argued that there really is no objective reality, only differing perspectives. In short, the study of global issues will challenge each thoughtful reader to examine her or his own values and beliefs.

Looking Ahead: Challenge Questions

Do the analyses of any of the authors in this section employ the assumptions implicit in the allegory of the balloon? If so, how? If not, how are the assumptions of the authors different?

All the authors point to interactions among different factors. What are some of the relationships that they cite? How do the authors differ in terms of the relationships they emphasize?

What are some of the assets that people have to solve problems that did not exist 100 years ago?

What major events during the twentieth century have had the greatest impact on shaping the world of today?

How will the world be different in the year 2030? What factors will contribute to these changes?

What do you consider to be the five most pressing global problems of today? How do your answers compare to those of your family, friends, and classmates?

Preparing for the 21st Century: Winners and Losers

Paul Kennedy

Paul Kennedy is Professor of History and Director of the International Security Program at Yale University. He is the author of The Rise and Fall of the Great Powers, *among many other books.* Preparing for the Twenty-First Century, *from which this article is drawn, is published by Random House.*

1.

Everyone with an interest in international affairs must be aware that broad, global forces for change are bearing down upon humankind in both rich and poor societies alike. New technologies are challenging traditional assumptions about the way we make, trade, and even grow things. Automated workplaces in Japan intimate the end of the "factory system" that first arose in Britain's Industrial Revolution and spread around the world. Genetically engineered crops, cultivated in biotech laboratories, threaten to replace naturally grown sugar, vanilla, coconut oil, and other staple farm produce, and perhaps undermine field-based agriculture as we know it. An electronically driven, twenty-four-hour-a-day financial trading system has created a global market in, say, yen futures over which nobody really has control. The globalization of industry and services permits multinationals to switch production from one country to another (where it is usually

cheaper), benefitting the latter and hurting the former.

In addition to facing these technology-driven forces for change, human society is grappling with the effects of fast-growing demographic imbalances throughout the world. Whereas birthrates in richer societies plunge well below the rates that would replace their populations, poorer countries are experiencing a population explosion that may double or even treble their numbers over the next few decades. As these fast-swelling populations press upon the surrounding forests, grazing lands, and water supplies, they inflict dreadful damage upon local environments and may also be contributing to that process of global warming first created by the industrialization of the North a century and a half ago. With overpopulation and resource depletion undermining the social order, and with a global telecommunications revolution bringing television programs like *Dallas* and *Brideshead Revisited* to viewers everywhere from Central America to the Balkans, a vast illegal migration is under way as millions of families from the developing world strive to enter Europe and North America.

Although very different in form, these various trends from global warming to twenty-four-hour-a-day trading are *transnational* in character, crossing borders all over our planet, affecting local communities and dis-

tant societies at the same time, and reminding us that the earth, for all its divisions, is a single unit. Every country is challenged by these global forces for change, to a greater or lesser extent, and most are beginning to sense the need to prepare themselves for the coming twenty-first century. Whether *any* society is at present "well prepared" for the future is an open question;[1] but what is clear is that the regions of the globe most affected by the twin impacts of technology and demography lie in the developing world. Whether they succeed in harnessing the new technologies in an environmentally prudent fashion, and at the same time go through a demographic transition, will probably affect the prospects of global peace in the next century more than any other factor. What, then, are their chances?

Before that question can be answered, the sharp contrasts among the developing countries in the world's different regions need to be noted here.[2] Perhaps nothing better illustrates those differences than the fact that, in the 1960s, South Korea had a per capita GNP exactly the same as Ghana's (US $230), whereas today it is ten to twelve times more prosperous.[3] Both possessed a predominantly agrarian economy and had endured a half-century or more of colonial rule. Upon independence, each faced innumerable handicaps in their effort to "catch up" with the West, and although Korea possessed a greater historical and cultural coherence, its chances may have seemed less promising, since it had few natural resources (apart from tungsten) and suffered heavily during the 1950–1953 fighting.

Decades later, however, West African states remain among the most poverty-stricken countries in the world—the per capita gross national products of Niger, Sierra Leone, and Chad today, for example, are less than $500[4]—while Korea is entering the ranks of the high-income economies. Already the world's thirteenth largest trading nation, Korea is planning to become one of the richest countries of all in the twenty-first century,[5] whereas the nations of West Africa face a future, at least in the near term, of chronic poverty, malnutrition, poor health, and underdevelopment. Finally, while Korea's rising prosperity is attended by a decrease in population growth, most African countries still face a demographic explosion that erodes any gains in national output.

This divergence is not new, for there have always been richer and poorer societies; the prosperity gap in the seventeenth century—between, say, Amsterdam and the west coast of Ireland, or between such bustling Indian ports as Surat and Calcutta[6] and the inhabitants of New Guinean hill villages—must have been marked, although it probably did not equal the gulf between rich and poor nations today. The difference is that the twentieth-century global communications revolution has made such disparities widely known. This can breed resentments by poorer peoples against prosperous societies, but it can also provide a desire to emulate (as Korea emulated Japan). The key issue here is: What does it take to turn a "have not" into a "have" nation? Does it simply require imitating economic techniques, or does it involve such intangibles as culture, social structure, and attitudes toward foreign practices?

This discrepancy in performance between East Asia and sub-Saharan Africa clearly makes the term "third world" misleading. However useful the expression might have been in the 1950s, when poor, nonaligned, and recently decolonized states were at-

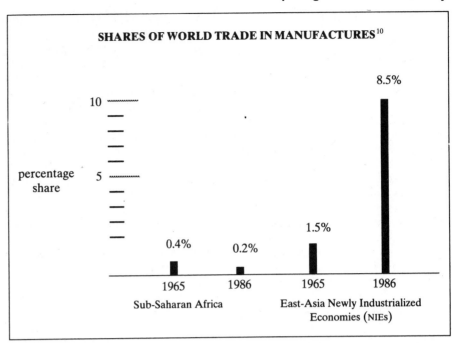

SHARES OF WORLD TRADE IN MANUFACTURES[10]

percentage share

Sub-Saharan Africa
1965 — 0.4%
1986 — 0.2%

East-Asia Newly Industrialized Economies (NIEs)
1965 — 1.5%
1986 — 8.5%

tempting to remain independent of the two superpower blocs,[7] the rise of super-rich oil-producing countries a decade later already made the term questionable. Now that prosperous East Asian societies—Korea, Taiwan, and Singapore—possess higher per capita GNPs than Russia, Eastern Europe, and even West European states like Portugal, the word seems less suitable than ever. With Taiwanese or Korean corporations establishing assembly plants in the Philippines, or creating distribution networks within the European Community, we need to recognize the differences that exist among non-Western economies. Some scholars now categorize *five* separate types of "developing" countries in assessing the varied potential of societies in Asia, Africa, and Latin America.[8]

Relative national growth in the 1980s confirms these differences. Whereas East Asian economies grew on average at an impressive annual rate of 7.4 percent, those in Africa and Latin America gained only 1.8 and 1.7 percent respectively[9]—and since their populations grew faster, the net result was that they slipped backward, absolutely and relatively. Differences of economic structure also grew in this decade, with African and other primary commodity-producing countries eager for higher raw-material prices, whereas the export-oriented manufacturing nations of East Asia sought

to keep commodity prices low. The most dramatic difference occurred in the shares of world trade in manufactures, a key indicator of economic competitiveness (see chart above). Thus, while some scholars still refer to a dual world economy[11] of rich and poor countries, what is emerging is increasing differentiation. Why is this so?

The developing countries most successfully catching up with the West are the trading states of the Pacific and East Asia. Except for Communist regimes there, the Pacific rim countries (including the western provinces of Canada and the United States, and in part Australia) have enjoyed a lengthy boom in manufacturing, trade, and investment; but the center of that boom is on the *Asian* side of the Pacific, chiefly fuelled by Japan's own spectacular growth and the stimulus given to neighboring economies and trans-Pacific trade. According to one source:

In 1962 the Western Pacific (notably East Asia) accounted for around 9 percent of world GNP, North America for 30 percent, and Western Europe for 31 percent. Twenty years later, the Western Pacific share had climbed to more than 15 percent, while North America's had fallen to 28 percent and Europe's to 27 percent. By the year 2000 it is likely that the Western Pacific will account for around one-quarter of world GNP, with the whole Pacific region increasing its share from just over 43 percent to around half of world GNP. [12]

East Asia's present boom is not, of course, uniform, and scholars distinguish between the different stages of economic and technological development in this vast region. Roughly speaking, the divisions would be as follows:

(a) Japan, now the world's largest or second largest financial center and, increasingly, the most innovative high-tech nation in the nonmilitary field;

(b) the four East Asian "tigers" or "dragons," the Newly Industrialized Economies (NIEs) of Singapore, Hong Kong, Taiwan, and South Korea, of which the latter two possess bigger populations and territories than the two port-city states, but all of which have enjoyed export-led growth in recent decades;

(c) the larger Southeast Asian states of Thailand, Malaysia, and Indonesia which, stimulated by foreign (chiefly Japanese) investment, are becoming involved in manufacturing, assembly, and export—it is doubtful whether the Philippines should be included in this group;

(d) finally, the stunted and impoverished Communist societies of Vietnam, Cambodia, and North Korea, as well as isolationist Myanmar pursuing its "Burmese Way to Socialism."

Because of this staggered level of development, economists in East Asia invoke the image of the "flying geese," with Japan the lead bird, followed by the East Asian NIEs, the larger Southeast Asian states, and so on. What Japan produced in one decade—relatively low-priced toys, kitchenware, electrical goods—will be imitated by the next wave of "geese" in the decade following, and by the third wave in the decade after that. However accurate the metaphor individually, the overall picture is clear; these birds are flying, purposefully and onward, to an attractive destination.

Of those states, it is the East Asian NIEs that have provided the clearest example of successful transformation. Although distant observers may regard them as similar, there are notable differences in size, population, [13] his-

tory, and political system. Even the economic structures are distinct; for example, Korea, which began its expansion at least a decade later than Taiwan (and democratized itself even more slowly), is heavily dependent upon a few enormous industrial conglomerates, or *chaebol*, of whom the top four alone (Samsung, Hyundai, Lucky-Goldstar, and Daewoo) have sales equal to half Korea's GNP. By contrast, Taiwan possesses many small companies, specializing in one or two kinds of products. While Taiwanese are concerned that their firms may lose out to foreign giants, Koreans worry that the *chaebol* will find it increasingly difficult to compete in large-scale industries like petrochemicals and semiconductors and shipbuilding at the same time. [14]

Despite such structural differences, these societies each contain certain basic characteristics, which, *taken together*, help to explain their decade-upon-decade growth. The first, and perhaps the most important, is the emphasis upon education. This derives from Confucian traditions of competitive examinations and respect for learning, reinforced daily by the mother of the family who complements what is taught at school.

To Western eyes, this process—like Japan's—appears to concentrate on rote learning and the acquisition of technical skills, and emphasizes consensus instead of encouraging individual talent and the habit of questioning authority. Even if some East Asian educators would nowadays admit that criticism, most believe that their own educational mores create social harmony and a well-trained work force. Moreover, the uniformity of the system does not exclude intense individual competitiveness; in Taiwan (where, incidentally, twelve members of the fourteen-member cabinet of 1989 had acquired Ph.D.s abroad), only the top one third of each year's 110,000 students taking the national university entrance examinations are selected, to emphasize the importance of college education. [15]

Perhaps nothing better illustrates this stress upon learning than the fact that Korea (43 million population) has around 1.4 million students in higher education, compared with 145,000 in Iran (54 million), 15,000 in Ethiopia (46 million), and 159,000 in Vietnam (64 million); or the further fact that

already by 1980 "as many engineering students were graduating from Korean institutions as in the United Kingdom, West Germany and Sweden combined." [16]

The second common characteristic of these countries is their high level of national savings. By employing fiscal measures, taxes, and import controls to encourage personal savings, large amounts of low-interest capital were made available for investment in manufacture and commerce. During the first few decades of growth, personal consumption was constrained and living standards controlled—by restrictions upon moving capital abroad, or importing foreign luxury goods—in order to funnel resources into industrial growth. While average prosperity rose, most of the fruits of economic success were plowed back into further expansion. Only when economic "take-off" was well under way has the system begun to alter; increased consumption, foreign purchases, capital investment in new homes, all allow internal demand to play a larger role in the country's growth. In such circumstances, one would expect to see overall savings ratios decline. Even in the late 1980s, however, the East Asian NIEs still had high national savings rates:

COMPARATIVE SAVINGS RATIOS, 1987 [17]	
Taiwan	38.8%
Malaysia	37.8%
Korea	37.0%
Japan	32.3%
Indonesia	29.1%
US	12.7%

The third feature has been a strong political system within which economic growth is fostered. While entrepreneurship and private property are encouraged, the "tigers" never followed a laissez-faire model. Industries targeted for growth were given a variety of supports—export subsidies, training grants, tariff protection from foreign competitors. As noted above, the fiscal system was arranged to produce high savings ratios. Taxes assisted the business sector, as did energy policy. Trade unions operated under restrictions. Democracy was constrained by the governor of Hong Kong, *dirigiste* administrations in Singapore, and the military regimes in Taiwan and Korea. Only lately have free elections and party politics been permitted. Defenders of this system argued that it was necessary to restrain libertarian impulses while concentrating on economic growth, and that democratic reforms are a "reward" for the people's patience. The point is that domestic politics were unlike those in the West yet did not hurt commercial expansion.

The fourth feature was the commitment to exports, in contrast to the policies of India, which emphasize locally produced substitutes for imports, and the consumer-driven policies of the United States. This was traditional for a small, bustling trading state like Hong Kong, but it involved substantial restructuring in Taiwan and Korea, where managers and workers had to be trained to produce what foreign customers wanted. In all cases, the value of the currency was kept low, to increase exports and decrease imports. Moreover, the newly industrialized economies of East Asia took advantage of favorable global circumstances: labor costs were much lower than in North America and Europe, and they benefitted from an open international trading order, created and protected by the United States, while shielding their own industries from foreign competition.

Eventually, this led to large trade surpluses and threats of retaliation from European and American governments, reminding us of the NIEs' heavy dependence upon the current international economic system. The important thing, however, is that they targeted export-led growth in manufactures, whereas other developing nations continued to rely upon commodity exports and made little effort to cater to foreign consumers' tastes.[18] Given this emphasis on trade, it is not surprising to learn that Asia now contains seven of the world's twelve largest ports.

Finally, the East Asian NIEs possess a local model, namely Japan, which Yemen, Guatemala, and Burkina Faso simply do not have. For four decades East Asian peoples have observed the dramatic success of a non-Western neighbor, based upon its educational and technical skills, high savings ratios, long-term, state-guided targeting of industries and markets, and determination to compete on world markets, though this admiration of Japan is nowadays mixed with a certain alarm at becoming members of a yen block dominated by Tokyo. While the Japanese domestic market is extremely important for the East Asian NIEs, and they benefit from Japanese investments, assembly plants, engineers, and expertise, they have little enthusiasm for a new Greater East Asia co-prosperity sphere.[19]

The benefits of economic success are seen not merely in East Asia's steadily rising standards of living. Its children are on average four or five inches taller than they were in the 1940s, and grow up in some of the world's healthiest countries:

A Taiwanese child born in 1988 could expect to live 74 years, only a year less than an American or a West German, and 15 years longer than a Taiwanese born in 1952; a South Korean born in 1988 could expect 70 years on earth, up from 58 in 1965. In 1988 the Taiwanese took in 50 percent more calories each day than they had done 35 years earlier. They had 200 times as many televisions, telephones and cars per household; in Korea the rise in the possession of these goods was even higher.[20]

In addition, the East Asian NIEs enjoy some of today's highest literacy rates, once again confirming that they are altogether closer to "first" world nations than poor, developing countries (see chart below).

Will this progress last into the twenty-first century? Politically, Hong Kong's future is completely uncertain, and many companies are relocating their headquarters elsewhere; Taiwan remains a diplomatic pariah-state because of Beijing's traditional claims; and South Korea still worries about the unpredictable, militarized regime in the north. The future of China—and of Siberia—is uncertain, and causes concern. The 1980s rise in Asian stock-market prices (driven by vast increases in the money supply) was excessive and speculative, and destined to tumble. Protectionist tendencies in the developed world threaten the trading states even more than external pressures to abandon price supports for local farmers. A rise in the value of the Korean and Taiwanese currencies has cut export earnings and reduced their overall rate of growth. Some Japanese competitors have moved production to neighboring low-cost countries such as Thailand or southern China. Sharp rises in oil prices increase the import bills. High wage awards (in Korea they increased by an average 14 percent in 1988, and by 17 percent in 1989) affect labor costs and competitiveness. The social peace, precarious in these recent democracies, is damaged by bouts of student and industrial unrest.[22]

On the other hand, these may simply be growing pains. Savings ratios are still extremely high. Large numbers of new engineers and technicians pour out of college each year. The workers' enhanced purchasing power has created a booming domestic market, and governments are investing more in housing, infrastructure, and public facilities. The labor force will not grow as swiftly as before because of the demographic slowdown, but it will be

COMPARATIVE LIVING STANDARDS[21]			
	Life Expectancy at Birth (years), 1987	Adult Literacy Rate (%), 1985	GNP per capita, 1988 US$
Niger	45	14	300
Togo	54	41	310
India	59	43	340
SINGAPORE	73	86	9,070
SOUTH KOREA	70	95	5,000
Spain	77	95	7,740
New Zealand	75	99	10,000

better educated and spend more.[23] A surge in overseas investments is assisting the long-term balance of payments. As the populous markets of Indonesia, Thailand, and Malaysia grow at double-digit rates, there is plenty of work for the trading states. A hardening of the currency can be met by greater commitment to quality exports, high rates of industrial investment, and a move into newer, high-technology manufacture—in imitation of the 1980s re-tooling of Japanese industry when its currency hardened swiftly. Nowhere else in the world would growth rates of "only" 5 or 6 percent be considered worrying, or a harbinger of decline. Barring a war in East Asia, or a widespread global slump, the signs are that the four "tigers" are better structured than most to grow in wealth and health.

2.

For confirmation of that remark, one need only consider the present difficult condition of Latin America, which lost ground in the 1980s just as East Asia was gaining it. Here again, distinctions have to be made between various countries within the continent, with its more than 400 million people in an area almost 7 million square miles stretching from the Rio Grande to Antarctica, and with a range of political cultures and socioeconomic structures. Argentina, which around 1900 had a standard of living suggesting that it was a "developed" economy, is very different from Honduras and Guyana. Similarly, population change in Latin America occurs in three distinct forms: such nations as Bolivia, the Dominican Republic, and Haiti have high fertility rates and lower life expectancies; a middle group—Brazil, Colombia, Mexico, Venezuela, Costa Rica, and Panama—is beginning to experience declines in fertility and longer life expectancy; and the temperate-zone countries of Argentina, Chile, and Uruguay have the demographic characteristics of developed countries.[24]

Despite this diversity, there are reasons for considering Latin America's prospects as a whole: the economic challenges confronting the region are similar, as are its domestic politics—in particular, the fragility of its recently emerged democracies; and each

PER CAPITA GDP OF LATIN AMERICAN COUNTRIES[27]
(1988 US Dollars)

Country	1960	1970	1980	1988
Chile	1,845	2,236	2,448	2,518
Argentina	2,384	3,075	3,359	2,862
Uruguay	2,352	2,478	3,221	2,989
Brazil	1,013	1,372	2,481	2,449
Paraguay	779	931	1,612	1,557
Bolivia	634	818	983	724
Peru	1,233	1,554	1,716	1,503
Ecuador	771	904	1,581	1,477
Colombia	927	1,157	1,595	1,739
Venezuela	3,879	4,941	5,225	4,544
Guyana	1,008	1,111	1,215	995
Suriname	887	2,337	3,722	3,420
Mexico	1,425	2,022	2,872	2,588
Guatemala	1,100	1,420	1,866	1,502
Honduras	619	782	954	851
El Salvador	832	1,032	1,125	995
Nicaragua	1,055	1,495	1,147	819
Costa Rica	1,435	1,825	2,394	2,235
Panama	1,264	2,017	2,622	2,229
Dominican Republic	823	987	1,497	1,509
Haiti	331	292	386	319
Jamaica	1,610	2,364	1,880	1,843
Trinidad & Tobago	3,848	4,927	8,116	5,510
Barbados	2,000	3,530	3,994	4,233
Bahamas	8,448	10,737	10,631	11,317

is affected by its relationship with the developed world, especially the United States.

Several decades ago, Latin America's future appeared encouraging. Sharing in the post-1950 global boom, benefitting from demand for its coffee, timber, beef, oil, and minerals, and enjoying foreign investments in its agriculture, industry, and infrastructure, the region was moving upward. In the thirty years after 1945, its production of steel multiplied twenty times, and its output of electric energy, metals, and machinery grew more than tenfold.[25] Real gross domestic product (GDP) per person rose at an annual average of 2.8 percent during the 1960s and spurted to an annual average increase of 3.4 percent in the 1970s. Unfortunately, the growth then reversed itself, and between 1980 and 1988

Latin America's real GDP per person steadily fell by an annual average of 0.9 percent.[26] In some states, such as Peru and Argentina, real income dropped by as much as one quarter during the 1980s. With very few exceptions (Chile, Colombia, the Dominican Republic, Barbados, the Bahamas), most Latin American countries now have per capita GDPs lower than they were a decade earlier, or even two decades earlier (see chart above).

The reasons for this reversal offer a striking contrast to the East Asian NIEs. Instead of encouraging industrialists to target foreign markets and stimulate the economy through export-led growth, many Latin American governments pursued a policy of import substitution, creating their own steel, cement, paper, automobiles, and electronic-goods industries, which were given protective tariffs, government

GROWTH OF LATIN AMERICAN INDEBTEDNESS (SELECTED COUNTRIES)[31]

Country	Total External Debt (billion US $)			Long-Term Public Debt As A Percentage of GNP		
	1977	1982	1987	1977	1982	1987
Argentina	8.1	32.4	53.9	10	31	62
Brazil	28.3	68.7	109.4	13	20	29
Chile	4.9	8.5	18.7	28	23	89
Guyana	0.4	0.9	1.2	100	158	353
Honduras	0.6	1.6	3.1	29	53	71
Jamaica	1.1	2.7	4.3	31	69	139
Mexico	26.6	78.0	93.7	25	32	59
Venezuela	9.8	27.0	29.0	10	16	52

subsidies, and tax-breaks to insulate them from international competition. As a result, their products became less attractive abroad.[28] Moreover, while it was relatively easy to create a basic iron and steel industry, it proved harder to establish high-tech industries like computers, aerospace, machine-tools, and pharmaceuticals—most of these states therefore still depend on imported manufactured goods, whereas exports chiefly consist of raw materials like oil, coffee, and soybeans.[29]

Secondly, economic growth was accompanied by lax financial policies and an increasing reliance upon foreign borrowings. Governments poured money not only into infrastructure and schools but also into state-owned enterprises, large bureaucracies, and oversized armed forces, paying for them by printing money and raising loans from Western (chiefly US) banks and international agencies. The result was that public spending's share of GDP soared, price inflation accelerated, and was further increased by index-linked rises in salaries and wages. Inflation became so large that it was difficult to comprehend, let alone to combat. According to the 1990 *World Resources* report, "in 1989, for example, annual inflation in Nicaragua was more than 3,400 percent; in Argentina inflation reached 3,700 percent, in Brazil almost 1,500 percent, and in Peru nearly 3,000 percent. Ecuador, with only 60 percent in-

flation, did comparatively well."[30] In such circumstances the currency becomes worthless, as does the idea of seeking to raise national savings rates for long-term capital investment.

Another result is that some Latin American countries find themselves among the most indebted in the world, as the chart below shows. Total Latin American indebtedness now equals about $1,000 for every man, woman, and child. But instead of being directed into productive investment, that money has been wasted domestically or disappeared as "capital flight" to private accounts in United States and European banks. This has left most countries incapable of repaying even the interest on their loans. Defaults on loans (or suspension of interest payments) then produced a drying up of capital from indignant Western banks and a net capital *outflow* from Latin America just when it needed capital to aid economic growth.[32] Starved of foreign funds and with currencies made worthless by hyperinflation, many countries are in a far worse position than could have been imagined twenty-five years ago.[33] For a while, it was even feared that the region's financial problems might undermine parts of the international banking system. It now appears that the chief damage will be in the continent itself, where 180 million people (40 percent) are living in poverty—a rise of 50 million alone in the 1980s.

Given such profligacy, and the conservative, "anti–big government" incumbents in the White House during the 1980s, it was predictable that Latin America would come under pressure—from the World Bank, the IMF, private bankers, Washington itself—to slash public spending, control inflation, and repay debts. Such demands were easier said than done in the existing circumstances. Islands of democracy (e.g., Costa Rica) did exist, but many states were ruled by right-wing military dictatorships or social revolutionaries; internal guerrilla wars, military *coups d'état*, labor unrest were common. Even as democracy began to reassert itself in the 1980s, the new leaders found themselves in a near-impossible situation: inheritors of the high external debts contracted by the outgoing regimes, legatees in many cases of inflationary index-linked wage systems, targets of landowner resentment and/or of guerrilla attacks, frustrated by elaborate and often corrupt bureaucracies, and deficient in trained personnel. While grappling with these weaknesses, they discovered that the Western world, which applauded the return to democracy, was unsympathetic to fresh lending, increasingly inclined to protectionism, and demanding unilateral measures (e.g., in the Amazon rain forests) to stop global warming.

Two other weaknesses have also slowed any hoped-for recovery. One is the unimpressive accomplishments of the educational systems. This is not due to an absence of schools and universities, as in parts of Africa. Many Latin American countries have extensive public education, dozens of universities, and high adult literacy rates; Brazil, for example, has sixty-eight universities, Argentina forty-one.[34] The real problem is neglect and underinvestment. One citizen bemoaned the collapse in Argentina as follows:

Education, which kept illiteracy at bay for more than a century, lies in ruins. The universities are unheated and many public schools lack panes for their window frames. Last summer [1990] an elementary school teacher with ten years' experience earned less than $110 a month. An associate professor at the Universidad de Buenos Aires, teaching ten hours a week, was paid $37 a month. A doctor's salary at a municipal hospital was $120 a month.... At times, teachers took turns teaching, or cut their class hours, because they and their students could not afford transportation.[35]

Presumably, if resources were available, those decaying educational and health-care structures could be resuscitated, helping national recovery; but where the capital can be raised in present circumstances is difficult to see. Moreover, in the strife-torn countries of Central America there is little education to begin with; in Guatemala, the latest census estimated that 63 percent of those ten years of age and older were illiterate, while in Honduras the illiteracy rate was 40 percent.[36] Unfortunately, it is in the educationally most deprived Latin American countries that resources are being eroded by swift population increases.

Despite these disadvantages, recent reports on Latin America have suggested that the "lost decade" of the 1980s will be followed by a period of recovery. The coming of democratic regimes, the compromises emerging from protracted debt-recycling talks, the stiff economic reforms (cutting public spending, abandoning indexation) to reduce inflation rates, the replacement of "state protectionism with import liberalization and privatization,"[37] the conversion of budget deficits into surpluses — all this has caused the Inter-American Development Bank to argue that "a decisive and genuine takeoff" is at hand, provided the new policies are sustained.[38] Growth has resumed in Argentina, Mexico, and Venezuela. Even investment bankers are reported to be returning to the continent.

Whether these changes are going to be enough remains uncertain, especially since the newly elected governments face widespread resentment at the proposed reforms. As one commentator put it, "Much of Latin America is entering the 1990s in a race between economic deterioration and political progress."[39] Whereas Spain, Portugal, and Greece moved to democracy while enjoying reasonable prosperity, Latin America (like Eastern Europe) has to make that change as its economies flounder — which

places immense responsibilities upon the political leadership.

Although it can be argued that the region's future is in its own hands, it will also be heavily influenced by the United States. In many ways, the US–Latin America leadership is similar to that between Japan and the East Asian NIEs, which are heavily dependent upon Japan as their major market and source of capital.[40] Yet there is more to this relationship than Latin America's economic dependence upon the United States, whose banking system has also suffered because of Latin American indebtedness. United States exports, which are fifty times larger to this region than to Eastern Europe, were badly hurt by Latin America's economic difficulties, and they would benefit greatly from a resumption of growth. The United States' own environment may now be threatened by the diminution of the Amazon and Central American rain forests. Its awful drug problem, driven by domestic demand, is fuelled by Latin American supplies—more than 80 percent of the cocaine and 90 percent of the marijuana entering the United States are produced or move through this region.

Finally, the population of the United States is being altered by migration from Mexico, the Caribbean, and Central America; if there should be a widespread socioeconomic collapse south of the Rio Grande, the "spillover" effects will be felt across the United States. Instead of being marginalized by the end of the cold war, Latin America may present Washington with formidable and growing challenges—social, environmental, financial, and ultimately political.[41] Thus, while the region's own politicians and citizens have to bear the major responsibility for recovery, richer nations—especially the United States—may find it in their own best interest to lend a hand.

3.

If these remarks disappoint readers in Brazil or Peru, they may care to glance, in grim consolation, at the world of Islam. It is one thing to face population pressures, shortage of resources, educational/technological deficiencies, and regional conflicts, which would challenge the wisest governments. But it is another when

regimes themselves stand in angry resentment of global forces for change instead of (as in East Asia) selectively responding to such trends. Far from preparing for the twenty-first century, much of the Arab and Muslim world appears to have difficulty in coming to terms with the nineteenth century, with its composite legacy of secularization, democracy, laissez-faire economics, industrial and commercial linkages among different nations, social change, and intellectual questioning. If one needed an example of the importance of cultural attitudes in explaining a society's response to change, contemporary Islam provides it.

Before analyzing the distinctive role of Islamic culture, one should first note the danger of generalizing about a region that contains such variety. After all, it is not even clear what *name* should be used to describe this part of the earth. To term it the "Middle East"[42] is, apart from its Atlantic-centered bias, to leave out such North African states as Libya, Tunisia, Algeria, and Morocco. To term it the "Arab World"[43] is to exclude Iran (and, of course, Israel), the Kurds, and the non-Muslim tribes of southern Sudan and Mauritania. Even the nomenclature Islam, or the Muslim world, disguises the fact that millions of Catholics, Copts, and Jews live in these lands, and that Islamic societies extend from West Africa to Indonesia.[44]

In addition, the uneven location of oil in the Middle East has created a division between super-rich and dreadfully poor societies that has no equivalent in Central America or sub-Saharan African.[45] Countries like Kuwait (2 million), the United Arab Emirates (1.3 million), and Saudi Arabia (11.5 million) enjoy some of the world's highest incomes, but exist alongside populous neighbors one third as rich (Jordan, Iran, Iraq) or even one tenth as rich (Egypt, Yemen). The gap is accentuated by different political systems: conservative, anti-democratic, traditionalist in the Gulf sheikdoms; demagogic, populist, militarized in countries such as Libya, Syria, Iraq, and Iran.

The 1990 Iraqi attack upon Kuwait, and the different responses of the Saudi elites on the one hand and the street masses in Amman or Rabat on the other, illustrated this divide between "haves" and "have-nots" in the Muslim world. The presence of millions of Egyptian, Yemeni, Jordanian, and Palestinian *Gastarbeiter* in the oil-rich states simply increased the mutual resentments, while the Saudi and Emirate habit of giving extensive aid to Iraq during its war against Iran, or to Egypt to assist its economic needs, reinforces the impression of wealthy but precarious regimes seeking to achieve security by bribing their larger, jealous neighbors.[46] Is it any wonder that the unemployed, badly housed urban masses, despairing of their own secular advancement, are attracted to religious leaders or "strongmen" appealing to Islamic pride, a sense of identity, and resistance to foreign powers and their local lackeys?

More than in any other developing region, then, the future of the Middle East and North Africa is affected by issues of war and conflict. The region probably contains more soldiers, aircraft, missiles, and other weapons than anywhere else in the world, with billions of dollars of armaments having been supplied by Western, Soviet, and Chinese producers during the past few decades. In view of the range and destructiveness of these weapons, another Arab-Israeli war would be a nightmare, yet many Muslim states still regard Israel with acute hostility. Even if the Arab-Israeli antagonism did not exist, the region is full of other rivalries, between Syria and Iraq, Libya and Egypt, Iran and Iraq, and so on. Vicious one-man dictatorships glare threateningly at arch-conservative, antidemocratic, feudal sheikdoms. Fundamentalist regimes exist from Iran to the Sudan. Terrorist groups in exile threaten to eliminate their foes. Unrest among the masses puts a question mark over the future of Egypt, Algeria, Morocco, Jordan.[47] The recent fate of Lebanon, instead of serving as a warning against sectarian fanaticism, is more often viewed as a lesson in power politics, that the strong will devour the weak.

To the Western observer brought up in Enlightenment traditions—or, for that matter, to economic rationalists preaching the virtues of the borderless world—the answer to the Muslim nations' problems would appear to be a vast program of *education*, not simply in the technical, skills-acquiring sense but also to advance parliamentary discourse, pluralism, and a secular civic culture. Is that not the reason, after all, for the political stability and economic success of Scandinavia or Japan today?

If that argument is correct, then such an observer would find few of those features in contemporary Islam. In countries where fundamentalism is strong, there is (obviously) little prospect of education or advancement for the female half of the population.[48] Where engineers and technicians exist, their expertise has all too often been mobilized for war purposes, as in Iraq. Tragically, Egypt possesses a large and bustling university system but a totally inadequate number of jobs for graduates and skilled workers, so that millions of both are underemployed. In Yemen, to take an extreme example, the state of education is dismal. By contrast, the oil-rich states have poured huge resources into schools, technical institutes, and universities, but these alone are insufficient to create an "enterprise culture" that would produce export-led manufacturing along East Asian lines. Ironically, possession of vast oil reserves could be a disadvantage, since it reduces the incentive to rely upon the skills and quality of the people, as occurs in countries (Japan, Switzerland) with few natural resources. Such discouraging circumstances may also explain why many educated and entrepreneurial Arabs, who passionately wanted their societies to borrow from the West, have emigrated.

It is difficult to know whether the reason for the Muslim world's troubled condition is cultural or historical. Western critics pointing to the region's religious intolerance, technological backwardness, and feudal cast of mind often forget that, centuries before the Reformation, Islam led the world in mathematics, cartography, medicine, and many other aspects of science and industry; and contained libraries, universities, and observatories, when Japan and America possessed none and Europe only a few. These assets were later sacrificed to a revival of traditionalist thought and the sectarian split between Shi'ite and Sunni Muslims, but Islam's retreat into itself—its being "out of step with History," as one author termed it[49]—

was probably also a response to the rise of a successful, expansionist Europe.

Sailing along the Arab littoral, assisting in the demise of the Mughal Empire, penetrating strategic points with railways, canals, and ports, steadily moving into North Africa, the Nile Valley, the Persian Gulf, the Levant, and then Arabia itself, dividing the Middle East along unnatural boundaries as part of a post–First World War diplomatic bargain, developing American power to buttress and then replace European influences, inserting an Israeli state in the midst of Arab peoples, instigating coups against local popular leaders, and usually indicating that this part of the globe was important only for its *oil*—the Western nations may have contributed more to turning the Muslim world into what it is today than outside commentators are willing to recognize.[50] Clearly, the nations of Islam suffer many self-inflicted problems. But if much of their angry, confrontational attitudes toward the international order today are due to a long-held fear of being swallowed up by the West, little in the way of change can be expected until that fear is dissipated.

4.

The condition of sub-Saharan Africa—"the third world's third world," as it has been described—is even more desperate.[51] When one considers recent developments such as perestroika in the former Soviet Union, the coming integration of Europe, and the economic miracle of Japan and the East Asian NIEs, remarked a former president of Nigeria, General Olusegun Obasanjo, and "contrasting all this with what is taking place in Africa, it is difficult to believe that we inhabit the same historical time."[52] Recent reports upon the continent's plight are extraordinarily gloomy, describing Africa as "a human and environmental disaster area," as "moribund," "marginalized," and "peripheral to the rest of the world," and having so many intractable problems that some foreign development experts are abandoning it to work elsewhere. In the view of the World Bank, virtually everywhere else in the world is likely to experience a decline in poverty by the year 2000 *except* Africa, where things will only get worse.[53] "Sub-Saharan Africa," concludes one economist, "suffers from a combination of economic, social, political, institutional and environmental handicaps which have so far largely defied development efforts by the African countries and their donors."[54] How, an empathetic study asks, can Africa survive?[55]

The unanimity of views is remarkable, given the enormous variety among the forty-five states that comprise sub-Saharan Africa.[56] Nine of them have fewer than one million people each, whereas Nigeria contains about 110 million. Some lie in the desert, some in tropical rain forests. Many are rich in mineral deposits, others have only scrubland. While a number (Botswana, Cameroun, Congo, Gabon, Kenya) have seen significant increases in living standards since independence, they are the exception—suggesting that the obstacles to growth on East Asian lines are so deep-rooted and resistant to the "development strategies" of foreign experts and/or their own leaders that it may require profound changes in attitude to achieve recovery.

This was not the mood thirty years ago, when the peoples of Africa were gaining their independence. True, there was economic backwardness, but this was assumed to have been caused by decades of foreign rule, leading to dependency upon a single metropolitan market, monoculture, lack of access to capital, and so on. Now that Africans had control of their destinies, they could build industries, develop cities, airports, and infrastructure, and attract foreign investment and aid from either Western powers or the USSR and its partners. The boom in world trade during the 1950s and 1960s, and demand for commodities, strengthened this optimism. Although some regions were in need, Africa as a whole was self-sufficient in food and, in fact, a net food exporter. Externally, African states were of increasing importance at the United Nations and other world bodies.

What went wrong? The unhappy answer is "lots of things." The first, and perhaps most serious, was that over the following three decades the population mushroomed as imported medical techniques and a reduction in malaria-borne mosquitoes drastically curtailed

infant mortality. Africa's population was already increasing at an average annual rate of 2.6 percent in the 1960s, jumped to 2.9 percent during the 1970s, and increased to over 3 percent by the late 1980s, implying a doubling in size every twenty-two years; this was, therefore, the highest rate for any region in the world.[57]

In certain countries, the increases were staggering. Between 1960 and 1990, Kenya's population quadrupled, from 6.3 million to 25.1 million, and Côte d'Ivoire's jumped from 3.8 million to 12.6 million. Altogether Africa's population—including the North African states—leapt from 281 to 647 million in three decades.[58] Moreover, while the majority of Africans inhabit rural settlements, the continent has been becoming urban at a dizzying speed. Vast shanty-cities have already emerged on the edges of national capitals (such as Accra in Ghana, Monrovia in Liberia, and Lilongwe in Malawi). By 2025, urban dwellers are predicted to make up 55 percent of Africa's total population.

The worst news is that the increase is unlikely to diminish in the near future. Although most African countries spend less than 1 percent of GNP on health care and consequently have the highest infant mortality rates in the world—in Mali, for example, there are 169 infant deaths for every 1,000 live births—those rates are substantially less than they were a quarter century ago and will tumble further in the future, which is why demographers forecast that Africa's population in 2025 will be nearly three times that of today.[59]

There remains one random and tragic factor which may significantly affect all these (late 1980s) population projections—the AIDS epidemic, which is especially prevalent in Africa. Each new general study has raised the global total of people who are already HIV positive. For example, in June 1991, the World Health Organization abandoned its earlier estimate that 25–30 million people throughout the world would be infected by the year 2000, and suggested instead that the total could be closer to 40 million, and even that may be a gross underestimate.[60] Without question, Africa is the continent most deeply affected by AIDS, with entire families suffering from the disease. Tests of pregnant

women in certain African families reveal that 25–30 percent are now HIV positive.[61] Obviously, this epidemic would alter the earlier projections of a doubling or trebling of Africa's total population over the next few decades—and in the worst possible way: family sizes would still be much larger than in most other regions of the globe, but tens of millions of Africans would be dying of AIDS, further crushing the world's most disadvantaged continent.

The basic reason why the present demographic boom will not otherwise be halted swiftly is traditional African belief-systems concerning fecundity, children, ancestors, and the role of women. Acutely aware of the invisible but pervasive presence of their ancestors, determined to expand their lineage, regarding childlessness or small families as the work of evil spirits, most Africans seek to have as many children as possible; a woman's virtue and usefulness are measured by the number of offspring she can bear. "Desired family size," according to polls of African women, ranges from five to nine children. The social attitudes that lead women in North America, Europe, and Japan to delay child-bearing—education, career ambitions, desire for independence—scarcely exist in African societies; where such emerge, they are swiftly suppressed by familial pressures.[62]

This population growth has not been accompanied by equal or larger increases in Africa's productivity, which would of course transform the picture. During the 1960s, farm output was rising by around 3 percent each year, keeping pace with the population, but since 1970 agricultural production has grown at only half that rate. Part of this decline was caused by the drought, hitting countries south of the Sahara. Furthermore, existing agricultural resources have been badly eroded by overgrazing—caused by the sharp rise in the number of cattle and goats—as well as by deforestation in order to provide fuel and shelter for the growing population. When rain falls, the water runs off the denuded fields, taking the top-soil with it.

None of this was helped by changes in agricultural production, with farmers encouraged to grow tea, coffee, cocoa, palm oil, and rubber for export rather than food for domestic consumption. After benefitting from high commodity prices in the early stages, producers suffered a number of blows. Heavy taxation on cash crops, plus mandatory governmental marketing, reduced the incentives to increase output; competition grew from Asian and Latin American producers; many African currencies were overvalued, which hurt exports; and in the mid-1970s, world commodity prices tumbled. Yet the cost of imported manufactures and foodstuffs remained high, and sub-Saharan Africa was badly hurt by the quadrupling of oil prices.[63]

These blows increased Africa's indebtedness in ways that were qualitatively new. Early, postcolonial borrowings were driven by the desire for modernization, as money was poured into cement works, steel plants, airports, harbors, national airlines, electrification schemes, and telephone networks. Much of it, encouraged from afar by international bodies like the World Bank, suffered from bureaucratic interference, a lack of skilled personnel, unrealistic planning, and inadequate basic facilities, and now lies half-finished or (where completed) suffers from lack of upkeep. But borrowing to pay for imported oil, or to feed half the nation's population, means that indebtedness rises without any possible return on the borrowed funds. In consequence, Africa's total debt expanded from $14 billion in 1973 to $125 billion in 1987, when its capacity to repay was dropping fast; by the mid-1980s, payments on loans consumed about half of Africa's export earnings, a proportion even greater than for Latin American debtor nations. Following repeated debt reschedulings, Western bankers—never enthusiastic to begin with—virtually abandoned private loans to Africa.[64]

As a result, Africa's economy is in a far worse condition now than at independence, apart from a few countries like Botswana and Mauritius. Perhaps the most startling illustration of its plight is the fact that "excluding South Africa, the nations of sub-Saharan Africa with their 450 million people have a total GDP less than that of Belgium's 11 million people"; in fact, the entire continent generates roughly 1 percent of the world GDP.[65] Africa's share of world markets has shriveled just as East Asia's share has risen fast.

Plans for modernization lie unrealized. Manufacturing still represents only 11 percent of Africa's economic activity—scarcely up from the 9 percent share in 1965; and only 12 percent of the continent's exports is composed of manufactures (compared with Korea's 90 percent). There is a marked increase in the signs of decay: crumbling infrastructure, power failures, broken-down communications, abandoned projects, and everywhere the pressure of providing for increasing populations. Already Africa needs to import 15 million tons of maize a year to achieve minimal levels of food consumption, but with population increasing faster than agricultural output, that total could multiply over the next decade—implying an even greater diversion of funds from investment and infrastructure.[66]

Two further characteristics worsen Africa's condition. The first is the prevalence of wars, *coups d'état*, and political instability. This is partly the legacy of the European "carve-up" of Africa, when colonial boundaries were drawn without regard for the differing tribes and ethnic groups,[67] or even of earlier conquests by successful tribes of neighboring lands and peoples; Ethiopia, for example, is said to contain 76 ethnic groups and 286 languages.[68] While it is generally accepted that those boundaries cannot be unscrambled, most of them are clearly artificial. In extreme cases like Somalia, the "state" has ceased to exist. And in most other African countries, governments do not attract the loyalty of citizens (except perhaps kinsmen of the group in power), and ethnic tensions have produced innumerable civil wars—from Biafra's attempt to secede from Nigeria, to the conflict between Arab north and African south in the Sudan, to Eritrean struggles to escape from Ethiopia, to the Tutsi-Hutu struggle in Burundi, to clashes and suppressions and guerrilla campaigns from Uganda to the Western Sahara, from Angola to Mozambique.[69]

These antagonisms have often been worsened by struggles over ideology and government authority. The rulers of many new African states rapidly switched either to a personal dictatorship, or single-party rule. They also embraced a Soviet or Maoist political

economy, instituting price controls, production targets, forced industrialization, the takeover of private enterprises, and other features of "scientific socialism" that—unknown to them—were destroying the Soviet economy. Agriculture was neglected, while bureaucracy flourished. The result was the disappearance of agricultural surpluses, inattention to manufacturing for the world market, and the expansion of party and government bureaucracies, exacerbating the region's problems.

The second weakness was the wholly inadequate investment in human resources and in developing a culture of entrepreneurship, scientific inquiry, and technical prowess. According to one survey, Africa has been spending less than $1 each year on research and development per head of population, whereas the United States was spending $200 per head. Consequently, Africa's scientific population has always trailed the rest of the world:

NUMBERS OF SCIENTISTS AND ENGINEERS PER MILLION OF POPULATION[70]	
Japan	3,548
US	2,685
Europe	1,632
Latin America	209
Arab States	202
Asia (minus Japan)	99
Africa	53

In many African countries—Malawi, Zambia, Lesotho—government spending on education has fallen, so that, after some decades of advance, a smaller share of children are now in school. While there is a hunger for learning, it cannot be satisfied beyond the secondary level except for a small minority. Angola, for example, had 2.4 million pupils in primary schools in 1982–1983, but only 153,000 in secondary schools and a mere 4,700 in higher education.[71] By contrast, Sweden, with a slightly smaller total population, had 570,000 in secondary education and 179,000 in higher education.[72]

Despite these relative weaknesses, some observers claim to have detected signs of a turnaround. With the excep-

15

tion of intransigent African socialists,[73] many leaders are now attempting to institute reforms. In return for "structural adjustments," that is, measures to encourage free enterprise, certain African societies have secured additional loans from Western nations and the World Bank. The latter organization has identified past errors (many of them urged on African governments and funded by itself), and encouraged economic reforms. Mozambique, Ghana, and Zambia have all claimed recent successes in reversing negative growth, albeit at considerable social cost.

Democratic principles are also returning to the continent: the dismantling of apartheid in South Africa, the cease-fire in Angola, the independence of Namibia, the success of Botswana's record of democracy and prosperity, the cries for reforms in Gabon, Kenya, and Zaire, the rising awareness among African intellectuals of the transformations in East Asia, may all help—so the argument goes—to change attitudes, which is the prerequisite for recovery.[74] Moreover, there are local examples of economic self-improvement, cooperative ventures to halt erosion and improve yields, and village-based schemes of improvement.[75] This is, after all, a continent of enormous agricultural and mineral resources, provided they can be sensibly exploited.

Despite such signs of promise, conditions are likely to stay poor. Population increases countered only by the growing toll of AIDS victims, the diminution of grazing lands and food supplies, the burdens of indebtedness, the decay of infrastructures and reduced spending on health care and education, the residual strength of animist religions and traditional belief-systems, the powerful hold of corrupt bureaucracies and ethnic loyalties... all those tilt against the relatively few African political leaders, educators, scientists, and economists who perceive the need for changes.

What does this mean for Africa's future? As the Somalian disaster unfolds, some observers suggest that parts of the continent may be taken over and administered from the outside, rather like the post–1919 League of Nations mandates. By contrast, other experts argue that disengagement by developed countries might have the positive effect of compelling

Africans to begin a *self-driven* recovery, as well as ending the misuse of aid monies.[76] Still others feel that Africa cannot live without the West, although its leaders and people will have to abandon existing habits, and development aid must be more intelligently applied.[77] Whichever view is correct, the coming decade will be critical for Africa. Even a partial recovery would give grounds for hope; on the other hand, a second decade of decline, together with a further surge in population, would result in catastrophe.

5.

From the above, it is clear that the developing countries' response to the broad forces for global change is going to be uneven. The signs are that the gap between success and failure will widen; one group enjoys interacting beneficial trends, while others suffer from linked weaknesses and deficiencies.[78]

This is most clearly the case with respect to demography. As noted earlier, the commitment of the East Asian trading states to education, manufacturing, and export-led growth produced a steady rise in living standards, and allowed those societies to make the demographic transition to smaller family sizes. This was in marked contrast to sub-Saharan Africa where, because of different cultural attitudes and social structures, improved health care and rising incomes led, *not* to a drop in population growth, but to the opposite. Just before independence in 1960, for example, the average Kenyan woman had 6.2 children, whereas by 1980 she had 8.2[79]—and that in a period when Africa's economic prospects were fading.

In Africa's case the "global trend" which drives all others is, clearly, the demographic explosion. It spills into every domain—overgrazing, local conflicts over water and wood supplies, extensive unplanned urbanization, strains upon the educational and social structures, reliance upon imported food supplies (at the cost of increasing indebtedness), ethnic tensions, domestic unrest, border wars. Only belatedly are some African governments working to persuade families to limit their size as people become aware that access to family planning, plus improved educational opportunities for women, produce sig-

nificant declines in birth rates. Against such promising indications stand the many cultural, gender-related, and economic forces described above that encourage large families. This resistance to change is aided by Africa's general lack of resources. Raising Somalia's female literacy rate (6 percent) to South Korea's (88 percent) to produce a demographic transition sounds fine until one considers how so ambitious a reform could be implemented and paid for. Unfortunately, as noted above, the projections suggest that, as Africa's population almost trebles over the next few decades, the only development curtailing it could be the rapid growth of AIDS.[80]

In many parts of Latin America, the demographic explosion will also affect the capacity to handle globally driven forces for change. While wide differences in total fertility rates exist between the moderate-climate countries and those in the tropics, the overall picture is that Latin America's population, which was roughly equal to that of United States and Canada in 1960, is increasing so swiftly that it will be more than double the latter in 2025.[81] Even if birth-rates are now declining in the larger countries, there will still be enormous increases: Mexico's population will leap to 150 million by 2025 and Brazil's to 245 million.[82] This implies a very high incidence of child poverty and malnutrition, further strain upon already inadequate health-care and educational services, the crowding of millions of human beings into a dozen or more "mega-cities," pollution, the degradation of grazing land, forests, and other natural resources. In Mexico, for example, 44 million people are without sewers and 21 million without potable water, which means that when disease (e.g., cholera) strikes, it spreads swiftly.[83] These are not strong foundations upon which to improve the region's relative standing in an increasingly competitive international economic order.

In this regard, many Muslim states are in a similar or worse position; in no Arab country is the population increasing by less than 2 percent a year,[84] and in most the rate is considerably higher. The region's total population of more than 200 million will double in less than twenty-five years and city populations are growing twice as fast as national averages. This puts enormous pressures upon scarce food, water, and land resources, and produces unbalanced populations. Already, in most Arab countries at least four out of every ten people are under the age of fifteen—the classic recipe for subsequent social unrest and political revolution. One in five Egyptian workers is jobless, as is one in four Algerian workers.[85] In what is widely regarded as the most turbulent part of the world, therefore, demography is contributing to the prospects of future unrest year by year. Even the Israeli-Palestine quarrel has become an issue of demography, with the influx of Soviet Jews seen as countering the greater fertility of the Palestinians.

There is, moreover, little likelihood that population growth will fall in the near future. Since infant mortality rates in many Muslim countries are still high, further improvements in prenatal care will produce rises in the numbers surviving, as is happening in the Gulf States and Saudi Arabia (see chart above).

As elsewhere, politics intrudes; many regimes are deliberately encouraging women to have large families, arguing that this adds to the country's military strength. "Bear a child," posters in Iraq proclaim, "and you pierce an arrow in the enemy's eye."[87] Countries such as Iraq and Libya offer many incentives for larger families, as do the Gulf States and Saudi Arabia, anxious to fill their oil-rich lands with native-born rather than foreign workers. Only in Egypt are propaganda campaigns launched to curb family size, but even if that is successful—despite resistance from the Muslim Brotherhood—present numbers are disturbing. With a current population of over 55 million Egyptians, six out of ten of whom are under twenty, and with an additional one million being born every eight months, the country is in danger of bursting at the seams during the next few decades.

6.

For much the same reasons, we ought to expect a differentiated success rate among developing countries in handling environmental challenges, with the newly industrializing East Asian economies way ahead of the others. This is not to ignore significant local

COMPARATIVE INFANT MORTALITY RATES[86] (Infant deaths per 1,000 live births)		
	1965–1970	1985–1990
Algeria	150	74
Egypt	170	85
Sudan	156	108
Yemen Arab Republic	186	116
Saudi Arabi	140	71
Kuwait	55	19
Iraq	111	69
Japan	16	5
US	22	10
Sweden	13	6

schemes to improve the ecology that are springing up in Africa and the interesting proposals for "sustainable development" elsewhere in the developing world,[88] or to forget that industrialization has caused environmental damage in East Asia, from choked roads to diminished forests. Yet the fact is that nations with lots of resources (capital, scientists, engineers, technology, a per capita GNP of over US $4,000) are better able to deal with environmental threats than those without money, tools, or personnel. By contrast, it is the poorer societies (Egypt, Bangladesh, Ethiopia) that, lacking financial and personnel resources, find it difficult to respond to cyclones, floods, drought, and other natural disasters—with their devastated populations augmenting the millions of refugees and migrants. Should global warming produce sea-level rises and heightened storm surges, teeming island populations from the Caribbean to the Pacific are in danger of being washed away.[89]

Finally, it is the population explosion in Latin America and South Asia and Africa that is the major cause for the overgrazing, soil erosion, salinization, and clearing of the tropical rain forests, which, while contributing to global warming, also hurts the local populations and exacerbates regional struggles for power. Elsewhere, in the Middle East for example, supplies of

water are the greatest concern, especially in view of growing demographic pressures. The average Jordanian now uses only one third the amount of domestic water consumed in Israel and has little hope of increasing the supply, yet Jordan's population, which is now roughly equal to Israel's, is expected to double during the next twenty years.[90]

With all governments in the region striving to boost agricultural output and highly sensitive to famine and unrest among their peasant farmers, the search for secure water influences domestic politics, international relations, and spending priorities. Egypt worries that either the Sudan or Ethiopia might dam the Nile in order to increase irrigation. Syria and Iraq have taken alarm at Turkey's new Ataturk dam, which can interrupt the flow of the Euphrates. Jordan, Syria, and Israel quarrel over water rights in the Litani, Yarmuk, and Jordan river valleys, as do Arabs and Jews over well supplies in the occupied West Bank. Saudi Arabia's ambition to grow wheat is draining its aquifers, and the same will occur with Libya's gigantic scheme to tap water from under the Sahara.[91] As more and more people struggle for the same—or diminishing—amounts of water, grand ideas about preparing for the twenty-first century look increasingly irrelevant; surviving *this* century becomes the order of the day.

What are the implications for these societies of the new technologies being developed by Western scientists? The revolution in biotech farming, for example, is of great relevance to developing countries, even if the consequences will be mixed. Improved strains of plants and more sophisticated pesticides and fertilizers could, potentially, enhance yields in the developing world, reduce pressures upon marginal lands, restore agricultural self-sufficiency, improve the balance of payments, and raise standards of living. Since much biotech does not involve expensive enterprise, we could witness farmers' groups experimenting with new seeds, improved breeding techniques, cultivation of gene tissue, regional gene-banks, and other developments.

Yet it is also possible that giant pharmaceutical and agro-chemical firms in the "first" world may monopolize much of the knowledge—and the profits—that this transformation implies. Surpluses in global foodstuffs caused by the biotech revolution could be used to counter malnutrition. They could also undermine commodity prices and hurt societies in which most inhabitants were employed in agriculture. Removing food production from the farm to the laboratory—which is what is implied by recent breakthroughs in biotech agriculture—would undercut agrarian societies, which is why some biotech experts in the development field call for serious planning in "agricultural conversion," that is, conversion into other economic activities.[92]

While the uses of biotechnology are relatively diverse, that is not the case with robotics and automated manufacture. The requirements for an indigenous robotics industry—capital, an advanced electronics sector, design engineers, a dearth of skilled labor—suggest that countries like Taiwan and Korea may follow Japan's example out of concern that Japan's automation will make their own products uncompetitive. On the other hand, automated factories assembling goods more swiftly, regularly, and economically than human beings pose a challenge to *middle-income* economies (Malaysia, Mexico), whose comparative advantage would be undercut. As for countries without a manufacturing base, it is difficult to see how the robotics revolution would have any meaning—except to further devalue the resource which they possess in abundance, masses of impoverished and under-educated human beings.

Finally, the global financial and communications revolution, and the emergence of multinational corporations, threatens to increase the gap between richer and poorer countries, even in the developing world. The industrial conglomerates of Korea are now positioning themselves to become multinational, and the East Asian NIEs in general are able to exploit the world economy (as can be seen in their trade balances, stock-markets, electronics industries, strategic marketing alliances, and so on). Furthermore, if the increasingly borderless world rewards en-trepreneurs, designers, brokers, patent-owners, lawyers, and dealers in high value-added services, then East Asia's commitment to education, science, and technology can only increase its lead over other developing economies.

By contrast, the relative lack of capital, high-technology, scientists, skilled workers, and export industries in the poorer countries makes it difficult for them to take part in the communications and financial revolution, although several countries (Brazil, India) clearly hope to do so. Some grimmer forecasts suggest the poorer parts of the developing world may become more marginalized, partly because of the reduced economic importance of labor, raw materials, and foodstuffs, partly because the advanced economies may concentrate upon greater knowledge-based commerce among themselves.

7.

Is there any way of turning these trends around? Obviously, a society strongly influenced by fundamentalist mullahs with a dislike of "modernization" is unlikely to join the international economy; and it does not *have* to enter the borderless world if its people believe that it would be healthier, spiritually if not economically, to remain outside. Nor ought we to expect that countries dominated by selfish, authoritarian elites bent upon enhancing their military power—developing world countries spent almost $150 billion on weapons and armies in 1988 alone—will rush to imitate Japan and Singapore.

But what about those societies that wish to improve themselves yet find that they are hampered by circumstances? There are, after all, many developing countries, the vast majority of which depend upon exporting food and raw materials. With dozens of poor countries seeking desperately to sell their cane sugar or bananas or timber or coffee in the global market, prices fall and they are made more desperate.[93] Moreover, although much international aid goes to the developing world, in fact far more money flows out of impoverished countries of Africa, Asia, and Latin America and *into* the richer economies of Europe, North America, and Japan—to the tune of at least $43 billion each year.[94] This outward flow of interest repayments, repatriated profits, capital flight, royalties, fees for patents and information services, makes it difficult for poorer countries to get to their feet; and even if they were able to increase their industrial output, the result might be a large rise in "the costs of technological dependence."[95] Like their increasing reliance upon Northern suppliers for food and medical aid, this has created another dependency relationship for poorer nations.

In sum, as we move into the next century the developed economies appear to have all the trump cards in their hands—capital, technology, control of communications, surplus foodstuffs, powerful multinational companies[96]—and, if anything, their advantages are growing because technology is eroding the value of labor and materials, the chief assets of developing countries. Although nominally independent since decolonization, these countries are probably more dependent upon Europe and the United States than they were a century ago.

Ironically, three or four decades of efforts by developing countries to gain control of their own destinies—nationalizing Western companies, setting up commodity-exporting cartels, subsidizing indigenous manufacturing to achieve import substitution, campaigning for a new world order based upon redistribution of the existing imbalances of wealth—have all failed. The "market," backed by governments of the developed economies, has proved too strong, and the struggle against it has weakened developing economies still further—except those (like Korea and Taiwan) which decided to join.

While the gap between rich and poor in today's world is disturbing, those who have argued that this gap is unjust have all too often supported heavy-handed state interventionism and a retreat from open competition, which preserved indigenous production in the short term but rendered it less efficient against those stimulated by market forces. "Scientific socialism for Africa" may still appeal to some intellectuals,[97] but by encouraging societies to look inward it made them less well equipped to move to newer technologies in order to make goods of greater sophistication and value. And a new "world communications order," as proposed a few years ago by UNESCO to balance the West's dominance, sounds superficially attractive but would in all likelihood become the pawn of bureaucratic and ideological interests rather than function as an objective source of news reporting.

On the other hand, the advocates of free market forces often ignore the vast political difficulties which governments in developing countries would encounter in abolishing price controls,

selling off national industries, and reducing food subsidies. They also forget that the spectacular commercial expansion of Japan and the East Asian NIEs was carried out by strong states which eschewed laissez faire. Instead of copying either socialist or free market systems, therefore, the developing countries might imitate East Asia's "mixed strategies" which combine official controls and private enterprise.[98]

Although the idea of a mixed strategy is intriguing, how can West or Central African countries imitate East Asia without a "strong state" apparatus, and while having a weak tradition of cooperation between government and firms, far lower educational achievements, and a different set of cultural attitudes toward family size or international economics? With the global scene less welcoming to industrializing newcomers, how likely are they to achieve the same degree of success as the East Asian NIEs did, when they "took off" a quarter-century ago?[99] Even if, by an economic miracle, the world's poorest fifty nations did adopt the Korean style of export-led growth in manufactures, would they not create the same crisis of overproduction as exists in the commodity markets today?

How many developing nations will be able to follow East Asia's growth is impossible to tell. The latest *World Development Report* optimistically forecast significant progress across the globe, provided that poorer nations adopted "market friendly" policies and richer nations eschewed protectionism.[100] Were Taiwan and Korea to be followed by the larger states of Southeast Asia such as Malaysia and Thailand, then by South Asia and a number of Latin American countries, that would blur the North-South divide and make international economic alignments altogether more variegated. Moreover, sustained manufacturing success among developing countries *outside* East Asia might stimulate imitation elsewhere.

At the moment, however, the usual cluster of factors influencing relative economic performance—cultural attitudes, education, political stability, capacity to carry out long-term plans—suggests that while a small but growing number of countries is moving from a "have-not" to a "have" status, many more remain behind. The story of winners and losers in history will continue, therefore, only this time modern communications will remind us all of the growing disparity among the world's nations and regions.

NOTES

[1]Discussed further in my new book, *Preparing For the Twenty-First Century* (Random House, 1993).

[2]For reasons of size and organization, China and India (containing around 37 percent of the world's population) are not treated here: for coverage, see Chapter 9, "India and China," of *Preparing For the Twenty-First Century.*

[3]*World Tables 1991* (Washington, DC: World Bank, 1991), pp. 268–269, 352–353.

[4]*World Tables 1991*, pp. 268–269, 352–353.

[5]See the World Bank publication *Trends in Developing Economies*, 1990, pp. 299–303, for Korea.

[6]For descriptions, see F. Braudel, *Civilization and Capitalism: Vol. 3, The Perspective of the World* (Harper and Row, 1986), pp. 506–511.

[7]See P. Lyon, "Emergence of the Third World," in H. Bull and A. Watson, editors, *The Expansion of International Society* (Oxford University Press, 1983), p. 229 ff.; G. Barraclough, *An Introduction to Contemporary History* (Penguin, 1967), chapter 6, "The Revolt Against the West."

[8]J. Ravenhill, "The North-South Balance of Power," *International Affairs*, Vol. 66, No. 4 (1990), pp. 745–746. See also, J. Cruickshank, "The Rise and Fall of the Third World: A Concept Whose Time Has Passed," *World Review*, February 1991, pp. 28–29. Ravenhill's divisions are high-income oil-exporting countries; industrializing economies with strong states and relatively low levels of indebtedness (Taiwan, etc.); industrializing economies with the state apparatus under challenge and/or with debt problems (Argentina, Poland); potential newly industrializing countries (Malaysia, Thailand); primary commodity producers (in sub-Saharan Africa, Central America).

[9]Ravenhill, "The North-South Balance of Power," p. 732.

[10]S. Fardoust and A. Dhareshwan, *Long-Term Outlook for the World Economy: Issues and Projections for the 1990s*, a World Bank report (February 1990), p. 9, Table 3.

[11]W. L. M. Adriaansen and J. G. Waardensburg, editors, *A Dual World Economy* (Groningen: Wolters-Noordhoff, 1989).

[12]P. Drysdale, "The Pacific Basin and Its Economic Vitality," in J. W. Morley, editor, *The Pacific Basin: New Challenges for the United States* (Academy of Political Science with the

1. A CLASH OF VIEWS

East Asian Institute and the Center on Japanese Economy and Business, 1986), p. 11.

[13]While Korea has a population of around 43 million and Taiwan about 20 million, Hong Kong possesses 5.7 million and Singapore only 2.7 million.

[14]See especially, "Taiwan and Korea: Two Paths to Prosperity," *The Economist*, July 14, 1990, pp. 19–21; also "South Korea" (survey), *The Economist*, August 18, 1990. There is a useful comparative survey in L. A. Veit, "Time of the New Asian Tigers," *Challenge*, July–August 1987, pp. 49–55.

[15]N. D. Kristof, "In Taiwan, Only the Strong Get US Degrees," *The New York Times*, March 26, 1989, p. 11.

[16]Figures taken, respectively, from J. Paxton, editor, *The Statesman's Yearbook 1990–1991* (St. Martin's Press, 1990); and from R.N. Gwynne, *New Horizons? Third World Industrialization in an International Framework* (New York/London: Wiley, 1990), p. 199.

[17]Lest this 1987 figure appear too distant, note that Korea's sixth Five-Year Plan calls for a national savings rate of 33.5 percent in the early 1990s: see *Trends in Developing Economies,* p. 300. This table is taken from p. 31 (Table 10) of T. Fukuchi and M. Kagami, editors, *Perspectives on the Pacific Basin Economy: A Comparison of Asia and Latin America* (Tokyo: Asian Club Foundation, Institute of Developing Economics, 1990).

[18]The table on p. 4 (Table 1) of Fukuchi and Kagami shows the different rates of growth, and of export's share of total GDP, of the Asian Pacific nations compared with those of Latin America. See also H. Hughes, "Catching Up: The Asian Newly Industrializing Economies in the 1990s," *Asian Development Review*, Vol. 7, No. 2 (1989), p. 132 (and Table 3).

[19]"The Yen Block" (Survey), *The Economist*, July 15, 1989; "Japan Builds A New Power Base," *Business Week*, March 20, 1989, pp. 18–25.

[20]"Taiwan and Korea: Two Paths to Prosperity," *The Economist*, p. 19; "South Korea: A New Society," *The Economist*, April 15, 1989, pp. 23–25.

[21]"Development Brief," *The Economist*, May 26, 1990, p. 81, for the first two columns; the GNP per capita comes from *World Development Report,* 1990, pp. 178–179.

[22]"When a Miracle Stalls," *The Economist*, October 6, 1990, pp. 33–34

(on Taiwan); *Trends in Developing Economies,* 1990, pp. 299–300 (Korea); R. A. Scalapino, "Asia and the United States: The Challenges Ahead," *Foreign Affairs*, Vol. 69, No. 1 (1989–1990), especially pp. 107–112; "Hong Kong, In China's Sweaty Palm," *The Economist*, November 5, 1988, pp. 19–22.

[23]See the detailed forecasts in "Asia 2010: The Power of People," *Far Eastern Economist Review*, May 17, 1990, pp. 27–58. On industrial retooling, see pp. 8–9 of "South Korea" (Survey), *The Economist*, August 18, 1990.

[24]N. Sadik, editor, *Population: The UNFPA Experience*, (New York University Press, 1984), chapter 4, "Latin America and the Caribbean," pp. 51–52.

[25]A. F. Lowenthal, "Rediscovering Latin America," *Foreign Affairs*, Vol. 69, No. 4 (Fall 1990), p. 34.

[26]Figure from "Latin America's Hope," *The Economist*, December 9, 1989, p. 14.

[27]Taken from page 5 of G. W. Landau et al., *Latin America at a Crossroads*, (The Trilateral Commission, 1990), which reports the source as being *Economic and Social Progress in Latin America: 1989 Report* (Washington, DC: Inter-American Development Bank, 1989), Table B1, p. 463.

[28]As mentioned earlier, Japan and its East Asian emulators also sought to protect fledgling domestic industries, but that was in order to create a strong base from which to mount an export offensive—*not* to establish an economic bastion within which their industries would be content to remain.

[29]For details, see the various national entries in *The Statesman's Year-Book 1990–91*; and *The Economist World Atlas and Almanac* (Prentice Hall, 1989), pp. 131–157. R.N. Gwynne's *New Horizons?* has useful comments on Latin America's "inward-oriented industrialization" (chapter 11), which he then contrasts with East Asia's "outward orientation" (chapter 12).

[30]World Resources Institute, *World Resources 1990–91* (Oxford University Press, 1990), p. 39.

[31]*World Resources 1990–91*, p. 246.

[32]In 1989, the net transfer of capital leaving Latin America was around $25 billion.

[33]For the above, see pp. 33–48 of *World Resources 1990–91*: "Latin America At a Crossroads," B.J. McCormick, *The World Economy: Patterns of Growth and Change* (Oxford University Press, 1988), chapter 13;

"Latin American debt: The banks' great escape," *The Economist*, February 11, 1989, pp. 73–74.

[34]For educational details, see *The Statesman's Year-Book 1990–91*, pp. 95, 236; for literacy rates, see especially those of Uruguay, Costa Rica, Argentina, and Venezuela in the table "Development Brief," *The Economist*, May 26, 1990, p. 81.

[35]T. E. Martinez, "Argentina: Living with Hyperinflation," *The Atlantic Monthly*, December 1990, p. 36.

[36]*The Statesman's Year-Book 1990–91*, pp. 584, 605.

[37]T. Kamm, "Latin America Edges Toward Free Trade," *The Wall Street Journal*, November 30, 1990, p. A10.

[38]C. Farnsworth, "Latin American Economies Given Brighter Assessments," *The New York Times*, October 30, 1990; "Latin America's New Start," *The Economist*, June 9, 1990, p. 11; N.C. Nash, "A Breath of Fresh Economic Air Brings Change to Latin America," *The New York Times*, November 13, 1991, pp. A1, D5.

[39]"Latin America's Hope," *The Economist*, December 9, 1989, p. 15; Nash, "A Breath of Fresh Economic Air Brings Change to Latin America."

[40]J. Brooke, "Debt and Democracy," *The New York Times*, December 5, 1990, p. A16; P. Truell, "As the U.S. Slumps, Latin America Suffers," *The Wall Street Journal*, November 19, 1990, p. 1.

[41]For these arguments, see especially Lowenthal's fine summary, "Rediscovering Latin America,"in *Foreign Affairs*; also G.A. Fauriol, "The Shadow of Latin American Affairs," *Foreign Affairs*, Vol. 69, No. 1 (1989–1990), pp. 116–134; and M.D. Hayes, "The U.S. and Latin America: A Lost Decade?" *Foreign Affairs*, Vol. 68, No. 1 (1988–1989), pp. 180–198.

[42]This is the subdivision preferred by *The Economist World Atlas and Almanac*, pp. 256–271, which discusses the North African states (except Egypt) in a later section, under "Africa."

[43]"The Arab World" (survey), *The Economist*, May 12, 1990.

[44]See "Religions," p. 21 of the *Hammond Comparative World Atlas* (Hammond, Inc., 1993 edition).

[45]The few oil-producing countries in Africa, such as Gabon and Nigeria, still have relatively low per capita GNPs compared with the Arab Gulf states.

[46]G. Brooks and T. Horwitz, "Shaken Sheiks," *The Wall Street Journal*, December 28, 1990, pp. A1, A4.

[47]"The Arab World," *The Economist*, p. 12.

[48]In 1985, adult female literacy in the Yemen Arab Republic was a mere 3 percent, in Saudi Arabia 12 percent, in Iran 39 percent. On the other hand, many women from the middle and upper-middle classes in Muslim countries are educated, which suggests that poverty, as much as culture, plays a role.

[49]M. A. Heller, "The Middle East: Out of Step with History," *Foreign Affairs* Vol. 69, No. 1 (1989–1990), pp. 153–171.

[50]See also the remarks by S. F. Wells and M. A. Bruzonsky, editors, *Security in the Middle East: Regional Change and Great Power Strategies* (Westview Press, 1986), pp. 1–3.

[51]D. E. Duncan, "Africa: The Long Good-bye," *The Atlantic Monthly*, July 1990, p. 20.

[52]J. A. Marcum, "Africa: A Continent Adrift," *Foreign Affairs*, Vol. 68, No. 1 (1988–1989), p. 177. See also the penetrating article by K. R. Richburg, "Why Is Black Africa Overwhelmed While East Asia Overcomes?" *The International Herald Tribune*, July 14, 1992, pp. 1, 6.

[53]C. H. Farnsworth, "Report by World Bank Sees Poverty Lessening by 2000 Except in Africa," *The New York Times*, July 16, 1990, p. A3; Marcum, "Africa: A Continent Adrift"; Duncan, "Africa: The Long Good-bye"; and "The bleak continent," *The Economist*, December 9, 1989, pp. 80–81.

[54]B. Fischer, "Developing Countries in the Process of Economic Globalisation," *Intereconomics* (March/April 1990), p. 55.

[55]J.S. Whitaker, *How Can Africa Survive?* (Council on Foreign Relations Press, 1988).

[56]As will be clear from the text, this discussion excludes the Republic of South Africa.

[57]T. J. Goliber, "Africa's Expanding Population: Old Problems, New Policies," *Population Bulletin*, Vol. 44, No. 3 (November 1989), pp. 4–49, an outstandingly good article.

[58]*World Resources 1990–91*, p. 254.

[59]*World Resources 1990–91*, p. 254 (overall population growth to 2025), and p. 258 (infant mortality). L.K. Altman, "W.H.O Says 40 Million Will Be Infected With AIDS by 2000," *The New York Times*, June 18, 1991, p. C3 (for percentage of GNP devoted to health care).

[60]L.K. Altman, "W.H.O. Says 40 Million Will Be Infected With AIDS Virus by 2000"; and for further figures, see Kennedy, *Preparing For the Twenty First Century*, chapter 3.

[61]K.H. Hunt, "Scenes From a Nightmare," *The New York Times Magazine*, August 12, 1990, pp. 26, 50–51.

[62]See Whitaker, *How Can Africa Survive?*, especially chapter 4, "The Blessings of Children," for a fuller analysis; and J.C. Caldwell and P. Caldwell, "High Fertility in Sub-Saharan Africa," *Scientific American*, May 1990, pp. 118–125.

[63]"The bleak continent," *The Economist*; Whitaker, *How Can Africa Survive?*, chapters 1 and 2; Goliber, "Africa's Expanding Population," pp. 12–13.

[64]Whitaker, *How Can Africa Survive?*; Duncan, "Africa: The Long Good-bye."

[65]"Fruits of Containment" (op-ed), *The Wall Street Journal*, December 18, 1990, p. A14, for the Africa-Belgium comparison; H. McRae, "Visions of tomorrow's world," *The Independent* (London), November 26, 1991, for Africa's share of world GDP.

[66]"Aid to Africa," *The Economist*, December 8, 1990, p. 48.

[67]In this regard, East Asian nations like Taiwan and Korea, possessing coherent indigenous populations, are once again more favorably situated.

[68]*The Economist World Atlas and Almanac* (Prentice Hall, 1989), p. 293.

[69]Apart from the country by country comments in *The Economist World Atlas and Almanac*, see also K. Ingham, *Politics in Modern Africa: The Uneven Tribal Dimension* (Routledge, 1990); "Africa's Internal Wars of the 1980s—Contours and Prospects," United States Institute of Peace, *In Brief*, No. 18 (May 1990).

[70]T. R. Odhiambo, "Human resources development: problems and prospects in developing countries," *Impact of Science on Society*, No. 155 (1989), p. 214.

[71]*The Statesman's Yearbook 1989*, p. 84; Goliber, "Africa's Expanding Population," p. 15.

[72]*The Statesman's Yearbook 1989*, pp. 1,159–1,160 (certain smaller groups of students are excluded from these totals).

[73]P. Lewis, "Nyere and Tanzania: No Regrets at Socialism," *The New York Times*, October 24, 1990.

[74]"Wind of change, but a different one," *The Economist*, July 14, 1990, p. 44. See also the encouraging noises made—on a country by country basis—in the World Bank's own *Trends in Developing Economies*, 1990, as well as in its 1989 publication *Sub-Saharan Africa: From Crisis to Sustainable Growth* (summarized in "The bleak continent," *The Economist*, pp. 80–81).

[75]See especially P. Pradervand, *Listening to Africa: Developing Africa from the Grassroots* (Greenwood, 1989); B. Schneider, *The Barefoot Revolution* (London: I. T. Publications, 1988); K. McAfee, "Why The Third World Goes Hungry," *Commonweal* June 15, 1990, pp. 384–385.

[76]See Edward Sheehan's article "In the Heart of Somalia," *The New York Review*, January 14, 1993. See also Duncan, "Africa: The Long Good-bye," p. 24; G. Hancock, *Lords of Poverty: The Power, Prestige, and Corruption of the International Aid* (Atlantic Monthly Press, 1989); G.B.N. Ayittey, "No More Aid for Africa," *The Wall Street Journal*, October 18, 1991 (op-ed), p. A14.

[77]Whitaker, *How Can Africa Survive?* p. 231.

[78]See, for example, the conclusions in B. Fischer, "Developing Countries in the Process of Economic Globalisation," pp. 55–63.

[79]Caldwell and Caldwell, "High Fertility in Sub-Saharan Africa," *Scientific American*, p. 88.

[80]"AIDS in Africa," *The Economist*, November 24, 1989, p. 1B; E. Eckholm and J. Tierney, "AIDS in Africa: A Killer Rages On," *The New York Times*, September 16, 1990, pp. 1, 4; C.M. Becker, "The Demo-Economic Impact of the AIDS Pandemic in Sub-Saharan Africa," *World Development*, Vol. 18, No. 12 (1990), pp. 1,599–1,619.

[81]*World Resources 1990–91*, p. 254. The US-Canada total in 1960 was 217 million to Latin America's 210 million; by 2025 it is estimated to be 332 million to 762 million.

[82]*World Resources 1990–91*, p. 254.

[83]Apart from chapters 2 and 4 above, see again *World Resources 1990–91*, pp. 33–48; T. Wicker, "Bush Ventures South," *The New York Times*, December 9, 1990, p. E17; T. Golden, "Mexico Fights Cholera But Hates to Say Its

1. A CLASH OF VIEWS

Name," *The New York Times*, September 14, 1991, p. 2.

[84]"The Arab World," *The Economist*, p. 4.

[85]"The Arab World," p. 6; Y.F. Ibrahim, "In Algeria, Hope for Democracy But Not Economy," *The New York Times*, July 26, 1991, pp. A1, A6.

[86]*World Resources 1990–91*, pp. 258–259.

[87]As quoted in "The Arab World," p. 5.

[88]See again Pradervand, *Listening to Africa*. Also important is D. Pearce et al., *Sustainable Development: Economics and Environment in the Third World* (Gower, 1990).

[89]F. Gable, "Changing Climate and Caribbean Coastlines," *Oceanus*, Vol. 30, No. 4 (Winter 1987–1988), pp. 53–56; G. Gable and D.G. Aubrey, "Changing Climate and the Pacific,"

Oceanus, Vol. 32, No. 4 (Winter 1989–1990), pp. 71–73.

[90]"The Arab World," p. 12.

[91]*World Resources 1990–91*, pp. 176–177; *State of the World 1990*, pp. 48–49.

[92]C. Juma, *The Gene Hunters: Biotechnology and the Scramble for Seeds* (Princeton University Press, 1989).

[93]D. Pirages, *Global Technopolitics: The International Politics of Technology and Resources* (Brooks-Cole, 1989), p. 152.

[94]McAfee, "Why the Third World goes Hungry," p. 380.

[95]See P.K Ghosh, editor, *Technology Policy and Development: A Third World Perspective* (Greenwood, 1984), p. 109.

[96]C.J. Dixon et al., editors, *Multina-

tional Corporations and the Third World* (Croom Helm, 1986).

[97]For a good example, B. Onimode, *A Political Economy of the African Crisis* (Humanities Press International, 1988), especially p. 310 ff.

[98]M. Clash, "Development Policy, Technology Assessment and the New Technologies," *Futures*, November 1990, p. 916.

[99]L. Cuyvers and D. Van den Bulcke, "Some Reflections on the 'Outward-oriented' Development Strategy of the Far Eastern Newly Industrialising Countries," especially pp. 196–197, in Adriaansen and Waardenburg, *A Dual World Economy*.

[100]*World Development Report 1991: The Challenge of Development*, a World Bank report (Oxford University Press, 1991). See also the World Bank's *Global Economic Prospects and the Developing Countries* (1991).

*The two axial principles of our age—tribalism and globalism—clash at every point
except one: they may both be threatening to democracy*

JIHAD VS. MCWORLD

BENJAMIN R. BARBER

*Benjamin R. Barber is the Whitman Professor of Political
Science at Rutgers University. Barber's most recent books
are* Strong Democracy *(1984) and* The Conquest of Politics
(1988): his new book, An Aristocracy of Everyone, *was published
in 1992.*

Just beyond the horizon of current events lie two
possible political figures—both bleak, neither democratic. The first is a retribalization of large swaths of
humankind by war and bloodshed: a threatened Leba-
nonization of national states in which culture is pitted against
culture, people against people, tribe against tribe—a Jihad in
the name of a hundred narrowly conceived faiths against
every kind of interdependence, every kind of artificial social
cooperation and civic mutuality. The second is being borne
in on us by the onrush of economic and ecological forces that
demand integration and uniformity and that mesmerize the
world with fast music, fast computers, and fast food—with
MTV, Macintosh, and McDonald's, pressing nations into one
commercially homogenous global network: one McWorld
tied together by technology, ecology, communications, and
commerce. The planet is falling precipitantly apart *and*
coming reluctantly together at the very same moment.

These two tendencies are sometimes visible in the same
countries at the same instant: thus Yugoslavia, clamoring just
recently to join the New Europe, is exploding into fragments; India is trying to live up to its reputation as the
world's largest integral democracy while powerful new
fundamentalist parties like the Hindu nationalist Bharatiya
Janata Party, along with nationalist assassins, are imperiling
its hard-won unity. States are breaking up or joining up: the
Soviet Union has disappeared almost overnight, its parts
forming new unions with one another or with like-minded
nationalities in neighboring states. The old interwar national
state based on territory and political sovereignty looks to be
a mere transitional development.

The tendencies of what I am here calling the forces of
Jihad and the forces of McWorld operate with equal strength
in opposite directions, the one driven by parochial hatreds,
the other by universalizing markets, the one re-creating
ancient subnational and ethnic borders from within, the other
making national borders porous from without. They have

one thing in common: neither offers much hope to citizens
looking for practical ways to govern themselves democratically. If the global future is to put Jihad's centrifugal
whirlwind against McWorld's centripetal black hole, the
outcome is unlikely to be democratic—or so I will argue.

McWorld, or the Globalization of Politics

FOUR IMPERATIVES MAKE UP THE DYNAMIC OF
McWorld: a market imperative, a resource imperative, an information-technology imperative,
and an ecological imperative. By shrinking the
world and diminishing the salience of national borders,
these imperatives have in combination achieved a considerable victory over factiousness and particularism, and
not least of all over their most virulent traditional form—
nationalism. It is the realists who are now Europeans, the
utopians who dream nostalgically of a resurgent England
or Germany, perhaps even a resurgent Wales or Saxony.
Yesterday's wishful cry for one world has yielded to the
reality of McWorld.

The market imperative. Marxist and Leninist theories of
imperialism assumed that the quest for ever-expanding
markets would in time compel nation-based capitalist
economies to push against national boundaries in search
of an international economic imperium. Whatever else
has happened to the scientist predictions of Marxism, in
this domain they have proved farsighted. All national
economies are now vulnerable to the inroads of larger,
transnational markets within which trade is free, currencies are convertible, access to banking is open, and contracts are enforceable under law. In Europe, Asia, Africa,
the South Pacific, and the Americas such markets are
eroding national sovereignty and giving rise to entities—
international banks, trade associations, transnational lobbies like OPEC and Greenpeace, world news services like
CNN and the BBC, and multinational corporations that
increasingly lack a meaningful national identity—that
neither reflect nor respect nationhood as an organizing or
regulative principle.

The market imperative has also reinforced the quest

for international peace and stability, requisites of an efficient international economy. Markets are enemies of parochialism, isolation, fractiousness, war. Market psychology attenuates the psychology of ideological and religious cleavages and assumes a concord among producers and consumers—categories that ill fit narrowly conceived national or religious cultures. Shopping has little tolerance for blue laws, whether dictated by pub-closing British paternalism, Sabbath-observing Jewish Orthodox fundamentalism, or no-Sunday-liquor-sales Massachusetts puritanism. In the context of common markets, international law ceases to be a vision of justice and becomes a workaday framework for getting things done—enforcing contracts, ensuring that governments abide by deals, regulating trade and currency relations, and so forth.

Common markets demand a common language, as well as a common currency, and they produce common behaviors of the kind bred by cosmopolitan city life everywhere. Commercial pilots, computer programmers, international bankers, media specialists, oil riggers, entertainment celebrities, ecology experts, demographers, accountants, professors, athletes—these compose a new breed of men and women for whom religion, culture, and nationality can seem only marginal elements in a working identity. Although sociologists of everyday life will no doubt continue to distinguish a Japanese from an American mode, shopping has a common signature throughout the world. Cynics might even say that some of the recent revolutions in Eastern Europe have had as their true goal not liberty and the right to vote but well-paying jobs and the right to shop (although the vote is proving easier to acquire than consumer goods). The market imperative is, then, plenty powerful; but, notwithstanding some of the claims made for "democratic capitalism," it is not identical with the democratic imperative.

The resource imperative. Democrats once dreamed of societies whose political autonomy rested firmly on economic independence. The Athenians idealized what they called autarky, and tried for a while to create a way of life simple and austere enough to make the polis genuinely self-sufficient. To be free meant to be independent of any other community or polis. Not even the Athenians were able to achieve autarky, however: human nature, it turns out, is dependency. By the time of Pericles, Athenian politics was inextricably bound up with a flowering empire held together by naval power and commerce—an empire that, even as it appeared to enhance Athenian might, ate away at Athenian independence and autarky. Master and slave, it turned out, were bound together by mutual insufficiency.

The dream of autarky briefly engrossed nineteenth-century America as well, for the underpopulated, endlessly bountiful land, the cornucopia of natural resources, and the natural barriers of a continent walled in by two great seas led many to believe that America could be a world unto itself. Given this past, it has been harder for Americans than for most to accept the inevitability of in-

terdependence. But the rapid depletion of resources even in a country like ours, where they once seemed inexhaustible, and the maldistribution of arable soil and mineral resources on the planet, leave even the wealthiest societies ever more resource-dependent and many other nations in permanently desperate straits.

Every nation, it turns out, needs something another nation has; some nations have almost nothing they need.

The information-technology imperative. Enlightenment science and the technologies derived from it are inherently universalizing. They entail a quest for descriptive principles of general application, a search for universal solutions to particular problems, and an unswerving embrace of objectivity and impartiality.

Scientific progress embodies and depends on open communication, a common discourse rooted in rationality, collaboration, and an easy and regular flow and exchange of information. Such ideals can be hypocritical covers for power-mongering by elites, and they may be shown to be wanting in many other ways, but they are entailed by the very idea of science and they make science and globalization practical allies.

Business, banking, and commerce all depend on information flow and are facilitated by new communication technologies. The hardware of these technologies tends to be systemic and integrated—computer, television, cable, satellite, laser, fiber-optic, and microchip technologies combining to create a vast interactive communications and information network that can potentially give every person on earth access to every other person, and make every datum, every byte, available to every set of eyes. If the automobile was, as George Ball once said (when he gave his blessing to a Fiat factory in the Soviet Union during the Cold War), "an ideology on four wheels," then electronic telecommunication and information systems are an ideology at 186,000 miles per second—which makes for a very small planet in a very big hurry. Individual cultures speak particular languages; commerce and science increasingly speak English; the whole world speaks logarithms and binary mathematics.

Moreover, the pursuit of science and technology asks for, even compels, open societies. Satellite footprints do not respect national borders; telephone wires penetrate the most closed societies. With photocopying and then fax machines having infiltrated Soviet universities and *samizdat* literary circles in the eighties, and computer modems having multiplied like rabbits in communism's bureaucratic warrens thereafter, *glasnost* could not be far behind. In their social requisites, secrecy and science are enemies.

The new technology's software is perhaps even more globalizing than its hardware. The information arm of international commerce's sprawling body reaches out and touches distinct nations and parochial cultures, and gives them a common face chiseled in Hollywood, on Madison Avenue, and in Silicon Valley. Throughout the 1980s one of the most-watched television programs in South Africa was *The Cosby Show*. The demise of apartheid was already in production. Exhibitors at the 1991 Cannes film festival expressed growing anxiety over the "homogenization" and "Americanization" of the global film industry when, for the third year running, American films dominated the awards ceremonies. America has dominated the world's popular culture for much longer, and much more decisively. In November of 1991 Switzerland's once insular culture boasted best-seller lists featuring *Terminator 2* as the No. 1 movie, *Scarlett* as the No. 1 book, and Prince's *Diamonds and Pearls* as the No. 1 record album. No wonder the Japanese are buying Hollywood film studios even faster than Americans are buying Japanese television sets. This kind of software supremacy may in the long term be far more important than hardware superiority, because culture has become more potent than armaments. What is the power of the Pentagon compared with Disneyland? Can the Sixth Fleet keep up with CNN? McDonald's in Moscow and Coke in China will do more to create a global culture than military colonization ever could. It is less the goods than the brand names that do the work, for they convey life-style images that alter perception and challenge behavior. They make up the seductive software of McWorld's common (at times much too common) soul.

Yet in all this high-tech commercial world there is nothing that looks particularly democratic. It lends itself to surveillance as well as liberty, to new forms of manipulation and covert control as well as new kinds of participation, to skewed, unjust market outcomes as well as greater productivity. The consumer society and the open society are not quite synonymous. Capitalism and democracy have a relationship, but it is something less than a marriage. An efficient free market after all requires that consumers be free to vote their dollars on competing goods, not that citizens be free to vote their values and beliefs on competing political candidates and programs. The free market flourished in junta-run Chile, in military-governed Taiwan and Korea, and, earlier, in a variety of autocratic European empires as well as their colonial possessions.

The ecological imperative. The impact of globalization on ecology is a cliché even to world leaders who ignore it. We know well enough that the German forests can be destroyed by Swiss and Italians driving gas-guzzlers fueled by leaded gas. We also know that the planet can be asphyxiated by greenhouse gases because Brazilian farmers want to be part of the twentieth century and are burning down tropical rain forests to clear a little land to plough, and because Indonesians make a living out of converting their lush jungle into toothpicks for fastidious Japanese diners, upsetting the delicate oxygen balance and in effect puncturing our global lungs. Yet this ecological consciousness has meant not only greater awareness but also greater inequality, as modernized nations try to slam the door behind them, saying to developing nations, "The world cannot afford *your* modernization; ours has wrung it dry!"

Each of the four imperatives just cited is transnational,

transideological, and transcultural. Each applies impartially to Catholics, Jews, Muslims, Hindus, and Buddhists; to democrats and totalitarians; to capitalists and socialists. The Enlightenment dream of a universal rational society has to a remarkable degree been realized—but in a form that is commercialized, homogenized, depoliticized, bureaucratized, and, of course, radically incomplete, for the movement toward McWorld is in competition with forces of global breakdown, national dissolution, and centrifugal corruption. These forces, working in the opposite direction, are the essence of what I call Jihad.

Jihad, or the Lebanonization of the World

OPEC, THE WORLD BANK, THE UNITED NATIONS, the International Red Cross, the multinational corporation . . . there are scores of institutions that reflect globalization. But they often appear as ineffective reactors to the world's real actors: national states and, to an ever greater degree, subnational factions in permanent rebellion against uniformity and integration—even the kind represented by universal law and justice. The headlines feature these players regularly: they are cultures, not countries; parts, not wholes; sects, not religions; rebellious factions and dissenting minorities at war not just with globalism but with the traditional nation-state. Kurds, Basques, Puerto Ricans, Ossetians, East Timoreans, Quebecois, the Catholics of Northern Ireland, Abkhasians, Kurile Islander Japanese, the Zulus of Inkatha, Catalonians, Tamils, and, of course, Palestinians—people without countries, inhabiting nations not their own, seeking smaller worlds within borders that will seal them off from modernity.

A powerful irony is at work here. Nationalism was once a force of integration and unification, a movement aimed at bringing together disparate clans, tribes, and cultural fragments under new, assimilationist flags. But as Ortega y Gasset noted more than sixty years ago, having won its victories, nationalism changed its strategy. In the 1920s, and again today, it is more often a reactionary and divisive force, pulverizing the very nations it once helped cement together. The force that creates nations is "inclusive," Ortega wrote in *The Revolt of the Masses.* "In periods of consolidation, nationalism has a positive value, and is a lofty standard. But in Europe everything is more than consolidated, and nationalism is nothing but a mania. . . ."

This mania has left the post–Cold War world smoldering with hot wars; the international scene is little more unified than it was at the end of the Great War, in Ortega's own time. There were more than thirty wars in progress last year, most of them ethnic, racial, tribal, or religious in character, and the list of unsafe regions doesn't seem to be getting any shorter. Some new world order!

The aim of many of these small-scale wars is to redraw boundaries, to implode states and resecure parochial identities: to escape McWorld's dully insistent imperatives. The mood is that of Jihad: war not as an instrument of policy but as an emblem of identity, an expression of community, an end in itself. Even where there is no shooting war, there is fractiousness, secession, and the quest for ever smaller communities. Add to the list of dangerous countries those at risk: In Switzerland and Spain, Jurassian and Basque separatists still argue the virtues of ancient identities, sometimes in the language of bombs. Hyperdisintegration in the former Soviet Union may well continue unabated—not just a Ukraine independent from the Soviet Union but a Bessarabian Ukraine independent from the Ukrainian republic; not just Russia severed from the defunct union but Tatarstan severed from Russia. Yugoslavia makes even the disunited, ex-Soviet, nonsocialist republics that were once the Soviet Union look integrated, its sectarian fatherlands springing up within factional motherlands like weeds within weeds within weeds. Kurdish independence would threaten the territorial integrity of four Middle Eastern nations. Well before the current cataclysm Soviet Georgia made a claim for autonomy from the Soviet Union, only to be faced with its Ossetians (164,000 in a republic of 5.5 million) demanding their own self-determination within Georgia. The Abkhasian minority in Georgia has followed suit. Even the good will established by Canada's once promising Meech Lake protocols is in danger, with Francophone Quebec again threatening the dissolution of the federation. In South Africa the emergence from apartheid was hardly achieved when friction between Inkatha's Zulus and the African National Congress's tribally identified members threatened to replace Europeans' racism with an indigenous tribal war. After thirty years of attempted integration using the colonial language (English) as a unifier, Nigeria is now playing with the idea of linguistic multiculturalism—which could mean the cultural breakup of the nation into hundreds of tribal fragments. Even Saddam Hussein has benefited from the threat of internal Jihad, having used renewed tribal and religious warfare to turn last season's mortal enemies into reluctant allies of an Iraqi nationhood that he nearly destroyed.

The passing of communism has torn away the thin veneer of internationalism (workers of the world unite!) to reveal ethnic prejudices that are not only ugly and deepseated but increasingly murderous. Europe's old scourge, anti-Semitism, is back with a vengeance, but it is only one of many antagonisms. It appears all too easy to throw the historical gears into reverse and pass from a Communist dictatorship back into a tribal state.

Among the tribes, religion is also a battlefield. ("Jihad" is a rich word whose generic meaning is "struggle"—usually the struggle of the soul to avert evil. Strictly applied to religious war, it is used only in reference to battles where the faith is under assault, or battles against a government that denies the practice of Islam. My use here is rhetorical, but does follow both journalistic practice and history.) Remember the Thirty Years War? Whatever forms of Enlightenment universalism might once have come to grace such historically related forms of monotheism as Judaism, Christianity, and Islam, in many of their modern incarnations they are parochial rather than cosmopolitan, angry rather than loving, proselytizing rather than ecumenical, zealous rather than rationalist, sectarian rather than deistic, ethnocentric rather than universalizing. As a result, like the new forms of hypernationalism, the new expressions of religious fundamentalism are fractious and pulverizing, never integrating. This is religion as the Crusaders knew it: a battle to the death for souls that if not saved will be forever lost.

The atmospherics of Jihad have resulted in a breakdown of civility in the name of identity, of comity in the name of community. International relations have sometimes taken on the aspect of gang war—cultural turf battles featuring tribal factions that were supposed to be sublimated as integral parts of large national, economic, postcolonial, and constitutional entities.

The Darkening Future of Democracy

THESE RATHER MELODRAMATIC TABLEAUX VI-vants do not tell the whole story, however. For all their defects, Jihad and McWorld have their attractions. Yet, to repeat and insist, the attractions are unrelated to democracy. Neither McWorld nor Jihad is remotely democratic in impulse. Neither needs democracy; neither promotes democracy.

McWorld does manage to look pretty seductive in a world obsessed with Jihad. It delivers peace, prosperity, and relative unity—if at the cost of independence, community, and identity (which is generally based on difference). The primary political values required by the global market are order and tranquillity, and freedom—as in the phrases "free trade," "free press," and "free love." Human rights are needed to a degree, but not citizenship or participation—and no more social justice and equality than are necessary to promote efficient economic production and consumption. Multinational corporations sometimes seem to prefer doing business with local oligarchs, inasmuch as they can take confidence from dealing with the boss on all crucial matters. Despots who slaughter their own populations are no problem, so long as they leave markets in place and refrain from making war on their neighbors (Saddam Hussein's fatal mistake). In trading partners, predictability is of more value than justice.

The Eastern European revolutions that seemed to arise out of concern for global democratic values quickly deteriorated into a stampede in the general direction of free markets and their ubiquitous, television-promoted shopping malls. East Germany's Neues Forum, that courageous gathering of intellectuals, students, and workers which overturned the Stalinist regime in Berlin in 1989, lasted only six months in Germany's mini-version of McWorld. Then it gave way to money and markets and monopolies from the West. By the time of the first all-German elections, it could scarcely manage to secure three percent of the vote. Elsewhere there is growing evidence that *glasnost* will go and *perestroika*—defined as privatization and an opening of markets to Western bidders—will stay. So understandably anxious are the new rulers of Eastern Europe and whatever entities are forged from the residues of the Soviet Union to gain access to credit and markets and technology—McWorld's flourishing new currencies—that they have shown themselves willing to trade away democratic prospects in pursuit of them: not just old totalitarian ideologies and command-economy production models but some possible indigenous experiments with a third way between capitalism and socialism, such as economic cooperatives and employee stock-ownership plans, both of which have their ardent supporters in the East.

Jihad delivers a different set of virtues: a vibrant local identity, a sense of community, solidarity among kinsmen, neighbors, and countrymen, narrowly conceived. But it also guarantees parochialism and is grounded in exclusion. Solidarity is secured through war against outsiders. And solidarity often means obedience to a hierarchy in governance, fanaticism in beliefs, and the obliteration of individual selves in the name of the group. Deference to leaders and intolerance toward outsiders (and toward "enemies within") are hallmarks of tribalism—hardly the attitudes required for the cultivation of new democratic women and men capable of governing themselves. Where new democratic experiments have been conducted in retribalizing societies, in both Europe and the Third World, the result has often been anarchy, repression, persecution, and the coming of new, noncommunist forms of very old kinds of despotism. During the past year, Havel's velvet revolution in Czechoslovakia was imperiled by partisans of "Czechland" and of Slovakia as independent entities. India seemed little less rent by Sikh, Hindu, Muslim, and Tamil infighting than it was immediately after the British pulled out, more than forty years ago.

To the extent that either McWorld or Jihad has a *natural* politics, it has turned out to be more of an antipolitics. For McWorld, it is the antipolitics of globalism: bureaucratic, technocratic, and meritocratic, focused (as Marx predicted it would be) on the administration of things—with people, however, among the chief things to be administered. In its politico-economic imperatives McWorld has been guided by laissez-faire market principles that privilege efficiency, productivity, and beneficence at the expense of civic liberty and self-government.

For Jihad, the antipolitics of tribalization has been explicitly antidemocratic: one-party dictatorship, government by military junta, theocratic fundamentalism—often associated with a version of the *Führerprinzip* that empowers an individual to rule on behalf of a people. Even the government of India, struggling for decades to model democracy for a people who will soon number a billion, longs for great leaders; and for every Mahatma Gandhi, Indira Gandhi, or Rajiv Gandhi taken from them

by zealous assassins, the Indians appear to seek a replacement who will deliver them from the lengthy travail of their freedom.

The Confederal Option

HOW CAN DEMOCRACY BE SECURED AND SPREAD in a world whose primary tendencies are at best indifferent to it (McWorld) and at worst deeply antithetical to it (Jihad)? My guess is that globalization will eventually vanquish retribalization. The ethos of material "civilization" has not yet encountered an obstacle it has been unable to thrust aside. Ortega may have grasped in the 1920s a clue to our own future in the coming millennium.

> Everyone sees the need of a new principle of life. But as always happens in similar crises—some people attempt to save the situation by an artificial intensification of the very principle which has led to decay. This is the meaning of the "nationalist" outburst of recent years. . . . things have always gone that way. The last flare, the longest; the last sigh, the deepest. On the very eve of their disappearance there is an intensification of frontiers—military and economic.

Jihad may be a last deep sigh before the eternal yawn of McWorld. On the other hand, Ortega was not exactly prescient; his prophecy of peace and internationalism came just before blitzkrieg, world war, and the Holocaust tore the old order to bits. Yet democracy is how we remonstrate with reality, the rebuke our aspirations offer to history. And if retribalization is inhospitable to democracy, there is nonetheless a form of democratic government that can accommodate parochialism and communitarianism, one that can even save them from their defects and make them more tolerant and participatory: decentralized participatory democracy. And if McWorld is indifferent to democracy, there is nonetheless a form of democratic government that suits global markets passably well—representative government in its federal or, better still, confederal variation.

With its concern for accountability, the protection of minorities, and the universal rule of law, a confederalized representative system would serve the political needs of McWorld as well as oligarchic bureaucratism or meritocratic elitism is currently doing. As we are already beginning to see, many nations may survive in the long term only as confederations that afford local regions smaller than "nations" extensive jurisdiction. Recommended reading for democrats of the twenty-first century is not the U.S. Constitution or the French Declaration of Rights of Man and Citizen but the Articles of Confederation, that suddenly pertinent document that stitched together the thirteen American colonies into what then seemed a too loose confederation of independent states but now appears a new form of political realism, as veterans of Yeltsin's new Russia and the new Europe created at Maastricht will attest.

1. A CLASH OF VIEWS

By the same token, the participatory and direct form of democracy that engages citizens in civic activity and civic judgment and goes well beyond just voting and accountability—the system I have called "strong democracy"—suits the political needs of decentralized communities as well as theocratic and nationalist party dictatorships have done. Local neighborhoods need not be democratic, but they can be. Real democracy has flourished in diminutive settings: the spirit of liberty, Tocqueville said, is local. Participatory democracy, if not naturally apposite to tribalism, has an undeniable attractiveness under conditions of parochialism.

Democracy in any of these variations will, however, continue to be obstructed by the undemocratic and antidemocratic trends toward uniformitarian globalism and intolerant retribalization which I have portrayed here. For democracy to persist in our brave new McWorld, we will have to commit acts of conscious political will—a possibility, but hardly a probability, under these conditions. Political will requires much more than the quick fix of the transfer of institutions. Like technology transfer, institution transfer rests on foolish assumptions about a uniform world of the kind that once fired the imagination of colonial administrators. Spread English justice to the colonies by exporting wigs. Let an East Indian trading company act as the vanguard to Britain's free parliamentary institutions. Today's well-intentioned quick-fixers in the National Endowment for Democracy and the Kennedy School of Government, in the unions and foundations and universities zealously nurturing contacts in Eastern Europe and the Third World, are hoping to democratize by long distance. Post Bulgaria a parliament by first-class mail. Fed Ex the Bill of Rights to Sri Lanka. Cable Cambodia some common law.

Yet Eastern Europe has already demonstrated that importing free political parties, parliaments, and presses cannot establish a democratic civil society; imposing a free market may even have the opposite effect. Democracy grows from the bottom up and cannot be imposed from the top down. Civil society has to be built from the inside out. The institutional superstructure comes last.

Poland may become democratic, but then again it may heed the Pope, and prefer to found its politics on its Catholicism, with uncertain consequences for democracy. Bulgaria may become democratic, but it may prefer tribal war. The former Soviet Union may become a democratic confederation, or it may just grow into an anarchic and weak conglomeration of markets for other nations' goods and services.

Democrats need to seek out indigenous democratic impulses. There is always a desire for self-government, always some expression of participation, accountability, consent, and representation, even in traditional hierarchical societies. These need to be identified, tapped, modified, and incorporated into new democratic practices with an indigenous flavor. The tortoises among the democratizers may ultimately outlive or outpace the hares, for they will have the time and patience to explore conditions along the way, and to adapt their gait to changing circumstances. Tragically, democracy in a hurry often looks something like France in 1794 or China in 1989.

It certainly seems possible that the most attractive democratic ideal in the face of the brutal realities of Jihad and the dull realities of McWorld will be a confederal union of semi-autonomous communities smaller than nation-states, tied together into regional economic associations and markets larger than nation-states—participatory and self-determining in local matters at the bottom, representative and accountable at the top. The nation-state would play a diminished role, and sovereignty would lose some of its political potency. The Green movement adage "Think globally, act locally" would actually come to describe the conduct of politics.

This vision reflects only an ideal, however—one that is not terribly likely to be realized. Freedom, Jean-Jacques Rousseau once wrote, is a food easy to eat but hard to digest. Still, democracy has always played itself out against the odds. And democracy remains both a form of coherence as binding as McWorld and a secular faith potentially as inspiriting as Jihad.

The New World Economic Order

Economic Time Zones: Fast Versus Slow

Alvin and Heidi Toffler

Futurists Alvin and Heidi Toffler are co-authors of Future Shock, The Third Wave, *and most recently* Powershift.

In the next century, the great danger for humanity will not be the conflict between East and West, or even between North and South. It will be the decoupling of the fast world from the slow world.

As time itself has become a critical factor of production, the wealth gap has grown rapidly between societies whose accelerative economies are driven by knowledge and advanced technology and those societies whose economies are mired in traditional agriculture or bureaucratic smokestack industry.

Economic processes in *third wave* knowledge-driven societies are accelerating, while those in *first wave* agricultural societies and *second wave* industrial societies are lagging or stagnating. This gap in relative speed is widening.

As Ryszard Kapuscinksi has written, "By the beginning of the next century, there may be completely different worlds on the same planet. Unlike the vision we all held thirty years ago,

the world is not converging, but spreading apart like the galaxies."

And time itself is a key force driving us apart. Because of the new information technologies, the old adage, "Time is money," is now obsolete. In the new accelerated system of wealth creation, it is being superseded by a new hidden law of economics in which time is no longer just money. Now each unit of saved time is actually worth more money than the last unit. The faster economic processes work, the more wealth is created in the same period with the same or even fewer resources.

The bar code on a pack of cigarettes, the computer in the Federal Express truck, the scanner at the supermarket checkout counter, robots with remote sensors on the assembly line, the electronic transfer of capital — all presage a twenty-first-century economy that will operate at nearly real-time, or instantaneous, speeds.

The feedback loop between producer and consumer is nearly immediate. Thus, overnight, mail companies can locate your package by computer anywhere at any time. Fickle fashion trends can be changed many times a year while

From *New Perspectives Quarterly,* Vol. 8, No. 4, Fall 1991, pp. 56-58. © 1991 by The Center for the Study of Democratic Institutions. Reprinted by permission.

keeping inventories low. For example, Haggar Apparel of Dallas is now able to restock its twenty-five hundred retail customers with slacks every three days instead of every seven weeks, as it once did.

This new system of wealth creation consists of an expanding global network of markets, banks, production centers, and laboratories in instant communication with one another, constantly exchanging huge flows of data and knowledge.

To be decoupled from this fast economy is to be excluded from the future.

If the poorer regions of the planet, from the third world to the post-communist East, continue to build economies based on cheap labor, raw materials, or clunky smokestack production, the future will pass them by.

Indeed, because of the acceleration of production, cheap labor is becoming expensive. Ford Motor Company recently brought a truck manufacturing plant back from Brazil to the United States because, despite the low labor costs, it took six months to manufacture a truck in Brazil compared to only forty-five days in the United States.

Similarly, a children's sleepwear designer based in Pennsylvania recently decided against manufacturing clothes in China because, despite paying the world's lowest wages, the Chinese ability to meet delivery deadlines is unreliable. The designer delivers hundreds of thousands of units of clothing to JC Penny, K-Mart and Sears, but if delivery is late by even one day the retailers refuse to accept the shipment. That is because one week small children want bunnies on their pajamas, and the next week they want bears. Consumer tastes, on which volume sales depend, change too rapidly to rely on China's slow and unreliable production.

But it is not only fashion that changes swiftly. So do high-technology products, from microchips to laser tools. As the new system of wealth creation spreads, labor costs shrink dramatically. In some advanced industries today, labor costs represent only 10 percent of the total cost of production. Far greater savings can be found through better technology, faster information flows, and streamlined organization than by squeezing workers. Low-wage muscle is no longer much of a competitive advantage in the emerging world economy.

Any slow country that wants to participate in tomorrow's global economy must make it a priority to couple electronically to the fast world.

The slow tempo of decision making in such places as China and the Soviet Union is also a reason for the collapse of many joint ventures. The endless negotiations and glacial pace of the bureaucratic chain of economic command kill deals regularly between fast and slow partners.

The slow world's raw materials are also devalued by accelerated production, which relies more on inputs of scientific innovation, knowledge, and organization than energy or other natural resources.

An example: In the future, superconductivity will radically reduce the need for energy by reducing losses during transmission. The experience of Japan's high-speed economy has already made this point clearly: In 1984 Japan consumed only 60 percent of the raw material required for the same volume of industrial output in 1973.

If catatonic agrarian societies and stagnant smokestack societies are to avoid becoming marginalized spectators of the future, perpetuating their misery, they will have to revolutionize their concepts of development.

Any slow country that wants to participate in tomorrow's global economy must make it a priority to couple electronically to the fast world. That not only means telephones but also computers, fax machines, satellites, fiber-optic communication systems, and other electronic networks. At least part of the population — the cities, the elites, and the manufacturing sector — must be linked electronically to the outside world.

Though this partial approach may be the most viable development strategy, and thus the one most likely to be followed, it raises another specter. In slow places like China or Africa, which are so weighed down by their agrarian masses, the global decoupling of fast and slow may be reproduced internally. While advanced sectors in Shanghai or Cairo may become coupled to the world economy, billions of peasants might remain technologically and politically decoupled in their own country.

But the problems of the slow world can never be completely decoupled from the well-being of the fast world. New links must be forged to avoid global conflict between those inside and those outside the accelerated economy.

The maldistribution of telecommunications in today's world is even more dramatic than the maldistribution of food. Of the 600 million telephones in the world, 450 million of them are located in nine countries. The lopsided distribution of computers, data bases, technical publications and research expenditures tells us more about the future potential of nations than all the gross national product figures ground out by economists.

The next century can be a promising one for all — but only if we see to it that the slow world is plugged into the fast one, closing the informational and electronic gap.

(United Nations Chen/jr)

The consumer market of western societies is demanding and fickle. The success of a product is most often a question of timing; if that product is manufactured in a country that is unable to meet a demanding delivery schedule, for whatever reason, marketers will not accept delivery. The shirts being made in this photo in China must reach their final destination on time or the manufacturer may suffer an economic disruption. The future of a new world economic order depends on a good working relationship between manufacturing and marketing.

Global Unemployment At 700 Million

Why global unemployment, and what to do about it

Jeremy Brecher

This September, hundreds of workers in the southern Italian town of Crotone, learning that their chemical factory would be closed, occupied the plant, poured barrels of phosphorous on roads and set it afire, stoned police officers who sought to storm the plant, and then barricaded themselves in the factory. The Roman Catholic Bishop of Crotone joined the workers and said, "We're becoming like dry branches, and every job lost is a great injustice." A 38-year-old electrician unfurled a banner from the plant's smokestack reading, "I have a family, I want work" and threatened to hurl himself off if his job was not restored. As in the past, so today unemployment is social dynamite.

No concept in Karl Marx' critique of capitalism was more bitterly ironic than the notion that the system produced a "relative surplus population." While the conventional economics of his day (as, once again, of ours) held that prolonged mass unemployment was a theoretical impossibility, Marx maintained that a "reserve army of labor" was a normal—indeed a necessary—feature of capitalism. That people could be "surplus" relative to the system underlined the perversity of a system which defined people who lacked property as "unproductive" unless they could serve as a means for those with property to make a profit.

It's too bad the heralded "global triumph of capitalism" can't consign to the dustbin of history the evils Marx described as readily as it does the beliefs he championed. Unfortunately, the fruit of the "global triumph of capitalism" has been a rapidly expanding "global surplus population." In Europe and Canada unemployment has surged to 11 percent; it is at historic highs in Japan; it probably runs from 20 to 40 percent in most ex-Communist countries. In the United States, unemployment remains near its recession peak after several years of "jobless recovery"; more than 400,000 layoffs have been announced since January 1; more than 60 percent of the new jobs that have been created in 1993 are part-time. For the 24 industrialized countries of the OECD, the official unemployment rate is 8.5 percent—a "reserve army" of 35 million. According to United Nations estimates, there are some 700 million people currently unemployed or underemployed in the "developing world."

This summer, President Clinton quite unexpectedly acknowledged that there was a "global crisis of unemployment." On his way to Tokyo for the annual meeting of the Group of Seven (the G-7 or "Rich Men's Club"), he noted that "All the advanced nations are having difficulty creating new jobs, even when their economies are growing... We have to figure out how to unlock the doors for people who are left behind in this new global economy."

The G-7 accepted his call for a "jobs summit" this fall to consider what to do about it.

When President Clinton called for such a conference, the *New York Times* reported that "Some officials fear that the meeting could prove risky" because it will "focus public attention on a nagging problem that the President cannot possibly solve quickly." The conference may also provide an opportunity for those who

From *Z Magazine*, November 1993, pp. 45-48. © 1993 by Jeremy Breecher. Reprinted by permission.

wish to "focus public attention" on the downsides of the "new global economy" and the needs and demands of its victims.

The Fruits of Triumph

Under such banners as "supply-side economics," "neoliberalism," "monetarism," "free trade," and "deregulation," countries all over the world have dismantled long-established vehicles for fighting unemployment. Over the past dozen years they have cut public employment, abandoned Keynesian growth management, forced poor countries to accept austerity "structural adjustment" plans, and promoted international economic agreements to impose world-wide deregulation.

These policies have proved a disaster. Global GNP growth has slowed from almost 5 percent per year from 1948-1973 to only half that in 1974-89 and to a mere crawl since then. The failure is even greater when we include such non-GNP factors as degradation of the world's earth, air, and water and the growing gap between rich and poor within and between countries. Unemployment is one "bottom line" of this disaster.

Mass unemployment is nothing new. The entire history of capitalist economies has been marked by rapid growth alternating with recessions and depressions—and unemployment. To counter these, capitalist governments created non-market structures, notably central banking to regulate money and credit and Keynesian policies of government spending to stimulate stagnating economies.

Such national non-market structures contributed to the unprecedented period of sustained growth from World War II to the early 1970s. But over the past two decades the nation as an economic unit has been undermined by the "globalization" of corporations, markets, finance, banking, transportation, communication, and production. As a result, classic problems of capitalism have reasserted themselves on a global scale—without the corrective of compensating national policies.

As Keynesian remedies failed in the face of a globalizing economy, a wide consensus formed around a simple but dubious formula: Each country should reduce costs for labor and government in order to become "more competitive" in the global economy. All will benefit because goods and services will be provided by those whose "comparative advantage" enables them to produce more cheaply.

The real result is that workers and communities all over the world are being put into ruinous competition. Transnational corporations invest where they are offered the lowest labor and environmental costs—causing a "race to the bottom" in wages and environmental conditions.

This in turn has generated a downward global spiral. As each workforce, community, or country seeks to become "more competitive" by reducing wages and social and environmental overheads, their incomes fall and their social and physical infrastructures deteriorate. Low wages and reduced public spending mean less buying power, leading to inadequate demand—and rising unemployment.

This "global crisis of unemployment" has a multitude of ramifications. Most obvious are the various forms of misery it generates. In poor communities in the United States, real unemployment often exceeds 40 percent and infant mortality surpasses that of many third world countries. In the former Communist countries, national incomes have generally fallen twice as far as the United States's did between the peak of the boom in 1929 and the pit of the Great Depression in 1933. In Africa, many families have stopped visiting relatives suffering from AIDS because they're ashamed that they can't afford to buy them aspirin to ease their pain.

The economic crisis is causing political crisis. It is doubtful that any of the leaders who came to the G-7 summit had support in the opinion polls from a majority of their own people. The various political crises and regime instabilities in Japan, France, Germany, Italy, Canada, the United Kingdom and the United States—seemingly due to unrelated local factors—are actually in considerable part results of the global economic crisis. They also make that crisis more difficult to resolve.

Mass unemployment is also generating racism and extremist nationalism around the world. From the skinheads of Germany to the "culture war" of Pat Buchanan, economic problems are being blamed not on the economic system or those who control it but on racial, ethnic, religious, and national scapegoats. Like fascism in the 1930s, this provides a threat not only to those directly attacked, but to the whole of society—including those politicians and business leaders who play footsie with it.

Non-Solutions

Official economists have begun to acknowledge that we are in a "jobless recovery" and that the very drives for "productivity" and "globalization" promoted by the free marketeers are also major causes of global joblessness. According to the *New York Times*, "officials on both sides of the Atlantic" say unemployment is high because "technical change is displacing so many workers" and because of "heightened foreign competition, especially from developing countries." Laura D'Andrea Tyson, head of President Clinton's Council of Economic Advisors, adds that "Globalization has depressed the wage growth of low-wage workers" and has been a reason for "the increasing wage gap between high-wage and low-wage workers."

Yet the "solutions" proposed at the G-7 Summit would leave these problems untouched or even aggravate them. Its communiques talked about greater investment in education and training—at a time when Ph.d's around the world struggle for the opportunity to drive a taxi and the graduates of elite U.S. colleges clean houses and wait on table. And they called for greater "wage flexibility" and the re-examination of social insurance programs that "unduly discourage employment creation." (Perhaps they should have gone further and called for the abolition of all wages and benefits—after all, employers would hire all the unemployed if they didn't have to pay them.)

Meanwhile, each country attempts to solve its own economic problems by increasing exports—with intensified global competition and global glut as the inevitable though unintended consequence. And despite the recession, most countries are attempting to deflate their own economies—witness this year's U.S. budget, which jettisoned even a modest "economic stimulus package" and instead devoted all resources to "deficit reduction."

Solutions

The solution to this downward spiral is neither austerity in pursuit of national competitiveness nor protectionism in pursuit of national autarky. Rather, just as national economies once developed non-market structures for economic governance at a national level, so today our global economy needs a new governance structure at the global level.

To design a new governance structure for the global economy we should look at three historical models:

(1) *Domestic economic regulation*. The tools of monetary and fiscal policy did much to counter recessions and depressions within national economies. So did minimum labor standards, welfare state programs, collective bargaining, and other means to raise the purchasing power of have-nots. Similar instruments for providing economic stimulus and increasing the buying power of those at the bottom are now required in the global economy.

(2) *The Bretton Woods system*. As World War II drew to a close the victorious powers, fearing a return of world depression, established the International Monetary Fund. It set exchange rates so as to allow member countries to use fiscal and monetary policy to pursue full employment—contributing to the nearly 5 percent growth rate of 1948-1973.

This system eventually failed because it was built around a single currency (the dollar)—a flaw that an updated "Bretton Woods" system would need to avoid. But it did succeed for more than 20 years in preventing the drive for international competitiveness from generating a global downward spiral of the kind we face today.

(3) *The North-South Dialogue*. As the Bretton Woods system was breaking down, the United Nations Conference on Trade and Development initiated a "North-South Dialogue" with the goal of establishing a "New International Economic Order." The third world countries which promoted the Dialogue did not propose to replace capitalism, but they did insist that global market forces be managed to support the development of poorer countries. After several rounds of North-South discussions, newly-elected U.S. President Ronald Reagan scuttled the entire process.

Whatever the weaknesses of its specific proposals, the North-South dialogue indicates the kind of international political process required to create a new governance structure for the global economy. This structure cannot simply represent the world's wealthiest; it must have a structured position for the overwhelming majority of the world who are poor, represented by their governments, popular movements, and other nongovernmental organizations.

The dilemma for national labor and social movements is that any national policy to increase employment will lead to negative consequences for a country's position in the global economy. Even if a political movement representing working and poor people came to power, it would face this same dilemma. If it attempted to break out of the global downward spiral by itself, it would face drastic trade imbalance, currency collapse, and capital flight. Our goal must be to transform the transnational, not just the national, economy.

The first step toward building a new structure to govern the global economy should be to junk the policies that have bred the global crisis of unemployment. The impending "jobs summit" could serve as a good vehicle for labor movements and other non-governmental organizations to focus public attention on the failure of present policies and to kick off the discussion of alternatives.

One model might be the gatherings of non-governmental organizations from around the world which have been held regularly at the G-7 Summit and the World Bank-IMF annual meetings for the past several years. At the same time as this summer's G-7 meeting, for example, 400 grassroots activists from many countries held an "alternative summit" in a Tokyo suburb. Speakers argued that the G-7 and international economic institutions like the International Monetary Fund, World Bank, and General Agreement on Tariffs and Trade served the interests of the wealthy and of multinational corporations at the expense of ordinary people.

A similar counter-meeting at the "global jobs summit" could serve as the starting point for dramatizing the global unemployment crisis—and for pointing out where real solutions lie. It could bring together labor movements, NGOs, and representatives of the unemployed themselves to redefine the issues both for their own countries and globally. For the labor movement it would provide an opportunity to build bridges—both internationally and to potential allies.

This April, almost unreported in the U.S. press, more than a million Europeans took part in coordinated demonstrations in 150 cities to protest rising unemployment. From London to Rome, workers staged work stoppages to call attention to the loss of jobs.

Could the G-7 summit on the global crisis of unemployment serve as the occasion to hold similar demonstrations on a global basis? Perhaps not. But it certainly can serve as an opportunity to challenge the policies that have bred this global crisis and to demand the building of a new structure to govern the global economy.

Population

The world's population situation is not restricted to rapid growth and too many people. In some areas, governments do not believe there are enough people. In the oil-rich Gulf states (e.g., Saudi Arabia), governments pursue a high birthrate policy. Large numbers of foreign workers have immigrated to these countries to work in the oil fields and at other, related projects. Consequently, the governments are pursuing policies that encourage large families so that eventually their own population will be able to replace the foreign workers.

Population demographics also vary a great deal from nonindustrial countries to the industrially developed nations. In North America and Western Europe, women, on the average, are having two children or less. Population in the United States is growing primarily because people are immigrating into the country, not because people are having large families.

In 1987 global population reached 5 billion, a gain of 2 billion people in just 27 years. The lead article in the section provides an overview of the dynamics of demography. Explosive population growth and massive migration from the countryside are creating cities that dwarf the great capitals of the past. By 2000 there will be several "megacities" with populations of 10 million or more. Most of these will be in developing countries.

The section continues with a discussion of contending perspectives on the implications of population growth. Some experts view population growth as the major problem facing the world, while others see it as secondary to social, economic, and political problems. This theme of contending views, in short, has been carried forward from the introductory section of the book to the more specific discussion of population.

This broad discussion is followed by a series of articles that examine specific issues such as the movement of people from the Third World to industrial nations. Much of contemporary international trade policy and the movement toward regional trading blocs has at its foundation a concern about this migration. The European Community's 1992 market integration and the North American Free Trade Agreement are both responses in varying degrees to this issue. In addition, the migration issue raises many questions that go beyond purely economic considerations. How does a culture maintain its identity when it must absorb large numbers of new people? Where will a government obtain the resources necessary to integrate these new members into the mainstream of society?

As the world approaches the next century, there are many population issues that transcend numerical and economic issues. The future of indigenous people is a good example of the pressures of population growth and the future of people who live on the margins of modern society. The loss of these distinct groups diminishes not only our cultural heritage but important knowledge also will be lost about native systems of health care and so forth. Finally, the spread of AIDS looms like a dark cloud over many regions of the world. Every person in the world needs to be well-informed about this growing epidemic.

Making predictions about the future of the world's population is a complicated matter, for there are a variety of forces at work and considerable variation from region to region. The danger of oversimplification must be overcome if governments and international organizations are going to respond with meaningful positions and policies.

Looking Ahead: Challenge Questions

What are the basic characteristics of the global population situation? How many people are there? How fast is the population growing?

How do population dynamics vary from one region to the next?

What regions of the world are attracting large numbers of international immigrants?

How does rapid population growth affect the environment, social structures, and the ways in which humanity views itself?

How does a rapidly growing population affect a Third World country's development plans?

How can economic and social policies be changed to reduce the impact of population growth on the quality of the environment?

In an era of global interdependence, is it possible for individual governments to have much impact on demographic changes?

What would be the political implications if the United States decided to end immigration?

Unit 2

MEGACITIES

By the millions they come, the ambitious and the downtrodden of the world drawn by the strange magnetism of urban life. For centuries the progress of civilization has been defined by the inexorable growth of cities. Now the world is about to pass a milestone: more people will live in urban ares than in the countryside. Does the growth of megacities portend an apocalypse of global epidemics and pollution? Or will the remarkable stirrings of self-reliance that can be found in some of them point the way to their salvation?

EUGENE LINDEN

KINSHASA, ZAIRE—HOME TO 4 million people—is no place to live. The city's social fabric has been fraying for years, but in September 1991 it started to unravel completely. The crisis began when a group of élite government troops, angry because they had not been paid for months, went on a looting spree that was quickly joined by civilians. During the next few days, nearly $1 billion worth of property, from clothes to computers, was pillaged. After the rampage, foreign businessmen—and foreign money—fled the city. The economy collapsed. Since the government now has almost no money to buy supplies and spare parts from abroad, all the services that make urban life bearable are breaking down. Buses and trains stall, fuel supplies are uncertain, electricity is unreliable and water quality is in jeopardy.

To the people of Kinshasa, the chaos brings much more than inconvenience and financial loss. The real threats are epidemics and starvation. Antibiotics and other medicines are scarce, and diseases such as malaria and tuberculosis are spreading rapidly. Strikes and sabotage by disgruntled workers hamper the flow of flour, vegetables and manioc to the city.

For Jonas Mutongi Kashama, whose well-kept, one-room home belies his desperate straits, the disintegration of Kinshasa means that for long periods his family must subsist on one meal every two days. Mutongi is actually one of the lucky ones, since, after six months of unemployment, he found work as an accountant. Even so, with the jobless rate at 80%, he must support out-of-work relatives on a tiny salary that is constantly eroded by an annual hyperinflation rate of more than 3,000%. "If things do not change, we will die," says Mutongi with quiet resignation.

"Is Kinshasa an aberration or rather a sign of things to come?" asks Timothy Weiskel, a Harvard anthropologist. His answer: Many of today's cities will go the way of Kinshasa. After all, he points out, the rise and fall of great cities has been part of civilization's cycle since humans first began to congregate in large numbers some 6,000 years ago.

Then there is Curitiba, Brazil, a surprisingly good place for 2.2 million people to live. It has slums and shantytowns, just like Kinshasa. But Curitiba's government has relied on imagination, commonsense planning and determination to deliver enviable services, including a bus system that quickly gets people where they want to go and public housing projects that are still immaculate 20 years after being built.

If Curitiba has a theme, it is self-reliance. The city is not rich, but it makes the most of the resources it has. Recycling, for example, is practically a religion. Jogging paths in the city's many parks are lit with lamps made from Fanta soda bottles, and the offices of Curitiba's environmental department were built in part with old telephone poles.

Most important, the government knows how to tap the energy of the people. In some communities of former squatters outside the routes of sanitation trucks, residents take their own garbage to designated sites and in exchange receive bags of surplus vegetables from the city. A woman named Lindamir Vas Floriano says that before this so-called green-exchange program, her hilly neighborhood was completely carpeted with trash and plagued by disease. Now the area is almost litter free, and the people are noticeably healthier.

Kinshasa or Curitiba: two visions of the future for most of the world's people. Which shall it be?

KINSHASA, ZAIRE

In a country blessed with gold, diamonds, copper, rich agricultural land, abundant clean water and inexpensive electric power, Kinshasa should be one of Africa's most prosperous capitals. Instead, the city has crumbled under corruption during the 27-year-reign of President Mobutu Sese Seko.

In this kleptocracy, looting sometimes exceeds even the anarchic standards of Somalia. On one occasion, officials pilfered all but 24 tons out of 369 tons of emergency food aid sent by the European Community. "It's not that officials do not know how to run ministries honestly," says a foreign diplomat, "but that there is no reason to do so."

The routine disappearance of fuel, manufactured goods, food and medical supplies has helped raise the price of almost everything. A sack of manioc that will barely feed a family for a month costs far more than the basic monthly salary of a clerk. If patients want operations at some public hospitals, they have to supply their own drugs.

Zaïrians have put their hopes in a national conference, which has chosen Mobutu's rival, Etienne Tshisekedi, as Prime Minister for a new government. Mobutu, however, continues to maneuver to keep control. Last December he dismissed the Tshisekedi government, though he had no power to do so, precipitating a crisis in the transition to democratic government. Even if Tshisekedi and Western pressure manage to inch Zaïre toward democracy, it could be several years before Kinshasa's economy recovers.

THE DAWNING AGE OF MEGACITIES

In the coming years, the fate of humanity will be decided in places like Kinshasa and Curitiba. Faster than ever before, the human world is becoming an urban world. Near the end of this decade, mankind will pass a demographic milestone: for the first time in history, more people will live in and around cities than in rural areas.

Explosive population growth and a torrent of migration from the countryside are creating cities that dwarf the great capitals of the past. By the turn of the century, there will be 21 "megacities" with populations of 10 million or more. Of these, 18 will be in developing countries, including some of the poorest nations in the world. Mexico City already has 20 million people and Calcutta 12 million. According to the World Bank, some of Africa's cities are growing by 10% a year, the swiftest rate of urbanization ever recorded.

Is the trend good or bad? Can the cities cope? No one knows for sure. Without question, urbanization has produced miseries so ghastly that they are difficult to comprehend. In Cairo, children who elsewhere might be in kindergarten can be found digging through clots of ox dung, looking for undigested kernels of corn to eat. Young, homeless thieves in Papua New Guinea's Port Moresby may not know their last names or the names of the villages where they were born. In the inner cities of America, newspapers regularly report on newborn babies dropped into garbage bins by drug-addicted mothers.

But cities remain the cradle of civilization's creativity and ambition. To focus on the degradation is to miss the deep well of pride and determination that inspire the urban poor to better their lives. In Bombay, high school girls learn about sanitation, nutrition and immunization so that they can pass on this information to illiterate neighbors. In Bangkok a program called Magic Eyes has reduced street trash by 85% through the gentle method of encouraging children to hum a jingle about sloppiness when they see their parents litter. In Mexico City cash-starved peasants band together to form cooperatives that guarantee credit for people who might otherwise never be able to afford a home.

History issues grim warnings about the future of cities. Since the beginning of civilization, they have risen to greatness only to collapse because of epidemics, warfare, ecological calamities, shifts in trade or social disorder. Calah, Tikal and Angkor are among the fabled places that disappeared into the sands or jungles of time. Surviving cities have undergone wild swings of fortune. Alexandria, Egypt, may have housed several hundred thousand people at its peak in Roman times, but

CURITIBA, BRAZIL

While mayors around the world spend their time making excuses for crime, drugs and urban decay, Jaime Lerner of Curitiba, Brazil, has the enviable problem of trying to be modest about his city's success. "Curitiba is different from other Third World cities because it has made an effort to be different," says Lerner. Beginning in 1970 he launched low-cost programs to build parks, control garbage, house the poor and develop a mass-transit system. Two decades ago, Curitiba had 0.46 sq m (5 sq. ft.) of open space for every citizen; now it has 51 sq m (550 sq. ft.). New York City, by contrast, has 14.5 sq m (156 sq. ft.) of open space per capita. Most astonishing, Curitiba has added parks and plazas even as its population increased 164% since 1970.

"Services like parks and high-quality public transportation give dignity to the citizen," says Lerner, "and if people feel respected, they will assume responsibility to help solve other problems." Lerner has used his high public approval ratings to mobilize support for such initiatives as the establishment of 40 centers that feed street children and teach them simple skills.

Some of Lerner's innovations have caught the attention of the developed world. Last spring, for instance, New York City began experimenting with a low-cost bus system invented in Curitiba as an alternative to subways. Curitiba's "speedy line" uses express street lanes from which cars are banned and loading platforms where passengers pay their fare before boarding the bus. The buses travel through the city at an average speed of 32 km/h (20 m.p.h.) and can transport 3.2 times as many passengers as standard buses can during a given interval. The system was installed in six months. That, says Lerner, "means you don't have to waste a generation building a subway." People all over Brazil respect Lerner's commonsense approach. He has been mentioned as a candidate to succeed former President Fernando Collor de Mello.

when Napoleon entered it in 1798, it had shrunk to 4,000 souls. Since then, it has again boomed to nearly 3 million and faces grave ecological threats. The gleaming city that Arab poet Ibn Dukmak compared to "a golden crown, set with pearls, perfumed with musk and camphor, and shining from East to the West," is slowly sinking into the unstable, sewage-contaminated Nile Delta.

During earlier periods of urban collapse, the fact that human society was largely rural tempered the effects of catastrophes. When the black death wiped out 80% of Europe's urban population, more than 95% of the people lived in the country. But if the world enters a new age of epidemics, few will escape unaffected.

CITIES AND CIVILIZATION

Workers laying a new sewer line in a Cairo suburb uncover foundations of a 4,600-year-old working-class neighborhood; a subway project in Rome reveals a long-dead Pope's toothbrush; improvements in Red Square during the twilight of the Soviet empire unearth wooden homes built before Moscow had its first prince in the 13th century. In the next millennium, construction workers in Cairo, Rome and Moscow will no doubt be puzzling over traces of current cultures. As the triumphant remake the world's cities, the shards of the vanquished are literally trodden into the ground.

These layers of sediment become pages in urban history, which, in large measure, is the history of civilization. The need to preserve foods and seeds at trading centers in ancient Mesopotamia and Anatolia focused human ingenuity on the problem of storage and led eventually to the development of armories, banks and libraries. Along a treacherous path paved with bloodshed and pestilence, cities evolved as the repositories of humanity's collective intelligence: the record of culture and science that enables a civilization to benefit from the lessons of the past.

But the development of cities fostered competition among humans and alienation from nature. The price of a city's greatness is an uneasy balance between vitality and chaos, health and disease, enterprise and corruption, art and iniquity. The Elizabethan London that nurtured Shakespeare, after all, was a fetid dump cloaked with coal dust.

This delicate balance always threatens to tip, and when it does, cities can spiral into an anarchy that defies all attempts at reversal. From Belfast, where religious hatred spawns terror, to Los Angeles, where the acquittal of four white policemen accused of beating a black motorist triggered last April's rampage of looting and arson, city dwellers have paid a horrible price when ethnic and political tensions boiled to the surface. When fighting began in Beirut in 1974, merchants spoke confidently of a return to normality within months. Few Lebanese expected that strife would still rule their lives 18 years later.

Yet the catalytic mixing of people that fuels urban conflict also spurs the initiative, innovation and collaboration that move civilization forward. The late social critic Lewis Mumford once remarked that "the city is a place for multiplying happy chances and making the most of unplanned opportunities." Curitiba's mayor, Jaime Lerner, bases his whole approach to urban planning on this idea. "If life is the art of encounter, then the city is the setting for encounter," he says. Curitiba has multiplied the chances for encounters by providing its citizens with an abundance of pedestrian walks and parks. Even the bus terminals make cozy and comfortable meeting places. The mayor's public housing program mixes both low- and middle-income people in a largely successful effort to discourage ghettos.

Ironically, the very programs that have made Lerner one of the most popular mayors in Brazilian history threaten Curitiba's future. Says Ashok Khosla, president of the New Delhi–based Society for Development Alternatives: "Each city contains the seeds of its own destruction because the more attractive it becomes, the more it will attract overwhelming numbers of immigrants." Luciano Pizzato, a federal Deputy from Curitiba, notes that during the next 10 years, Brazil's population will grow by 40 million people—an increase the size of Argentina's population. "You cannot create facilities for a new Argentina in 10 years," says Pizzato, who fears that Brazil's poor will make Curitiba their destination of choice.

It is easy to understand why Brazilians would migrate to Curitiba, but why do people keep streaming into a Kinshasa or a Karachi, Pakistan? What is the irresistible lure of the megacity? To the outsider, a neatly swept native village in Africa, Asia or Latin America may look more inviting than a squalid urban squatter settlement. But until recently even the most wretched city slums have offered better access to paying jobs, more varied diets, better education and better health care than what was available in rural communities.

THE MEDICAL AND ENVIRONMENTAL TOLL

No one knows how big some cities are or how rapidly they are expanding. Estimates of Mexico City's population vary from 14 million to 20 million, depending on whether demographers calculate the figure according to the 1990 census (which some believe drastically undercounted), or whether the number is determined by estimates of water use. Still, the fastest urban growth is in those areas

---

NEW YORK CITY

Urban experts often say that inside every First World city is a Third World city. In the case of New York City, that could be construed as an insult to the Third World. After a series of editorials depicting the city as "the New Calcutta," the *New York Times* ran a rebuttal pointing out that the poorest neighborhoods of the Indian city had less crime and more community spirit than the Big Apple.

A walk through the South Bronx fulfills every outsider's vision of urban decline. With their cracked façades and broken windows, abandoned tenements stare vacantly, like blind sentinels over street corners and rubble-strewn lots where drug dealers congregate openly.

Amid this blight, however, is evidence of resilience. In the Hunts Point district, rows of neat homes built by urban homesteaders testify to the determination of the poor to reclaim the most degraded blocks of the city. Many of New York's bravest urban pioneers are immigrants who, with the American Dream firing their ambition, come from Haiti, Russia, Ethiopia, Korea, Poland, Guatemala, India and many other nations. As New York's middle-class professionals exit, this new blood could provide an infusion of taxpayers.

In the past, New York has risen from its ashes. It lost its pre-eminence as a port and a manufacturing center, but still discovered new roles to fill. Now, when it needs to reinvent itself once more, the city can call on the energy of its immigrants and its unsurpassed intellectual resources in the fields of finance, industry, the media, design, advertising and the arts.

---

that are poorest and least prepared.

Karachi, for instance, may be swelling by 6% a year. Estimates of its population range from 8.4 million to 11 million, a figure that could rise to 19 million by the year 2002. That increase would be the same as adding on New York City's population in a decade. But Karachi makes do with a central sewer system not significantly improved since 1962. The city provides 30% less water than needed, forcing the poor to drink from untreated supplies often contaminated with hepatitis virus. An epidemic of the disease has been raging for more than a year. Those taking medicines often get sicker because unscrupulous local manufacturers sometimes boost profits by adulterating pills and potions with motor oil, sawdust and tainted tap water. Says Mohammad Farooq Sattar, 32, the former mayor, who started his career as an M.D.: "Karachi is a city very much in need of a doctor."

So are many other cities. The era of the megacity could bring the triumphant return of microbes that have toppled empires throughout history. Says Harvard public-health expert Jonathan Mann: "We only have a truce with infectious disease, and if a city's infrastructure gets overloaded, the balance can tip back to microbes at any time." The cholera epidemic that hit Latin American cities last year, hospitalizing more than 400,000 people and killing at least 4,000 in a few months, shows how quickly a disease can move when it finds a foothold in crowded slums.

Large cities are breeding grounds for novel, antibiotic-resistant strains of old germs and for entirely new kinds of microbes. Not since the bubonic plague has the world encountered anything like the

AIDS virus, which has infected at least 10 million people. No one knows exactly where AIDS originated, but it has become an epidemic in the cities of Africa, Europe, Asia, Latin America and the U.S. In addition to its own deadly impact, AIDS fosters the spread of other diseases. The tuberculosis germ, for example, attacks weakened AIDS victims and uses them as a beachhead for invading healthy populations.

The possibility that AIDS evolved in the African rain forests has raised the nightmare prospect that as humans continue to cut back tropical forests, other opportunistic new viruses may emerge to fasten on human hosts. "Imagine a virus like AIDS that was transmitted by droplets in the air rather than sexually, and which led to death in months rather than years. In these circumstances we might not have time to study the disease before it ravaged cities," says Uwe Brinkmann, a Harvard epidemiologist.

Inadequate sanitation often provides new pathways for infectious agents. In Mexico cysticercosis, caused by a tapeworm that invades the human brain, used to be transmitted primarily by improperly cooked pork. Now people are getting the disease from vegetables grown in fields irrigated by water containing effluent that flows into the Tula River from Mexico City. Brinkmann estimates that more than half of the 300 million urban poor in the developing world are in a permanently weakened condition because they carry one or more parasites.

The threat of disease is heightened by urban pollution. Brinkmann notes that in industrial countries, as much as 50% of the population will suffer from a rash or other skin disease during the course of a year, compared with maybe 2% in the 1950s. "Is this an indication that pollutants have weakened human immune defenses, leaving city dwellers more vulnerable to otherwise benign diseases?" the epidemiologist asks. Many of the effects of environmental degradation are far from benign. In Upper Silesia, Poland, indiscriminate dumping of toxic wastes has so poisoned the land and water that 10% of the region's newborns have birth defects, from missing limbs to brain damage.

Nowhere is pollution more palpable than in Mexico City. When the wind is still, the fumes of 3 million cars and 35,000 industrial sites become trapped by the high ring of mountains that surrounds the city. Last February a cloud of smog pushed ozone readings above 0.35 parts per million on some days, severe enough to harm even healthy people and four times the level considered safe under, say, California law. In recent years Mexico City has started to shut down polluting factories, introduce lead-free fuels, get rid of diesel-powered buses, mandate emission controls on new cars, and even decree that vehicles be driven only six days a week. But with the number of cars growing 7% a year, ozone pollution still worsened 22% between 1990 and 1991. Today the city is looking at electric cars and new pollution controls for buses and industry. The situation is desperate enough that the ordinarily sensible mayor, Manuel Camacho Solis, has entertained daffy ideas such as the installation of 100 giant fan complexes, each 13.3 hectares (33 acres) in size, to blow pollution out of the area.

Even the best-managed cities have trouble coping with the crush of population growth. Tokyo is overwhelmed by its own trash—22,000 tons each day—despite massive recycling and incineration programs. Ironically, Japanese fastidiousness is a big part of the problem. In a city where taxi drivers wear spotless white gloves, Tokyo consumers want wrappers around virtually anything they buy.

At the present discard rate, Tokyo will run out of dump sites by 1995. The city has been building artificial islands in Tokyo Bay to hold garbage, but cannot continue to do so without threatening both the fishing and shipping industries. Some critics argue that in its obsession with technology, the government has chosen the wrong tack. Notes Keisuke Amagusa, editor of the journal *Technology and People*: "The government is focusing on garbage collected and not doing anything to reduce the garbage created."

The pell-mell expansion of cities creates risks not just for their residents but for every human being. As cities grow, so does the demand for standardized, easily transportable foods. Farmers in the coun-

MEGACITIES		
Population of metropolitan areas* in millions	1992	2000
Tokyo	25.8	28.0
São Paulo, Brazil	19.2	22.6
New York City	16.2	16.6
Mexico City	15.3	16.2
Shanghai	14.1	17.4
Bombay	13.3	18.1
Los Angeles	11.9	13.2
Buenos Aires	11.8	12.8
Seoul	11.6	13.0
Beijing	11.4	14.4
Rio de Janeiro	11.3	12.2
Calcutta	11.1	12.7
Jakarta, Indonesia	10.0	13.4
Tianjin, China	9.8	12.5
Metro Manila	9.6	12.6
Cairo	9.0	10.8
New Delhi	8.8	11.7
Lagos, Nigeria	8.7	13.5
Karachi, Pakistan	8.6	11.9
Bangkok	7.6	9.9
Dacca, Bangladesh	7.4	11.5

* Urban area estimates vary widely, depending on area definitions and recency of census.
Source: Population Division of the U.N. Secretariat

tryside respond to this demand by planting a narrower range of crops, which in turn increases the likelihood of major disruptions of the food supply by pests and droughts. Particularly in the developing world, cities act as destructive parasites on the surrounding countryside. Urban thirst for fuel wood and building materials leads to deforestation, which can destroy an area's watershed and thus cause flooding and soil erosion. In many cases, the impact of urban centers extends across the seas. Demand for plywood building materials in Japanese cities drives the decimation of Borneo's forests.

With every kind of threat, the stakes are higher than ever before. A repeat of Tokyo's devastating 1923 earthquake today might cause worldwide economic stagnation as rebuilding the city soaked up hundreds of billions of dollars of Japanese capital. If global warming causes a sharp rise in sea levels during the next century, as many scientists predict, the coastal megacities may have to build giant dikes to prevent disastrous flooding, but only a few urban areas can afford such an undertaking.

Ideally, it might be better to disperse humanity more evenly around the countryside. But people have flocked to cities for thousands of years, and the lure of the bright lights runs so deep that it cannot easily be overcome by government policies. With the world's population growing by nearly 100 million a year, the forces driving urban expansion are irresistible.

WILL CITIES LOSE THEIR ALLURE?

Yet there are signs that urban growth can be slowed. Four decades ago, Mexico City was a relatively attractive place, with only 4 million people and not much traffic along its spacious boulevards. Since then the population has quadrupled, and the congestion has become stifling. In recent years the city's immigration rate has declined while the flow of people to smaller Mexican cities has increased. This trend suggests that the combination of crowding, poor sanitation, noise and pollution can eventually become intolerable.

In rich countries as well, many cities are not quite the magnets they used to be. In return for the highest combined city and state taxes in the U.S., residents of New York City get deteriorating bridges and roads, racial tension that frequently ignites violence, schools in which students must worry about gun battles erupting in the hallways, subway stations that double as public urinals, and streets full of panhandlers. Last summer one house in a middle-class neighborhood in Brooklyn was burglarized on five separate occasions, and the police did nothing to stop the robberies.

Not surprisingly, the city has been losing its middle class and is in danger of losing many of its professionals. A New York *Times* poll showed that 60% of the people sampled were thinking of leaving. "If the ability to believe in the future is what separates a growing from a dying civilization, then New York is in deep trouble," says Stephen Berger, a former executive director of the Port Authority of New York and New Jersey.

For all its problems, though, New York still has a superb infrastructure for housing, transporting and employing large numbers of people. "It's far easier to fix New York," says Berger, "than to rebuild it in Des Moines." More important, cities such as New York and Tokyo will never lose their role as marketplaces of ideas. Even as electronic communications increasingly link people over long distances, they still crave face-to-face encounters.

Kenzo Tange, the revered Japanese architect, points out that in his country there is no substitute for sizing up business associates in meetings and at social occasions. Tange thinks the Tokyo area, though choked with nearly 30 million people, will remain the focal point of Japan's economy simply because the city houses the headquarters of two-thirds of the country's major companies. In Japan and around the world, many of the most creative minds in business, finance, fashion, the arts and the media will keep wanting to brainstorm in the megacities.

THE REVIVAL OF SELF-RELIANCE

Experts began predicting the violent collapse of Third World megacities more than a decade ago. Urban planner Janice Perlman recalls the skepticism she encountered in the mid-1980s when she first proposed Mega-Cities, a project to promote the exchange of ideas and innovations among the world's biggest urban areas. She was told that her proposal was futile because such cities as Jakarta and Mexico City would be torn apart by disease and disorder within a few years.

The first modern urban apocalypse could easily have started at 7:18 a.m. on Sept. 19, 1985. That was when an earthquake measuring 8.1 on the Richter scale rocked Mexico City. Hundreds of thousands were left homeless, water mains broke, the threat of epidemics loomed, and the government fumbled helplessly in dealing with the crisis.

But instead of obliterating the city, the earthquake tapped a wellspring of self-reliance that astonished officials and outside observers alike. Neighborhoods and communities organized themselves to rescue those buried, clean up the rubble and restore services. Since then, a chastened government has tried to do a better job of harnessing local initiative. Says Mayor Camacho: "We have learned to take advantage of mass mobilization."

The awakening of self-reliance in the urban poor is a global phenomenon. In Karachi, architect Akhter Hameed Khan rallied the people of the Orangi district around a self-help initiative to upgrade their sanitation. With 800,000 residents from five of Pakistan's major ethnic groups, the neighborhood is periodically racked by violence. Still, working lane by lane, beginning in 1980, Hameed Khan and his co-workers in the Orangi Pilot Project proved to the district that with a tiny investment ($40 a house), it could install its own sewerage system. Since then, roughly 70% of the 6,347 lanes have been linked to the system. The people of Orangi can now see for themselves the difference between the neat lanes in the project and the garbage-strewn open sewers of neighboring alleys. Hameed Khan's programs, particularly initiatives to improve the role of women, have stirred some fundamentalist mullahs in this Islamic country to call for his death, but the 78-year-old social activist resolutely continues his efforts to make Karachi more livable.

The World Bank, which generally finances giant projects, increasingly supports small community-based initiatives. One such project is the Kampung Improvement Program in Jakarta. Its success grew out of a decision to give squatters title to plots of land. In return, the new landowners agreed to help build footpaths, improve drainage and reduce garbage. "Instead of thinking of themselves as temporary boarders, the poor began to look at their

MEXICO CITY

When Hernán Cortés gazed in 1519 on what is now called Mexico City, he saw a vast Aztec center of several hundred thousand souls that dwarfed any European city of his era. The city had grown by feeding on tribute from subdued tribes.

Though centuries have passed, Mexico City is still subsidized by the countryside. Its children, for instance, can ride to school for one-tenth the cost of a bus ticket in some rural areas. Education, health care and jobs are much more available. No wonder several thousand peasants flocked to Mexico City each week

throughout the 1980s. Exequiel Ezcurra, chairman of the National University's Ecological Center, is concerned that the capital has exceeded its sustainable limits. "In a city this large," he says, "a catastrophe such as a rash of deaths caused by air pollution can go unnoticed."

The city's great assets are its homogeneity and the determination of its citizens. Profound devotion to community saved it from collapse after the 1985 earthquake. The question is whether this spirit can prevent an urban apocalypse as the population inexorably increases.

community as their home," says Josef Leitmann, a World Bank urban planner. "A simple change in psychology produced a change in physical surroundings."

The cities obviously need more money. In many countries the help that urban areas receive from the national government has dwindled steadily. Moreover, during the past decade, foreign aid shifted more and more to rural problems even as people moved to the cities. Now, with urban areas producing half the world's income, and governments nervous about restive urban populations, agencies such as the World Bank have begun to focus more on cities once again.

But money by itself will not prevent the collapse of megacities. The troubles of a Karachi or a Jakarta will not disappear if planners from the World Bank rush in to build housing projects and a freeway system. Humanitarian aid in the form of food and medicine can be a godsend, but it will not give a city prosperity.

Ultimately, the responsibility for making cities livable rests with their governments and their people. Too often those governments, whether in New York City or Kinshasa, become corrupt systems for dispensing benefits to agencies, employees and political supporters. If, as in Curitiba, governments can learn again how to serve the public, they can regain a mighty power—the power that comes from harnessing the combined imaginations and enterprise of millions of human beings.

The historical cycle of urban growth and collapse will be hard to break, but hope can be found in the stubborn self-reliance shown by people in some of the world's poorest cities. Like the cumbersome bumblebee that flies in the face of aerodynamic theory, the megacities will have to defy gravity and invent a sustainable future for themselves. Since the fate of the world is entwined with the fate of its cities, humanity has no other choice.

TOKYO

During Japan's imperial era, Tokyo's planners built unexpected curves and dead ends into streets to confuse any invader who dared enter the capital. These mystifying turns still befuddle taxi drivers and lend a rare whimsical touch to a city that has evolved into a sprawling technopolis. There is nothing whimsical, however, about the problems that have accompanied Tokyo's metamorphosis into a colossus: traffic-choked streets, housing costs beyond the reach of young families and the overwhelming waste generated by 30 million people.

Still, the Japanese obsession with efficiency and technological wizardry may generate solutions. One scheme makes use of Tokyo's vast waste stream. Called the Urban Heat system, it extracts heat from sewage and then uses the energy to regulate temperatures in several Tokyo buildings, including the monumental new city hall. If such innovations were matched by programs that encouraged ordinary people to reduce waste, Tokyo's governor, Shunichi Suzuki, might yet live up to his commitment to make the capital an earth-friendly city.

THE NUMBERS GAME

**By the year 2000 the world will have more than
6 billion people. Are we doing ourselves in?
Or are we upping the odds of producing lots of Einsteins?**

DAVID BERREBY

*This is David Berreby's first DISCOVER
article. He lives in Brooklyn.*

In 1968, when Stanford biologist Paul
Ehrlich published *The Population Bomb,*
there were 3.5 billion human beings.
That was more, he warned, than the
planet could support. "In the 1970s," he
wrote, "the world will undergo famines—hundreds of millions of people are
going to starve to death." We now know
that didn't happen in the seventies. What
did happen was that food production
soared worldwide, prices dropped, and
growers who could not sell enough of
their surplus went bankrupt.

This month Ehrlich and his wife,
Anne, are coming out with *The Population Explosion,* a sequel to the 1968 best-
seller. The message is much the same;
the timetable, however, is revised. "The
human population is now 5.3 billion,
and still climbing," they write. "Yet the
world has hundreds of billions *fewer*
tons of topsoil and hundreds of trillions
fewer gallons of groundwater with which
to grow food crops than it had in 1968."
Now, they warn, our excess numbers
have overloaded both the environment

and human communities. Global warming, acid rain, the hole in the ozone
layer, rampant crime, viral epidemics,
homelessness—all these problems and
more stem from overpopulation. If we
don't heed the warning this time, they
write, we can look forward to "a billion
or more deaths from starvation and disease," and possibly "the dissolution of
society as we know it."

The Population Explosion, like the
original *Bomb,* is full of statistics to back
these claims. Like many sequels,
though, this new effort may not get as
friendly a reception as the original.
These days fear of overpopulation is not
what it used to be. Over the past 20 years
many social scientists, in particular,
have turned skeptical. "A good number
of true believers," says Dennis Ahlburg
of the University of Minnesota's Center
for Population Analysis and Policy,
"have become agnostics." They are now
framing new hypotheses to explain the
world's problems. "We're in a bit of a
predicament," says Ahlburg, "because

we can't keep saying that population is a
horrible thing. The evidence isn't
there."

In parts of Asia, Africa, and Latin
America, exploding populations are often blamed for poverty, famine, crowding in cities, deforestation, pollution,
and practically everything else that goes
wrong. But in case after case, says
Ahlburg, it's not population that causes
the problem: in general the resources
exist to support more people—the problem is that societies encourage waste.
There are countless ways to do this,
from misguided government policies to
spectacular blunders like wars. Population growth, Ahlburg argues, is an easy
scapegoat for political failures.

Such revisionism is clear in the changing stand of the National Academy of
Sciences. In a report issued in 1971 the
academy declared rapid population
growth a clear danger to the survival of
the human race. But in 1986 a new
report found that the effects of population growth had been exaggerated in

earlier studies. The academy noted that "despite rapid population growth, developing countries have achieved unprecedented levels of income per capita, literacy, and life expectancy." The report concluded that slower population growth is probably desirable in developing countries because it would give them more time to adjust—not because they are breeding themselves into oblivion.

As fear of the teeming billions has subsided, developed nations have reduced spending on contraceptive research. And the United States, in particular, has cut back its funding of international programs aimed at reining in reproduction in the Third World, where up to 90 percent of future population growth is expected.

Meanwhile, in much of the industrial world, birthrates have fallen so low that native populations are leveling off or actually declining. This drop in fertility surprised many planners, and it dramatically changed their projections. In the late sixties the United Nations estimated that the world's population in the year 2000 would be 7.5 billion; the projection now is 6.1 billion.

When a nation's birthrate drops, its population ages: the ratio of old people to young people grows larger. Some governments now worry about supporting growing numbers of retired people, and others fear that languages and cultures may die out. In the French-speaking province of Quebec, where the birthrate is lower than in the rest of Canada, the provincial government started offering cash bonuses this past year for babies. In Singapore, where the number of children born to the average woman dropped from 4.7 in 1965 to 1.4 in 1987, the government started a matchmaking service to coach career-driven nerds (as they are universally known) in the subtle arts of courtship.

Today's apparent lack of alarm over population growth compelled the Ehrlichs to title the first chapter of their new book "Why Isn't Everyone as Scared as We Are?" An important part of the answer to their question is the work of Julian Simon, a professor of business administration at the University of Maryland. For two decades Simon has pushed the idea that "population growth, along with the lengthening of human life, is a moral and material triumph." Although widely reviled in the seventies, Simon, like the Ehrlichs, persevered. His work has dealt the con-

ventional wisdom two severe blows: first, by challenging the widely held assumption that our numbers are driving the planet to the end of its rope; and second, by outlining a theory that gradual population growth not only doesn't harm us and the environment but actually accelerates our progress.

"I find it difficult to understand how they can see some things as only problems when I see them as miracles," says Simon. "The fact we can keep five billion people alive now is an incredible accomplishment. We've escaped nature's domination, and all they see is problems. 'Escaped' doesn't mean we've beaten it into submission. It means we've killed the mosquitoes and the smallpox germs."

The Ehrlichs are worse than wrong, says Simon; their efforts to persuade people to have fewer children are morally repugnant. "I'm unhappy about it when I get a letter from a guy saying, 'My wife and I believed, on the basis of what Ehrlich said, that to bring a baby into the world is a negative act against society. So I had myself sterilized and now I can't reverse it.' That makes me sad." He becomes even sadder when a government as powerful as China's campaigns to limit every couple to only one child. "The cost," he says, "is the second child for a hundred million Chinese couples. A hundred million human beings who would never enjoy life as you and I and Ehrlich enjoy it."

Much current thinking on population

> "It's beyond my comprehension that we should run an experiment to see how many people we can cram on the planet before all its systems collapse."

lies between Simon on one coast and Ehrlich on the other. They heartily despise each other, and each would have you believe that the other is scarcely able to understand, much less contrib-

ute to, the population debate. "If you were doing a story on the solar system, would you talk to someone who thinks the Earth is flat?" Ehrlich asks. Meanwhile the index to Simon's most influential work, *The Ultimate Resource*, includes the entry, "Ehrlich, Paul, respect for human life lacking in." Still, they share more than mutual contempt. Each is a gifted polemicist. Each sees himself as an island of sanity in a world that has gone over to the other side. And most important, each considers the other's discipline to be arrogantly wrong in its fundamental assumptions about human populations.

The National Academy of Science's "revisionist" report was prepared entirely by social scientists, says Ehrlich, and thus was "never reviewed by anybody who knew anything about the subject." Ehrlich belongs to the Club of Earth, which in its own report in 1988 reached a conclusion opposite that of the academy. Every one of those dissenting researchers, Ehrlich points out, also belongs to the academy, but they are all biologists rather than social scientists. As for Simon, he is now working on a paper titled "Why Are Biologists Usually the Most Vocal Doomsayers?"

In the 1960s Ehrlich was a young biology professor at Stanford. He had first noticed the effects of human population growth years before, when as an undergraduate at the University of Pennsylvania he gathered butterflies in New Jersey. "We found out we couldn't raise our butterflies because there was so much pesticide in everything that it killed the caterpillars, and my favorite places to collect were disappearing under Levittowns." In graduate school at the University of Kansas, he met and married Anne, who is now a biological researcher at Stanford. They have only one child— "a contribution you can make toward being socially responsible," he says.

When *The Population Bomb* came out in 1968, headlines were filled with news of Vietnam, protests, and riots. In that apocalyptic year, people were receptive to a book that began, "The battle to feed all of humanity is over." Johnny Carson was certainly receptive; he invited Ehrlich to appear on *The Tonight Show*. Despite a few qualms ("I'd be canceling my ticket with my colleagues"), Ehrlich decided to accept the invitation ("I don't care about glory in science. It's more important that I do this"). He has maintained two careers ever since—as academic scholar and population polemicist.

Ehrlich believes that human populations are subject to the same natural constraints as those of, say, checkerspot butterflies. The absolute limit on any species's success, he says, is the "carrying capacity" of its environment—the maximum number of individuals a habitat can support. "Humanity," Ehrlich argues, "will pay the price for exceeding the carrying capacity of its environment as surely as would a population of checkerspots."

According to Ehrlich, the key limit on the carrying capacity of the planet is photosynthesis—the ability of green plants, algae, and many kinds of bacteria to convert the energy of sunlight into living tissue. Some animals consume those plants and microbes, and bigger animals eat smaller ones. But no matter how high or low on the food chain any species may dine, its numbers are ultimately limited by photosynthesis.

In their new book the Ehrlichs estimate that human beings and their domestic animals now consume 4 percent of the solar energy that photosynthesis captures on land. Adding the amount of this

energy we don't directly consume but destroy (such as plants killed when forests are burned) and the amount we prevent from growing (as when we pave productive land) raises the human share to nearly 40 percent. But even 4 percent, in the Ehrlichs' opinion, is a disproportionate share for only one of Earth's 30 million species.

How do the Ehrlichs know we are crowding other species? A population exceeds carrying capacity, they write, when it "can't be maintained without rapidly depleting nonrenewable resources." And by this standard, they declare, "the entire planet and virtually every nation is

1989 POPULATION

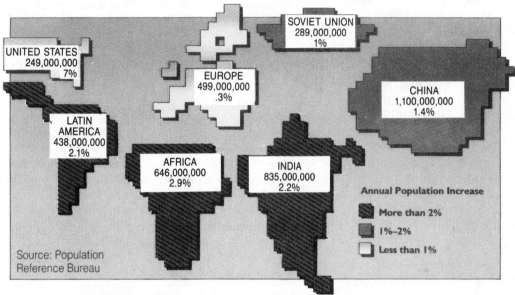

The Third World dominates a map drawn so that land area is proportional to population. The top figures represent total population; the bottom figures, annual growth rate.

ANNUAL ENERGY CONSUMPTION

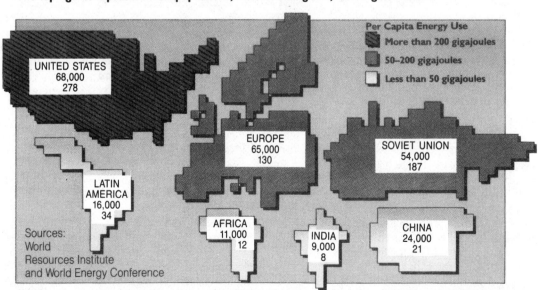

The United States and Europe loom large on a global energy map, drawn so that land area is proportional to energy use. The top figures represent total energy consumption (in petajoules, or 10^{15} joules); the bottom figures, annual consumption per capita (in gigajoules, or 10^9 joules). These figures are based on 1986 data for commercial energy and 1987 data for firewood and charcoal.

already vastly overpopulated." Humans are different from butterflies, however, in one important ecological respect: they have more control in choosing what to eat and how to live. This is why the planet's carrying capacity for humans is not a fixed number. The world can support more vegetarian Indians on bicycles than hamburger-eating Americans in cars. Yet the limit on our species, says Ehrlich, is nonetheless real. "And it's beyond my comprehension," he says, "that we should run an experiment to see how many people we can cram on the planet before all its systems collapse."

That concept is essentially the one British economist Thomas Malthus advanced in 1798. In his famous "dismal essay" on the principle of population, Malthus wrote that humans will increase their numbers beyond their means of subsistence until famine, war, and disease wipe out the excess. History may not have worked out the way Malthus expected, but that's only because of what Ehrlich calls a onetime bonanza based on the use of coal and oil to power our industrial civilization. "Malthus," he says, "wasn't wrong."

The problem for this argument—and the foundation of Simon's—is that things haven't yet given way. "Every one of these prophets' dire predictions has failed to come to pass," Simon says. "They've been wrong on food, on energy, on resources, on the environment, on everything."

Simon believes that the most relevant measure of human well-being is life span. Our average life expectancy has increased dramatically, he argues, and this tells you right away that everything we need to sustain us is also increasing. He notes that food production per capita has increased since World War II and says the same holds true for every other resource people worry about.

Global 2000, a projection of global environmental trends to the end of the century, is one of the "doom and gloom" reports that Simon relishes attacking. "The report came out in 1980 saying there was a plateau in world fisheries," he says. "Since then the amount of increase in the world fish catch has been astounding." To refute the report's analysis, Simon refers to statistics compiled by marine biologist John Wise from United Nations reports. In 1979, Wise finds, the world fish catch totaled 78 million tons; in 1987 it was 102 million tons. "Sure, you can say it's

because of new methods of extraction," says Simon, "but that doesn't alter the fact that they said it was going to be the other way around."

What such statistics mean, Simon argues, is not that we've been lucky so far. "They mean we're on a permanent roll," he says, "with no limit yet in sight. If the biologists don't see this, it's because they've left something out of their theories."

In 1968, when Ehrlich was taking to the airwaves to promote *The Population Bomb,* Simon was teaching economics at the University of Illinois. Simon's main claim to fame was having written the basic how-to book on running a mail-order business. By 1968 he had already read about the population explosion, become duly concerned, and turned his attention to possible solutions.

One beautiful spring day in 1969, while on the way to an appointment in Washington, Simon had an epiphany. He described it twelve years later in his book *The Ultimate Resource:* "I thought, Have I gone crazy? What business do I have trying to help arrange it that fewer human beings will be born, each of whom might be a Mozart or a Michelangelo or an Einstein—or simply a joy to his or her family and community, and a person who will enjoy life?" His nagging doubts about the way economic data did not square with the prevailing view of the world's "population crisis" kindled into a crusade to correct the idea.

During the 1970s Simon was denounced as a religious maniac, an emotional wreck, a mere mail-order specialist, and a shabby scholar. At the very first Earth Day in 1970, a fellow faculty member at the university ridiculed him before 2,000 students at a teach-in. (Simon retaliated at a faculty party with three well-aimed gin and tonics.)

But in 1981, the year that Simon published *The Ultimate Resource,* political currents were changing. Ronald Reagan had been elected president in a landslide; vigorous economic development, skepticism of environmentalism, and "family values" were back in style. In the opinion-influencing game of newspaper editorials, seminars, symposia, and government reports, Simon's star began to rise. At the same time, more and more social scientists were becoming convinced by their own data that there

> "There is no meaningful physical limit—even the commonly mentioned weight of the earth—to our capacity to keep growing forever."

was something to his critique of the standard assumptions.

Simon now lives just outside Washington, where he is a figure of some influence. He and his wife, sociologist Rita Simon, have decorated their comfortable, middle-class house with sculptures and framed posters—many of which depict a mother and child. They have three children.

The concept of carrying capacity, Simon argues, shouldn't be applied to human beings at all. Malthus and all who follow in his footsteps pay too little attention to an important fact: humans are producers as well as consumers. As a resource becomes more difficult to obtain, people find ways to get more of it or to use it more efficiently. Or they develop substitutes. Firewood yields to coal, which yields to oil, which yields to nuclear, solar, or some other source of power. Simon argues that our resources expand rather than shrink, because we don't really want coal or oil—we want energy. The same holds true even for apparently fixed resources like soil. Farmland isn't just dirt; it's wilderness that was cleared, desert that was irrigated, swamps that were drained. We don't really want dirt—we want nutrition. And humans are the one species that can invent more ways of applying energy (not only the sun's) to materials (not only today's crops and farmland) to get nutrition—as well as all the other things we enjoy in life.

So people are constantly escaping the Malthusian trap. In fact, Simon argues, population growth applies a needed spur. In the short run, new people are a burden: more babies mean more mouths to feed, so the parents work harder and have less of everything for themselves. But in the long run, Simon contends that those babies are the solution to the apparent problem: as adults they add more to our stock of resources than they consume. "It is your mind that matters economically, as much or more so than your mouth or hands," he says.

"Taken in the large," Simon writes, "an increased need for resources usually leaves us with a permanently greater capacity to get them, because we gain knowledge in the process. And there is no meaningful physical limit—even the commonly mentioned weight of the earth—to our capacity to keep growing forever."

This is the economist's vision at its purest. To Simon it is the lesson of the past few centuries. To most any biologist it's beyond strange. "The physical and biological systems are prior," says Ehrlich. "You can change economics, but the laws of nature are out there." Moreover, he argues that Simon's faith in technology is misguided. "It's usually economists or social scientists who expect science to be able to do all these wonderful things. Scientists don't."

That's the sort of argument to the future that gets Simon's goat. He doubts anyone's ability to predict the limits of technology, whether it's genetic engineering or just ordinary farming done more efficiently. In 1968 Ehrlich wrote, "I have yet to meet anyone familiar with the situation who thinks India will be self-sufficient in food by 1971, if ever." Now, despite a population jump from 500 million in 1966 to 835 million today, Simon points out that India has managed to feed itself.

And *that's* the sort of argument from the past that irritates Ehrlich. India's impressive achievement, he says, was bought at the expense of its future. "They managed to up their grain production by throwing away their soil and their groundwater, and that makes the long-term situation worse." The same is true, he argues, for most of the other encouraging statistics. When there are too many people, technology doesn't really solve our problems—it only postpones them. "Electricity was going to be too cheap to meter because of nuclear power, remember. Many technological rabbits that have been pulled out of hats in the past have had nasty droppings."

In short, Ehrlich has not conceded the past. And neither he nor Simon is conceding the present. In their book, the Ehrlichs use every bit of bad news—children starving in Africa, malaria on the rise again in Asia—as ammunition for their claim that our bubble is finally bursting. "We've got 5.3 billion people on the planet now," says Ehrlich. "At least a billion of them are living at a standard that you wouldn't trade for in a million years. The estimates are that at least two hundred million people have died of hunger-related diseases over the past twenty years." Can the Einsteins or Mozarts that Simon is counting on develop their talents, he asks, in utter destitution and misery?

Simon dismisses that distressing information as old news. Some people have always struggled even while the average situation was improving. "Their paradigm," he says of the other side, "is that the present and the future will be unlike the past, that we're at a turning point in history. But you find that sentiment in every generation. There is absolutely no way to tell if we are at a turning point in history."

Accordingly, Simon has made a one-man cottage industry of assaulting alarming reports. He is a relentless sifter of statistics. "When people say, for instance, 'The world is being deforested,'" he says, "I go look for the aggregate data. I found that in fact the world is *not* being deforested; it is being reforested in general. Yes, there are some tropical countries where deforestation is taking place. Is that bad? Is that good? Who knows?"

New Scientist, a British weekly, published Simon's article on deforestation in 1986. He gets a hearing for such contrary views because there are no precise, comprehensive data for many global trends. Current opinion is often based on spot surveys rounded out by estimates, which can be argued up or down. With forests, for instance, not even the record of photographs from satellites shows enough of the globe for enough years to prove whether the loss of a forest in, say, the Philippines has been offset by a gain in Finland.

Researchers debate everything, Ehrlich acknowledges, from the rate of deforestation to the rate of global warming. Nonetheless, he adds, "there isn't a competent scientist who doesn't believe that the world is facing these problems." As long as the data are still coming in, there will always be need for revision. But "you can't wait for absolute proof before acting."

On and on they go, each confident that the other's statistics distort the truth about what our growing population means to our future well-being. Meanwhile, in the most private and secret places, humanity in its billions is deciding for itself how many people to add to the planet, without reference to either Simon or Ehrlich.

Sixty million on the move

Alan B. Simmons

Alan B. Simmons is a Canadian sociologist based at York University in Toronto, where he is a Fellow of the Centre of Research on Latin America and the Caribbean and a member of the Centre for Refugee Studies. He has published many articles on globalization and international migration, and is the author (with A. Laquian and S. Diaz-Briquets) of Social Change and Internal Migration *and (with R. Cardona) of* Destino La Metropoli.

The modern scientific community takes pride in providing answers to world problems, yet, paradoxically, it often makes a greater contribution by the perspicacity with which it continues to ask questions. The premature proposal of simple solutions to difficult problems often does no more than reveal ignorance.

The complex emerging patterns of international migration are a case in point. Efforts by Europe, North America and other developed regions to shut the door on the rising tide of migrants from the Third World are not only questionable on ethical grounds but may also turn out to be impractical as well. Many migrants will find ways round all but the most costly, vigorous and harsh control systems. This is because the very logic of social and economic change tends to create new avenues and opportunities for migrants. Just how this works is only now beginning to be understood.

Equally misguided is the argument that coordinated international development efforts and economic growth in the countries of out-migration will soon lead to a reduction in South-to-North migration. There is a considerable body of historical evidence to contradict this argument. After a long period of economic growth in the South, pressures promoting current migration trends are indeed likely to ease or stop, but in the short to medium term—over twenty to thirty years or even longer—development efforts will probably tend to increase South-North migration. This is because the mechanization and increased efficiency required to boost productivity will mean that large numbers of workers will lose their jobs. As unemployment rises, so too will the numbers of people seeking refuge elsewhere. The process may run over several decades, since even in the best possible circumstances development is gradual.

It is estimated that some 60 million people in the world are currently "on the move". This figure includes people displaced by war, civil strife, political repression, environmental catastrophe, the threat of starvation, economic hardship or the desire to better their circumstances. Some 16 million of these people are political refugees within the definition of the United Nations Charter, that is, they are individuals seeking asylum from a well-founded fear of persecution.

Potential migrants are heavily concentrated in the poor regions of the South—in the previously colonized nations of Africa, Asia, the Caribbean and Latin America, and in the southern regions of the Soviet Union. They not only move to neighbouring countries within their own regions, but, more and more, they are seeking to move to industrially advanced regions such as Europe, North America and Australia.

The Northern nations (and some migrant-receiving nations in the South) are reacting with alarm. In the north, this alarm has been fed by graphic images in the press of Haitian, Albanian and Sri Lankan "boat people" arriving in Florida, Italy and Canada. Some leaders are calling for the expulsion of unwelcome migrants, while others are calling for increased efforts to solve the economic problems in the sending regions so that migrant flows will be stopped at source. In some countries pressure is mounting to stop virtually all immigration.

The concerns underlying these attitudes are complex, ranging from fear that migrants will steal jobs or be a burden on social services, to xenophobia and even racism.

THE "GLOBALIZATION" OF TRADE

There is a tendency to blame current South-to-North migration on development failures in the South and, indeed, the 1980s, the "Decade of Development", were marked by economic stagnation and declining levels of real per capita income in Africa, the Caribbean and Latin America. The decade will also be viewed historically as a period of dramatic shift towards "globalization" of markets and a related global co-ordination of national economic policies.

Key trends, which are still under way, include: globalization of production (final assembly based on parts manufactured in various parts of the world); globalization of consumer markets (goods assembled in one nation are sold in many others); the spread of "structural adjustment" programmes (to favour export-oriented development); the rise of international trading blocs (Europe, the North American Free Trade Agreement, the Southern Cone trading bloc in Latin America, etc.). Clearly globalization is not an accident. It is the result of deliberate policies promoted by the developed nations, by major international institutions and by many less developed countries that have taken their lead from one of the major players.

One of the principal effects of globalization has been to differentiate more sharply between the "winners" and the "losers" in economic development. Globalization and the policies supporting it have, for example, worked to benefit the fast-growing economies of the Pacific Rim (The Republic of Korea, Hong Kong, Taiwan, Singapore, Malaysia and Thailand) because they combined political stability, progressive policies on education, low wages and other elements to attract investors and promote exports. Mexico may gain in the near future from globalization due to the size of its labour force, industrial infrastructure and access to the United States.

Other regions have clearly been losers in the new global trade and development game. Africa, for example, has such poorly developed economic infrastructures and such underdeveloped labour force skills that even its very low wages and geographic proximity to Europe did not attract many new investors in the 1980s. Development aid has been insufficient to fill this gap. Foreign direct investment in Africa actually declined over the 1980s, as it did in most countries of Latin America.

Third World countries that have experienced economic growth in recent decades have also generally experienced long periods of high unemployment and significant out-migration, although there are some exceptions. Puerto Rico since the 1950s, Mexico in the 1960s and 1970s, and Korea in the 1970s and 1980s, all experienced rather spectacular economic growth, while at the same time losing large numbers of workers and their families through international migration. High rates of natural population growth and the impact of mechanization in agriculture and industry created far more workers in these countries than could be absorbed in the local economy. In the late 1970s, on the other hand, Malaysia's economic growth was so fast that it actually suffered from labour shortages. This, however, was an exceptional case and cannot be taken as a general model.

Over the 1980s, a much larger number of countries lost ground economically, and rising unemployment and falling real incomes in these nations generated political crises and rising pressure for emigration. We have no crystal ball to indicate which countries will be tomorrow's winners and losers in the global development game. What does seem clear is that development in the new era of globalization will be inherently uneven and will inevitably continue to generate large pressures for international migration. The places of origin of the migrants will shift as global circumstances change.

THE ENVIRONMENTAL IMPACT

Poor nations with limited capital and technology are obliged to seek economic growth through export of those products they can produce cheaply and, when wood and minerals are key exports, control over the negative environmental impacts of forestry and mining tends to become lax. Similarly, the drive to be competitive lowers the State's revenues for environmental programmes, so that deforestation, brought about as poor people seek fuel or new land to cultivate or as entrepreneurs turn jungle into grazing land for cattle, continues unabated.

Environmental degradation is but one element in the interconnected web of forces tending to generate new patterns of South-to-North movement. High unemployment, the rise of an underground economy in illicit drugs, animal skins or ivory, and international migration are all linked in this web.

The developed nations are also involved. Not only do the wealthy nations promote structural adjustment and export-driven trade policies in Third World countries (through their central role in the International Monetary Fund and other international financial institutions), but the logic of internal development patterns in countries of the North creates opportunities for migrants from the South.

AN INTERNATIONAL DIVISION OF LABOUR

Globalization of production has reinforced an international division of labour in which scientific, technological, design, finance, management and control jobs are concentrated in the North, while labour-intensive and manual manufacturing jobs are concentrated in the South. Economic growth in the North leads to an expanding demand for low-cost service and support activities in the developed countries themselves. These are jobs which workers in the developed countries do not want, or will not take at the prevailing wage level – in building, cleaning, gardening, garbage collection, etc. This situation lends itself to the sub-contracting of services to smaller companies which in turn may hire foreign-born workers, including illegal immigrants.

The demand for drugs and other illicit international commodities arises mainly in the North. This has led to a globalization of underground commerce, creating further employment opportunities in both the exporting and importing countries. Illicit commercial opportunities in the importing countries favor migrants since they are well placed to work across languages and to link vendors in their home countries with buyers in their new countries of residence.

A further effect of the globalization of trade and international commerce has been to bring about a dramatic fall in travel and communications costs. Information flows across international boundaries have increased enormously and have given rise to an unprecedented level of information in the South about informal job niches and economic opportunities in the North. This, together with the globalization of consumer products and advertising, has generated a rising demand for income and purchasing power, all of which fuels motivation of potential migrants in poor countries.

An additional level of complexity arises in some major migrant-receiving regions in the North, where the presence of large ethnic communities changes the politics of immigration. Families and ethnic groups originating in Third World countries press the State to open the door to ethnic kin. These pressures are most evident in the multi-ethnic receiving countries—the United States, Canada and Australia.

A CHANGING SOCIAL AND ECONOMIC WORLD

The conclusion that current trends in South-North migration are part of a global system of changing social and economic relationships, favoured and promoted by the North, will not please those who see the current migration crisis as a process that can be stopped by stiff migration controls or by short-term development programmes.

Solutions to the current crisis must include a longer-term perspective. It must be recognized that, although international development efforts will probably reduce migration in the longer term, these same efforts will almost certainly increase pressures for South-to-North migration in the short to intermediate term.

The overall international system, and the way in which the economies of the Northern countries function within it, imply at least moderate levels of international migration. Levels that are too low will be opposed internally as well as externally and will work against economic development and co-operation in the international system.

It is difficult to imagine how economic growth can take place in the South without extensive and rising trade, technical exchange and co-operation with the North. Similarly, it is difficult to imagine how the North can achieve greater security without fair and just co-operation with the South. This mutuality of interest in the new global context will require legitimate procedures to permit the short- and long-term movement of rather substantial numbers of people from South to North as new international institutions and arrangements are forged and strains arising from uneven international development are compassionately dealt with. To imagine otherwise is to go back to a state of greater isolation of nations, conflict between States and international chaos.

THE WAR ON ALIENS

The Right calls the shots

RUTH CONNIFF

The story begins with fleets of ships anchored off the coasts of Europe and the United States. Crammed with ragged, starving refugees from the Third World, and trailing a terrible stench of human waste, the rusty, creaking vessels form the front lines in a massive invasion of the North. The European and American governments are paralyzed by the emergency—unable to fire a shot at the unarmed invaders, and hopelessly mired in political debates about what to do. To make matters worse, the Western liberal media denounce as "racists" all those who propose defending the borders, and issue utopian proclamations of brotherly love, thus preparing the way for an unprecedented assault on Western civilization. . . .

This is a scene from *The Camp of the Saints,* a French white-supremacist novel by Jean Raspail. Left-wing antiracists are the villains of the story—traitors who throw open the doors and make it possible for the "invasion" of the West to take place:

"One would empty out all our hospital beds so that cholera-ridden and leprous wretches could sprawl between their clean white sheets. Another would cram our brightest, cheeriest nurseries full of monster children. Another would preach unlimited sex, in the name of one, single race of the future. . . . Still another would turn our supermarkets over to the barefoot, swarthy horde: 'Can't you see it now! Hundreds of thousands of women and children, smashing their way through those gigantic stores, stuffing their mouths with food, beside themselves with pleasure.'"

Raspail wrote his book in 1973—well before news stories about Haitian and

Ruth Conniff is Associate Editor of The Progressive.

Chinese refugees spurred a flurry of concern over "uncontrolled migration," before Europe tightened its asylum policies, before polls showed that most Americans think immigration is "bad for the country."

In July, *Newsweek* illustrated what it called the "immigration backlash" with a cover depicting the Statue of Liberty up to her nose in a rising tide of boat people. Earlier in the summer, a similar graphic appeared on the cover of the right-wing magazine *Chronicles,* with a horde of pointy-eared, demonic creatures scaling a wailing Liberty, under the headline BOSNIA, U.S.A. Pictures of the Statue of Liberty in distress have rapidly become an op-ed-page cliché, as have water metaphors, with so many waves of immigrants flooding, inundating, leaking in, seeping through, and drowning the nation.

In just the last few months, what were once considered right-wing views on immigration—that the United States is being "invaded" by the Third World, that immigrants pose a threat to the American economy and way of life, and that the borders need military fortification—have become

part of the accepted wisdom. Politicians are running to get ahead of the trend. Senator Barbara Boxer, the liberal Democrat from California, has proposed bringing in the National Guard to help seal the border with Mexico. California's Republican governor, Pete Wilson, has proposed a constitutional amendment that would deny U.S. citizenship and social services to the children of illegal immigrants. And President Clinton has announced a plan to tighten the asylum process and beef up the Border Patrol.

In the current anti-immigration climate, America's newcomers have become the lightning rod for almost all of our nation's anxieties and ills.

How has Raspail's dystopian vision moved from the lunatic fringe into the mainstream of the immigration debate?

Part of the backlash against immigrants results from the simple facts of increased worldwide migration, a constricting U.S. economy, and a series of high-profile news stories showing refugees and terrorists coming into the United States. But the current anti-immigration climate also owes

From *The Progressive,* October 1993, pp. 22-29. Reprinted by permission from *The Progressive,* 409 East Main Street, Madison, WI 53703.

'The melting pot is melting down.
The ethnic strife is tearing the country apart....
This is destroying the social fabric of America.
It's causing ethnic warfare.'

a lot to the calculated efforts of conservative individuals and groups.

John Tanton has probably done more than any other individual to shape the current anti-immigration movement in the United States. An ophthalmologist who lives in Petoskey, Michigan, Tanton provokes strong reactions. Friends describe him as "eclectic" and "brilliant." Opponents consider him a menace. A conservationist who was once president of Zero Population Growth, Tanton has built a network of more than a dozen organizations whose overlapping aims include conservation, population control, restricting immigration, and making English the official language of the United States.

In 1978, Tanton broke with Zero Population Growth to pursue his interest in the connection between population and immigration, and set out for Washington to found the Federation for American Immigration Reform (FAIR)—the most visible group in his network.

Regularly cited in the media as an expert source on immigration, FAIR provides statistics and data on immigration to members of Congress. The group lobbies for tighter security on the borders and a cap on annual legal immigration, and it was a driving force behind the 1986 legislation mandating employer sanctions for those who hire undocumented workers.

In July, the media watchdog group with the same acronym, Fairness and Accuracy in Reporting—which has taken to calling itself "the good FAIR" to distinguish itself from the anti-immigration group—issued a report pointing out that Tanton's Federation for American Immigration Reform receives hundreds of thousands of dollars from the Pioneer Fund, a group founded in 1937 by a millionaire who advocated sending American blacks back to Africa, and who promoted the work of Nazi eugenicists in Germany. Today, the Pioneer Fund bankrolls most of the major eugenics research in North America—including a study at the University of Western Ontario of comparative cranium and gonad size and IQ distribution among blacks, whites, and Asians.

FAIR's executive director, Dan Stein, is irked by the suggestion that receiving money from the Pioneer Fund compro-

mises his group. "I don't give a shit what they do with their money," he says. "My job is to get every dime of Pioneer's money. . . . And if they don't like what Pioneer is doing with the other grantees—you know, whatever their name is [Fairness and Accuracy in Reporting]—why don't they take it up with Pioneer? Why are they picking on us?"

The news about the Pioneer Fund is not the first scandal to plague Tanton's groups. In 1988, trouble erupted at U.S. English—a group he helped found to press for English as the official language of the United States—over a memo in which Tanton posed a series of hypothetical questions, referring to what he called "the Latin onslaught." "Will Latin American immigrants bring with them the tradition of the *mordida* (bribe), the lack of involvement in public affairs, etc.?" Tanton wrote. "Will the present majority peaceably hand over its political power to a group that is simply more fertile? . . . On the demographic point: Perhaps this is the first instance in which those with their pants up are going to get caught by those with their pants down!"

Then-director of U.S. English Linda Chavez and board member Walter Cronkite both quit, citing what Chavez called Tanton's "repugnant" and "anti-Hispanic" remarks. Chavez was also upset to discover that Cordelia Scaiffe May, the heiress who supports the Tanton network, had paid for the first U.S. reprint of Raspail's *The Camp of the Saints,* which some staff at U.S. English were reading. Chavez called the novel "without doubt the most vehemently racist book I have ever read."

Today, Tanton stands by everything he wrote in his memo. "In fact, it seems mild given what has happened since then," he says. Charges of racism annoy Tanton—they distract attention from what he considers to be the urgent issues of population growth and environmental degradation confronting Americans. "The charge of racism is really a move for cloture," he says. "That is, it's designed to silence people and to cut off debate."

But it is precisely the racial aspect of Tanton's work, and of the current anti-immigration climate, that is so troubling. To argue that we should bar the door against the Third World "onslaught" is just

a short step from the outright racism Raspail unabashedly expresses in his novel.

"You'd almost have to say he was prescient," says John Tanton, who read *The Camp of the Saints* around the same time he founded the Federation for American Immigration Reform. "I remember seeing pictures of the Albanians in their boats about two years ago, and it was just like Raspail described, with people hanging off the sides and spilling overboard. And the images of the boatloads of Chinese refugees were the same thing. . . . As revolting and disgusting as some of his descriptions were, Raspail was ahead of his time in that he was able to see the results of demographic trends. "

Flipping through a glossy FAIR publication entitled "Crowding Out the Future," Stein, who often appears as the group's spokesman on television and radio shows, points to charts, graphs, and computer-enhanced satellite photographs that illustrate connections among immigration, population growth, and the depletion of the United States' natural resources.

FAIR's central argument, that immigration is causing overpopulation in the United States and wreaking havoc on our environment, has broad appeal. Well-known ecologist Garrett Hardin is on FAIR's board of directors, Stein points out. And a number of sister organizations with names like Negative Population Growth and Carrying Capacity Network are pushing for immigration restrictions. Even the Sierra Club is currently divided over whether or not to adopt a "replacement-level" immigration policy along the lines that FAIR promotes, to stabilize U.S. population.

"Extreme Right ideology has been sifting into the environmental movement for some time," says Chip Berlet of Political Research Associates in Cambridge, Massachusetts. "It doesn't surprise me, because within the environmental movement there has always been a kind of Malthusian wing. In the last few years in Germany there's been a rebirth of what we call the Green Nazis. The problems they talk about are real. But their solution is to put rifles on the border. It is essentially a military, white-supremacist solution."

'The indomitable American spirit is being awakened....
White American citizens got guns
to fight back against the illegal aliens
and the criminals.'

Over the summer, FAIR ran a series of radio advertisements in major cities around the United States connecting immigration to a variety of urban problems. In Chicago, the ads provoked a response from the Chicago Coalition for Immigrant and Refugee Protection. "By attributing economic ills and environmental degradation to immigrants, FAIR is playing on people's most basic fears and prejudices," says David Marzahl, the coalition's executive director.

In 1990, a pilot ad in Houston caused a similar stir among Latino leaders there. According to the *Houston Chronicle,* the ads linked the flow of immigrants to homelessness, drug smuggling, and traffic congestion. "In one ad, a man stuck in a traffic jam wonders aloud, 'Look at all these people, where do they come from?'" the *Chronicle* reported. "His companion answers, 'Traffic is awful, and it will get worse if those politicians have their way. The paper says they want to let in millions more immigrants. Millions!'

"'WHAT?' says the man. 'Where are we going to put them? Who's going to feed them? Look at this traffic!'

"'Yes, millions more immigrants,' a woman says. 'We have got more homeless than we can feed now! What about jobs, health-care costs? Where's the housing? It is just not fair!'"

When I asked Stein about the ads, he confirmed that a new version was playing in radio markets around the country. He called the ads "innocuous" and dismissed criticisms of them. "It was the usual coalition for whatever—they were just bitching—the usual complaints. They just want to silence all voices but their own. Their opinion is all that matters and everything else is un-American." But Stein declined to let me hear the new ads or see transcripts of them.

Frank Sherry, executive director of the National Forum for Immigrant and Refugee Rights, sees FAIR's talk about protecting America as divisive. "When you get through all the sound bites and statistics," he says, "you get to the theme: There are too many people in the world. Too many of 'them,' and 'we' have got to do something about it."

This "us-versus-them" theme—the idea that "we" must protect America before the immigrants destroy it—runs through

the anti-immigration movement. Senator Alan Simpson, Republican of Wyoming, the author of legislation restricting immigration, says Americans suffer from "compassion fatigue." As resources become scarce and times get hard, Simpson and other conservatives argue, Americans have grown tired of embracing the downtrodden; they realize it's time to draw the wagons in a circle.

Along with resource depletion, among the most frequently invoked arguments against immigration is the idea that American culture is falling apart. A theme that emerges over and over is the ethnic warfare raging in the former Yugoslavia. Bill Anderson, the current director of U.S. English, uses Bosnia as an argument for having an official language in the United States.

"Certainly there are people in Sarajevo who wish someone had thought about language a long time ago," he says. "Had they had a common language they would have been able to talk those things through and resolve them by conversation rather than by confrontation and guns."

This point is dampened somewhat by the fact that people in the former Yugoslavia actually do share a common language. Still, the idea that Bosnian-style ethnic warfare threatens the United States has captured the imaginations of many Americans who oppose immigration.

"The melting pot is melting down," says Robert Goldsborough, founder and president of the far-right Americans for Immigration Control in Virginia. "The ethnic strife is tearing the country apart. Now you have Asian and Hispanic gangs in Long Beach, California, doing drive-bys and killing each other. . . . You've got Chinese heroin and cocaine gangs being operated by a major drug lord out of Red China. This is destroying the social fabric of America. It's causing ethnic warfare."

Nowhere has this feeling reached a more fevered pitch than in California.

Bette Hammond is a resident of Marin County, California, who sells New Age products for a mail-order company. Last January, she and a group of her neighbors, disgruntled by the migrant workers standing around on the street corners of San Rafael, formed a group called STOP-IT— Stop the Out-of-control Problems of Immigration Today.

STOP-IT's headquarters are in Hammond's home—a modest apartment in suburban Novato, where Hammond has a separate STOP-IT phone line and fax machine, and a letterhead that shows a weeping Statue of Liberty holding up a stop sign. Lately, Hammond has become something of a local celebrity, entertaining a steady stream of reporters in her living room. When I visited in August, she was cordial and eager to talk—showing me her cats, and chatting while she poured me a cup of coffee. But when she began talking about "the illegals" her expression hardened and her voice rose to an alarming pitch—punctuating every few sentences with the words "stop," "stop the insanity," and "stop it."

"We're against illegal aliens. They don't belong in our country. Just by being here they are criminals," she says. "We believe we're being invaded and we're out to stop it."

As Hammond sees it, illegal aliens have caused a range of problems for California, from the Los Angeles riots to crime, pollution, and the drought. Her group is part of a movement that is responding to this crisis.

"The indomitable American spirit is being awakened," Hammond says. "Americans don't like the graffiti in their neighborhoods. They don't like the traffic and overcrowding and the crime. American citizens don't like some of the neighborhoods in Southern California being taken over by illegals. . . . I have to stop our members from taking up weapons," she says. "We're out to *stop* the bloodshed. But I'll tell you, I have a feeling the reason there haven't been any more riots in L.A. is because so many people lined up to buy guns. White American citizens got guns to fight back against the illegal aliens and the criminals."

The whole state of California is facing an almost existential crisis, as military bases close and military contractors cut back their work forces. Fear, resentment, and social pathology are on the rise in white, middle-class communities as optimism about the future recedes. Violent antipathy toward immigrants is one result of this decline.

STOP-IT's membership has doubled over the last six months, and now includes 483 people, according to Hammond. She attributes the increase to publicity about

'**P**eople are coming to understand Vietnam now.
Public opinion has changed.
And I think in the same way they're coming
to understand the immigration problem.'

illegal immigration. Articles in *Time* and *Newsweek,* as well as a blurb on STOP-IT in *Borderwatch*, a magazine associated with the Americans for Immigration Control, all brought in new members.

Dan Stein's FAIR—in spite of its moderate reputation—has also been of assistance in organizing the group, Hammond says. "They help us out. If we have a meeting, they'll distribute notices. We all work hand-in-hand. It's good."

At Hammond's suggestion I visited San Rafael. She scribbled a map for me that took me past suburban houses with manicured lawns and palm trees, a few well-maintained apartment complexes with Mercedes and Saabs parked outside, and acre upon acre of strip malls—picture-perfect white America.

Except that along the curb by the freeway entrance, a group of about five Latino men in baseball caps sat waiting for work trucks. And further in, among the apartment complexes, a Mexican woman in a frilly white dress carried a pail in one hand, holding onto a small child with the other. These are the migrants invading suburban California.

On May 4, someone broke into the eleventh-floor offices of the Coalition for Immigrant and Refugee Rights and Services in downtown San Francisco, and wrote on the walls in black marker, USA—Love It or Get the - - - - Out Bitch.

Emily Goldfarb, the director of the office, had already received a series of threatening faxes in April. The most menacing came from a group called the California Coalition for Immigration Reform, to which STOP-IT belongs, and which claims a total membership of more than 10,000 "from the Bay Area to the Border."

"It may take some time," the fax stated, "but eventually you, the illegal, the devious, the underhanded who hold the laws of this great nation in contempt, will be purged from our midst as will the treacherous elected officials who have betrayed our trust!"

Such threats call to mind the messages distributed by paramilitary groups in Latin America—a comparison not lost on the Salvadoran refugees in the office.

"Of course, we are from countries where we have experienced political per-

secution," says Clara Luz Navarro, "so it is very alarming." Navarro was a nurse in her home town in El Salvador. She fled to the United States in the 1980s when the death squads began targeting health-care workers. Today, she organizes a Latina women's group called *Mujeres Unidas y Activas* in San Francisco. Navarro is proud of her group's community projects, such as a gardening class and beautification effort in the public parks, for which the city has donated land. With support from the Coalition, the group also conducts education and job training, sponsors entrepreneurial projects, and works to strengthen families, prevent child abuse, and improve life for immigrant women and their children.

"I came here just like them, and I had the same problems," Navarro says of the women in her group. "When you come to a new country and you don't speak the language, you feel very isolated and fearful."

Members of Mujeres are particularly concerned about Governor Wilson's announcement that he plans to shut off social services for illegal immigrants and deny citizenship to their children. "We're going to give a class and talk about what people can do if they decide to exclude the undocumented from health care." says Navarro. "What will happen to sick children? That is something that worries us."

Emily Goldfarb is also worried. Sitting in her office conference room, she fidgets and taps her feet. "It's been incredible the last few months," she says. "In the political arena, it's one thing after another. Each plan is more drastic than the one before. What worries us is that the statements by the governor and other political leaders are fueling resentment toward immigrants, and letting people know that it's okay to blame the person next door for all of your problems."

Goldfarb believes that efforts to crack down on illegal immigrants by cutting off social services will only make matters worse in California, creating an impoverished, outlaw underclass. "People need to understand the phenomenon of global migration," she says. "Immigrants come here because of conditions in their home countries, for reasons having to do with politics, economics, and war. . . . No one really believes that if we take away all their rights and services, that will change immigration."

Goldfarb also challenges the notion that immigrants are responsible for the problems with the California economy. "The problems the state is facing are very complex," she says. "It's obvious to me that this is just cynical, political rhetoric."

The economic data on immigration are hard to sort out. Figures produced by immigration advocates claim that all immigration, legal and illegal, is a net economic benefit to the United States; anti-immigration groups say that immigrants are costing taxpayers billions of dollars.

The economic statistics cited by FAIR, and by almost every other anti-immigration group, come from a study by Dr. Donald Huddle, an economist at Rice University. Huddle's figures, which show that immigrants cost the United States $54 billion a year in social services, have been widely cited in the news as facts.

"We've been trying to get the full report that Don [Huddle] did, but all we get is a kind of press kit from a group called the Carrying Capacity Network," says Dimitri Papadimitriou, a senior associate at the Carnegie Endowment for International Peace. "I cannot evaluate the figures until I see the full report."

Papadimitriou authored a recent Labor Department report on the economic impacts of immigration. "The assumptions about illegal immigration are extraordinary," he says of FAIR's claims. "The analysis is geared toward making a political statement. The real experts in the field make much more guarded and nuanced statements than FAIR."

The Carnegie Endowment is now working on another report on immigration, due out in November, Papadimitriou says. But the stodgy and careful analysis Carnegie's economists produce will not likely compete with FAIR's media campaign. "They are the only game in town," says Papadimitriou. "What I would hope journalists would stop doing is parking their judgment at the door and accepting any figure as legitimate unless it is dismissed by a legitimate person."

As for arguments about immigrants taking jobs away from Americans, "all of the evidence, both real world and econometric, suggests that there is virtually no displacement of American workers by immi-

France to Immigrants: Go Home

From Sweden to Portugal to Austria, doors are slamming shut. As the recession worsens in Western Europe and unemployment climbs to 12 per cent, attitudes toward immigration—and the laws governing it—are changing dramatically.

Germany no longer promises asylum to "people persecuted on political grounds." Greece recently expelled more than 25,000 Albanians. The number of racial incidents in Britain nearly doubled in just four years. And France, once a relatively welcoming new home, now offers a vivid example of the harsh new approach to immigration.

The view from a park bench in the Belleville gardens is classic Paris: charming rooftops, church spires, the coquettish peak of the Eiffel Tower. But even this world-renowned panorama won't persuade Chechene Coulibaly of the beauties of France. After seven years—and numerous short stays in prison because he doesn't have working papers—the twenty-two-year-old native of Mali is ready to give up life as an illegal immigrant and return to his poverty-stricken village.

"The police ask for our papers every day—on the street, on the Metro, right here in the gardens," he says, lowering his voice as a gendarme passes by the pansies and begonias in full bloom. "My family is very poor. I wanted to get money to help them buy food—that's the only reason I came here. I never stole, I never sold drugs, but they ask for my papers every day and now I want to leave France."

If the new conservative-dominated government of France has its way, a package of tough new immigration laws may prod other foreigners here to make the same decision as Coulibaly. The laws, which were passed earlier this year, tighten the screws on legal and illegal immigrants by restricting access to citizenship, allowing the police to make random identity checks, and speeding up deportations.

While a few of the laws were recently declared unconstitutional, the general trend is clear: France is no longer a haven for foreigners.

The laws are the fulfillment of the conservatives' campaign promises last spring to crack down on clandestine immigrants. The most vocal proponent is Interior Minister Charles Pasqua, the pit bull of a politician who oversees the police.

"The goal we have set, given the seriousness of the situation," he told the daily newspaper *Le Monde*, "is to tend toward zero immigration."

With a grim recession kicking in, the new measures appear to have general support from the French public: Many are quick to make a correlation between France's three million unemployed and the country's 3.6 million foreign residents.

Yet opposition is building. National protests organized by SOS Racism, an antiracist group, rallied mid-sized crowds, including about 15,000 in Paris, and such prominent intellectuals as Nazi-hunter Serge Klarsfeld and writer Marguerite Duras have denounced the laws. "With these measures," Duras says, "we sully the image of France."

The new government's first public feud emerged after Justice Minister Pierre Mehaignerie and Social Affairs Minister Simone Veil wrote to the prime minister protesting the wording of a section of the law authorizing spot identity checks by the police. It stated that the checks could be made on the basis of "all elements that allow the presumption of foreignness, with the exception of racial appearance."

This awkward turn of phrase inspired much public debate, with editorial writers noting that targets for identity checks could include people wearing African head scarves or speaking Arabic—as well as those listening to British rock bands or reading American newspapers.

"If you are reading *The New York Times* in the street, you may be presumed to be a foreigner," confirmed Gaullist Deputy Alain Marsaud, the author of the text, when asked in a radio interview what criteria the police should use to pinpoint foreigners.

"I don't want yellow people to be checked because they are yellow, or blacks to be checked because they are black," he added. "It will be up to the police to use their imagination."

But some observers say that new creativity by the police could have dangerous results. "The mind-set of these laws is one of suspicion," says Catherine Wihtol de Wenden, an immigration expert at France's Institute for Political Science. "Suspicion of allegiance, suspicion of fraud, suspicion about the possibilities for plurality. I fear they will aggravate tensions and encourage the emergence of violence as a new form of political expression." And, she adds, because the laws fail to target employers who provide jobs for illegal immigrants in the garment-making, building, and cleaning trades, they probably won't stem the tide of newcomers.

"These laws were made for the French public to say we are doing something," de Wenden says. "They are a series of linked, symbolic measures more than a real and effective policy. The voters will see in six months that it has not stopped anything, and that will create feelings of discontent and aggravate demands for a still stronger policy."

For immigrants in France, the situation is distressing. "It's not people on the street making remarks—it's the government that made these laws," says Hamouda Hertelli, the director of a federation of eighteen immigrant-workers' groups. Born in Tunisia, he has lived in France for decades and raised two children here, but he now fears for their future. "We are in a grave phase," he adds. "Our national discourse is one of xenophobia and racism."

Sometimes, though, it's difficult to spot the xenophobia among images of a multiracial France. In the Belleville gardens, on the edge of an immigrant neighborhood in eastern Paris, five young black girls wearing African-print dresses with bows at the back sit on a railing singing "Frère Jacques" at the top of their lungs on a sunny afternoon. Nearby, Africans, Europeans, Arabs, and Orthodox Jews stroll among the terraced gardens while children play in the soccer field, wading pool, tree huts, and fountains, all built by the city.

None of this impresses Chechene Coulibaly, however. Anticipating his return to his dust-bitten village of 500 inhabitants, he shrugs. "I've gotten nowhere here," he says.

—Lisa Glazer

(Lisa Glazer, former editor of City Limits magazine, is an American free-lance writer living in Paris.)

'They called us all kinds of nasty things.
We were racists.
We were bigots.
Then the Chinese landed and Washington panicked.'

grants," says Papadimitriou. "This is the consensus of the discipline."

While there are temporary displacements in given localities, Papdimitriou explains, there is no trend toward Americans becoming unemployed due to immigrant labor.

Similarly, costs in social services are disproportionately incurred in communities where there are large numbers of immigrants. But the net economic effect of all immigration—both legal and illegal—is to add wealth to the country, according to the Labor Department study. The solution, Papadimitriou and others argue, is not to clamp down on immigration, but rather for the Federal Government to redistribute the wealth in taxes and income from immigrant labor, and compensate localities that pay the costs.

With the national trend toward limiting immigration, and the political clout wielded by California, Washington is clearly moving to the Right on immigration policy.

"What pleases me is to see the liberals and conservatives finally getting together," says Senator Simpson, who has long advocated a more restrictive immigration policy. "I know someone from one of the [immigration advocacy] groups and I used to say to him, 'Button your shirt, your heart fell out.' He said to me, 'You know, it's really no fun to defend terrorists anymore.'"

One member of the Clinton Administration, a former advocate himself, told me that public perceptions have had a powerful effect on the Administration's immigration and asylum policy. "If we didn't introduce the legislation that we introduced, they would now be working on the Simpson bill," he says, "and if you don't think our Democratic friends in the Senate read us that message loud and clear, then you don't understand what's going on here."

The same official, who declined to be identified, seemed tormented by charges that the Administration is bowing to political pressure to adopt a conservative line on immigration. Rather, he says, it is the advocacy groups who are making the Administration's job hard: "My only plea to them is to recognize some of the good things we are doing," he said, "because if you don't, part of the incentive to fight for those things is diminished."

Duke Austin, the spokesman for the Immigration and Naturalization Service appointed under President Reagan, is pleased with the way the immigration debate is working out.

"Just a few years ago, it wasn't politically correct to talk about immigration," he says. "Now not only are they talking about it, they're fighting about whose partisan issue it is."

Austin, who is considering going to work for FAIR when he retires, is gratified by Clinton's plan to give more funding and staff to the INS.

An Army colonel in the Vietnam war, he feels a special affinity for the Border Patrol. A large poster hanging next to his desk shows uniformed agents on horseback, wielding guns, and driving motorcycles and speedboats. The public misunderstands the Border Patrol in the same way Americans misunderstood the troops in Vietnam, Austin says. "People are coming to understand the war now. Public opinion has changed. And I think in the same way, they're coming to understand the immigration problem," he says. "It's not the Border Patrol's fault."

Roberto Martinez, who runs the U.S.-Mexico border program for the American Friends Service Committee, is appalled by this shift in public perception. Martinez has monitored Border Patrol abuse over the years, including beatings and shootings of border crossers and harassment of U.S. citizens who simply look Latin.

"There are some real psychopaths in the Border Patrol," Martinez says. "And they already have M-16s. Now they want to send in the National Guard, who would bring bazookas. . . . It's insane."

Muriel Watson, the widow of a Border Patrolman in San Diego who devotes herself to the agency's cause, had me follow her out to the border at night. Suit jacket flapping as she dashed out of her car, she raced back to where I was pulling in behind her. "Turn off your lights, honey," she said as I got out. She pointed up the hill to a bonfire. "The aliens are massing up there," she said. "They're getting ready to charge." I could see a few figures silhouetted against the border wall—not the thousands I'd been told come over the border every night—perhaps ten people milling around in the dark.

Watson, who is running for the State Senate, is the founder of a group called Light Up the Border. At one time she organized hundreds of cars to drive out here and shine their headlights into Tijuana. "I call it the silent invasion," she says. "The hemorrhage of Mexico into the United States. My family in Minnesota calls to ask me, 'Gee, what's going on down there, Muriel?'" She let out a short laugh and waved at the darkened hills around her. "All hell is breaking loose!"

Light Up the Border was disbanded last year after people in the community did not respond favorably to the idea of targeting the Latin Americans coming across the border and shining headlights in their eyes. "They called us all kinds of nasty things—we were racists, we were bigots," says Watson. "Then the Chinese landed and Washington panicked."

Today, Watson is feeling more optimistic about her efforts. After she started Light Up the Border, stadium lights went up along the fence that closes off San Diego's border area. Watson would like to see a bigger fence, more patrol cars, and lights all along the border.

Many of Watson's fellow protesters are ranchers who feel abandoned by the Government, alone on the frontier, at the mercy of the smugglers and illegal immigrants who cross the border every day.

"The state of California estimates that they spend $2 billion on the illegal alien problem—that includes invasion of our hospitals, our schools, and welfare," says Ted Power, who took part in Light Up the Border. "In San Diego, known illegals have received assistance costing $1.4 million last year."

The ranchers are used to watching illegal immigrants come across their land, and they see it as an example of Government negligence that the border isn't better guarded. "The problem is higher up. The U.S. Government doesn't want to stop the illegals," says Kim Silva, a member of the citizens' group. "They like all the cheap labor coming into the United States."

"The inevitable result is it's going to be a border war," says Power. "We're very serious about our sovereignty here and our families. If our government don't do something, by God we will."

Far from the U.S.-Mexico border, on the shores of Lake Michigan, Dr. John Tanton runs U.S. Inc., a non-profit foundation he set up to handle the phone-calling and paperwork for his various interests. To the extent that other people are now paying attention to the issues he's been working on for so long, "that's all to the good," says Tanton. But his outlook, like Raspail's, is still not optimistic. "This is not a fairy tale that has some happy ending," he says. "It's going to be a very difficult time for mankind."

Raspail's story ends, inevitably, with racial warfare. A few courageous whites are the doomed heroes, holding out in the last unoccupied village of France until they are finally overrun by the "swarthy hordes." Before the final assault, an assimilated Indian who lives in Europe tries to warn the Western governments not to open their borders. "You don't know my people," he says. "The squalor, the superstitions, the fatalistic sloth they've wallowed in for generations. You don't know what you're in for if that fleet of brutes ever lands in your lap! Everything will change in this country of yours. . . . They'll swallow you up." Which is exactly what happens at the end of the book.

The same apocalyptic nightmare looms in America's future, according to anti-immigration groups—unless we shut our doors. "We've always said if reasonable people can't sit down and solve these problems, it will end up in the streets," says Stein.

But the idea of saving ourselves by building a higher wall around our borders, fortifying it with more guns, and hunting down the "aliens" in our midst is a lost cause. It will not change the global economic and political problems that send people fleeing here from other countries.

And it will certainly not win us a more peaceful society. It is ironic that the anti-immigration groups invoke the example of Yugoslavia. With its divisive rhetoric and undercurrent of racial hate, the anti-immigration movement promotes the very ethnic divisions its members warn about.

Immigrants have always been part of this country. In the end, what we do about immigration depends upon what kind of society we envision for ourselves. If we want to live in a humane society, we must resist our worst impulses to turn our backs on the rest of the world.

"We're at the beginning of having to organize a movement strong enough to withstand the fear of foreigners and people of color building in this country," says Frank Sherry. "It's an enormous challenge. Right now a betting person would bet for the restrictionists and the racists."

Hobson's Choice for Indigenous Peoples

Stuck between cultural extinction and misery

L'EXPRESS

GILBERT CHARLES

They put on their Sunday dresses, their pretty braided bracelets, and the only shoes they had. Clarinda was 12; Gervina was 14. Then they went out to the forest and hanged themselves. Ataliba, a 40-year-old farmworker, poisoned himself by swallowing pesticide as he set out for work. He died, writhing in pain, in the middle of a sugar-cane field, under the terrified gaze of his companions. Pedro, 17, hanged himself at home. Nena, 13, put her neck through a piece of cord she had tied to a tiny tree behind the church where her parents were attending a service and choked herself by simply falling to her knees.

The Guarani Indians of Brazil seem to have decided to exterminate themselves. For five years, men, women, and children have been systematically committing suicide, one after another. They never leave a note, and those who survive their suicide attempts refuse to give the slightest explanation and take shelter in silence. First noticed in 1987, this epidemic has grown steadily: 21 dead in 1990 and 31 in 1991. Almost all the victims belong to the Guarani Kaiowa tribe, a group of 6,300 descendants of communities colonized by the Jesuits' famous "missions," which were dismantled in the 18th century. With a reputation for being peaceful and religious, the Kaiowa formerly occupied a territory of about 7,700 square miles near Brazil's border with Paraguay. Gradually driven out by giant soybean and sugar-cane plantations, they have been tucked into an 8,750-acre reservation near the town of Dourados, where they live in a state of overcrowding and misery.

"The young are killing themselves to recover their freedom," says Carlito de Oliveira, one of the tribal chiefs. "They prefer to go over to the 'other side,' because we have lost everything: our lands, our traditions, our dignity." Brazil's Indians numbered 5 million about five centuries ago; according to official figures, only 200,000 remain. Slaughtered by the conquistadors, converted by the missionaries, ravaged by alcohol, driven away by settlers, and decimated by disease, they are in desperate straits. They have little choice but to give up their ancient cultures and blend into the great market system that now holds sway around the world. To disappear as Indians or to succumb to misery—that is the choice. But either way, the result is the same: pauperism.

Give or take a few nuances, this scenario is being repeated the world over for most of the so-called primitive peoples. Australia had 300,000 Aborigines before the English arrived in the 18th century, compared with 60,000 a century later. In 1960, there were about 5,000 Pygmies living in Uganda; now there are only 300. There were more than 10,000 Punan nomads in the forest of Borneo in the early 1980s; now only 500 are left. The rest have wandered to towns, as logging companies have methodically deforested their island. This time, there is no doubt about it: The world's "savages" are about to vanish, buried with their feathers and their myths beneath the steamroller of civilization. And, with them, a part of humankind's memory will disappear.

It was not until 1982 that the United Nations recognized the existence of "indigenous peoples." They are defined as descendants of the original inhabitants of conquered territories possessing a minority culture and recognizing themselves as such. Still, that description covers some 200 million people spread unevenly across 70 countries. Indigenous people account for less than 1 percent of the population of Brazil or the U.S., for example, but 66 percent of the population in Bolivia and 40 percent in Peru. In Greenland, 90 percent of the population is Inuit. It is in Asia that indigenous people are the most numerous: 86 million in China (particularly the Uighurs, Tibetans, and Mongols) and 51 million in India.

The status of indigenous peoples varies considerably from one state to another, but they are often treated as second-class citizens or even considered sub-human. For example, under Brazilian law, Indians are treated as legal minors under the guardianship of the Indian-affairs agency, which is charged with protecting them from themselves. The Pygmies of the Central African Republic and Uganda are not included in these countries' censuses, because they are not considered part of the population.

After centuries of domination, the indigenous peoples are

From the newsmagazine "L'Express" of Paris.

Reprinted from *World Press Review*, September 1992, pp. 26-28.

starting to wake up and get organized. A constellation of tribal associations has cropped up in recent years, bringing together mainly American Indians but also the Papuans of New Guinea, the Sarawaks of Malaysia, and the Pygmies of Rwanda. Most of them stick to grass-roots activism, but international meetings are increasing. Last February, for example, the Indians of South America's five Amazonian countries met to discuss self-determination. A few weeks later, representatives of some 50 American, Asian, and African tribes met in Penang, Malaysia, and issued a "Charter of the Forest Peoples," which singles out deforestation as a "crime against humanity." In May, an event titled "500 Years of Resistance" (to colonization) was held in Rio de Janeiro as a prelude to the UN's Earth Summit.

We are still far from seeing anything like a "global liberation movement," but indigenous peoples are less and less fearful of laying claim to their history and heritage. A group of Mexican Indians recently demanded the return of the crown of an Aztec emperor that has been preserved in a Vienna museum. The Krahos Indians of Brazil have already succeeded in recovering a sacred hatchet that had lain in the Indian museum in Rio de Janeiro since 1949. In Canada, the Attikamek-Montagnais people are demanding sovereignty over one third of Quebec, while the Inuit propose to create a nation to be called Nunavut (Our Land) out of half of the Northern Territories—an area three times the size of France. "Those people underwent a conquest that they have never accepted," says anthropologist Pierre Grenand. "Now they want their space and their status redefined."

Many governments are beginning to accept the idea of some form of self-determination for native peoples. The Canadian constitution has recognized the "ancestral rights of indigenous peoples" since 1982, and the government has accepted the outlines of the Inuit plan for Nunavut. Australia and Colombia recently adopted articles along the same lines as the Canadian constitution. And Brazil's President Fernando Collor de Mello has granted a reservation of 23 million acres to some 9,500 Yanomami Indians of the Amazon and has promised to lay out boundaries around the spaces of all other tribes within a year.

But the problems of indigenous peoples are much more complex than they seem and do not all result from the constraints imposed by governments. Native groups' positions are often very different, and their interests sometimes conflict. North America's Algonquin Indians and Inuit, enemies for thousands of years, have little in common. The same goes for Africa's Bantus and Pygmies, the latter of whom live under the domination of the former.

It may be a mistake to look on all indigenous peoples as victims: Some are more victimized than others. In Brazil, for example, side by side with impoverished peoples such as the Guarani and Yanomami, one finds relatively prosperous Indians. Some of the Kayapo Indians, in southern Brazil, have built a comfortable fortune by selling gold and lumber from their reservation, where 70,000 trees have been felled since 1986 for a profit of $43 million, according to estimates by a Brazilian environmental institute. That has enabled the chiefs to fly hundreds of painted warriors to Brasília whenever they are unhappy with government policy. "The Indians can no longer live without money," says Chief Tutu Pombo, who owns two airplanes, a sizable cattle

ranch, and a respectable bank account. True, but the money earned from the Indians' common heritage is far from being equitably distributed among all the Kayapos.

That kind of story puts a serious dent in the somewhat angelic image of the Indian living in harmony with the universe, a living symbol of environmentalism and of the purity of early man. Unfortunately, folklore is often the only means by which Westerners express any interest in the fate of native peoples, and the native peoples may understandably try to strike that sentimental chord.

"The world's 'savages' are about to vanish, buried beneath the steamroller of civilization."

Who can speak for the native peoples? That question has been the subject of heated debate, and the Indians themselves have trouble agreeing on the answer. This was seen in the chaotic disagreements that arose over the commemoration of "500 Years of Resistance" at Rio. Intended as an example of unity among native groups, the event was more reminiscent of the building of the tower of Babel.

Even more serious is the fact that most of the grass-roots organizations decided to boycott the event. Orlando Melgueiro, the spokesman for a federation of 36 indigenous Amazonian associations, called the gathering "a pointless media event." Melgueiro, who speaks mainly for the Indians of the forest, generally criticizes the "city Indians" for their "opportunist" strategies. But Marcos Terena, leader of Brazil's Terena Indians, feels that minorities must emancipate themselves by adopting the "methods and language of the white man." He says, "Why should we be doomed to cutting lumber with axes when there are chain saws? We, too, are entitled to refrigerators, cars, video, and the right at the same time to preserve our traditional culture."

This is the inescapable dilemma: Can native peoples adapt to civilization without giving up their values? "That debate is ridiculous," says anthropologist Jean-Claude Jeffreys. "The real problem of the indigenous people is material survival with dignity. Whether or not it involves preserving their culture has become secondary." Jean-Patrick Razon, director of the French section of Survival International, a kind of Amnesty International for indigenous people, adds: "They are entering the white man's system, in any event. But many of them manage to get by with one foot in each world."

Saving the "savages" before it is too late means saving the last remnants of nature with which they live. Although human rights may have no price, the forests are becoming a commodity quoted on the world market. From 30–40 percent of modern medicines contain ingredients extracted from exotic flora and fauna, ranging from curare, a muscle relaxant used by Indians to tip their arrows, to the Mexican sweet potato, which contributed to the development of birth-control pills.

2. POPULATION

The Third World is now calling for full sovereignty over these resources, which have until now been considered the common heritage of mankind. Westerners, in their own interest, are prepared to recognize that sovereignty and to allocate the funds needed to create biodiversity preserves. The tropical countries will thus be able to exploit their ecosystems as other countries exploit their oil reserves.

What will be the role of the Indians in the ecological market now taking shape? Some past examples do not augur well. Bolivia and Ecuador have plundered the nature reserve inhabited by the Chimane and Waorani Indians, whose protection had been paid for by American environmentalists. The Indians have a card up their sleeves: No one knows the wild plants and animals better than they do. But they will have to learn to market their knowledge. American anthropologist Darell Posey, a specialist on the Kayapo Indians, is campaigning for recognition of the "intellectual rights of the forest peoples," urging them to make agreements with entrepreneurs and demand compensation for the information they supply for research. The result is that the Xavantes, the Tukaramais, the Tucanos, and the Kayapos are now obtaining legal counsel when they have business deals with the white man.

Five hundred years ago, the conquistadors landed in the New World in search of gold, which became synonymous with death for the Indians. Today, it is green gold that is luring the Westerners to the tropics. This time, the effort is aimed at protecting the Indians by pointing to their knowledge, their culture, and their mythology, which could disappear forever. But do we need logical reasons for saving these peoples? A good Indian is a live Indian.

The AIDS Pandemic in Africa

"By the year 2000, approximately 25 million Africans" could be infected with HIV, the virus that causes AIDS. "How can one begin to discuss the broad implications of HIV infection and AIDS for the poorest continent on earth, where average annual government health-care expenditures are about $2 for each man, woman, and child?"

DENNIS C. WEEKS

DENNIS C. WEEKS, *the president of Sweet Hill Associates, has served as a consultant to the United States Agency for International Development and is currently working on AIDS and other health-care projects in Africa.*

Does AIDS represent a cataclysm for Africa? The fatal disease has spread throughout the continent quickly in the last ten years, and the potential impact over the next decade is nothing short of devastating—given no development of a vaccine, no cure, and no dramatic increase in the availability of life-extending medications and treatment.

The numbers themselves are frightening. In July 1990, the World Health Organization (WHO) estimated that there were approximately 8 million HIV-infected adults worldwide, of whom approximately 3 million were women and 5 million were men. In July 1991 the agency estimated the total at between 10 million and 12 million HIV-positive individuals. Seven months later, on February 12, 1992, revised WHO figures put the global total at 12 million, of whom 1 million are children who are not yet sexually active.[1] Of this global total, 7.5 million, or 62.5 percent, are Africans. Among the world's infected female population, at least 81 percent, or more than 3.7 million, reside in Africa, while approximately 52 percent, or 3.8 million, of the world's HIV-infected males are Africans.

WHO estimates that within the next five years the number infected globally will at least double and possibly triple; it further estimates that by the year 2000 at least 30 million people will be infected throughout the world, with some experts expecting closer to 40 million. Infants and children will account for up to 10 million of the total, and there will be approximately 10 million AIDS orphans—children whose parents have died from AIDS.

If the gender ratios remain constant, more than 15 million females and 25 million males will be infected with HIV by the year 2000. Furthermore, if the same geographical distribution patterns hold, the number of infected African females could exceed 12 million while infected African males could reach 13 million. Thus by the year 2000 approximately 25 million Africans, representing five out of every eight global infections, or nearly 63 percent, could be expected.[2]

CHARTING THE IMPACT OF AIDS

Uganda is the African country that has been hardest hit by AIDS.[3] An ongoing study of pregnant women in the capital city of Kampala, begun in the mid-1980s, shows that the infection rate increased from nearly 11 percent of pregnant women in 1985 to more than 25 percent today. The women studied are considered a low-risk group; those in a high-risk group—prostitutes and others with many sexual partners—had a 75 percent infection rate. Outside major cities in Uganda, current infection rates approximate the 1985 major city rate,

THE PATHOLOGY OF AIDS

AIDS (acquired immune deficiency syndrome) results from infection with HIV (human immunodeficiency virus). A person who is infected with HIV is commonly referred to as being HIV-positive, which means that antibodies to HIV are present in that person's blood. This does not mean that the person has AIDS. A significant period of time will elapse, usually many years, from the time of infection with HIV until the person develops AIDS. General exceptions to that statement are infants who are born infected and usually die within 24 months after birth.

The time between initial HIV infection, followed by symptomatic HIV illness such as thrush or Kaposi's sarcoma, and a subsequent diagnosis of AIDS varies widely and depends on many factors, some of which are related to location. In the United States and Western Europe, the time span between HIV infection and diagnosis of AIDS is approximately seven years and lengthening. In Africa the period can be shorter, and further studies will offer a clearer timeframe.*

There is currently no cure for or vaccine against AIDS, which gradually debilitates an individual by reducing the body's natural ability to fight diseases such as pneumonia, tuberculosis (TB), and diarrhea, for which there are common, effective therapies. The prospects for developing a vaccine are not encouraging, and most experts do not expect one until the end of the century.

Several strains of the virus have been discovered, and the two strains that account for nearly all infection in Africa are referred to as HIV-1 and HIV-2. While both strains are found to some extent in most African countries, HIV-1 is predominant in eastern and southern Africa, and HIV-2 is responsible for virtually all infection in western Africa. (HIV-1 is the strain almost exclusively found in the United States and Europe.)

HIV can be transmitted three different ways:

- via infected blood through transfusions or unsterilized surgical instruments and hypodermic needles;
- from mother to infant, either through intrauterine transfer of blood or fluids or through mothers' milk by breast-feeding;
- transfer of bodily fluids, primarily semen and vaginal secretions generated by sexual activity.

Infection through the transfer of blood or blood products usually occurs because they have not been cleansed of the virus before transfusion or injection. (A common practice that many Africans believe provides energy is receiving a pint of blood from another person.) Transmission through unsterilized needles occurs most often through reuse or group-use of needles that should be disposed of after one use. This method of transmission is not a major concern in Africa, since intravenous drug use on the continent is extremely rare, although it is a major problem in the United States, Europe, and some parts of Asia and Latin America.

Surgical instruments, which in Africa include knives and razor blades, can also become sources of transmission when there is inadequate sterilization, and when the same instrument is used on many people in succession without sterilization. In Africa this occurs during semiannual or annual village circumcision rites that can include as many as 100 youths. Scarification ceremonies, frequently associated with puberty, also include many individuals. However, transmission through blood or blood products accounts for perhaps as little as 5 percent of total African AIDS cases.

Another form of transmission occurs from mother to infant.** Although most infections occur at birth, a small proportion are caused by breast-feeding. Although numerically insignificant at this time—less than 5 percent of the total—there has been recent speculation that transmission through breast-feeding might be more efficient than thought earlier. If true, this could have serious implications for the successful campaigns to promote breast-feeding as the best means of providing biological immunization and high nutrition, a natural method of child spacing with positive health implications for mothers, and a reduction in consumption of infant formula, which is often mixed with contaminated water. Panic could drive mothers to resist breast-feeding, whether or not they are HIV-positive.

More than 90 percent of HIV transmission worldwide is the result of transfer of bodily fluids between sexual partners through sexual intercourse. Since homosexuality and bisexuality appear to be rare in Africa, and have not been well researched, there is wide agreement among experts that nearly all HIV transmission in Africa is the result of heterosexual activity.

---

*Many think that in Africa a combination of factors such as water-borne diseases, malaria, tuberculosis, sexually transmitted diseases, parasites, lack of proper medical care, and a dearth of the most basic medicines, account for the shorter period between infection with HIV, diagnosis of AIDS, and death.

**Transmission from mother to infant occurs when the mother is either HIV-positive or has AIDS. The rate at which infants are infected through contact with the bodily fluids of their infected mothers ranges between 25 and 50 percent, which means that of every 100 infants born to mothers with either HIV infection or AIDS, as many as 50 will themselves be infected at or shortly after birth.

with a wave of infection moving toward the rural areas.

Other countries with seriously high rates of HIV infection among low-risk populations in major cities include Burundi, Malawi, Rwanda, Tanzania, and Zambia. Among these countries, Burundi appears to have the lowest rate of infection of low-risk groups in major cities, at nearly 18 percent, while the others show rates in excess of 22 percent, with Rwanda and Zambia at or above 25 percent. High-risk urban populations in those same countries have infection rates ranging from 18 percent in Burundi to 80 percent in Rwanda; most have rates between 40 and 60 percent. Other African countries that appear to have infection rates between 5 and 10 percent in low-risk urban populations include the Central African Republic, Congo, Ivory Coast, Kenya, Sierra Leone, and Senegal.

The available data describing African HIV infection rates are not very reliable, and probably underestimate infection levels. Most African governments have denied AIDS is a problem in their countries, fearing that tourists would abandon plans to visit, which would disrupt the flow of hard currency. The denial is so extensive that data for rates of HIV infection and/or AIDS are not available from many African countries.

Statistics from some African countries show a reduction in the rate of increase of infection and death. Often this merely demonstrates that hospitals are already operating beyond capacity and are not accepting more patients. After being rejected by hospitals and clinics, many people stricken with AIDS simply return home, so their illnesses and deaths are not included in the data. Conversely, initially high rates of infection might reflect implementation of data-gathering systems, followed by a more accurate accounting of morbidity and mortality.

The governments that have been the most aggressive in acknowledging the presence of AIDS in their country were also the first to receive technical and financial assistance from WHO's Global Program on AIDS. WHO's assistance in most cases led to the development of plans to fight AIDS in those countries. The earlier the assistance was received and plans developed, the more extensive are the data-reporting systems now in place. Two examples are Uganda and Zambia, which allowed the development of AIDS education and prevention strategies.

Data are the foundation on which successful programs are built. Because some countries have shown early initiative in acknowledging the presence of AIDS, their relatively well-developed reporting systems give the appearance that they have higher rates of infection than their neighbors. But a more realistic assumption is that countries bordering other countries with highly infected populations also have high rates of infection.

Only a handful of African governments have reliable data on infection rates in rural populations. The rural data that do exist, however, show a worrisome trend toward higher and growing rates of transmission. Most Africans live in rural areas—as much as 85 percent of the total population in many countries—which means that the spread of AIDS into the rural population will heighten the tragedy. Most programs have targeted urban-based Africans, with specific emphasis on locations where many people are in one place at the same time, such as workplaces. With the exceptions of religious institutions and some agriculturally oriented cooperative societies, opportunities for informing large groups at one time about the facts of AIDS, and its transmission and prevention, are relatively limited in rural Africa. Compounding the difficulties are the linguistic and tribal barriers to communicating with large numbers of rural residents.

HEALTH CARE AND AIDS

How can one begin to discuss the broad implications of HIV infection and AIDS for the poorest continent on earth, where average annual government health-care expenditures are about $2 for each man, woman, and child? How does a continent cope with nearly 10 million AIDS orphans by the turn of the century, of which

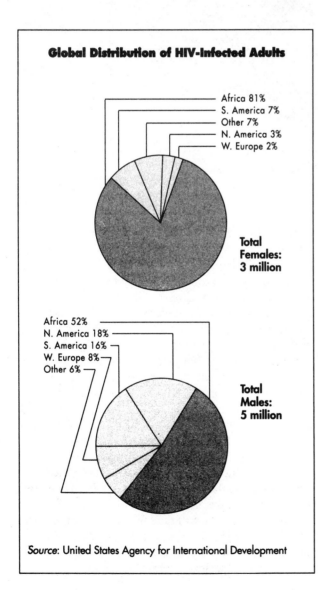

Global Distribution of HIV-Infected Adults

Africa 81%
S. America 7%
Other 7%
N. America 3%
W. Europe 2%

Total Females: 3 million

Africa 52%
N. America 18%
S. America 16%
W. Europe 8%
Other 6%

Total Males: 5 million

Source: United States Agency for International Development

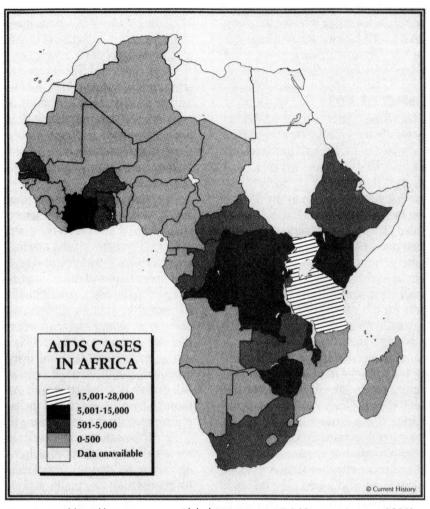

Source: World Health Organization, Global Program on AIDS (Geneva, January 1992).

there are already nearly 500,000 in Uganda alone, and the number is growing rapidly in areas surrounding Lake Victoria in Tanzania? How will countries cope with the possible decimation of the extended African family? How can these orphaned and abandoned children sustain their physical and mental health if there is no one to take care of them? What means exist to help these children care for their parents, many of whom are dying of AIDS?

The hopelessness of the situation can be seen by looking at conditions at Kampala's Mulago hospital, where for several years the only AIDS clinic in Uganda has had no medication to offer those who are diagnosed with the disease, and where the staff has refused to assist women to deliver their infants because of a lack of rubber gloves and footwear. Most AIDS sufferers, already in poor health by the time they are diagnosed, simply drift back to their village or to the village where their father or mother was born, to die. Many are not taken in by their relatives because of the stigma and fear of the disease, and after they die their children are often left to fend for themselves.

A broader look at African health issues is helpful in

understanding the context in which AIDs is viewed by Africans. In countries where malaria is a constant scourge and new strains continue to resist available drugs and weaken immunity developed over decades, and where diarrheal disease kills hundreds of thousands of both young and elderly each year, it has been reasonable for governments to pay more attention to traditional health threats than to a new, relatively unknown or unheard-of disease. For example, at the height of the recent drought, as many as 500,000 people were expected to die in a year from the drought's effects. At the same time, more than 500,000 children in Nigeria alone were dying each year from malaria and water-borne disease. Conditions similar to those in Nigeria, although with fewer deaths, are common throughout the continent. AIDS is just another disease in the eyes of Africans, policymaker and simple citizen alike, until the rate of infection reaches the point that members of their families, coworkers and next-door neighbors start dying. In many cities in eastern, central, and southern Africa, most people have already experienced those situations.

Governments and individual leaders have reacted predictably to pressures from long-established social and religious institutions that have argued against the development and implementation of AIDS education and prevention programs that emphasize open discussion of sexual behavior, long a taboo even between parent and child. In many countries where AIDs education and prevention programs have proposed the use of condoms as one way of slowing transmission, responses have included open hostility from both political and religious leaders. Such programs have also generated confusion among Africans who have neither seen nor heard of condoms, who are embarrassed and angry when they are first exposed to them, and who interpret condom promotion as an attempt to develop a profitable market for an unpopular and unwanted item.

Two other health-care problems closely related to AIDS are traditional sexually transmitted disease (STDs) and tuberculosis (TB). HIV and other STDs amplify each other's effects. Experts estimate that there is a very low likelihood of transmitting HIV from a single episode of vaginal intercourse. If, however, one of the parties is already infected with another STD at the time of that single episode—especially chancroid or syphilis, both of which can cause lesions—the risk of transmitting HIV is up to 50 times greater. WHO collected data from women visiting prenatal clinics in 10 African countries and found that the prevalence of syphilis ranged between 10 and 20 percent. Rapid increases in HIV infection in the neighborhoods of those clinics and escalating rates of fetal death and infant mortality will no doubt follow.

Tuberculosis, perhaps the world's leading killer and certainly among the top three, has resurfaced in areas long considered safe. The link between TB and AIDS is clear and made more critical by a new, drug-resistant strain occurring in some populations with high levels of HIV infection. In Africa the number of current cases of active TB has created an epidemic similar in size to that of AIDS. The potential impact of TB is dramatized by the fact that most practicing health-care professionals have no experience with TB except through textbooks, there has been little research on it, and the disease is spread through coughs and sneezes. Health-care professionals in the United States, which is also experiencing an increase in TB, have begun discussing whether to reopen sanitariums once used for TB patients and to quarantine people with active TB. Africa, too, must prepare for potentially devastating effects of the disease.

THE ECONOMIC IMPACT OF AIDS

Quantitative studies of the economic impact AIDS has had on Africa are generally unavailable. However, broad areas of impact are obvious, including both the direct and indirect costs associated with AIDS in the workplace and the health-care and psychological costs to society.

The private sector's economic health in the African countries hardest hit by AIDS had been marginal at best even before the malady became a problem. Except for the banking and insurance industries, corporations are just beginning to emerge from prolonged retrenchment and the debt accumulated through borrowing for capital improvements and expansion during the 1970s and 1980s. It is now time for most industries to rebuild or replace their plants and equipment, and the lack of financial resources prevents them from doing so.

American reluctance to invest in Africa, in spite of the fact that investment codes are the most lenient in nearly 25 years and that return on investment is greater across Africa than it has been since the early 1960s, leads to the conclusion that Africa is not attractive to American investors for reasons other than standard calculations of return on investment. European investment in Africa, historically bolder and more effective than American investment on the continent, also seems to be on hold. Asian investment on the continent continues at the most rapid pace, but in the face of slowing economies at home, it is not likely to remain as rapid, with the exception of the export markets targeted by Asian manufacturers of vehicles and spare parts.

An example of the position Africa holds in the minds of non-African investors becomes clear from a mid-February 1992 announcement in major financial publications that the treasurer of the World Bank, Donald C. Roth, will soon resign in order to form the Emerging Markets Corporation, a private venture.[4] He will be joined by a former chairman of Salomon Brothers and a former senior vice president of the World Bank, with financing partly provided by the United States–based Bankers Trust Company. The announcements listed the targets of the new venture as eastern Europe, Latin America, and Asia. Not one word was mentioned about Africa, even though approximately $100 billion is expected to be invested in developing country firms worldwide by the year 2000, up from approximately $20 billion at the end of 1990.

When AIDS is introduced into the profit picture of African industry, the disease covers it like a dark cloud. The loss of industry's top layer of African managers—often the only layer of African managers—compounded by the persistent reduction of members of the most energetic component of the nonmanagement workforce, carries high direct and indirect costs. After years of careful selection and training, the loss of managers can leave an organization without leadership and unable to remain competitive. High prospective death rates for nonmanagement workers, especially those between 18 and 35 years of age, could create a labor shortage resulting in bidding wars for those able to work, thereby escalating labor costs.

Hospital, clinic, and pharmaceutical expenses, death benefits to surviving family members, burials, transport costs, time off for coworkers to attend funeral services, grief leave, recruitment and training costs associated with a replacement workforce, and higher insurance premiums are examples of direct costs due to AIDS that must be absorbed by organizations just barely able to function without it. In addition, there are indirect costs that may prove even more important over the long run. Among them are decreasing productivity because of fear and sadness associated with death and dying; dissension and discrimination at the workplace because of the incorrect belief that HIV infection and AIDS are transmitted through casual contact; and the lack of a clearly stated organizational policy concerning infected workers.

As AIDS continues to spread throughout Africa and the rest of the world, business decision makers must recognize that the disease can make their organizations dysfunctional and, eventually, defunct. Parent companies based in the United States, Europe, and Asia need to protect their investments and most important resource—human capital—through aggressive AIDS education and prevention programs, with follow-up activities directed at counseling and treatment of the sick and dying and their survivors. Government decision makers must incorporate similar tactics to ensure that civil services and state-owned businesses remain viable.

HOPE IN MANY FORMS

Relative wealth will define the long-term, global distribution of HIV infection and AIDS-related deaths. While there is neither a vaccine against nor a cure for AIDS, state-of-the-art treatment is approaching the point that within a short time, perhaps as soon as two years, the availability of and access to medical and psychological treatment for those who are HIV-positive or have AIDS could sustain life indefinitely.

Most developed countries now provide the health care and medications that can slow the progression from HIV infection to AIDS and eventual death. There is little likelihood that those at the lower end of the global socioeconomic scale will benefit from life-prolonging treatment in the foreseeable future. This is especially true for the countries of Africa. Human vaccine trials set to begin within two years in at least two African countries (one of which is Uganda) might offer some hope, but a vaccine will not be available globally until early in the next century. Thus simple economic truths ensure that Africa will bear an increasingly disproportionate share of the impact of AIDS.

Given the relatively bleak picture painted so far, is there hope for Africa? Yes, in many forms, one of which comes from outside the continent. Donor countries and organizations have always provided assistance, and in the case of the AIDS pandemic assistance has appeared from throughout the world in a bewildering array of goods and services. The efficiency with which foreign assistance is offered and delivered, however, is frustrating. At times the requirements of donors are as confusing to recipients as the range of aid offered. Competing interests and overlap have meant

that delivery and management of assistance is reduced, sometimes dramatically.

Of all the sources of AIDS assistance given to Africa, none comes close to the financial and technical inputs provided by the United States. Although other countries dedicate larger portions of their gross domestic product to foreign assistance, the amount of aid distributed by the United States dwarfs that of most others. In terms of AIDS assistance, WHO received more than $77 million from donor contributions in 1990, nearly $21 million of which was donated by the United States Agency for International Development (AID). Since 1986, AID, the largest financial supporter of WHO's Global Program on AIDS, has also donated more than $91 million through bilateral assistance programs and another $10 million from assorted AID accounts.

Another source of hope is that as medications for AIDS and AIDS-related illnesses are developed, they will eventually be made available for mass consumption at prices affordable to all, including Africans. But there will be a considerable time lag from initial availability of the medications until the research and development costs are recovered and prices thus decrease. The development costs of new products are high, but there are indications that firms with products now available are assessing areas where they can make contributions toward alleviating AIDS-related problems.

The most important source of hope rests with Africans themselves. Innovative AIDS projects have been under way for several years in many African countries, funded in part by foreign donors. In many cases the projects have been "indigenized" as Africans have assumed decision-making roles and developed new programs. This ability to sustain projects is an important part of all AIDS activities.

African corporations that have agreed to develop AIDS-in-the-workplace programs that educate workers about the disease and its prevention have realized the importance of allowing employees time off for training and have donated space for meetings, provided transportation to training programs, and have even allowed and encouraged their executives to take the lead in work-based sessions.

Africans have shown an initial reluctance to embrace those parts of the training programs that focus on sensitive subjects never before discussed by them publicly, such as sexual practices and their related risks, or the merits of using condoms along with graphic descriptions of their proper use and disposal. Yet according to the AID Office of Population, the demand for condoms has increased more than five times since AIDS education programs began including descriptions of safer sex practices; in 1990 more than 176 million condoms were shipped to Africa by AID, up from 34 million in 1987. The increased demand must reflect a change in behavior on the part of Africans.

Another important objective of many AIDS programs is to change high-risk behavior, such as having many sexual partners, to low-risk behavior, such as having only one. Education that clearly discusses modes of transmission, including the use of unsterilized cutting instruments, has led village leaders to change the ways group circumcisions are performed. Africans have also taken the lead in developing messages about AIDS in effective formats, such as through films, dramas, music festivals, and competitions in dance, drama, and music. Some African leaders have aggressively led discussions about AIDS and have encouraged their political bodies to enact legislation to eliminate AIDS discrimination in jobs, education, and housing, and to encourage national education and prevention activities. Not all countries have openly joined the fight, but there is great hope that as the impact of AIDS on Africa is increasingly felt, Africans will demonstrate their resilience and insist on the development of innovative, effective ways of preventing AIDS from becoming the single greatest killer of Africans in the next 20 years.

[1]WHO's data estimates are released too infrequently to be realistic and are inadequate for purposes of intervention program planning because of the speed at which the AIDS pandemic is progressing. Applying the 1990 global ratio of 3 infected women for every 5 infected men to the July 1991 WHO estimates of infected adults would mean that at least 4,125,000 women and 6,875,000 men are HIV-positive, along with another million children, approximately half boys and half girls.

[2]There are reasons to suspect that the African experience could become more extreme than current ratios indicate. Merely extrapolating current data gives too low an impression because the data themselves are too low, among other reasons discussed in the next section.

[3]This assessment is based on the most recent figures available from the United States Bureau of the Census, Health Studies Branch of the Center for International Research; they were released in November 1991 and cover data collected through 1990.

[4]*The New York Times*, February 13, 1992, p. D4.

Natural Resources

- **International Dimensions (Articles 11–14)**
- **Raw Materials (Articles 15 and 16)**
- **Food and Hunger (Articles 17 and 18)**
- **Energy (Articles 19–22)**

In the eighteenth, nineteenth, and early twentieth centuries, the idea of the modern nation-state was developed and expanded. These legal entities were conceived of as separate, self-contained units, which independently pursued their national interests. Scholars envisioned the world as an international political community of independent units, which "bounced off" each other (a concept that has often been described as a billiard ball model).

This concept of self-contained and self-directed units, however, has undergone major rethinking in the past 20 years, primarily because of the international dimensions of the demands being placed on natural resources. National boundaries are becoming less and less valid. The Middle East, for example, contains a majority of the world's known oil reserves, yet Western Europe and Japan are very dependent on this source of energy. Neither resource dependency nor such problems as air pollution recognize political boundaries on a map. There-

fore, the concept that independent political units control their own destiny is becoming outdated. In order to understand why it is so, one must look at how Earth's natural resources are being utilized today.

The articles in the first subsection of this unit discuss the international dimensions of the uses and abuses of natural resources. The central issue has to do with whether or not human activity is bringing about basic changes in the functioning of the biosphere. The lead article explores this issue and the debate within the scientific community about the likely impact on the climate resulting from the buildup of greenhouse gases. Central to this analysis is the fact that these problems transcend national boundaries. Global changes in the climate will affect everyone, and international efforts will be required to respond to these changes. A single country or even a few countries cannot have a significant impact on these problems.

Unit 3

The following articles examine other transnational dimensions of natural resources utilization. The collapse of communism in Central Europe has revealed a region-wide pollution problem that creates all kinds of social questions regarding economic and environmental priorities.

Many environmental problems are truly international in scope. The consequences of human activity are profound and no one country or even a small group of countries can remedy these problems by themselves. Solutions will have to be conceived that are truly global in scope. Just as there are shortages of natural resources, there are also shortages of new ideas for solving many of these problems.

The second subsection begins with a discussion of the issues involved in moving from a perspective of the environment as simply an economic resource to be used to a perspective that has been defined as "sustainable development." This change is easily called for, but in fact it goes to the core of social values and basic economic activities. Implementing it, therefore, will be a challenge of great magnitude. This broad discussion is then followed by a case study that illustrates this challenge. "Facing a Future of Water Scarcity" looks at water resources and how wasteful practices need to be changed in order to encourage conservation and greater efficiency.

The third subsection focuses on the most fundamental relationship between society and nature: food production and hunger. Included is a description of how environmental problems such as deforestation negatively affect food production. In addition, an overview is provided of the modern food production system along with efforts to make this system sustainable.

Another critical relationship between social structures and the environment is the subject of the final subsection of this unit: the production and consumption of energy. Since 1973, the fluctuations in the price and supply of energy in general and oil in particular have had a major impact on everyone. The initial price shocks of 1973 (which resulted from an Arab oil boycott of Israel's political allies) have been followed by many ups and downs. At one point, the Organization of Petroleum Exporting Countries (OPEC) was perceived to be a major new force in the international political arena. In the mid-1980s OPEC's control of global oil markets dramatically declined. This was a result of new sources coming onstream along with the lack of discipline among the different factions within OPEC in terms of keeping their production at prescribed quotas. Those with the most oil (such as Kuwait) wanted to keep prices low so the industrial nations would have no incentive to develop alternatives to oil. As a result, Kuwait and a couple of other Gulf producers produced well beyond their quotas, leading to an oil glut. Iraq, on the other hand, wanted higher oil prices. Increased revenues were necessary to pay for its imports, debts, and the damage incurred in its 8-year war with Iran. Iraq wanted the quotas to be observed in order to raise prices. Its gamble to quickly solve many of its economic problems by annexing Kuwait led first to dramatic increases in oil prices and then to war. These events once again demonstrated that the supply and price of oil remain at the core of the global political economy. However, many predict that the heavy dependence on oil will change as supplies dwindle and new technologies are developed. This prospect creates special problems for developing countries, for they will have to develop alternative energy sources and more efficient technologies than what is currently available.

Nature is not some object "out there" to be visited at a national park. It is the food we eat and the energy we consume. Human beings are joined in the most intimate of relationships with the natural world in order to survive from one day to the next. It is ironic how little time is spent thinking about this relationship. The pressures that rapidly growing numbers of people are placing on Earth's carrying capacity suggest that this oversight will not continue much longer.

Looking Ahead: Challenge Questions

How is the availability of natural resources affected by population growth?

In what ways has the international community responded to problems of pollution and threats to the common heritage?

What is the natural resource picture going to look like 30 years from now?

How is society, in general, likely to respond to the conflicts between economic necessity and resource conservation?

How is agricultural production a function of many different aspects of a society's economic and political structure?

Are there any similarities between the global energy and food shortages?

What is the likely future of energy supplies in both the industrial world and the Third World?

What transformations will societies that are heavy users of fossil fuels have to undergo in order to meet future energy needs?

THE GREENHOUSE EFFECT:
APOCALYPSE NOW OR CHICKEN LITTLE?

Is Earth's complex climate machine on the blink—or is it just having a bad century?

Robert Silverberg

The world's temperature has been rising lately, just as apocalypse-minded "greenhouse effect" scientists have predicted. And there's no doubt that the levels of carbon dioxide, methane, and other heat-retaining "greenhouse gases" in our atmosphere are also climbing. We seem to be well along our way toward the torrid, sultry, terrifying future that the climatologists say is coming—a world of melting polar ice caps, drowned coastal cities, and vast migrations as new patterns of drought and heat make great sections of the globe uninhabitable.

Or are we? Some scientists are not so sure that the recent doomsday scenarios ought to be taken so readily at face value. They call for cautious examination of the whole greenhouse concept before we plunge into any sort of crash program for purifying our atmosphere—a program that the congressional Office of Technology Assessment estimates could cost as much as $150 billion a year over the next 25 years, simply to reduce carbon dioxide emissions to about 65 percent of today's levels.

While the scientists bicker, what's the public to make of the baffling mass of seemingly conflicting data on global warming? History provides few clues; our climate records have proved an imperfect tool for prediction at best. It's enough to tempt even the most scientifically savvy among us to dismiss the issue altogether.

But that's just what we cannot afford to do. Crisis or not, it's time for a rational approach to unveiling the mysteries of the global climate machine. Whether the greenhouse effect foreshadows a cataclysmic event or a mere blip on the climatic time line, the current debate deserves close attention.

The greenhouse-effect theory of climate is nothing new. The concept dates back to 1822, when the French mathematician Jean Fourier likened the earth's atmosphere to the glass walls of a plant conservatory. A greenhouse's walls allow solar energy to enter, then trap its component of heat by blocking the outward radiation of infrared waves. Later in the nineteenth century scientists discovered that the heat-trapping component of our atmosphere is carbon dioxide (CO_2); and in 1897 the Swedish chemist S. A. Arrhenius, studying the relationship between global temperatures and the quantity of CO_2 in the atmosphere, calculated that a doubling of the present amount of atmospheric CO_2 would produce a mean global warming of 4° to 6°C or 7° to 11°F—with accompanying catastrophic environmental changes.

The amount of CO_2 in the atmosphere is minute: a little more than 300 parts per million, or one thirtieth of one percent. But that percentage has been growing rapidly in the century since Arrhenius. Vast quantities of CO_2 were locked up long ago in the "fossil fuels"—coal, oil, natural gas—that were created by the decay of organic matter at a time when the earth's climate was much warmer than it is today. We are now busily unlicking that treasure house of energy and our rate of consumption is rising from year to year,

with the liberation of CO_2 rising in proportion as well.

Between 1860 and 1959 the combustion of coal and other fossil fuels released an amount of CO_2 equal to 14 percent of the total already in the atmosphere. Some of this was absorbed by the oceans; the rest remained in the air. By 1960 the quantity of atmospheric CO_2 was about 7 percent greater than it had been in the middle of the nineteenth century.

But that was only the beginning. Between 1958 and 1962 alone, the CO_2 content of the atmosphere grew by 1.15 percent. In those five years, the burning of fossil fuels released 53 billion tons of CO_2, and 26 billion tons of that accumulated in the atmosphere. And the CO_2 level has risen in each year since: In the past 30 years it has gone from 315 parts per million to 355, an increase of more than 20 percent in the past century and more than 10 percent in a single generation.

Nor is CO_2 the only gas that produces the greenhouse effect. Methane (CH_4), which is released by decaying matter in marshes and tundra, the actions of termites, and cattle breaking wind, has some 20 times the heat-trapping quality of CO_2. Methane is increasing in our atmosphere at a rate of about 1 percent a year. So, too, are the various nitrogen oxides thrown off by factory smokestacks, automobile exhausts, and the breakdown of agricultural fertilizers. Then there are the sinister chlorofluorocarbons (CFCs) emitted by refrigerators, air conditioners, aerosol devices, and other products of twentieth-century inge-

Reprinted by permission of *Omni*, July 1991, pp. 50-54, 86, 88. © 1991 Omni Publications International, Ltd.

nuity. Neither methane nor nitrogen oxide nor CFCs played any part in Arrhenius's original greenhouse-effect calculations.

With all four kinds of greenhouse gases piling up in the atmosphere at a rate unprecedented in the planet's history, then we must be right on course for the catastrophic warming that the Arrhenius data indicate. A rise of 7° to 11°F in the mean global temperature may not sound like very much. But in fact just such a drop, some 25,000 years ago, sent glaciers down across Europe and North America and plunged the world into an ice age lasting thousands of years. An increase of little more than that magnitude 200 million years ago created the muggy, swampy, tropical world in which the dinosaurs flourished.

If a temperature increase of the Arrhenius magnitude were to happen now, floods caused by the melting of the polar ice caps would submerge thousands of miles of low-lying coastline within a matter of 40 or 50 years. The rising oceans would cover all of Florida south of Lake Okeechobee, and Washington, DC, would be covered almost to the White House and the Capitol steps. Low-lying islands throughout the world would disappear. Rainfall patterns would shift, turning the grain-belt districts in the interiors of our continents into dust bowls and bringing devastating torrential deluges elsewhere. Some rivers would become virtually dry; others would rise to the point of becoming unnavigable. Millions would starve.

The climate crisis would disrupt the living habits of entire nations. No wonder that Roger Revelle and Hans Suess of the Scripps Institution of Oceanography, contemplating the steady increase in atmospheric CO_2 levels, declared as far back as 1957 that humanity is performing a "great geophysical experiment"—with the entire planet as its lab.

And all the evidence indicates that the globe is warming just as the theory predicts. 1987 and 1988 were the two warmest years since reliable record-keeping began in the late nineteenth century, and the summer of 1988 saw not only scorching temperatures almost everywhere but a horrendous drought in most agricultural regions. "We can state with ninety-nine percent confidence," James Hansen of NASA's Goddard Institute told the U.S. Senate during testimony that fierce summer, "that current temperatures represent a real global warming trend, rather than a chance fluctuation. We will surely have many more years like this—more droughts and many more days above a hundred degrees [F]—in the Nineties." Indeed the average temperature for 1989 was warmer than that of record-breaking 1988; and 1990 was hotter still, coming in with a mean global temperature of just under 60°F.

Hansen's dire warnings set off a political uproar. Environmental-minded legislators called for immediate cutbacks in fossil fuel usage, changes in agricultural practices, restrictions on CFCs beyond those already agreed to for minimizing ozone layer damage, a halt to the destruction of the world's forests, a worldwide treaty covering atmospheric pollution, and a host of other drastic corrective measures. World leaders issued statements and urged action. Petitions were signed; placards were waved; considerable panic was generated among ordinary citizens.

But very little of a substantive nature has been done so far to ward off the coming environmental catastrophe. Mainly, two big conferences have been held in Washington, DC, one in April 1990 and a second in February 1991 at which scientists and government officials from 130 nations got together to discuss the problem of global warming. What came out of both conferences were the expectable expressions of deep concern—an "action agenda" but no real action—and resolutions calling for continued study, plus plans for four more conferences, culminating with a June 1992 conference in Rio de Janeiro at which representatives would sign an international treaty.

Meanwhile, greenhouse gases continue to pour into the atmosphere ev-

ery day. But while environmentalists, their dismay growing hour by hour, continue to call for strict and immediate regulatory action, climatologists argue over whether there is a crisis at all. The austere pages of *Science,* the nation's foremost scientific journal, have rung with accusations that the advocates of a crash antigreenhouse program are practicing "junk science" and "science by consensus." The more conservative scientists claim that their apocalyptic-minded colleagues have succumbed to a Chicken Little syndrome, crying out that the sky is falling when in fact nothing of the sort seems to be taking place. They say that what greenhouse alarmists are doing is sorting through the evidence looking for data that will advance their own research agendas.

"There is a selective use of facts," said S. Fred Singer, an atmospheric and space physicist with the Washington Institute, at the global-warming conference last winter. "Nobody tells an untruth, but nobody tells the whole truth, either. It all depends on the ideological outlook. . . . My nuclear friends are happy to promote the greenhouse effect. My natural gas friends are happy to promote the greenhouse effect. A lot of scientists promote the greenhouse effect because of increased funding." *Forbes* magazine ran a cover story entitled "The Global Warming Panic: A Classic Case of Overreaction."

What's going on? Are we doomed or aren't we?

There are three points to bear in mind as we contemplate the possibility of a world transformed by rising temperatures:

•Changes in greenhouse-gas levels aren't the only factor involved in worldwide temperature fluctuations.

• Feedback processes that we barely understand today may serve to counteract the worst of the greenhouse-effect problems caused by rising atmospheric gas content.

• Warmer global temperatures don't necessarily spell doom, especially if upward changes turn out to be less severe than some climatologists predicted.

Scientists, moreover, need to place the unquestionable statistics on global warming in the Eighties in a larger historical context. The world indeed saw a general pattern of warming temperatures around 1890, just as the modern era of industrial expansion was hitting its first great peak and greenhouse gas emissions began to climb. A steady pattern of rising temperatures was recorded over the succeeding decades.

But the rate of temperature increase between 1920 and 1940 exceeded the level that could be accounted for by greenhouse-effect calculations alone. And then in 1940 global temperatures began to turn *cooler* again—precisely at the time when World War II was spurring another tremendous expansion in industrial activity. For the next thirty years, *as atmospheric pollution increased year by year,* mean world temperatures dropped steadily. The winter of 1962–63, for instance, brought England its coldest winter since 1740, averaging 32°F for three consecutive months. Not until 1970 did temperatures start climbing again, a rise that so far has gone on unchecked.

Climatological history reveals all manner of sharp temperature fluctuations during eras utterly unaffected by human environmental meddling. The ice ages that periodically afflict this planet are the most spectacular examples. The temperature increase during the era of the dinosaurs constitutes another. Prehistoric shifts in rainfall distribution stimulated the development of extraordinary human cultures in prehistoric Egypt and Mesopotamia and wiped out one in the Sahara. More recently, a period of climate cooling lasting from the fifteenth to the eighteenth century brought a "little ice age" to preindustrial Europe that killed the rich vineyards of England and destroyed the colonies that the Norsemen had planted in Greenland. In Queen Elizabeth's time, people skated on the frozen Thames in winter. By 1800 the climate was turning warmer again; the Thames has not frozen over since 1814. And so it has gone, up and down, through all the billions of years of our planet's existence.

Many forces affect Earth's climate, not all of which we understand. The chief climatic factor is the energy we receive from the sun. But the amount of solar radiation we get is not necessarily consistent throughout time. The sun has undergone many changes in size and radiative power in the last few billion years. Its output seems to vary, furthermore, in relation to the 11-year sunspot cycle—the low-temperature points of the "little ice age" period in medieval and Renaissance Europe coincided with prolonged periods of low sunspot activity recorded in 1280–1350, 1450–1550, and 1645–1715. Larger changes in solar activity, the result of forces we don't really comprehend (and certainly could never hope to control), may correlate with the severe glacial periods in the remote past and with periods of above-average warmth during the icy interludes.

Volcanic activity, moreover, can produce cooling phases. The giant eruption of Krakatoa, near Java, in 1883, spewed 13 cubic miles of debris into the air and reduced the sunlight falling on distant European observatories from 10 to 20 percent for the following three years. Other great eruptions in 1902 (in the West Indies) and 1912 (in Alaska) had the same effect. An almost total absence of major volcanic blasts between 1920 and 1940 may have been responsible for the period of unusually rapid warming that was recorded then, rather than the increase in atmospheric greenhouse-gas levels that was going on at the same time. We just don't know.

Changes in the earth's position relative to the sun, movements of the earth along its own axis, and the migration of the continents over long periods of time, must all be considered possible causes of the great temperature shifts that are evident in the geological and fossil records. Against such immense geophysical upheavals, a rise in the level of greenhouse gases may turn out to be a very small factor indeed.

Then, too, we have no assurance that the undeniable increase in atmospheric CO_2 and the other greenhouse gases will have the predicted severe consequences. Large-scale feedback processes may protect us against the folly of our own pollutions.

Atmospheric CO_2, for example, stimulates plant growth. Plants absorb CO_2 in the course of the process of photosynthesis. The more plants there are, the more CO_2 they will take in, thereby helping to reduce the atmospheric oversupply. This is *negative feedback*—a self-correcting mechanism in which a problem generates its own solution.

Another kind of negative feedback that may ease our greenhouse problem: Clouds reflect sunlight back to space, thus cooling the climate. Increased ocean evaporation caused by rising temperatures may enhance cloud cover, helping to bring temperatures back down. (On the other hand, clouds can also serve as traps for infrared radiation; thus an increase in cloud cover could strengthen the warming trend. This would be an example of *positive* feedback, which amplifies a situation rather than correcting it.)

What's more, warmer temperatures hasten the breakdown of methane into the less damaging CO_2, a beneficial process. But a rise in ocean temperature might foster the release of oceanic methane into the atmosphere, further heating it—another positive-feedback event. The warming of the seas would also reduce their capacity to absorb CO_2, making more trouble for us, since the ocean swallows up much of the CO_2 we put into the atmosphere now. This is balanced, however, by the likelihood that the oceans—which are vast thermal sinks that keep planetary temperatures stable—would absorb much of the increase in heat produced by greenhouse effects, thereby minimizing or even canceling out any global warming that might occur. Similarly, the emergence of immense forests in areas now too cold for vegetation—particularly the Arctic and subarctic tundra—might lead to a net planetary gain in the amount of CO_2 absorbed during photosynthesis. Or the warming of the frigid tundra could release the CO_2 and methane now stored in its soil in the form of peat, making matters worse.

Adding to the general perplexity is the argument raised by University of East Anglia climatologist T. M. Wigley in the British scientific journal *Nature* last winter. Wigley points out that the burning of fossil fuels releases not only the dreaded greenhouse gases, but also sulfur dioxide particles, or "aerosols," which serve to reflect sunlight and moderate the temperature of the planet. A sudden and radical reduction in fossil fuel consumption, Wigley maintains, would diminish the cooling effect of the aerosols that the fossil fuels produce. And so a cutback in the use of greenhouse-effect fuels might actually *increase* the global warming trend.

The consequent rise in temperature could more than compensate for any cooling that a reduction in greenhouse gases would create, leaving us in even bigger trouble than we might be heading for otherwise. Robert Charlson, an atmospheric chemist at the University of Washington, calls this problem "a sleeping giant of a sort" and "something that has been missed, and the consequences are not trivial. It is going to complicate matters in setting policy."

These feedback forces illustrate just how tricky the whole problem is, and just how uncertain our climatologists really are about what is likely to happen. Even after two centuries of serious study, we have only an approximate understanding of the forces that drive our climate. In many cases, we are not sure which is the cause and which the effect. During a 10,000-year warm spell in the last ice age, for instance, atmospheric CO_2 and methane levels were far higher than they were in the surrounding colder periods. But did that increase in greenhouse gases create the warm spell, or was it the other way around? No one can say. And a study of the Alaskan permafrost conducted by the U.S. Geological Survey shows a thawing of several degrees in the past 100 years but a drop in temperature of more than a degree for the period 1984–87 alone. One suggested explanation is that the shrinkage of the Arctic snow cover during the warming period of the Eighties has reduced the amount of insulation that the snow provides, allowing greater radiation of heat from the permafrost. So a warming produces a cooling: negative feedback at work again.

Whether all these intricate processes will cancel each other out, leaving our climate more or less unscathed, is something that only time is going to tell. We are indeed conducting a geophysical experiment with the planet as our laboratory, and the outcome is far from certain, despite the confidence that various theorists express. At the moment there are no facts, only speculations, when we talk about global warming. We have had no experience with greenhouse effects from which we can predict what's ahead.

Computer simulations alone won't give us the answers, nor are our meteorological records accurate enough over a long period of time to provide us with a clear view of what has actually been going on. Scientists can measure CO_2 concentrations in ancient times by looking at ice cores brought up from polar depths, but the weather bureau records of 1850 and 1900 and even 1950 are statistically unreliable because the samplings tended to be too small, and the methods of measurement often had built-in inaccuracies that make comparisons with today's weather misleading. If we aren't sure where we have been, how can we be certain about where we are going?

The middle-of-the-road scientific position, though, seems to be that *some* climatic warming will happen during the first half of the twenty-first century as a result of the changes in the atmosphere that we have already brought about—though it may be a mean increase of only a degree or so, rather than the 5° to 10° that the most extreme environmentalists are predicting.

A minor warming of that sort would require some local readjustments. Low-lying coastal settlements in marginal areas where flooding has traditionally been a problem might have to be abandoned. Rainfall patterns would probably change to some extent, and some of today's productive agricultural regions may experience water shortages.

Middle-latitude zones might become too warm for efficient farming.

But these negatives would be balanced by corresponding positive changes elsewhere. Vast areas in Canada, the Soviet Union, and the northern United States, their development now hampered by cold weather much of the year, would experience a beneficial access of warmth. What farmers in Arkansas might lose, those in Saskatchewan would gain.

The same with rainfall patterns: Regions now blighted by chronic drought would become fertile. All over the planet, the increase in CO_2 levels would make plant growth more vigorous. Seas now blocked by ice much of the year would be open to navigation. And so forth: not catastrophe but change. And we are an adaptable species.

Part of the problem of knowing whether global warming will be good or bad is our geophysical ignorance. "We don't even know within a factor of ten how much total biomass there is on Earth," said NASA scientist Gerald Soffen at a greenhouse effect discussion at the 1991 meeting of the American Association for the Advancement of Science. "Is life expanding or not? We can't say." Another AAAS panelist, botanist Lynn Margulis of the University of Massachusetts, added, "We have millions of species, each processing carbon differently, and we don't understand any of them perfectly. If we try to guess how life will respond [to global warming] we'd really be fools rushing in."

We should not, of course, rule out the possibility that we are indeed heading for catastrophic climatic events. But the conservative climatologists, who deny that these events will be apocalyptic, hold that it's unwise to launch crash programs of industrial cutback that might well have economic consequences for many countries far more serious than any climatic change that's in the cards. We need to wait for further evidence that a severe global warming is actually coming.

Meanwhile, as we await that further evidence, what can we do to ward off the worst-case scenarios? One smart move would be to try—within the limits of economic realities—to reduce industrial emissions and the use of fossil fuels in general. Not in any panicky way, with visions of the oceans covering our

coasts and our forests turning into tropical jungles, but with a calm, clear-eyed resolve, based on the understanding that it's a dumb idea for any creature to foul its own nest. The junk we've been putting into the atmosphere can't possibly do us any good, and there's a reasonable chance that it can do us great harm. Therefore we should clean up our act, not by closing down the factories and switching overnight from cars to bicycles, but by zeroing in on the chief causes of pollution and finding rational ways of eliminating them, and by putting programs of energy conservation into use.

A halt in the indiscriminate destruction of forests in Third World countries would help, too. Those trees—the lungs of the planet—are one of the most powerful climatic moderators we have, and once they're gone, implacable deserts will replace them; tropical soils are surprisingly infertile and undergo dismaying changes once their forest cover is stripped away.

Another wise move would be systematic reforestation of areas already denuded. It isn't just that trees are pretty. They soak up CO_2—a forest the size of Alaska would take in a billion tons of it a year—and give off oxygen. Having them around is a fundamentally good idea.

These conservation measures, none of them so stringent that they will unsettle any nation's economy, may of themselves succeed in stabilizing our atmosphere. The worst-case greenhouse world isn't necessarily on the way. Prudent planetary housekeeping is in order right now. Hysteria isn't.

Because even now many of the processes that rule our climate are mysteries to us, many scientists are uncomfortable with the recent outcries for radical environmental reform. "Whenever you try to do this quickly, you run up against our ignorance and the quality of the data," says Michael Schlesinger, a climatologist at the University of Illinois, and his caution is echoed in many other quarters. We have greatly changed the face of our planet; but whether those changes have set a devastating climatic change in motion is something we simply don't know. For once, more studies really *are* needed. What we have to do now is to watch and wait.

Trouble on, in, and around the oceans...

CAN WE SAVE OUR SEAS?

Ron Chepesiuk

Ron Chepesiuk, a free-lance writer and member of the faculty of Winthrop College, Rock Hill, South Carolina, U.S.A., writes regularly about international political and environmental topics.

The pattern is worldwide and disturbing.

On 5 January 1993, the oil tanker *Braer* loses power off Scotland's Shetland Islands. Gale-force winds drive the ship aground, then batter it for more than a week, breaking the ship apart, and spilling its 98 million litres (26 million gallons) of light crude oil into the ecologically fragile waters and blowing a sheen of oil for long distances inland.

• In April 1992, the Maltese-registered ship *Katina P* grounds on a sandbar off the coast of Mozambique. The ship is carrying 73.4 million litres (19.4 million gallons) of oil, almost double the amount spilled from the *Exxon Valdez* into Alaska's Prince William Sound in 1989. Leaking oil from the tanker fouls Mozambique's unspoiled beaches.

• In the Gulf of Mexico, sea turtles mistake floating plastic bags for jellyfish, their natural prey. The bags twist in the turtles' stomachs, catch in their throats, or block their digestive tracts. The sea turtles suffocate.

• In the North Pacific, seals and otters seek food among plastic debris like beverage holders and discarded fishing nets and become entangled. The animals strangle and die.

• Near Corpus Christi, Texas, U.S.A., Atlantic bottlenose dolphins are dying at an unprecedented rate. In March 1992 more than 79 were found dead. Environmentalists believe the dolphins died because of changes in their habitat.

• Meanwhile, off the coast of New Jersey, U.S.A., the population of several of the most popular species of edible fish, including fluke, weakfish, and bluefish tuna, are so depleted that the state government and national agencies are drafting regulations to reduce the size of the catch for commercial and recreational

fishermen. National Marine Fisheries Service statistics show that while commercial fluke catches generated between 1.8 and 3.1 million kilograms (four and 6.8 million pounds) in New Jersey from 1980 to 1988, the catches had declined to 681,000 kilos (1.5 million pounds) by 1990.

"Before the end of the decade, every fish species in New Jersey will have some kind of regulation on it," says Thomas P. Fote, president of the 25,000-member New Jersey Coast Anglers Association, a group of recreational fishermen.

As these globe-spanning incidents show, something is going wrong with the oceans. Just a few years ago, the planet's oceans and seas were thought of as limitless resources, impervious to human abuse. Stretching over 70 percent of the Earth's surface, they contain an endless variety of plants, fish, and other animals that scientists say can be harvested for the world's needs. The oceans hold the promise of keeping mankind prosperous, of feeding desperately poor developing countries, and helping to propel them into the modern world.

But because they are vast, mankind has also considered them a bottomless garbage pit for sludge, trash, chemicals, and debris. As Anne W. Simon, author of "Neptune's Revenge: The Oceans of Tomorrow," says: "Our concept of the ocean has always been: Use it, enjoy it, take what you want from it."

Today, no part of the oceans is free from pollution. James A. Coe of the U.S. National Oceanic and Atmospheric Administration has calculated that Styrofoam alone litters the middle of the Pacific Ocean in concentrations of 50,000 particles per square kilometre (0.39 square mile). "It's true some parts of the oceans are more polluted than others," says Rod Fujita, staff scientist at the Environmental Defense Fund (EDF). "But pristine parts, as in the South Pacific, which don't have many people, are starting to have problems, too. That is scary."

Marine debris has no geographical boundaries. As famed ocean explorer Jacques Cousteau explains, "Wa-

From *The Rotarian*, March 1993, pp. 18-21, 59. © 1992 by Rotary International. Reprinted by permission.

ter moves. That's why pollutants like DDT are found in the livers of penguins in Antarctica, where there's no pollution. To show how water moves: In 90 years there will not be one drop of water in the Mediterranean that is there today. The pollutants in that sea will finally come to pollute the rest of the oceans. The same is true of the Caribbean, the North Sea, the Gulf of Finland, and so on."

The deterioration of the oceans, which interact with the rest of the planet's ecology, is a serious threat to human survival. The oceans serve as the world's lungs and profoundly influence climatic change, both because they can moderate concentrations of atmospheric constituents believed to control average global temperatures.

Pollution can have an effect not only on fish and other sea animals, but on plankton as well. Plankton is a single-celled ocean plant that feeds higher forms of life. Through conversion of carbon dioxide, plankton may provide the world with as much oxygen as all land plants combined. If water-borne pollution kills the plankton, much of the oxygen we rely on will be depleted.

Ninety percent of all pollutants reaching the ocean come from land-based sources flowing through ground water and rivers into seashore water. Some of it is unintentionally discharged. For instance, when it rains, gutters and sewers fill up with oil, grease, litter, fertilizers, and pesticides, all of which eventually make their way into the ocean.

Most land-based ocean pollution, however, is intentional, created by sanitary sewage and industrial waste water and urban runoff either passing through sewage treatment plants or conveyed directly into coastal systems through "combined sewer overflows" (CSOs). These waste streams often contain toxic pollutants and sewage sludge that make their way to coastal areas, contaminating the water and killing the aquatic life.

In the U.S., thousands of CSOs line coastal areas, into which they discharge untreated waste every time it rains. "CSOs represent uncontrollable sources of water pollution that are preventing coastal areas from attaining even marginal water quality," says EDF's Tod Fujita. "They are the single most important reason why shellfish beds remain closed, why beaches are closed due to high bacterial counts after summer storms, and why 'floatable' items like tampons and plastic debris wash up on beaches."

A concerted effort to conserve water and develop new means of treating sanitary waste water is urgently needed to accommodate increasing population growth along the coasts of most countries. Some demographers project that by the year 2010, a fourth of the U.S. population will live within an hour's drive of the coast.

In addition to land-based sources of ocean pollution, an estimated 6.4 billion kilos (14 billion pounds) of garbage and waste is purposely dumped into the sea each year. "You name it, and we have dumped it into the oceans," says Suzanne Iudicello, program counsel for the Washington, D.C.-based U.S. Center for Marine Conservation (CMC).

This offshore dumping often has unpredictable consequences. Between 1946 and 1970, the U.S. dumped 90,000 concrete-lined drums of low-level radioactive waste off San Francisco, California, and Sandy Hook, New Jersey. Recent searches located only a few hundred of the drums. Some had collapsed; others were leaking.

But of all the items dumped into the oceans, plastics are the most destructive. Radioactive waste sinks, but plastic floats and can stay around for centuries, killing sea life and washing up on beaches. A typical plastic holder for beer and soft drink cans will not degrade for about 450 years. Each year, 44.9 million kilos (99 million pounds) of plastic is dumped from oceangoing vessels or flows from storm sewers into the sea.

Some experts estimate the annual death toll from plastics may exceed two million seabirds and 100,000 sea mammals. A recent U.S. Office of Technology report warned that plastic pollution is a greater threat to marine mammals and birds than are pesticides, oil spills, or even contaminated runoff from the land.

The estimated 135 million kilos (298 million pounds) of plastic nets and lines let loose on the high seas each year highlights the problem that overfishing poses for the oceans. Fish stocks—from the haddock off the eastern seaboard of the U.S. to the cod in the North Sea, from the pilchard off the Namibian coast to the ice fish around Antarctica—are in decline worldwide. The Food and Agriculture Organization, the international body monitoring world fisheries, reports that at least 40 percent of the world's fish stocks are considered to be in a declining state. The reason: High technology has revolutionized fishing methods.

Today, enormous fishing factories equipped with kilometre-long nets, vast holds and freezers, and sophisticated instruments are taking fish from the ocean much faster than the fish can reproduce. A net called the "purse seine" is one example of the ruthlessly efficient modern fishing methods. The net is pulled into a circle and "purse strings" are drawn to enclose the catch. Entire shoals of oceanic fish (herring, pollack, sardine, tuna) can be scooped up after detection by sonar. The drift net, another high-tech method used to catch tuna, squid, and salmon mainly in the Pacific, is nicknamed "the wall of death" because it accidentally traps and suffocates seals, dolphins, porpoises, and turtles. (A number of major U.S. tuna-packing corporations have banned the use of this net since 1991.)

"Many countries see the oceans as something to be mined rather than conserved for long-term sustainability," says Andy Palmer of the American Oceans Campaign, based in Santa Monica, California, and Washington, D.C. "We can't keep building fishing fleets that operate well beyond the capacity of the oceans to sustain such frenetic effort."

The human population growth, expected to double by the next century, will certainly put further pressure on the ocean's resources. But the problem of overfishing is more immediate, given that, today, fishing is the only source of protein for a billion people worldwide.

Oil spills also pose a threat, for oil is a potent toxin that can kill zooplankton and phytoplankton, the source of the food chain and most of the world's oxygen. And as the Valdez spill dramatized, oil can kill mammals and sea birds in large numbers. The American Oceans Campaign says that more oil was spilled in the oceans in 1991 than ever before. "Oil spills represent a small percentage of the totality of ocean pollution, but we shouldn't ignore them," Andy Palmer explains. "They tend to concentrate in specific areas, and ecologically, can completely destroy those places."

Land-based pollutants, dumping, overfishing, and oil spills have all taken a toll on the oceans, but fortunately, the problems of ocean abuse and pollution are preventable. "There is a lot of hope that we can get the problem under control," says Tod Fujita. "It appears that damage inflicted on the oceans is decreasing; however, we can't be satisfied with that."

Some evidence of improvement:
• On 1 January 1989, an international law called MARPOL V (for marine pollution) made it illegal to dump plastics in the ocean. More than 29 countries, representing half the gross tonnage of the world's merchant fleet, have signed the agreement. Public vessels are exempt from the treaty, but the U.S. Congress has decided to restrict all navy vessels as well. Congress voted that by 1993, the U.S. Navy will not be allowed to throw plastics overboard. Instead, Navy vessels will be equipped with shipboard trash compactors and sterilizers.
• Also in 1989, the United Nations adopted a resolution banning drift-net fishing, worldwide, starting in 1993. Japan, Taiwan, and South Korea, which opposed such a ban in the past, agreed to abide by the resolution.
• A number of major oil companies are building a new generation of double-hulled oil tankers, to decrease the likelihood of spills.
• Researchers are finding new technologies to replace plastics or make them biodegradable. Giant corporations like Dow Chemical and Du Pont now market plastics for beverage packs that degrade after 60 days of exposure to sunlight.

Another turning point is the move toward increased regional cooperation. Some environmentalists consider this a necessary and positive step that will help control ocean dumping and pollution–but add that the trash will still have to go somewhere. Moreover, such cooperation doesn't usually address the major cause of marine pollution–the land-based sources like CSOs and river discharges laden with excess nutrients and floatable debris.

"Rather than figure how much mistreatment the ocean can take before we wreck it entirely, governments and scientific and environmental groups are now saying: 'Let's start reducing toxins and pollutants in the first place,'" says Suzanne Iudicello. "That approach is real pollution prevention." She suggests recycling, reducing waste, and reclaiming sewage and upgrading and routinely inspecting sewage treatment plant infrastructure as important ways to reduce ocean pollution at the source.

Citizen participation and education are also important. "The ocean debris problem stems from old habits," explains marine biologist Kathryn J. O'Hara, who directs the marine debris and entanglement program at the CMC Chesapeake Bay Field Office. "That is why education is essential. People need to realize that tossing trash over the rail is no longer acceptable."

Environmental groups have organized community projects to get people involved in cleaning up beaches and teach them about ocean pollution. The Sea Grant Program at the Massachusetts Institute of Technology calculates that volunteers collect 77.2 kilos (170 pounds) of trash per person on clean-up days along Massachusetts beaches.

Each year dozens of such cleanups are held in U.S. coastal states. The CMC has a program called National Beach Cleanup, which in 1990 had 108,749 cleanup volunteers worldwide–including Rotary clubs. The volunteers removed at least 25,000 metric tons (about 28,000 U.S. tons) of trash from beaches. In 1992, Canadian members of the International Fellowship of Canoeing Rotarians cleaned debris from waterways in Ontario. The Fellowship hopes to expand the program to other countries in 1993.

Environmentalists are encouraged by both the heightened public awareness of the plight of the oceans and other waterways and efforts by industry and governments to improve the situation. Cautious optimism is a common attitude. "We have enough time to take action," says Andy Palmer of the American Oceans Campaign. "We will never be able to get the oceans to where they were, say, 1,000 years ago. They are changed systems now, but they *can* be made sustainable."

Sacrificed to the Superpower

The Soviet drive to achieve nuclear dominance left lives and the land in ruins

Michael Dobbs

Washington Post Foreign Service

SEMIPALATINSK, Kazakhstan
It was the happiest day of Sergei Davydov's life: Aug. 29, 1949.
The retired engineer still remembers the blinding flash and his
"feverish joy" at the sight of a huge, mushroom-shaped cloud
erupting over the desert of northern Kazakhstan. The Soviet
Union, the world's first Communist state, had become a nuclear
superpower—and he had pressed the button.

In a squalid wooden hut 600 miles away in southern Russia,
by the bank of the Techa River, Mavzhida Valeyeva remembers
1949 for a different reason. It was the year her health began to
deteriorate dramatically. Along with practically all her neighbors, she now suffers from violent headaches and constant
nosebleeds. Her blood is anemic. Her four children and five
surviving grandchildren are all invalids.

It took Valeyeva more than four decades to make a connection between her family's devastating health problems and the
Soviet Union's nuclear bomb project. In 1990, the Soviet
government finally acknowledged that millions of tons of highly
toxic radioactive waste had been secretly dumped in the Techa
by a plutonium plant 49 miles upstream from Valeyeva's village,
Muslyumovo. The river the villagers saw as a source of life was
in fact a source of death.

"It would be better if they had never discovered this nuclear
energy," says Valeyeva, who visited the river daily to collect
drinking water and wash her family's clothes. "It would be
better to be poorer, but at least to be healthy and give our
children and grandchildren a chance of living a normal life."

The Communist politicians who launched the Soviet
Union on a program of breakneck industrialization and
transformed the country into a military and political rival
of the United States, believed that the natural resources under
their control were inexhaustible. Yet future generations of
Russians and Tatars, Balts and Ukrainians, Czechs and Poles
will pay a heavy price for the hubris of their leaders. There
came a point when nature simply rebelled.

A two-month journey from the center of Europe to the
Russian Far East to review the legacy of Marx, Engels, Lenin
and Stalin revealed the destructive impact that communism had
on the environment in Russia—one of the scars left by the
combination of totalitarian rule and socialist economics that will
almost certainly take generations to heal.

The environmental catastrophe left behind by 70 years of
Communist rule is visible in poisoned rivers, devastated forests,
dried-up lakes and smog-polluted cities. Some of these disasters, such as the evaporation of the Aral Sea after the diversion
of rivers for an irrigation project, have permanently changed
the contours of the vast Eurasian landmass. But, according to
Russian scientists and ecologists, the most lasting physical
damage will probably have been caused by the unleashing of
nuclear power.

"Radioactive contamination is the number one environmental
problem in this country. Air and water pollution come next,"
says Alexei Yablokov, a biologist who serves as President Boris
Yeltsin's chief adviser on environmental matters. "The way we
have dealt with the whole issue of nuclear power, and particularly the problem of nuclear waste, was irresponsible and
immoral."

The scale of nuclear contamination in the former Soviet
Union has only become clear over the last few years, with the
advent of free speech and the lifting of censorship restrictions.
In the wake of the 1986 Chernobyl catastrophe, Russians
learned about other disasters, including a series of accidents at a
plutonium-producing plant near the southern Urals city of
Chelyabinsk between 1948 and 1967. They also learned about
dozens of ad hoc nuclear dumps, some of which could begin
seeping radioactivity at any moment. The seas around Russia—
from the Baltic to the Pacific—are littered with decaying hulks
of nuclear submarines and rusting metal containers with tens of
millions of tons of nuclear waste. Russia itself is dotted with
dozens of once secret cities with names like Chelyabinsk-70,
Tomsk-7 and Krasnoyarsk-26, where nuclear materials have

been stockpiled. Unmarked on any map, they hit the headlines only when there is an accident. Vast areas of the country have been treated as a nuclear dump, the result of four decades of testing.

"We were turned into human guinea pigs for these experiments," says Bakhit Tumyenova, a senior health official in the Semipalatinsk region, the main Soviet nuclear test site until 1989. "They kept on telling us that it was for the good of the people, the Communist Party, the future. The individual never counted for anything in this system."

The testing of the Soviet Union's first atomic bomb in 1949 represented a huge achievement for a backward, semi-Asiatic country. It had mobilized vast economic and human resources, from the team of elite scientists who designed the bomb to the army of slave laborers who mined the uranium and disposed of the nuclear waste.

The two sides of the Soviet nuclear project—the epic achievements and the disregard for human life—are symbolized by the man initially in charge of it. Lavrenti Beria, the chief of Stalin's secret police, was a great organizer. But he was also a great destroyer, willing to obliterate any obstacle to achieve his goal.

"It was a heroic epoch," recalls Igor Golovin, a leading scientist and biographer of Igor Kurchatov, the head of the nuclear project. "We worked days and nights and really believed in what we were doing. The propaganda instilled the idea that the United States had the bomb and wanted to enslave us, so it was vital that we acquired our own nuclear weapons as soon as possible, whatever the cost."

Few of the scientists and engineers working on the project gave much thought to the dangers of radioactive fallout. After pushing the button that triggered the first nuclear device, Davydov rushed to the site of the explosion without any protective clothing or gas mask. He was later sick with leukemia for about 20 years.

"They gave me special injections, and it somehow stabilized. Now I feel all right," says the 76-year-old pensioner, proudly displaying a chestful of medals. "Personally, I think that all those people who demand privileges from the government because their health suffered as a result of these tests are just crooks and swindlers."

The idea that any sacrifice was justified in the effort to turn the Soviet Union into a superpower was a fundamental part of the Communist ethos. ("You can't make an omelette without cracking eggs," Lenin liked to remark.) It permeated the nuclear project right from the start, and still exists to some extent among older people. The system elevated the state above ordinary individuals—and this was its basic flaw.

"The postwar generation was brought up with the idea that they should be ready to sacrifice themselves for the state. This was the philosophy of the time. It was a pernicious philosophy because it prevented any thought being given to ecological problems," says Natalya Mironova, an environmental activist in Chelyabinsk. "For many years we were unable even to discuss such matters."

Little attention was paid to such issues as nuclear safety and the training of responsible personnel. The manager of the Chernobyl plant at the time of the 1986 disaster had previously been in charge of a heating plant. According to officials, roughly 50 percent of the accidents in nuclear power stations and 75 percent of accidents on nuclear submarines are due to "human error."

This year alone, there have been at least three accidents at nuclear facilities in Russia involving the release of radioactivity. The government has been inundated with dozens of letters from scientists at both military and civilian nuclear facilities warning of "further Chernobyls" because of rapidly deteriorating working conditions and the departure of many highly qualified workers.

For the 1,000 inhabitants of Muslyumovo in the southern Urals, the Soviet Union's experiments with the atom are a curse that will blight the lives of many generations. According to the local doctor, Gulfarida Galimova, four of every five villagers are "chronically sick." She says the effects of radiation have altered the genetic code of the local Tatar population, with the result that babies are often sick from birth.

"We do not have a future," says Galimova. "We have been so genetically harmed that our descendants will not be able to escape this curse. Patients come to me, and I know I can never cure them. Radiation has entered the food chain. Our cows eat radiated grass. The potatoes we grow in our back yards are poisoned. The only solution is to close this entire region off—and not let anyone come here for 3,000 years. But they won't do that, because there isn't enough money."

The 2.75 million curies of radioactive waste flushed into the shallow Techa was equivalent to half the fallout from the bomb that fell on Hiroshima, but nobody bothered to inform local inhabitants. In the late 1950s, signs were posted along the Techa warning people not to bathe in the river. The nature of the danger was never explained, so most villagers paid little attention.

In the early 1980s, Galimova first started noticing that something was terribly amiss with the health of Muslyumova residents. Nearly 10 percent of births in the village were premature. Many of her patients were anemic. There was a high incidence of cancer. When she reported her findings to her superiors in Chelyabinsk, the problems were blamed on bad food and a lack of hemoglobin. She was accused of being a bad doctor.

What local people refer to as "the river illness" is now affecting the third and even fourth generation of Muslyumovo residents. Valeyeva's eldest son, Ural, 33, is mentally retarded. His three children—aged 6, 4 and 18 months—can barely summon up the energy to get out of bed. Another daughter, Sazhida, 29, has a chronic craving for chalk that has destroyed all her teeth. Her oldest son, Vadim, 11, has been sick from birth. Timur, 6, has chronic bronchitis and anemia.

It was not until April 1986 that Galimova finally guessed what was the matter. Chernobyl played a crucial role in convincing Mikhail Gorbachev and other Soviet leaders that the country's problems could not be solved without *glasnost,* openness. Discussion of ecological problems was no longer taboo.

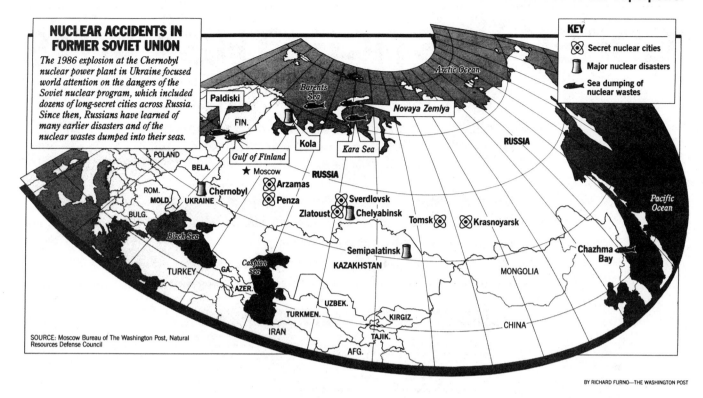

NUCLEAR ACCIDENTS IN FORMER SOVIET UNION

The 1986 explosion at the Chernobyl nuclear power plant in Ukraine focused world attention on the dangers of the Soviet nuclear program, which included dozens of long-secret cities across Russia. Since then, Russians have learned of many earlier disasters and of the nuclear wastes dumped into their seas.

KEY

☣ Secret nuclear cities

⚗ Major nuclear disasters

🐟 Sea dumping of nuclear wastes

SOURCE: Moscow Bureau of The Washington Post, Natural Resources Defense Council

BY RICHARD FURNO—THE WASHINGTON POST

When they finally came clean about the contamination of the Techa, the authorities also admitted two disasters involving the Mayak plutonium-producing plant at Kyshtym, about 60 miles northwest of Chelyabinsk. In 1957, a waste storage tank exploded at the plant, releasing 20 million curies of radiation. A decade later, a drought dried up nearby Lake Karachai, which had been used as a storage tank for 120 million curies of waste products from Mayak. High winds scattered radioactive dust over a wide area.

According to an official Russian government report released earlier this year, the three disasters at Mayak affected 450,000 people living in a contaminated region roughly the size of Maryland. The amount of radioactivity still stored at Mayak—much of it in insecure conditions—is equivalent to the fallout from 20 Chernobyl disasters.

Nearly 20,000 residents of the Chelyabinsk region were evacuated from their homes. By a tragic twist of fate, some of these people were moved from one high-risk region to another.

Valentina Lazareva, for example, was evacuated from a village near Mayak in 1957 as a 9-year-old orphan. There were rumors of an "explosion" at the plant, but nobody knew anything for sure. She spent the rest of her childhood in an orphanage in Brodokalmak, a village a few miles downriver from Muslyumovo. The children crossed the Techa every day on their way to school and drank water from a nearby well. In the summer, they would swim in the village.

"Now we are all sick," says Lazareva, who is 46 but looks much older. "There were 32 people in my class. We have already buried five of my classmates. Another 10 are dying. But all are invalids, in one way or another."

Today, there is no shortage of glasnost about the manmade environmental disaster confronting the former Soviet Union. But there is a desperate shortage of resources to do much about it. The amount of money the government has earmarked to clean up the Chelyabinsk region—roughly $20 million—is minuscule compared to the $40 billion to $60 billion cost the United States has projected for the cleanup of its main plutonium-producing facility, the Hanford nuclear reservation in Washington state.

In Kazakhstan, which declared itself an independent state in December 1991 after the breakup of the Soviet Union, health officials say they are unable to provide even basic medical care to villages exposed to four decades of nuclear tests. The lack of basic health services has encouraged many people to turn to charlatans and faith healers for help. In Semipalatinsk—the site of 470 nuclear explosions, including 116 in the atmosphere, between 1949 and 1989—a Muslim preacher named Sary-Aulie has been attracting crowds of 10,000 with his promise to cure aches and pains through "vibrations."

"We can't do much for these people, so it's not surprising that they put their trust in charlatans," says Tumyenova, the regional health administrator. "The Semipalatinsk test site served the entire Soviet Union. Now the other republics have gone their own way—and we have been left alone, sitting on top of a gigantic nuclear rubbish heap."

GREEN JUSTICE: THE FACTS

THE EARTH DEVOURED

Who is polluting the world and consuming its resources? The New Internationalist tots up the environmental bill per head, North and South.

IN THE SOUTH:[1]

LIVE THREE QUARTERS OF THE WORLD'S PEOPLE

WHO CONSUME JUST ONE SIXTH OF THE WORLD'S RESOURCES

WITH AVERAGE INCOMES 18 TIMES LOWER THAN THOSE IN THE NORTH.

Throw-away energy

Australians and Bangladeshis both live in relatively warm climates, but Australians get through one hundred times more energy than Bangladeshis.
    Western industrialized countries use roughly half the world's energy, while the Third World uses just one sixth.

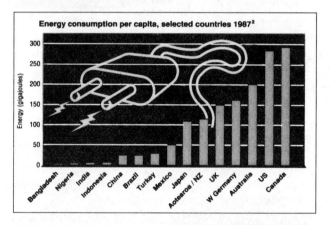

Energy consumption per capita, selected countries 1987[2]

Tree pulp

From diapers to doors, from wrapping to writing paper, the average Canadian gets through 100 times more trees than the average Indian – and recycles less.

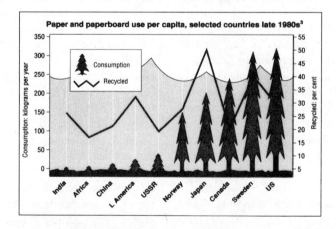

Paper and paperboard use per capita, selected countries late 1980s[3]

1 *Environment and Development: Towards a Common Strategy for the South in the UNCED Negotiations and Beyond*, South Centre – the Follow-up Office of the South Commission, Geneva, 1991. **2** *World Resources 1990-91*, World Resources Institute. **3** *State of the World 1990*, Worldwatch Institute. **4** *Human Development Report 1991*, UNDP. **5** 'Toxic waste for a small planet' by David Weir in *Consumer Lifelines*, IOCU, April 1989. **6** *State of the World 1991*, Worldwatch Institute. **7** US Department of Agriculture, 1989 figures. **8** Australian Board of Statistics 1989 figures. **9** New Zealand Meat Board 1989 figures. **10** Statistics Canada 1989 figures. **11** UK Meat Livestock Commission 1990 figures.

Unfair exchange

Between 1983 and 1989 a net total of $241 billion was transferred from South to North, mostly in the form of repayments on debts.

Trade protectionism in the North costs the South an estimated $100 billion a year in lost revenue from agricultural products and a further $50 billion a year for textiles.[2]

About 125,000 tons of toxic waste are sent to the Third World from Europe each year, and this is likely to increase with attempts to clean up Eastern Europe.[5]

IN THE NORTH:[4]

LIVE ONE QUARTER OF THE WORLD'S PEOPLE
WHO PUMP OUT FOUR FIFTHS OF THE WORLD'S GREENHOUSE GASES
WITH FACTORIES, CARS, AIR CONDITIONERS AND AEROSOL SPRAYS
THAT ALSO RELEASE ALMOST 90 PER CENT OF THE CFC GASES THAT
DESTROY THE OZONE LAYER.

Greenhouse greed

The average US citizen produces 170 times more pollution from burning fossil fuels like oil and coal (which causes 'global warming') than the average citizen of Zaire.

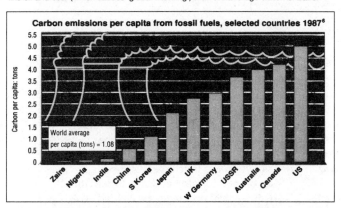

Carbon emissions per capita from fossil fuels, selected countries 1987[6]

Animal fat

There are three rungs on the ladder of the world's food consumption: at the bottom, 630 million people do not have enough to eat; in the middle, 3.4 billion grain eaters get most of their protein from plants; at the top, 1.25 billion meat eaters consume three times as much animal fat per person as the remaining four billion – and use 40 per cent of the world's grain to fatten the livestock they eat.

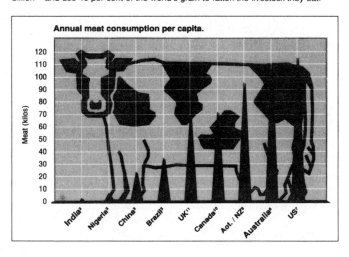

Annual meat consumption per capita.

A Planet in Jeopardy

Despite increased attention to the environment, the health
of the earth is deteriorating at an unprecedented rate.
Time itself is our scarcest resource as we struggle to create
a sustainable society.

Lester R. Brown,
Christopher Flavin,
and Sandra Postel

Lester R. Brown is president of the Worldwatch Institute, and Christopher Flavin and
Sandra Postel are vice presidents for research with the Institute. Their address is
1776 Massachusetts Avenue, N.W., Washington, D.C. 20036.

Bruce Wallace, a biology professor at
Virginia Polytechnic Institute and State
University, offers this story from the
past that reflects on our own times:
"Five days after departing from South-
hampton, England, the *Titanic* grazed
an iceberg in the North Atlantic. The
incident passed unnoticed by most
passengers—a mere trembling, according to one.

"Having heard reports of water entering the hold, Captain Edward J.
Smith and Mr. Thomas Andrews, a
ship designer who was aboard representing the *Titanic*'s builders, went below to conduct an inspection. Upon
returning to the bridge, Mr. Andrews
made some rapid calculations, then
broke the news to the captain: 'The
ship is doomed; at best you have one
and a half hours before she goes
down.' An immediate order was issued: Uncover the lifeboats!

"The *Titanic*'s passengers were not
seasoned sailors. The ship was large
and reassuring; it had been their home
for the better part of a week. Bankers
still intent upon returning to their
New York offices continued to plan
upcoming business deals. Professors

returning from sabbatical leaves still
mulled over lesson plans. Eventually,
many preferred to stay on board rather
than disembark on a tiny lifeboat.

"Grasp of an altered reality comes
slowly, not as much the result of denial
as of not comprehending. When the
truth could no longer be denied, the
passengers exhibited the entire range
of human qualities—from bravery and
heroism to cowardice. Some panicked
and gave up hope entirely. Others
achieved comfort by maintaining the
status quo: Third-class passengers
were prevented by many crew members from leaving the flooded steerage
quarters for the temporary haven of
the upper, higher-priced decks.

"In the end, reality could not be
denied. Early on the morning of April
15, 1912, the *Titanic* sank with a loss of
over 1,500 lives."

As the twentieth century nears a
close, the tale of the *Titanic* comes un-
comfortably close to describing the
perceptual gap we now face: our inability to comprehend the scale of the
ongoing degradation of the planet and
how it will affect our future. Few understand the magnitude of the poten-

tial tragedy; fewer still have a good
idea of what to do about it.

The *Titanic*'s passengers were mainly innocent victims, but the dilemma
now facing society is largely of our
own making. And for us, there is still
hope. But saving Planet Earth—and its
human passengers—will require going
beyond the denial of reality that still
characterizes many of our political and
business leaders. It also hinges on the
collective capacity and will to quickly
make the transition from perception to
policy change—an unprecedented
challenge.

Success Stories Are Few

The first step—waking up to the dimensions of the world's environmental problems—has in a sense been
under way for more than two decades.
At the global level, a milestone was the
U.N. Conference on the Human Environment held in Stockholm, Sweden,
in 1972. The 20 years since that meeting have seen the birth of a worldwide
environmental movement, the emergence of thousands of grass-roots environmental organizations, and the
proliferation of environmental laws

and regulations in nations around the world.

Now, as the world prepares for another global environmental summit, this time in Rio de Janeiro, Brazil, major speeches of prime ministers and presidents are incomplete without mention of the environment. Dozens of corporate executives have declared themselves committed environmentalists. And more than 115 nations have established environment agencies or ministries since 1972.

Laws and ministries are one thing. Real environmental progress is another. The two decades since the Stockholm conference have seen only scattered success stories. The Cuyahoga River in Cleveland, Ohio, no longer catches fire, and swimming has resumed in some of the Great Lakes. Air quality has improved in Tokyo and in many northern European cities as well. Soil erosion has slowed on U.S. cropland.

But outside of the "post-industrial" North, progress is rarer: Some regions of eastern Europe now face virtual epidemics of environmental disease, misuse of water resources is reducing the agricultural potential of wide sections of South Asia, and soil erosion is undermining the food prospects of much of Africa. Peru's inability to provide clean water for its people became evident when it was struck in 1991 by the world's worst cholera epidemic in decades. In Mexico City, coin-operated oxygen stations are being planned to help people cope with air pollution that has become life threatening.

At the global level, almost all of the indicators are negative. Each year now, the level of greenhouse gases in the atmosphere reaches a new high, and the ozone layer grows thinner. These fundamental assaults on the atmosphere are caused almost entirely by rich nations that use most of the fossil fuels and ozone-depleting chemicals. Yet, the long-term costs will be borne by humanity as a whole. Ozone depletion may cause skin cancer among Andean peasants who never used aerosol spray cans, while global warming could flood the homelands of Bangladeshis who have never used electricity.

Environmental concerns were viewed by many Third World leaders in 1972 as "luxury problems" that only rich nations could afford to deal with. Although this view is still espoused by some, it has a thoroughly unconvincing ring. In the wattle-and-daub villages and urban shantytowns where most Third World people live, environmental quality is more than a question of the quality of life; it is often a matter of life or death. In many nations, environmental degradation is now recognized as a key barrier to governments' ability to meet basic needs and sustain living standards.

Winning Battles, but Losing the War?

But despite increased awareness, the health of the planet has deteriorated at an unprecedented rate. Since 1972, the world has lost nearly 200 million hectares of trees, an area the size of the United States east of the Mississippi. Deserts have expanded by 120 million hectares, claiming more land than is planted to crops in China and Nigeria combined. The world's farmers lost about 480 million tons of topsoil, roughly equal to that which covers the agricultural land of India and France. And thousands of plant and animal species with which we shared the planet in 1972 no longer exist.

In the past 20 years, human numbers have grown by 1.6 billion—the same number of people that inhabited the planet in 1900. Each year now, the annual addition of more than 90 million people is equivalent to the combined populations of Denmark, Finland, the Netherlands, Norway, Sweden, and the United Kingdom. Meanwhile, world economic output, which historically has paralleled demands on the earth's resources, has increased by nearly 75% over the same two decades.

Denis Hayes, chairman of Earth Day 1990, raised the essential paradox when he asked, "How could we have fought so hard, and won so many battles, only to find ourselves now on the verge of losing the war?" Part of the answer lies in the failure to alter the basic patterns of human activity that cause environmental deterioration—from our reproductive behavior to our dependence on fossil fuels. Like the *Titanic*'s passengers, most of whom were unable to grasp the fundamental nature of their predicament, we are still struggling to understand the dimensions of the changes we are causing.

National governments have focused on building water-treatment facilities, controlling air pollutants from power plants, cleaning up toxic-waste sites, and trying to find new places to put their garbage. While much of this is necessary, such efforts cannot by themselves restore the planet's environmental health. Stabilizing the climate, for example, depends on restructuring national energy policies. Getting the brakes on population growth requires fundamental changes in social values and services. So far, only a handful of countries have undertaken such initiatives.

Economists vs. Ecologists

The still widely held belief that the global economy can continue along the path it has been following stems in part from a narrow economic view of the world. Anyone who regularly reads the financial papers or business weeklies would conclude that the world is in reasonably good shape and that long-term economic prospects are promising. Even the apparent problems—the U.S. budget deficit, Third World debt, and gyrating oil prices—are considered minor by most economic planners. They call for marginal course corrections as they pursue business as usual. To the extent that constraints on economic expansion are discussed on the business pages, it is in terms of inadequate demand growth rather than limits imposed by the earth's resources.

Lacking an understanding of the carrying capacity of ecological systems, economic planners are unable to relate demand levels to the health of the natural world. If they regularly read the leading scientific journals, their faith might be shaken. Every major indicator shows deterioration in natural systems.

These different views of the world have their roots in economics and ecology—disciplines with intellectual frameworks that contrast starkly. From an economist's perspective, ecological concerns are but a minor subdiscipline of economics—to be "internalized" in economic models and dealt with at the margins of economic planning. But to an ecologist, the economy is a narrow subset of the global ecosystem. Humanity's expanding economic activities cannot be separated from the natural systems and resources from which they ultimately derive, and any activity that undermines the global ecosystem cannot continue indefinitely. Modern societies, even with their technological sophistication, ignore dependence on nature at their own peril.

Environment and Development

The health of the planet is ultimately about the health of its people, and from this perspective as well, disturbing trends emerged during the past two decades. Despite soaring economic output, the ranks of the world's poor have increased. Some 1.2 billion people now meet former World Bank President Robert McNamara's 1978 definition of absolute poverty: "a condition of life so limited by malnutrition, illiteracy, disease, squalid surroundings, high infant mortality, and low life expectancy as to be beneath any reasonable definition of human decency."

In the 1980s, average incomes fell by 10% in most of Latin America; in sub-Saharan Africa, they were down by 20%. Economic "development" is simply not occurring in many countries. And even a large portion of the industrial world is no longer moving forward. In the former Soviet Union, the economy is in a state that economists describe as "free fall." Real income dropped 2% in 1990 and an estimated 10%–15% in 1991.

The ranks of the poor are concentrated among the rapidly growing populations of sub-Saharan Africa, Latin America, the Middle East, and South Asia. The growth in Third World jobs has fallen short of population growth, leaving tens of millions unemployed and hundreds of millions underemployed. Even more people lack access to clean water, adequate health care, and a full and balanced diet.

The rising tide of world poverty has many roots. Rapid population growth is one; another is the failure of many governments to reform their economic and political systems. Meanwhile, foreign-aid donations have stagnated since the mid-1980s,

and $1.2 trillion worth of foreign debt has accumulated, sapping financial earnings and undermining the credit-worthiness of low-income countries. The $950 billion spent on the military in 1990 was the biggest drain on resources of all.

The once separate issues of environment and development are now inextricably linked. Environmental degradation is driving a growing number of people into poverty. And poverty itself has become an agent of ecological degradation, as desperate people consume the resource bases on which they depend. Rather than a choice between the alleviation of poverty and the reversal of environmental decline, world leaders now face the reality that neither goal is achievable unless the other is pursued as well.

Unsustainable Economies

Our economies are engaged in a disguised form of deficit financing: Processes such as deforestation and overpumping of groundwater inflate current output at the expense of long-term productivity. In sector after sector, we violate fundamental principles of environmental sustainability. Relying on an incomplete accounting system, one that does not measure the destruction of natural capital associated with gains in economic output, we deplete our productive assets, satisfying our needs today at the expense of our children. As economist Herman Daly puts it, "there is something fundamentally wrong in treating the earth as if it were a business in liquidation."

To extend the analogy, it is as though a vast industrial corporation quietly sold off a few of its factories each year, using an accounting system that did not reflect these sales. As a result, its cash flow would be strong and profits would rise. Stockholders would be pleased with the annual reports, not realizing that the profits were coming at the expense of the corporation's assets. But once all the factories were sold off, corporate officers would have to inform stockholders that their shares were worthless.

To reverse this process, industries and governments will need to alter their world views—focusing less on

the short-term financial bottom line and more on the long-term sustainability of the economies they invest in. If we do not change our ways, we may find that the lifeboats are rapidly filling up and that it is too late for many to get aboard. While the rich may congregate on the upper decks and protect themselves for a while, they too are ultimately threatened.

The effort required to create a sustainable society is more like mobilizing for war than any other human experience. Time itself is the scarcest resource as we begin preparing for the struggle that will unfold in this decade and beyond. Indeed, we have only a few short years to overcome the political, social, and economic impediments to real progress—to lay the foundations for a fundamentally improved society. Once the self-reinforcing trends of environmental degradation and deepening poverty are too deeply established, only a superhuman effort could break the cycle and reverse the trend.

If the struggle for a sustainable society is to succeed, we must have some vision of what we are aiming for. If not fossil fuels to power society, then what? If forests are no longer to be cleared to grow food, then how is a larger population to be fed? If a throwaway culture leads inevitably to pollution and resource depletion, how can we satisfy our material needs? In sum, if the present path is so obviously unsound, what vision of the future can we use to guide our actions toward a global community that can endure?

A sustainable society is one that satisfies its needs without jeopardizing the prospects of future generations. Just as any technology of flight, no matter how primitive or advanced, must abide by the basic principles of aerodynamics, so must a lasting society satisfy basic ecological principles. At least two preconditions are undeniable: If population growth is not slowed and climate stabilized, there may not be an ecosystem on Earth we can save.

The 1990s will be the environmental decade—whether we want it to be or not. Already, it is a lost decade for many ecosystems and people, but it is also a last chance to begin turning things around.

Facing a Future of
WATER
SCARCITY

Enormous savings of the precious liquid are being thwarted by policies and laws that encourage wastefulness and misuse, rather than efficiency and conservation.

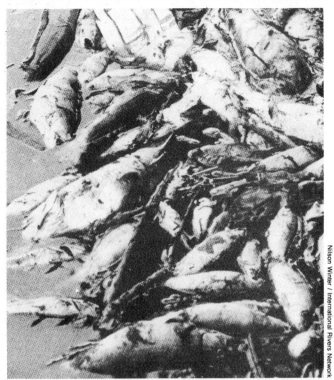

Rampant river pollution is wiping out millions of fish in Brazil.

Sandra Postel

Ms. Postel, vice president for research, Worldwatch Institute, Washington, D.C., is the author of Last Oasis: Facing Water Scarcity.

BENJAMIN FRANKLIN once pointed out that, "When the well's dry, we know the worth of water." Much of the world is in danger of learning Franklin's lesson the hard way. For decades, water has been wasted, mismanaged, and overused—and the consequences are beginning to hit home.

Water scarcity typically conjures up visions of drought, the temporary dry spells that nature inflicts from time to time. Yet, while droughts capture headlines, the far greater threat posed by escalating water consumption goes largely unnoticed. Despite 1993's floods, water tables are falling, lakes are shrinking, and wetlands are disappearing. Around water-short cities, competition is brewing between city-dwellers and farmers who lay claim to the same limited supply.

In each major area of water use—agriculture, industry, and cities—demands have increased rapidly. Global water use has more than tripled since 1950, and what is removed from rivers, lakes, and ground-water amounts to 30% of the world's stable renewable supply. People actually rely on a far larger share since water bodies dilute pollution, generate electricity, and support fisheries and wildlife. Because of improved living standards, demand has been growing faster than population—per capita use is nearly 50% higher than it was in 1950 and continues to climb in most of the world.

For decades, planners have met this rising demand by turning to ever more and larger water development projects, particularly to dams and river diversions. Engineers have built more than 36,000 large dams around the globe to control floods and provide hydroelectric power, irrigation, industrial supplies, and drinking water to an expanding population and economy. Rare is the river that now runs freely toward the sea, and many that still do are slated to come under control soon.

Limits to this ever-expanding supply are swiftly coming to light, however. Engineers naturally first selected the easiest and least-costly sites for water development. Over time, water projects have become increasingly complex, expensive to build, and more damaging to the environment. Fewer dams and diversion projects are making it off the drawing boards, and most that do will deliver water at a far higher price than in the past.

Meeting human needs while facing up to water's limits—economic, ecological, and political—entails developing an entirely new relationship to the precious liquid. Historically, it has been managed with a frontier philosophy, manipulating natural systems to whatever degree engineering know-how would permit. Modern society has come to view water as a resource that is there for the taking, rather than a life-support system that underpins the natural world humans depend on. Instead of continuously reaching out for more, people must begin to look within their regions, communities, homes, and themselves for ways to meet their needs while respecting water's life-sustaining functions.

Although water is a renewable resource, it also is a finite one. The water cycle makes available only so much each year in a given location. That means supplies per person, a first-order indicator of water security, drop as population grows. Thus, per capita water supplies worldwide are one-third lower than in 1970, due to the 1,800,000,000 people added to the planet since then.

One of the clearest signs of scarcity is the increasing number of countries in which population has surpassed the level that can be sustained comfortably with the water available. As a rule of thumb, hydrologists designate water-stressed countries as those with annual supplies of about 725-1,450 gallons per person a day. When the figure drops below 725 gallons, nations are considered water-scarce—its lack becomes a severe constraint on food production, economic development, and protection of natural systems. Today, 26 countries—collectively home to 232,000,000 people—fall into the water-scarce category. As many of them have very high population growth rates, their problems are deepening fast. Africa has the largest number of water-scarce countries, 11; by 2010, six others will join the list. At that time, the total number of Africans living in water-scarce nations will climb to 400,000,000, approximately 37% of the continent's projected population.

Nilson Winter / International Rivers Network

Nine of the 14 countries in the Middle East face water-short conditions, making this the most concentrated region of scarcity in the world. With populations in several of them projected to double within 25 years, a rapid tightening of supplies is inevitable. Since virtually all Middle East rivers are shared by several nations, tensions over water rights are a potent political force throughout the region and could ignite before the end of the century.

Although the population-water equation suggests where to expect trouble, numerous physical symptoms of stress already exist—not just in water-scarce areas, but in parts of water-wealthy ones as well. Among the most pervasive problems is that of declining water tables, which results when groundwater is used faster than nature replenishes it. If pumping is not brought into balance with recharging, the underground supply eventually becomes too expensive to keep tapping, too salty to use as it is pulled up from greater depths, or simply too depleted to serve as a supply. Overuse of groundwater is now ubiquitous in parts of China, India, Mexico, Thailand, the western U.S., North Africa, and the Middle East.

Some of the most troubling cases of unsustainable groundwater use involve "fossil" aquifers, underground reservoirs that hold water hundreds or thousands of years old and receive little replenishment from rainfall. Like oil reserves, these aquifers essentially are nonrenewable—pumping water from them depletes the supply in the same way that extractions from an oil well do. Farms and cities that depend on this water eventually will face the dilemma of what to do when the well runs dry.

Shrinking groundwater reserves, falling water tables, and projected demands that far exceed available supplies are clear signals of water stress. Perhaps the most worrying sign of trouble comes from examining the health of aquatic environments. The damming, diverting, and polluting of watercourses with little regard for the environmental services they provide and the species they support has wreaked havoc on the planet's wetlands, deltas, lakes, and riverine habitats. Of all the threatened forms of biological diversity on Earth, aquatic life may be the most in jeopardy.

A distressing conflict has emerged over two of water's roles—as a commodity serving the economic aims of greater agricultural productivity, industrial expansion, and urban growth, and as a key life support for all species and natural communities. Mounting scarcity has thrown this friction into sharp relief. More water devoted to human needs means less for sustenance of ecosystems—and, in many areas, nature is losing out fast.

The infamous shrinking Aral Sea in central Asia is the most dramatic in a long list of natural areas destroyed, degraded, or at grave risk from human use and abuse of water. Among them are many unique wild places—including California's Mono Lake, south Florida's Everglades, Spain's Doñana wetlands, and Sudan's Sudd swamps—that are home to astounding numbers and varieties of bird and wildlife species.

In many areas, there is a tug-of-war between the demands of conventional economic development and those of aquatic ecosystems. A more pervasive sign of the severely compromised health of the water environment is the number of aquatic species now in jeopardy. In North America, for example, the American Fisheries Society lists 364 species of fish as endangered, threatened, or of special concern—the vast majority of them at risk because of habitat destruction. An estimated one-third of the continent's fish, two-thirds of its crayfish, and nearly three-fourths of its mussels are rare or imperiled. They often reach such status by way of incremental human actions that end up undermining their basic habitat requirements—be it the timing, quantity, or quality of water's flow.

Of the many varieties of native fish species at risk in North America, perhaps the most notable for their cultural and recreational values are several species of salmon in the western U.S. The winter run of the chinook salmon in California's Sacramento River declined from 120,000 in the 1960s to 400 today, and the species was added to the Federal endangered list in 1989. In 1991, just four adult sockeye salmon made it from the Pacific Ocean past eight Federal dams in the Columbia River basin to their primordial spawning ground at Idaho's Redfish Lake. On the brink of extinction, the Snake River sockeye was listed as endangered in November, 1991.

Each wetland, lake, or aquatic species at risk presents a crucial test of whether a region's people and economy can adapt to the ecological needs of a healthy aquatic system. Only in rare instances are public values and future generations winning out over private rights to dam and divert natural watercourses. A growing movement to protect property rights from government actions to safeguard the environment could tip this balance even further away from ecosystem protection. Unfortunately for the future, protecting aquatic environments and their species still often is viewed as a luxury that can be traded off against pressing economic goals, rather than as essential to preserving the environmental foundation all else rests upon.

Water-thrifty food production

With agriculture claiming two-thirds of all the water removed from rivers, lakes, streams, and aquifers, making irrigation more efficient is a top priority in moving toward more sustainable use. The possible savings—ranging from 10 to 50%—constitute a large and mostly unexploited new source of supply. Reducing irrigation needs by 10%, for instance, would free up enough water roughly to double domestic water use worldwide.

A wide variety of measures exist to boost agriculture's water productivity, including new and improved irrigation technologies, better management practices by farmers and water managers, and changes in the institutions that govern the distribution and use of irrigation water. While gains have been made in each area, there remains a vast untapped potential.

Some of the biggest technological successes in improving irrigation efficiency have occurred where water scarcity poses serious threats to farming. In Texas, for example, many farmers have adapted old-fashioned furrow systems to a new surge technique that reduces percolation losses at the head of the field and distributes water more uniformly. This has cut their water use by 15-50% while reducing their pumping costs. For those in the Texas Plains, where savings have averaged 25%, the initial investment of about $30 per hectare (2.47 acres) normally is recouped within the first year.

Many irrigators in northwest Texas have moved from high-pressure sprinklers, which typically register efficiencies of 60-70%, to low-pressure ones that boost efficiency to around 80%. A relatively new sprinkler design, known as low-energy precision application (LEPA), offers even greater savings. LEPA sprinklers deliver water closer to crops by means of drop tubes extending vertically from the sprinkler arm. When used with water-conserving land preparation methods, LEPA can achieve efficiencies as high as 95%. Adapting an existing sprinkler for LEPA costs Texas farmers $60-160 per hectare; the water, energy, and yield gains typically pay back the initial investment in two to four years.

Elsewhere, Israel has brought about what widely is perceived as an agricultural miracle over the last three decades. Although it remains to be seen whether that nation's success in making the desert bloom will prove sustainable, Israel has developed technologies, methods, and scientific capabilities in irrigation that could prove invaluable to much of the world as the era of water constraints unfolds.

Among the most heralded of its accomplishments is the development of drip irrigation, whereby water is delivered directly to crops' roots through a network of porous or perforated piping installed on or below the soil surface. This keeps evaporation and seepage losses extremely low. Because water is applied frequently at low doses, optimal moisture conditions are maintained for the crop, boosting yields, and salt does not accumulate in the root zone. Modern Israeli farms often have highly automated drip systems, with computers and monitors sensing when and how much water to apply and determining the precise amount of nutrients to add. Israeli farmers liken their irrigation practices to "feeding the plant with a teaspoon."

New technologies that build efficiency into their designs—such as surge, LEPA, and drip irrigation—can help make crop production less demanding of the world's water supply. Equally important is raising the efficiency of the extensive surface canal systems that dominate the world's irrigated lands. Much land slated for irrigation, and often counted as receiving it, gets insufficient water or none at all because irrigation works are poorly maintained and operated.

Many problems with large canal systems arise because irrigation officials rarely have any incentive to improve the performance of projects they administer. Their operating budget may come from a state or national treasury and bear no relation to how well the system functions. Irrigation fees collected from farmers may go back into a general treasury, rather than being used to operate and maintain the local system. Since farmers have little say in how their projects are managed and are not charged for water according to their use, they, too, have few incentives to use water wisely. In short, there is barely any accountability of those in control, and little control by those who are supposed to benefit.

Especially in government-run projects, some form of "water users association" is necessary for farmers to have a say in management decisions. Such an organization also provides a mechanism for collecting fees to cover operation and maintenance costs and involving farmers directly in maintenance activities. Many studies have shown that, when farmers actively participate in projects and have some responsibility for the operation, canals and other infrastructure function better, a greater proportion of the project area gets irrigated, and crop yields rise.

Another way to stretch freshwater supplies is to use treated municipal wastewater for irrigation. Farmers worldwide spend heavily on chemical fertilizers to give their crops the nitrogen, phosphorus, and potassium that domestic wastewater contains in large amounts. By using municipal water supplies twice—once for domestic use and again for irrigation—would-be pollutants become valuable fertilizers, rivers and lakes are protected from contamination, the irrigated land boosts crop production, and the reclaimed water becomes a reliable, local supply.

By not making wastewater reuse a part of water planning and management, developing countries put their urban and rural populations at risk. As World Bank wastewater specialists Carl Bartone and Saul Arlosoroff note, "Examples abound of local farmers breaking into sewer interceptors both within and on the outskirts of urban areas to steal the effluents for watering their crops. These are often

vegetable crops destined for local markets that will be consumed raw. In addition . . . highly polluted rivers serve as major water sources for large-scale irrigation projects."

When designed and operated properly, waste stabilization ponds that biologically treat wastewater offer a low-cost way to keep sewage out of rivers and streams, safeguard human health from disease-causing organisms, and produce a nutrient-rich source of irrigation water. Studies have shown them capable of treating wastewater up to the World Health Organization's standards for irrigation of crops not eaten raw. Care always must be taken to prevent heavy metals from getting into wastewater destined for irrigation. Cadmium, copper, nickel, zinc, and other heavy metals can accumulate in crops and soils or percolate to groundwater and contaminate a drinking supply. A key to safe reuse is preventing untreated industrial effluent—often containing heavy metals—from mixing with domestic wastewater.

Finally, producing enough food for the world's expanding population while economizing on water will require boosting yields on the 84% of the planet's cropland watered only by rainfall. The drylands of Africa, western India, north-central China, and southwestern Latin America present formidable challenges to crop production. Altogether, arid and semi-arid lands cover about one-third of the Earth's land surface and are home to 600,000,000 people, including many of the world's poorest farmers. For them, conservation and more efficient use of scarce water quite literally is a matter of life and death.

Attention is turning to the potential of smaller-scale projects—micro dams, shallow wells, low-cost pumps, moisture-conserving land techniques, and a wide variety of rainwater harvesting methods—to make food production more secure for dryland dwellers. Many of these efforts have proved more cost-effective and less disruptive to local communities than the massive schemes that dominated development efforts during the past few decades. Their smaller size and use of local resources tend to make them less damaging to the environment.

Industrial recycling

Collectively, industries account for nearly one-quarter of the world's water use. In most industrial countries, they are the biggest user—frequently accounting for 50-80% of total demand, compared with 10-30% in much of the Third World. As developing countries industrialize, however, their water demands for electric power generation, manufacturing, mining, and materials processing are rising rapidly.

In contrast to that used in agriculture, only a small fraction of industrial water actually is consumed. Most of it is utilized

for cooling, processing, and other activities that may heat or pollute water, but do not use it up. This allows a factory to recycle its supplies. American steelmakers, for example, have reduced their water intake to 14 tons per ton of steel, securing the remainder from recycling.

So far, the main impetus for industrial water recycling has come from pollution control laws. Most of the world's wealthier countries now mandate that industries meet specific water quality standards before releasing wastewater into the environment. The most effective and economical way to comply with these requirements often is to treat and recycle water, thereby discharging less. Pollution control laws, therefore, not only have helped clean up rivers, lakes, and streams, they have promoted conservation and more efficient water use.

Given the proper incentives, industries of many types have shown they can cut their water needs 40-90% with available technologies and practices, while at the same time protecting water from pollution. Industrial conservation offers cities facing shortages a large untapped new supply. Ensuring that new factories incorporate conservation and recycling from the outset would help delay costly investments in urban water supplies, reduce overpumping of aquifers, lessen competition for water, and help prevent pollution from reaching levels hazardous to people and wildlife. Closing the industrial water and wastewater cycle not only is technically possible, it increasingly makes good economic and environmental sense.

Homes, apartments, small businesses, and other municipal enterprises account for less than one-tenth of the world's total water use. However, their demands are concentrated in relatively small geographic areas, and in many cases are escalating rapidly. As cities expand, they strain the capacity of local water bodies and force engineers to reach out to ever more distant sources.

In addition, the reservoirs, canals, pumping stations, pipes, sewers, and treatment plants that constitute a modern water and wastewater system require huge sums of money to build and maintain. Collecting and treating water and wastewater also takes large amounts of energy and chemicals, adding to environmental pollution and the over-all costs of a community's water system. Under such constraints, many cities are having difficulty meeting the needs of their residents, and large numbers of low-income households in developing countries get no service at all.

Conservation, once viewed as just an emergency response to drought, has been transformed in recent years into a sophisticated package of measures that offers one of the most cost-effective and environmentally sound ways of balancing urban water budgets. Just as energy planners have discovered that it often is cheaper to save energy than to build more power plants, water planners are realizing that an assortment of efficiency measures can yield permanent savings and thereby delay or avert the need for expensive new dams and reservoirs, groundwater wells, and treatment plants. The idea slowly is spreading that managing demand, rather than continuously striving to meet it, is a surer path to water security while saving money and protecting the environment at the same time.

Raising the price of water to reflect its true cost better is one of the most important steps any city can take. Water consistently is undervalued and, as a result, chronically is overused. The water rate structure of many utilities actually reward waste by charging less the more that is consumed.

Many residences in both industrial and Third World cities are not equipped with water meters, making it impossible to charge people appropriately for their water use. Metering not only is a prerequisite to the success of most conservation measures, it encourages savings in and of itself simply by tying the water bill to the amount used.

Raising water prices often can be politically difficult to do. Yet, if accompanied by public outreach explaining the need for the hike and steps consumers can take to keep bills down, higher prices can have a strong positive effect. When faced with dire water supply conditions in the mid 1970s, for instance, officials in Tucson, Ariz., raised rates sharply to make them reflect the true cost of service better. They also ran a public education campaign called "Beat the Peak" with a goal of curbing water use on hot summer afternoons, when the supply was most in danger of running short. The result was a 16% drop in per capita use within a few years, which, along with the lowered peak demand, allowed the Tucson water utility to cut its expansion expenses by $75,000,000.

Since economic incentives and public outreach will not motivate everyone to conserve, setting water-efficiency standards for common fixtures—toilets, showerheads, and faucets—can be a critical component of a reliable conservation strategy. Legislation that would set national standards passed Congress in October, 1992, as part of a broad energy bill. It requires that all new homes and major remodeling nationwide incorporate water-efficient fixtures and appliances.

Effective pricing, regulations, and public outreach also can help curb water use outdoors. In many dry regions, the sprinkling of lawns accounts for one-third to half of residential water demand. Many communities in the U.S. have turned to Xeriscape landscaping that draws on a wide variety of indigenous and drought-tolerant plants, shrubs, and ground cover to replace the thirsty green lawns found in most suburbs. A Xeriscape yard typically requires 30-80%

less water than a conventional one and can reduce fertilizer and herbicide use as well.

In addition to cutting indoor and outdoor use, a comprehensive urban conservation effort will curb waste in the water distribution system itself. As urban water systems deteriorate because of age or lack of maintenance, large amounts can be lost through broken pipes and faults in the distribution network. In most cases, finding and fixing leaks rewards a city not only with water savings, but with a quick payback on the investment. At a cost of $2,100,000, the Massachusetts Water Resources Authority's leak detection program cut system-wide demand in the greater Boston area by about 10%, making it one of the most cost-effective measures in a successful conservation strategy.

What does water cost?

Many of the shortages cropping up around the world stem from the widespread failure to value water at anything close to its true worth. Pricing it properly is especially important in agriculture because wasteful irrigation constitutes the single largest untapped new supply. Yet, water subsidies are larger and more pervasive in agriculture than in any other sector. Governments often build, maintain, and operate irrigation systems with public funds, then charge farmers next to nothing for these expensive services.

Undercharging not only fosters waste and the planting of water-intensive crops, it also deprives government agencies of the funds needed to maintain canals and other irrigation works adequately. Correcting the situation requires bucking deeply entrenched and politically influential special interests, instilling irrigation bureaucracies with a broader sense of mission, and decentralizing water management so that local water suppliers and users have more responsibility and accountability for the performance of their operations.

With the pace of development slowing and supplies no longer expanding in places, new demands increasingly must be met by shifting water among different users—irrigators, industries, cities, and the natural environment. In the western U.S., competition for scarce supplies has spawned an active water market. During 1991, 127 water transactions of various kinds were reported in 12 western states. Almost all the water sold or leased came from irrigation, and two-thirds of the trades resulted in cities getting more water for immediate or future use.

Exactly how far U.S. water trading ultimately will go in reallocating supplies remains unclear. According to some estimates, redirecting seven percent of western agriculture's water to cities could meet the growth in urban demand projected for the end of the decade. After that, larger shifts would be needed. Unless cities

stabilize their water use through conservation, reuse, and, where necessary, limits on the size of their populations and economies, agriculture ultimately could lose more water—and land—than is socially desirable, given the challenge that lies ahead of feeding a much larger world population.

Wherever pricing and marketing fail to take into account the full social, environmental, and intergenerational costs of water use, some additional correction is necessary. In areas with declining groundwater levels, for instance, governments can limit the total amount pumped to the average rate of aquifer recharge. In the case of fossil aquifers, a depletion tax might be levied on all groundwater extractions. In this way, those profiting from draining one-time reserves at least partially would compensate society.

Public action also is required to ensure that ecological systems get the water they need to remain healthy. One option is to limit the total amount that can be diverted from a river, lake, or stream. Protecting water systems also depends on regulating the use of those critical areas of land that help moderate its cycling through the environment. Degradation of the watershed—the sloping land that collects, directs, and controls the flow of rainwater in a river basin—is a pervasive problem in rich and poor countries alike. Besides contributing to flash floods and loss of groundwater recharge, which can exacerbate the effects of drought, it leads to soil erosion that prematurely fills downstream reservoirs with silt, shortening the useful life of expensive water projects.

Many of the measures that can help safeguard water supplies enhance crop production in upland areas. Terracing, mulching, agroforestry (the combined production of crops and trees), and planting vegetative barriers on the contour are a few of the ways soil and water can be conserved while improving agricultural output. On lands unsuitable for cultivation, the menu of options for watershed protection includes revegetating deforested slopes, reducing grazing pressures, and altering timber practices. The challenge for governments is to plan the use of watershed lands with soil and water conservation in mind, recognizing that the way uplands are managed greatly affects the livelihoods of people and the integrity of water systems downstream.

The idea is to devote as much human ingenuity to learning to live in balance with water as has been put into controlling and manipulating it. Conservation, efficiency, recycling, and re-use can generate a new supply large enough to get mankind through many of the shortages on the horizon. However, the pace of this transition needs to quicken if the planet is to avert severe ecological damage, economic setbacks, food shortages, and international conflicts. In the end, the time available to adjust may prove as precious as water itself.

THE LANDSCAPE

OF

HUNGER

We have seen the victims of mass starvation. We have shuddered at the images of millions of people arriving at remote camps for aid. Many of the world's famines result from wars or civil strife. But we rarely see that hunger also grows from environmental ruin.

BRUCE STUTZ

Bruce Stutz is features editor at Audubon. *He is the author of* Natural Lives, Modern Times.

The numbers alone are staggering: In 1990, 550 million people worldwide were hungry, 56 million more than in the early 1980s. During that time, the number of malnourished children in the developing world increased from 167 million to 188 million. And experts predict that the situation will only get worse as food production in the poorest countries continues to decline.

Deforestation, desertification, and soil erosion have devastating effects on food production. Where forests are cut down, the soils are washed or blown away. Where land is planted too often or grazed too long, it can no longer support crops or cattle.

Ironically, modern agriculture—the science of growing food—has had the greatest impact on the decline in the food supply. In the 1960s governments began encouraging nomads to settle in one place, to raise one cash crop instead of several, to herd only one kind of livestock, and the soils quickly became exhausted.

This "green revolution"—intensified farming of "improved crop varieties" with irrigation, chemicals, and pesticides—at first raised productivity, but the long-term results were just the opposite. According to Mostafa K. Tolba, former executive director of the United Nations' Environment Programme, the process "made agroecosystems increasingly artificial, unstable, and prone to rapid degradation."

Population growth and refugee migration add to the problems of environmental degradation. When the land becomes too crowded and the soil too exhausted to support life, farmers move into forests, slashing and burning new farms. As the land gives out, the people move on, again and again. Eventually, they find their way to the refugee camps.

At the 1972 United Nations Conference on the Human Environment in Stockholm, environmental issues were considered secondary to issues of economic development. But the 1968–74 drought in Ethiopia and the Sahel made it evident that the environmental costs of traditional economic development might be too high.

The Ethiopian government estimated that its highlands were then losing ap-

From *Audubon*, Vol. 95, No. 2, March/April 1993, pp. 54-63. Reprinted by permission.

proximately 1 billion tons of soil a year through water and wind erosion. So when development experts convened at the United Nations Conference on Environment and Development (UNCED) last June, the agenda had changed. The environment had to be protected, it was decided. The diplomats finally recognized the simplest truth: The land that produces the food must be preserved.

The food web inextricably connects plants, animals, and people with the water, soil, and atmosphere of the planet; the hunger web begins as those connections are severed. Air and water pollution contaminate and ruin food sources. The predictions are that global warming will also have an effect, changing planting times, growing seasons, even the ability of crops to survive in their present ranges.

On the following pages *Audubon* examines the environmental causes of mass hunger and some possible solutions. Most do not involve high-tech, grand-scale megaprojects; the best of them are low-tech, local, modest in scale. The solutions may not be as dramatic as scenes of armies massing to feed millions. But they are sustainable—which means that in the future hunger may be defeated without the help of armies.

DEFORESTATION

Slash, Burn, Plow, Plant, Abandon

Forests now cover 27.7 percent of all ice-free land in the world. In 1990 wood was the main energy source for 9 out of 10 Africans, providing more than half of their fuel. By the end of this decade, according to Mostafa Tolba, 2.4 billion people will be unable to satisfy their minimum energy requirements without consuming wood faster than it is being grown.

As human beings encroach on the world's remaining woodlands, deforestation will exacerbate the problems of hunger. For when hillsides are denuded, soil erosion sets in.

In Haiti, where forests once covered most of the land, 40 to 50 million trees are cut each year to supply firewood, cropland, and charcoal. At the current rate of deforestation, Haiti's forests will cease to exist within two or three years.

Already, loss of forests has caused massive soil erosion, and when drought strikes, the quality of the remaining soil will decline. When rain finally *does* fall, runoff will be too rapid and farmers will be forced to abandon cultivation. Since the 1970s, food aid to Haiti has risen sevenfold.

In Bangladesh and India, deforestation has caused another kind of problem, increasing the frequency and force of floods. Bangladesh used to suffer a catastrophic flood every 50 years or so; by the 1980s the country was being hit with major floods—which wash away farms and rice paddies—every four years. Between the late 1960s and late 1980s, India's flood-prone areas grew from approximately 25 million hectares to 59 million. (One hectare equals 2.4 acres.)

PROTECT AND PRESERVE

Although some countries, notably Brazil and Costa Rica, have preserved tracts of their forested land, less than 5 percent of the world's remaining tropical forests are protected as sanctuaries, parks, or reserves.

Regenerating woodlands by replanting them would provide some measure of relief. Over the past 10 years, China has reforested some 70 million hectares of endangered landscape. The U.N. Food and Agriculture Organization estimates that 1.1 million hectares of trees are successfully planted each year worldwide.

Modifying wood stoves to make them more efficient and increasing use of solar cooking would slow the decline of forests by decreasing reliance on wood for fuel.

Using the forests sustainably—by tapping trees for rubber, for example, or developing environmentally sound tourism—would provide more revenue than slash-and-burn agriculture.

DESERTIFICATION
The Spreading Barrens

Every year nearly 6 million hectares of previously productive land becomes desert, losing its capacity to produce food. The United Nations defines desertification as "land degradation in arid, semiarid, and dry subhumid areas [drylands] resulting mainly from adverse human impact." Translated into human suffering, that phrase means that by 1977, 57 million people had seen their lands dry up. By 1984 the number had risen to 135 million worldwide. Today, one-sixth of the total world population is threatened with desertification.

When drylands—which make up about 43 percent of the total land area of the world—revert to desert, hunger follows almost axiomatically. Most crops can't survive in the parched landscape, and harvests fail. Further, withered root systems can't hold the soil, and winds finally erode whatever topsoil remains.

Arid landscapes are so fragile that they break down quickly. A drought can mean catastrophe. In Mozambique, for instance, civil war combined with a worsening drought last year to leave 3.1 million people in need of food aid, 1.2 million more than in 1991.

But Africa is not the only place where food supplies are threatened by desertification. In Russia, annual desertification and sand encroachment northwest of the Caspian Sea were estimated to be as high as 10 percent. Around the drying Aral Sea, the desert has been growing at some 100,000 hectares per year for the last 25 years, an annual desertification rate of 4 percent.

STAVING OFF DISASTER

Agroforestry—planting trees as windbreaks and shade to protect pastureland—contributes to the maintenance of hard-used fields. In Kenya, for example, the Green Belt Movement has embarked on a large-scale tree-planting program.

Massive irrigation projects, such as those tried in Nigeria (see "Death of an Oasis," *Audubon* May-June 1992), are less practical, benefiting only a few at great cost to the environment. Small-scale projects, as low-tech and low-cost as collecting and managing rainwater, are often slow and laborious, but according to the Bread for the World Institute on Hunger and Development, they have succeeded in reclaiming hundreds of hectares of degraded land.

SOIL EROSION
A Worldwide Dust Bowl

Worldwide, erosion removes about 25.4 billion tons of soil each year. Deforestation and desertification both leave land open to erosion. In deforested areas, water washes down steep, naked slopes, taking the soil with it. In desertified regions, exposed soils, cleared for farming, building, or mining, or overgrazed by livestock, simply blow away. Wind erosion is most extensive in Africa and Asia. Blowing soil not only leaves a degraded area behind but can bury and kill vegetation where it settles. It will also fill drainage and irrigation ditches.

When high-tech farm practices are applied to poor lands, the result is often a combination of soil washing away and chemical pesticides and fertilizers polluting the runoff.

In Africa, soil erosion has reached critical levels, with farmers pushing farther onto deforested hillsides. In Ethiopia, for example, soil loss occurs at a rate of between 1.5 billion and 2 billion cubic meters a year, with some 4 million hectares of highlands considered "irreversibly degraded."

In Asia, in the eastern hills of Nepal, 38 percent of the land area consists of fields that have been abandoned because the topsoil has washed away. In the Western Hemisphere, Ecuador is losing soil at a rate 20 times what would be considered acceptable by the U.S. Soil and Conservation Service.

And even in the United States, 44 percent of cropland is affected by erosion.

DEFEATING THE ELEMENTS

According to the International Fund for Agricultural Development (IFAD), traditional labor-intensive, small-scale efforts at soil conservation—which combine maintenance of shrubs and trees with corp growing and cattle grazing—work best.

In the Barani area of Pakistan, a program begun by IFAD in 1980 to control rainfall runoff, erosion, and damage to rivers from siltation has resulted in a 20 to 30 percent increase in crop yields and livestock productivity.

POPULATION GROWTH

More Mouths to Feed

With a population growth rate of 1.7 percent, the world added almost 100 million people in 1992; an increase of some 3.7 billion is expected by 2030. Since 90 percent of the increase will occur in developing countries in Africa, Asia, and Latin America, the outlook is bleak: None of those countries can expect to produce enough food to feed a population increasing at such rates.

Population growth and environmental damage go hand in hand with poverty and hunger. In sub-Saharan Africa, for example, as colonial governments replaced pastoral lifestyles with sedentary farming, populations grew and farming and grazing intensified. Today, 80 percent of the region's pasture- and rangelands show signs of damage, and overall productivity is declining. Yet during the next 40 years the sub-Saharan population is expected to rise from 500 million to 1.5 billion.

Today only Bangladesh, South Korea, the Netherlands, and the island of Java have population densities greater than 400 people per square kilometer. (By comparison, the population density of the United States works out to 27 per square kilometer.)

By the middle of the next century, one-third of the world's population will probably live in overcrowded conditions. Bangladesh's population density could rise to 1,700 per square kilometer.

In Madagascar, population pressures have forced farmers to continuously clear new land. Virtually all the lowland forests in the country are gone. But cleared soil wears out quickly. Per capita calorie supply in Madagascar has fallen by 9 percent since the 1960s, probably the greatest decline anywhere in the world.

In Nepal, one of the world's poorest nations, increased population (700 people per square kilometer of cultivable land, the world's highest average) has forced villagers to expand their farm plots onto wooded hillsides. Marginal farmers rely on livestock, which they allow to graze in the remaining forests. Terraced soil once used for crop production has been abandoned for lack of nutrients, putting more pressure on ever-diminishing forest resources.

CHOOSING THE FUTURE

If a fertility rate of slightly more than two children per couple can be achieved by the year 2010, the world's population will stabilize at 7.7 billion by 2060. If that rate is not reached until 2065, world population will reach 14.2 billion by 2100.

According to a 1992 World Bank report, improving education for girls is an important long-term policy in the developing world. The more educated a woman is, the more likely she is to work outside the home and the smaller her family is likely to be. Choice also plays a role here: The United Nations' World Fertility Survey has found that women would have an average of 1.41 fewer children if they were able to choose the size of their family. Access to birth control methods could help lower the world's population by as many as 1.3 billion people over the next 35 years. During the Reagan-Bush years U.S. funding to programs offering such information was cut back; but President Bill Clinton has reversed that stand.

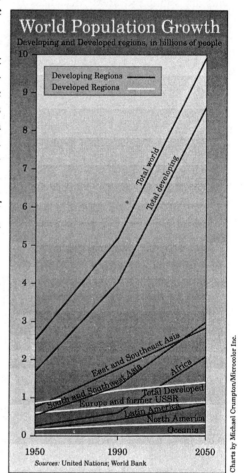

World Population Growth
Developing and Developed regions, in billions of people

Developing Regions
Developed Regions

Total world
Total developing
East and Southeast Asia
South and Southwest Asia
Africa
Europe and former USSR
Total Developed
Latin America
North America
Oceania

1950   1990   2050

Sources: United Nations; World Bank

Charts by Michael Crumpton/Microcolor Inc.

Somalia: An Ecopolitical Tragedy

Somalia's breakdown of law and order has created new waves of famine in recent months, but the groundwork for civil strife was laid by years of misuse of the nation's precious grazing lands and water resources.

Almost the entire country is categorized by the United Nations Environment Programme as susceptible to soil degradation, and most of the country is overgrazed.

Over the years the degradation was accelerated by the parceling out of communal grazing lands to private owners, which undermined traditional systems of land management. Private herds—which are generally larger than those owned communally—have stripped the hillsides bare, causing wind erosion during droughts and runoff during rains.

Building dams across valleys to halt water runoff in the north of the country has made matters worse by disrupting the natural drainage systems.

In the south the productivity of irrigated fields has been lessened by poor water management, which has created saline, waterlogged soils on the edge of the desert. There the salt will render the soil useless for food production in the decades to come.

—*Fred Pearce*

ENVIRONMENTAL REFUGEES
A Moveable Famine

The cycle of overpopulation, poverty, environmental ruin, and famine begins all over again when those trying to find a better life flee their ruined homelands. Land degradation is the largest cause of environmental-refugee movements.

According to Jodi L. Jacobson, a senior researcher at Worldwatch Institute, in Washington, D.C., 135 million people live in areas undergoing severe desertification.

But when those refugees move into areas that are already stressed by overpopulation or too intense agriculture, they place an added burden on the environment. Refugees need wood for fuel, water to drink, land on which to graze their livestock, and grain to eat—all of which are already scarce.

Jacobson estimates that some 10 million people worldwide are refugees from environmental ruin. "Competition for land and natural resources is driving more and more people to live in marginal, disaster-prone areas," she says, "leaving them more vulnerable to natural forces. Hence, millions of Bangladeshis live on *chars*, bars of silt and sand in the middle of the Bengal delta, some of which are washed away each year by ocean tides and monsoon floods."

CLIMATE CHANGE
Global Warning

Since 1800 atmospheric concentration of carbon dioxide (CO_2) has increased by about 25 percent and continues to rise each year. Over the same period atmospheric methane concentrations have doubled. Since the 1960s more than 100 separate studies have confirmed that a doubling of the CO_2 concentration would raise average surface temperatures by one to four degrees centigrade; three degrees is the figure used by the United Nations' Intergovernmental Panel on Climate Change.

Although a small number of scientists dispute these findings, weather and climate remain the biggest concern for farmers as warming begins to change growing seasons, irrigation needs, and land use. These changes will be especially serious in tropical regions, where farmland is already marginal and crops are growing near the limits of their temperature tolerance.

Those who live along shorelines will be hardest hit: The greenhouse effect could cause a global mean sea level rise of about six centimeters per decade. At that rate, many islands would become uninhabitable, and currently productive lowlands would be flooded. The developing countries that now experience the worst food shortages can expect to be hurt most by global warming. A study conducted by the University of Oxford and the Goddard Institute for Space Studies, funded by the U.S. Environmental Protection Agency, found that with an increase in average temperatures of three to four degrees centigrade, grain production in developing countries would decline by 9 to 11 percent by the year 2060, putting between 60 and 360 million people at risk from hunger—10 to 50 percent more than the currently predicted 640 million.

CLOSING THE GREENHOUSE

The use of renewable, or nonfossil, fuels—and more efficient use of all fuels—would go far to control the buildup of CO_2.

The World Bank recommends that governments remove energy subsidies and that they tax the use of carbon fuels. Maintenance of the world's large remaining forests would also help: Tropical deforestation accounts for 10 to 30 percent of the CO_2 released into the atmosphere.

The Oxford–Goddard Institute study found that slowing population increases could allow developing nations to cope more readily with the changing climate by changing land use and farming practices.

Hunger and the Ozone Hole

In early 1992 researchers from five U.S. marine-science institutes reported a drop of 6 to 12 percent in phytoplankton production under the Antarctic ozone hole. It appears that tiny marine organisms, which constitute more than half of all biomass on earth, may not be able to withstand harmful wavelengths of ultraviolet light—UV-B radiation—that penetrate the earth's thinning ozone layer.

When ozone holes form in the spring, most of the fish, shellfish, and crustaceans that humans harvest are in their larval, planktonic stages—floating in the topmost layer of the ocean. "Increasing intensities of UV-B radiation near the surface could negatively impact the reproductive potential of some of our most valuable marine resources, including tuna, pollock, cod, halibut, and flounder," wrote John Hardy, an associate professor at Huxley College, Western Washington University, in the November 1989 issue of *Oceanography*. Juvenile crabs, lobsters, shrimp, and anchovies are also vulnerable.

Just how such damage might move up the food chain is not known, but in Newport, Oregon, the Environmental Protection Agency's stratospheric ozone–depletion team found preliminary evidence of retarded growth in amphipods fed with phytoplankton that had been exposed to UV-B.

Although the leading industrial nations have agreed to halt production of the worst ozone-destroying compounds by 1996, ozone depletion is expected to continue for several decades as existing chemicals seep into the stratosphere. An ozone hole is likely to appear over the Northern Hemisphere, where ozone is dwindling at an estimated 1 percent per year. Each 1 percent decline in ozone is thought to increase exposure to biologically harmful ultraviolet light by at least 2 percent.

The United Nations Environment Programme warns that a 16 percent reduction in stratospheric ozone (which could occur in the next few years) would trigger a 6 to 9 percent drop in seafood production. Oceans now provide more than 30 percent of the animal protein eaten by humans.

—*Brad Warren*

A New Strategy for
Feeding a Crowded Planet

David Norse

DAVID NORSE is a research associate for the Overseas Development Institute in London and a research fellow at the Environmental Change Unit at the University of Oxford.

How many is too many? Is planet Earth really in danger of collapsing because of overpopulation? How valid is the recent joint statement by the U.S. National Academy of Sciences and the U.K. Royal Society that, "If current predictions of population growth prove accurate and patterns of human activity on the planet remain unchanged, science and technology may not be able to prevent either irreversible degradation of the environment or continued poverty for much of the world"?[1]

Similar warnings were given by the British economist Thomas Malthus in 1798, when Earth's population was only about 1 billion;[2] yet 5.3 billion people are now supported, albeit inadequately in many cases, by Earth's bounty. Malthus's warning of collapse was wrong because he had a static view of science and technology and of how they could compensate for the lack of land by raising agricultural productivity, for example, through irrigation and fertilization.

More recent assessments have taken account of technology to a greater or lesser extent. Some of them, however, surpassed Malthus's perception of the problem to introduce technology itself as an additional factor that could lead to collapse.[3] For instance, such production inputs as mineral fertilizers and pesticides have been cited for causing environmental damage when they are applied incorrectly or excessively.[4]

Earlier estimates of the maximum human population that Earth could support were methodologically weak and primarily concerned with the ratio of humans to land. More recent estimation techniques are more sophisticated and commonly use the concept of Earth's human-carrying capacity (or potential population-supporting capacity) to introduce agroecological and other factors into the analysis. The carrying capacity of a particular region is the maximum population of a given species that can be supported indefinitely, allowing for seasonal and random changes, without any degradation of the natural resource base that would diminish this maximum population in the future.[5]

The concept was first used by ecologists and zoologists to describe the ability of natural ecosystems to support wildlife populations. If wildlife populations exceed the natural food supply available locally or through migration, population collapse is inevitable. But, whereas the carrying capacity of natural ecosystems is essentially static, that of managed agroecosystems is dynamic. A region's human-carrying capacity can be increased by raising land and labor productivity or through trade with better endowed regions.[6]

Prior to about 1850, the world's human population could be fed, clothed, and otherwise supported by relatively limited modifications to natural ecosystems. Since then, however, and at an accelerating pace since about 1945, the food supply—and hence the carrying capacity—has become increasingly dependent on science-based agriculture and on external inputs of nonrenewable resources (notably fossil fuels and rock phosphate). Thus has arisen the critical question of sustainable agricultural development and the role of the United Nations Conference on Environment and Development (UNCED), to be held in Rio de Janeiro this June, in effecting the necessary changes to achieve it.

The preparatory process for UNCED has highlighted a number of critical uncertainties regarding sustainable development and the long-term carrying capacity of the globe. The first uncertainty concerns the human population growth rate and whether Earth's natural resource base and technological prospects will be adequate to sustain future populations. In particular, is the planet's carrying capacity threatened, on the one hand, by climate change caused primarily by the developed countries and their wasteful consumption patterns[7] and, on the other, by irreversible land degradation in the developing countries?[8] The second uncertainty is the link between population pressure, poverty, and environmental degradation, which has both national and international dimensions and involves positive as

From *Environment*, Vol. 34, No. 5, June 1992, pp. 6-11, 32-39. Reprinted with permission of the Helen Dwight Reid Educational Foundation. Published by Heldref Publications. 1319 Eighteenth St., NW, Washington, DC 20036-1802.

3. NATURAL RESOURCES: Food and Hunger

Land reforms are needed to reduce poverty and malnutrition in Guatemala.

WORLD BANK

well as negative impacts on carrying capacity.[9] The third issue is the different attitudes of developed and developing countries toward the tradeoffs that must be made between the environment and development.[10] Developed countries tend to give priority to environmental conservation in spite of the high economic and social costs that may be associated with such measures. Developing countries, however, tend to emphasize the need to ensure that environmental measures do not have adverse economic effects on their development, in part because eliminating poverty is a prerequisite for limiting certain forms of land degradation that undermine carrying capacity.

Of course, a region's human-carrying capacity is not always defined in terms of food production potential; in some situations, the principal constraint on carrying capacity may be the lack of water or fuelwood.[11] In addition, the lack of food production potential can often be offset by other economic activities, but these factors are beyond the scope of this discussion. Nevertheless, even a general assessment of the major threats to Earth's long-term carrying capacity reveals the need for a new strategy for sustainable agriculture.

Before addressing these issues, however, it should be stated that asking what the human-carrying capacity is or asking how many people can be fed is dodging the issue in two important respects. First, it is posing the problem as a supply problem stemming from the lack of production potential, whereas the demand problem is more serious and its analysis should take precedence over any theoretical estimates of carrying capacity.[12] The 500 million to 1 billion people who go hungry each day do so because they are too poor to buy all of the food they need.[13] Thus, the central issues

should be the elimination of poverty, the resolution of the debt crisis, and the removal of developed countries' trade barriers that prevent developing countries and their people from raising their incomes.[14] Second, the momentum of human population growth is so great and so insensitive to minor changes in mortality, migration, and fertility rates that world population will grow by some 3 billion between now and 2025, the year chosen as UNCED's development horizon, unless the AIDS pandemic goes out of control or unless socially unacceptable forms of family size limitation are adopted.[15] Thus, the issue is not whether Earth can support a population of 8.6 billion or so in 2025—it will have to—but, rather, whether it can do so sustainably.

The Global Picture

Almost 200 years have passed since Malthus first raised doubts about the global carrying capacity, and the global population has increased fivefold. Still, the debate continues, with estimates of carrying capacity ranging from 2 billion to 30 billion people. The issue was widely discussed in the aftermath of World War II and came back into prominence in the late 1960s and early 1970s, when various

individuals and computer modeling groups, particularly those supported by the Club of Rome, argued that projected population growth, excessive demands on the natural resource base, and pollution would overburden the biosphere and cause its collapse.[16] This was the basic message of the club's *The Limits to Growth* report that shocked many people into examining the whole question of growth in a finite world.[17] Other analysts, however, while not denying the seriousness of present population and pollution trends, have concluded that collapse is avoidable with relatively minor and equally realistic changes in the assumptions about the rate of technological growth (that is, faster), and about how prices and demand respond to scarcity of natural resources.[18]

Dutch scientists belonging to one of the modeling groups set up by the Club of Rome produced the first comprehensive assessment of global carrying capacity.[19] The scientists disaggregated the world's land resources into 222 broad soil regions with known climatic, vegetative, and topographic characteristics and irrigation potential. Maximum production potential per hectare was calculated in units of "cereal equivalents" for each of these soil regions and then summed

96

to give a total maximum production of some 50 billion tonnes of cereal equivalent per year. However, this estimate is a theoretical maximum assuming the use of all of the land potentially suitable for farming (3.4 billion hectares compared with the 1.5 billion hectares that are currently farmed), no pests and diseases, no plant nutrient shortages, and no water constraints. Acknowledging that such assumptions are unrealistic, the scientists later applied a range of reduction factors for land availability, average attainable yields, seed requirements, storage losses, and so on to arrive at estimates of potential production of consumable grain.[20] A comparison was also made between potential production using the full package of modern inputs and that from labor-oriented agriculture without the use of tractors, modern machines, pesticides, or fertilizers. Table 1 on this page shows more than an eightfold difference between the production potentials of the two systems.

These output figures were roughly transformed into carrying capacity terms by assuming an average grain consumption of 800 kilograms per capita per year. The resulting global carrying capacities were 6.7 billion people for the modern system and 2.7 billion for the labor-oriented production system.[21] It is interesting to compare these results with some other, back-of-the-envelope estimates. F. Baade, for example, assuming that the arable land area was between 2 billion and 3 billion hectares and that average yields could rise to 5 tonnes of cereal equivalent per hectare, estimated the potential carrying capacity at some 30 billion.[22] No consideration was given to whether production could be sustained at this level; to whether all arable land would be used for agriculture; or to the increase in indirect demands for cereals as people switch to higher value but lower calorie-content foods when their income grows.

Roger Revelle and Bernard Gilland made assumptions similar to Baade's regarding potential crop yields, that is, about 5 tonnes of cereal equivalent per hectare.[23] Revelle also assumed

that much of the potentially arable land would be used for food production, whereas Gilland doubted whether the area available for sustainable agriculture would be much greater than the present one. At an average per-capita grain consumption of 800 kilograms per year, Baade's carrying capacity estimate becomes more than 18 billion, Revelle's becomes 14 billion, and Gilland's is 8.8 billion. These estimates exclude the output of rangelands, pastures, and fisheries, which could raise carrying capacity by more than 10 percent at the global level and by considerably more in certain regions.[24]

Critical Countries?

Methodological sophistication was taken a step further in a study completed in 1982 by the UN Food and Agriculture Organization (FAO) and the International Institute for Applied Systems Analysis (IIASA).[25] The study, on agroecological zones and

their population-supporting capacity, moved away from global and regional estimates to identify not just critical countries but also critical zones within countries. The analysis was completed on 115 developing countries, excluding China, North and South Korea, and some very small nations because of the lack of data. The land area within countries was subdivided into zones according to the length of the growing season, which was determined by the number of days in each year with temperature, rainfall, and soil moisture conditions suitable for crop growth. Each of these zones was further subdivided on the basis of soil characteristics, slope, and other factors influencing the suitability of land for crop growth. And, unlike most previous studies that estimated production potential only in terms of cereal equivalents, production was determined for 15 major crops: rice, wheat, maize, millet, sorghum, barley, cassava, sweet potato, white potato, banana and plantain, soybean, *Phaseolus* bean, peanuts, oil palm, and sugar cane.

Potential yields under rain-fed conditions were constrained according to the length of the growing season and were estimated for three different assumptions regarding the level of management and input use: a low level,

TABLE 1
PRODUCTION POTENTIALS OF DIFFERENT AGRICULTURAL SYSTEMS

Agricultural system	GRAIN PRODUCTION						
	South America	Australia	Africa	Asia	North America	Europe	World[a]
			(millions of tonnes)				
Modern agriculture on all potential agricultural land[b]	2,932	623	2,863	3,770	1,870	1,100	13,156
Modern agriculture on present agricultural land[b]	379	100	636	2,929	712	582	5,338
Labor-oriented agriculture on maximum agricultural land[c]	241	57	236	426	391	256	1,606

[a]World totals do not reflect row totals because of rounding.
[b]Allows for seed requirements and storage losses amounting to 20 percent of total production.
[c]Assuming that only two-thirds of the land is cropped with grains.
SOURCE: P. Buringh and H. D. J. van Heemst, *An Estimation of World Food Production Based on Labour-Oriented Agriculture* (Wageningen, the Netherlands: Agricultural Press, 1977).

3. NATURAL RESOURCES: Food and Hunger

with traditional varieties, no mineral fertilizers or pesticides, and no specific soil conservation measures; an intermediate level, with a basic package of inputs and limited soil conservation measures; and a high level, involving optimum use of mineral fertilizers, pesticides, and improved crop varieties, plus long-term soil conservation measures regardless of the costliness of these inputs. Soil conservation measures were assumed to be totally effective at the high level, but, at the other levels, land and productivity loss from soil degradation were taken into consideration. Irrigation was not addressed in detail, nor were nonfood cash crops, although land was allocated to them. Allowance was also made for livestock production from rangelands unsuitable for crop production.

A computer program determined the optimum cropping pattern to maximize calorie production and then calculated the number of people that could be fed at the minimum calorie intake level for each country. Estimates were made, using the UN "medium variant" population projections, for each of the input levels and for the years 1975, 2000, and 2025. The resulting projections suggested that global carrying capacity is adequate for the year 2000 even at low input levels, provided that much of the potentially arable land can be used for food crop production instead of livestock or forest.[26] At the regional level, however, the picture is bleak, with only South America's developing countries having adequate carrying capacity under the assumption of minimal input use. It is not, of course, a realistic assumption; with the exception of sub-Saharan Africa, present input use is generally at the intermediate level or higher.

The crunch comes at the country level. At the low input level, 64 of the 117 countries studied would be unable to feed their projected populations in 2000 even if they use all of their arable land for food production. With greater input use at the intermediate level, the number of critical countries falls to 36, but 18 remain critical even at the high input level (see Table 2 on this page). Such estimates, however, assume that the countries concerned wish or have to be self-sufficient in food, whereas this is seldom the case. Most countries wish to exploit any comparative advantage they have regarding other natural resource endowments, like mineral deposits and fossil fuels, or in the production of manufactured goods. For example, the 18 critical countries include a number of oil producers in the Middle East, which, with little but desert for food production, can import their needs much more cheaply than they can grow them, and, if they use their resources wisely, could establish sustainable economies in spite of their limited carrying capacity in terms of food production. There are some countries, however, such as Burundi, Niger, and Rwanda, that have few natural resource endowments to exploit and,

TABLE 2

DEVELOPING COUNTRIES ABLE TO SUPPORT LESS THAN HALF OF THEIR PROJECTED POPULATION IN 2000

Level of agricultural inputs	Level of economic dependence on agriculture	Medium risk	Higher risk	Highest risk
High	High	Netherlands Antilles Barbados Cape Verde		Rwanda Democratic Yemen Yemen
	Significant exports of manufactured goods	Lebanon Israel Mauritius Singapore	Jordan	
	Significant fossil fuel resources	Kuwait Qatar United Arab Emirates Oman Saudi Arabia Bahrain		Afghanistan
Intermediate	High	Réunion Martinique Antigua	Lesotho Mauritania	Haiti Burundi Somalia
	Significant exports of manufactured goods		El Salvador Kenya	
	Significant fossil fuel resources		Iraq Niger Algeria	
Low	High	Guadeloupe Windward Islands	Namibia	Comoros Ethiopia Uganda
	Significant exports of manufactured goods			
	Significant fossil fuel resources			Nigeria

SOURCE: UN Food and Agriculture Organization, *Land, Food and People* (Rome: FAO, 1984).

Although Kenya exports some manufactured goods, the country may not be able to feed even half of its population by 2000.

because of their land-locked situation, have no comparative advantage in the production of low-cost, labor-intensive goods. These countries seem destined to remain on the critical list.

Limitations to the Concept

Refinements of the type introduced by FAO allow policy planners to go beyond global and regional generalities by helping identify where population pressures are most acute. Nevertheless, there are important limitations to the utility of the carrying capacity concept. As the saying goes, man does not live by bread alone, and people and countries are seldom entirely dependent on food production, agriculture, or their natural resource base for the means to ensure adequate access to basic needs. It is becoming increasingly clear, however, that at least part of this reduced dependence is a response to population pressures on the natural resource base. Poor farm families are diversifying their income sources to cope with population pressures and food production instability. Farmers may be able to meet their basic needs in a more sustainable way by producing export crops, for example, and buying their food requirements. Thus, in the Ivory Coast, oil palm production is four to five times more profitable than maize production. Moreover, oil palm cultivation is generally a more ecologically sound form of land use in tropical areas with high rainfall than is monocultural maize production.

Countries are seldom totally dependent on agriculture. Even in highly agrarian countries like Bangladesh, agriculture accounts for only 50 percent of the gross domestic product. At the other extreme, in countries like Switzerland and Singapore, the agricultural resource base no longer plays a significant role. As long as these countries use their capital bases well,

the carrying capacity of their own lands will be of secondary importance. Thus, many of the critical countries identified by the FAO/IIASA study are not in danger of collapse because they can buy their way out of trouble,[27] provided, of course, that the major food-exporting countries avoid serious land degradation and thus maintain their export potential.

Some of these limitations have been addressed in the second generation of natural resource models developed by FAO and IIASA. A case study of Kenya, for example, was developed to provide a district- and national-level planning tool rather than carrying capacity estimates.[28] Land resources were assessed at the district level, as was the potential for food production. Land requirements for and the potential productivity of export crops, primarily coffee, tea, cotton, sisal, pineapple, and pyrethrum, were estimated. Soil degradation was considered in detail, including erosion and loss of fertility through inadequate fallows. Livestock production and fuelwood supply were also assessed.

Such refinements allow a more precise assessment of local carrying capacity in physical terms, but several limitations remain. Risk is not taken into consideration, nor is the articulation between agroecological zones, migration, market infrastructure, and

the all-important economic dimension. Risk, for example, particularly that stemming from drought and unreliable rainfall, can be a major constraint to the adoption of yield-raising technologies. Purchased inputs such as mineral fertilizers may be profitable given the average rainfall assumed in carrying capacity studies but waste farmers' money in unpredictable drought years. Thus, the use of long-run averages for weather assumptions can result in overestimates of carrying capacity.

The importance of the economic dimension, migration, and market infrastructure is well illustrated by a recent study of the Machakos district of Kenya.[29] Large parts of the district were virtually uninhabited at the beginning of this century. Yet, by the 1930s, substantial areas were so degraded by agricultural activities that it was thought to be on the edge of ecological collapse.[30] Nonetheless, the population has increased more than fivefold during the past 60 years.[31] In terms of the per-capita food requirement assumed by Revelle and Baade (800 kilograms of cereal equivalents per year), the district's carrying capacity was exceeded in the 1940s. Using the lower food requirement assumed by the FAO/IIASA study (2,320 calories per capita per day), the carrying capacity was exceeded about 10

TABLE 3 ▀▀▀▀▀▀▀▀▀▀
SHARE OF HARVESTED LAND USED FOR EXPORT CROPS FROM 1987 TO 1989

Country	Importance of agricultural exports[a]	Percentage of harvested area used for export crops[b]
Burkina Faso	High	5
Ivory Coast	High	44
Ethiopia	High	4
Honduras	High	22
India	Low	1
Indonesia	Low	18
Kenya	High	8
Malawi	High	5
Rwanda	High	5
Uganda	High	7

[a]Defined in terms of share of primary agricultural commodity exports in total merchandise exports in 1989. High = 85–99 percent; Low = 19–21 percent.
[b]After an allowance for the area used to meet domestic requirements for those crops is subtracted.
SOURCE: Importance of agricultural exports estimated from data in World Bank, *World Development Report 1991: The Challenge of Development—World Development Indicators* (New York: Oxford University Press, 1991). Percentages derived from Supply Utilization Tables for 1987/89, FAO AGROSTAT Data Bank, FAO, Rome.

years later. Reality, however, has been quite different, and the district has continued to flourish.

A number of factors account for this inconsistency: emigration to urban areas and internal migration to more marginal lands in response to land shortages and rising land prices;[32] a reduction of the fallow period;[33] intensification of land use through multiple cropping and, particularly, through the use of manure (the supply of which is heavily dependent on intensified livestock production) and mineral fertilizers (in the case of export crops);[34] the adoption of soil conservation measures to rehabilitate land, notably conservation tillage, contour farming, and terracing (the terraced area rose from about 52 percent in 1948 to 96 percent in 1978;[35] and finally, the introduction of coffee, fruit, and other horticultural crops that provide higher incomes than do the basic staples and thus make soil conservation more profitable.[36] The introduction of

these crops was a response more to improvements in local processing facilities and market access than to population pressure per se. Thus, migration to marginal lands was probably less than that which would have occurred in the absence of agricultural intensification and export crops.

The Machakos experience and the example of palm oil production in the Ivory Coast are clear rebuttals to the argument that the competition for land between export crops and food crops is a threat to development, to food security, to the poor, and, implicitly, to carrying capacity.[37] Export crops seldom occupy more than 10 to 20 percent of a country's arable land, and, even then, it is not necessarily the best land (see Table 3 on this page). Most countries can compensate for the diversion of land to export crops by modestly increasing productivity on the remaining food-crop land and still achieve approximate self-sufficiency. Under careful management, both carrying capacity and food security will rise. Moreover, export crops can provide a range of economic benefits. Locally, their greater profitability means that the growers and their employees can both raise and diversify their food intake. The extra income also increases farmers' ability to pay for the education of their children. Education is a priority expenditure in much of the developing world and generally results in slower population growth. Nationally, the gains in foreign exchange earnings from export crops can eliminate or lower the need for food aid and can help to consolidate a country's political independence.

Environmentally, the threat to sustainability can be much less than with staple food crops.[38] The tree canopy of the oil palms in the Ivory Coast, for example, protects the soil surface from erosion almost as well as the original forest did. And the palms' deep roots raise mineral nutrients from the subsoil. Thus, oil palm production is often an ecologically sounder use of the land than is food crop production. Coffee trees in the Machakos district also protect the soil

from erosion better than do most annual food crops. With their extensive root systems, the citrus, mango, and other tropical fruit trees introduced into the district help to hold the soil in place on the terraces and provide greater economic incentives to farmers to construct and maintain the terraces. Other cash crops, such as cotton and pyrethrum, yield high returns that can make the use of mineral fertilizers profitable. These crops leave behind fertilizer residues that benefit the staple food crops that follow them in the production rotation and, hence, help to limit nutrient mining and soil degradation.[39] Finally, by providing greater employment and incomes, cash crops discourage migration into environmentally fragile marginal areas.

In light of these studies and assuming that recent growth rates in technology continue, it appears that most countries have adequate land or other resources to carry their projected populations for 2025. Land and resources may even be sufficient over the very long term, when Earth's population is expected to stabilize at around 11 billion after about 2100, provided that the wasteful consumption patterns of the developed countries are not taken as the universal model and that satisfactory answers can be found to the following questions:

• Can agricultural production be increased fast enough to keep ahead of population growth?
• Will some of the carrying capacity potential be lost because of land degradation and other factors?
• What changes are required to shift from the present unsustainable development path?

Production vs. Population

Most carrying capacity studies make three major assumptions regarding the first question—namely that crop production will win the competition for land against livestock and forestry, and losses from urban and industrial development will not be serious; that crop yields can increase fast enough; and that food prices will not rise beyond people's ability to pay.

Historically, crop production has almost always won the competition for land.[40] Increased desertification caused by crop production displaces livestock onto more and more marginal land and causes high rates of tropical deforestation, of which from one-half to two-thirds results from shifting cultivation. Competition for land from urban and industrial development, however, could become increasingly serious. Much of this development will involve the expansion of existing conurbations, which are often located on coastal plains and in river valleys with some of the best soils. Once these soils are built on, they are lost forever. Few of the developed countries had effective land-use policies to protect such soils before the 1960s and 1970s.[41] It is not surprising, therefore, that many developing countries are finding it difficult to introduce the necessary policies, and so, nearly 300 million hectares—one-quarter of all highly arable land—are at risk.

The expansion of crop production through 2025 seems likely to cause the loss of some 180 million hectares of rangeland and forests, whose soils are only marginally suitable for annual crop production and need very careful management if degradation is to be avoided.[42] Such losses are likely to have spill-over effects in terms of greater risks of overgrazing and intensification of the fuelwood crisis. Thus, it is vital for policymakers to focus on raising the productivity and employment requirements of the existing crop land so as to reduce the pressure for the cultivation of and migration onto these marginal lands.

Two facts cast doubt on whether it is possible for the rate of crop-yield increase to keep pace with population growth. First, staple crop yields in many sub-Saharan countries have been essentially static for the past 10 years or more.[43] The reasons are complex. In part, static yields stem from weak government policies that have failed to give adequate price incentives and infrastructural support to producers. But they also reflect the widespread lack of appropriate technologies and the failure of research systems to develop sustainable technologies that match the perceptions and resources of small farmers.[44]

Second, although other regions have been more successful than sub-Saharan Africa at raising yields, there is growing concern that the future production potential may be insufficient. In parts of Asia, for example, experimental yields for irrigated wheat and rice fields seem to have reached a plateau.[45] Maximum yields have been static for some 10 to 20 years. Meanwhile, average yields still fall well short of experimental yields and are unlikely to match them entirely, but there is still a yield gap to be closed. Thus, it seems possible that recent trends in yield growth will continue for another one or two decades. Thereafter, however, the evidence suggests that it will become increasingly difficult to prevent a slow decline in yield growth unless research achieves another shift on the production frontier.[46] Whether advances in biotechnology will provide the solution is still an open question.

There remains the assumption regarding affordability. Current estimates of the number of malnourished people range from 500 million to 1 billion.[47] The numbers are not expected to decline appreciably, at least in the mid term.[48] By and large, people are malnourished because they are too poor to buy all of their needs. Purchasing power, however, has not been considered by a carrying capacity study conducted to date.

Projections suggest that future food prices will remain more or less constant in real terms for the next decade or so, as long as market mechanisms operate efficiently and the apparent crop yield ceiling is breached. If these projections are correct, the strains on carrying capacity will stem primarily from income growth. In the middle-income countries where people are consuming increasing amounts of livestock products, carrying capacity ceilings are already being breached because of the lack of grazing land and the greater cost-efficiency of raising dairy cattle, pigs, and poultry on feed grains. Many countries are currently or will soon be unable to produce these feed grains in adequate quantities. They will become increasingly dependent on feed grain imports, and part of the environmental costs of production will be transferred to exporting countries like the United States, Canada, Argentina, and Thailand.[49]

The Effects of Soil Degradation

After *The Limits to Growth* was published and the 1973 oil crisis, many countries became concerned about the constraints on the raw materials for fertilizer and the energy supply. Neither concern withstands close analysis, however. The reserves of the main raw materials for fertilizer are adequate for well more than 200 years at projected levels of use, but prices will rise. If the global population is more or less stable in 100 years, agricultural production systems should be able to evolve so that a sustainable balance is reached between soil nutrient removal by crops and replacement by humans.[50] Fossil fuel energy resources will eventually run out, but, with greater policy and research emphasis on renewable energy systems and greater energy efficiency, agriculture's carrying capacity should be maintainable. Agriculture's share of primary energy use is only 3 to 5 percent of total use. Therefore, safeguarding its supply of energy is a question more of sociopolitical priorities than of resource scarcity per se.

There are other threats, however, that cannot be dismissed, particularly those from land degradation and climate change. Over the past millennium, humanity has degraded about 2 billion hectares of land, though only a small proportion of this area is too degraded to remain in agricultural use.[51] More recent estimates suggest that the present situation is much worse. For example, a recent study for the UN Environment Programme called the Global Assessment of Soil Degradation (GLASOD) concludes that people have degraded about 25 percent of the occupied land, and much of this damage has been caused in the past 50 years (see Table 4 on this page).[52] The most serious causes of degradation are water erosion through deforestation (43 percent), overgrazing (29 percent), and poor farming practices (24 percent). Population pressure on marginal lands plus mismanagement of the better soils may have acclerated land degradation over the past 20 years to reach some 5 million to 6 million hectares annually.[53]

Much of this degradation has stripped the land of soil. The quantities involved are immense. The current rate of soil erosion in excess of new soil production has been estimated at some 23 billion tonnes per year.[54] If the global soil reservoir is declining at about 0.7 percent annually, between 20 and 25 percent of the total could be lost by 2025.

These soil losses sound disastrous, but scientists and economists are unsure of their long-term implications. Estimating the consequences of this degradation for soil productivity and, hence, for human-carrying capacity is very difficult. There have been few well-conducted experiments on the relationship between soil degradation and crop yield losses, and most of them apply only to conditions in developed counties. Consequently, such estimations rely heavily on subjective judgements. Nonetheless, the GLASOD study concludes that some 295 million

hectares are so degraded that restoration of the land to full productivity is beyond the normal means of a farmer but that these hectares could be restored with major investments. (There is, of course, substantial uncertainty about the cost of land restoration. The GLASOD estimates are based largely on formal project costs, but the Machakos example given earlier and a number of NGO and community-based actions show that quite extreme degradation can be corrected profitably and at modest costs.)[55] An even greater area—910 million hectares—is moderately degraded to the point that the original biotic functions are partly destroyed and agricultural productivity is greatly reduced. If these estimates are correct, human-carrying capacity has already been seriously undermined, and the present trend is for even greater damage in the future unless corrective actions are given much greater priority.

Substantiating evidence for this view comes from two other directions. Studies of soil nutrient balance in which rates of nutrient removal by crops, soil erosion, leaching, and other factors are set against nutrient inputs from natural soil processes, dust, rain, manures, and mineral fertilizers indicate that widespread soil nutrient mining is taking place, particularly in sub-Saharan Africa, where food production has failed to keep up with population growth for the past 20 years.[56] This conclusion is supported by a number of other ex-

periments that have compared declining yields and fertilizer response ratios over time. It appears that one of the consequences of nutrient mining has been unfertilized base yields. In areas of Ghana, Malawi, Kenya, and Java, for example, the base yields of cereals have been falling by 2 to 10 percent per year for the past 10 to 20 years. Such losses are clearly unsustainable over the long term. The reasons are complex. Contributing factors include nutrient mining, as well as physical and chemical damage to the soil through erosion, loss of organic matter and soil moisture-holding capacity, and the buildup of soil pests and diseases caused by reduced fallows. Mineral fertilizers can compensate for such damage to a substantial degree, but they are too expensive for poor farmers or often simply unprofitable. And sometimes, mineral fertilizers are insufficient to restore fertility. Inputs of organic manures are required to achieve fertility, but the supply is commonly inadequate.

Attempts have been made to place these physical losses from land degradation in their national economic contexts.[57] Recent estimates suggest that, if remedial action is not taken, Ghana could lose 7 percent of its gross national product because of land degradation and that Nigeria could lose more than 17 percent of its gross national product because of deforestation, soil degradation, water contamination, and other environmental problems over the long term. Again the message is clear: Land degradation at current rates will reduce carrying capacity both by lowering agricultural production potential and by lowering the ability of countries to import food.

These losses seem destined to be compounded by climate change. A scientific concensus has emerged during the past five years or so that the threat to food production is real, though the timing and regional pattern of climate change's impacts is still uncertain.[58] Climate change could seriously threaten carrying capacity and sustainable agriculture in certain regions, though there may be both win-

TABLE 4
AREAS OF MODERATE TO EXCESSIVE SOIL DEGRADATION

Region	Water erosion	Wind erosion	Chemical degradation (millions of hectares)	Physical degradation	Total
Africa	170	98	36	17	321
Asia	315	90	41	6	452
South America	77	16	44	1	138
North and Central America	90	37	7	5	139
Europe	93	39	18	8	158
Australasia	3	1	1	2	6
Total	**748**	**280**	**147**	**39**	**1,214**

SOURCE: L. R. Oldeman, R. T. A. Hakkeling, and W. G. Sambroek, *Global Assessment of Soil Degradation* (Wageningen, the Netherlands: ISRIC/UNEP, 1990).

ners and losers from climate change. Some regions and countries may benefit from greater agricultural productivity because of temperature and rainfall increases and because of carbon dioxide's enhancement of plant growth.

Two major concerns are that some of the countries most at risk are already very vulnerable to food shortages and close to their human-carrying capacity if crop yields cannot be raised and that population pressure's negative impacts on the environment may increase both the intensity of and the land's vulnerability to climate change.[59] In the case of some Sahelian countries, for example, the analog approach to impact analysis suggests that the potential human-carrying capacity from domestic agriculture could fall by some 30 percent if climate change causes a decline in rainfall similar to that experienced in the 1965 to 1985 drought.[60]

A more recent analysis for Senegal that built on a carrying capacity model developed by the U.S. Geological Survey and on crop models from the Institut Senegalais de Recherche Agricole came to similar conclusions. Rain-fed production potential is projected to decrease 30 percent in spite of adaptive responses to climate change—a reduction equivalent to the food needs of 1 million to 2 million people.[61] Related impact analyses focusing on maize production in Zimbabwe, where conditions are not so arid as in Senegal, have projected a smaller impact.[62] Rain-fed yields should fall by less than 20 percent, in part because the positive effect of higher atmospheric carbon dioxide concentrations compensates partially for the negative impact of higher temperatures. What is more worrying, however, is the projected increase in the variability of rainfall and, hence, crop yield, which could seriously lower food security and increase the financial risk of using the mineral fertilizers essential for maintaining soil fertility.

A New Strategy

A new strategy is required that is the opposite in many respects to current policies. Present strategies tend to focus on four aspects of agricultural development—incentives, inputs, institutions, and infrastructures—and on the investments required by them and tend to give inadequate attention to sustainability. The new strategy should be more concerned with decentralized natural resource management by the farmers and communities that will ultimately decide the strategy's appropriateness and success. The strategy should therefore focus on local-level husbandry and development controlled by local community or user-based institutions, such as grazing associations and water-user groups, rather than on sophisticated institutional structures for national or regional land-use planning, for example, or for investment allocation. Of course, such structures do have an important role to play, provided that they are economically sustainable by the nations concerned and that they provide incentives rather than top-down directives for resource development and management. The issue is not top-down versus bottom-up; both approaches are needed, but they must be consistent with each other, and they must promote a convergence of national goals and local priorities.

The decentralization of decision-making can only lead to a socially desirable and sustainable allocation of productive and environmental resources if other requirements are met. For example, the responsibilities and entitlements of farmers and rural communities must also be decentralized through the clear allocation of property rights and environmental resources. User groups and similar bodies must have the power to raise revenues from resource users for operation, maintenance, and further development of those resources. Commodity prices must reflect as much as possible the full environmental costs of a given resource use, besides providing adequate incentives to producers.[63] Once governments have provided the infrastructure to ensure market access and have set appropriate environmental standards and taxes on discharges to protect public goods, government intervention should be kept to a minimum so that markets can function efficiently.

The strategy should be built around four critical components of resource management—soil fertility management; integrated pest management; water management; and integrated crop, livestock, and tree management—and around their greater integration. Past efforts by public and private development organizations, however, have often followed a relatively uniform approach centered on encouraging the use of one or a limited number of purchased production inputs.

Many past conservation measures that have failed were not profitable, except possibly in the long term. Priority should be given to resource conservation actions that quickly raise productivity and farmers' incomes. Some of the required conservation techniques are already available. In many cases, however, new technologies must be developed for, or existing ones adapted to, specific ecological conditions. This development and adaptation will take several years, substantial research funding, and a change in research and extension techniques.

More emphasis is required on biological approaches to resource management, including

• biological (as opposed to engineering) approaches to soil and moisture conservation, such as maintaining continuous ground cover with live mulches;

• biological inputs to integrated pest management systems to minimize pesticide inputs; and

• biological sources of nitrogen to replace or, in most instances, to complement mineral sources (phosphorus and other nutrients commonly have to come from mineral sources).

This emphasis on biological approaches would not contradict efforts to promote the use of mineral fertilizers and other off-farm inputs. These will continue to be a prime contribu-

103

3. NATURAL RESOURCES: Food and Hunger

tor to increased agricultural production for the foreseeable future, but there are situations where such inputs are too costly and are therefore not a viable solution. In these situations, biological approaches can complement or substitute for off-farm inputs to reduce production costs and maximize environmental sustainability. It is this balance that the proposed strategy seeks to achieve.

The new strategy differs from past ones in that it addresses sustainability problems through their social and cultural determinants or through the institutional constraints that have previously blocked such approaches, rather than treating them as environmental problems to be addressed by technical solutions developed in isolation from the ultimate users. Consequently, it stresses the evolutionary approach in which changes in farming practices build on indigenous knowledge, rather than the prevailing step-wise or single-component approach, and focuses on improvements in both the levels and the stability of yields instead of just maximum yields. This evolutionary approach concentrates on highly informed but low-risk and low-cost measures to minimize the need for credit-demanding technologies involving extensive use of off-farm inputs that are more suited to large-scale farmers, but it does not ignore the needs of the latter nor the fact that such technologies can be equally suited to small farmers in very fertile areas. Large farms will continue to play a critical role in producing food for urban populations and other net food buyers and as major suppliers of export crops. Most farmers need better support regarding water supply management and integrated pest management and help in minimizing or preventing some of the environmental problems commonly associated with large-scale, intensive farming systems.

Three main conclusions can be drawn from this discussion. First, there are some grounds for optimism regarding humanity's ability to raise and sustain agriculture's carrying capacity at the global and regional levels. This optimism, however, is contingent on major policy changes regarding international equity and the ecological soundness of technological growth. It is difficult, however, to see how some countries can sustain their projected populations through agriculture or other economic activities. The pressure for international migration may therefore be substantial.

Second, and further tempering optimism, there are a number of uncertainties about the future that support the increasing calls for the adoption of the precautionary principle to provide "a scientifically sound basis for policies relating to complex systems that are so poorly understood that the consequences of disturbances cannot yet be predicted. According to this principle, highest priority should be given to reducing the two greatest disturbances to Planet Earth: the growth of human population and overconsumption of resources."[64] These uncertainties include: the rate of deceleration in population growth, given that policy inaction could seriously delay the achievement of a stable population; the loss of arable land to urban development; the long-term consequences of soil degradation; the impacts of climate change; and the ability of science to continue to raise agricultural productivity.[65]

Third, if the concept of carrying capacity is to be introduced more centrally into the debate on sustainable development, it has to be widened to embrace economic as well as environmental considerations and complemented by a new strategy for sustainable agriculture.[66] Many poor farmers are forced to use unsustainable agricultural practices for a variety of institutional and economic reasons. In their struggle to satisfy current food needs, they have to place at risk the long-term carrying capacity of their land. Fine ecological words and appeals on behalf of future generations will not sway them unless the required changes in land management practices will also raise present-day household security.

ACKNOWLEDGMENTS

The author wishes to thank Tom Downing, Hartwig de Haen, and Mary Tiffen, as well as the reviewers, for their helpful comments on the first draft of this article.

NOTES

1. U.S. National Academy of Sciences and the Royal Society of London, "Population Growth, Resource Consumption, and a Sustainable World" (Joint statement released on 27 February 1992).

2. T. R. Malthus, *First Essay on Population 1798* (London: Macmillan, 1966).

3. E. Goldsmith et al., *Blueprint for Survival* (London: Penguin Press, 1972).

4. R. Carson, *Silent Spring* (Boston, Mass.: Houghton Mifflin, 1962).

5. G. Ledec, R. J. A. Goodland, J. W. Kirchner, and J. M. Drake, "Carrying Capacity, Population Growth and Sustainable Development," in D. J. Mahar, ed., *Rapid Population Growth and Human Carrying Capacity: Two Perspectives*, working paper no. 690 (Washington, D.C.: World Bank, 1985).

6. Mahar, ed., note 5 above.

7. Intergovernmental Panel on Climate Change, *Climate Change: The IPCC Impacts Assessment* (Canberra, Australia: Australian Government Publishing Service, 1990); and M. Parry, *Climate Change and World Agriculture* (London: Earthscan, 1990).

8. E. Eckholm, *Losing Ground: Environmental Stress and World Food Prospects* (New York: W. W. Norton, 1976); L. R. Brown, *The Changing World Food Prospect: The Nineties and Beyond*, Worldwatch Paper no. 85 (Washington, D.C.: Worldwatch Institute, 1988); and D. Norse, C. James, B. J. Skinner, and Q. Zhao, "Agriculture, Land Use and Degradation," in J. C. I. Dooge et al., eds., *An Agenda of Science for Environment and Development into the 21st Century* (Cambridge, England: Cambridge University Press, 1992).

9. R. W. Kates and V. Haarmann, "Where the Poor Live: Are the Assumptions Correct?" *Environment*, May 1992, 4.

10. D. Norse, "Trade-Offs Between the Environment and Agricultural Development," in *Proceedings of the European Association of Agricultural Economists Seminar on Environment and Agricultural Management* (Viterbo, Italy: European Association of Agricultural Economists, January 1991).

11. N. B. Ayibotele and M. Falkenmark, "Fresh Water Resources," in Dooge et al., note 8 above.

12. Even during famines, it is the collapse of household incomes, rather than the lack of food availability, that is the main cause of starvation. See A. Sen, *Poverty and Famines: An Essay in Entitlements and Deprivation* (Oxford, England: Clarendon Press, 1981).

13. R. W. Kates et al., *The Hunger Report: 1988* (Providence, R.I.: Brown University, Alan Shawn Feinstein World Hunger Program, 1988); and World Bank, *World Bank Development Report 1990* (Washington, D.C.: Oxford University Press, 1990).

14. Kates and Haarmann, note 9 above.

15. L. Arizpe, R. Costanza, and W. Lutz, "Primary Factors Affecting Population and Natural Resource Use," in Dooge et al., note 8 above; and R. M. Anderson, R. M. May, M. C. Boily, G. P. Garnett, and J. T. Rowley, "The Spread of HIV-1 in Africa: Sexual Contact Patterns and the Predicted Demographic Impact of AIDS," *Nature* 352 (15 August 1991):581.

16. F. Osborne, *Our Plundered Planet* (Boston, Mass.: Little, Brown & Co., 1948); W. Vogt, *Road to Survival* (Washington, D.C.: Population Reference

Bureau, 1948); H. Brown, *The Challenge of Man's Future: An Inquiry Concerning the Condition of Man During the Years That Lie Ahead* (New York: Viking Press, 1954); G. F. White, "Speculating on the Global Resource Future," in K. R. Smith, F. Fesharaki, and J. P. Holdren, eds., *Earth and the Human Future: Essays in Honour of Harrison Brown* (Boulder, Colo., and London: Westview Press, 1985); and D. H. Meadows, J. Richardson, and G. Bruckmann, *Groping in the Dark* (Chichester, England: John Wiley for the International Institute for Applied Systems Analysis, 1982).

17. D. H. Meadows, D. L. Meadows, J. Randers, and W. W. Behrens, *The Limits to Growth* (New York: Universe Books, 1972). The authors were not, as is commonly suggested, forecasters of doom proposing zero growth. They were considering alternative futures open to humanity, including sustainable futures. They returned to the issue in their recent sequel to the 1972 book. The dangers of rapid population growth and prolific resource use are again analyzed, as are the dangers of overshooting the limits imposed by finite resources and the ability of the environment to absorb emissions and waste. But in this new book, they consider in more detail the possible content of a sustainable future and the technological and other changes since 1972 that could facilitate the achievement of such a future. See D. H. Meadows, D. L. Meadows, and J. Randers, *Beyond the Limits: Global Collapse or a Sustainable Future* (London: Earthscan Publications, 1992).

18. H. S. D. Cole, C. Freeman, M. Jahoda, and K. L. R. Pavitt, *Models of Doom* (New York: Universe Books, 1973); H. Kahn, *The Coming Boom* (New York: Simon & Schuster, 1982); and J. Simon, *The Ultimate Resource* (Princeton, N.J.: Princeton University Press, 1981).

19. P. Buringh, H. D. J. van Heemst, and G. J. Staring, *Computation of the Absolute Maximum Food Production of the World* (Wageningen, the Netherlands: Agricultural Press, 1975). Their results were used in the development of the MOIRA model described in H. Linneman and M. A. Keyzer, eds., *MOIRA: A Model of International Relations in Agriculture* (Amsterdam: Economic and Social Institute, Free University, 1977).

20. P. Buringh and H. D. J. van Heemst, *An Estimation of World Food Production Based on Labour-Oriented Agriculture* (Wageningen, the Netherlands: Agricultural Press, 1977).

21. Carrying capacity estimates are highly sensitive to the assumptions regarding per-capita food requirements. There can be a twofold or greater difference in them, depending on whether food requirements are based on a primarily vegetarian diet or on one rich in grain-fed livestock products. See Kates et al., note 13 above.

22. F. Baade, *Der Wettlauf zum Jahre 2000* (Oldenburgh, Germany, 1960).

23. R. Revelle, "The Resources Available for Agriculture," *Scientific American* 235, no. 3 (1976):165; and B. Gilland, "Considerations on World Population and Food Supply," *Population and Development Review* 9, no. 2 (June 1983).

24. UN Food and Agriculture Organization, *The Fifth World Food Survey* (Rome: FAO, 1987).

25. UN Food and Agriculture Organization, United Nations Fund for Population Activities, and the International Institute for Applied Systems Analysis, *Po-*

tential Population Supporting Capacities of Lands in the Developing World (Rome: FAO, 1982); and P. A. Oram, "Building the Agroecological Framework," *Environment*, November 1988, 14.

26. UN Food and Agriculture Organization, *Land, Food and People* (Rome: FAO, 1984).

27. Ibid., 28.

28. UN Food and Agriculture Organization and the International Institute for Applied Systems Analysis, *Agroecological Land Resources Assessment for Agricultural Development Planning: A Case Study of Kenya* (Rome: FAO/IIASA, 1991).

29. Overseas Development Institute (ODI), *Environmental Change and Dryland Management in Machakos District, Kenya 1930–90* (London: ODI, 1991).

30. Ibid., 31; and M. Mortimore, ed., *Environmental Profile*, ODI working paper 53 (London: ODI, 1991).

31. See note 29 above, page 31; and M. Tiffen, *Population Profile*, ODI working paper 54 (London: ODI, 1991).

32. See note 29 above, page 33.

33. Overseas Development Institute, note 31 above; and R. S. Rostom and M. Mortimore, *Land Use Profile*, ODI working paper 58 (London: ODI, 1991).

34. Overseas Development Institute, note 31 above; and M. Mortimore and K. Wellard, *Profile of Technological Change*, ODI working paper 57 (London: ODI, 1991).

35. Overseas Development Institute, note 31 above; and F. N. Gichuki, *Conservation Profile*, ODI working paper 56 (London: ODI, 1991).

36. Overseas Development Institute, note 31 above; and M. Tiffen, *Farming and Income Systems*, ODI working paper 59 (London: ODI, 1991).

37. S. George, *How the Other Half Dies* (Totowa, N.J.: Rowman and Allanheld, 1977); and F. M. Lappe and J. Collins, *Food First: Beyond the Myth of Scarcity* (Boston, Mass.: Houghton Mifflin, 1977).

38. M. Tiffen and M. Mortimore, *Theory and Practice in Plantation Agriculture: An Economic Review* (London: ODI, 1990).

39. E. M. A. Smaling, "Two Scenarios for the Sub-Sahara: One Leads to Disaster," *Ceres: The FAO Review* 22, no. 2 (1991).

40. Norse et al., note 8 above.

41. Organization for Economic Cooperation and Development, *Land Use Policies and Agriculture* (Paris: OECD, 1976).

42. Norse et al., note 8 above.

43. UN Food and Agriculture Organization, *African Agriculture: The Next 25 Years* (Rome: FAO 1986); and World Bank, *The Population, Agriculture and Environment Nexus in Sub-Saharan Africa* (Washington, D.C.: World Bank, Africa Region, December 1991).

44. World Bank, page 45, note 43 above; S. J. Carr, *Technology for Small-Scale Farmers in Sub-Saharan Africa* (Washington, D.C.: World Bank, 1989); and D. Merril Sands, *The Technology Applications Gap: Overcoming Constraints to Small-Farm Development* (Rome: FAO, 1986).

45. P. L. Pingali, P. F. Moya, and L. E. Velasco, *The Post-Green Revolution Blues in Asian Rice Production: The Diminishing Gap Between Experiment Station and Farmer Yields* (Los Banos, Philippines: IRRI Social Sciences Division, 1990).

46. Y. Hayami and K. Otsuka, "Beyond the Green Revolution: Agricultural Development into the New

Century" (Paper prepared for the World Bank conference on Agricultural Technology: Current Policy Issues for the International Community and the World Bank, Virginia, October 1991).

47. Kates et al., note 13 above.

48. N. Alexandratos, ed., *World Agriculture: Toward 2000* (Rome and London: FAO and Belhaven Press, 1988).

49. M. P. Burton and T. Young, *Agricultural Trade and Sustainable Development* (Manchester, England: University of Manchester, 1990).

50. V. Smil, "Nitrogen and Phosphorus," in B. L. Turner II et al., eds., *The Earth As Transformed by Human Action* (Cambridge, England: Cambridge University Press, 1990); and Gilland, note 23 above.

51. Q. Zhao, "Land Degradation," *Acta Pedologica Sinica* 25, no. 4.

52. L. R. Oldeman, R. T. A. Hakkeling, and W. G. Sombroek, *Global Assessment of Soil Degradation* (Wageningen, the Netherlands: ISRIC/UNEP, 1990).

53. UN Food and Agriculture Organization, "Issues and Perspectives in Sustainable Agriculture and Rural Development" (Document prepared for the FAO/Netherlands Conference on Agriculture and the Environment,'s-Hertogenbosch, the Netherlands, April 1991).

54. L. R. Brown, "Conserving Soils," in L. R. Brown et al., eds., *State of the World 1984* (New York: W. W. Norton, 1984).

55. W. V. C. Reid, "Sustainable Development: Lessons from Success," *Environment*, May 1989, 6; and C. Reijk, *Soil and Water Conservation in Sub-Saharan Africa: Towards Sustainable Production by the Rural Poor* (Rome: International Fund for Agricultural Development, 1992).

56. Smaling, note 39 above; and Norse et al., note 8 above.

57. W. Magrath and P. Arens, *The Cost of Soil Erosion on Java: A Natural Resource Accounting Approach* (Washington, D.C.: World Bank, August 1989); J. Bishop, *The Cost of Soil Erosion in Malawi* (Washington, D.C.: World Bank, Malawi Country Operations Division, November 1990); and D. Pearce, "Conserving Global Natural Wealth: Economics and Politics," in J. Ball, ed., *The Creation of Wealth* (London: Edward Elgar, forthcoming).

58. See note 8 above.

59. D. Norse, "Population and Global Climate Change," in J. Jäger and H. L. Ferguson, eds., *Climate Change: Science, Impacts and Policy—Proceedings of the Second World Climate Conference* (Cambridge, England: Cambridge University Press, 1991).

60. The analog approach is described in M. H. Glantz, "The Use of Analogies in Forecasting Ecological and Societal Responses to Global Warming," *Environment*, June 1991, 10. The results of the Sahelian study were displayed at the Second World Climate Conference, see note 59 above.

61. T. E. Downing, "Climate Change and Vulnerable Societies: Case Studies in Zimbabwe, Kenya, Senegal and Chile," in *Climate Change and International Agriculture* (Oxford, England: University of Oxford, Environmental Change Unit, 1992).

62. Ibid., 26.

63. Burton and Young, note 49 above.

64. Dooge et al., note 8 above.

65. Arizpe et al., note 15 above.

66. Kates and Haarmann, note 9 above.

OIL: THE STRATEGIC PRIZE

Daniel Yergin

Daniel Yergin is president of Cambridge Energy Research Associates, a leading energy consulting firm, and best-selling author of The Prize: The Epic Quest for Oil, Money, and Power. *This article is excerpted from Yergin's prologue to* The Prize.

Winston Churchill changes his mind almost overnight. Until the summer of 1911, the young Churchill, Home Secretary, was one of the leaders of the "economists," the members of the British Cabinet members critical of the increased military spending that was being promoted by some to keep ahead in the Anglo-German naval race. That competition had become the most rancorous element in the growing antagonism between the two nations. But Churchill argued emphatically that war with Germany was not inevitable, that Germany's intentions were not necessarily aggressive. The money would be better spent, he insisted, on domestic social programs than on extra battleships.

Then on July 1, 1911, Kaiser Wilhelm sent a German naval vessel, the *Panther*, steaming into the harbor at Agadir, on the Atlantic coast of Morocco. His aim was to check French influence in Africa and carve out a position for Germany. While the *Panther* was only a gunboat and Agadir was a port city of only secondary importance, the arrival of the ship ignited a severe international crisis. The buildup of the German Army was already causing unease among its European neighbors; now Germany, in its drive for its "place in the sun," seemed to be directly challenging France and Britain's global positions. For several weeks, war fear gripped Europe. By the end of July, however, the tension had eased—as Churchill declared, "the bully is climbing down." But the crisis had transformed Churchill's outlook. Contrary to his earlier assessment of German intentions, he was now convinced that Germany sought hegemony and would exert its military muscle to gain it. War, he now concluded, was virtually inevitable, only a matter of time.

Appointed First Lord of the Admiralty immediately after Agadir, Churchill vowed to do everything he could to prepare Britain militarily for the inescapable day of reckoning. His charge was to ensure that the Royal Navy, the symbol and very embodiment of Britain's imperial power, was ready to meet the German challenge on the high seas. One of the most important and contentious questions he faced was seemingly technical in nature, but would in fact have vast implications for the twentieth century. The issue was whether to convert the British Navy to oil for its power source, in place of coal, which was the traditional fuel. Many thought that such a conversion was pure folly, for it meant that the Navy could no longer rely on safe, secure Welsh coal, but rather would have to depend on distant and insecure oil supplies from Persia, as Iran was then known. "To commit the Navy irrevocably to oil was indeed 'to take arms against a sea of troubles,' " said Churchill. But the strategic benefits—greater speed and more efficient use of manpower—were so obvious to him that he did not dally. He decided that Britain would have to base its "naval supremacy upon oil" and, thereupon, committed himself, with all his driving energy and enthusiasm, to achieving that objective.

There was no choice—in Churchill's words, "Mastery itself was the prize of the venture."[1]

With that, Churchill, on the eve of World War I, had captured a fundamental truth, and one applicable not only to the conflagration that followed, but to the many decades ahead. For oil has meant mastery throughout the twentieth century.

At the beginning of the 1990s—almost eighty years after Churchill made the commitment to petroleum, after two World Wars and a long Cold War, and in what was supposed to be the beginning of a new, more peaceful era—oil once again became the focus of global conflict. On August 2, 1990, yet another of the century's dictators, Saddam Hussein of Iraq, invaded the neighboring country of Kuwait. His goal was not only conquest of a sovereign state, but also the capture of its riches. The prize was enormous. If successful, Iraq would become the world's leading oil power, and it would dominate both the Arab world and the Persian Gulf, where the bulk of the planet's oil reserves is concentrated. Its new strength and wealth and control of oil would force the rest of the world to pay court to the ambitions of Saddam Hussein. With the resources of Kuwait, it would be able to make itself into a formidable nuclear weapons state and, perhaps, even move down the road toward becoming a superpower. The result would be a dramatic shift in the international balance of power. In short, mastery itself was once more the prize.

But the stakes were so obviously large that the invasion of Kuwait was not accepted by the rest of the world as a fait accompli, as Saddam Hussein had expected. It was not received with the passivity that had met Hitler's militarization of the Rhineland and Mussolini's assault on Ethiopia. Instead, the United Nations instituted an embargo against Iraq, and many nations of the Western and Arab worlds dramatically mustered military force to defend neighboring Saudi Arabia against Iraq and to resist Saddam Hussein's ambitions. There was no precedent for either the cooperation between the United States and the Soviet Union or for the rapid and massive deployment of forces into the region. Over the previous several years, it had become almost fashionable to say that oil was no longer "important." Indeed, in the spring of 1990, just a few months before the Iraqi invasion, the senior officers of America's Central Command, which would be the linchpin of the U.S. mobilization, found themselves lectured to the effect that oil had lost its strategic significance. But the invasion of Kuwait stripped away the illusion. In early 1991, when peaceful means failed to secure an Iraqi withdrawal from Kuwait, a coalition of thirty-three nations, led by the United States, destroyed Iraq's offensive capability in a five-week air war and one hundred hours of ground battle, which forced Iraq out of Kuwait. At the end of the twentieth century, oil was still central to security, prosperity, and the very nature of civilization.

Though the modern history of oil begins in the latter half of the nineteenth century, it is the twentieth century that has been completely transformed by the advent of petroleum. In particular, three great themes underlie the story of oil.

The first is the rise and development of capitalism and modern business. Oil is the world's biggest and most pervasive business, the greatest of the great industries that arose in the last decades of the nineteenth century. Standard Oil, which thoroughly dominated the American petroleum industry by the end of that century, was among the world's very first and largest multinational enterprises. The expansion of the business in the twentieth century—encompassing everything from wildcat drillers, smooth-talking promoters, and domineering entrepreneurs to great corporate bureaucracies and state-owned companies—embodies the twentieth-century evolution of business, of corporate strategy, of technological change and market development, and indeed of both national and international economies. Throughout the history of oil, deals have been done and momentous decisions have been made—among men, companies, and nations—sometimes with great calculation and sometimes almost by accident. No other business so starkly and extremely defines the meaning of risk and reward—and the profound impact of chance and fate.

As we look toward the twenty-first century, it is clear that mastery will certainly come as much from a computer chip as from a barrel of oil. Yet the petroleum industry continues to have enormous impact. Of the top twenty companies in the Fortune 500, seven are oil companies. Until some alternative source of energy is found, oil will still have far-reaching effects on the global economy; major price movements can fuel economic growth or, contrarily, drive inflation and kick off

recessions. Today, oil is the only commodity whose doings and controversies are to be found regularly not only on the business page but also on the front page. And, as in the past, it is a massive generator of wealth—for individuals, companies, and entire nations. In the words of one tycoon, "Oil *is* almost like Money."[2]

The second theme is that of oil as a commodity intimately intertwined with national strategies and global politics and power. The battlefields of World War I established the importance of petroleum as an element of national power when the internal combustion machine overtook the horse and the coal-powered locomotive. Petroleum was central to the course and outcome of World War II in both the Far East and Europe. The Japanese attacked Pearl Harbor to protect their flank as they grabbed for the petroleum resources of the East Indies. Among Hitler's most important strategic objectives in the invasion of the Soviet Union was the capture of the oil fields in the Caucasus. But America's predominance in oil proved decisive, and by the end of the war German and Japanese fuel tanks were empty. In the Cold War years, the battle for control of oil between international companies and developing countries was a major part of the great drama of decolonization and emergent nationalism. The Suez Crisis of 1956, which truly marked the end of the road for the old European imperial powers, was as much about oil as about anything else. "Oil power" loomed very large in the 1970s, catapulting states heretofore peripheral to international politics into positions of great wealth and influence, and creating a deep crisis of confidence in the industrial nations that had based their economic growth upon oil. And oil was at the heart of the first post-Cold War crisis of the 1990s—Iraq's invasion of Kuwait.

Yet oil has also proved that it can be fool's gold. The Shah of Iran was granted his most fervent wish, oil wealth, and it destroyed him. Oil built up Mexico's economy, only to undermine it. The Soviet Union—the world's second-largest exporter—squandered its enormous oil earnings in the 1970s and 1980s in a military buildup and a series of useless and, in some cases, disastrous international adventures. And the United States, once the world's largest producer and still its largest consumer, must import half of its oil supply, weakening its overall strategic position and adding greatly to an already burdensome trade deficit—a precarious position for a great power.

With the end of the Cold War, a new world order is taking shape. Economic competition, regional struggles, and ethnic rivalries may replace ideology as the focus of international—and national—conflict, aided and abetted by the proliferation of modern weaponry. But whatever the evolution of this new international order, oil will remain the strategic commodity, critical to national strategies and international politics.

3. NATURAL RESOURCES: Energy

A third theme in the history of oil illuminates how ours has become a "Hydrocarbon Society" and we, in the language of anthropologists, "Hydrocarbon Man." In its first decades, the oil business provided an industrializing world with a product called by the made-up name of "kerosene" and known as the "new light," which pushed back the night and extended the working day. At the end of the nineteenth century, John D. Rockefeller had become the richest man in the United States, mostly from the sale of kerosene. Gasoline was then only an almost useless by-product, which sometimes managed to be sold for as much as two cents a gallon, and, when it could not be sold at all, was run out into rivers at night. But just as the invention of the incandescent light bulb seemed to signal the obsolescence of the oil industry, a new era opened with the development of the internal combustion engine powered by gasoline. The oil industry had a new market, and a new civilization was born.

In the twentieth century, oil, supplemented by natural gas, toppled King Coal from his throne as the power source for the industrial world. Oil also became the basis of the great postwar suburbanization movement that transformed both the contemporary landscape and our modern way of life. Today, we are so dependent on oil, and oil is so embedded in our daily doings, that we hardly stop to comprehend its pervasive significance. It is oil that makes possible where we live, how we live, how we commute to work, how we travel—even where we conduct our courtships. It is the lifeblood of suburban communities. Oil (and natural gas) are the essential components in the fertilizer on which world agriculture depends; oil makes it possible to transport food to the totally non–self-sufficient megacities of the world. Oil also provides the plastics and chemicals that are the bricks and mortar of contemporary civilization, a civilization that would collapse if the world's oil wells suddenly went dry.

For most of this century, growing reliance on petroleum was almost universally celebrated as a good, a symbol of human progress. But no longer. With the rise of the environmental movement, the basic tenets of industrial society are being challenged; and the oil industry in all its dimensions is at the top of the list to be scrutinized, criticized, and opposed. Efforts are mounting around the world to curtail the combustion of all fossil fuels—oil, coal, and natural gas—because of the resultant smog and air pollution, acid rain, and ozone depletion, and because of the specter of climate change. Oil, which is so central a feature of the world as we know it, is now accused of fueling environmental degradation; and the oil industry, proud of its technological prowess and its contribution to shaping the modern world, finds itself on the defensive, charged with being a threat to present and future generations.

Yet Hydrocarbon Man shows little inclination to give up his cars, his suburban home, and what he takes to be not only the conveniences but the essentials of his way of life. The peoples of the developing world give no indication that they want to deny themselves the benefits of an oil-powered economy, whatever the environmental questions. And any notion of scaling back the world's consumption of oil will be influenced by the extraordinary population growth ahead. In the 1990s, the world's population is expected to grow by one billion people—20 percent more people at the end of this decade than at the beginning—with most of the world's people demanding the "right" to consume. The global environmental agendas of the industrial world will be measured against the magnitude of that growth. In the meantime, the stage has been set for one of the great and intractable clashes of the 1990s between, on the one hand, the powerful and increasing support for greater environmental protection and, on the other, a commitment to economic growth and the benefits of Hydrocarbon Society, and apprehensions about energy security.

These, then, are the three themes that animate the story that unfolds in these pages. The canvas is global. The story is a chronicle of epic events that have touched all our lives. It concerns itself both with the powerful, impersonal forces of economics and technology and with the strategies and cunning of businessmen and politicians. Populating its pages are the tycoons and entrepreneurs of the industry—Rockefeller, of course, but also Henri Deterding, Calouste Gulbenkian, J. Paul Getty, Armand Hammer, T. Boone Pickens, and many others. Yet no less important to the story are the likes of Churchill, Adolf Hitler, Joseph Stalin, Ibn Saud, Mohammed Mossadegh, Dwight Eisenhower, Anthony Eden, Henry Kissinger, George Bush, and Saddam Hussein.

The twentieth century rightly deserves the title "the century of oil." Yet for all its conflict and complexity, there has often been a "oneness" to the story of oil, a contemporary feel even to events that happened long ago and, simultaneously, profound echoes of the past in recent events. At one and the same time, this is a story of individual people, of powerful economic forces, of technological change, of political struggles, of international conflict and, indeed, of epic change. It is the author's hope that this exploration of the economic, social, political, and strategic consequences of our world's reliance on oil will illuminate the past, enable us better to understand the present, and help to anticipate the future.

1. Randolph S. Churchill, Winston Churchill, vol, 2, Young Statesman, 1901–1914 (London: Heinemann, 1968), p. 529 ("bully"); Winston S. Churchill, The World Crisis, vol. 1 (New York: Scribners, 1928), pp. 130–36.
2. Interview with Robert O. Anderson.

Paradise Islands or an Asian Powder Keg?

Lured by up to $1 trillion in oil and gas, six nations claim at least part of the South China Sea's Spratly chain

Clayton Jones

Staff writer of The Christian Science Monitor

Kuala Lumpur, Malaysia

In satellite photos, the tiny atoll called Layang-Layang hardly seems the stuff over which a war might be waged.

The atoll's four miles of tree-less beaches and undefiled coral reefs lie about 100 miles off Borneo in the South China Sea and seem better suited to tourists than soldiers. But Layang-Layang is just one of about 60 islands known as the Spratlys chain that are claimed in part or whole by six countries: China, Vietnam, Taiwan, Malaysia, Brunei, and the Philippines.

As much as $1 trillion in oil and gas may lie in geological structures beneath the Spratly seabed, according to some analysts.

The lure of such economic riches has turned these once-forgotten shoals and reefs into Asia's potential powder keg for major conflict. "It's well known that there is a gold mine there," says Derek da Cunha, a security analyst in Singapore.

Since 1991, after the cold war ended and the United States Navy withdrew from the Philippines, the six nations have become more anxious about defending and prosecuting their overlapping claims. "During the cold war, it was too dangerous to force a claim," says Lee Taito, an expert on the Spratlys at the National University of Singapore. "Now all the claims are coming out."

Another reason for concern is that the Chinese Navy killed about 70 Vietnamese soldiers in 1988 while invading seven islands occupied by Vietnam. This ominous projection of China's new naval power set off alarms among its southern neighbors.

"Whoever controls the Spratlys can monitor sea traffic between the Pacific and Indian oceans," Dr. Lee says. "In World War II, Japan used the islands to attack the Philippines and Southeast Asia. They are a watchtower on two seas."

DAVE HERRING – STAFF

Most of the six states have put soldiers, airstrips, or ships on the islands that they now hold, helping to turn the Spratlys into a potential flash point for conflict in Asia. "The Spratlys is a global issue," Lee says. "If anything goes wrong, all trading nations will be affected."

Malaysia, which controls Layang-Layang and other islands, also took the unusual step this year of reinforcing its claim by opening a tourist resort on the atoll.

For $1,400 per person, a group of divers can hire a 150-foot-long luxury boat for an eight-day cruise to the island. A chalet for visiting divers has been built on the beach, according to Susan Leong of Sabah Holiday tour agency. The only permanent residents on Layang-Layang are Malaysian Army soldiers who guard the island against foreign invaders. The diving trip is advertised for those "who crave intrigue."

Vietnam has taken Malaysia's lead and plans to set up a lighthouse on one Spratly island and a fishing port on another to fend off further Chinese advances. In a provocative move last year, China gave permission to the Colorado-based Crestone Energy Corp. to explore for oil in a section of the South China Sea claimed by Vietnam. China backed up the project by landing troops on a reef to set up a "sovereignty post."

China also appears to be building a military landing strip on one of the Paracel Islands in the waters near Vietnam, which would allow it to back up its claims to the Spratlys with more force. Beijing took the Paracels from Vietnam in 1974.

"There are different opinions among China's leaders on whether to use peaceful or violent means," Lee says. "Nonetheless, the Chinese can never think of China without the South China Sea."

For the time being, Dr. da Cunha suggests, Beijing may be just using its interest in the Spratlys to gain political influence. "The claims are one way for China to say, 'Look, you have to take us into account on all issues.' "

To help defuse rising tensions over the Spratlys, Indonesia, which does not claim any of the islands, has hosted a series of informal, semi-academic workshops since 1991 among the six nations to discuss possible joint development of the seabed resources.

The workshops appear to be based on a general consensus that each nation should freeze its interests in oil exploration to allow talks on joint ventures.

And at the least, Lee says, the talks "prevent people from shooting at each other." So far, he says, most of the ideas put forward in the workshops are really ways for each country to stake its individual claim.

But more importantly, says Bilahari Kausikan, director of Singapore's East Asia and Pacific bureau, "the workshops help to integrate China into a network of relationships." Other analysts see the workshops as potential trouble.

"Suppose someone strikes oil? How do you share the goodies?" asks Tommy Koh, former Singapore ambassador to Washington. "Then the real bargaining begins."

Another worry is a rising thirst for oil among these fast-growing nations. "They all need capital, so shelving [the issue] for one or two generations is an act of self-denial that would be very difficult to observe," says former Singapore Prime Minister Lee Kuan Yew. "At the moment the self-denial is enforced because of the stalemate. China hasn't got the capability to start drilling without interference, and neither has anybody else. . . . China has said 'joint development, we can talk and share.' But do we share by population size, or do we share by proximity to shore line, or what? That will depend on the ingenuity of the negotiators and a sense of fairness."

Vietnam, Brunei, and Malaysia are already pumping oil on their continental shelf, but they all see the day in about 20 to 30 years when they might need oil from under their Spratlys claims. Taiwan, according to a Taipei newspaper, will begin oil exploration near Taiping, its heavily fortified Island in the chain.

The waters around this archipelago are deep, making oil exploration a costly proposition suitable only for Western nations with advanced drilling technology.

Indonesia Foreign Minister Ali Alitas wants to upgrade the workshop to official talks, but China opposes such a move.

"It's difficult to see the sincerity of the countries in the workshop when they are beefing up their maritime defenses," says Professor Lee. "I'm not optimistic of a solution. Managing this conflict will be most difficult. The Spratlys is just an example of other potential conflicts in Asia."

So far, the workshops have found some common ground on proposals to deflect conflict. One idea calls for turning the largely untouched islands into a marine park for fishing, bird-watching, and diving. Another is to conduct joint scientific research on wave patterns, biodiversity, typhoons, and other nonpolitical topics.

Canada Is Ready to Exploit Huge Oil Reserves Locked in Sands

T. R. Stauffer

Special to The Christian Science Monitor

EDMONTON, ALBERTA

Alberta's tar sands, long recognized as a potential source of massive amounts of oil, may in a few years become a notable factor in the world oil market.

Recent tests of a new technique for exploiting the underground resource indicate costs can be brought down to a competitive level with recovery of deposits of liquid oil at present world prices, government experts say. The Athabasca tar sands are located in the flat, featureless terrain at the northern end of this province.

These deposits contain "greater volumes than the entire Middle East oil reserves," states the 1993 report of the Alberta Oil Sands Technology & Resource Authority, the agency mandated to promote exploitation of this vast energy resource. Official estimates record a volume of at least 1 trillion barrels of oil enmeshed in gritty, tarry masses of bitumen, sand, clay, and shale, equal to six times the reported reserves of Saudi Arabia.

To date, oil sand production is minor. Development has been disappointing because of the high costs of extracting the oil. One problem is weather. Winter temperatures drop well below zero degrees F., when tempered steel mining equipment can snap like dry noodles. Second, the oil does not flow. The tarry agglomerations must be mined and the bitumen separated from the sand. The tar then must be upgraded to a salable product.

Total costs for this process run about $20 per barrel (Canadian, US$15), leaving little margin for government royalties, federal taxes, or company profits. Even with royalty and tax breaks, the projects eke out a modest rate of return. Saudi oil can be produced for less than $2 a barrel.

"We are the Saudi Arabia of the North," says Dr. Rick Luhning, vice chairman of AOSTRA. "We now believe that we have developed the key to these riches." That key is a new mining/extraction process. It worked at the pilot stage and is now poised for commercial-scale development.

The tar sands are not new discoveries. Peter Pond, when first exploring the area more than 200 years ago, found Indians waterproofing canoes with bitumen from natural seeps.

Two multibillion-dollar "mega-projects" have been completed and produce almost 300,000 barrels per day (bpd)—as much as the smallest OPEC members. Four other follow-on schemes are on

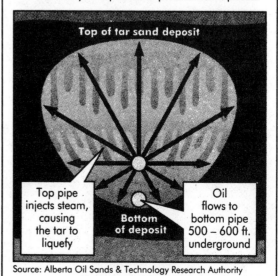

DAVE HERRING – STAFF

Extracting Oil From Tar Sands

By injecting steam through the top pipe, oil that is caught in sand, clay, or shale flows down into the bottom pipe. Recent tests show that extraction costs can be brought down to a competitive level with recovery of liquid oil at present world prices.

Top of tar sand deposit

Top pipe injects steam, causing the tar to liquefy

Bottom of deposit

Oil flows to bottom pipe 500 – 600 ft. underground

Source: Alberta Oil Sands & Technology Research Authority

hold. The technology, still too costly, leaves little scope for future refinement: The tarry masses are mined using oversize equipment including huge excavators and draglines. They are then frothed and centrifuged to separate the oil bitumen. The viscous residues are then upgraded to a low-sulphur "synthetic" crude oil in refinery-like plants. The process is capital intensive and promised savings from large-scale operations were not realized.

The new method reverses the conventional logic. First, it starts from the bottom up, rather than from the top down. Instead of surface mining the sands, the "steam-assisted gravity drainage" technique starts from mining shafts 500 to 600 feet down into hard rock underlying the tar beds. The surface is barely disturbed. Then pairs of parallel horizontal wells are drilled from the shaft into the sands. The top horizontal wells are pumped full of medium-pressure steam. That fluidizes the viscous tars, which flow into the lower horizontal well. The tar is then easily pumped to the surface.

The second advantage of the new approach is its small scale: The optimal size is 30,000 bpd, a fraction of the size of the existing megaprojects.

The savings are dramatic. No overburden must be removed, no land reclamation costs whatsoever are incurred, and by far the bulk of the sand and waste rock is left undisturbed. Instead of excavating tons of sand and rock, the process pumps out tons of hot bitumen. The process is economically and environmentally much simpler.

The final technical breakthrough came as horizontal drilling techniques were perfected. The process only works if the pairs of pipes are properly positioned—about 8 to 14 vertical feet apart. If the pipes are too close, there is a "short-circuit," and the steam bypasses part of the sands. If too far apart, the yield is much reduced. Pipes now can be positioned within one to two feet of a target over almost 1,800 feet. This permits 50 percent to 60 percent of the contained oil to be recovered. These wells are prolific, flowing at 10 times the average for conventional ones in this area. The production cost for bitumen before upgrading to crude oil is US$6 per barrel, about $4 to $5 per barrel less than present projects and enough to make the process viable.

A consortium is mobilizing to launch the commercial project, although realization will take three to four years. The Alberta government has shared the costs and the technology with a clutch of North American oil companies, but two unexpected partners have recently joined. The Chinese National Petroleum Corporation hopes to use the techniques to exploit tar deposits in the eastern Gobi Desert.

The Japanese government is also represented. JAPEX, its agent, has spent billions of dollars searching for large-sized, reliable, and economic oil sources outside of the Middle East, a goal which has eluded them.

A New Energy Path for the Third World

Nicholas Lenssen

NICHOLAS LENSSEN, a senior researcher at Worldwatch Institute in Washington, D.C., is coauthor of The Coming Energy Revolution, *W.W. Norton (1994). From 1984 to 1987, he worked on rural development in Ecuador with the Peace Corps. This article is adapted from his Worldwatch paper "Empowering Development: The New Energy Equation."*

In their efforts to improve the lives of the 4 billion people who live in Africa, Asia, and Latin America, development agencies have clung to a questionable assumption: that a growing energy supply is the necessary foundation for expanding industries, providing jobs, and raising standards of living in the Third World. On the face of it, that assumption seems logical enough, since high energy use is a conspicuous trait of the most developed nations. In practice, the notion of equating energy consumption with economic health has begun to unravel.

Developing countries have more than quadrupled their energy use since 1960, doubling their per capita use. Yet the strategies that have been so successful in achieving this growth have left these nations staggering from oil price shocks, struggling with foreign debt, and suffering from serious environmental and health problems—while still facing severe energy shortages.

Despite more rapid energy development in the South than in the North, the income gap between the hemispheres has been growing, not shrinking. In 1960, the richest fifth of the world's countries produced 30 times more income per person than the poorest fifth, according to the United Nations Development Programme. By 1989, the disparity had widened to 60 to 1. Over the past decade, per capita incomes have declined in some 50 countries. In Latin America, where some of the world's largest energy projects have been built, three-quarters of the population saw its income fall in the 1980s.

This occurred partly because developing economies were saddled with back-breaking debts to foreign banks and governments—debts totaling $1.43 trillion in early 1993. And as debt deepened poverty by siphoning off state funds, rising energy use deepened the debt. In Brazil and Costa Rica, for example, one of every four borrowed dollars went to pay for giant electric power projects.

At the same time, environmental and health costs associated with energy use and production are taking a mounting toll. In coal-dependent China, acid rain falls on at least 14 percent of the country, damaging forests, crops, and water ecosystems, and cities have 14 times the level of suspended particles found in the United States.

Elsewhere, urban air is choked with pollution from motor vehicles. Mexico City, where ozone levels violated international standards 303 days in 1990, is joined by Bangkok, Nairobi, Santiago, and São Paulo in the growing list of cities whose people suffer lung damage despite per capita levels of energy consumption far below those of Northern cities.

Conventional energy development has also increased the threat of global warming. Although industrial countries are responsible for 79 percent of the fossil fuel–derived carbon dioxide emitted since 1950, and still accounted for 69 percent of the total in 1990, future growth in fossil-fuel use is predicted to be greater in the South than in the North. If recent trends continue, emissions in the developing world will grow from 1.8 billion tons of carbon in 1990 to 5.5 billion tons in 2025, according to the U.N.'s Intergovernmental Panel on Climate Change (IPPC). China alone is expected to emit more carbon dioxide by 2025 than the current combined total of the United States, Japan, and Canada. Such increases would boost global emissions by half at a time when, according to the IPPC, they should be cut by at least 60 percent if the atmospheric concentration is to be stabilized and climate change minimized.

For all the ills brought on by expanded energy use, many developing countries are still contending with shortages of electricity. India's shortfall averages 9 percent, rises to 22 percent during peak periods, and is worsening. China's shortfall results in regular shutdowns of industry; it idled one-fourth of the country's industrial capacity in 1987. According to World Bank estimates, electricity shortages are costing Latin America's industry as much as $15 billion per year in lost

From *Technology Review*, October 1993, pp. 42-51. Adapted from *Worldwatch Paper III*, "Empowering Development: The New Energy Equation" by Nicholas Lenssen, Worldwatch Institute, Washington, DC. Reprinted by permission.

output. And then there are the 2.1 billion people world-wide who live in areas with no electricity at all.

With such a gulf between supply and demand, funding agencies and Third World government planners can be expected to continue their efforts to expand energy supplies for years to come. After all, people in the developing world still use just one-ninth as much commercial energy on average as those in industrial countries *(see the table on next page)*. Yet if developing countries are to achieve the hoped-for gains in living standards, they need to meet their energy demand in a way that allows them to close the economic gap between North and South and maintain the health of their people, forests, cropland, and waterways.

Developing countries can achieve sustainable energy development by following a two-part strategy. First, they will need to emphasize the use of more energy-efficient technologies in everything from industrial processes to consumer products. Over the next 35 years, $350 billion invested in efficiency improvements could eliminate the need for $1.75 trillion worth of power plants, oil refineries, and other energy infrastructure by reducing growth in energy demand, according to a study at the Lawrence Berkeley Laboratory (LBL). This would free up money for vastly larger investments in food production, health, education, and other neglected needs. Second, the Third World will need to develop its own alternatives to costly oil and polluting coal. Many developing countries have extensive untapped reserves of natural gas, which could supplant oil and coal in buildings, transport, industry, and power generation. And all have enormous potential to rely on solar, wind, biomass, or geothermal energy. Through a combination of efficiency and alternative energy sources, developing countries can "leapfrog" to the advanced technologies being commercialized in industrial countries today, avoiding billions of dollars of misdirected investments in infrastructure that is economically and environmentally obsolete.

Using Energy Wisely

Since the 1973 Arab oil embargo, industrial countries have made large gains in using energy economically. Energy use by the 24 member nations of the Organization for Economic Cooperation and Development (OECD) rose only one-fifth as much as economic growth between 1973 and 1989. However, these gains have largely bypassed developing countries, where energy use expanded 20 percent faster than economic growth during the same period.

Developing-country economies now require 40 percent more energy than industrial ones to produce the same value of goods and services. This is mainly because they are using outdated technologies that squander energy. The gross inefficiency of these technologies—whether wood stoves, cement plants, light bulbs, or

trucks—offer innumerable opportunities to limit energy consumption and expenditures while expanding the services they provide. For example, the congressional Office of Technology Assessment estimates that nearly half of overall electricity use in the South can be cut cost-effectively.

Half of Third World commercial energy consumption goes to industry, yet for each ton of steel or cement produced, the typical factory in the global South uses far more energy than its Northern counterpart. Steel plants in developing countries consume roughly one-quarter more energy than the average plant in the United States, and about three-quarters more than the most efficient plant. Fertilizer plants in India use about twice as much oil to produce a ton of ammonia as a typical British plant. Pulp and paper facilities consume as much as three times more energy for the same amount of output. Such records are often the result of poor maintenance and operating procedures and can be readily improved—given sufficient information and incentive to do so. A study by Indonesian researchers, for example, found that that country's industries could cut energy use 11 percent without *any* capital investment, simply by changing operating procedures. Similarly, a Ghanaian survey found potential savings of at least 30 percent in medium- to large-scale industries.

Some of the biggest opportunities to save energy and money can be found in the electric power industry. Third World power plants typically burn one-fifth to two-fifths more fuel for each kilowatt-hour generated than those in the North, and they experience far more unplanned shutdowns for repairs, as they are often operated by undertrained staff and poorly maintained, according to the World Bank.

Because the developing world is still in the early stages of building its industrial infrastructure, it has opportunities to base future development not just on more efficient processes but also on more efficient products. Building a $7.5 million factory for making compact fluorescent light bulbs, for example, would eliminate the need to construct $5.6 billion worth of coal-fired power plants, if the bulbs (which need 75 percent less power than incandescent ones) were used domestically, calculates Ashok Gadgil of LBL.

In agriculture, too, there is an urgent need for movement toward greater energy efficiency: farming is likely to become more energy-intensive as population growth drives up the demand for food. Besides requiring large amounts of chemicals, agriculture in developing countries is often a major consumer of electricity. India's 8 million irrigation pumps, which use nearly one-quarter of the country's electricity, employ inefficient motors and poorly designed belts, and are plagued by leaky foot valves and high friction losses. Using more efficient pumps could cut electricity consumption by roughly half, at a cost of only 0.1 cent per kilowatt-hour saved, according to Jayant Sathaye of LBL.

Although industry and agriculture still consume most of the commercial energy in developing countries, the urban residential and commercial sectors are growing much faster. In China, for example, only 3 percent of Beijing's households had refrigerators in 1982; six years later, 81 percent did. Unfortunately, a typical Chinese refrigerator uses 365 kilowatt-hours of electricity per year, whereas a South Korean model of the same size uses 240 kilowatt-hours and a Danish one needs less than 100 kilowatt-hours. Industrial planners and manufacturers in developing countries are rarely concerned with the energy efficiency of their products—only with producing and selling more of them by keeping the initial cost as low as possible.

The same can be said of architects and civil engineers. Much of the developing world relies on air conditioning in commercial buildings. Improved building designs—including insulation, better windows, and natural ventilation—could cut cooling needs and costs, but such designs are not widely used. In Bangkok, for example, large offices typically use windows made of a single sheet of glass. By substituting advanced double-paned windows with a special low-emissivity coating (which filters out infrared rays but passes visible light), builders would reduce not only the subsequent electricity costs but the initial costs of construction, since they would then be able to install smaller, less expensive air conditioners.

Efficiency improvements can even be made in the use of biomass—wood, charcoal, or agricultural residues—for cooking, allowing women to spend less time or money acquiring fuel. Although energy-efficient stoves promoted by development agencies in the 1970s were costly and unreliable, an improved charcoal stove—the ceramic jiko—has become a major success in Kenya and other African countries. In India, a government program had distributed some 6 million advanced cookstoves by early 1989.

A third venue of rapidly growing energy consumption is transportation. In China, transportation doubled its percentage of national oil consumption between 1980 and 1988. In most developing countries, this sector accounts for over one-half of total oil consumption, and one-third of commercial energy use. Congestion in Bangkok has dropped the average vehicle speed from 7 miles per hour in 1980 to about 3 today. Although major improvements are needed in traffic management, mass transportation, and land-use planning, just promoting wider use of bicycles and other nonmotorized vehicles would stem automotive ills while increasing the mobility of the poor.

In combination, the efficiency potential now within reach for industry, agriculture, construction, and transportation could provide an enormous boost to the economies of developing countries. By investing $10 billion a year, these countries could cut future growth of their energy demand in half, lighten the burden of pollution on their environments and health, and stanch

COMMERCIAL ENERGY CONSUMPTION

REGION	1970		1990	
	ENERGY CONSUMPTION[1]	PER CAPITA[2]	ENERGY CONSUMPTION	PER CAPITA
DEVELOPING COUNTRIES	30	12	84	21
—LATIN AMERICAN	8	26	16	37
—ASIAN	19	10	59	20
—AFRICAN	4	10	9	14
INDUSTRIAL COUNTRIES	129	180	154	185
CENTRALLY PLANNED ECONOMIES	44	120	71	167
WORLD	203	55	310	59

[1] EXAJOULES   [2] GIGAJOULES

Higher energy use has failed to bring prosperity to developing countries. Even though their consumption rate has grown far faster than that of the industrialized world, the income gap between rich and poor nations continues to widen.

the flow of export earnings into fuel purchases. Gross savings would average $53 billion a year for 35 years, according to the LBL study.

Although such large-scale savings remain paper prophecies, some countries have achieved notable successes. In 1980, China launched an ambitious program to improve energy efficiency in major industries. By directing roughly 10 percent of its energy investment to efficiency over five years, the nation cut its annual growth in energy use from 7 percent to 4 percent, without slowing growth in industrial production. Efficiency improvements accounted for more than 70 percent of the energy savings, with shifts toward less energy-intensive industries yielding the remainder. And efficiency gains were found to be one-third less expensive than comparable investments in coal supplies. One result was that China's energy consumption expanded at less than half the rate of economic growth from 1980 through 1988.

Brazil's National Electricity Conservation Program has catalyzed impressive savings of energy and money. Over four years, it spent $20 million on more than 150 efficiency projects and programs, for which local governments and private industry provided matching funds. Most of the money went to education and promotion programs to increase awareness of the savings efficiency could generate. The program also encouraged the National Development Bank to offer low-interest loans to businesses willing to invest in efficiency. These efforts yielded electricity savings worth between $600 million and $1.3 billion in reduced need for power plants and transmission lines, estimates Howard Geller, executive director of the American Council for an Energy-Efficient Economy, who has intensively studied the Brazilian energy sector.

Brazil and China need not be anomalies: similar potential exists throughout the developing world. Halving the rate at which Third World energy demand grows over the next 30 years would hold the overall increase to a doubling of consumption rather than a tripling. That difference could have profound consequences for environmental and human health worldwide—and for the ability of the developing world to meet the basic needs of its growing population.

Developing Alternatives

If Third World countries squeeze all the waste they can out of the way they use energy, they will greatly reduce the need for larger supplies. But in the long run, it will still be necessary to develop new energy sources. Unfortunately, government planners and international institutions still assume that developing countries have to follow the energy path the North blazed a century ago—a strategy that relies primarily on expanding supplies of coal and oil. These two fossil fuels already provide 51 percent of all energy used in developing countries *(see the table below)*, and more than 75 percent of commercial energy.

While a few developing nations have improved their export-import balance sheets through oil sales, most face a continual drain on their economies as a result of their dependency on oil. Scarce foreign exchange earned through exports of agricultural products or minerals is spent to import oil for domestic consumption, draining resources away from development. Three-fourths of developing countries are oil importers. And of the 38 poorest countries, 29 import more than 70 percent of their commercial energy—nearly all of it in the form of oil.

Although energy planners have promoted alternatives to fossil fuels, these pose problems of their own. Hydroelectric power provides a third of developing countries' electricity, and less than 10 percent of its technical potential has been tapped. Yet efforts to exploit the rest have run into roadblocks, and orders for large dams have declined in recent years as the real costs—both in capital and in displacement of people—of building them have become more apparent. Nuclear power, too, has fallen short of its promise to supply cheap electricity in developing countries, just as it has elsewhere. The Third World accounts for only 6 percent of the world's nuclear generating capacity, with many programs—including those of Argentina, Brazil, and India—over budget, behind schedule, and plagued by technical problems. Because of its high cost and complex technology, nuclear power is not a viable option for the vast majority of developing countries.

But other, more manageable energy sources are available and waiting to be put to wider use. Natural gas is an obvious example. When oil companies operating in developing countries find natural gas in an exploratory well, they usually cap the well and write the venture off as a tax loss.

ENERGY SUPPLIES IN DEVELOPING COUNTRIES, 1991

SOURCE	SHARE
BIOMASS	35
OIL	26
COAL	25
NATURAL GAS	8
RENEWABLES	6
NUCLEAR	<1

Oil and coal provide over half the energy used in the developing world, but underutilized sources like natural gas and renewables could relieve shortfalls without imposing the economic and environmental burdens of fossil fuels.

Such gas reservoirs are simply too small to develop for export markets. Yet locally, the gas in these so-called noncommercial wells could be used for cooking and producing electricity, and could replace coal and oil in factories and motor vehicles. A natural gas well just one-hundredth the size needed for commercial export would be cost-effective for local use, according to Ben W. Ebenhack, a petroleum engineer at the University of Rochester who heads a project to tap previously drilled wells in Africa for local use. The key is building the infrastructure needed to bring natural gas to the large markets awaiting it.

Petroleum geologists have already found substantial reserves of natural gas in some 50 developing countries, and many other countries hold great promise. Most of these stocks are in oil-producing countries such as Algeria, Indonesia, Mexico, Nigeria, and Venezuela, many of which have burned off gas as a waste byproduct of petroleum production without capturing any useful energy.

Nevertheless, the revival of natural gas that has taken place in North America and Europe in recent years has also occurred to some extent in the South. Government and private engineers have drawn up plans for vast networks of gas pipelines that would connect developing countries. In Latin America, Argentina could soon be piping gas over the Andes to smog-choked Santiago, Chile. Another network, which received its initial go-ahead in 1992, will feed Bolivian gas to southern Brazil and northern Argentina. And in southeast Asia, Thailand hopes to build a gas grid with neighboring Malaysia and Myanmar (formerly Burma).

Even China is reconsidering natural gas as part of its effort to slow growth in oil and coal use. The government formed a gas research institute in 1986 and decided in early 1992 to build a pipeline from a large offshore gas field discovered earlier during an unsuccessful search for oil. Gas commonly accompanies coal as well as oil. It is therefore likely that China, with its enormous coal reserves, is well endowed with natural gas, too.

Developing countries also have abundant supplies of renewable energy resources, such as sunlight, wind, biomass, and heat from deep within the earth, which are becoming more economical. The past decade has seen dramatic technological improvement in tapping these renewables—the costs of solar and wind energy systems, for example, have been slashed by 66 to 90 percent. Electricity sources such as solar thermal power and photovoltaics could be the least expensive route for developing countries, predicts World Bank economist Dennis Anderson. The availability of land is not a problem: for solar energy to double the Third World's energy consumption, only 0.2 percent of the acreage in these countries would be needed.

Many renewables are already less expensive than fossil fuels or nuclear power, once social and environmental costs—such as air pollution, resource depletion, and government subsidies—are included. But even if social and environmental costs are not included, it still makes sense for energy planners to take immediate advantage of renewable energy's potential. Investments in uses that are viable today can stimulate development of the technological and business infrastructure and the domestic expertise, both private and public, needed to apply renewables on a large scale in the future.

Using the sun to heat water is already a cost-effective way to save electricity. Total capital costs for solar hot water are, on average, nearly 25 percent lower than those for electric hot water when the cost of building power plants is included, according to data collected by the Office of Technology Assessment. Solar heating industries have already sprung up in many developing countries. Residents of Botswana's capital, Gaborone, have purchased more than 3,000 solar water heaters, displacing nearly 15 percent of residential electricity demand. Some 30,000 of these heaters have been installed in Colombia, and 17,000 in Kenya. In Jordan, 12 percent of the urban water heating systems are solar.

Villagers in some rural areas use photovoltaic cells to power lights, radios, and even televisions, needs that are usually met with kerosene lamps and disposable or rechargeable batteries. With the help of nongovernmental organizations and private businesses, more than 100,000 photovoltaic lighting units have been installed in developing countries such as Colombia, the Dominican Republic, Mexico, and Sri Lanka. In Africa, photovoltaic lighting has undergone a virtual boom since the mid-1980s: Kenya has 10 private companies selling photovoltaics, with as much as 1,000 kilowatts installed.

For grid-connected power supplies, geothermal power plants and new wind generators based on variable-speed turbines and advanced blades can produce electricity at a cost comparable to that from coal-fired power plants. India leads the developing world in wind energy, with 38 megawatts of capacity installed by the beginning of 1992. Aided by Danish companies, the country plans to install 1,000 megawatts of domestically manufactured wind turbines by the end of the decade. According to Worldwatch Institute estimates, wind could provide more than 10 percent of developing countries' electricity.

Geothermal energy already plays a major role in some countries; in 1990 it produced 21 percent of the electricity in the Philippines, 18 percent in El Salvador, and 11 percent in Kenya. Yet this resource is abundant—and still largely untapped—in Bolivia, Costa Rica, Ethiopia, India, and Thailand. Another two dozen countries, including Brazil and Pakistan, appear to have equally good, though less explored, potential.

Another advanced technology suitable for developing countries is fuel cells. With even higher efficiency and lower pollution than combined-cycle gas turbines, these battery-like devices convert natural gas, biomass, or hydrogen to electric power and heat. Industrial countries, including Japan and the United States, are commercializing fuel-cell technologies that could be useful in developing countries, especially since fuel cells are modular and require less maintenance than standard electric power plants. India has funded a fuel-cell demonstration project, though investment throughout the developing world has so far been low.

Biomass supplies 35 percent of developing countries' energy but could contribute more if existing agricultural and industrial wastes were better utilized and if more energy crops were produced. Efficient electric power can be generated by gas turbines fired with agricultural residues or with forestry wastes that would otherwise be burned at paper and pulp factories. If sugar mills burned all their residues in advanced gas turbines, they would produce more than a third as much electricity as is now consumed in developing countries, according to Robert H. Williams and Eric D. Larson of Princeton University.

Hundreds of millions of acres of degraded lands could be returned to productivity by planting fast-growing trees and other crops suitable for energy use, according to the United Nations Solar Energy Group for Environment and Development. Any such attempt to boost biofuels production, however, would require major investments by governments and private companies. Past efforts to entice villagers to plant more trees have failed more often than not, particularly if the undertaking is packaged as an energy project instead of as a timber- or food-producing venture.

One key may be to integrate biomass energy production with a comprehensive agricultural development strategy that produces marketable items. Agroforestry techniques, for example, offer a way to boost both food yields and wood harvests. Research in Kenya and Nigeria has shown that mixing corn and leucaena trees can produce 39 to 83 percent more corn than does growing corn by itself, while yielding at least 2 tons of wood per acre. Of course, this approach can do little to help the poorest of the poor, who are landless; indeed, it is difficult to disentangle rural energy problems, and their solutions, from the problems of land ownership and economic equity. But agroforestry could be a boon to landed farmers.

Together with efficiency improvements on the demand side, an energy system run on renewable energy resources and natural gas has the potential to meet all the new energy needs of developing countries, according to Amulya Reddy and his colleagues at the Indian Institute of Science in Bangalore. Reddy's group crafted a plan that could meet the state of Karnataka's electricity needs in the 1990s for only $6 billion of invest-

ment, rather than the $17.4 billion a government committee had proposed to spend on large hydroelectric, coal-fired, and nuclear power plants.

Among the new supplies in Reddy's plan are natural gas, solar hot water, and more efficient use of sugar mill wastes and other biomass. Unlike the state's plan, which foresees continuing power shortages despite the enormous investment, Reddy's proposal would electrify all homes in the state and employ more people. At the same time, it would boost carbon-dioxide emissions by only one-fiftieth the amount the government plan envisions.

Sustainable Strategies

Even if piecemeal attempts to improve efficiency and exploit alternative sources are successful, comprehensive changes will be needed to ensure that a country's energy development is sound. The kinds of policies that can help make this happen include expunging destructive subsidies from energy prices, so that users will have incentives to conserve; shifting emphasis in energy planning from building new power plants and supplies to providing more efficient energy services; and shifting supply-end investment from coal and oil to more benign sources.

Implementing these policies will require major institutional changes, from international development agencies, governments, electric utilities, individual industries, and nongovernmental organizations advocating sustainable development. And it is critical that support from the North include not only the billions of dollars annually provided in foreign assistance but also the power of example. That has already occurred to some degree in the development of more energy-efficient industrial processes and consumer products, but the example will become far more persuasive when it includes more substantial shifts to renewable, nonpolluting energy sources and less energy-intensive lifestyles.

Abundant opportunities for promoting end-use efficiency can be found in industrial equipment, home appliances, buildings, and transportation. Some measures are relatively simple: adopting product efficiency standards, putting efficiency labels on products, and publicizing the benefits of efficient products to consumers.

Other measures are more complex but no less effective. Utilities, for example, can adopt a policy known as integrated resource planning. Originally pioneered by U.S. utilities and regulators, and now spreading to Canada, Japan, and Western Europe, this policy requires power companies considering new generating capacity to compare the cost of expansion with the cost of improvements in customer energy efficiency. If efficiency measures prove less expensive, utilities invest money in those, instead of in new generating capacity. They also have the option of investing in alternative technologies, such as solar water heaters, that cost-effectively reduce power consumption. Integrated resource planning was recently adopted in Thailand, where utilities expect as a result to save at least $180 million by 1997.

To encourage such policies, lending agencies need to shift their priorities. The World Bank has started to show more interest in energy efficiency and new energy sources—it recently formed an alternative energy unit in its Asian section, for example, and in 1991 gave India a $450 million loan to expand its use of natural gas. But like most other multilateral development banks, it still tends to equate energy with expanding centralized electric power. When lending agencies do attempt to promote efficiency, they usually rely on politically difficult price hikes. Instead, the banks could encourage the use of integrated resource planning—as the Asian Development Bank, which operates much like the World Bank, has recently started to do—while investing directly in energy efficiency.

A step in the right direction is the Global Environment Facility (GEF), an international fund set up in 1990 and administered by the World Bank, the United Nations Development Programme, and the United Nations Environment Programme. The GEF finances efficiency and renewables projects by making grants designed to slow global warming. It has supported some promising initiatives, including a $7 million project for household photovoltaics in Zimbabwe and a $3.3 million project for energy from sugarcane residues in Mauritius. And it is considering several other worthy ideas: installing efficient lighting in Mexico, capturing methane from coal mines in China, financing improvements in electricity end-use in Thailand, developing biomass-fueled gas turbines in Brazil, and promoting a variety of renewables in India.

But GEF has two limitations. First, its total funds—$1.3 billion for three years, of which only 40 to 50 percent can be energy-related—are not enough to reform energy development worldwide. The multilateral development banks lend 30 times as much per year on traditional energy projects. Second, the inclusion of efficiency and renewables projects in its portfolio sustains the false notion that they are not economical on their own, but simply a means to reduce carbon-dioxide emissions. The institution's real impact will be felt once the development banks' entire energy loan portfolios follow the pattern of today's GEF grants.

The GEF's shortcomings expose a glaring weakness of the United Nations: there is no central U.N. energy office other than the International Atomic Energy Agency. A new, broader agency could take the lead role in promoting efficient energy systems. Such an institution could be decentralized, incorporating research stations in key regions around the world that could design and demonstrate renewable and efficient technologies, gather and disseminate information, and train technicians and professionals in developing countries. The centers would be particularly useful to smaller developing countries that do not have the resources of nations such as Brazil or India.

At the national level, government programs can be funded by energy taxes or carbon taxes, which are based on the carbon content of the fuel. In early 1992, the Thai parliament levied a tax on petroleum products and natural gas, equivalent to just over 1 cent per liter of petroleum product, that will provide $50 million to $60 million a year for investments in efficiency and renewables. Ghana already funds its independent energy board with a small tax on fossil fuels, and Tunisia originally funded its efficiency program through a modest tax on oil. More general application of carbon taxes would encourage research and investment in efficiency and renewables. The Italian government, for example, has recommended that part of the revenue from a proposed European Community carbon tax go to sustainable energy investments in the South.

Such proposals underscore the gradual realization in the North that energy and environmental stability are closely linked. But developing countries need a new energy path for reasons quite apart from threats to the earth's climate. Cutting the cost of energy services, as well as the environmental and health costs of air pollution, would allow developing countries to invest in more pressing areas. In Brazil, for example, about 30 percent of children are malnourished and 78 percent do not complete primary school. With the technologies of efficiency and renewables, and with the policies for their dissemination that have already proved effective, Brazil could shift $2 billion to $3 billion a year out of the power sector and roughly double its funding for nutrition, preventive health care, and water and sanitation programs. Throughout the South, investments in transportation and communication systems, health and education infrastructure, water supplies, and shelter could be stepped up.

Indeed, an energy strategy based on clean and efficient sources is a cornerstone of sustainable development and is essential if the countries of the South are to improve their living standards. As countries move to this new strategy, their energy economies will shift from obstructing development to enabling it.

Development

- Nonindustrial Nations (Articles 23–27)
- Industrial Nations (Articles 28–33)

One of the terms most frequently used in descriptions of the world today is "development." Television talk shows, scholarly publications, political speeches, and countless other forums echo this term. Yet, if we gathered together a group of experts, it would soon be apparent that each one uses the word "development" in a somewhat different manner. To some, development means becoming industrialized—like the United States or Japan, for example. To others, development means having a growing economy; this is usually measured in terms of the expansion of Gross National Product (GNP). To still others, development is primarily a political phenomenon. They question how a society can change its economy if it cannot establish collective goals and successfully administer their implementation. And to still others, development means attaining a certain quality of life, based on the establishment of adequate health care, leisure time, and a system of public education, among other things. It is obvious, then, that the term must be defined before a discussion of the issue of development can begin.

Because this book includes both industrial and nonindustrial countries in its discussion of development, a broad definition will be used. Development will mean improvement in the basic aspects of life: lower infant mortality rates, greater life expectancy, lower disease rates, higher rates of literacy, healthier diets, and improved sanitation. While it is obvious that, judged by these standards, some groups of people are more developed than others, the process of development is an ongoing one for all nations. This unit, therefore, is divided into two parts. It looks first at the development process in nonindustrial countries, then focuses on the industrial countries of North America and Europe, and on Japan and Russia. Although the economy of Russia differs from the consumer-oriented economies of the West, the structure of its industrial system is in the midst of a dramatic transformation. The outcomes of this historic change are difficult to predict, but the significance of these changes is recognized by all. This change, along with a variety of associated changes in the Russian social system, is likely to dominate much of the world news for the remainder of the 1990s.

Nonindustrial Nations. The decade of the 1980s was a period of considerable economic growth in the industrial nations of the world; but for the nonindustrial nations it was a period of stagnation and even decline. The gap between the rich and poor countries widened. Furthermore, the burden of this growing inequality fell most heavily on women and children. Of the illiterate people in the nonindustrial nations, three out of every four are women. What is to be done about this situation is a question that is widely debated. The demise of the planned economies of the old Soviet Union and its allies no longer provides this approach as a model for development. There are also considerable doubts about the appropriateness of the capitalist model. Many argue that this system simply transfers wealth from the poor to the rich without any benefits flowing back to those who need the advantages of economic progress the most.

The articles in the nonindustrial nations section have been selected with the development debate as the focal point. The nature of the international economic system and how it rewards some and not others is examined from a number of perspectives, using numerous case studies.

Industrial Nations. Only a few years ago, industrialization was considered by many to be the end point of the development process. Industrialization, however, is not necessarily synonymous with improvement in the quality of life. When the industrial sector of the West's economy was thrown into deep recession after the oil price shocks of the 1970s, many experts joined the growing chorus of those calling for the development of industrial societies into a new, postindustrial structure, where knowledge, information, and space-age technologies would take over. Others believed that the "greening" of society, rather than a high-tech future, should become the new goal of development. This second group of people maintained that new, clean energy resources and an appreciation of the fragile nature of the environment would lead to a decentralized economy. As yet, neither of these visions has come to pass. The industrial countries, like the nonindustrial countries, are in the midst of a development process with no single blueprint to guide them.

The articles in this subsection that focus on the development of industrial countries offer a variety of contending viewpoints. Some observers predict an increase in economic cooperation and further integration of national economies. Others warn that trading blocs are going to replace failing efforts at an international trading system that was established after World War II. This new international economic system, they go on to say, is likely to be highly competitive, and not all will have an equal chance at being successful.

The United States, Japan, and Germany are each viewed by various experts as the potential leader of the

global economy in the next century. Each has problems as well as unique assets. Optimism and pessimism about these contenders tend to vary from year to year as they individually and collectively grapple with their own problems. However, if this contest for leadership is to be understood over the long run, it is essential to understand the core structural issues confronting each: increases in productivity, governmental reform, labor relations, political unrest, levels of investment in research and development, and so forth.

Finally, the future of the republics that comprised the former Soviet Union looms large on the horizon. There are no historical models for making the transition from planned economies to market economies. The former communist countries of Central Europe began this process a few years prior to Russia and the other members of the new Commonwealth of Independent States, but these various experiments in economic/political processes have not yielded a clear formula for success.

Industrial nations, like their nonindustrial counterparts, are in a period of transition. Many forces are at work, and as yet there is no widely accepted vision of where this is all going to lead. While so much divides the First and Third Worlds, uncertainty about the future and a lack of consensus about the policies necessary to improve the quality of life are two dimensions that they ironically have in common.

Looking Ahead: Challenge Questions

How are the social structures of traditional societies different from those of the consumer-oriented societies of the West?

How are the Third World countries dependent on the First World?

What are some of the barriers that make it difficult for nonindustrial countries to develop?

How has the role of the United States in the international economy changed in recent years?

The international economic system is faced with unprecedented problems. What are these, and what are some of the proposals for solving these problems?

How are the United States, Japan, Russia, and other industrial countries trying to alter their economies to meet new economic challenges? Are they likely to succeed?

China Sees 'Market-Leninism' as Way to Future

Nicholas D. Kristof

The writer of this article recently completed nearly five years as chief of the Beijing bureau of The New York Times.

Ever since the Opium War erupted 150 years ago, China has been groping for a way to regain the edge over the West that it enjoyed for most of recorded history.

Now, in the 1990's, China's leaders seem to think that they have found the Way.

The plan is to jettison Communism—but not Communist Party rule—and move China's nearly 1.2 billion people into the East Asian tradition of free-market authoritarianism. Pioneered in the 1960's and 1970's by South Korea and Taiwan, this East Asian model combines harsh single-party rule with competition in the marketplace.

In short, dissidents are zapped with cattle prods and the economy is prodded with market incentives.

After Deng Xiaoping, China's current paramount leader, was purged in 1976, the People's Daily quoted Mao Zedong as saying that Mr. Deng "knows nothing of Marxism-Leninism." Mao may have been half-right, for the 89-year-old Mr. Deng has even advised visitors from developing countries not to bother with Marxism.

At the same time, Mr. Deng and other Chinese leaders retain a fondness for Leninism, in the sense of highly disciplined one-party rule with centralized decision-making. Their aim, in other words, is Market-Leninism.

In some ways, China already resembles Brezhnev's Soviet Union or Honecker's East Germany less than it does modern Indonesia: a nepotistic and corrupt dictatorship that presides over a booming market economy with both state and private sectors. Mao once talked of China's becoming another Soviet Union; Mr. Deng reserves his highest praise not for a socialist country but for that bastion of capitalism, Singapore.

Paramount Leader's Paradise

The attraction of Singapore is that it has achieved Western living standards without being infected by Western political standards. Singapore is a paramount leader's paradise, for it is populated by clean-cut, law-abiding citizens who obligingly use their ballots to keep their rulers in power.

"China's dream is to become another Singapore," a Western diplomat noted the other day. A few feet away, a foreign ambassador responded without a pause, "It'll never happen."

Whether China will succeed in transforming itself into another Singapore—or even Indonesia—is one of the fundamental international questions for the next decade or two.

If China can make that metamorphosis, a new superpower could emerge in the 21st century. If it fails to transform itself economically and politically, perhaps collapsing under popular resentments and ethnic and geographical divisions, then many Chinese officials believe that civil war and massive chaos are possible. In that case, more than one-fifth of humanity could be caught in the upheavals, new states with nuclear weapons could pop up in the center of Asia, and a tidal wave of tens of millions of boat people could engulf distant shores.

Police Sell Cattle Prods

But whatever the future holds, it is already pretty clear that China is no longer a Communist country in any meaningful sense.

No Communist country, at least, has ever so fully embraced stock markets, satellite television, private colleges, Avon ladies, music video and radio talk shows. The Communist Party is still in command, but its branches no longer devote much energy to controlling ideology. Instead, in the 1990's the business of the party is business.

The State Security Ministry runs a bakery, the Police Ministry sells electric cattle prods, and—until it was caught—the party's official women's organization ran a brothel.

Misleading Froth
The Underside Of a Boom

The party's avarice and materialism tend to impress foreign visitors,

 From *New York Times*, September 6, 1993, pp. 1, 5. © 1993 by The New York Times Company. Reprinted by permission.

who are dizzied by aggressive quasi-capitalism: the glitzy discos that keep everyone bopping until the wee hours, the 30 Rolls Royces sold so far this year in China, the luxury restaurants that sprinkle bits of 24-karat gold into their dishes because rich patrons think it is good for longevity.

Yet all this is froth, and misleading froth at that. When foreigners rave at the sight of all the gleaming new high-rises under construction in Beijing, local people sometimes respond with a cynical old folk saying: On the outside, even donkey droppings are shiny.

Visitors who travel only to major cities learn about as much about China as a foreigner would learn about the United States from a few days spent next to the pool of an elegant hotel in Beverly Hills. In the countryside, where three-quarters of the population lives, the peasants are far more likely to inhabit caves than discos, and for every Chinese who eats gold there are millions who cannot afford meat.

Just as important, this scramble to get rich may be undermining China's value system. Many Chinese worry that the social contract is collapsing, for the old glue that held society together—Communism—has lost its adhesive qualities. The Chinese have a saying: "yi fang, jiu luan"—as soon as control eases, there is chaos.

"All the time in Chinese history, when you don't have strong rule, you get chaos and warlords," said a military official in an extremely sensitive post. "If we try to get too much democracy, it'll all fall apart again. China will disintegrate, and it'll be worse than in the Soviet Union."

Selling Military Secrets

The official complained that social order is disintegrating because of an almost universal desire to make money, and he seemed to know something about that. His purpose in arranging the meeting was to try to sell a reporter top-secret information about Chinese missile sales to Pakistan.

His forehead glistening with sweat as he contemplated the executioner's bullet that would rip apart his skull if he were caught, he provided evidence of his role in the missile program. He said that China was continuing to sell M-11 ballistic missiles to Pakistan, and he offered to provide the dates of shipments, quantities and other specific data in exchange for cash.

The United States formally concluded late last month that China was selling M-11 missile technology to Pakistan, in violation of international agreements, and imposed economic sanctions as a punishment. But the United States has not formally determined whether China has sold the complete missiles themselves to Pakistan.

Told that reporters do not pay for information, the military official asked for an introduction to an American diplomat who would pay. When that request was turned down as well, he declined to provide detailed information about M-11 shipments.

In the course of two lengthy meetings, in which a reporter tried to persuade him to give the information for free, and he continued to press for an introduction to a diplomat, the military official explained how he decided after months of agonizing to betray his country.

"If my neighbor's kid gets a toy, then my kid wants it too," he reflected during a tense meeting under a lamppost late one night. "Life's a competition now. Everybody's trying to make money. Everyone! Hey, I'm just trying to cash in on what I have."

The no-holds-barred capitalism shows in all kinds of ways. Children regularly die, for example, after drinking fake medicines that fly-by-night entrepreneurs churn out without regard to effectiveness or safety. Restaurant owners in at least half a dozen provinces have been caught lacing their dishes with opium pods in an effort to make their food literally addictive. The Ministry of Public Security became so alarmed that it recently ordered a crackdown on the use of opium as a spice.

In the village of Haotou, in southern China's Guangdong Province, the peasants figured out an easy way to join the market economy. They began kidnapping girls and young women from other areas, hauling them back to the village and forcing them into prostitution. Many of the peasants turned their homes into brothels employing more than 100 sex slaves.

Corruption has grown to such huge proportions that President Jiang Zemin warned last month that it threatened to ruin the Communist Party itself. A few years ago, the problem was petty bribery of a few dollars; now officials steal millions or billions.

In June, the Agricultural Bank of China disclosed that officers of one of its branches had issued fraudulent letters of credit for $10 billion. The fraud was revealed only because the bank wanted to make clear that it would not honor the documents.

Minor graft has turned into Mafia-style organized crime. Particularly in coastal areas of southern China, local party and army officials have joined forces with criminal gangs in Hong Kong and in Chinatowns abroad to engage in massive smuggling and other rackets.

More than 90 percent of the videocassette recorders sold in China have been smuggled in, often with the help of the police, the army or border guards. In the first four months of this year, South Korea exported 26,000 cars to China, but only 166 were reported to Chinese customs officials so that duties could be paid.

Police officials in Beijing run a prostitution racket out of an army-owned hotel. Doctors routinely demand bribes of hundreds of dollars before performing major surgery, and journalists demand payoffs for attending corporate news conferences.

Failed Experiment
A Crisis Of Legitimacy

"Corruption is much worse now than it ever was under the Nationalists," said an octogenarian former senior official, in a reference to the Government that the Communists overthrew in 1949. It is a bold statement, for corruption was so rampant under the Nationalists that the Government had virtually rotted away by the time the Communists overthrew it.

The old man was eating dinner in the spacious apartment that the Communist Government gave him as a reward for many decades of faithful service to the party. He has enjoyed all the perquisites of power in China and has even played bridge with Mr. Deng. But, largely because of the corruption, the party's esteem for him is not reciprocated.

"I'll tell you, in 1949, I hated the Nationalists," the old man said. "I went to welcome the Communists when they entered Beijing and I cheered for them. When a Communist soldier was shot, I went to get help for him. At a meeting in my office to discuss what to do, I was the first to speak out. I said we should support the Communist Party."

"Now, I would welcome the Nationalists back," he added bitterly. "In fact, I would go out and lead them into Beijing."

That sentiment is not unusual, particularly among intellectuals. Even many Communist leaders are said to acknowledge privately that the grand experiment to which they have devoted their lives has in many respects been a failure.

In the United States, many college radicals of the 1960's have changed their views and become bankers. The thinking of many Chinese leaders appears to have undergone a parallel evolution, but it is always easier for members of a congregation to slip out than for the high priests to stand at the altar and admit to atheism.

"None of them really believe in Communism any more," said the child of one Politburo member. The widow of a top leader says: "He stopped believing all that long ago, but what could he do? The only person he could admit it to was me."

Some Chinese—including the old man who would welcome back the Nationalists—believe that the Communist Party is a collapsing dynasty, just like all the other dynasties that have disintegrated in the past. They point to the irrelevance of its ideology, just like that of Confucianism at the end of the Qing Dynasty a century ago.

Confronted with a crisis of legitimacy during a period of widespread alienation and corruption, the Qing rulers responded with the same combination of repression and reform that the Communist Party has repeatedly tried.

The New Revolution
Economic Forces Remold a Nation

There is a huge difference, however, between China at the end of the Qing Dynasty and China today: In the 1990's, China has the fastest growing economy in the world. Instead of disintegrating into floods and famines, the former sick man of Asia is enjoying the fruits of the world's latest economic miracle.

Prof. Thomas B. Gold, a sociologist at the University of California at Berkeley, agrees that China resembles a disintegrating dynasty, but he argues that the economic boom makes a crucial difference. It may have the momentum to keep the country going, he says.

"In many ways, what is happening in China today is more revolutionary than what the Communists did," Professor Gold said. He notes that change used to come from the top in China, dictated by political campaigns. But now it is the nation's economic forces that are remolding the nation.

The emerging China, Professor Gold and other scholars suggest, will look increasingly like Taiwan and South Korea. On other continents, the parallels may be Spain under Franco in the 1960's or Chile under Gen. Augusto Pinochet in the 1970's.

Among the crucial changes in Taiwan, and in the other East Asian countries, were a rise in educational and income levels, greater interaction with the outside world and the emergence of a technocratic elite in the bureaucracy. The economic boom nurtured a growing urban middle class that was able, after the passing of the old guard, to demand what might be called stable change: far-reaching political and economic liberalization achieved without spilling too much blood.

The same processes are under way in China. It is an open question whether the Communists would allow them to work if it meant the party would be presiding over its own demise. Moreover, it is far more complicated to choreograph the transformation of a nation of 1.2 billion people—including minorities like Tibetans—than it is to transform a city-state like Singapore or an island like Taiwan.

The uncertainty about China's prospects reflects a long debate about whether a market for goods can flourish for long if there is no companion market for ideas. Particularly in the West, many people assume that China will be unable to liberalize its economy successfully if it does not liberalize its political system.

Yet in Asia, many people draw the opposite conclusion. They see democracies like the Philippines where economic growth is anemic and conclude that industry grows best in tightly controlled political greenhouses like China. The Soviet Union under Mikhail S. Gorbachev emphasized "glasnost" more than "perestroika"—openness more than economic restructuring—while China has churned up some impressive statistics by trying perestroika more than glasnost.

If China continues to thrive, it will offer a lesson to the third world that the West may find profoundly unsettling: Political repression is the grease that can lubricate an economic boom.

For students of the Soviet Union, one of the longest arguments was between those who foresaw the state's collapse and those who predicted convergence with the non-Communist world. In the case of the

Soviet Union, those who took the bleakest view were proved right.

Now the same argument is raging about China. One of the most talked-about books in China in recent years was a prediction of the collapse of the Communist world, written by Zbigniew Brezezinski in the 1980's and published in Chinese in a limited edition for senior officials.

Some young Chinese intellectuals worry that the Communist Party will survive the collapse of Communism, and that what the leadership is really trying to build is fascism. Mao himself was the first to warn of this risk.

"We are afraid that we will stop being a revolutionary country and will become a revisionist one," the Chairman said in 1963. "When that happens in a socialist country, it becomes worse than a capitalist country. A Communist Party can turn into a fascist party."

And so, some argue, it has. There are parallels, for example, with Italy under Mussolini and especially with Spain under Franco, in the sense that China is an authoritarian, militarized and disciplined society in which state-controlled corporations compete in market conditions.

A Huge Improvement

Even if what is emerging in China is fascism, however, in practice it represents a huge improvement for most Chinese. The Government still smashes those who challenge it—the authorities sentenced a Chinese journalist to life in prison on Aug. 30 for leaking an official document—but it no longer tries to regulate every aspect of daily life.

When China had a redder tint, its people could not wear lipstick, listen to rock music, have foreign friends, dress in colorful clothes, or use "bourgeois" expressions like "Miss." Now Chinese have reclaimed their private lives from the Communist Party; once again, they can display personalities.

In short, China seems to be in an immensely important transition from totalitarianism to authoritarianism. Dissidents are still brutalized, but life for the average peasant or worker—who knows that politics, like explosives, are to be avoided—is relatively free.

It may be no more than the freedom of a bird cage. But most birds probably would prefer to be able to fly around in a cage than be skewered on a rotisserie, which is what life in China used to be like.

New Tally of World's Economies Catapults China Into Third Place

Steven Greenhouse

Special to The New York Times

WASHINGTON, May 19 — Saying that traditional measures underestimate the economies in developing countries, the International Monetary Fund has concluded that China's economy is more than four times as large as previously measured. That makes it the third largest, behind the United States and Japan.

The new study, to be released next week, also greatly increases estimates of the economies of India, Indonesia, Mexico, Brazil and other developing countries.

Until now, most studies have measured each country's output by valuing its goods and services in dollars, using international exchange rates. Thus, it China's currency weakened, its economy appeared to shrink.

But in the new method, national output is calculated by what goods and services a country's currency will buy, compared with the purchasing power of other countries' currencies.

By this method, the I.M.F. found, China produced about $1.7 trillion in goods and services last year, far greater than most previous estimates of about $400 billion.

An Influence on Foreign Aid

The recalculation means that China's economy, one of the fastest

growing in the world, is just slightly smaller than Japan's—and not No. 10, as previously calculated. It is less than half the size of the United States economy.

Many economists say the new calculation is long overdue and gives a much more accurate picture of the developing world's economy. The study could have far-reaching repercussions in international aid programs, where per-capital income is crucial in determining assistance.

In China's prodigious growth continues, the World Bank said, the combined economies of China, Hong Kong and Taiwan will be larger than the United States economy in less than a decade.

"The main importance of this is geo-political," said Paul Krugman, an economist at the Massachusetts Institute of Technology. "It's a reminder that China is a great power already, which is something many people haven't quite grasped yet."

The new estimates, many economists say, will push policymakers to stop thinking of the world economy as having just three poles—the United States, Europe and Japan—and encourage them to add a fourth: China.

"You have over a billion people there, and even with per-capita income that's pretty modest, you have a pretty big overall economy and a growing market for imports," said C. Fred Bergsten, director of the Institute of International Economics.

With China playing a larger role on the economic stage, some economists are wondering whether it should be invited to join the Group of Seven industrial democracies.

"China will have a very different viewpoint from the Group of Seven," said Mr. Bergsten. "It's a developing country; its per-capita income is just an eighth or so of that of the G-7 nations. Besides, China is neither industrial nor a democracy."

All That Non-Money Can Buy

In its new study, the I.M.F. does not measure an economy's size in the traditional way, by translating the local-currency value of output into dollars. Instead, the fund uses purchasing-power parity, which compares currencies according to what they buy at home.

The measure looks at prices of a bundle of goods and services, including food, clothing, housing and transportation, using that yardstick to compare the total value of output in different countries.

Many economists favor this measure, noting that if a country's exchange rate drops 10 percent against the dollar, this should not automatically reduce the size of the nation's economy by 10 percent.

"It's a great triumph that the I.M.F. has made this change, because it gives a more accurate reflection of the world economy," said Robert

Summers, an economics professor at the University of Pennsylvania, a leading authority on this measuring method. "Purchasing-power parity has long been the accepted method in the academic community. This measure helps change people's perception of the world, although we should remember that all the distended bellies are still there."

Car Is Not a Car Is Not a Car

Some economists say they will still measure economies using current exchange rates because they do not fully trust purchasing-power parity. They say it is hard to compare the value of goods in different countries, for instance, to weigh the value of a Chinese car with that of an American car, or of a one-bedroom apartment in Manhattan with one in Beijing or Tokyo.

I.M.F. officials said they would now rely mostly on purchasing-power parity in measuring economies, but added that they would not abandon use of exchange-rate measures.

Using the fund's new measure, per-capita income in China was about $1,600 last year, compared with $370 using estimates based on exchange rates. Based on purchasing-power parity, per-capita income in the United States was $22,204 in 1991, the last year for which a range of comparable figures is available.

Using the new measure India's economy soared in 1991 to $996 billion, the sixth largest, from $285 billion using exchange rates. India's per-capita income in 1991 was $1,150, rather than the $330 calculated using exchange rates.

Analysts count potatoes and cars instead of dollars.

World Bank economists apply the purchasing-power parity somewhat differently, and their estimate of China's total output is even higher than reckoned by I.M.F. The bank puts the figure at $2.2 trillion in 1990. If one allows for China's brisk growth over the last two years, its output reached $2.35 trillion in 1991 and the $2.6 trillion in 1992, pushing it past Japan to No. 2 position.

Using the new measure, the share of the developing world in global output almost doubled in 1991, to 34 percent, from 18 percent under the older reckoning.

Officials from some developing countries object to using purchasing-power parity because World Bank rules state that countries with annual per-capita income of more than $765 cannot qualify for loans under the most favorable terms, usually 35 years with no interest.

But the World Bank continues to measure economies by exchange rates, and officials said that if they adopted purchasing-power parity, they might have to raise the per-capita ceiling for cheap loans.

The new measure is contained in the annex to the I.M.F.'s World Economic Outlook, which was released in April. The annex, which is to be published next week, puts China's economy at more than 6 percent of worldwide output in 1990, the last year for which global figures are available, up from slightly under 3 percent in 1970. In comparison, the United States represented 22.5 percent of world output, Japan 7.6 percent and Germany 4.3 percent.

The former Soviet Union accounted for 8.3 percent of world output in 1990, but the annex gave no separate figures for Russia's economy.

After several years of internal debate, I.M.F. officials have begun using purchasing-power parity because they are convinced that traditional measures produced invalid results. For example, measuring output by exchange rates indicated that China's economy had shrunk to slightly less than 2 percent of global output, from slightly more than 2 percent two decades ago, even though its economy had grown twice as fast as the world economy.

AFRICA
IN THE BALANCE

Summary: The Cold War and superpower leveraging are dead, and the heyday of the African dictators is over. In fact, so many nations are beating back repression that some Africans are calling the nineties a second era of independence. Recent talk of also opening up to foreign capital could make for some interesting competition.

Henrik Bering-Jensen

The seventies and eighties were the heyday of the mad African dictators. Who was worst is debatable.

There was Idi Amin of Uganda, the butcher of Kampala, whose closest collaborators had a way of suddenly disappearing. He was rumored to keep their remains in his refrigerator. Atrocious though he was, he was not without humor: Once at a summit of African leaders, he let himself be carried in by four white businessmen, with a fifth holding a parasol over his head.

There was Jean-Bedel Bokassa of the Central African Republic, another suspected cannibal, who had his uniforms reinforced to carry his medals, declared himself emperor and modeled his coronation on that of Napoleon Bonaparte — an extravaganza that cost his dirt-poor country one-quarter of its annual foreign earnings.

There was Lt. Col. Mengistu Haile Mariam of Ethiopia, who smothered the country's old emperor, Haile Selassie, with a pillow and under whose policies millions starved to death.

And that only begins the list. Until very recently, African despots could carry on pretty much as they pleased. The Soviets had no qualms about propping up murderous regimes, as long as they were "progressive," which is to say anti-American. As for the United States and its allies, guilt over colonialism and the necessities of the Cold War meant that, qualms or not, they also propped up dubious regimes. To ease their conscience, they often cited political scientists who claimed that one-party rule was natural for African culture and alone could mold tribal communities into modern nation-states.

According to Smith Hempstone, the outspoken U.S. ambassador to Kenya, African rulers could trade on this tension between East and West, playing one superpower against another. With the end of the Cold War, that game is over. Superpower rivalry no longer ensures the grip on power of corrupt regimes. Says Hempstone, "With the Soviets out of the game, we no longer can be blackmailed into giving money to projects which we know are not beneficial to the countries concerned." Or as Omar Bongo, president of Gabon, put it recently, noting the turn of events in Eastern Europe: "The wind from the East is shaking the coconut trees."

Not since independence have so many African countries moved toward more representative government as have done so in the past two years. In Zambia, the leader for the past 27 years, Kenneth Kaunda, was voted out of office, much to his surprise. In Nigeria, Africa's most populous state, the ruling military regime has created political parties along American lines in a phased move toward democracy.

In Angola, there was a negotiated settlement last year between the Soviet-supported People's Movement for the Liberation of Angola and the U.S.-backed National Union for the Total Independence of Angola, led by Jonas Savimbi, with the old colonial power Portugal assuming the role of mediator. In Ethiopia, the hated regime of Mengistu, whose forced resettlement policies caused the famine of 1985, collapsed and the colonel had to flee and seek refuge in Zimbabwe. Not only do former Soviet clients no longer have material support from the Soviets, they no longer have ideological or philosophical patrons.

This has provoked rethinking by African leaders, one sign of which came at the recent summit of the Organization of African Unity in Dakar, Senegal. President Frederick Chiluba of Zambia hammered away at his colleagues for having poured money into absurd, self-aggrandizing political monuments to themselves and for having tolerated massive violations of human rights. Chiluba stressed the need to break the group's tacit agreement of not speaking critically about conditions in neighboring countries. During this salvo, some of the other members of the organization, which once was described as a "trade union for tyrants," looked less than comfortable.

Some Africans are now calling the nineties a second era of independence, the first having gone sour through three decades of misrule, incompetence and internal repression. According to Michael Chege of the Ford Foundation in Harare, Zimbabwe, people have finally realized that domestic repression can be just as cruel as colonial repression. "What people in Africa talk about today," he says, "are individual liberties, freedom of speech, First Amendment guarantees," as in the United States.

What people are also talking about is reopening their economies to foreign investment, after decades of official hostility to private capital from abroad. Unfortunately for Africans, this opening comes at a most inopportune moment in history, for they will now be in direct competition with Eastern Europe and the former Soviet Union for foreign investment. Given the current state of their economies, and the woeful neglect of the population by the departing dictators, this is not a competition they look likely to win. As an often-quoted French diplomat put it recently in *Le Monde*, in most undiplomatic fashion: "Economically speaking, if all of black Africa, with the exception of South Africa, were to disappear in a flood, the global cataclysm would be approximately nonexistent."

A number of theories have been advanced to explain the failures of the first independence. For most African states that won independence during this period, the transition from colonialism was a messy and hurried affair. The old powers for the most part left quickly. In some cases, as with Portugal and Belgium, they left behind anarchy and civil war; in others, notably Britain, the legacy was too much of a good thing — an intricate bureaucratic structure that lent itself too readily to central control of the economy.

At the same time, the period was one when socialism was seen as the wave of the future: Many African leaders were trained in European and American universities, where confidence in planned economies was at an all-time high, and where many professors were disaffected by the political systems of their own countries. "The untold story of Africa is how American intellectuals influenced African intellectuals to take the wrong path," says Thomas Henriksen of the Hoover Institution.

Instead of embarking on an export-oriented economic strategy, as did newly independent Asian states, most African nations chose a route of so-called African socialism, which was inward-looking and heavy on regulation and nationalization.

To make matters worse, the fragile young states were taking root just as the Soviet Union under Khrushchev and Brezhnev turned its attention to worldwide expansion. Moscow's policy of supporting so-called wars of liberation in the Third World had the effect of turning many of the newly independent countries into proxy battlefields between East and West.

Nor were matters helped by the reluctance of the ex-colonial powers to criticize, even minimally, human rights violations by the new generation of African leaders. Many Westerners accepted at face value the self-justifying arguments of these

rulers — that only one-party governments were strong enough to protect their fledgling nations from the ethnic and religious rivalries that threatened to split them apart and retard economic development. In many cases, of course, these new ruling parties were thinly disguised vehicles for the continued dominance of one tribe over its traditional rivals.

The tendency of Western diplomats to tolerate the sins of the new rulers as trivial compared with the sins of colonialism led to curious double standards in the international arena. South Africa, where oppression was white on black, became a cause celebre for human rights activists around the globe. But elsewhere on the continent, powerful groups could wreak havoc on the less powerful with relative impunity. There was no public outcry over the battles in Ruanda-Urundi (now Rwanda and Burundi), for example, when the Tutsi massacred the Hutus or the Hutus massacred the Tutsi.

Many African leaders adroitly exploited this indifference. Similarly, they became virtuosos in exploiting superpower competition, quickly dropping hints that they could switch their allegiance at the first sign that their current superpower patron was reluctant to deliver aid, economic or military. Such maneuvering lay behind the intricate politics on the Horn of Africa in the seventies. In 1969, Gen. Siad Barre came to power in Somalia and offered Moscow the use of his country's warm-water ports. The U.S. at the time was supporting Ethiopia, Somalia's traditional rival. When pro-Western Ethiopian emperor Haile Selassie was overthrown in the revolution of 1974, the alliances were reversed. Somalia allied itself with the United States. And by the time Mengistu consolidated his power in 1977, he was the Soviet Union's most reliable client in Africa.

Most adept at exploiting the Cold War for his own purpose may have been Mobutu Sese Seko of Zaire, the former Belgian Congo. Because of its strategic location, Zaire has received more U.S. support than any other sub-Saharan state. Mobutu is the founder and leading practitioner of the cult of Mobutuism. Born Joseph Mobutu, his adopted full name, Mobutu Sese Seko kuku Ngbenbu wa za Banga, can be loosely translated as the "all powerful warrior who through endurance and inflexible will goes from conquest to conquest, leaving fire in his wake."

As head of the army, Mobutu proclaimed himself president in 1965, and in the decades since he has sys-

tematically plundered his country, which with its rich stores of copper, cobalt, diamonds, gold and uranium could have been one of the richest in Africa. Besides 11 palaces in his own country, one known as the African Versailles, Mobutu also owns chateaus and estates in France, Belgium and Switzerland. In euphemistic economese, this is referred to as a "blurring of public and private finances." In more direct speech, Mobutu has established a "kleptocracy" that benefits himself and his family and allows him to buy off potential enemies.

Apart from keeping Zaire itself from falling under Soviet domination, Mobutu allowed the transit of U.S. covert assistance to the UNITA forces in Angola who were fighting Cuban proxy troops, thereby letting the U.S. avoid the embarrassment of relying on South Africa. In 1983, he sent 2,000 Zairian troops to support the pro-Western regime of Chad's president, Hissene Habre, against rebels loyal to Libya's Col. Muammar Qaddafi. Since the end of the Cold War, however, the United States and international organizations have suspended all aid to Mobutu, and it now seems only a matter of time before he is toppled. He is reported to spend most of his time tooling up and down the Congo on his presidential yacht, fearful of entering his own capital of Kinshasa.

Absent the imperative to block the Soviets, the West now has some leverage of its own against the Mobutus of Africa. It can push for reform by demanding accountability and democracy in return for aid. According to the Ford Foundation's Chege, a native Zimbabwean, it is crucial that the Western nations, in return for friendship and aid, insist on the same political standards they require elsewhere in the world. Countries like Portugal and Spain, for example, were not considered worthy of membership in the European Community until they got rid of their dictators. Human rights, he says, are universal.

Such has been the approach of Ambassador Hempstone in Kenya. Among the most outspoken U.S. diplomats on the continent, Hempstone is a political appointee who has skipped the niceties of diplomacy and spent three years as an irritant, constantly pressing a kicking and screaming President Daniel T. arap Moi to allow political parties to form and to free imprisoned dissidents. In a recent example of the efficacy of this approach, the Scandinavian ambassadors in Zimbabwe, whose countries are among the largest aid donors there, let the government of Robert Mugabe know that the flow of aid would dry up if it did not release the handful of political prisoners it held. As if by magic, the prisoners were released.

Another sign of the new, less forgiving attitude by aid donors came in a 1989 World Bank report on Africa. Though not ignoring colonialism, weather and disease — the factors habitually invoked by African strongmen for their poor economic performance — these explanations were no longer emphasized. Instead the report homed in on harmful internal government policies like collectivization of agriculture and bloated bureaucracies. Many of these policies, points out American Enterprise Institute scholar Nicholas Eberstadt, had been tolerated or even subsidized by the bank in the past, despite its professed support for sound investment.

But pressure from abroad and conditional foreign aid can only be a catalyst, not a solution. In order to succeed, according to Chege, African leaders must admit something many of them still deny: Since the Cold War, their importance in the eyes of the West has dropped dramatically. The leaders of these states further have to face the unpleasant fact that most of their countries are in worse shape today than they were at the time of independence, a fact that was underscored recently in Zimbabwe, where many people now mutter about the good old days under Ian Smith, the leader of the white minority government forced out of power in 1980. Just a few months ago, Smith drove into the small town of Gweru in his old battered truck. A crowd of hundreds who had been waiting outside a supermarket to buy maize meal, the staple in their diet and unavailable for weeks, seized the leader, hoisted him and carried him through town shouting "We want Smith back, we want Smith back."

To escape from their position as aid mendicants, say analysts, a new generation of African leaders must make their peace with private foreign investment. Creating an attractive climate for such investors, one that allows them to earn profits commensurate with the risks they take, is the only sure way to modernize African economies. This will mean reducing corruption and red tape for starters. But more important, it will mean a change in some of the continent's most fundamental beliefs and attitudes. Until now, foreign investment has been regarded as part and parcel of the bad old days, inextricably entwined with colonialism.

Indeed, recognizing that Africa is so far behind, some economists have made so bold as to call for a "new colonialization" — meaning free commerce with foreign capitalists. John Robertson, chief economist with the First Merchant Bank of Zimbabwe Ltd., is an open advocate of this course. This new colonialism, he says, would be a benevolent one, beneficial to the host country and to foreign investors and without political masters.

Thus Robertson advocates rolling out the red carpet for investors, allowing them to settle with their families and put their ideas to work. Only in this fashion, he believes, can African economies quickly be modernized.

An important element in successful economic reform, according to Robertson, will be firm guarantees to the investors that they can take money out of the country. Distrust of the profit motive and fear of the flight of capital are invariably counterproductive. This showed in Zimbabwe after independence, when the government of Robert Mugabe immediately moved to limit dividends paid to shareholders, which caused many to disinvest in a hurry for fear of what might come next. The profits Mugabe targeted turned out to be tiny compared with the money those investors had made available by paying taxes, paying into medical health funds and pension funds on behalf of employees, and by being customers of other enterprises in the country, which also paid salaries, taxes and pensions. Besides, notes Robertson, if things go well, investors will want to plow some of their profits back in and that reinvested capital will stoke the fires of economic growth.

The kind of investment Robertson has in mind is exemplified by people like Volle Kirk, who runs a model farm of 12,500 acres in Zimbabwe, raising cattle and growing tobacco. The farm has its own butchery, shop, dairy and school for the children of the 200 families that live on Kirk's land. Having left his native Denmark in 1972, Kirk brought the newest ideas in agriculture and breeding techniques and put them to work. He has not received a cent in aid and carefully stays out of politics. "I don't care whether they bury people standing up, lying down or on the side," he says, "as long as they let me go about my business."

The question remains how long the present trend toward multiparty systems and more open economies is going to last and whether it will take root. A functioning democracy normally requires a substantial middle class, working institutions and reliable public officials, all things that are in short supply in Africa.

Apart from these universal prerequisites, there are some distinctly African obstacles to overcome. One is the tradition of tribal loyalties and enmities, a problem magnified by the colonial powers. The existing national borders on the continent often represent the cavalier decisions made by officers and explorers for the colonial powers over brandy and cigars. People might wake up one day to the announcement that they were now the privileged underlings of her majesty the queen of England, or the king of Belgium. As a result, ethnic groups are divided by many borders, creating all sorts of mischief.

According to Africa specialist Peter Duignan of the Hoover Institution, one of the reasons socialism swept Africa was its adaptability to age-old African ideas. For instance, a ruler who does not give preferential treatment to his own people will not be seen as an honest and upright man, only as a poor provider. And the huge bureaucracy of a socialist state was a convenient vehicle for a leader wishing to favor the members of his tribe or clan with jobs and perquisites. Furthermore, Duignan notes, the old system of communal farming and grazing rights on the continent represents a form of collectivism that tends to inhibit individual initiative.

All of these features are intrinsic to a system not geared to change. But they are also the sorts of difficulties best solved by the people themselves. And this is the opportunity, thanks to events far away, that may now be afforded them.

"In ancient Britain," notes Henriksen of the Hoover Institution, "the Romans built aqueducts and bridges, and when they left the whole place went to hell. Yet nobody today blames the Romans for the injustices they did the Brits. It is too long ago. I think Africans have got to get over that too, and start thinking about what comes next."

The Burden of Womanhood

Too often in the Third World, a female's life is hardly worth living

John Ward Anderson and Molly Moore

Washington Post Foreign Service

GANDHI NAGAR, India

When Rani returned home from the hospital cradling her newborn daughter, the men in the family slipped out of her mud hut while she and her mother-in-law mashed poisonous oleander seeds into a dollop of oil and forced it down the infant's throat. As soon as darkness fell, Rani crept into a nearby field and buried her baby girl in a shallow, unmarked grave next to a small stream.

"I never felt any sorrow," Rani, a farm laborer with a weather-beaten face, said through an interpreter. "There was a lot of bitterness in my heart toward the baby because the gods should have given me a son."

Each year hundreds and perhaps thousands of newborn girls in India are murdered by their mothers simply because they are female. Some women believe that sacrificing a daughter guarantees a son in the next pregnancy. In other cases, the family cannot afford the dowry that would eventually be demanded for a girl's marriage.

And for many mothers, sentencing a daughter to death is better than condemning her to life as a woman in the Third World, with cradle-to-grave discrimination, poverty, sickness and drudgery.

"In a culture that idolizes sons and dreads the birth of a daughter, to be born female comes perilously close to being born less than human," the Indian government conceded in a recent report by its Department of Women and Child Development.

While women in the United States and Europe—after decades of struggling for equal rights—often measure sex discrimination by pay scales and seats in corporate board rooms, women in the Third World gauge discrimination by mortality rates and poverty levels.

"Women are the most exploited among the oppressed," says Karuna Chanana Ahmed, a New Delhi anthropologist who has studied the role of women in developing countries. "I don't think it's even possible to eradicate discrimination, it's so deeply ingrained."

PHOTO BY JOHN WARD ANDERSON—THE WASHINGTON POST

Rani, 31, with Asha, 2, says she killed another daughter 3½ years ago. "I wanted to kill this child also . . . . Now I have killed, I still haven't had any sons."

From *The Washington Post National Weekly Edition,* March 22–28, 1993, pp. 6-7. © 1993 by The Washington Post. Reprinted by permission.

4. DEVELOPMENT: Nonindustrial Nations

This is the first in a series that will examine the lives of women in developing countries around the globe where culture, religion and the law often deprive women of basic human rights and sometimes relegate them to almost subhuman status. From South America to South Asia, women are often subjected to a lifetime of discrimination with little or no hope of relief.

As children, they are fed less, denied education and refused hospitalization. As teenagers, many are forced into marriage, sometimes bought and sold like animals for prostitution and slave labor. As wives and mothers, they are often treated little better than farmhands and baby machines. Should they outlive their husbands, they frequently are denied inheritance, banished from their homes and forced to live as beggars on the streets.

The scores of women interviewed for this series—from destitute villagers in Brazil and Bangladesh, to young professionals in Cairo, to factory workers in China—blamed centuries-old cultural and religious traditions for institutionalizing and giving legitimacy to gender discrimination.

Although, the forms of discrimination vary tremendously among regions, ethnic groups and age levels in the developing world, Shahla Zia, an attorney and women's activist in Islamabad, Pakistan, says there is a theme: "Overall, there is a social and cultural attitude where women are inferior—and discrimination tends to start at birth."

In many countries, a woman's greatest challenge is an elemental one: simply surviving through a normal life cycle. In South Asia and China, the perils begin at birth, with the threat of infanticide.

Like many rural Indian women, Rani, now 31, believed that killing her daughter 3½ years ago would guarantee that her next baby would be a boy. Instead, she had another daughter.

"I wanted to kill this child also," she says, brushing strands of hair from the face of the 2-year-old girl she named Asha, or Hope. "But my husband got scared because all these social workers came and said, 'Give us the child.'" Ultimately, Rani was allowed to keep her. She pauses. "Now I have killed, and I still haven't had any sons."

Amravati, who lives in a village near Rani in the Indian state of Tamil Nadu, says she killed two of her own day-old daughters by pouring scalding chicken soup down their throats, one of the most widely practiced methods of infanticide in southern India. She showed where she buried their bodies—under piles of cow dung in the tiny courtyard of her home.

"My mother-in-law and father-in-law are bedridden," says Amravati, who has two living daughters. "I have no land and no salary, and my husband met with an accident and can't work. Of course it was the right decision. I need

a boy. Even though I have to buy clothes and food for a son, he will grow on his own and take care of himself. I don't have to buy him jewelry or give him a 10,000-rupee [$350] dowry."

Sociologists and government officials began documenting sporadic examples of female infanticide in India about 10 years ago. The practice of killing newborn girls is largely a rural phenomenon in India; although its extent has not been documented, one indication came in a recent survey by the Community Services Guild of Madras, a city in Tamil Nadu. Of the 1,250 women questioned, the survey concluded that more than half had killed baby daughters.

In urban areas, easier access to modern medical technology enables women to act before birth. Through amniocentesis, women can learn the sex of a fetus and undergo sex-selective abortions. At one clinic in Bombay, of 8,000 abortions performed after amniocentesis, 7,999 were of female fetuses, according to a recent report by the Indian government. To be sure, female infanticide and sex-selective abortion are not unique to India. Social workers in other South Asian states believe that some communities also condone the practice. In China, one province has had so many cases of female infanticide that a half-million bachelors cannot find wives because they outnumber women their age by 10 to 1, according to the official New China News Agency.

The root problems, according to village women, sociologists and other experts, are cultural and economic. In India, a young woman is regarded as a temporary member of her natural family and a drain on its wealth. Her parents are considered caretakers whose main responsibility is to deliver a chaste daughter, along with a sizable dowry, to her husband's family.

"They say bringing up a girl is like watering a neighbor's plant," says R. Venkatachalam, director of the Community Services Guild of Madras. "From birth to death, the expenditure is there." The dowry, he says, often wipes out a family's life savings but is necessary to arrange a proper marriage and maintain the honor of the bride's family.

After giving birth to a daughter, village women "immediately start thinking, 'Do we have the money to support her through life?' and if they don't, they kill her," according to Vasanthai, 20, the mother of an 18-month-old girl and a resident of the village where Rani lives. "You definitely do it after two or three daughters. Why would you want more?"

Few activists or government officials in India see female infanticide as a law-and-order issue, viewing it instead as a social problem that should be eradicated through better education, family planning and job programs. Police officials say few cases are reported and witnesses seldom cooperate.

"There are more pressing issues," says a top police official in Madras. "Very few cases come to our attention. Very few people care."

Surviving childbirth is itself an achievement in South Asia for both mother and baby. One of every 18 women dies of a pregnancy-related cause, and more than one of every 10 babies dies during delivery.

For female children, the survival odds are even worse. Almost one in every five girls born in Nepal and Bangladesh dies before age 5. In India, about one-fourth of the 12 million girls born each year die by age 15.

The high death rates are not coincidental. Across the developing world, female children are fed less, pulled out of school earlier, forced into hard labor sooner and given less medical care than boys. According to numerous studies, girls are handicapped not only by the perception that they are temporary members of a family, but also by the belief that males are the chief breadwinners and therefore more deserving of scarce resources.

Boys are generally breast-fed longer. In many cultures, women and girls eat leftovers after the men and boys have finished their meals. According to a joint report by the United Nations Children's Fund and the government of Pakistan, some tribal groups do not feed high-protein foods such as eggs and meat to girls because of the fear it will lead to early puberty.

Women are often hospitalized only when they have reached a critical stage of illness, which is one reason so many mothers die in childbirth. Female children, on the other hand, often are not hospitalized at all. A 1990 study of patient records at Islamabad Children's Hospital in Pakistan found that 71 percent of the babies admitted under age 2 were boys. For all age groups, twice as many boys as girls were admitted to the hospital's surgery, pediatric intensive care and diarrhea units.

Mary Okumu, an official with the African Medical and Research Foundation in Nairobi, says that when a worker in drought-ravaged northern Kenya asked why only boys were lined up at a clinic, the worker was told that in times of drought, many families let their daughters die.

"Nobody will even take them to a clinic," Okumu says. "They prefer the boy to survive."

For most girls, however, the biggest barrier—and the one that locks generations of women into a cycle of discrimination—is lack of education.

Across the developing world, girls are withdrawn from school years before boys so they can remain at home and lug water, work the fields, raise younger siblings and help with other domestic chores. By the time girls are 10 or 12 years old, they may put in as much as an eight-hour work day, studies show. One survey found that a young girl in rural India spends 30 percent of her waking hours doing household work, 29 percent gathering fuel and 20 percent fetching water.

Statistics from Pakistan demonstrate the low priority given to female education: Only one-third of the country's schools—which are sexually segregated—are for women, and one-third of those have no building. Almost 90 percent of the women over age 25 are illiterate. In the predominantly rural state of Baluchistan, less than 2 percent of women can read and write.

In Islamic countries such as Pakistan and Bangladesh, religious concern about interaction with males adds further restrictions to females' mobility. Frequently, girls are taken out of school when they reach puberty to limit their contact with males—though there exists a strong impetus for early marriages. In Bangladesh, according to the United Nations, 73 percent of girls are married by age 15, and 21 percent have had at least one child.

Across South Asia, arranged marriages are the norm and can sometimes be the most demeaning rite of passage a woman endures. Two types are common—bride wealth, in which the bride's family essentially gives her to the highest bidder, and dowry, in which the bride's family pays exorbitant amounts to the husband's family.

In India, many men resort to killing their wives—often by setting them afire—if they are unhappy with the dowry. According to the country's Ministry of Human Resource Development, there were 5,157 dowry murders in 1991—one every hour and 42 minutes.

After being bartered off to a new family, with little education, limited access to health care and no knowledge of birth control, young brides soon become young mothers. A woman's adulthood is often spent in a near constant state of pregnancy, hoping for sons.

According to a 1988 report by India's Department of Women and Child Development: "The Indian woman on an average has eight to nine pregnancies, resulting in a little over six live births, of which four or five survive. She is estimated to spend 80 percent of her reproductive years in pregnancy and lactation." Because of poor nutrition and a hard workload, she puts on about nine pounds during pregnancy, compared with 22 pounds for a typical pregnant woman in a developed country.

A recent study of the small Himalayan village of Bemru by the New Delhi-based Center for Science and the Environment found that "birth in most cases takes place in the cattle shed," where villagers believe that holy cows protect the mother and newborn from evil spirits. Childbirth is considered unclean, and the mother and their newborn are treated as "untouchables" for about two weeks after delivery.

"It does not matter if the woman is young, old or pregnant, she has no rest, Sunday or otherwise," the study said, noting that women in the village did 59 percent of the work, often laboring 14 hours a day and lugging loads 1 1/2 times their body weight. "After two or three . . . pregnancies, their stamina gives up, they get weaker, and by the late thirties are spent out, old and tired, and soon die."

Studies show that in developing countries, women in remote areas can spend more than two hours a day carrying water for cooking, drinking, cleaning and bathing, and in some rural areas they spend the equivalent of more than 200 days a year gathering firewood. That presents an additional hazard: The International Labor Organization found that women using wood fuels in India inhaled carcinogenic pollutants that are the equivalent of smoking 20 packs of cigarettes a day.

Because of laws relegating them to a secondary status, women have few outlets for relaxation or recreation. In many Islamic countries, they are not allowed to drive cars, and their appearance in public is so restricted that they are banned from such recreational and athletic activities as swimming and gymnastics.

In Kenya and Tanzania, laws prohibit women from owning houses. In Pakistan, a daughter legally is entitled to half the inheritance a son gets when their parents die. In some criminal cases, testimony by women is legally given half the weight of a man's testimony, and compensation for the wrongful death of a woman is half that for the wrongful death of a man.

After a lifetime of brutal physical labor, multiple births, discrimination and sheer tedium, what should be a woman's golden years often hold the worst indignities. In India, a woman's identity is so intertwined and subservient to her husband's that if she outlives him, her years as a widow are spent as a virtual nonentity. In previous generations, many women were tied to their husband's funeral pyres and burned to death, a practice called *suttee* that now rarely occurs.

Today, some widows voluntarily shave their heads and withdraw from society, but more often a spartan lifestyle is forced upon them by families and a society that place no value on old, single women. Widowhood carries such a stigma that remarriage is extremely rare, even for women who are widowed as teenagers.

In some areas of the country, women are forced to marry their dead husband's brother to ensure that any property remains in the family. Often they cannot wear jewelry or a *bindi*—the beauty spot women put on their foreheads—or they must shave their heads and wear a white sari. Frequently, they cannot eat fish or meat, garlic or onions.

"The life of a widow is miserable," says Aparna Basu, general secretary of the All India Women's Conference, citing a recent study showing that more than half the women in India age 60 and older are widows, and their mortality rate is three times higher than that of married women of the same age.

In South Asia, women have few property or inheritance rights, and a husband's belongings usually go to sons and occasionally daughters. A widow must rely on the largess of her children, who often cast their mothers on the streets.

Thousands of destitute Indian widows make the pilgrimage to Vrindaban, a town on the outskirts of Agra where they hope to achieve salvation by praying to the god Krishna. About 1,500 widows show up each day at the Shri Bhagwan prayer house, where in exchange for singing "Hare Rama, Hare Krishna" for eight hours, they are given a handful of rice and beans and 1.5 rupees, or about 5 cents.

Some widows claim that when they stop singing, they are poked with sticks by monitors, and social workers allege that younger widows have been sexually assaulted by temple custodians and priests.

On a street there, an elderly woman with a *tilak* on her forehead—white chalk lines signifying that she is a devout Hindu widow—waves a begging cup at passing strangers.

"I have nobody," says Paddo Chowdhury, 65, who became a widow at 18 and has been in Vrindaban for 30 years. "I sit here, shed my tears and get enough food one way or another."

THIRD-WORLD DEBT
The disaster that didn't happen

Ten years ago Mexico announced to the world that it could no longer service its external debt. Similar news from Brazil and Argentina came soon afterwards. The Latin American debt crisis had begun. William R. Rhodes, **vice chairman of Citibank, is the commercial banker most closely identified with managing the crisis. He looks back at the evolution of events and the lessons to be learned.**

THE philosopher William James once said that "great emergencies and crises show us how much greater our vital resources are than we had supposed". As we now look back on the events of the past ten years, I would point to three aspects of the third-world debt crisis that bear that out.

First, despite all the gloom and doom that surrounded the early stages of the crisis, the international financial system did not collapse. I don't think I have ever been in a more collectively pessimistic setting than the IMF/World Bank meetings of September 1982 in Toronto. The standing joke was that the efforts to contain the crisis amounted to no more than "rearranging the deck chairs on the Titanic".

Such gallows humour was not unfounded. Among the money-centre banks in New York, for example, the exposure to troubled debtor countries exceeded their capital. The real threat was the possibility that a major bank would encounter funding problems in the markets, which in turn could have set off a chain reaction that would have severely shaken the international financial system. It did not happen.

The banks were given the time to raise capital and increase reserves, and the debtor countries began reforming their economies.

Second, in the early years, all the major parties—the commercial banks, the debtor countries, the creditor countries and the international financial institutions—temporarily put aside their own interests and worked for a collective purpose. If greed drives people apart, fear brings them together. That was certainly the case then. It was perhaps best exemplified by the then leader of Mexico's economic team, Jesus Silva Herzog, and his chief debt negotiator, Angel Gurria. Both believed that the best interests of all could be achieved by co-operation, rather than confrontation.

Third, the long-term response to the crisis did more than just allow the major countries of Latin America to cope with their debt. It also provided time to put in place the structural adjustments such as trade liberalisation, privatisation, deregulation and tax reform that have now brought both growth and investment to several countries in the region. Success was due in large part to political leaders who rose to the occasion,

as in the reform programme implemented by the economic team in Mexico, under presidents Miguel de la Madrid and Carlos Salinas, and the programme for opening the economy enacted by two successive Chilean governments. Chile's reform has succeeded to the point where one of the leading American credit-rating agencies recently gave the country an investment-grade rating, much improving its standing in international capital markets. Argentina, under the leadership of President Carlos Menem and his finance minister, Domingo Cavallo, is containing inflation, returning to growth and recovering access to capital markets.

A vacation cut short

I was on holiday in 1982 when I was called back to New York with the ominous warning that "the Mexicans are in trouble". At a meeting on August 20th at the New York Federal Reserve Bank, the commercial banks learned that Mexico could no longer service its debt. I was struck by two overriding thoughts. First, we had to assume that the crisis could be managed, and, to contain any panic, we had to convince the world's financial community that we could manage it. Second, we were entering entirely uncharted waters. True, there had been earlier debt crises, and several countries were in various stages of restructuring their debt. But with the announcement by Mexico and expectations of more bad news from Argentina and Brazil, we had no formula for dealing with a crisis of this size.

With hindsight, that may have been a blessing in disguise. Not being bound by any conventional wisdom, we were able to respond to the crisis in a much more flexible and focused manner.

One of the principles that came to the fore in the early days is still very applicable: the need for a case-by-case approach. While that is today taken for granted, some bankers and academics at the time were pressing for "global solutions"—a kind of "one-size-fits-all" answer to the debt problem. A look

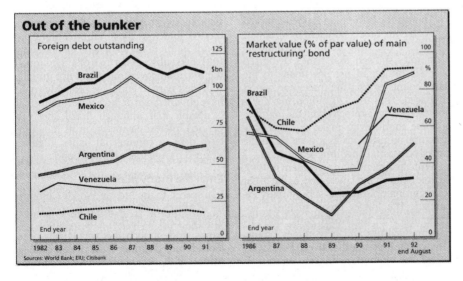

Out of the bunker

Foreign debt outstanding

Brazil
Mexico
Argentina
Venezuela
Chile

End year

1982 83 84 85 86 87 88 89 90 91
Sources: World Bank; EIU; Citibank

Market value (% of par value) of main 'restructuring' bond

Brazil
Chile
Venezuela
Mexico
Argentina

End year

1986 87 88 89 90 91 92
end August

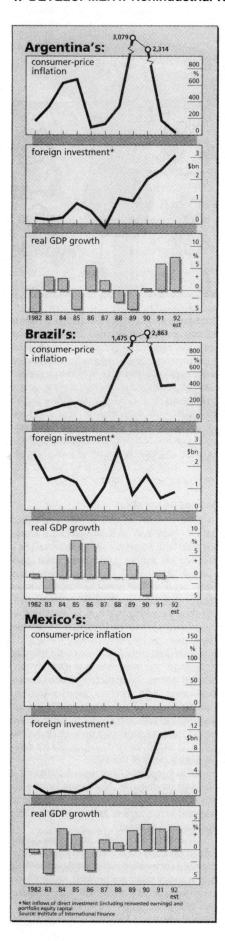

Argentina's:
consumer-price inflation

foreign investment*

real GDP growth

Brazil's:
consumer-price inflation

foreign investment*

real GDP growth

Mexico's:
consumer-price inflation

foreign investment*

real GDP growth

*Net inflows of direct investment (including reinvested earnings) and portfolio equity capital
Source: Institute of International Finance

at the distinctive varieties of the Brady plan employed over the past three years in Mexico, Venezuela, Argentina, Brazil, the Philippines and Uruguay shows how ill-suited a generic response would have been.

The steps to safety

The crisis passed through several phases. In the first, commercial banks assembled short-term emergency financing packages whereby debt due to mature over the next two years or so was stretched out over five to seven years. In addition, new money was committed to meet borrowers' immediate cash needs, as in the 1982-83 restructurings of Mexico, Argentina and Brazil.

The second phase was aimed at buying time; time for the countries to implement reforms and for the banks to build capital and reserves. At the heart of this was the agreement that the IMF would monitor a country's economic performance over periods substantially longer than it normally does under stand-by arrangements, and that the resultant information would be made available to the commercial banks.

During this phase, in 1984, Mexico and its creditor banks agreed on the first multi-year restructuring agreement. The Mexican restructuring also featured the first use of debt/equity swaps, a concept that the Chileans took even greater advantage of in a deal negotiated the following year.

The third phase began in October 1985, at the IMF/World Bank meeting in Seoul, when America's Treasury secretary, James Baker, announced his plan for world debt. It emphasised growth-oriented structural economic reforms in debtor countries. In return for these reforms, commercial banks were asked to continue to make new loans available—Mr Baker suggested $20 billion over three years. At the same time, the World Bank was brought into the fray; until then, the debt strategy had been dominated principally by the IMF. This phase also saw Mexico and Chile begin to emphasise structural adjustments in the areas of trade and privatisation.

Though the Baker plan is often attacked for not having raised sufficient new money, a study by the Institute for International Economics showed that banks disbursed over $13 billion in net new loans to the Baker countries over the three-year period envisaged. That the $20 billion mark was not reached says as much about the inability of some countries to make the necessary structural adjustments as it does about the banks' occasional unwillingness to lend.

With the Argentinian agreement in 1987, the role of the market increased, as the list of restructuring options was substantially expanded. The longer menu included co-financings with the World Bank, trade financing facilities and new-money bonds. This was the first time that an exit bond with a fixed, below-market interest rate was of-

fered in an attempt to stimulate debt-reduction. Though this Argentinian bond was a failure, it helped set the stage for the next phase, voluntary debt-reduction.

In the same year Citibank, motivated by Brazil's moratorium on its medium- and long-term commercial-bank debt, raised its reserves (provisions) against doubtful third-world debts. Many American, British and Canadian banks followed suit. These higher reserves gave banks greater flexibility to manage their loan portfolios, through such debt-reduction options as exchanges of debt for equity and cash buy-backs of debt.

1987 also saw the deal between J.P. Morgan and Mexico, which attempted debt-reduction by offering banks the chance to exchange loans for bonds, at a discount, with the principal collateralised by United States Treasury zero-coupon bonds. This did not produce the results that some had hoped for, but it did become one of the bases of the Brady plan, named after Nicholas Brady, who succeeded Mr Baker at the Treasury.

In September 1988 Brazil signed a medium-term financing package to bring it out of its moratorium. Although the Brazilians never fully implemented this agreement, it demonstrated for the first time that new money and voluntary reduction of existing debt were not mutually exclusive. Both the banks and the debtor countries were now looking to voluntary debt-reduction as a big part of these financial packages. The package itself contained $5.2 billion of new money. As with Argentina, the original debt was exchanged at par for fixed-rate bonds paying below-market rates. Unlike the comparable Argentinian bonds, these ones succeeded; they were the forerunner of the par bonds in the Brady-plan agreements. Some 100 banks subscribed a total of $1.1 billion. If the Brazilian government had not initially restricted participation, we probably could have obtained two or three times as much. It is notable that, although Brazil later suspended interest payments on its medium-term debt to commercial banks, it never stopped paying interest on its bonds.

Enter the Brady plan

In a speech to the Bretton Woods Committee in March 1989, Mr Brady proposed voluntary debt-reduction by commercial banks, and—though this was largely overlooked—urged further flows of new money. As part of the Brady plan, the IMF and the World Bank agreed to offer resources to back debt-reduction programmes for countries with viable economic programmes.

All this set the stage for the Mexican debt package that was signed in February 1990. It included most of the debt-reduction techniques used earlier, such as debt/equity conversions, interest-rate reductions and principal-reduction bonds. It also incorporated many of the new-money techniques, including bonds, trade finance and on-

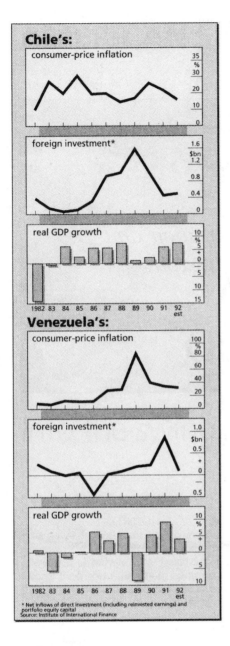

Chile's:
consumer-price inflation
foreign investment*
real GDP growth

Venezuela's:
consumer-price inflation
foreign investment*
real GDP growth

* Net inflows of direct investment (including reinvested earnings) and portfolio equity capital
Source: Institute of International Finance

mercial bank debt of Venezuela, Uruguay, the Philippines, Costa Rica and Nigeria. It also forms the basis of the debt agreements with Brazil and Argentina.

Back to normal?

Some people have been suggesting that the debt crisis in Latin America will be wrapped up almost exactly ten years after it started. Certainly there has been a fair amount of progress. Signing of the Argentinian package is expected some time in October, and, despite the political volatility in Brazil, the Brazilian senate is still expected to approve that country's restructuring by the end of September, after which it can be sent to its creditor banks. The completion of these two agreements will signal the phase-out of the debt saga among the major economies of Latin America. Although it is outside the region, the signing of a Brady-style agreement by the Philippines this July was another very positive sign.

There are still Latin American countries, however, that have yet to put the problem behind them, notably Peru and Ecuador (though Ecuador's new government has already announced a new economic-reform plan and initiated discussions with individual members of the bank steering committee). And, beyond Latin America, several countries in Africa and in Central and Eastern Europe need to address both their debt problems and the issue of structural reform.

Compelling motivation

In any circumstances there are good reasons for a country to regularise relations with its international creditors. Foremost is the need for access to capital markets, access that is severely limited for countries not meeting their external obligations.

In today's world there are still more compelling reasons. A rough estimate of the amount of capital needed for privatisations in Latin America, South-East Asia and Central and Eastern Europe is $500 billion, and as much again for the former Soviet Union. The resulting $1 trillion is all the more striking when one considers that privatisations in the developing world are financed, in large part, through just one type of capital, risk capital. At the same time, both developed and developing economies also have a broad range of other capital needs, adding to the overall demand. Meanwhile, two of the largest providers of risk capital in the past decade, Japan and Germany, have their hands full in their own backyards.

Given the strong demand for capital around the world, the countries best positioned to get it are those that have become genuinely competitive and creditworthy. It was no coincidence that the pace of the Mexican privatisation programme was accelerated after President Salinas spent a state visit to Europe listening to senior officials there talk about the direct-investment opportunities in Central and Eastern Europe. That same motivation also accounted, in part, for his decision to initiate discussions on the inclusion of Mexico in the North American Free Trade Agreement.

Lessons for reformers

Just as great crises reveal the full extent of our resources, they also hold important lessons. A close look at the experiences of Mexico, Chile and, to a great extent, Argentina shows that all three met the following criteria in successfully implementing their respective economic-reform programmes.

• A head of state who demonstrates political will and strong leadership.

• A viable, coherent and comprehensive economic plan that is implemented in a proper sequence.

• A motivated and competent economic team, working together, not in rivalry.

• Belief in the plan from the head of government, his cabinet and other senior officials involved, who must have the conviction to stay the course.

• An integrated programme to sell the plan to all levels of society through the media. The plan is often difficult to implement, but people will accept it, if they see that there is light at the end of the tunnel.

• Continuity in implementation of reform from one administration to the next.

These criteria are notable for two reasons. They are drawn from the actual experiences of the countries involved. Second, they are applicable not only to the countries of Latin America, but elsewhere in the developing world as well. Adherence to them will help greatly, in any country, in implementing economic reform.

Only time, though, will tell if the trend toward reform in Latin America is permanent. I am confident that much of the progress made so far will stick, in most countries. But reform can be fragile. The cost of economic adjustment should never be underestimated, and there is still a great need to convince all levels of society that opening up the economy will bring with it the long-term benefits of sustained growth.

lending facilities. In addition, the package introduced two new techniques: collateralised interest for debt-reduction bonds, and value-recovery, which allowed the banks to receive additional payments if the price of Mexico's oil exceeded an agreed level. At the same time as the Salinas administration was negotiating this agreement with the commercial banks, it was also accelerating the pace of structural reform.

Since the Mexican agreement, the Brady plan has been used to restructure the com-

*An open letter to the G-7 leaders—the
Presidents and Prime Ministers of the United
States, Japan, Germany, France, Britain,
Italy, and Canada—from a leading Japanese
industrialist, the chairman of Sony*

TOWARD A NEW WORLD ECONOMIC ORDER

AKIO MORITA

GENTLEMEN:

You will soon assemble in Tokyo for the next G-7 summit. You will be asked to consider many important questions. I would like to add one more to your agenda—one that I believe has an overarching significance to your task as stewards of the world economy.

I am a businessman, not a statesman or a politician. However, I know that all of you share a belief in the new importance of business and economics as dynamic forces underpinning the peace and prosperity of our world.

So perhaps you will be willing to listen to an ordinary businessman whose company does a great deal of business in each of your countries, and hear out my argument for how all of us in North America, Europe, and Japan might be able to work together to remove barriers to the free-market system and make it more open, more inclusive, and freer than it is at present.

The proposal I ask you to consider is that we begin to seek the ways and means of lowering *all* economic barriers between North America, Europe, and Japan—trade, investment, legal, and so forth—in order to begin creating the nucleus of a new world economic order that would include a harmonized world business system with agreed rules and procedures that transcend national boundaries. You, as political leaders, have the power to take the steps necessary to make the increasing de facto globalization of business the most creative, positive, and beneficial force it can be, rather than the source of new

From *The Atlantic*, June 1993, pp. 88-90, 92-94, 96-98. © 1993 by Akio Morita, Chairman of the Board, Sony Corporation. Reprinted by permission.

international conflict. I believe that if we can go down this road together, we will also establish the basis for a much more equitable sharing of the burdens, responsibilities, and costs of international leadership.

Perhaps you will find it surprising that such a proposal comes from a Japanese businessman. Many people are skeptical about Japan's commitment to free and fair trade. Let me assure you that I recognize the reasons why outsiders consider Japan "unfair." My proposal to you is closely connected to proposals I am making inside Japan that action be taken to break down the walls of what often appears to outsiders to be a "Fortress Japan." It is clear that Japan has much work to do to open its domestic market and to help create a favorable climate for harmonization of the global trading system. Japan cannot and should not deny that reality.

During the Gulf War, U.S. President George Bush spoke about the need for a "new world order." What he meant by that was a new political and military-security order to deal with the challenges of the post–Cold War period. Certainly we need that. But the world also needs a new economic order, focused on international economic security.

Some will say the program outlined here is overly idealistic. But new appeals for greater global cooperation almost always sound too idealistic at first, with critics rushing to point out the likelihood that they will founder on contradictory national politics, reflecting contradictory national interests.

As we are increasingly discovering, however, all our nations have a "national interest" in doing what is best for the global economic interest. My proposal is offered in that spirit.

At the Edge of the Twenty-first Century

JUST AS WE HAVE ARRIVED IN SIGHT OF THE TWENTY-first century, the leading economies of the world find themselves at a startling and unexpected juncture. The Cold War is over. What used to be called the Soviet threat is disappearing, and the triumph of democratic values and free-market economics is taking place worldwide.

And yet . . . Amid what might have been considered near-utopian conditions just a generation ago, we face new and complex challenges that threaten the peace and prosperity we have achieved. Throughout the "Triad" (the developed economies of North America, Europe, and Japan) recent economic downturns have revealed troubling long-term structural questions. Some big corporations have lost their way. Political systems are ossified and corroded, unable to deal with new challenges and suffering declining popular trust. Meanwhile, the extreme nationalisms that are splintering many countries and societies with such tragic results threaten to influence the world to move in a more nationalist direction.

We all pay lip service to the notion that we live in an increasingly interdependent global village. Yet we seem willing to forget about interdependence when it comes to problems that require national governments to emphasize the "give" part of the give-and-take equation. We all talk about how we favor global growth and ever-freer world trade, and yet we rarely comment on what we are willing to give up to achieve those aims.

All of us are also paying for the mistakes of the past decade. As it turned out, the 1980s were a bit like Alice's descent into Wonderland. The border between economic reality and fantasy was blurred. To differing degrees this is true of the "Roaring Eighties" of America, the wave of "Europhoria" that swept the European Community, and the "Bubble Economy" in Japan.

The 1990s have emerged as a decade of sober awakenings. Economic growth rates for the industrialized world as a whole have plunged from an average of four percent in 1988 to less than two percent in 1992. The need to pay off excessive debts taken on in the past, the downsizing of large corporations, the demographics of graying populations, the shift away from manufacturing economies to service businesses in which productivity gains are often elusive, and other factors combine to suggest that average annual economic growth in the Triad may continue to hover in the two percent range over the next few years— unless creative action is taken to nurture and stimulate sustainable growth.

True, we are witnessing some cyclic economic recovery in the United States. Europe and Japan will probably follow. But many indicators suggest that while we will have growth, it may be slow. We face not just a cyclic challenge but a systemic one that requires an overall rethinking of some long-held views on global business.

Slow growth constrains the financial resources of governments and the investment plans of business. When business lacks confidence, it is hard to invest for the sake of long-term objectives. Under such conditions it is doubly hard to find the investment capital needed to tackle our huge responsibilities to help less developed countries and the emerging market economies trying to rebuild after decades in communist straitjackets.

In truth, many of the biggest security challenges are no longer primarily military in nature. The fact that the total output of Eastern Europe and the former Soviet Union has shrunk by a third since the fall of the Berlin Wall is a dangerous early-warning signal of possible threats to democracy and stability. Today's international security requires economic peacekeeping as well as traditional military peacekeeping. But to do our job as economic peacekeepers—to be able to provide the kind of aid that Russia and other countries emerging from communism need over the long term—we must have both the political will and a positive economic climate in our own countries to back it up.

The atmosphere of slow growth also highlights the pre-

The right prescription for restarting global growth on

a new, sustainable basis must involve an intensi-

fication of efforts to harmonize the inner workings of

major economies and business systems.

carious balance between the economic and political clocks of history. The inspiring drive toward a single Europe slowed down significantly in the past year. Superficially, the cause appeared to be public fear of ceding too much power to a supranational European Community. But underneath, public concerns were fueled by poor economic performance in key countries. Similarly, the North American Free Trade Agreement (NAFTA) has faced a series of new obstacles even after having been agreed to and signed by the leaders of Canada, the United States, and Mexico. In U.S.-Japan relations both sides have found it more convenient to focus on their own domestic problems than to consider what kind of new, cooperative initiatives befit two such interdependent economies. And the General Agreement on Tariffs and Trade (GATT), the world's most far-reaching multilateral economic institution, has experienced a wrenching, traumatic period of conflict as some small but powerful national lobbies have managed to stall progress on a new framework for freer global trade.

This bit of recent history underscores the fact that we cannot count on market mechanisms alone to create a new economic order. We also need political vision, organized discussion and debate, and new institutions that are capable of pressing on toward the goal of a borderless economy even in difficult times and even when dealing with difficult questions about how to allocate benefits and sacrifices.

Although structured political efforts to enhance cross-border free trade and establish workable global economic rules have encountered difficulty of late, we must not abandon them. In my view, the right prescription for restarting global growth on a new, sustainable basis, as well as for coping with the new challenges of our times, must involve an intensification of efforts to harmonize the inner workings of major economies and business systems.

Economic Harmonization

THE FREE-MARKET SYSTEM HAS CLEARLY SHOWN itself to be superior to the failed system of centrally planned socialism. About this there can be no doubt. However, the United States, the European Community, and Japan practice somewhat different types of free-market capitalism, and each has its own strengths and weaknesses. What is needed to cope with new challenges is not a replacement of the free-market system but a strengthening of it through the harmonization of business practices.

By making the whole of the developed world essentially one big market, the harmonization of major economies can provide the stimulus needed to emerge from what otherwise might be a prolonged period of slow growth worldwide. This is particularly true for the increasingly technology-intensive manufacturing sector, which requires global markets to justify its huge investment needs. A thriving high-tech manufacturing sector, generating ever newer and more innovative products, is the key to a growing positive spiral of market demand and employment. Harmonization is also crucial to the expansion of the advanced, innovative service sector of the economy, where few international rules now exist. Financial, information, and telecommunications services, for example, have inherently global markets, yet face a myriad of conflicting regulations and standards in different countries which prevent them from growing efficiently on a global scale.

All business people desire a level playing field on which to compete. But it has become clear that a level playing field cannot be declared into existence, even when tariffs are removed and even when certain of the obvious non-tariff barriers disappear. The history of each country and region generates political, social, economic, and cultural factors that result in a business environment unique to that nation or region. This in turn gives rise to a variety of competitive factors unique to each market, any of which can be seen as nontariff barriers by those seeking to enter from outside.

I believe that, as the engines of the world economy, the G-7 countries should commit themselves to the goal of eliminating the barriers that now stud the playing field of global competition. Over time we should seek to create an environment in which the movement of goods, services, capital, technology, and people throughout North America, Europe, and Japan is truly free and unfettered. In such an environment international businesses could minimize waste and bureaucracy. Companies could focus their competition on the truly creative areas of enterprise which yield innovation, new technology, and improved service. When business is allowed to focus on these creative areas, quantum leaps in productivity, output, and quality of life are possible.

To achieve meaningful harmonization, a variety of government regulations, along with business practices on issues from trade and cross-border investment to patents, currency rates, financial and securities regulation, tax treatment, and environmental protection, would need to be brought into rough parity. Practical agreements on particularly controversial issues—dumping, transfer pricing, and local content, to name but a few—should be developed. Multilateral institutions capable of enforcing such agreements would need to be established.

As a result, markets would become open to the full force and benefit of global competition—not just in theory but in practice. Japanese rice farmers would not be able to keep their market closed, nor would Japanese *keiretsu* be allowed to exclude foreign suppliers from their production systems or imported goods from retail shelves. But neither would Americans be able to deal with perceived unfairness through methods such as unilateral tariffs. And Europeans would not be able to sit in unilateral judgment on what is or isn't a "European" car.

The European Example

"HARMONIZATION" APPEARED AS AN IMPORTANT international economic concept several years ago, during the European Community's debate over how best to create a single internal market among its twelve member nations. It arose as an idea distinct from standardization. Even in Europe, where geography and history closely link many countries, it was understood that trying to standardize varying business practices would be impossible. But "harmonizing" them—bringing key laws, rules, and procedures into general conformity—was deemed possible.

After an exhaustive period of discussion and debate the EC eventually agreed on nearly 300 specific areas of harmonized rules, on issues from baking to banking. Every country has made concessions; every interest group has given up something it wanted in order to keep the process going and to achieve the broader benefits. Through this process of cross-border give and take, the exit path from the conflicts bred by the era of nationalism has begun to take shape.

Today, of course, there are still those who focus on the difficulties the European Community faces in achieving greater unification. I believe, however, that history will eventually show that the Europeans are on the right road in creating an economy without national borders. Indeed, buried amid news about the EC's well-publicized difficulties is the bigger story: supranational institutions have been created to govern many aspects of European business and economic affairs—and these institutions are actually working rather well.

The EC experience with harmonization is the most advanced. But a similar process is taking place in North America, through NAFTA. In East Asia discussions about regional coordination are also ongoing at a variety of levels. While there has been concern that these regional agreements could turn into closed "fortresses" and mutually exclusive economic blocs, I take an alternative view. Particularly with regard to the EC and NAFTA, countries have already made many sacrifices and accepted certain limits on their national sovereignty. They have transcended their national boundaries and taken concrete measures to open up their markets.

What I am proposing is not at all in opposition to these regional agreements. Rather, it is the next logical step—the interregional harmonization of these three dynamic parts of the world, using groundwork already laid by the existing agreements.

Beginning the Process

TO SOME ECONOMISTS, THE WORD "HARMONIZAtion" may connote simply a lot of bureaucratic intervention in the private sector. As that is certainly not my goal, it might be useful to look more specifically at the kinds of efforts I have in mind when thinking about the harmonization of the global business infrastructure.

Market access. All the major economies have taken important steps to reduce tariffs and to liberalize and deregulate their marketplaces over the past generation. Even in Japan, often criticized by foreigners as "closed," huge strides forward have been taken, so that Japan now imports more than $230 billion worth of goods annually from around the world—up more than 80 percent since 1985—including more than $50 billion from the United States.

Yet market access remains a highly contentious issue. Whether a market is open or closed, and whether foreign companies are treated fairly or unfairly, is often in the eyes of the beholder. This is especially true when it comes to product health-and-safety standards, differing rules on intellectual property, and differing systems of distribution. In addition to clearer rules and greater multilateral consultation, couldn't we benefit from the establishment of a supranational arbitration panel that would investigate quickly and independently complaints about practices in specific industries, and propose specific remedies to facilitate foreign entry in areas found to be unfair or insufficiently open?

In all our countries government has emerged as a very large sector of the economy. Yet most government procurement policies provide the last bastion of a protected market for "national champion" and domestic companies. From supercomputers to automobiles, there is a strong tendency for governments to buy domestic, rather than using government's powerful platform to encourage buying global. Can't we start with this field, which government controls directly, and make a sweeping change quickly?

Anti-dumping laws. Because of the nature of the Japanese production system, companies can accept razor-thin profit margins that Western competitors find intolerable. This fact alone often leads to charges of dumping against Japanese companies when, technically speaking, they are not actually engaging in dumping. Structural, legal, and accounting differences between the Japanese business system and others add to the confusion. Currency fluctuations distort even the most objective efforts to establish whether or not a company is selling a certain export product below its domestic price or cost of manufacture. The inefficiency of the Japanese retailing system—which ends up charging *Japanese* consumers unfairly high prices for many goods—further complicates matters.

I am not arguing that no Japanese company has ever been guilty of dumping. On the whole, though, I believe that the culprit here is not any Japanese desire to undermine the competitive framework in other countries but rather the extent of the differences between the business systems. Even in cases where American or European companies have been unfairly victimized by dumping practices, the adjudication process is usually so long and drawn out that by the time a determination is made, the companies have suffered irreparable losses. The only sure beneficiaries of this process are lobbyists and lawyers who get involved in these issues and are paid whether they win or lose.

In a world where ever more products are globally traded, new, harmonized anti-dumping laws are needed to take better account of the many complexities of product pricing in domestic and foreign markets. In addition, it would seem we need an enforcement system somewhere between the slow-moving GATT and the sometimes arbitrary or at least unilateral decision-making practiced by individual government bodies. Isn't this an area where an ombudsman-type system could be set up to get quick, fair, objective rulings, as well as practical solutions to structural differences among different business systems?

Antitrust law. The United States, the European Community, and Japan have their own sets of laws in this area. What is called antitrust law in America is called competition policy in Europe and anti-monopoly law in Japan. The objectives are generally the same, but the actual practice is very different in each part of the world.

American business has been highly critical of the Japanese *keiretsu* system, which is seen by outsiders as a cartel-like approach to production and distribution. But the *keiretsu* system also has many virtues, some of which are readily recognized even by American and European critics. Similarly, the American antitrust approach, while it obviously has great benefits in spurring competition and promoting the interests of consumers, also has noticeable shortcomings with respect to the difficulties

companies face in sharing research and development, carrying out joint manufacturing, or forming various kinds of beneficial partnerships and alliances.

The basic principles of American antitrust law were developed in the first half of the twentieth century, when "competition" meant mainly competition in the domestic market among domestic companies. The laws as they were written did not foresee the day when U.S. companies would need to compete with those from other countries. Japanese attitudes, on the other hand, were shaped in a period when Japanese companies were trying desperately to recover from the ruins of war and compete in world markets.

Our systems need to be brought up to date. It would seem to be common sense that the Japanese approach to antitrust problems is probably too lax, while the American approach is probably too severe and narrow to reflect the needs of business in today's global economy. Couldn't joint study and discussion of this problem lead to simultaneous reforms of differing systems throughout the Triad, so that the gulfs between them would be narrowed? Couldn't some sort of joint arbitration panel be established to respond to complaints?

Patent rights. In a technology-driven economy, patent rights become an increasingly important issue. Discussions are in progress on harmonizing patent systems. The United States appears willing, as part of a concrete package of tradeoffs being proposed in current multilateral world patent negotiations, to consider replacing its traditional "first inventor rights" with the "first application rights" to which both Japan and Europe subscribe. This progress should become the cornerstone for broader trilateral harmonization, in which Japan and the EC would change a number of their laws in order to arrive at a global system that equally and fairly protected inventors and innovators in each country.

Environmental protection. A new issue coming to the fore is the environmental regulations under which products are manufactured in different countries. If one country has stringent environmental regulations that add costs to manufacturing a certain product, should companies from another country be able to export directly competing products made under less stringent environmental rules? This issue has been central to the recent NAFTA negotiations and must be seen as an increasingly important part of all trade negotiations. The goal of the harmonization process here should be to harmonize "up," not "down"—to encourage raising all concerned to the level of those countries with the most effective environmental regulations.

The free-floating exchange-rate system. Requiring not just harmonization but active and ongoing policy coordination is the problem of the volatility of currency values in today's free-floating exchange-rate system, which acts as a kind of nontariff barrier preventing greater cross-border investment and business development. This system is a factor that keeps the global playing field in a permanently unlevel state, although one never knows to whose advantage the field will tilt.

Manufacturers who import raw materials and parts can never be sure of final production costs; those who sell in global markets can never be confident of future selling prices or profit margins. As a businessman, I find nothing more frustrating than discovering that our product, which was designed with a certain target price in mind, must now suddenly sell for a much higher price simply because currency rates have changed. I find it incredible that our investments in a certain country can lose 10 percent, 25 percent, or even more of their value almost overnight, just because a few currency traders have turned bearish on a certain currency. Consumers, naturally, cannot escape the burden of these exchange-rate-induced price distortions.

Certainly, big companies are capable of dealing with some of this volatility through currency hedging. But when industrial companies become wrapped up in financial-engineering stratagems, there is both a financial cost to be paid and a nonquantifiable cost in terms of loss of focus and efficiency. The high volatility of currency rates becomes another factor to promote short-termism, because the vast bulk of currency-futures trading is focused on the next contract, usually no more than a few months away. The huge volume of funds flowing through the system of currency speculation dwarfs the value of what flows through the trading system in physical goods and services. As a result, it is the speculators' opinions and biases that become the arbiters of value, in place of more-objective indices such as purchasing-power parity and real production costs.

It is said that free-floating currencies promote economic efficiency. Nothing could be further from the truth. What they really do is impose the irrationality of the speculator's culture on the daily lives of business people and consumers everywhere.

What is needed here is an evolutionary harmonization of the dollar, the major European currencies represented by the European Currency Unit, and the yen, so that over time we could create a common currency system throughout the Triad. We need not get rid of national currencies or lock rates in permanently. We could start with target zones, coupled with close policy coordination on the part of the major countries to keep currencies within those zones. This kind of approach has been successful at various points in taming some of the excessive volatility in currency markets, but it has yet to be truly institutionalized. Alternatively, we could move to a system of flexible currency fixing, in which values could be locked in for a certain period of time and readjusted according to agreed-upon criteria (such as purchasing-power parity) only during set review periods. Many other solutions are also possible.

The point is, we need leadership to take us out of ex-change-rate anarchy and toward some kind of sustainable order that will again allow currency to play its true role in the international system: as a public-utility means of exchange for goods and services, not a commodity unto itself to be controlled for profit by a handful of speculators.

The above areas are only illustrative highlights. Many others need to be addressed—taxation and accounting systems, labor law, securities and banking law. Because the goal I propose is only a kind of rough parity, not a completely unified market, we do not need a program as comprehensive as the European Community harmonization agenda. But all the same, there is a vast amount of work to do just to establish the broad outlines of a harmonized system across the Triad.

An End to "Fortress Japan"

TO ACHIEVE GLOBAL HARMONIZATION, EVERY country must adapt. But there is no question that the greatest burden of change would fall on Japan. The Japanese business system is more different from the United States and Europe than the United States and Europe are from each other. Although there is much to commend in Japan's economic system, it is simply too far out of sync with the West on certain essential points.

Before worrying that the EC will establish a "Fortress Europe," or NAFTA a "Fortress North America," Japanese business and political leaders should look at our situation in Japan, which is perceived by outsiders as the biggest fortress of all. Japan has been late in opening its markets to the world and in ensuring the transparency of those markets. Change has come piecemeal, and often only under intense foreign pressure. Although overt protectionism has been curbed, it is clear that many foreign products still have trouble with entry into and distribution in the Japanese market.

But there are more subtle—and perhaps more important—ways in which Japan stands apart from the world. I have been writing and speaking about these problems in recent months, encouraging my fellow Japanese to understand that despite our great success, we now need nothing so urgently as to "reinvent Japan"—to change fundamentally many of our ways of doing things. I have called into question, for example, the long hours and short holidays of Japanese workers. The fact that the average Japanese work year is still nearly 20 percent longer in hours than the average American work year not only detracts from the quality of Japanese life but also constitutes a subtle kind of advantage in the global competition between Japanese manufacturers and their foreign counterparts. A similar advantage is found in the low dividend-payout ratios of major Japanese companies, the way in which suppliers can be squeezed in the production system, and many other facets of the relationship be-

The greatest burden for change would fall on Japan.

Although there is much to commend in Japan's

economic system, it is simply too far out of sync with

the West on certain essential points.

tween Japanese companies and their broader network of "stakeholders."

Inside Japan, moreover, there continues to be a producer bias, rather than the shift toward a consumer emphasis which many of our political leaders and economists have called for. Japan's great wealth remains primarily corporate wealth, and the benefits have not sufficiently filtered down to the average Japanese in terms of such things as better housing and a better material standard of life. This situation not only causes frustration among the Japanese people but also accounts for at least some of the difficulties foreign companies have in competing.

A good illustration of the problem is the way in which since the Plaza Agreement of 1985 the distribution system has worked to minimize the positive impact for consumers of the strong yen. The prices of imported goods in the Japanese domestic market have not come down in tandem with the lowered values of foreign currencies. If we were to see true price competition in some of the highly protected sectors—and a fair, sustainable method of determining currency rates on an ongoing basis—the retailers of many kinds of Japanese goods would be forced by market mechanisms to find ways to bring their prices down. In the process we would likely see increased consumer demand, a rise in imports, and the invigoration of the whole economy.

It is no longer heresy inside Japan to point out what foreign experts have long said: the Japanese system regulates excessively. According to one estimate, government regulation affects economic activities composing 40 percent of Japan's GNP. The consumer-oriented, competition-enhancing kind of deregulation that we have seen in areas such as transportation, broadcasting, telecommunications, and financial services in the United States and to some degree in Europe has not taken place as fully in Japan.

In short, certain parts of the same political and economic system that provided the foundation for developing Japan's economic power over the past forty years are today hindering progress toward free and unobstructed competition. And this outmoded system continues to present the image of a Fortress Japan to outsiders.

I have called for making nonregulation the rule rather than the exception. And I have made the case that to-

day's Japan will not lose its competitive advantage by giving up some of the aspects of its system which it has inherited from the past. Japan's industrial and business fundamentals will become stronger if we allow the dynamics of the free market to affect our economy more forcefully. Thus we will help ourselves at the same time that we rid ourselves of the "unfair" label that keeps Japan apart from the rest of the world. And if Japan can make such changes, it will show Americans and Europeans that harmonization, with all its market-enlarging and stimulating benefits, is possible.

Not everything can be accomplished overnight. I have stressed that the right place to begin is with harmonizing concrete rules and procedures involving business and economic practices. But business harmonization must take place alongside another kind of harmonization—a kind of geo-economic, geopolitical harmonization in which Japan continues to assume more burdens of world leadership. Many commentators have pointed out that the competitiveness of American business has paid a price for America's outsized responsibility in keeping world peace, and that Japan, with many fewer responsibilities and obligations, has been able to focus more narrowly on what is best for its own economy.

Of course, Japan is making progress in shouldering its global political responsibilities. Our Diet has finally passed legislation that allows limited numbers of Japanese Self-Defense Forces to be dispatched as peacekeepers to world trouble spots, for example. In those areas where Japan has been willing to assume leadership (and where other major countries have supported a larger Japanese role), the record is generally quite good. Individual Japanese who have assumed high-visibility positions—among them Sadako Ogata, the UN High Commissioner for Refugees—have been able to inspire much greater Japanese awareness of global issues, and the commitment of Japanese resources to them. Inside Japan people are beginning to talk about the need for our country to play a more active role in the UN and to find a way to qualify for a permanent seat on the Security Council. But in the years ahead there must be greater harmonization of costs, burdens, responsibilities, and powers for maintaining the peace and stability of a global system from which Japan benefits so directly.

Helping Each Other Do the Right Thing

JAPAN IS NOT THE ONLY COUNTRY THAT NEEDS TO change in order to promote economic harmonization and lay the basis for a new world economic order. Indeed, change and adaptation are incumbent on every country.

European leaders, for example, have a huge responsibility to ensure that their countries continue to evolve on the path of economic harmonization and unification. They need to respond with creative, flexible solutions to the objections and problems that have arisen. What is more, Europeans must resist the impulse to become narrow, inward-looking, and protectionist. This has not always been so clear. For example, the EC has resisted American efforts to liberalize European agricultural markets and has taken positions on automobile imports which Japanese business people have trouble seeing as anything other than blatantly protectionist.

Europe faces trade deficits with both Japan and the United States, and many large European companies are in the throes of major structural changes and downsizing. The political pressures on European governments are obvious. But I believe that the EC has chosen its road carefully and that EC leaders will continue to show that a borderless internal European market means one in which companies from the United States, Japan, and elsewhere can also compete fairly and freely.

As for the United States, the election of Bill Clinton last year signaled the American people's serious desire to renew the U.S. economic base in order to become more competitive. A deep recognition of the challenges involved is now unfolding, and a consensus is beginning to form on tackling problems like the budget deficit, health care, infrastructure, education, capital formation, productivity, and manufacturing quality. Nevertheless, the road is not easy and many difficult choices must be made and sustained—including a measure of what President Clinton has termed "sacrifice."

America's success at reinventing its competitive prowess is crucial to the rest of the world, because the $6 trillion U.S. GNP is still the most powerful single engine of world economic growth, and America still plays the primary leadership role in maintaining global security. America's ability to provide global leadership is truly exceptional. No other single country can now perform that critical function so well. But since no one can expect the United States to continue to bear such outsized international responsibilities without a strong, vibrant economy at home, it is in the interests of all concerned for the United States to succeed at renewing its economic vitality.

President Clinton must find a way to steer the U.S. economy in the direction of competing harder, smarter, and better, without succumbing to the false temptation of protectionist solutions. It would be a severe setback to the growing momentum of international cooperation if the United States, so long the world's most open market and the prime proponent of free trade, were to seek a politically popular but economically dangerous course along the path of protectionism. Although I think it is worth pointing out the dangers of following such a course, that is not the course that I believe the United States will take.

It is interesting to note that Bill Clinton is not just the first American Baby Boom President; he is one of the first of his generation to emerge as the chief political leader of a major country. His election was motivated by a deep-seated desire for fundamental change on the part of the American people. But that desire for change—particularly for innovative solutions commensurate with the demands of the fast-approaching twenty-first century—is becoming a worldwide phenomenon. And over time we may find that the next generation of political leaders in the major countries will be better able to bridge the culture gap, more aware of new approaches to global economic issues, and more able to work collectively toward meaningful consensus and action.

We should help one another to see the right thing to do—and to do it. None of us should be afraid to point out the shortcomings of others. And all should be prepared to respond constructively to such criticism. I do not think this is a utopian notion. In the U.S.-Japan dialogue known as the Structural Impediments Initiative we have seen an example of a process that allows detailed criticisms and observations about the basic structures of one another's societies to be put on the table.

Changes that are difficult for one country to make on its own may be easier to make in the context of a Triad in which each economy is undergoing a specified program of change. The moral force of an arrangement in which we become responsible to one another can serve as a kind of supranational conscience to the process.

In that spirit, let us not shrink from the task of developing a bold vision of what we can do together to promote the best interests of our own economies and the global order as a whole. For the G-7 leadership to miss the opportunity presented at this historic juncture would be nothing short of tragic. If we, the wealthy and successful nations of the world, cannot find the vision and action to steer the world back on the track of global growth and increased cooperation, history will judge our collective failure harshly.

■ AFTER NAFTA

Global Village or Global Pillage?

JEREMY BRECHER

Jeremy Brecher is a historian and co-editor of Global Visions: Beyond the New World Order *(South End).*

For most of the world's people, the "New World Economy" is a disaster that has already happened. Those it hurts can't escape it. But neither can they afford to accept it. So many are now seeking ways to reshape it.

When I first started writing about the destructive effects of globalization three years ago, The North American Free Trade Agreement was widely regarded as a done deal. The near defeat of NAFTA reveals pervasive popular doubt about the wisdom of an unregulated international market. The struggle against NAFTA represented the first major effort by Americans who have been hurt by global economic integration to do something about it. Like many mass movements, it included contradictory forces, such as the Mexico-bashing bigotry of Pat Buchanan, the populist grandstanding of Ross Perot and the nationalistic protectionism of some in the labor movement.

But other elements of the struggle against NAFTA prefigure a movement that could radically reshape the New World Economy. Out of their own experiences and observations, millions of Americans have constructed a new paradigm for understanding the global economy. Poor and working people in large numbers have recognized that NAFTA is not primarily about trade; it is about the ability of capital to move without regard to national borders. Capital mobility, not trade, is bringing about the "giant sucking sound" of jobs going south.

For the first time in many years, substantial numbers of people mobilized to act on broad class interests. I haven't seen a movement for years in which so many people at the grass roots took their own initiative. Typical was the unexpectedly large, predominantly blue-collar anti-NAFTA rally in New Haven, where a labor leader told me, "We didn't turn these people out."

The New Global Pillage

NAFTA became a symbol for an accumulation of fears and angers regarding the place of working people in the New World Economy. The North American economic integration that NAFTA was intended to facilitate is only one aspect of the rapid and momentous historical transformation from a system of national economies toward an integrated global economy. New information, communication, transportation and manufacturing technologies, combined with tariff reductions, have made it possible to coordinate production, commerce and finance on a world scale. Since 1983, the rate of world foreign direct investment has grown four times as fast as world output.

This transformation has had devastating consequences. They may be summarized as the "seven danger signals" of cancerous, out-of-control globalization:

Race to the bottom. The recent quantum leap in the ability of transnational corporations to relocate their facilities around the world in effect makes all workers, communities and countries competitors for these corporations' favor. The consequence is a "race to the bottom" in which wages and social and environmental conditions tend to fall to the level of the most desperate. This dynamic underlies U.S. deindustrialization, declining real wages, eradication of job security, and downward pressure on social spending and investment; it is also largely responsible for the migration of low-wage, environmentally destructive industries to poor countries like Mexico and China.

> **N**ational governments have lost much of their power to direct their own economies.

Global stagnation. As each work force, community or country seeks to become more competitive by reducing its wages and its social and environmental overheads, the result is a general downward spiral in incomes and social and material infrastructures. Lower wages and reduced public spending mean less buying power, leading to stagnation, recession and unemployment. This dynamic is aggravated by the accumulation of debt; national economies in poor countries and even in the United States become geared to debt repayment at the expense of consumption, investment and development. The downward fall is reflected in the slowing of global GNP growth from almost 5 percent per year in the period 1948-1973 to only half that in the period 1974-89 and to a mere crawl since then.

Polarization of haves and have-nots. As a result of globalization, the gap between rich and poor is increasing both within and between countries around the world. Poor U.S. communities boast world-class unemployment and infant mortality. Meanwhile, tens of billions of dollars a year flow from poor to rich regions of the world, in the form of debt repayment and capital flight.

Loss of democratic control. National governments have lost much of their power to direct their own economies. The ability of countries to apply socialist or even Keynesian techniques in pursuit of development, full employment or other national economic goals has been undermined by the power of capital to pick up and leave. Governmental economic power has been further weakened throughout the world by neoliberal political movements that have dismantled government institutions for regulating national economies. Globalization has reduced the power of individuals and communities to shape their destinies.

Walter Wriston, former chairman of Citicorp, recently boasted of how "200,000 monitors in trading rooms all over the world" now conduct "a kind of global plebiscite on the monetary and fiscal policies of the governments issuing currency. . . . There is no way for a nation to opt out." Wriston recalls the election of "ardent socialist" François Mitterrand as French President in 1981. "The market took one look at his policies and within six months the capital flight forced him to reverse course."

Unfettered transnational corporations. Transnationals have become the world's most powerful economic actors, yet there are no international equivalents to national antitrust, consumer protection and other laws that provide a degree of corporate accountability.

Unaccountable global institutions. The loss of national economic control has been accompanied by a growing concentration of unaccountable power in international institutions like the International Monetary Fund, the World Bank and the General Agreement on Tariffs and Trade (GATT). For poor countries, foreign control has been formalized in the World Bank's "structural adjustment plans," but I.M.F. decisions and GATT rules affect the economic growth rates of all countries. The decisions of these institutions also have an enormous impact on the global ecology.

Global conflict. Economic globalization is producing chaotic and destructive rivalries. In a swirl of self-contradictory strategies, major powers and transnationals use global institutions like GATT to impose open markets on their rivals; they pursue trade wars against one another; and they try to construct competing regional blocs like the European Community and NAFTA. In past eras, such rivalries have ultimately led to world war.

In sum, the result of unregulated globalization has been the pillage of the planet and its peoples.

Transnational Economic Programs

What are the alternatives to destructive globalization? The right offers racism and nationalism. Conventional protectionism offers no solution. Globalization has also intellectually disarmed the left and rendered national left programs counterproductive. Jimmy Carter's sharp turn to the right in 1978; François Mitterrand's rapid abandonment of his radical program; the acceptance of deregulation, privatization and trade liberalization by poor countries from India to Mexico; and even the decision of Eastern European elites to abandon Communism—all reflect in part the failure of national left policies.

But the beginnings of a new approach emerged from the anti-NAFTA movement itself. Rather than advocate protectionism—keeping foreign products out—many NAFTA opponents urged policies that would raise environmental, labor and social standards in Mexico, so that those standards would not drag down those in the United States and Canada. This approach implied that people in different countries have common interests in raising the conditions of those at the bottom.

Those harmed by the New World Economy need not be passive victims.

Indeed, the struggle against NAFTA generated new transnational networks based on such common interests. A North American Worker-to-Worker Network links grass-roots labor activists in Mexico, the United States and Canada via conferences, tours, solidarity support and a newsletter. Mujer a Mujer similarly links women's groups. The Highlander Center, Southerners for Economic Justice, the Tennessee Industrial Renewal Network and a number of unions have organized meetings and tours to bring together Mexican and U.S. workers. There are similar networks in other parts of the world, such as People's Plan 21 in the Asian-Pacific and Central American regions and the Third World Network in Malaysia.

These new networks are developing transnational programs to counter the effects of global economic restructuring. Representatives from environmental, labor, religious, consumer and farm groups from Mexico, the United States and Canada have drawn up "A Just and Sustainable Trade and Development Initiative for North America." A parallel synthesis, "From Global Pillage to Global Village," has been endorsed by more than sixty grass-roots organizations. Related proposals by the Third World Network have recently been published as "Towards a New North-South Economic Dialogue."

Differing in emphasis and details, these emerging alternative programs are important not only because of the solutions they propose but also because those solutions have emerged from a dialogue rooted in such a diversity of groups and experiences. Some require implementation by national policy; some by international agreement; some can be implemented by transnational citizen action. Taken together, they provide what might be described as "seven prescriptions" for the seven danger signals of the unregulated global economy:

International rights and standards. To prevent competition from resulting in a race to the bottom, several of these groups want to establish minimum human, labor and environmental rights and standards, as the European Community's "social charter" was designed to do. The International Metalworkers Federation recently proposed a ten-point "World Social Charter," which could be incorporated into GATT.

"A Just and Sustainable Trade and Development Initiative for North America" spells out in some detail an alternative to NAFTA that would protect human and worker rights, encourage workers' incomes to rise in step with productivity and establish continental environmental rights, such as the right to a toxics-free workplace and community. Enforcement agencies would be accessible to citizens and could levy fines against parties guilty of violations. The initiative especially emphasizes the rights of immigrants. Activists from nongovernmental organizations in all three countries have proposed a citizens' commission to monitor the human, labor and environmental effects of trade and investment.

Upward spiral. In the past, government monetary and fiscal policy, combined with minimum wages, welfare state programs, collective bargaining and other means of raising the purchasing power of have-nots, did much to counter recession and stagnation within national economies. Similar measures are now required at international levels to counter the tendency toward a downward spiral of inadequate demand in the global economy. The Third World Network calls on the I.M.F. and World Bank to replace their ruinous structural adjustment plans with policies that "meet the broad goals of development . . . rather than the narrower goal of satisfying the needs of the creditors." It also demands a reduction of developing country debt. "A Just and Sustainable Trade and Development Initiative" proposes that the remaining debt service be paid in local currency into a democratically administered development fund. Reversing the downward spiral also ultimately requires a "global Keynesianism" in which international institutions support, rather than discourage, national full-employment policies.

An upward spiral also requires rising income for those at the bottom—something that can be encouraged by international labor solidarity. Experiments in cross-border organizing by U.S. unions like the Amalgamated Clothing and Textile Workers and the United Electrical Workers, in cooperation with independent unions in Mexico, aim to defeat transnationals' whipsawing by improving the wages and conditions of Mexican workers.

Redistribution from haves to have-nots. "A Just and Sustainable Trade and Development Initiative" calls for "compensatory financing" to correct growing gaps between rich and poor. A model would be the European Community funds that promote development in its poorer members. The Third World Network calls for commodity agreements to correct the inequities in the South's terms of trade. It also stresses the need to continue preferential treatment for the South in GATT and in intellectual property protection rules.

Strengthened democracy. NAFTA, GATT and similar agreements should not be used—as they now can be—to preempt the right of localities, states, provinces and countries to establish effective labor, health, safety and environmental standards that are higher than the guaranteed minimum in international agreements. Above all, democratization requires a new opportunity for people at the bottom to participate in shaping their destiny.

Codes of conduct for transnational corporations. Several transnational grass-roots groups call for codes of conduct that would, for example, require corporations to report investment intentions; disclose the hazardous materials they import; ban employment of children; forbid discharge of pollutants; require advance notification and severance pay when operations are terminated; and prohibit company interference with union organizing. United Nations discussions of such a code, long stymied by U.S. hostility, should be revived.

While the ultimate goal is to have such codes implemented by agreements among governments, global public

pressure and cross-border organizing can begin to enforce them. The Coalition for Justice in the Maquiladoras, for example, a group of religious, environmental, labor, Latino and women's organizations in Mexico and the United States, has issued a code of conduct for U.S. corporations in Mexico and has used "corporate campaign" techniques to pressure them to abide by its labor and environmental provisions.

Reform of international institutions. Citizens should call on the U.N. to convene a second Earth Summit focusing on democratizing the I.M.F. and the World Bank, and consider formation of new institutions to promote equitable, sustainable and participatory development. International citizen campaigns, perhaps modeled on the Nestlé boycott and the campaign against World Bank–funded destruction of the Amazon, could spotlight these institutions.

Multiple-level regulation. In place of rivalry among countries and regions, such programs imply a system of democratically controlled public institutions at every level, from global to local.

After NAFTA: Globalization From Below

These proposals provide no short-term panacea; they are objectives to organize around. The New World Economy is not going to vanish from the political agenda. Neither will the passions and political forces aroused by the NAFTA debate. Many of the same issues will resurface in connection with the Asia-Pacific Economic Cooperation Forum and with GATT. As the fiftieth anniversaries of the I.M.F. and World Bank approach, calls for their reform are being sounded all over the world.

The struggle against NAFTA has shown that those harmed by the New World Economy need not be passive victims. So many politicians were so unprepared for the strength of the anti-NAFTA movement because it represented an eruption into the political arena of people who have long been demobilized. But to influence their economic destinies effectively, they need a movement that provides an alternative to the Ross Perots and Pat Buchanans. Such a movement must act on the understanding that the unregulated globalization of capital is really a worldwide attack of the haves on the have-nots. And it must bring that understanding to bear on every affected issue, from local layoffs to the world environment. "From Global Pillage to Global Village" suggests a vision to guide such a movement:

> The internationalization of capital, production and labor is now being followed by the internationalization of peoples' movements and organizations. Building peoples' international organizations and solidarity will be our revolution from within: a civil society without borders. This internationalism or "globalization from below" will be the foundation for turning the global pillage into a participatory and sustainable global village.

The organizations that have led the fight against NAFTA have a responsibility not to retreat to parochial concerns. They must regroup and begin addressing the broader impact of economic globalization on people and planet.

Push comes to shove

Western Europe is ailing, angry and afraid of the future

The gloomy cadences of Henryk Gorecki's Third Symphony are out-selling Madonna in parts of Europe this year. *Verdrossenheit,* connoting contempt and peevishness, captures the German mood. France has taken on a grayish *fin de siècle* hue. Italy is convulsed by scandal and cynicism. One Spanish worker in 5 is jobless. In Britain, a smash-hit BBC television series, "One Foot in the Grave," which stars a cantankerous whiner, captures the atmosphere better than a hundred opinion polls.

Western Europe emerged from the cold war victorious but utterly unprepared for the upheavals ahead. Now it is a mess. The drive for political and monetary union has stalled. Instead of taking its place as America's equal, Europe continues to dither over Bosnia and other security issues, reflexively looking to Washington for leadership only to find America turning inward again. Secretary of State Warren Christopher will travel to Europe again this week to consult with allied foreign ministers—but not to assert American leadership on the Bosnian conflict, which last month he called a "European problem." Instead, he wants to stick to a sundry list of trans-Atlantic issues, including trade differences and aid to Russia.

Global recession, technological change, the high cost of German unification and a surge of immigration have dashed hopes that 1993 would bring economic growth and new jobs. Figures released last week showed that Germany's gross domestic product plunged 3.2 percent during the first quarter of this year compared with a year ago, the sharpest drop since 1975. From Sweden to Spain, West Europeans are losing faith in their leaders, their political parties and the ideals of social democracy that have guided them for half a century or more.

Last week, xenophobia in Germany and France spilled over in murderous arson attacks on Turkish immigrants. More than 3,000 such incidents have been recorded in Germany alone in the past 18 months. At least 21 foreigners have died. Yet these assaults are merely the most obvious manifestations of anger and racism that have reached such a crescendo that the Turkish victims were moved to demand United Nations protection from their German neighbors.

Drift and disintegration are the common denominators in this "new" Europe. The impotence, divisiveness and paralysis that have been on display in Western Europe's attempts to cope with the collapse of Yugoslavia have captured the head-lines. But the malaise is much deeper. "A sense pervades that communities are falling apart, values are collapsing, institutions are crumbling, nation-states weakening," says David Howell, a respected member of the British Parliament. "High expectations after the end of the cold war have given way to bitter disappointments. People feel misled."

Rightist groupings in Britain, Germany, Greece and Sweden, leftist parties in France, Norway and Spain and centrist coalitions in Belgium, Italy and the Netherlands have rarely stood lower in popular esteem. Longtime leaders such as Germany's Helmut Kohl and France's François Mitterrand are openly mocked. Yet alternatives fare little better, and idealism about the future is nonexistent. "What is the situation in Europe today?" asked Danish Prime Minister Poul Nyrup Rasmussen recently. "Uncertainty, uncertainty, uncertainty. That's a disaster."

Although northern Europe is habitually as melancholy as its weather, this time the despondency is not misplaced.

■ **Slow growth.** For the first time since 1975 all but one of Europe's major economies are contracting. Growth for the 12-nation European Community this year is forecast to be between zero and −1 percent. Industrial production is falling sharply in Germany, France and Italy. Only Britain is bucking the trend. Recovery, if and when it comes in 1995–96, will be anemic.

■ **Joblessness.** Unemployment is reaching levels not seen since the 1930s. Nearly 18 million people in the EC, 10.2 percent of the work force, are jobless. EC unemployment is expected to reach 11 percent this year—50 percent higher than in the United States and almost five times the Japanese level—and to continue rising until 1996. In April, mass protests erupted in 150 cities across the EC, and last week, the Paris-based Organization for Eco-

---

NATIONALISM

You're dealing with very weak governments and a genuine leadership problem in the three main West European countries [Britain, France and Germany]. The main fear I see is tied to recession and the growing xeno-phobia it has touched off. It's not limited to Germany, though it's depress-ing it should reappear there after 45 years of democratic experiment.

STANLEY HOFFMANN, 64, CHAIRMAN OF THE CENTER FOR EUROPEAN STUDIES AT HARVARD UNIVERSITY

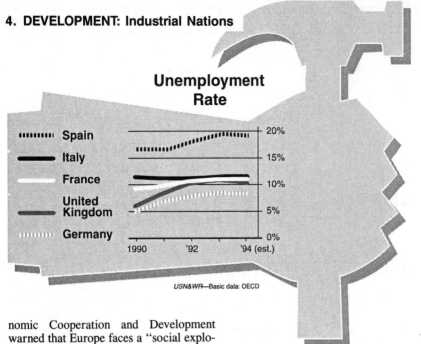

Unemployment Rate

- Spain
- Italy
- France
- United Kingdom
- Germany

20%
15%
10%
5%
0%

1990   '92   '94 (est.)

USN&WR—Basic data: OECD

INTOLERANCE

You will never be able to eliminate very basic differences of cultures and histories. This is the stuff of human progress. It's not differences that cause conflict, it's the intolerance of differences.

IMMANUEL JAKOBOVITS, 72, FORMER CHIEF RABBI OF
THE BRITISH COMMONWEALTH

nomic Cooperation and Development warned that Europe faces a "social explosion" if more jobs are not created.

■ **Losing out.** Europe is losing its ability to compete in the global marketplace. In 1980, the EC accounted for 21 percent of world exports. Today, it accounts for 16 percent. Last year, the EC ran a $90 billion trade deficit with the rest of the world—three times the 1985–90 average. Labor costs are twice as high in Germany as they are in America and one third higher than in Japan. That is one reason the EC generated jobs at less than one third the U.S. rate during the 1980s.

■ **Losing faith.** Corruption scandals threaten to engulf long-serving governments in half a dozen countries. Limp and uninspiring leaders wring their hands in frustration. Alienation is widespread. In Britain, John Major's government, re-elected in April 1992, is now the least popular since political opinion polls began in the 1940s. One Briton in 2 would like to emigrate. Six of 10 Germans regard the Kohl government as "incapable." Half of all Italians have lost faith in democracy. The corollary: a surge of support for

neofascist, racist and separatist groups.

Nowhere is the Continent's malaise more apparent than in its industrial heartland, Germany's Ruhr valley. Not long ago, the word *stahl,* which means steel, was synonymous with Teutonic efficiency. Now, it stands for a series of failures that are turning the steel industry into a millstone around Europe's neck. Sixty thousand jobs could be lost this year in Germany alone as companies such as Thyssen and Krupp lose millions of dollars to shrinking markets, low-wage competition from Eastern Europe and upmarket challenges from East Asia.

This spring, as steelworkers in eastern Germany went on strike for higher wages, 2,000 workers at the 100-year-old Krupp Hoesch plant in Rheinhausen were told that their plant in the western part of the country is closing. "A job at Krupp was supposed to be a lifetime position," says Hans Oyen, one of a group of workers

gathered in a dingy tent outside the factory gates. "No one can understand why the plant has to be dismantled."

For Oyen and tens of thousands of other West European workers facing early retirement or retraining, part of the answer lies in the cosseted past. At Daimler-Benz, Volkswagen and dozens of other industrial giants in the Ruhr and elsewhere, costs soared out of control in the 1980s, when growth seemed endless and the competition weak. Legislative interference also grew apace; a new Daimler-Benz factory in southwest Germany, opened in 1992, had to be shrouded in trees to hide it from the view of people flying over it.

A year later, the business environment is so different as to be unrecognizable. In the 12 months before April 1993, German car output—a key component of Europe's industrial health—fell by 26 percent. Volkswagen, which lost $773 million in the first quarter of 1993, claims it must run its plants in Germany at more than 100 percent capacity to make any profit. Daimler-Benz, Germany's biggest industrial company, is shedding 15,000 jobs this year on top of the 18,000 lost in 1992.

Yet as the Hamburg newspaper *Die Zeit* said recently, in a comment with Europe-wide relevance, much of German industry is still "too fat, too heavy, too costly." Some firms are trying to slim down. Mercedes-Benz used to buy only German parts for its car production. Now, it is purchasing abroad. It also has decided to build a factory in the United States, where costs are one-third lower. Other firms are axing bloated managements. "We have 11 levels between me and the person selling the car," Volvo boss Soren Gyll said last year, when he unveiled plans to close two of the company's three plants in Sweden. "Many will have to go."

But scaling back will not be easy. Six-week vacations, generous sick-pay provisions, short workweeks and high social security costs are deeply engrained in West European culture. Labor unions, too, retain muscle in much of Europe. Nor is there much sign that the EC understands

DISILLUSIONMENT

The origins of the dictatorships in Europe in the 1920s and 1930s varied, but the common thread was a mixture of fear and resentment. Now we're disillusioned. We've become used to prosperity. Europe is quarrelsome today, and there's a lot of alienation and depression. But from a historical perspective, the "new" Europe is about at the stage of development Western Europe was at in 1947. There's still a long way to go before we can say it is a failure.

HISTORIAN ALAN BULLOCK, 78, FORMER
VICE CHANCELLOR OF OXFORD UNIVERSITY AND A MEMBER OF BRITAIN'S HOUSE OF LORDS

THE DEATH OF NATIONS

European nation states were born in the 19th century as part of a process of nation building. Today we're witnessing a reverse process: ethnicization and the disintegration of nation-states. This is virgin territory for security thinking. The test bed is how we cope with events in Yugoslavia. It's very difficult to see how international organizations would operate if ethnicity supersedes the logic of traditional nation-states.

FRANCOIS HEISBOURG, 43, FORMER FRENCH DIPLOMAT AND DIRECTOR OF THE
INTERNATIONAL INSTITUTE FOR STRATEGIC STUDIES

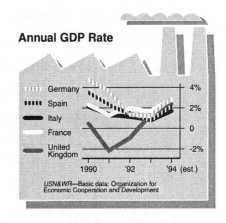

Annual GDP Rate

Germany · Spain · Italy · France · United Kingdom

4% · 2% · 0 · -2%

1990 · '92 · '94 (est.)

USN&WR—Basic data: Organization for Economic Cooperation and Development

that it is living in a more competitive era; last week, the group, with Britain alone dissenting, agreed to impose a 48-hour maximum workweek in the community by 1996.

Lost jobs. Decisions such as this seem bound to boost unemployment as firms

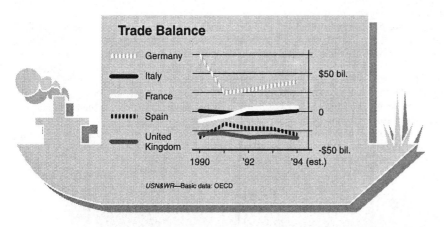

Trade Balance

Germany · Italy · France · Spain · United Kingdom

$50 bil. · 0 · -$50 bil.

1990 · '92 · '94 (est.)

USN&WR—Basic data: OECD

struggle to shore up profits. In Ireland and Spain, the two hardest-hit EC states, the jobless level is already above 20 percent, and even once immune countries such as Denmark are hurting. In eight of the 12 EC states, more than half of those out of work have been unemployed for more than a year; 6 percent of jobless Americans fall into this category. In Britain, a quarter of all workers are estimated to have lost their jobs since recession began there in 1990. Not surprisingly, 79 percent of Britons say unemployment is the most important issue facing their country.

The human frustrations generated by this situation are evident at a "job club" for the long-term unemployed in the Lancashire town of Bolton in northwest England. "My experience, my qualifications count for nothing," says Mike Brewer, a 52-year-old engineer who has been out of work for two years. "My age is against me and so is being a man. All employers want these days are part-time female staff."

No easy solutions exist. A recent edition of the *Lancashire Evening Telegraph* indicates why. One story reported the closure of a debt-ridden, U.S.-owned textile works in Accrington—the largest employer in that town for 140 years but the victim of low-cost competition from the developing world. A second story described the closure on environmental grounds of an inefficient coal-burning power plant in Burnley. A third examined the local future of British Aerospace De-

fense Ltd. as military orders dry up following the end of the cold war.

These broader issues may be of little interest to Mike Brewer. As he puts it: "Today I look in the mirror and wonder why anyone should want me. My whole life has narrowed. I know the price of a single potato now." Yet it is the wider context that is determining his future and those of millions of Europeans like him.

Gilbert Zara knows this only too well. Thirty years ago, he arrived in the Paris suburb of Sarcelles from Tunisia and opened a food shop selling ethnic fare. For a time he prospered. But then a tide of black African and Arab immigrants flooded in from former French colonies to sweep streets and do other menial chores in the capital.

Robbed and beaten. Today, Sarcelles has become a synonym in France for racial unrest, overcrowding, drugs and crime. Thugs have robbed Zara's shop five times in the past year, beating him, his wife and his sons. "I'd sell and get out, but no one will buy this shop," he laments. Half of Sarcelles's inhabitants are immigrants from Third World nations. Unemployment hovers around 40 percent, four times France's national average. Crime

UNIFICATION

The West has not been able to take advantage of the great victory over communism. It is in Russia that the process of decomposition of the international order began. It is a reality that has unleashed all the religious and racial hatreds that have always characterized that society. Now the contagion westward seems unstoppable. The only medicine against these ferments is the rapid construction of genuine European unification.

GIOVANNI SPADOLINI, 67, PRESIDENT OF THE ITALIAN SENATE,
TWICE PRIME MINISTER OF ITALY

ALIENATION

The industrial revolution is now paralyzed by bureaucracy. That's the most basic evil. I see a real danger in the alienation of people from parliamentary politics and from government. This flatulence of nationalism we see all over Europe is the result of the leveling process of the industrial revolution.

HANS-GEORG GADAMER, 93, ONE OF GERMANY'S BEST-KNOWN PHILOSOPHERS

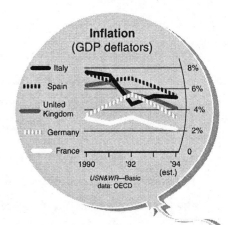

Inflation
(GDP deflators)

Italy
Spain
United Kingdom
Germany
France

8%
6%
4%
2%
0

1990   '92   '94 (est.)

USN&WR—Basic data: OECD

rates are high, syringes litter stairwells, graffiti cover walls, rubbish lines the streets. "The only good news is that guns are not as readily available as in America, but that is only a matter of time," says Pierre Lellouche, the town's newly elected deputy to parliament.

Unhappily for France, and for Europe, Sarcelles may be a nightmare vision of tomorrow's reality in scores of other West European cities. Already the region is facing its biggest refugee influx since World War II, sparked by Yugoslavia's implosion and Eastern Europe's shaky transition from communism to democracy. This year, 1 million outsiders are expected to seek asylum, two thirds of them in Germany. Millions more people, especially young males from North Africa, the Mideast and the Indian subcontinent, are clamoring to get in as "economic migrants" from no-hope economies.

In reaction, an increasingly violent backlash is in full swing in every West European country except Ireland. Attacks on foreigners in Germany, where immigrants form 8 percent of the population (twice the EC average), rose 10-fold in 1992 and continue to increase. Britain, France, Italy and Spain have all witnessed murderous assaults on racial minorities this year as frustrations about jobs start to boil over.

Earlier this month, the EC unveiled measures designed to make mass immigration into the community all but impossible without saying as much. The new French government is blunter: It no longer welcomes Third World immigrants and will limit them with a new close-to-zero policy. "Either we fix the immigration problem, or it explodes," says Lellouche.

Western Europe's handling of its racial and employment problems, like its approach to economic change and political integration, is fragmented and inconsistent. "We have not often had such a combination of personal, political and ideological immobility as is seen today," says Martin Woollacott, a leading British journalist. The temptation for the richer, northwestern part of the Continent to insulate itself is growing. But even staunch advocates of Fortress Europe concede that isolation, even if it were practical, is not the answer to the region's difficulties.

Nearly 60 years ago, Winston Churchill attacked leaders of his day over their head-in-the-sand attitude toward Hitler's Germany: "So they go on in strange paradox, decided only to be undecided, resolved only to be irresolute, adamant for drift, solid for fluidity, all-powerful to be impotent." Much has changed in Europe since Churchill's day. Much has not.

BY ROBIN KNIGHT IN ENGLAND WITH JOHN MARKS IN GERMANY AND FRED COLEMAN IN FRANCE

Number One Again

As Europe and Japan struggle, fundamental changes put the U.S. economy back on top

Clay Chandler

Washington Post Staff Writer

For a president whose greatest passion seems to be winning the global economic competition, the recent news must be awfully sweet.

A flurry of economic indicators announced two weeks ago shows the U.S. economy surging, even as Europe and Japan remain mired in recession. U.S. unemployment has fallen sharply and consumer confidence has shot up—and all in a week that began with the free fall of the Tokyo stock market.

Beyond these short-term numbers, some economists see a fundamental shift of America's position in the global economy.

They argue that the United States has emerged from a period of economic "restructuring"—a polite term for the brutal layoffs and cost-cutting—as the most vigorous and competitive economy in the world—and it may be poised to retain that distinction for years to come.

In the hypercompetitive global economy, suddenly everything seems to be going America's way.

You could almost imagine President Clinton running to the White House balcony and shouting: "We're Number One!"

CERTAINLY, THERE'S A LOT worth shouting about. Consider some of the recent signs of the U.S. economic renaissance:

■ The U.S. economy is expected to grow faster than any other industrial nation this year and outpace growth in every nation except Canada in 1994.

Economists polled by Consensus Economics Inc., a business research group, said the U.S. economy will expand 2.7 percent this year and 2.8 percent next year.

The Japanese and German economies, by contrast, are expected to shrink this year and limp along with growth of less than 1 percent in 1994.

■ Economic indicators suggest that the U.S. economy has moved from recovery into a period of sustained expansion.

Interest rates and inflation remain at their lowest levels in two decades. Business investment has been rising strongly for months, industrial production is climbing and consumer spending has revived. Meanwhile, Wall Street has been strong.

■ The job outlook is brightening too. On Dec. 3, the Labor Department said the November unemployment rate fell to 6.4 percent, its biggest one-month improvement in a decade.

In most European countries, by contrast, unemployment is in double digits and climbing.

In Japan, the nominal unemployment rate remains below 3 percent, but economists expect that number to deteriorate sharply because Japanese firms are keeping millions of idle workers on the payroll despite slow sales.

The cheery news contrasts sharply with the gloomy fate many had envisioned for the U.S. economy just a few years ago. Back then, when Japanese companies were gobbling up office buildings and Western European nations were busy forging the world's largest single market, many experts lamented the decline of the United States as an industrial power.

❏

NOW IT IS THE JAPANESE AND Europeans who nurse wounded economies and fret about falling behind in the global competitiveness race.

Japanese firms, bracing for a fourth straight year of falling profits, are slashing investment and paring workers. Europe's attempt at unity has bogged down. And high interest rates, rigid labor practices and protective trade laws are crippling European exports.

"Fears are spreading that the European Community is suffering a

From *The Washington Post National Weekly Edition*, December 13–19, 1993, p. 20. © 1993 by The Washington Post. Reprinted by permission.

second attack of Eurosclerosis," worried a recent issue of Europe, a magazine published by the European Community Council.

In part, the current strength of the U.S. economy relative to its major international trade rivals is a matter of timing.

"No doubt part of what we're seeing now is cyclical," says Robert Barbera, chief economist at Lehman Brothers Inc. "We went into recession first and now we're the first out of it. But Japan and Germany grew fast while we were in the soup, and may again when we slow down."

Now the key question, however, is whether the United States can sustain its current capacity for higher growth over the long term after the slumps in Japan and Europe have run their course.

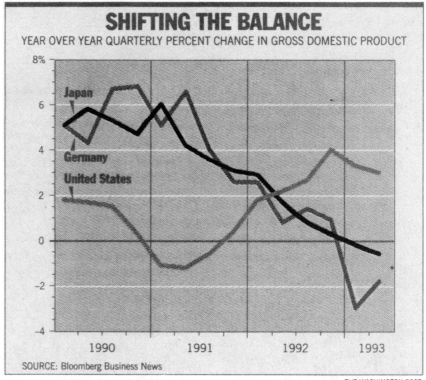

SHIFTING THE BALANCE
YEAR OVER YEAR QUARTERLY PERCENT CHANGE IN GROSS DOMESTIC PRODUCT

SOURCE: Bloomberg Business News

THE WASHINGTON POST

A clear sign of America's competitive strength is that many big foreign companies are rushing to invest here.

"We've seen a long-term structural shift" in the U.S. economy's productive capacity, argues Thomas Duesterberg, director of the Hudson Institute's Competitiveness Center.

"The competitive position of the Japanese and German economies has been impaired for the next five years," contends Barbera.

There is much evidence to support this view of a resurgent U.S. economy:

■ U.S. labor costs are about 30 percent below the weighted average foreign level, according to the Paris-based Organization for Economic Cooperation and Development.

America's "international cost competitiveness remains very strong," concluded the OECD in its annual economic survey for 1993. "The United States is well-positioned to expand export volumes once the cyclical downturn in Europe and Japan is over."

■ The United States regained its traditional position as the world's largest exporter in 1989, and since 1986 has increased its relative share of exports in manufactured goods among industrialized nations to 18 percent from 14 percent.

Nearly a quarter of all U.S. merchandise exports in 1992 were in high-technology products, and this year the United States regained its spot as the world's leading exporter of semiconductors.

■ The U.S. merchandise trade deficit is rising, but economists say that simply reflects the greater demand for imports as the U.S. economy surges.

What is more surprising, however, is that U.S. exports of goods are growing as well. They are up more than 2 percent in the year to Sept. 31—in the face of recessions in all of America's major overseas markets.

■ A recent study of labor productivity by McKinsey & Co. found overall U.S. labor productivity in manufacturing to be 17 percent higher than in Japan and 21 percent higher than in Germany. An earlier study by the group found that U.S. workers have a similar edge in the service sector.

■

SOME ECONOMISTS, THOUGH, are skeptical of the notion that there has been a long-term improvement in the U.S. economy's growth potential.

Massachusetts Institute of Technology economist Paul Krugman warns against writing off the productive capabilities of U.S. trading partners on the basis of recent developments.

"Japan is in a slump because of a bursting of its speculative bubble," he argues. "In Europe, the welfare state has run amok and they have messed up monetary policy coordination."

Other economists, however, ascribe the resilience of America's economy to its willingness to endure wrenching change, to keep its markets open and to confront foreign competition head on.

"The U.S. has met the competition from Japan in a very direct and brutal way," says William Lewis, head of the McKinsey Global Institute. In most industries, says Lewis, "U.S. manufacturers have gotten as good as the Japanese or they have gone out of business."

■

A CLEAR SIGN OF AMERICA'S competitive strength is that many big foreign companies are rushing to invest here, to take advantage of low labor costs, high productivity and a robust consumer market.

Two of the biggest German automakers—BMW and Mercedes-Benz—recently announced plans to build new production facilities in the Southeast, following the lead of Japan's Toyota and Nissan, and Honda in Ohio.

One senior Daimler-Benz executive says that the United States now has a roughly 30 percent cost advantage in manufacturing over Germany.

The recent success of America's freewheeling capitalist economy hasn't come without costs. A prominent Canadian economist notes that the U.S. improvement comes at a time of sharp decline in what she calls "civitas"—the sense of community that holds nations together.

And the "restructuring" revolution that has swept through the U.S. economy has embittered workers and managers who have been brushed aside.

Those resentments surfaced in the debate over the North American Free Trade Agreement, which many Americans saw as a threat to the jobs of ordinary work-

ers. They fear that the price of winning a global economic competition with countries such as Mexico and China will be lower wages and less job security.

President Clinton has not actually mounted the White House balcony to trumpet the good news. But he has made it clear that he is playing a long game in the global economic league—and that he intends to win.

"This country is dealing with structural economic challenges of 20-year duration," he said at a recent speech to the Democratic Leadership Council. "We are dealing with social challenges that have been building for 30 years. We are reversing economic policies that were in place for 12 years. We will not be able to turn this around overnight."

Japan's Non-Revolution

Karel van Wolferen

Karel van Wolferen, president of the Institute for Independent Japanese Studies, has lived in Japan since 1962. He is the author of The Engima of Japanese Power.

THE AGE OF UNCERTAINTY

The recent and ubiquitous speculation in the world's media that Japanese society has reached a watershed is based more on wishful thinking than on an understanding of the forces at work in the Japanese body politic. It is a curious phenomenon, indicative of Western apprehensions, that almost every time Japanese developments gain international attention they are accompanied by assertions that the Japanese people are making choices that will change the way they live and work. In reality, the saddest aspect of Japan is that the Japanese people are not in a position to make such choices.

It is true that Japan has entered what can properly be described as an age of uncertainty. The recent fracturing of the Liberal Democratic Party (LDP) and the parliamentary crisis are symptoms of a disorientation without precedent in postwar Japan. International reality has changed for Japan's elite administrators. Its dominant element, the relationship with the United States, has lost the underpinnings that kept it in place for over four decades. With the disappearance of Cold War certainties from American foreign policy, and Japan's emergence as a discomforting economic force, American indulgence toward Japan is shrinking to a point where the basic guarantees that Japan's political elite could count on for four decades have disappeared.

Changes in domestic reality have been less abrupt and are less easily singled out for analysis, but a pervasive sense of unease about Japan's economic future has left its elites disoriented. Although often deceived by their own propaganda, many of Japan's elite know that Japan's ability to export the costs of its postwar strategy of unlimited industrial expansion has been fundamental to that strategy's success. They doubt that Japan can much longer shift such costs as

unemployment, environmental degradation and industrial obsolescence to other countries. During the deflation of the "bubble economy" these past three years, the Ministry of Finance has again demonstrated its genius in disproving prophets of Japanese economic doom. But the officials are now confronting forces so enormous, and international hostility to Japan's "torrential exports" has made the future effectiveness of rescue actions so unpredictable, that continued confidence in their ability to control economic outcomes can no longer be taken for granted.

Japan's age of uncertainty reached an important moment on June 18 when two prominent members of the LDP joined non-LDP politicians in a routine no-confidence vote against Prime Minister Kiichi Miyazawa. Four days later 44 LDP members resigned, forming two new parties. Along with the year-and-a-half-old Japan New Party, they have overturned what Japanese political commentators called "the 1955 setup." This political system, crucial to the shaping of postwar Japan, rested on two pillars: the guaranteed incumbency of the LDP, and a Socialist Party that for 38 years was mired in internal squabbles and unrealistic priorities, guaranteed to keep it out of power.

Since the early 1960s Japan's politicians have not played a significant role in determining national policy.

For over a quarter of a century, informed Japanese and foreigners alike have readily expressed doubts about the authenticity of Japanese democracy. A vote in the countryside could be worth up to four times as much as one in the cities. The Supreme Court, although recognizing that this system violated the constitution, has refused to endorse corrective action that might "cause confusion." By the second half of the 1960s the urban electorate had by and large stopped supporting the LDP, and in successive elections switched what were widely understood to be "protest votes" from one minor party to another. The electorate outside the cities has to a large extent been bribed or subtly coerced into keeping the LDP in power. The Diet has hardly ever been used for genuine parliamentary debates on public issues because the socialist-led opposition indulged in utterly ritualistic politics, regular boycotts of Diet proceedings being its major weapon.

The July 18 elections to the House of Representatives have knocked over one pillar of the 1955 setup. The socialists have been punished for betraying the electorate for 38 years through the loss of half their seats. The politicians who now occupy those seats are not expected to follow the socialist example of marginalizing themselves, raising the possibility that the Diet will become less the rubber-stamp outfit than it has been. Japan's one-party system may well be dead.

POLITICIANS WITHOUT POWER

But the one-party aspect of the 1955 setup, on which doubts concerning Japanese democracy have usually centered, has obscured a more fundamental defect that is likely to remain even now that the 1955 setup is defunct. Since the early 1960s Japan's politicians have not played a significant role in determining national policy, with the sole exception, perhaps, of the brilliant and controversial Kakuei Tanaka. Despite periodic efforts by such talented politicians as Yasuhiro Nakasone, there has not been effective political oversight over bureaucratic decision-making. This bureaucratic decision-making has almost exclusively been restricted to administrative matters. A major shift in national priorities—the need for which is often conceded by independent members of the political elite—cannot come from the bureaucracy, because there is no single entity with the mandate to make decisions that are binding on the entire governing apparatus. The single most powerful entity, the Ministry of Finance, is ultimately guided by the course of action its institutional memory indicates will serve it best, which means that it continues to support the unlimited expansion of Japan's productive capacity.

It is unlikely that this arrangement could have continued for as long as it did without the strategic and diplomatic shield provided by the United States. As Japan concentrated solely on unlimited industrial expansion, there was almost no need to cope with a capricious world; no need to develop acrobatic skills in international diplomacy. These unusual conditions fulfilled the vision held by Japan's first important postwar prime minister, Shigeru Yoshida, of how the Japanese political elite could make the best of the unfortunate circumstances of the late 1940s.

In return for American protection, the LDP accommodated the United States in what Washington cared about most until the Berlin Wall collapsed. Security arrangements, giving the Pentagon unconditional use of whatever military bases it wished to maintain in Japan, were safe as long as the conservatives kept the

socialists out of power. But the LDP failed the United States in a way that no one in Washington ever anticipated. By abdicating responsibility for the national agenda to the bureaucracy, the LDP deprived the American government (and that of any other country) of an effective means to discuss any major issue requiring Japanese action. It has not been possible for an American president to discuss the future with a representative of Japan whose mandate reaches further than adjusting technicalities. As things stand, no matter how often Bill Clinton talks with the Japanese prime minister, or how cordial their relationship may be, these two cannot even begin to come to grips with what is threatening to rupture their two countries' crucial relationship.

Japanese ministries come closer to being states unto themselves than any other government institution in the industrialized world.

For some time American trade representatives and other emissaries have been attempting to identify "the right people to talk with." And if there are not any individuals who could make a difference, so it is thought, there must be groups with access to "the right buttons." They do not exist. By leaving overall policymaking in the hands of an unelected and self-appointed group of officials, Japan's elected representatives turned over the core functions of government to men of great but limited competence. Since the 1950s, this bureaucracy has understood limitless industrial growth to be the unquestioned primary goal for Japan, a goal to which all other domestic concerns, such as education and general welfare, as well as international relations must remain subservient. Bureaucrats everywhere judge themselves by their efforts to gain prestige or power for their own institutions. Unless changes could conceivably bring further advantage to their own bureaus, bureaucrats will endeavor to work for the status quo. Japanese bureaucrats are no exception, which results in the institutional paralysis with which foreign negotiators have become familiar.

THE PERMANENT GOVERNMENT

The LDP's abdication of political responsibility fits in with previous forms of Japanese governance, and is connected with the major political flaw of twentieth-century Japan: the absence of a center of political accountability. This is fundamentally different from what has frequently been diagnosed as a "leadership problem," rooted in temporary weaknesses of political will on the part of Japan's highest elected officials. It must be understood that Japan's government agencies do not for practical purposes represent a real government—a core of the state entrusted with the right and duty of decision-making on behalf of the national interest, a core that Japanese citizens could get a grip on if they so desired. Japan poses major conceptual challenges to the West. Americans and Europeans, who take for granted that countries have centers of political accountability (as is clear from the frequent exhortations that "Japan should do this" or "Japan should accept that"), cannot easily understand the workings of a political system lacking a core that can explain to foreigners, to its own population and to the political elite itself what it is doing and why.

Japanese ministries come closer to being states unto themselves than any other government institutions in the industrialized world. Besides their responsibilities for administration, they also monopolize the lawmaking capacities and jurisdiction within their own bailiwicks. For all practical purposes they themselves are not subject to the rule of law. There exists no system of informal power in the world so vast as that of Japan. The system has, however, formal supports in laws that are purposely kept extremely vague to allow for the widest possible bureaucratic discretion. The only significant formal curb on the ministries would be the constitution, which is almost ignored by Japan's bureaucracy. This foreign document—bestowed upon Japan by General Douglas MacArthur—contains a number of articles designed to ward off, in one way or another, arbitrary bureaucratic rule, but these are consistently and systematically violated.

The Ministry of Finance is strongest among these semi-independent governing bodies, since the other government agencies depend on its budget bureau, which judges their annual requests. The banking law assumes that the banks will always follow the ministry's widely varying interpretations of the law. As the 1991 financial scandals demonstrated, ministry officials are not held accountable for violating the securities laws through their informal instructions. The ministry engineered a massive transfer of wealth from the household sector to the industrial sector during the "bubble economy" years, but no one thought to protest. Effective means for holding Ministry of Finance bureaucrats accountable do not exist. Japan's main financial and economic newspaper, the *Nihon Keizai Shimbun,* functions as an amplifier for what ministry officials want players in the Japanese economy to think and believe, preventing it from monitoring ministerial action with critical eyes.

Cabinet ministers are generally not even considered part of the ministries they ostensibly lead. Hence the actual coordination of the Japanese bureaucracy does not take place at cabinet level, and a prime minister's leverage over the entire governing apparatus is virtually nonexistent. To ensure a measure of stability and coordination, and to minimize turf battles, ministries exchange personnel. These bureaucrats on loan double as diplomats and spies, and one of their main tasks is coordinating measures to keep at bay politicians with ambitions to make policy.

The changed circumstances that have ushered in Japan's age of uncertainty demand political adjustments from Japan that the bureaucracy cannot possibly deliver. This is understood by the main figures in the non-LDP ranks whose actions precipitated the recent political upheaval. Two of the new "reformers," now in the Japan Renaissance Party, Ichiro Ozawa and Tsutomo Hata, have for some years made clear that they are eager to apply their considerable political skills to national policymaking. They were protected by Shin Kanemaru, the single most powerful LDP boss, until an internal LDP power struggle one year ago resulted in his removal (with the help of the most recent political scandal in the press). Their loss of a solid political base inside the LDP and failure to get the LDP behind their program for electoral reform gave them an incentive to try their luck at establishing what the three had frequently mentioned as being good for Japan—a two-party system. The third major "reformer," Morihiro Osokawa, deserted the LDP the year before to form his own Japan New Party and has drawn attention with his advocacy of reviewing certain areas of bureaucratic power. The leader of a group of breakaway socialists, Satsuki Eda, also understands that new directions for Japan can only come from politicians.

An unknown number of senior officials in the ministries, as well as prominent retired bureaucrats, also believe in the need for political oversight. Some officials, understanding from personal experience their own ministries' limitations, privately worry that Japan will blunder into catastrophe, as it did in the 1930s, for lack of strong political guidance. But the flaw in Japan's political system is self-perpetuating. In the absence of a center of political accountability these concerned powerholders cannot take preventive action without losing their dignity and creating the impression that they are disloyal to the institutions in which they have made their careers.

A coalition government of reform-minded politicians fully intent on wresting political control from the bureaucracy would face phalanxes of the real powerholders in Japan who are highly skilled in sabotaging projects not to their liking. Drastic interference with bureaucratic personnel appointments would be required. Such steps would probably be followed by an uproar, with the activist politician pilloried among his colleagues and in the media as being un-Japanese for breaking the unwritten rules of Japanese "harmony." Ozawa, who is without a doubt the strongest of the politicians, has already gained a reputation as being too pushy for a Japanese politician. Someone of his caliber who takes a truly courageous stand in the face of bureaucratic opposition becomes very vulnerable, because it is not difficult to launch a scandal that can bring him down. As part of the new coalition parties, an ambitious group of "reformers" might actually assist officialdom in realizing bureaucratic schemes that would have been more difficult to accomplish under the old 1955 setup. It is entirely possible that the upheaval will eventually make the Japanese governmental system even less responsive to international interests and those of the Japanese citizenry. It is conceivable that future coalitions composed of the existing splitters of the LDP, new splitters, what is left of the LDP and the older, minor parties could become indistinguishable from what the LDP has been–a passive and secondary player in Japan's government.

THE SELF-CENSORING PRESS

Admiration for Japan's undoubted economic successes and for its putative supremacy in managerial skills has blinded many Westerners to the profound failures of the Japanese political system. The general assumption, which was again very much in evidence between the lines of most press commentary, assured us that when it really became necessary this political system would respond and repair itself. This may, of course, still happen. But there are good reasons for pessimism. Major obstacles to self-repair are not fully understood in the West, because they are entirely unexpected. But they could provide clues as to what the rest of the world, especially the United States, can do to help salvage what is salvageable of Japanese democracy.

The single biggest impediment to Japanese political reform is probably the Japanese press. It is monolithic, since the five large daily newspapers speak with one voice–their commentary on the issues of the day is almost indistinguishable, and their selection of what to report and what to ignore is virtually identical. The systematic and heavy self-censorship the newspapers engage in is without parallel in the industrialized world. Hence the press directly and decisively determines what others conceive of as political reality, and as such it should be considered Japan's most powerful political–as distinct from administrative–entity.

The vast informal Japanese power structure provides ample opportunity to flay politicians with corruption scandals. Almost any politician can be implicated in such scandals at any time, because gaining political stature in Japan requires raising large sums of money. The easiest means of raising this money stems from the discretionary licensing powers of the bureaucracy. Relatively new or rapidly expanding businesses must protect themselves against arbitrary treatment. Businesses turn to politicians and

offer them very lucrative roles as influence brokers. Without ever distinguishing between unethical bribery and generally accepted political funding, the newspapers consistently denigrate the motives and character of politicians, thus helping to keep alive a general sense that Japan's politicians should not be entrusted with more real power.

No newspaper doubts the need for political reform. But their standard preachings on this subject are placed safely in the context of alleged moral deficiencies of politicians and never concern the shortcomings and abuses of unchecked bureaucratic power. Senior Japanese newspaper editors view themselves as public guardians, entrusted to help maintain a disciplined society with a maximum of order and a minimum of conflict. Since politicians cause political disturbance, and cannot hide the fact that they want power–as opposed to bureaucrats, who are thought to be selfless and dedicated servants of the people–editors protect the bureaucrats and wage regular campaigns against politicians. The newspapers are effectively allied with the police, the public prosecutor, the ministries of finance, justice, education and the *Keidanren* (the umbrella organization of the business bureaucrats, a de facto public organization).

A very difficult aspect of Japanese political reality to fathom is the absence of public opinion. What passes for it is manufactured by the media, especially the five national dailies, and often bears little resemblance to what the Japanese people actually think. They are as capable as people anywhere of discussing a great variety of subjects with indignation and candor, but Japan lacks the institutions to turn these privately expressed opinions into a shared public opinion.

When, prompted by events, a "national debate" emerges concerning fundamental issues, it is immediately filtered by the press to conform to bureaucratic goals, in particular the overriding aim of preserving the status quo. It is therefore not surprising that the burning question in Japan's age of uncertainty, how to accomplish political direction over bureaucratic power, and the fact that this is central to the current parliamentary crisis, are not widely discussed.

Japanese civil society is extremely weak and politically ineffectual. In fact, the press can be said to have supplanted civil society. Genuine labor unions were crushed long ago and have a tradition of serving management. Japan's famous "company loyalty" precludes political activism (which would certainly destroy an employee's career in the company) and has prevented the emergence of a politically significant middle class. Political action and interest groups are not nationally coordinated and are invariably tied to single causes, making them unfit to serve as the foundation for sustained reasoned opposition to the status quo. The judiciary is not independent. With few exceptions, Japanese intellectuals are servants of the bureaucracy, indulging in a type of verbal political opposition that allows them to maintain an image of independence but is harmless because it remains unconnected with political reality.

Attributing Japan's parliamentary crisis to a Japanese public disgusted with political corruption, as the Western press has done, is therefore highly inaccurate. The widespread notion that the upheaval will lead to a shift from Japan's exclusive concern with producer interests to those of consumers is equally ill-conceived.

CAN JAPAN CHANGE?

Japan's true national interest cannot be discussed and served unless politicians gain ascendancy. If, instead, a succession of weak coalitions leads to the further consolidation of unaccountable bureaucratic and business-bureaucratic power, this would not only be tragic for the Japanese people, but highly problematic and perhaps even dangerous for the rest of the world.

As commentators such as R. Taggart Murphy and Christopher Wood have pointed out, endless additions to productive capacity without regard to profitability could create the conditions for global depression.[1] The gradual transformation of countries belonging to the Association of Southeast Asian Nations into "subcontracted economies" headquartered in Tokyo raises new questions about long-range Japanese security arrangements for the protection of these foreign assets.

Japan is today one of the world's most powerful political entities. Coping with it requires more than three days a year of the president's time and the attention of third- and fourth-rank American bureaucrats. Even though President Clinton has shown some understanding of the problem, there are very few people who understand how to deal with Japan effectively. They will be utterly overwhelmed with the magnitude of the task.

As experience shows, conventional diplomacy can achieve only limited goals in Japan. But the rest of the world does have levers to change Japan, while avoiding punitive sanctions. The greatest leverage comes from the desperate hankering on the part of Japan's elite administrators for acceptance of their country as a full political equal of the world's other major democratic states. The implied message from the American president and other governments should be that this is not possible unless Japan establishes a system of politi-

cal accountability. An appropriate context in which to send this message is Tokyo's ardent desire to be given permanent membership on the U.N. Security Council. The Security Council veto power should be made conditional on Japan demonstrating a functioning civilian control mechanism over its own security apparatus. The well-known apprehensions of Korea, Russia and the Southeast Asian countries will strengthen America's case in this matter.

Such concern will actually dovetail with latent and deep-seated fears of large segments of the Japanese political elite, notably the economic ministries. They continue to treat Japan's military (by budget allocation standards the third or fourth biggest in the world) as if it hardly existed—partly because they are unsure as to where in the scheme of Japan's informal power system a fully rehabilitated army and navy would come to rest.

A convincing civilian control mechanism over the defense bureaucracy would foster the development of control mechanisms over other powerful entities, particularly the Ministry of Finance and the business-bureaucratic establishment. Large Japanese companies are—in their behavior and incentive structure—effectively bureaucratic entities, not ultimately driven by considerations of profit making.

A well-informed, imaginative approach ready to engage in unconventional "diplomacy" can achieve much vis-à-vis Japan. Washington could start by urging the Japanese people to write their own constitution. The political/intellectual turbulence this would engender in Japan could only have a salutary effect on the growth of Japan's civil society. It would also end any lingering impression of the United States as postwar parole officer—a role Washington no longer cares to play or understands how to play in any case. Some of the "reformist" politicians, notably Ozawa, need no convincing that Japan needs a constitution giving it unambiguous sovereignty and legitimizing its armed forces.

Contrary to fashionable opinion, the way in which the Japanese have organized their sociopolitical system is very much the business of foreigners. Japanese journalists, many of them moved by feelings of guilt about their systematic self-censorship, frequently solicit and print opinions of foreigners on subjects they dare not touch themselves. Newspapers will prominently feature well-known Americans who direct themselves to the Japanese public with sympathy and genuine understanding. Constant reminders that the people of a great nation must wield power through their politicians and cannot leave fundamental questions of their lives undiscussed would have a far greater positive impact than Westerners now imagine.

R. Taggart Murphy, "Power Without Purpose: The Crisis of Japan's Global Financial Dominance," *Harvard Business Review,* March/April 1989; Christopher Wood, *The Bubble Economy,* New York: Atlantic Monthly Press, 1992.

Privatization in the Former Soviet Empire
The Tunnel at the End of the Light

Stephen S. Cohen and Andrew Schwartz

Stephen S. Cohen is co-director and Andrew Schwartz is a research associate at the Berkeley Roundtable on the International Economy at the University of California at Berkeley.

In the former Soviet empire, the collapse of Communism created an opportunity for the victims of one failed utopian ideology to find another. The evaporating Soviet system left an ideological vacuum that was quickly filled as legions of Western advisers arrived to help translate the goals of political democracy and a market economy into an action agenda: "democracy" translated quickly into elections; a "market economy" into privatization.

As in many hurried translations, the bare essentials were grasped, but much was missed. Elections are essential to democracy, but functioning democracies are built on much more than just elections. And private ownership is only one element of a modern market economy. But it was fundamentalist capitalism that poured in—the simple, universal program that all could understand: free prices, free trade, and, above all, privatize.

The fate of small enterprises like shops, restaurants, or farms was never at issue. Everyone agreed that rapid small-scale privatization was the best way to energize private sector growth and to develop a capitalist ethic and an entrepreneurial class.

The thornier question was how, and how fast, to privatize the clunking state enterprises that employed thousands and thousands. Supposedly, only an abrupt and ruthless privatization could clear the stage of the remnants of a command economy—the perverse incentives, the incompetent and corrupt apparatchiks, the endless subsidies, the mindless production of the wrong goods. Delay risked permitting those who stood to lose the most from privatization—the old-line bureaucrats and the managers and workers of the giant state enterprises—to undermine the privatization process, thereby jeopardizing the transition to a market economy. According

to Harvard University economist Jeffrey Sachs:

> The need to accelerate privatization in Eastern Europe is the paramount economic policy issue facing the region. If there is no breakthrough in privatization in large enterprises in the near future, the entire process could be stalled for political and social reasons for years to come, with dire consequences for the reforming economies of the region.

The *Economist* agreed, calling "the growing acceptance of...gradualism...the greatest peril now facing the countries of Eastern Europe."

But there is an alternative to radical privatization, and it is not just a smokescreen put forward by nostalgics for the old system. It is rather the safest and sanest approach to building a market economy and democratic society.

Rapid privatization will backfire, for few of the newly privatized big companies can survive in a competitive market environment. The structures of both supply and demand for these giant firms have been shattered; the industrial linkages among Eastern Europe and the former Soviet republics are severed. The abrupt political change separated enterprises from their traditional customers the way the movement of rivers into new channels left medieval entrepots high and dry on silted streams. The economic collapse resulting from sudden privatization would result in extensive layoffs, massive bankruptcies, and social unrest. In a climate of chaos, the state would eventually have to support the failing enterprises, one way or another.

Markets can't regulate monopolies. A heritage of monopolies implies active regulation. Who shall regulate monopoly and oligopoly industries? Who shall oversee the liquidation of the losers, the temporary subsidy of restructurings, and the re-employment of workers? For a prolonged period, newly privatized firms won't be able to compete in their home markets against superior imported goods. Who shall oversee international trade and

ration foreign exchange, as West European governments had to do after World War II? Further, such essential preconditions for modern capitalist economies as an established legal system or tax code, financial institutions, and effective capital markets do not exist. These shortcomings increase the odds that a "big bang" privatization will turn into a "big bust."

This essay develops the argument for a pragmatic approach to privatization. It boils down to three basic contentions.

First, the creation of capitalist institutions takes time. Privatizing ownership will not by itself make large, uncompetitive enterprises operate efficiently. Nor will distributing ownership of shares create a market system or a capitalist culture. Giant corporations need internal capabilities in organization, pricing, labor relations, accounting, and marketing in addition to productive incentives. The repair of severed domestic and international linkages—among existing plants, between suppliers and users, between firms and their traditional markets—will also take time.

Second, private ownership, even in the Western context, makes sense only in the context of embedded socioeconomic institutions. Big companies don't exist in an institutional vacuum. Nor do markets. Both require external structures of law, finance, and regulation. Erecting a system of domestic finance with efficient capital markets is but one important example of such needed institutions.

Third, the state will inevitably play the major role in industrial development in most of the countries of the former Soviet empire, especially Russia, for a long interim. It will help create and regulate markets; it will control imports and oversee the flow of capital; and, irrespective of the chosen privatization strategy, it will effectively control substantial portions of major industrial assets. The competitive vulnerability of existing industry allows no other alternative for the near future. The creation of an honest and effective public administration—not the broad distribution of shares in uncompetitive giant firms—is the key step toward the creation of a successful capitalistic market system and a functioning democracy.

Varieties of Capitalism, or Who Owns Mitsubishi?

Radical capitalists ignore the great differences in the institutions of private ownership of big firms in such successful capitalist countries as the U.S., Japan, Germany, France, and Italy, as well as the other enormous institutional differences that distinguish the competing capitalisms. They strip away the complex variety and reduce private ownership to the simple model of textbook economics. They neglect history, they discard experience. Any remotely appropriate historical experience—such as Europe after World Wars I and II—points in a quite different direction.

Radical capitalists insist that only a system of privately owned firms linked together by markets provides the right incentives and the right constraints, a set of signals that promotes social dynamism and optimal allocation. Moreover, market signals are prompt and unrelenting. Adaptation is fast and permanent. One of the impressive aesthetics of capitalism is the perfect match between efficiency in capital formation and efficiency in production. Moreover, newly privatized industries are likely to attract foreign investors—the main sources of modern technology and management skills—more readily than state counterparts. Finally, competition will relentlessly downsize the old industrial monsters into more productively sized companies.

At first glance, the radical capitalist argument is appealing. The problem, of course, is that the textbook caricatures of the institutions of modern capitalism obscures an understanding of how the different systems actually function. Take the two critical institutions—price-driven, "free" capital markets and private ownership of giant corporations. Neither is simple in practice; and neither is universal in form.

In France, as in Japan, Germany, and Korea, for more than a generation after World War II, capital markets were neither "free" nor price-driven. To a critical extent, especially where giant corporations were concerned, capital was allocated less by price (as in the proposed capital markets for Eastern Europe) than by administrative systems of priorities.

Nor does the pragmatic experience of forms of ownership correspond to the simplistic radical capitalist model. In Japan, the most successful case ever of rapid development, ownership is "private," but only if one defines private as not owned by the state. Interlocking shareholding and finance within the industrial groups known as *keiretsu* created something far removed from the simple ownership model of the radical capitalists. Keiretsu have no obvious analogy in the rest of the First World, and no place whatsoever in Econ 101 textbooks. Who owns Mitsubishi? Perhaps the most accurate functional answer is "Mitsubishi owns Mitsubishi."

The form of ownership is an important element in modern capitalism, but it is less a unifying than a differentiating characteristic; and it takes its real world meaning only within the complex institutional context that defines a particular capitalist system. There is more than one variety of successful capitalism.

Structural Constraints and Realistic Choices

Just as it is dangerous to apply narrowly naive concepts of capitalist institutions to the different countries of the former Soviet realm, so it is dangerous to generalize about this region. The several countries have different political systems, legal traditions, ownership patterns, educational levels, industrial structures, languages, ethnic cleavages, religions, and, of course, sizes. It is little wonder that of the countries most actively engaged in privatization—the Czech Republic, Slovakia, Poland, Hungary, Slovenia, and Russia—each has a different privatization strategy. Nonetheless, the Communist system left a shared legacy that constrains the prospects for rapid privatization. At least seven of these troubling legacies will shape the results of privatization.

1. Shortage of entrepreneurial experience; surplus of criminal experience. More than 40 years of Communism have produced a managerial class ill-equipped to function in a capitalist market. The best of the technical-managerial leadership is lodged in the military-industrial complex, a declining market. Most of the market experience comes from the "second economy," and it is dubious that such experience will translate into competent large company ownership or management.

Besides petty black marketeers, the other likely new ownership stratum is those who made money illegally—big-time black marketeers or corrupt bureaucrats—or both working together, as they always have. They are best positioned to cash in on abrupt privatizations. They can split enterprises into valuable and potentially negative parts, shift labor across those parts, maintain control of the good bits, and reap a capital gain at the moment of privatization—millionaires in one quick shot. They can reap a windfall gain no matter how the enterprise performs. Even where assets are auctioned to the highest bidder, these networks of officials and plant managers, with their underground allies (most often called, locally, "the Mafia"), typically have the cash and insider knowledge to bid. This potential was not lost on sophisticated foreign advisers: bars in foreigners-only hotels are filled with International Monetary Fund and World Bank officials explaining how the late medieval capitalists in Europe were considered, in their time, to be criminal elements. Likewise, the winners of the American bootlegging wars have now become solid, corporate capitalists. Privatization ideally would transform the criminal mafia into normal organizations—unless, of course, the Southern Italian model were to prevail.

2. Shortage of companies ready for a market economy. Most of the giant enterprises are burdened with obsolete product and process technology and mountains of debt. The debt will be written off by the state one way or another. But even with newly cleaned balance sheets, they are poor candidates for market viability. Finding real private owners to run them, without permanent subsidy and protection, will be difficult. Even the German privatization agency the *Treuhandanstalt*, despite an infusion of about $100 billion, had only privatized about half of the eastern German industries by 1992, representing the best of Communist enterprise. Some 1.6 million workers remain under Treuhand jurisdiction. Despite its ferocious determination to the contrary, it would not be surprising if the Treuhand found itself slowly transformed into a new German version of Italy's much maligned I.R.I. (the giant state holding company).

3. Poor work habits. This report from the *New York Times* is typical: "Managers of new private companies say they must dismiss dozens of people to find one not afflicted by the lackadaisical work ethic fostered by the Communist system. Private hotels in Warsaw do not even accept applications from former state employees." In addition, a hierarchical mentality still pervades enterprises. In the past, incentive structures in Communist enterprises discouraged managers from acting with initiative. In most cases, managers were better off playing along with the system than risking their position by exercising discretion.

4. Shortage of domestic and international capital. The previous regimes left the economies virtually without savings. The rebuilding of the industrial capacity in the region cannot rely on small contributions from the accumulated savings of the domestic population. Newly privatized firms will need debt financing from domestic banks or from institutions based abroad. Yet none of the governments has yet established a banking system ready to make the loans. Moreover, real and/or nominal rates are high, and credit is generally very tight throughout the region. The major source of capital is likely to remain the state, or in very selected circumstances, foreigners.

The newly privatized firms, striving to become competitive, will not be the only large claimants on the small capital pool. Indeed, they will most likely find themselves at the end of the queue. The best candidates for privatization, and for capital infusions, are the classic infrastructural industries: telecommunications, road building, railways, airlines, and the like, not to mention electric power generation—the handling of those dangerous nuclear power plants on West Europe's doorstep. The Western Europeans want those stations rebuilt for safety, and their nuclear power industry is hurting from a lack of orders. They will provide massive investment to the newly privatizing electric utilities, thus combining safety and capitalist development in the East along with safety and the generation of business for state-supported industry in the West.

Privatizing infrastructural industries would also have the advantage of producing tradable shares with which to generate capital markets. Moreover, they would be acceptable vehicles for international aid and investment institutions that are obligated to make a substantial portion of their financing to private firms. All in all, such industries present an ideal set of financeable and potentially privatizeable activities, protected from the vicissitudes of markets and competition. They are not, however, very likely, to be particularly generative of a new capitalist culture.

Those who expect a major capital injection from the West are likely to be disappointed. A "Marshall Plan" for the former Soviet empire is not in the cards. For one thing, recession and high government deficits have drained public coffers in the West. For another, there are alternative targets for scarce Western and Japanese capital, in Asia and Latin America. To date, inbound private investment has been quite small. For instance, in 1990 and 1991, Poland received $1.3 billion, Czechoslovakia $800 million, and Hungary $2.3 billion. World Bank commitments to the region for 1991 amounted only to a little over $3 billion. The EBRD (European Bank for Reconstruction and Development) put in only about $800 million, about half for telecommunications loans. Over the same period, as noted, East Germany, a territory of some 17 million souls, received almost $100 billion. Multiply that amount by ten to get a comparable infusion for Russia alone, and one can see that the German experience, a new intra-German Marshall Plan, is not a model for the region. Finally, there will be dramatic

differences among the host nations in the role of foreign capital. Foreign capital and foreign markets will be major shapers of the Czech economy; they will necessarily have only a small impact on the Russian economy.

5. Risky business conditions. Marko Simonetti, director of privatization for Slovenia, argues that the challenge of privatization is to find active owners willing to lead companies through the transition period. But why should new owners restructure their enterprises when there may be an immediate payoff if they simply liquidate the assets? Domestic producers won't be able to compete effectively in open markets, at home or through exports. A quick taste of what lies ahead is the case of large state enterprises in eastern Germany. Unable to compete abroad, these firms lost their home market when products and companies from the western part of the country moved in.

The temptation to liquidate rather than to invest is heightened by the asset value of many companies. The company's land, buildings, and the right to do business may be worth more in the marketplace than its productive potential, lying in often dubious and difficult assets like machinery or the labor force. A common story is that of CKD Tatra—until recently the world's largest maker of tram cars, but last year the manufacturer of only 300—which has attracted investment interest mostly because its factory sits on valuable land in central Prague. This is simple rent-seeking, not entrepreneurship.

6. Weak links between labor, suppliers, manufacturers, and consumers. First World countries like Japan and Germany were able to get back on their feet quickly after World War II partly because reconstruction meant the reconstitution of forms of economic organization established years earlier rather than the creation of completely new relationships. For instance, keiretsu, the centralized forms of ownership in Japan, were antedated by *zaibatsu* which originated a century ago in the Meiji era. German business and unions reached durable working arrangements long before the postwar German miracle. Eastern Europe won't be able to manufacture those relationships overnight.

7. Fragmented markets; broken international linkages; ethnic hostility. The countries emerging from the former Soviet empire are fractured by unresolved differences in ethnicity, language, and religion. In many cases these differences have not been politically or economically resolved. Divisions between Czechs and Slovaks, Hungarians and Romanians, Armenians and Asseris, Russians and Ukranians, to name a few, are likely to stymie economic

rationalization. Perhaps the most poignant example is most of Yugoslavia, where civil war has halted economic reform.

The long-run economic choices of Eastern European countries will be restricted by the poverty and small size of most of the national markets in the region. To be competitive, industries in small countries must be active participants in foreign markets. Ideally, industries in small countries operate in a very open international market, buy where value is best, and sell internationally in niches. They must be outward-looking and dynamic: exactly the opposite of Eastern European large enterprises.

The industrial structures of Eastern Europe did not develop according to classic economic logic; they were defined by planned linkages within the regions of the ex-Soviet empire. Isolated from world markets, large firms produced goods made better and cheaper abroad. They operated in captive markets and exported on a large scale to similarly noncompetitive markets. They learned to operate with constant output and input prices and virtually unlimited access to credit. Sooner or later, many of those companies must be eliminated as national resources are channelled into products where the Eastern European countries are likely to have a competitive advantage, not just compared with one another but compared with the entire world. As one big firm in the region tries to improve itself by buying quality components from the world market, it dries up the markets for the other large firms, its traditional suppliers. When local consumers get a little real money and the chance to buy coveted imported goods rather than generally lower quality local products, the entire system collapses.

These old networks are now completely severed. As a result, Eastern European companies have lost the only conceivable buyers for much of what they produce. The problem is not simply one of price efficiency: it is one of political borders and disruption. Even a substantial increase in efficiency will not make up for the tattered regional industrial structure. It takes years to build a new structure, and a new structure cannot be built until the political uncertainty is overcome. Private investment—obtained in a real capital market—won't be readily forthcoming in newly privatized companies that are unsure of where their markets lie, where their sources of supply are located, or who their competitors are.

These seven obstacles would deter the most ardent reformers from attempting a program of drastic and potentially all-or-nothing industrial change. But the radical capitalists argue that it is essential to privatize quickly precisely because of such problems. That prescription might be tenable given a stable institutional setting with stable national boundaries and political systems, functioning tax codes, financial and legal systems, and broad-based capital markets, as well as plausible networks of international markets and industrial linkages. But there are few credible tested institutions. Without them, rapid privatization won't provide a solid base for prosperity, nor will it aid the development of independent entrepreneurs.

The Crucial Role of Capital Markets

Capital markets, just one of the absent institutions, invite particular attention. Price-driven capital markets are dear to the hearts of privatizers. Capital markets remove power, in giant dollops, from the hands of entrenched bureaucracies. They are fast, powerful, and provide invisibility for the market movers. It is difficult for a public bureaucracy to close down the only industry in a midwestern American town; that now-familiar objective is more easily achieved by a twitch on the Tokyo or New York stock exchange.

In capitalist economies, broad-based equity markets serve both investors and corporations in several ways. First, equity markets signal the underlying value of securities. Theoretically, this facilitates the proper allocation of resources by providing both investors and companies opportunities to raise cash as well as to spread resources among businesses that vary by product line and investment risk. Accurate share valuations provide stockholders with a de facto evaluation of management, which may sometimes precipitate corrective action. Second, equity markets provide avenues for companies to raise capital (equity or debt) from a wide net of investors. By the same token, equity markets enable investors to control risk in their portfolio more easily. Finally, equity markets ease the costs of investment and corporate restructuring by providing liquidity to both investors and corporations.

Because they are so powerful, capital markets are dangerous, especially when they lack proper safeguards and depth. In the lands of the ex-Soviet empire, the hazards are particularly acute because of the complete lack of experience in using these markets. Additionally, capital markets are likely to attract more attention than usual because of their novelty in the region and their significance as a capitalist symbol. Radical capitalists assume, correctly in our view, that capital markets will arise concurrently with privatization and the issuance of shares. Despite few viable companies, public stock markets are being organized in most of the countries.

Unfortunately, in spite of good intentions, these equity markets probably won't be able to perform efficiently—and just may perform with delegitimating perversity. It will be virtually impossible to establish fair market value for the exchange's listed companies given the shortage of capital in the region and the unstable business conditions. The lack of well-established, highly capitalized market participants implies that there will be a lack of liquidity in the equity markets. This will produce thin equity markets and wild price swings. The inexperience of the traders may also increase the likelihood of price gyrations.

Corruption is sure to become a big problem. Inexperienced market regulators will not be able to police markets that are moving quickly and without apparent reason. Market rigging and stock manipulation are inevitable. As most experienced traders will attest, financial market operations are very complex and enforcing fair rules can be nearly impossible. The first rounds of stock market activity are sure to see managers and their invisible partners in the administration cash in big. A crop of instant millionaires—whom everyone knew as the old *nomenklatura*—will become conspicuous symbols to be manipulated by potential demagogues.

If the resentment against black marketeers in Russia is any indication, there will be a groundswell against the "excessive" greed and corruption in the equity markets. Legitimate operators could get caught up in the popular outrage; so might the whole reform movement, especially in the context of large-scale economic misery and uncertainty experienced "by honest, hard working, native people."

Until a viable equity market is operational, companies will go elsewhere to raise capital or sell assets—by privately placing equity or raising capital through debt rather than equity. However, whereas in the West, market valuations can be made quickly due to the relatively free flow of information and the efficiency of markets, in the East, market valuations will be much more problematic. The lack of accepted accounting standards and a credible tax system will exacerbate the problem. These added uncertainties will make it much tougher to raise capital. Under these conditions, big firms will have no choice but to rely on the state, or in special cases private banks or foreigners, for their capital requirements. The investment policy of the newly privatized enterprise is likely to become dependent on the state. Independent active ownership may become an illusion, despite rapid privatization.

Public Enterprises Reconsidered

Radical capitalists insist that state ownership and capitalism don't mix, nor do state ownership and rapid development. In their view, the Communist economic malaise is just another failure of state ownership. Throughout the world, and in the Third World in particular, they argue, stated-owned industries are notoriously inefficient and corrupt. Little wonder that many poor nations, as diverse as India, Turkey, and Mexico, have embarked quite successfully on massive privatization programs in recent years.

Yet state ownership makes sense at certain times under certain conditions. For instance, when markets are imperfect and capital scarce, institutional malfunctions may channel investment away from industries that are key to long-term development. In several countries, a sudden implosion of whole sectors, sometimes whole sets of sectors, has resulted in the state finding itself forced to step in and nationalize the losers. Hence the typical state sector, with its portfolio of coal mines, steel mills, railways, and shipbuilding docks. Italy and Spain have lavish government portfolios so acquired. This history of nationalizing dying industries in response to political pressures or more simply of managing the difficult task of restructuring and downsizing as painlessly as possible has given state-owned enterprises their bad name. They are, most often, collections of basket cases that no one else would take. This is what makes their experience particularly relevant to the former Communist realm.

There are, however, other examples of state-owned companies, nationalized for one reason or another, that were not already dying. France provides the best examples, and the history has been anything but negative. As late as 30 years after World War II, the French state still owned all or major firms in steel, coal, oil distribution, transportation, automobiles, cigarettes, electronics, ocean shipping, aircraft, skyscraper office development, radio and television broadcasting, telephone services, gas, electricity, plus, horrid as it may seem, most big banks and insurance companies. This is a partial list. The postwar modernization, restructuring, and growth of the French economy has been, by anyone's standards (except Japan's) extraordinarily successful. What is more, state-owned firms played a leading role, not simply a shock-absorbing role, in that transformation and modernization.

In Japan and Korea, the giant industrial groupings that dominate the economy defy simple classification as private or public. Nor is there any compelling reason to make the distinction. Surely the great Japanese keiretsu are not public firms; the government does not own them. But it is extremely difficult to assimilate the Sumitomo or Mitsubishi groups into the traditional category of a private firm. The market is not the opposite of the government; the firm is not in opposition to the state. There are many varieties of institutional arrangements, and they change with time and circumstance. The all-or-nothing dichotomy of public bureaucracy or private (capital market based) firm is dangerously simplistic—especially as a guide for Eastern Europe, where capitalism does not yet exist. It pops out of textbook economics, not out of the history of successful economic development, especially "catch-up" development. That is the relevant genre: the people of Eastern Europe do not have to invent their positive future—just catch up with it.

What determines the success of state-owned enterprises? State-operated industries can be operated efficiently or inefficiently, using technologically advanced production techniques or backward ones. Empirically, the answer is clear. Good performance is a function of the domestic political economy and its institutions, not just of the nature of ownership. Drawing from a cross-national collection of case studies of privatization, Raymond Vernon in *The Promise of Privatization* concluded:

"Where governments have been reasonably competent and responsible, and where comparisons between private enterprises and state-owned enterprises have been possible, the technical performance of state-owned enterprises has not appeared much different from that of private enterprises. Here and there a strikingly efficient performance by a state-owned enterprise has cast doubt on the simple stereotypes of the public enterprise as a perennial wastrel."

In certain circumstances, reliance on the public sector and public ownership, in particular, may actually be good strategy. State ownership is certainly not to be sought as an end in itself; nor for the matter is private ownership of large enterprises. It all depends on the context in which choices must be made. Where private ownership seems doomed to fail—as in the case of many large enterprises in the ex-Soviet empire—the failure will result in a sudden implosion of the economy and society. In these cases, alternatives to simple privatization should be sought.

Further, the recent surge of privatization throughout Europe, Japan, and the Third World indicates that state ownership need not be permanent. Those trying to design new systems might profitably sift the rich varieties of institutional experience of other countries to see what made for better or worse performance: from state-owned, state-regulated, state-controlled, or state-in-cahoots-with. Ownership is a complex concept, contingent on embedded institutions. Given current conditions for big industry in the former Communist realms, some state ownership may be more desirable than simple "private ownership." Indeed, the logic of privatization in those lands does not ensure a dynamic market economy dominated by private firms. More likely, rapid privatization would precipitate state re-intervention sooner or later.

The Faulty Institutional Logic of Rapid Privatization

The focus on privatization, especially rapid privatization, diverts attention from implementation of policies and creation of market firms and institutions that encourage the development of competitive industries and an effective state bureaucracy to ensure viable democratic societies.

More than increasing efficiency expected from privatization, these troubled nations need the benefit of rebuilding the networks of industrial linkages and trade within the region. They need outlets for goods—such as steel, ships, coal, and especially agriculture—to Western Europe; this will not be easy to obtain. They will need import controls so all savings won't wash out quickly in a wave of consumer buying, and most likely controls on capital outflows too. More than anything, they need a competent and honest public administration to recreate those international linkages, administer those controls, negotiate those trade agreements, regulate the new and wildly imperfect markets, and buffer the shocks of industrial restructuring.

To the radical capitalists, rapid privatization is a shortcut. Eliminate the state, and voila, economic growth. But this is myth, ideology. The state will not whither away despite the dreams of radical capitalists any more than it did despite the dreams of Karl Marx. The state will run things for a long time, if not as owner, then as regulator.

Ironically, the logic of rapid privatization does not make the dependence of industry on the state any less likely. The state is destined to be the key economic player for the foreseeable future, whether privatization be rapid or gradual. Newly privatized giant enterprises will depend on the state for financing and for establishing rules and regulations. The state will also maintain a heavy hand in the industrial core of the economy because the inherited industrial structure provides most industries with too few firms for successful self-regulation by competition. And regulation by foreign competition may prove fatal.

Just as the state will necessarily be interventionist, given rapid privatization, so it will be protectionist. Assisted by their new armies of shareholders, the newly privatized enterprises, unfit to meet foreign competition, are likely to press for protectionist measures, especially since competing in an open economy would be suicidal. Free competition would open the field for Japan, the newly industrialized countries, and other low-cost, high-quality producers and leave little chance for inefficient domestic producers. They are inefficient now, and by world standards, they will be inefficient and uncompetitive for the near term. One must recall that Japan, Korea, France, and Germany never exposed their "infant industries" to the rigors of foreign competition; nor will most of the struggling new nations of the ex-Communist bloc.

Finally, rapid privatization plans aren't necessarily conducive to narrow, active, and independent ownership. Some rapid privatization plans envision ownership through mutual funds or through national distribution of share vouchers. In either case, there is no guarantee that active, independent ownership pressing for dynamic restructuring will emerge. Mutual funds owning shares in many firms, as in the Czech plan, may react to poor performance by selling shares, not necessarily by restructuring industry. If they don't, or are not allowed to, they become more like Italy's I.R.I. than a Wall Street fund. More important, the mutual funds (even with foreign advisers) are likely to advocate conservative measures for change due to the dependence of enterprises on the state and perhaps ultimately on the workers.

Grand designs are associated with great risk. So it was with Communism, so it will be with capitalism. The radical capitalists' fallacy is that pragmatism will ultimately result in the loss of discipline as local interests forestall change. Their concern is valid, but their prescription is not. The risks associated with rapid privatization skew the odds toward failure and ultimately toward disenchantment with capitalism and a democratic, more liberal state.

The big, inefficient state enterprises will not succeed as private enterprises. But they cannot simply be abolished. Building the structures of capitalism, the institutions of a functioning market system, will take time and breathing room. Radically pure markets won't build them; they will destroy those structures and risk ending the capitalist experiment before it has had a chance to develop into something worthwhile. It was no less than Joseph Schumpeter, the great advocate of entrepreneurial capitalism, in his brilliant case for maintaining less-than-perfect markets, who remarked: "You put brakes on a car so that it can go faster, not slower."

An uncut version of this article, with 72 footnotes, is available from BRIE, University of California, Berkeley, California 94720.

Conflict

In the international arena, governments are sometimes able to fulfill their goals by making mutually agreeable exchanges (i.e., giving up something in order to gain something they value more). This exchange process, however, often breaks down. When threats and punishments replace mutual exchanges, conflict ensues. Neither side benefits, and there are costs to both. Each side may hope the other will capitulate, but if efforts at coercion fail, the conflict may escalate into violent confrontation.

With the end of the cold war, the issues of national security are changing for the world's major powers. Old alliances are changing, not only in Europe but in the Middle East as well. These changes not only have major policy implications for the major powers but for participants in regional conflicts as well. Agreements between the leadership of the now-defunct Soviet Union and the United States led to the elimination of support for participants in low-intensity conflicts in Central America, Africa, and Southeast Asia. Fighting the cold war by proxy is now a thing of the past. Nevertheless, there is no shortage of conflicts in the world today.

The section begins with a broad overview of the major forces at work shaping the international politics of the twenty-first century. Included is a discussion of the types of conflicts that are likely to result and how these present new challenges to keeping them from escalating into warfare. This lead article is then followed with specific case studies: ethnic violence, terrorism, regional arms races, and the spread of nuclear weapons.

This unit concludes by examining one of the most important issues in history—the avoidance of nuclear war. Many experts initially predicted that the collapse of the Soviet Union would decrease the threat of nuclear war. However, many now believe that the threat has increased as control of nuclear weapons has become less centralized and the command structure less reliable. What these dramatically different circumstances mean for strategic weapons policy in the United States is also a topic of considerable debate. With this changing political context as the backdrop, the prospects for arms control and increased international cooperation are reviewed in the areas of nuclear and conventional weapons. Methods to reduce the risk of accidental nuclear war are also examined.

Like all the other global issues described in this anthology, international conflict is a dynamic problem. It is important to understand that it is not a random event, but there are patterns and trends. Forty-five years of cold war established a variety of patterns of international conflict as the superpowers contained each other with vast expenditures of money and technological know-how. The consequence of this stalemate was a shift to the Third World for the arena of conflict. With the end of the cold war, these patterns are already changing. Will there be more nuclear proliferation or will there be less? Will the emphasis be shifted to low-intensity conflicts related to the interdiction of drugs? Or will economic problems for the industrial world have them turn inward and allow a new round of ethnically motivated conflicts to turn brutally violent as we have seen in Yugoslavia? The answers to these and related questions will determine the patterns of conflict in the post–cold war era.

Looking Ahead: Challenge Questions

Is violent conflict and warfare increasing or decreasing today?

What changes have taken place in recent years in the types of conflicts that occur and in who participates?

How is military doctrine changing to reflect new political realities?

How is the role of the United States in global security likely to change?

Are nuclear weapons more or less likely to proliferate in the post–cold war era?

What institutional changes can be instituted to reduce the danger of nuclear war?

Unit 5

In this era, when keeping track of the number of times the superpowers can destroy the world is obsolete, attention has shifted to the number of brushfires cropping up in the world. As Michael Klare points out, it remains to be seen whether international organizations are up to the challenge of extinguishing them or whether they will be allowed to rage because of international inattention, inactivity, and indecision.

The New Challenges to Global Security

MICHAEL T. KLARE

MICHAEL T. KLARE is the Five College Associate Professor of Peace and World Security Studies, a joint appointment at Amherst, Hampshire, Mount Holyoke, and Smith Colleges and the University of Massachusetts at Amherst. He is the author of American Arms Supermarket (Austin: University of Texas Press, 1984) and co-editor of Low-Intensity Warfare (New York: Pantheon, 1988) and World Security: Trends and Challenges at Century's End, 2d ed.(New York: St. Martin's Press, 1993).

For 45 years, from World War II's finish to the end of the cold war, most agreed that the greatest threat to global security was an all-out war between the two superpowers that would culminate in the use of nuclear weapons. Fearing this, government officials and concerned citizens sought to diminish the risk of nuclear conflict through intensive diplomacy, improved crisis management, arms control, and cultural and other exchanges. Because of these efforts and the reforms that Soviet President Mikhail Gorbachev set in motion in 1985, the risk of a superpower conflict has largely vanished, and the world no longer dreads a nuclear conflagration.

The post–cold war era, however, is by no means free of the threat of armed conflict, as demonstrated by continuing warfare in areas as diverse as Afghanistan, Angola, Burma, Indonesia, Kashmir, Liberia, Peru, Somalia, Sri Lanka, the Caucasus (Georgia, Armenia, and Azerbaijan), and the former Yugoslavia. While these conflicts do not have the potential to erupt into a nuclear holocaust, they do pose a threat of widespread regional fighting with fearsome death tolls and destruction. Moreover, as weapons of mass destruction be-

come more widely diffused, a growing number of these regional wars will entail a risk of chemical and even nuclear attack. Preventing, controlling, and resolving these conflicts, and impeding the spread of advanced weaponry will, therefore, constitute the principal world security tasks of the 1990s and beyond.

THE SHIFTING POLITICAL LANDSCAPE

A metaphor popular among analysts thinking about the current reshaping of the world is that of "tectonic motion," or the movement of the giant "plates" that make up the earth's rocky crust. Because this movement can reshape continents and alter climates—sometimes cataclysmically—through the earthquakes and volcanoes it produces, it serves as an apt analogy for the end of the cold war and other dramatic changes now occurring throughout the world.[1]

The geological metaphor conveys the scale of the changes now under way around the globe and illustrates how surface events are the product of deeper sociohistorical forces. Thus we sense that the drive for democracy and human rights in Russia and eastern Europe is related to similar pressures in Myanmar, Chile, China, Haiti, Mexico, the Philippines, and Thailand. The image of tectonic motion also suggests the havoc wreaked by the breakup of large empires and federations (notably the Soviet empire and the old Yugoslavia) and the fracturing of established alliances such as the Warsaw Pact and, to a lesser degree, NATO.

But to adequately describe the security environment of this era after the cold war, the tectonics metaphor must be supplemented by an additional image—one that captures the profusion of ethnic, tribal, religious, and national conflicts that we are witnessing today. Imagine a piece of glass laid over a map of the world and then struck by a large, heavy weight: the result would be an intricate web of cracks across the world, with heavier concentrations in some areas but with none left entirely unscathed.

These cracks represent the many fissures in our multiethnic, multiclass, and multilingual societies—

---

[1]As the historian John Lewis Gaddis has observed, "Like the tectonic forces that move continents around on the surface of the earth," the end of the cold war and other recent developments suggest a massive shift in the "historic tectonics" of human civilization. John Lewis Gaddis, "Tectonics, History, and the End of the Cold War" (Columbus, Ohio: Occasional Paper from the Mershon Center of the Ohio State University, 1992), p. 4.

the divisions between rich and poor, black and white, Hindu and Muslim, Muslim and Jew, Czech and Slovak, Serb and Croat, Azeri and Armenian, and so on. The fissures are stressed by the tectonic shifts occurring beneath the surface, but it is along their jagged lines that the battles of the post–cold war era are being fought.

The fractured-glass analogy suggests the multiplicity of conflictual relationships in the world. Just consider for a moment the situation in the Middle East, which is not just a conflict between the Arab states and Israel, or between Iran and Iraq, but rather a far more elaborate configuration of animosities. In Lebanon, for instance, it involves Maronite Christians, Sunni and Shiite Muslims, the Druze, and Palestinians; in Syria, the Alawites and other Muslims; and in Iraq, Kurds, Sunnis, and Shiites. A similar diversity in the conflictual pattern is found in the former Yugoslavia, and in the Caucasus region of what was once the Soviet Union.

Each of these images—tectonic motion and fractured glass—is helpful in identifying features of the current world security environment. However, to best describe this environment it is useful to combine the images: tectonic movements causing massive shifts beneath the surface that in turn accentuate and extend the cracks appearing on the surface. By assessing both the tectonic movements and networks of cracks, we can arrive at a comprehensive picture of current world security issues.

FIVE FORCES THAT SHAKE THE WORLD

It is risky, of course, to attempt an analysis while the world is still undergoing transformation. But enough has already occurred on the surface for us to be able to begin to understand what is happening below. Five tectonic shifts in particular are worthy of discussion:

The Pull of Economic Forces

There was a time, not so long ago, when the "fate of nations" was determined largely by political and military factors—most significantly, the ability of the state to marshal a country's resources for war, conquest, or defense. Today the state remains a major international actor, but its capacity to organize resources for its purposes has been circumscribed by what has been called "supranational capitalism." As the economist Robert Heilbroner sees it, the global nexus of multinational corporations and international financial institutions has accumulated vast power and influence at the expense of national capitalism and state agencies. This, Heilbroner notes, endows supranational capitalism with the ability "to rearrange the global division and distribution of political and economic power"—a capacity that, when exercised, is often "seismic" in its impact.[2]

Obviously it is impossible to establish a one-to-one correlation between broad economic phenomena and specific world events. But that the failure of the Soviet Union and its eastern European satellites to keep pace with economic growth in the West contributed to the debilitation of Communist regimes is certain. Unable to generate funds for investment in economic and social revitalization, these regimes stagnated and lost what remained of their political legitimacy. The eventual result was a rapid slide from power, with what had become a corrupt and demoralized ruling class putting up little resistance.

The same economic forces are now exacerbating intergroup conflicts around the globe. Because some groups and societies have adapted more successfully than others to the competitive pressures of global capitalism, socioeconomic divisions in multinational states are becoming more visible and pronounced, provoking increased conflict between those on opposite sides of these rifts. Thus, the dissolution of Yugoslavia can be partially attributed to the desire of the country's stronger economic units, Croatia and Slovenia, to break away from their less advantaged fellow republics and integrate more closely with the western European economies. Similarly, the breakup of Czechoslovakia can be explained in part by growing resentment in Slovakia over the faster pace of economic activity in the Czech Republic.

Perhaps even more destabilizing is the widening economic gap between the industrialized "North" and underdeveloped "South." Although some third world countries have in recent years managed to join the ranks of the more affluent nations—one thinks especially of the newly industrialized countries of the Pacific Rim—most of the less developed countries of Asia, Africa, and Latin America have seen the difference between their standard of living and that of the wealthier nations widen over the past decade. At the same time, the global spread of Western culture and consumption patterns via the mass media have inculcated an appetite for goods and services not attainable by the masses of the poor and unemployed. The result is increased North-South tensions ranging from the growing militancy of political and religious movements with anti-Western themes (movements, for example, like the Maoist Shining Path in Peru and the Islamic Jihad in Egypt) to more South-to-North drug smuggling. Depressed economies in the South are also behind the rise in migration to the nations of the North—itself a growing cause of violence in the destination countries.

[2]Robert L. Heilbroner, "The Future of Capitalism," in Nicholas X. Rizopoulus, ed., *Sea Changes: American Foreign Policy in a World Transformed* (New York: Council on Foreign Relations, 1990), pp. 114–115.

5. CONFLICT

The Global Diffusion of Power

The rise of supranational capitalism has been accompanied by a diffusion of political, military, and economic power away from the United States and the Soviet Union, the two main poles of the cold war era, to other actors in the international order. This has been in progress since the 1950s and 1960s, when the western European countries and Japan began to recover from the devastating effects of World War II and many third world nations secured their independence; it gained further momentum in the 1970s and 1980s with the slowdown of economic growth in the United States and the Soviet Union and the acquisition of major military capabilities by emerging third world powers. The process culminated in 1989–1991 with the collapse of the Soviet Union, the dissolution of the Warsaw Pact, and the resulting disappearance of the bipolar world.

As of yet, no clearly defined system of power relationships has developed in place of the bipolar system and the tight alliances of the cold war period. Rather, a number of regional power centers—Japan in Asia, Germany in Europe, Russia in central Euroasia, the United States in North America—have emerged, each surrounded by a cluster of associated states. These centers cooperate with each other in some matters and compete in others; states not aligned with any of the principal clusters manage as best they can.

The diffusion of political and military power and the realignment of global power relationships have multiple implications for world security. With the erosion of superpower influence and the proliferation of modern weapons, newly strengthened regional powers see an opportunity to pursue their hegemonic ambitions, often provoking fierce conflict in the process (as in the case of Iraq's 1980 invasion of Iran and its 1990 invasion of Kuwait). Furthermore, the collapse of central control over the periphery of what was the Soviet Union has resulted in a series of ethnic and territorial clashes between former components of the empire. And the worldwide diffusion of nonnuclear weapons has contributed to the duration and intensity of insurgencies and civil and ethnic conflicts.

Increased Popular Assertiveness at the Grass-Roots Level

Paralleling the growth of globalized economic institutions and the diffusion of political power among international players is the increased assertion at the local and national level of "people power." Wherever we look in the world today, we find grass-roots citizens movements striving for fundamental change in key social, economic, and political structures. In some areas, including the Philippines, China, Haiti, eastern Europe, and the former Soviet Union, this assertiveness has entailed a drive for democratic rights; it has also, however, appeared as anti-foreigner sentiment in Germany and increased anti-Semitism in Russia.

By far the most potent manifestation of this grass-roots assertiveness is the militant expression of ethnic, national, linguistic, and religious affiliations by peoples who have previously lived peacefully in multinational, multicultural societies. This expression takes many forms: the calls for secession by the constituent nationalities of the former Soviet Union and Yugoslavia; the militant assertion of Hindu fundamentalism in India and Islamic fundamentalism in Egypt; the Kurdish rebellion in Iraq and the Tamil rebellion in Sri Lanka; and the Palestinian intifada. As suggested by Myron Weiner of the Massachusetts Institute of Technology, "Peoples'—however they identify themselves by race, religion, language, tribe, or shared history—want new political institutions or new relationships within existing institutions"; when accommodation is not forthcoming, they are likely to escalate their demands.

The growing assertion of populist claims, whether of a political or an ethnic nature, has significant implications for world security. At the very least it is jeopardizing the ability of current leaders from North and South, East and West, to hold on to power. In many areas it has led to violent clashes between members of opposing groups. And in Yugoslavia it has created a maelstrom of ethnic fury that threatens to engulf much of southeastern Europe.

The Diminishing Power and Authority of the Nation-State

Caught between ever more powerful supranational capitalism on one side and restive populations on the other is the modern nation-state. Although still among the actors with the most clout on the international stage, the state is steadily losing ground to international financial institutions and well-organized ethnic and religious constituencies. This is evident both in the ability of the International Monetary Fund to dictate government spending practices in many third world and eastern European countries, and in that of Muslim clerics to affect foreign policy in Iran and Saudi Arabia.

To a great extent, the decline in the power of the nation-state is a product of a global revolution of rising expectations at a time of increased international economic competition. As Stanley Hoffmann of Harvard University observes, people still "count on their state to play the game of wealth effectively," and thus attain or protect high standards of living. But state authorities have less control over their economies than ever before, and when they fail to satisfy popular expectations invite popular revolt—through electoral channels where that option exists, through rioting and civil strife where it does not.

The replacement of older, unrepresentative regimes by new, popularly backed governments in the Soviet bloc and elsewhere has not, unfortunately, always resulted in greater social stability. In many cases the new regimes have played the game of wealth with even less success than their predecessors, resulting in widespread discontent and a risk of coups and mob action. To retain their hold on power, some of these regimes—most notably that in Serbia—have turned to ultra-nationalism as a solution, thereby provoking fresh outbreaks of ethnic violence. In other cases, such as Afghanistan, Mozambique, and Peru, the state has lost control over wide areas, ceding authority to local warlords and sectarian forces; in extreme cases, the state has simply withered away, giving free rein to the sort of gang warfare seen in Liberia and Somalia.

Population Growth and Environmental Decline

The erosion of the state's power and authority has been accelerated, in many instances, by a fifth tectonic force: rapid population growth and the emergence of harsh environmental limits. Population growth is not by itself a cause of instability—historically, it has often contributed to the health and vigor of societies, as in the case of the United States. But when population increases exceed the rate of economic growth (as in many third world countries today), and when they contribute to the depletion of valuable resources (such as tropical forests and tillable soil), the ability of states to engage in long-term economic and social development is impaired—thus ensuring worse hardship and unrest in the future.

The world's population now stands at about 5.5 billion people, and this figure is expected to double by the middle of the twenty-first century. Such a jump could theoretically be sustained if the planet's resources were evenly distributed, and if new products were developed to replace those natural substances being depleted. But resources are not evenly distributed, and new products might not be available at an affordable price to all who need them. As things stand now, many states in Asia, Africa, and Latin America (where population growth rates are at an all-time high) are not able to provide for burgeoning numbers of young people, and will be even less able to do so in the future. The consequences include a rising incidence of hunger and malnutrition, increased migration from the impoverished countryside to urban shantytowns, soaring unemployment (especially among youths), and the growing appeal of extremist movements.

[3]These findings emerge from the Project on Environmental Change and Acute Conflict, a joint study of the American Academy of Arts and Sciences and the Program on Peace and Conflict Studies of the University of Toronto. See Thomas Homer-Dixon, Jeffrey Boutwell, and George Rathjens, "Environmental Change and Violent Conflict," *Scientific American,* February 1993, pp. 38–45; Homer-Dixon, "Environmental Scarcity and Intergroup Conflict," in Michael Klare and Daniel Thomas, *World Security,* 2d ed. (New York: St. Martin's Press, 1993).

Even if population growth is stabilized, the world must still contend with the problems arising from human-induced degradation of the environment. Much has been written about the long-term effects of global warming and the depletion of the atmosphere's ozone layer, and on their implications for human, plant, and animal populations; much less, however, is known about the impact of environmental decline on intergroup and interstate relations. Preliminary research suggests that environmental decline, especially when it occurs in environmentally stressed areas of the third world (deserts, rainforests, hillsides, coastal lowlands) will exacerbate intergroup competition and conflict and drive yet more people into crowded urban shantytowns where the prospects for meaningful employment are dim and the danger of unrest is high.[3]

BREAKUP, BREAKDOWN, AND BLOW-UP

These tectonic forces act on the peoples, states, and societies of the world in such a way as to exacerbate existing tensions between groups and in many cases to provoke or intensify conflict. The resulting struggles take several forms, all of which have become all-too-common features of the global environment.

One manifestation is the world's decomposing empires and superstates. By far the most striking products of the cold war's end and communism's demise have been the dissolution of the Soviet Union and Yugoslavia. The Soviet Union was both an empire, assembled through centuries of conquest by the Russian czars and their Communist successors, and a modern superstate, uniting many individual nations in one centrally administered, confederated system. Yugoslavia also possessed attributes of empire and confederation. Systems of this sort can survive only when the center possesses enough strength to subdue separatist pressures in the periphery, and when there are sufficient social, economic, and political links between the disparate parts to resist the centrifugal forces that inevitably tear at such an assemblage.

With the collapse of communism—the binding agent in both the Soviet Union and Yugoslavia—and the growing impact of tectonic forces, these two superstates broke up in 1991, and the individual groups that had constituted them sought to establish full sovereignty over (what they viewed as) their rightful territory. As suggested by past instances of imperial decomposition, such as the breakup of the Austro-Hungarian and Ottoman Empires after World War I, the process inevitably spawns discord and conflict. Pieces of the decomposing empire fight over the demarcation of new international boundaries (hence the fighting between Croatia and Serbia, and between Armenia and Azerbaijan), and ethnic minorities find themselves trapped within alien and inhospitable states (hence the struggles of the Abkhazians and South Ossetians in Georgia, the Ingush and Chechens in Russia, the ethnic Russians in Moldova, and the ethnic Albanians in the Kosovo region of Serbia).

Such struggles are not limited to the former Soviet Union and Yugoslavia; other multinational superstates are feeling the vibrations of tectonic forces. Hence the survival of Canada remains in doubt as the French-speaking people of Quebec continue to seek greater autonomy from the English-speaking provinces, while India has experienced significant separatist pressures in Kashmir, the Punjab, and Assam. Ethiopia, once an imperial kingdom, has long been troubled by armed separatist movements in the provinces of Eritrea and Tigre, and is likely to experience renewed conflict if these pressures are not relieved. Two other third world superstates, China and Indonesia, continue to encounter resistance on their peripheries (the former in Tibet, the latter in East Timor) and will likely come under intensified pressure from separatists in the future.

Accompanying the breakup of large multinational states has come a surge in ethnonationalist and irredentist struggles as ethnic groups that have been denied a state (or have had theirs submerged in a larger multinational entity) seek to establish one, and as other groups already in possession of a state seek to enlarge it so as to incorporate adjacent territories occupied by large numbers of their kinsmen. Such impulses have long sparked fighting, but seem to have gained renewed vigor in recent years as the bipolar system broke and the balance of power between state authorities and populist elements shifted in favor of the latter.

As has been noted, ethnonationalist forces are evident in the separatist struggles in the former Yugoslavia, Georgia, India, China, and Indonesia. Other groups engaged in like struggles include the Kurds in Iraq and Turkey, the Palestinians in the West Bank and Gaza Strip, the Tamils in Sri Lanka, the Shan and Karen peoples of Burma, and the Basques of France and Spain.

Major irredentist struggles include the Serbians' campaign to create a "Greater Serbia" out of the remnants of Yugoslavia, Armenia's push to gain control over Nagorno-Karabakh (now controlled by Azerbaijan), Russia's drive to repossess the Crimean peninsula (which was ceded to Ukraine in 1954 by Nikita Khrushchev), and China's continuing efforts to repossess Taiwan. Many fear that irredentists in Hungary will press for the incorporation of Hungarian-speaking regions of Slovakia, Romania, and the former Yugoslavia in a "Greater Hungary."

REGIONAL RIVALRIES

The rivalries engendered by the breakup of larger states will be paralleled by regional rivalry. The breakdown of the bipolar system and concomitant diffusion of political power have given added impetus to rivalries between regional states, especially in East Asia, South

Asia, and the Middle East. Of particular concern are the ongoing rivalries between China and Taiwan, North Korea and South Korea, India and Pakistan, India and China, Iran and Iraq, Iran and Saudi Arabia, and Israel and Syria. These have all flared up periodically in the past, but they seem to have gained renewed intensity in recent years as the inhibiting influence of the superpowers declined and the regional power equation became more unsettled. Several of these contests could experience a fresh outbreak of fighting in the latter 1990s.

Factors that will come to bear on such rivalries include: the degree of progress (or lack of it) in regional peace negotiations, especially the Middle East peace talks; the degree to which these states are hobbled by internal power struggles; the ability of the United States—now the world's sole superpower—to discourage adventurism on the part of regional powers; and the impact of global economic conditions on these states' inclinations to engage in external conflict. No one can predict how these factors will play out in the years ahead, but it is reasonable to assume, for example, that a breakdown in the Mideast peace talks, coupled with a decline in United States influence and/or the emergence of aggressive-minded leaders in one or more states would increase the risk of a new regional conflagration.

Another key factor in all of this is the effect of weapons proliferation on the dynamics of conflict between regional rivals. All the states named above are engaged in major military buildups—in many cases involving weapons of mass destruction—and thus each has reason to fear the arms acquisition programs of its adversaries. Should any of these powers achieve a sudden and unexpected increase in its military capability—through, say, the acquisition of nuclear weapons or ballistic missiles—it could invite a preemptive strike by a rival. Such strikes have taken place before—for example, the 1981 Israeli attack on Iraq's Osirak reactor—and are all too likely to occur again.

REVOLUTIONARY AND FUNDAMENTALIST CRUSADES

Though the appeal of Soviet-style communism has largely dissipated, revolutionary and millenarian movements continue to hold an attraction for downtrodden and dispossessed peoples. Such movements promise not merely a change of leaders but a sweeping transformation of society, typically involving the elimination of existing institutions and their replacement by more "righteous" or egalitarian structures. Movements of this sort appear to be gaining strength in areas where economic conditions have worsened for the majority (or for particular groups) and where the capacity or inclination of state authorities to overcome widespread impoverishment and inequity has diminished. Revolutionary and millenarian groups in such areas appear increasingly willing to employ violence in their efforts to reform society.

At present two main types of revolutionary crusade can be discerned: ideological or political movements, usually attempting to end exploitation of the poor by the middle class and the rich; and religious fundamentalism, entailing a drive to subject all societal interactions to religious law and practice. Examples of the first type include the Shining Path in Peru, the Farabundo Martí National Liberation Front of El Salvador, Cambodia's Khmer Rouge, and the New People's Army in the Philippines; examples of the second category would be the Hindu fundamentalist Bharatiya Janata party in India, the Islamic Salvation Front in Algeria, the Islamic Jihad in Egypt, and the various Islamic fundamentalist forces in Afghanistan.

Finally, the world is confronted with an assortment of pro-democracy and anti-colonial movements, which tend to erupt periodically in strikes or civil disorders and/or to provoke repressive violence by the authorities. All these movements reflect the tectonic increase in grass-roots activism described earlier, and while they may experience setbacks in the short term are not likely to disappear anytime soon.

They include: popular drives for Western-style electoral democracy and human rights, as have been working themselves out in Burma, China, Haiti, the Philippines, South Korea, Thailand, and Zaire; struggles by disenfranchised minorities and majorities to abolish unrepresentative or discriminatory governments, from Northern Ireland to South Africa; and efforts by subject peoples to cast off what is viewed as colonial rule (even though the "colonizers" involved may be other third world countries), as in East Timor, Kashmir, the Western Sahara, and the West Bank and Gaza. Paralleling these movements are the increasingly vigorous efforts of indigenous people to reclaim rights and lands that have long been denied them by the dominant cultures.

WILL WEAPONS INHERIT THE EARTH?

Adding to the dangers posed by all the factors described above is the global proliferation of modern weapons and the technologies for producing them. Such proliferation entails not only the spread of nuclear, chemical, and biological weapons—the so-called weapons of mass destruction—but also a wide range of "conventional" arms—the tanks, planes, guns, and missiles used by regular military forces. Both sorts of weapons are finding their way into the arsenals of more and more nations, thereby stimulating local arms races and ensuring that future wars will be fought with ever-ascending lethality and destructiveness.

In the nuclear realm, the five declared nuclear weapons powers (the United States, Russia, Great Britain, France, and China) have been joined by three undeclared nuclear ones (Israel, India, and Pakistan), while Iran, Iraq, and North Korea continue their efforts to develop such weapons and Argentina, Brazil, South Africa, South Korea, and Taiwan retain a capacity to do so in the future. (Belarus, Kazakhstan, and Ukraine inherited some nuclear weapons from the former Soviet Union, but have pledged to turn them over to Russian authorities. Still, many analysts worry about the possible spread of former Soviet nuclear materials and technology.)

As for chemical weapons, American intelligence officials have identified 14 third world countries believed to possess an offensive chemical warfare capability: Burma, China, Egypt, India, Iran, Iraq, Israel, Libya, North Korea, Pakistan, South Korea, Syria, Taiwan, and Vietnam. Many of these nations have also engaged in research on biological weapons, and have acquired ballistic missiles that can be used to deliver nuclear, chemical, and biological warheads. We have already witnessed the extensive use of chemical weapons in the Iran-Iraq war, and in Iraq's subsequent campaign to liquidate Kurdish villages in strategic border areas. Iraq also threatened chemical attacks against Israel in 1990 and 1991, and Israeli officials responded with threats of possible nuclear retaliation. Central Intelligence Agency officials have reported that India and Pakistan were prepared to use nuclear weapons in 1990, when it was feared the fighting in Kashmir would spark a full-scale conflict.

The proliferation of advanced conventional arms has proceeded apace with that of weapons of mass destruction. According to estimates by the Congressional Research Service, third world countries spent $339.5 billion on imported weapons from 1983 to 1990 (in constant 1990 US dollars)—which translates into (among other things) some 13,010 tanks and self-propelled guns, 27,430 pieces of heavy artillery, 2,920 supersonic combat planes, 38,430 surface-to-air missiles, and 53,790 surface-to-surface missiles. These weapons sustained the Iran-Iraq war of 1980–1988 and other regional conflicts, and swelled the arsenals of emerging powers in Africa, Asia, and Latin America.

Security analysts are also worried about the growing diffusion of advanced conventional weapons. As military spending in NATO and the former Warsaw Pact falls, arms manufacturers in these countries, whether state-owned or private, are increasingly disposed to export their products to the third world, where the demand for modern weapons is high and the likelihood of their being used in combat is growing. The stockpiles built up by the Soviet Union and its Warsaw Pact allies during the cold war era constitute a vast reservoir of surplus arms that are increasingly finding their way into the black market—and thence into the hands of terrorists, guerrillas, separatist forces, and other irregular formations that threaten the peace in many areas of the world.

Proliferation of arms of all types is certain to figure as a primary security concern in the 1990s and beyond because it helps increase the number, length, and duration of conventional conflicts and also increases the risk that future wars will involve the use of weapons of mass destruction, whether deliberate or accidental.

KEEPING THE PEACE

The tectonic forces currently in motion and the growing tempo of internal, local, and regional conflict have placed enormous strain on the international community, forcing world leaders to consider new and enhanced methods of conflict control. The development and application of these to actual conflicts are likely to remain a central issue in security affairs for the foreseeable future.

With the cold war over and the superpowers no longer assuming responsibility for maintaining peace and stability within their respective spheres of influence, a greater burden has naturally fallen on the United Nations, which has responded by greatly expanding its peacemaking and peacekeeping operations around the world. Between 1991 and 1992 the United Nations established 13 new peacekeeping operations—exactly the number initiated by the world body in the entire previous 42 years of its existence. At the start of 1993, United Nations peacekeeping forces were serving in Angola, Cambodia, Cyprus, El Salvador, the Golan Heights, Kashmir, along the Kuwait-Iraq border, in Lebanon, Mozambique, the Sinai, Somalia, the former Yugoslavia, and the Western Sahara; all told, some 60,000 military and police personnel were involved in these operations, with the number expected to increase substantially in the months ahead.

These operations have contributed to stability in many parts of the globe and given the United Nations enhanced international visibility and respectability. And while some of the operations have run into difficulties, most observers agree that conditions in these areas would probably be much worse without the presence of the blue helmets. Nevertheless, world leaders generally agree that the United Nations' current capabilities and methods are inadequate for the wide range of conflicts and security challenges expected in the years to come. The Security Council has called on Secretary General Boutros Boutros-Ghali and his staff to suggest ways in which the organization's peacemaking activities can be improved, and development and implementation of these suggestions is likely to be the organization's top priority in the mid-1990s.

To inform the discussion on peacemaking, Boutros-Ghali published *An Agenda for Peace* last June.[4] In this document, the secretary general identifies five key areas in need of improvement: preventive diplomacy, or the negotiated termination of conflicts; peacemaking; peacekeeping, or the use of United Nations forces to monitor cease-fires and to prevent the re-ignition of hostilities;

peace enforcement, or the use of force to prevent or resist aggression by a belligerent in violation of United Nations resolutions; and post-conflict peace-building designed to alleviate human suffering and thus eliminate conditions that might contribute to the renewal of fighting. Boutros-Ghali proposed a number of initiatives in each of these areas, and broke new ground by calling for the formation of a permanent peacekeeping force under United Nations control (the current system staffs such units with contingents drawn from national forces on an ad hoc basis).

The development of new approaches to local and regional conflict has also been a matter of great concern in the United States, which has been under great pressure to step in and resolve certain ongoing crises (notably those in Bosnia and Herzegovina and Somalia). While some American leaders would prefer to delegate all such activities to the United Nations, others, including both Presidents George Bush and Bill Clinton, contend that the United States has an obligation to act in certain cases where no other option appears viable. Thus in December Bush, with only six weeks left in his term, ordered United States forces to Somalia in order to restore order in a country torn by factional warfare and to protect the delivery of relief supplies to starving Somalis.

In announcing Operation Restore Hope, the president indicated that the United States cannot assume such responsibility in every instance of regional disorder, but that it must be prepared to act when the survival of many human beings is at stake and when no other entity is available to do the job. "I understand [that] the United States cannot right the world's wrongs, but we also know that some crises in the world cannot be resolved without American involvement [and that] American action is often necessary as a catalyst for broader involvement of the community of nations." These comments, and the dispatch of American troops to Somalia, have sparked a heated debate in the United States over where and under what circumstances United States forces should be employed in such operations abroad.

Whatever the outcome in the United States and at the United Nations on the use of force in humanitarian and peacekeeping operations, it is apparent that the problem of preventing and controlling local, ethnic, and regional conflict has become the premier world security concern of the post–cold war era. Because such conflicts are likely to proliferate in the years ahead, and because no single power or group is willing and able to guarantee global peace and stability, United States and world leaders will be forced to enhance existing peacemaking instruments and to develop new techniques along the lines suggested by Secretary General Boutros-Ghali. How peaceful a world we inhabit in the twenty-first century will depend to a great extent on these endeavors.

---

[4]Boutros Boutros-Ghali, *An Agenda for Peace* (New York: The United Nations, 1992), p. 28.

The disintegration of Yugoslavia has led to a reevaluation of the idea that a multi-ethnic state is a viable entity. The factors that led to the dismantling of such a state in Yugoslavia are many and are open to revision, but one of the lessons that can be drawn from the process is clear: "The wars in the former Yugoslavia [show] that the principles and practices that provided a stable framework for international security in the era of the cold war are no longer sufficient to preserve the peace."

Why Yugoslavia Fell Apart

STEVEN L. BURG

STEVEN L. BURG *is associate professor of politics at Brandeis University. This article is part of a larger project,* Nationalism and Democracy in Post-Communist Europe: Challenges to American Foreign Policy, *supported by The Twentieth Century Fund.*

The disintegration of the Yugoslav federation and its descent into atavistic interethnic violence cannot be attributed to any single factor. Internal political conflicts in the 1980s, and the effort by Serbian leader Slobodan Milosevic to mobilize Serb nationalism on behalf of a strengthened federation, destroyed the cohesion of the country's regional Communist leaderships and weakened their control over society. Deteriorating economic conditions—especially plummeting living standards—eroded the benefits of sustaining the Yugoslav state and stimulated the rise of mass nationalisms and interethnic hostilities. The conflicting nationalist aspirations of the Yugoslav peoples and their leaders' efforts to maximize power, led to conflict over the control of disputed territories.

The end of the cold war left both Soviet and Western policymakers believing that Yugoslavia no longer held the strategic significance, or merited the attention, it had enjoyed in a world divided between East and West. This mistaken belief, as well as the attention commanded by the Persian Gulf War, led to neglect of the brewing crisis in Yugoslavia until the cost of meaningful action had risen beyond the point acceptable to Western policymakers and their publics. Even when less costly but still effective action remained possible, Western policymakers were deterred from acting by the fear that the dissolution of Yugoslavia, even if achieved through peaceful negotiation, would hasten the disintegration of the Soviet Union.

The fall of Yugoslavia thus can be attributed to internal conflict and the international community's failure to respond to the crisis effectively. However, forceful action by either Yugoslav leaders or American and European administrations would have required innovative thinking about some of the most basic principles of the international system and the post–cold war security framework in the Euro-Atlantic community. No political leadership—Yugoslav, American, or European—was then ready to confront these tasks. The only positive outcome of the Yugoslav debacle, therefore, may be the stimulus it has provided for such new thinking.

THE DOMESTIC CONTEXT OF DISINTEGRATION

By the mid-1970s, Yugoslavia had become a highly decentralized federation in which the constituent republics dominated the central government. Regional leaderships carefully protected the interests of their territorial constituencies at the expense of other regions and the federation. The regional leaders shared a common interest in preserving the Communist political order that shielded them from responsibility and popular accountability but little else. Ethnic and political integration processes had only modest impact. The proportion of the population that declared itself to be "Yugoslav" rather than an ethnic identity in the national census, for example, increased from 1.3 percent in 1971 to 5.4 percent in 1981. For the vast majority of the population, distinct ethnic or national identities continued to command emotional loyalties and provide the most powerful bases for political mobilization.

The ethnically defined territorial structures of the Yugoslav system reinforced the political strength of ethnic identities and intensified political divisions in the leadership. Federal political bodies, including the collective state presidency and the Communist party leadership, were composed of representatives of the republics and provinces, selected by the regional leaderships. Individual positions in these bodies, including the country's prime ministership and presidency, rotated among the regions according to an explicit agreement. Only the army remained a unified, all-Yugoslav, organization.

5. CONFLICT

While the political regions of Yugoslavia were defined in ethnic terms, in most cases they were not ethnically homogeneous. With the exception of Slovenia, their leaderships could not mobilize ethnic nationalism in support of political ambition or fulfill the nationalist aspirations of their ethnic majorities without alienating substantial minority populations and raising the prospect of severe ethnic conflict. The vast majority of ethnic Slovenes were concentrated in Slovenia and made up the majority of the population. Efforts by ethnically Slovene regional leaders to advance Slovene national-cultural interests and to strengthen Slovenian autonomy effectively encompassed all Slovenes. At the same time, these efforts neither threatened the status of a large minority inside Slovenia nor challenged the power of any other group over its own republic by encouraging a large Slovene minority population outside the republic to demand autonomy.

In Croatia, however, Serbs constituted a large minority or even a majority of the population in several areas of the republic. Croat leaders thus could not pursue exclusionary nationalist ambitions inside the Croatian state without risking the alienation of a large and territorially compact Serb minority that enjoyed strong links to Serbs outside the republic's borders. At the same time, a nationalistic Croatian government would stimulate unrest among the large, territorially compact population of ethnic Croats in adjacent areas of neighboring Bosnia and Herzegovina.

No single group could claim the overall majority in Bosnia and Herzegovina. While Muslims constituted the largest group (about 44 percent of the population in the 1991 census), they did not represent a majority. Serbs (over 31 percent) and Croats (more than 17 percent) constituted large minorities in the republic's

THE NEW BALKAN STATES

◎ National capitals
⊗ Yugoslav republic capitals
◉ Yugoslav autonomous regions capitals
• Other cities

0   25   50   75   100 Miles

© Current History, Inc.

population. In many areas of Bosnia there was no single ethnic majority. In the larger cities, those who took the nonethnic "Yugoslav" identity constituted from 20 to 25 percent of the population. Thus the pattern of ethnic settlement in Bosnia was highly complex. No ethnic leadership could advance exclusionary nationalist ambitions on behalf of its ethnic constituency without alienating vast portions of the population—including substantial numbers of its own group who had adopted the multiethnic civic culture associated with "Yugoslavism."

By the mid-1980s, the collective leaderships of the country were divided between those who supported a looser association among the regions and those who continued to support a strengthened federal government. This division was reinforced by differences over the scope and pace of further economic and political reform. The Yugoslav economy had gone into sharp decline in the 1980s. Living standards fell and regional economic differences widened. In the 1960s and 1970s, for example, per capita national income in Slovenia had been about six times that in Kosovo province and about three times that in Macedonia and Bosnia and Herzegovina. Income in Croatia had been about four times that in Kosovo and about twice that in Macedonia and Bosnia. By 1988, income in Slovenia was more than eight times that in Kosovo and income in Croatia was approximately five times higher. The frictions introduced by these growing inequalities were intensified by the ethnic differences between the regions, and especially by the increasingly violent conflict between Serbs and ethnic Albanians in Kosovo.

KOSOVO AND MILOSEVIC

The 1980s began with the outbreak of nationalist demonstrations by the Albanian people in Kosovo.

THE BREAKUP OF YUGOSLAVIA

1990

Jan. 22—The Communist party votes to allow other parties to compete in a new system of "political pluralism."

Feb. 5—Slobodan Milosevic, president of the republic of Serbia, says he will send troops to take control of Kosovo, a province where ethnic violence has entered its 2d week.

April 8—The republic of Slovenia holds parliamentary elections—the 1st free elections since World War II.

April 22—The 1st free elections in more than 50 years are held in the republic of Croatia.

July 5—The parliament of the Serbian republic suspends the autonomous government of the Kosovo region. On July 2, ethnic Albanian members of the Kosovo legislature declared the region a separate territory within the Yugoslav federation.

July 6—The state president orders Slovenia's parliament to rescind its July 2 declaration that the republic's laws take precedence over those of the Yugoslav federation.

Sept. 3—In Kosovo, more than 100,000 ethnic Albanians strike, closing factories, offices, stores, and schools to protest Serbian takeovers of formerly Albanian-controlled enterprises and the dismissal of Albanian workers.

Sept 13—The Yugoslav press agency reports that ethnic Albanian members of the dissolved parliament of Kosovo have adopted an alternative constitution and have voted to extend the mandate of parliament until new elections are held. The Serbian government has called the alternative constitution illegal.

Nov. 11—The republic of Macedonia holds its 1st free elections since 1945.

Nov. 18—Parliamentary elections are held in the republic of Bosnia and Herzegovina.

Dec. 9—The 1st free parliamentary elections in Serbia since 1938 are held.

1991

Feb. 20—The Slovenian parliament approves laws allowing the republic to take over defense, banking, and other government functions from the central Yugoslav government; the parliament also approves a resolution to divide Yugoslavia into two separate states; Slovenia has warned that it will secede if the other republics do not approve the plan.

Feb. 21—The Croatian parliament adopts measures giving the republic government veto power over central government laws it considers threatening to the republic's sovereignty; the parliament also adopts resolutions that support the dissolution of the Yugoslav federation.

March 2—After reports of violent clashes between Serb villagers and Croatian security forces, Borisav Jovic, the leader of the collective presidency, orders federal army troops to the Croatian village of Pakrac.

March 16—Milosevic declares that he is refusing to recognize the authority of the collective presidency; with this act he effectively declares Serbia's secession from Yugoslavia.

March 17—Milosevic proclaims Krajina, an area in Croatia where 200,000 ethnic Serbs live, a "Serbian autonomous region."

June 25—The parliaments of Slovenia and Croatia pass declarations of independence. The federal parliament in Belgrade—the capital of Serbia as well as of Yugoslavia—asks the army to intervene to prevent the secessions.

June 27—Slovenian Defense Minister Janez Jansa says, "Slovenia is at war" with the federal government.

July 18—The federal presidency announces that it is ordering all federal army units to withdraw from Slovenia.

Sept. 8—Results of yesterday's referendum in Macedonia show that about 75% of voters favor independence; ethnic Albanians boycotted the referendum.

Oct. 1—Heavy fighting in Croatia between Croatian militia and rebel Serbs (aided by the federal army) continues near the Adriatic port city of Dubrovnik.

1992

March 1—A majority of voters approve a referendum on independence in Bosnia; Serb citizens, who comprise 32% of Bosnia's population but control 60% of the territory, have threatened to secede if the referendum is passed.

March 25—Fighting between Serb militias—backed by the federal army—and Bosnian government troops begins.

April 5—After the Bosnian government refuses to rescind a call-up of the national guard, Serb guerrillas shell Sarajevo, the Bosnian capital.

April 27—Serbia and Montenegro announce the establishment of a new Yugoslavia composed of the 2 republics.

May 19—At a news conference in Washington, D. C., Haris Silajdzic, the foreign minister of Bosnia, says his country is being subjected to "ethnic cleansing" by Serb forces.

May 24—In an election in Kosovo termed illegal by Belgrade, ethnic Albanians vote overwhelmingly to secede from the rump Yugoslav state.

July 2—Croat nationalists living in Bosnia declare an independent state that includes almost one-third of the territory of Bosnia; Mate Boban, head of the 30,000-strong Croatian Defense Council militia, says the name of the new republic is Herzeg-Bosna.

Nov. 3—*The New York Times* reports the Serbian-dominated Yugoslav army has quit the siege of Dubrovnik, Croatia, and has withdrawn its forces from the surrounding area.

1993

Jan. 22—Croatian army units attack Serb-held positions in Maslenica and the port city of Zadar; Ivan Milas, a Croatian vice president, says the attacks came after Serbs delayed returning the areas to Croatian control as called for in the January 1992 UN-sponsored cease-fire agreement; state radio in Belgrade says the self-declared Serbian Krajina Republic has declared war on Croatia.

April 7—The Security Council approves UN membership for Macedonia under the provisional name "the Former Yugoslav Republic of Macedonia" as a compromise with the Greek government; Greece has objected to the new country using the same name as Greece's northernmost province.

May 16—In the Bosnian town of Pale, Bosnian Serb leader Radovan Karadzic announces that in a 2-day referendum, at least 90% of Serb voters rejected the provisional peace plan put forward by UN mediator Cyrus Vance and EC mediator Lord Owen; the plan called for a UN-monitored cease-fire; the establishment of a central government composed of 3 Muslims, 3 Croats, and 3 Serbs; the creation of 10 partially autonomous provinces with proportional representation of ethnic groups in the provincial governments; and the return of forcibly transferred property. Karadzic says the world should now recognize that a new state—Republika Srpska—exists in the Serb-controlled territory in Bosnia.

Aug. 28—The mainly Muslim Bosnian parliament votes 65 to 0 to reject a peace plan devised by the UN and the EC that would divide the country into 3 separate republics based on ethnicity; in the mountain town of Grude, the parliament of the self-declared Croat state approves the plan and officially declares the Croat republic of Herzeg-Bosna; the self-declared Bosnian Serb parliament also accepts the plan.

5. CONFLICT

Kosovo is viewed by Serbs as the "cradle" of their nation, but is populated by a demographically robust majority (over 80 percent in 1991) of ethnic Albanians. The demonstrations were initially suppressed by military force. But the decade saw almost continuous and often violent confrontations in the province between Serbs and Albanians. The Serbian leadership in Belgrade responded with increasingly repressive measures against the Albanians and their indigenous leaders.

Violence against Serbs in Kosovo contributed to the growth of nationalist sentiment among Serbs in Serbia and the other regions of Yugoslavia. But the movement received its most important support from Serbian Communist party President Slobodan Milosevic. Motivated at least in part by genuine personal outrage over the treatment of Serbs in Kosovo and by the failure of other Serbian leaders to defend them, Milosevic ousted a key proponent of interethnic accommodation with the Albanians of Kosovo and seized control of the Serbian leadership in September 1987. He then escalated his public defense of Serbian ethnic and political interests. He exploited the situation in Kosovo to further stimulate popular nationalism among Serbs all across Yugoslavia, and used that nationalism as leverage against the leaders of other republics and provinces. The intensity of popular emotions among Serbs was demonstrated by a series of large-scale, openly nationalist demonstrations across Vojvodina, Serbia, and Montenegro in the fall of 1988, and by a mass gathering of Serbs in Kosovo in June 1989.

The growing force of Serbian nationalism allowed Milosevic to oust independent leaders in Vojvodina and Montenegro, replacing them with more subservient ones, and to intensify repressive measures against the Albanians of Kosovo while placing that province, heretofore a relatively autonomous territory within the Serbian republic, under direct rule from Belgrade. These changes gave Milosevic effective control over four of the eight regional leaderships represented in the collective state presidency, the most authoritative executive body in the country. However, the disproportionate Serbian influence contributed to the de-legitimation of central authority and accelerated the political dissolution of the country.

Milosevic represented a powerful synthesis of Serbian nationalism, political conservatism, support for centralism, and resistance to meaningful economic reform. Developments in Serbia under his leadership stood in stark contrast to those in Slovenia, where the growth of popular nationalism took the form of demands for political democracy and rapid economic reform, the pluralization of group activity in the republic, and support for further confederalization of the Yugoslav regime. In Serbia the republic remained under the control of the unreformed Communist party. The Serbian Communists renamed themselves the Socialist party and co-opted some formerly dissident intellectuals into their leadership, but remained under Milosevic's control. The Slovenian Communist leadership, in contrast, cooperated with emergent social and political forces in their republic to move rapidly toward a more pluralistic order. The Slovenian leadership, rather than seeing organized popular pressure only as a threat, also viewed it as an important and necessary asset in its struggle for economic and political reform in Belgrade.

THE DISINTEGRATION BEGINS

Relations between Serbia and Slovenia began to grow tense at both the elite and mass levels. In October 1988 the Slovenian representative to the central party presidium resigned because of increasingly acrimonious relations with Milosevic. In February 1989 the use of federal militia to suppress a general strike in Kosovo raised widespread concern among Slovenes that, if such force could be used against more than 1 million Albanians, it could also be used against the 2 million Slovenes. This fear was not entirely unfounded. A year earlier an independent Slovenian journal, *Mladina,* revealed that federal Yugoslav military leaders had met to discuss emergency plans for the takeover of the republic.

After the suppression of the strike, the president of the Slovenian Communist party, Milan Kucan, publicly condemned the repression in Kosovo. This marked the beginning of open conflict between the Ljubljana and Belgrade leaderships—the former having embarked on a secessionist strategy calling for internal democratization, and the latter having begun an effort to re-centralize power and authority in the entire country while constructing a new, nationalist authoritarian regime in Serbia.

The escalation of conflict in Yugoslavia reached crisis proportions in the fall of 1989. The Slovenian leadership adopted constitutional amendments in September asserting the economic and political sovereignty of the republic, denying the right of the federation to intervene, and claiming the right to secede. In December it blocked an attempt by Serbian nationalists supported by Milosevic to pressure the Slovenian government into abandoning its strategy by bringing Serbs to Ljubljana for a mass demonstration. Milosevic responded to Slovene resistance by breaking off economic relations between the two republics. Democratic activist groups in Slovenia pressed for a complete break with Serbia. That move came the following month, at the January 1990 extraordinary congress of the ruling League of Communists of Yugoslavia.

Originally conceived by Milosevic and the Serbian leadership as a means of imposing greater central authority, the congress instead became the occasion for the collapse of the old regime. Unwilling and politically unable to support a draft platform calling for greater party unity, the Slovenian delegation walked out of the congress. The military and other regional party delegations, unwilling to surrender their own independence, refused to continue the congress. The congress then adjourned indefinitely, marking the de facto breakup of the nationwide party organization. This left each of the republic party organizations to respond independently to conditions in its own region. It also left the military (the Yugoslav People's Army, or JNA) the only organization still committed to, and dependent on, the continued survival of the federation.

The electoral victories of independence-oriented coalitions in Slovenia and Croatia in the spring of 1990, and the former Communists' victory in Serbia in December of that year, deepened political divisions among the regional leaderships of the Yugoslav federation. At the same time, political support for maintaining the federation evaporated almost completely. Federal Prime Minister Ante Markovic's attempt to create a countrywide political party committed to preserving the federation, for example, generated little support. And his effort to accelerate the holding of free elections for the federal parliament as a means of democratizing and legitimizing the federation failed completely.

In August 1990, Serbs in the central Dalmatian region of Croatia began an open insurrection against the Zagreb government. Already fearful of the nationalist campaign themes of the governing Croatian Democratic Community, and mindful of the violently anti-Serb character of the most recent episodes of extreme Croatian nationalism, the Serbs of Dalmatia viewed the government's effort to disarm ethnically Serb local police forces and replace them with special Croatian police units as a portent of further repression to come.

The Dalmatian Serbs declared their intention to remain part of a common Yugoslav state or, alternatively, to become an independent Serb republic. Their uprising should have been a clear warning to all concerned: the republic borders established by the Communist regime in the postwar period were extremely vulnerable to challenges from ethnic communities that did not share the identity on which new, nationalist post-Communist governments sought to legitimate themselves. Such communities were alienated or even threatened by the nationalistic legitimation of these new governments. If existing borders were to be preserved, substantial political guarantees had to be provided for the ethnic minority enclaves in the republics.

The overwhelming declaration of support for a sovereign and independent state by 88 percent of the Slovenian electorate in a December 23, 1990, referendum made the republic's secession look inevitable. The decision by Yugoslav leaders in February 1991 to begin determining how to divide the country's assets among the regions suggested still more clearly that the breakup of the country was at hand. But the threat by the Yugoslav minister of defense in December to use force to prevent Slovenia or Croatia from seceding signaled the possibility that a breakup of Yugoslavia would not be peaceful.

The most explosive conflict in Yugoslavia has been between the political aspirations of Croats and Serbs, whose historical and imagined national homelands and claims to sovereignty overlap. This is the conflict that destabilized the interwar regime and threatened to destabilize the Communist government in 1971. In December of that year, the Yugoslav leader, Josip Broz Tito, used the military to suppress the mass nationalist movement and to purge the leadership in Croatia. As a result, in the 1980s Croatian Communist leaders remained more conservative than their Slovenian counterparts. More important, because Croatian leaders traced their origins to the anti-nationalist purges of the early 1970s, they enjoyed little popular legitimacy. With the breakup of the Yugoslav Communist party in January 1990 and the onset of competitive elections in the republics, they were decisively defeated by the Croatian Democratic Union, a nationalist coalition led by Franjo Tudjman. The CDU's electoral victory polarized relations between Croats and Serbs in that republic and set the stage for a renewed confrontation between Croat and Serb nationalisms.

THE BATTLE OVER THE ETHNIC MAP

By 1990, definition of the emerging post-Communist order became the object of open conflict among several competing, and even mutually contradictory, nationalist visions. The Serbian vision allowed for two fundamentally different outcomes: either the federation would be sufficiently strengthened to assure the protection of Serb populations everywhere in the country, or the dissolution of the federation would be accompanied by the redrawing of boundaries to incorporate Serb populations in a single, independent Serb state. This did not preclude the accommodation of the Slovenian vision of an entirely independent Slovenian state, but it did contradict Croatian aspirations for an independent state defined by the borders inherited from the old regime.

Serb and Croat nationalist aspirations might both still have been accommodated by creating independent states that exercised sovereignty over their respective ethnic territories. But such a solution would have required the redrawing of existing borders that would call into question the continued existence of Bosnia as a multinational state of Muslims, Serbs, and Croats. Moreover, any agreement openly negotiated by Serbia that legitimated claims to self-determination based on the current ethnic composition of local populations would strengthen the Albanian case for an independent Kosovo, and raise the prospect for Serbia of either giving up that province peacefully or having to escalate the level of repression.

The increasing autonomy of the republics and the

growing interregional conflict stimulated fears among Serb nationalists that large portions of the Yugoslav Serb community might be "cut off" from Serbia. The repeated use of military force to suppress Albanian demonstrations in Kosovo in the 1980s, and changes in the Serbian constitution that revoked provincial autonomy, suggested that Milosevic and other Serb nationalists might take similar actions in retaliation for any effort to separate the Serb populations of either Croatia or Bosnia from Serbia. At the very least it suggested that any claim by Croats or Muslims to the right of national self-determination would lead to Serb demands for self-determination, and for the redrawing of internal borders to permit the consolidation of Serb-populated territories under the authority of a single Serbian national state.

Serbs, however, were not the only ethnic group in the former Yugoslavia that might exploit the redrawing of borders. Albanians in Kosovo had already declared their independence and adopted their own constitution in the summer and fall of 1990. Redrawing borders might lead them to claim several western counties of Macedonia where ethnic Albanians constituted the majority or a plurality of the local population. They might even lay claim to the bordering Serbian county of Presevo, where ethnic Albanians also constituted the majority. Radical nationalist elements in Kosovo had already called for the unification of all ethnically Albanian territories. Similarly, Muslim nationalists in Bosnia might lay claim to the several counties of the Sandzak region that lie across the Serbian-Montenegrin border in which Muslims make up the majority.

AN INEPT INTERNATIONAL RESPONSE

A narrow window of opportunity to negotiate a peaceful solution to the growing dispute among the republics and to address the demands raised by ethnic communities appeared to remain open until March 1991. The West's inaction in late 1990 and early 1991 can be partly attributed to preoccupation on the part of western European leaders with negotiations over European integration. Collective action through the European Community was further stymied by clear differences in perspective among the British, French, and Germans. United States policymakers, on the other hand, consciously chose to distance themselves from the issue. United States inaction may even have been due to a cynical calculation on the part of Secretary of State James Baker that this conflict should be left for the Europeans to handle, precisely because the difficulty of the issues and the internal divisions among them assured that they would fail, thus reaffirming the need for American leadership in Europe.

As noted earlier, the attention of Western policymakers was also diverted by two other issues: the military effort to reverse the Iraqi invasion of Kuwait, and the continuing political crisis in the Soviet Union. Any effort to facilitate the breakup of Yugoslavia appeared to have been precluded by fear that it might create an undesirable precedent for the Soviet Union. As a result, the political responses of the United States and other Western states to events in both the Soviet Union and Yugoslavia ignored the fundamental commitments to human rights for which they had pressed in meetings of the Commission on Security and Cooperation in Europe (CSCE) for more than a decade. Yugoslav policy was shaped almost entirely by the desire to preserve the territorial integrity of the Soviet Union.

Western states remained firmly committed to the status quo in Yugoslavia. No effort was made to encourage Yugoslav leaders to hold the federation together by devising new political arrangements that addressed the special interests and concerns of the territorially compact communities of ethnic minorities in the republics. Even more important, in an unprecedented and ill-advised extension of the Helsinki principles of territorial integrity and the inviolability of state borders, the West extended its political support to the borders between the republics of the Yugoslav federation. Neither the United States nor its European partners acknowledged that the growing nationalism of the various peoples of Yugoslavia not only called into question the survival of the federation—they also raised doubts about the political viability of multiethnic republics. The same principle of self-determination that the Slovenes and Croats might use to justify their independence could also be used to justify Dalmatian Serbs' demands for separation from Croatia. Moreover, any reference to the principles of sovereignty and territorial integrity to defend the Croats' claims to Croatia could be used just as easily by Serbs in Belgrade to justify defending the integrity of the former Yugoslavia. International actors made no attempt, however, to confront these issues. They failed to address the growing probability that the Serbian leadership in Belgrade and its Serb allies in the military would use the JNA either to prevent the secession of Slovenia and Croatia or to detach Serb-populated territories of Croatia and Bosnia and annex them to Serbia.

By taking a more comprehensive approach, the international community might have been able to mediate among the several contradictory values and goals of local actors. Extreme demands for the right to self-determination on the part of Serbs in Croatia and Bosnia might have been counterbalanced, for example, by Serbian concerns that adoption of the principle of the right to self-determination might lead to the loss of Kosovo. Croatian ambitions with respect to western Herzegovina might similarly have been moderated by the desire to hold on to the Krajina region.

Under these circumstances, it might have been possible to achieve an overall settlement based on trade-offs among the parties involved. But such an approach would have required the international community to place the peaceful settlement of conflicting demands for self-determination above the principle of territorial integrity of states. At the very least, it would have required the United States and the European Community to abandon their support for the borders of the republics as the basis for establishing new states within the boundaries of the former Yugoslavia. However, this approach stood the best chance of success before the cycle of interethnic violence had set in. By mid-1991 it already was too late.

THE LESSONS OF YUGOSLAVIA

The wars in the former Yugoslavia have made it clear that the principles and practices that provided a stable framework for international security in the era of the cold war are no longer sufficient to preserve the peace. The principles of state sovereignty, territorial integrity, human rights, and self-determination embedded in the United Nations Charter and other United Nations documents, and developed in detail in the documents of the CSCE, have proved contradictory, or at least subject to contradictory interpretation. Moreover, the mounting human tragedy in Bosnia has revealed the inadequacies of the decision-making principles, operational guidelines, and conflict-management capabilities of Euro-Atlantic institutions such as the CSCE, NATO, and the European Community, as well as the UN.

New diplomatic and political mechanisms must be developed to cope with demands for self-determination in ways that do not undermine the basic foundation of international stability—the system of sovereign states. The development of such mechanisms requires reconsideration of the meaning of self-determination in the contemporary era and the careful reconsideration of the indivisibility of state sovereignty. At the very least, it requires limiting the ability of states to use their claim to sovereignty to shield abuses from international inquiry. For any mechanisms to be effective, however, individual states and international organizations alike must become more proactive, undertaking preventive diplomatic and political efforts to solve interethnic and other conflicts before they threaten international peace.

International engagement in the Yugoslav crisis as early as 1990 would have remained futile if the Western states had continued to refuse to support the redrawing of borders as a possible path to a peacefully negotiated solution to the crisis. The declaration of independence by a territorially compact ethnic community, such as that of the Serbs in Croatia or any other group in Yugoslavia, could have been recognized as a legitimate demand for self-determination. By recognizing the equal rights of all peoples in the country to self-determination, international mediators might have been able to lead local actors toward mutual concessions. The key to such negotiations, however, lay in the recognition that international principles, and the rights derived from them, were equally applicable to all parties, as well as in a willingness to undertake the renegotiation of borders. This the international community failed to do.

Early insistence by outside powers on the democratic legitimation of existing borders might have encouraged greater concern for the protection of human rights and avoided the escalation of ethnic tensions in Croatia and Bosnia. The Communist order that held Yugoslavia together began to disintegrate as early as 1986. It entered into crisis in December 1989. This left sufficient opportunity for international actors to influence events. The importance in such a situation of clearly and forcefully articulating and enforcing the human rights standards to which states seeking recognition will be held cannot be overemphasized. By doing so international actors may affect popular perceptions and politics. In Yugoslavia, for example, the regional elections held in 1990 might have produced more moderate governments if the human rights standards of potential ruling parties had been at issue.

The existence of competing claims to territory complicated the Yugoslav crisis. But it does not by itself account for the magnitude of human destruction that has occurred. The extreme violence in Yugoslavia must also be attributed to the establishment of ethnically defined governments that failed to provide democratic safeguards for the human rights of minority communities. This reinforces the conclusion that if the international community is to facilitate the peaceful settlement of such conflicts elsewhere, it must devise the means to prevent ethnic domination and safeguard human rights. In short, the principles of sovereignty, territorial integrity, and national self-determination must be integrated into a single framework for determining the legitimacy of claims to political authority. And that framework must be based on the superiority of principles of human rights and democracy.

Who'll Stop the Next 'Yugoslavia'?

In oil-rich Central Asia, 'modern' and fundamentalist Islam vie for influence. Ethnic groups spar. Nuclear weapons stir concern. But parts of the region could become as petro-wealthy as Kuwait. The outcome may rest on 'the greatest Tajik commander in a millennium'—and the West's willingness to pay attention.

Boris Rumer and Eugene Rumer

Boris Rumer is a fellow at Harvard University's Russian Research Center. Eugene Rumer is an analyst at the Rand Corporation in Santa Monica, California. They specialize in regional developments in the former Soviet Union and have recently returned from Central Asia.

THE NEXT "Yugoslavia"—a much bigger one—threatens to erupt in the former Soviet states bordering Iran, Afghanistan, and China. In Central Asia, ethnic, religious, and territorial tensions are growing. If not resolved, they could exceed the rivalries that have plunged the peoples of Yugoslavia into a bloody civil war. Europe and the US can still take diplomatic and economic steps to forestall an explosion in these lands that were jerry-built by Stalin's planners for economic exploitation and that now have been suddenly set free by the demise of the USSR. But Western leaders have their hands full. Few in their foreign ministries are paying close attention.

Not many surrounding countries are in position to intervene in Central Asia, even to the degree that the international community has in Yugoslavia, to help create a new equilibrium and civil peace.

Why should outside powers—already stretched by difficult peacekeeping in the Mideast, Yugoslavia, Somalia, South Africa, and Cambodia—care about this landlocked region in the heart of the Eurasian continent?

There are positive and negative reasons. First—and most easily grasped—parts of the region contain huge gas and oil reserves. And the industrial democracies will need new sources in the next century as old sources shrink. If you extend a line north and east from the greatest oil pool on earth (Saudi Arabia-Kuwait-Iran-Iraq) through the Caspian Sea into the heartland of the Islamic republics, you encounter other great petroleum reserves. Among the three Islamic nations vying for influence in the region, two—Saudi Arabia and Iran—are OPEC powers. (The third is NATO ally Turkey.) This leads some planners to worry about a potential Islamic oil colossus if the Arab and Persian rivals should ever make common cause.

Second, nuclear weapons are still deployed in part of the region (Kazakhstan).

Third, the region may help to decide whether a more modern, confident, globally cooperative version of Islam or a fundamentalist, chauvinist version gains influence in the world.

A KEY figure in the future of these three matters, as we shall see in a moment, is a powerful warlord from the war against Moscow's control of Afghanistan: Ahmed Shah Massoud. The Afghan war, Western leaders would do well to remember, provided the most important early blow in the cracking of the Soviet empire. World attention has moved on now to other matters. But Massoud may pull it back as he starts to make his mark on a larger strategic canvas.

The five new independent states that make up this region still seem exotic and irrelevant to many Western eyes. Their names—Kazakhstan, Uzbekistan, Turkmenistan, Kyrgyzstan, Tajikistan—conjure up half-remembered history lessons starring Genghiz Khan, Tamburlaine, and Alexander the Great. Their strategic and economic importance are recognized more by neighboring powers vying for influence than by Western planners. As already noted, these rivals are:

TURKEY, which has centuries-old ethnic, linguistic, and cultural links to the peoples of Central Asia and would like to establish itself as the preeminent political and economic power in the region. The Turkish government envisions a "Turkish Com-

From *World Monitor*, November 1992, pp. 36-42, 44. © 1992 by Boris Rumer and Eugene Rumer. Reprinted by permission.

mon Market" and is already planning to facilitate free travel and business activity by introducing one single identification document in the Central Asian countries.

IRAN, which has close ethnic, language, and cultural ties to Tajikistan and seeks to expand the presence of its version of Islam in the region. It is competing with Turkey for political influence and economic opportunities.

SAUDI ARABIA, which, according to local Central Asian sources, is spending large sums of money for Islamic religious and educational activities. It has been offering Central Asian young people fellowships for study in Muslim countries and sponsoring traditional pilgrimages to Mecca for local Muslims who cannot afford it otherwise. Considerations of power balance in the Persian Gulf practically mandate Saudi involvement in Central Asia to counter possible Iranian advances in an area that could become a strategic rear to the Gulf, as well as in the Islamic community at large.

Prospects of change for good or ill are illustrated by Turkmenistan, where many would like to think of their country as the "second Kuwait" in the making. It is potentially the wealthiest state in the region, thanks to large deposits of natural gas. Independence gave Turkmenistan the ability to dispose of such resources at its own discretion.

Nearby Tajikistan remains poor, indeed the poorest in the Commonwealth of Independent States and least stable in Central Asia. It is the fuse that could set off the regional explosion. Internal strife, which most recently led to the resignation in September (by some accounts literally at gunpoint) of President Rakhmon Nabiyev has resulted in a power vacuum not likely to be filled by any of the warring factions in Tajikistan.

Threats to regional stability emanate not only from Tajikistan's domestic turmoil, but from the presence of a large Tajik population across a very porous border with Afghanistan. One possible scenario being discussed, and feared, in all of Central Asia entails unification of all Tajiks in a greater Tajikistan under the leadership of the man talked about in Dushanbe, Tajikistan's capital, as the greatest Tajik military commander in this millennium. He is the previously mentioned Ahmed Shah Massoud, the powerful warlord and leader of minority Tajiks in Afghanistan.

Iran's money, people, and religious and political influence are feared more than those of any other external source and are seen in the shadow of every mosque and behind every outburst of Islamic political activism in Central Asia.

Given the growing vacuum of power in Tajikistan—and the lack of a common ideological platform to reverse the fracturing of society—it may well take an outside political personality, such as Massoud, to bring a degree of stability to Tajikistan. But such stabilization would be short-lived and, were it to occur along with the rise of a Tajik state reuniting ethnic kin from the two sides of the border, would come at the terrible price of regional destabilization, for it would likely split Afghanistan and upset the fragile equilibrium in Uzbekistan with its own sizeable Tajik minority.

The Tajiks are the fastest-growing ethnic group in Central Asia and in the entire former Soviet Union. Their country is a patchwork quilt of regional, ethnic, and tribal fiefdoms where rivalries, suspicions, and territorial claims do not stop at the state border. Tajiks have long complained about the arbitrary and unfair borders drawn by Moscow in the 1920s, which gave Uzbekistan most of the fertile valleys (along with millions of Tajik subjects) and left Tajikistan with 90% of its territory consisting of mountains.

The logic and dynamics of internal rivalries in Tajikistan may appear incomprehensible to an outside observer. But the course of events there appears to be the prototype nightmare scenario that may

haunt more than one Central Asian leader. Ethnic, religious, regional, and clan divisions have combined to pose a threat of geopolitical eruption that could upset the fragile peace in all of Central Asia.

THE FALL of the

Moscow-backed Najibulla government in Afghanistan earlier this year crystallized the attention of Central Asian leaders. Much has been written about factional politics and rivalries in the coalition that has succeeded in ridding the country of the last vestiges of Soviet occupation only to turn on each other. One thing is becoming increasingly clear: The dividing line between the internal politics of Afghanistan and their spillover across the former Soviet border may soon disappear. The shifting fortunes of coalition warfare in Afghanistan are becoming closely tied to the politics of ex-Soviet Central Asia.

The connection is two-way. For the newly victorious ethnic warlords of Afghanistan, like Massoud, the leader of Afghanistan's Tajiks, the struggle for power in the battered Afghan capital, Kabul, is only beginning. The Tajiks' kin across the crumbling Soviet border in Tajikistan represent an important strategic rear in the struggle against the traditionally dominant Pashtun majority in Afghanistan.

Unification of Tajiks from the two sides of the former Soviet-Afghan border—an idea that has been raised on both sides—would, needless to say, alter the ethnic and power balances in Afghanistan. This, in turn, raises the specter of a partitioning of Afghanistan and mobilization of Pashtuns. And that would be a development that could not be ignored by Pakistan in the light of its own Pashtun population. Renewed pressure for a separate Pashtun state would threaten Pakistan's territorial integrity.

Tribal and regional violence in Tajikistan has generated a strong demand for weapons, which the local black market has not been able to satisfy through theft and illegal sales from Soviet Army warehouses. Border crossings by Tajiks from Tajikistan into Afghanistan in search of weapons have become commonplace. Many residents of Tajikistan, fearing for their safety, see personal weapons as their only protection against the threat of attack from neighboring villages or rival gangs.

According to one estimate, during the first three weeks of July smugglers brought into Tajikistan 5,000 AK-47 assault rifles, scores of grenade launchers, anti-tank rifles, hand grenades, and various kinds of ammunition. It is not unreasonable to assume that these weapons, available in abundance in Afghanistan, are being supplied by local militias at cut-rate prices and possibly free of charge, creating an important constituency north of the border.

And "brotherly help" from Afghan Tajiks does not end with supplying weapons and ammunition. According to information supplied by the Commonwealth of Independent States (CIS) military authorities in Central Asia, camps have been set up in Afghanistan for training of guerrillas, referred to there as "brother mujahideen from Tajikistan."

Many in Central Asia are convinced that the "Afghan-Tajik" connection does not begin in Afghanistan. Rather, they maintain, it originates in Iran, whose money, people, and religious and political influence are feared more than those of any other external source and are seen in the shadow of every mosque and behind every outburst of Islamic political activism in Central Asia.

Although most, if not all, of these suspicions have yet to be borne out, Tajikistan does represent a target of opportunity for Iran because of linguistic and cultural closeness. Tajikistan is the only country in Central Asia where the official state language does not belong to the Turkic group. Tajik is a close relative of Farsi, the national language of Iran.

The spillover of Afghan politics into Central Asia is undoubtedly a cause of major concern for all leaders in the region. The prospect of a greater Tajikistan would be enough to endanger the shaky political and territorial status quo. It would generate political momentum, intellectual rationale, and conceivably even precedent for further territorial revisions in the region. It would also be a likely catalyst for penetration of politically active fundamentalist Islam into the region, contributing to instability there along with other possible developments.

Nobody understands and fears such a prospect more than Uzbek President Islam Karimov. His country, with its sizable Tajik enclave and territory still claimed by many in Tajikistan, would be most vulnerable to revisionist demands from a future greater Tajikistan.

Relations between Uzbekistan and Tajikistan have deteriorated steadily. Uzbek refugees have been fleeing violence in Tajikistan. President Karimov has resorted to increasingly tough measures against what he apparently perceives as

the Tajik "fifth column" in Uzbekistan. In mid-July Tajik-language schools in Samarkand were closed. Rail traffic from Tajikistan has been tightly controlled and Tajik passengers traveling to Uzbekistan have been ordered off the trains at the border.

EVENTS IN Tajikistan

(alleged to have been precipitated by help from Afghanistan) clearly haunt President Karimov. Recently, he accused the opposition of taking the country along the "Tajik path" and warned about the threat of Islamic fundamentalism emanating from Tajikistan. Karimov swore that he would not stop at anything to maintain stability in the country and would be willing to "go down on his knees" to plead to his people for calm.

Inviolability of borders has become the cornerstone of Karimov's policies in the region and outside, shared vigorously by other leaders in Central Asia. Karimov has sought to suppress potential challenges to Uzbekistan's territorial integrity by cracking down on Samarkand Tajiks. At the same time he has categorically rejected separatist rumblings in the Uzbek community of Tajikistan, where the idea of unification with Uzbekistan has been raised.

Territorial integrity is also the most important issue on the domestic and foreign policy agenda of the other major regional power—Kazakhstan. Its geography and ethnic make-up leave President Nursultan Nazarbayev with little room to maneuver in avoiding breakup and cementing the independence so recently gained. Forty-five percent of Kazakhstan's 17 million inhabitants are of Turkic origin, predominantly Kazakh; 45% are Slavs—mostly Russians, but also Russified Ukrainians. The remaining 10% are "miscellaneous"—the Volga Germans and Crimean Tartars deported by Stalin, Koreans, and other minorities.

ANY ATTEMPT

by President Nazarbayev to introduce economic reforms involving significant privatization of state assets is likely to be tainted with allegations of ethnic bias owing to the uneven ethnic representation in various sectors of Kazakhstan's economy. Russians and other non-Kazakh minorities, which together constitute the majority of Kazakhstan's population, play the pivotal role in every sector of the econo-

my. These include the ex-Soviet space launch complex and the vast agricultural areas in the North developed in the late 1950s during Khrushchev's rule and known as the "virgin lands." "Russians make Kazakhstan run," many of them openly tell visitors, adding that, when it comes to privatizing industry and agriculture, they will lay claim to what they run now. And if the Kazakhs tell them to leave (as some Kazakh nationalists have) they will secede and split the country, taking their half and joining the Russian Federation.

The relative political calm in Kazakhstan is undoubtedly the greatest accomplishment of President Nazarbayev. He presides over a political process that so far has been much more tolerant than any other in Central Asia. The key to his success has been a publicly articulated desire of the government to avoid perceptions of ethnic bias in favor of one or the other major group. If the president is Kazakh, the prime minister is a Slav. If Kazakh is the official state language, Russian is the "language of interethnic communication."

However, Kazakhstan's veneer of stability and civility may turn out to be thin. The rough substance of Kazakhstan's domestic politics and the question of control of the economy lies close to the surface, and no politician, not even Nazarbayev, may be able to smooth it out if it breaks out in the open.

There can be little doubt that the leaders of the other two Central Asian states, Kyrgyzstan and Turkmenistan—Presidents Askar Akayev and Saparmurat Niyazov, respectively—also share this commitment to territorial status quo. Given their countries' size, economic constraints, uncertain national identity, and questionable boundaries, any territorial dispute would likely spell the end of them as independent states.

The tragedy and weakness of Central Asia's position after over a century of Russian and Soviet rule is reflected in its distorted pattern of economic development. Moscow exploited the region as a source of raw materials and agricultural goods with little or no regard for the environment and traditional ways of life. And Central Asia became dependent on Moscow for deliveries of key industrial and consumer commodities and for heavy subsidies to sustain uneconomic and resource-consuming agriculture and mineral industries.

Politically, Central Asia is, in the words of one senior Russian official, a "semi-feudal, semi-Communist structure." Indeed, with the notable exception of Kyrgyzstan's President Akayev, current Central Asian leaders are former Communist Party bosses who have managed to keep old party structures and power, albeit under different names. They have preserved all the essential features of the old Soviet system in Central Asia: autocratic regimes (admittedly, of varying degree of intolerance); tightly controlled public life; virtually absent independent news media; old entrenched Soviet elites; a predominant state sector in the economy; and little, if any, evidence of the economic and social reforms that have triggered radical changes elsewhere in the former Soviet Union.

ONE THING, however, has changed in Central Asia—Islam. In just a few years it has been transformed from a semi-underground, anemic religious movement controlled by Soviet secret police into an authoritative and influential religious, social, and political force—still gathering strength but already challenging the existing power structures. The growing influence of Islam in Central Asia is manifested in the fact that the presidents of Uzbekistan and Turkmenistan,

both former Communist Party bosses, have recently performed a *hajj*—the traditional Muslim pilgrimage to Mecca.

It would be too simplistic to assume that Islam is sweeping Central Asia. But Islam is perhaps the most profound polarizing issue in the region today.

And, as often happens, politics has produced strange bedfellows. Opponents of the Islamization of political and social life in Central Asia include local political and cultural elites, many of whom are Russian-educated and/or Western-educated and who, in their outlook and geopolitical orientation, associate with Russia and the West. This coalition includes the ex-Communist Party establishment still in power in Central Asia, local democratic dissident movements, local intelligentsia, cultural personalities, and the academic elite. It also includes broad segments of the urban population, many of whom have been Russified and Sovietized.

For members of this broad and odd coalition the specter of politically active Islam is frightening. They share a willingness to resort to any measures, including violence, to prevent its growth in their societies. To the entrenched political elite, Islamic power would mean the end of their predominant position. To the intelligentsia,

it would mean a radical change of ideology, perhaps even more pervasive than the old Communist ideology. And it would mean abandonment of cultural values and artistic freedoms they have enjoyed to a degree even before, and especially after, Gorbachev's perestroika. To the average urban citizen—Central Asia's quasi-middle class—it would also mean a fundamental departure from a way of life shaped by the shared values of consumer society.

On the other side of the Islamic divide are the masses: (1) the uneducated rural poor in areas where Islam has always been more resilient, even during the worst years of Soviet oppression; (2) the urban poor; (3) the fast-growing class of unemployed young who cannot find work in cities or in the countryside; and (4) a segment of nationalist and/or Islamic fundamentalist intelligentsia, including a growing number of clerics. Rural population amounts to 60% of the total population in the region.

IN MOST Central Asian countries there are as yet few overt signs of Islamic-based political mobilization among these segments of the population. But the economic and social conditions in

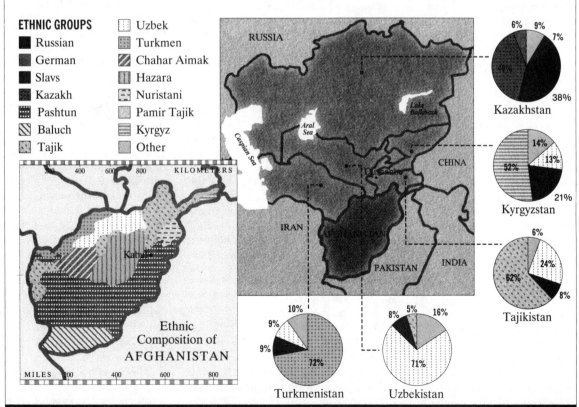

ETHNIC GROUPS

- Russian
- German
- Slavs
- Kazakh
- Pashtun
- Baluch
- Tajik
- Uzbek
- Turkmen
- Chahar Aimak
- Hazara
- Nuristani
- Pamir Tajik
- Kyrgyz
- Other

Ethnic Composition of AFGHANISTAN

Kazakhstan 6% 9% 7% 40% 38%

Kyrgyzstan 14% 13% 52% 21%

Tajikistan 6% 24% 62% 8%

Turkmenistan 10% 9% 9% 72%

Uzbekistan 8% 5% 16% 71%

Graphic by Dave Herring

Frontiers to watch: Central Asia's need for stabilization is dramatized by arms traffic to Tajikistan from fellow Tajiks clustered just across the border in Afghanistan. Ethnic tensions require effective governments everywhere in region no longer controlled by Moscow.

the countryside create a fertile environment for dissemination of Islam and its transformation from religious dogma into political ideology as the answer to all ills.

Fear of external and internal challenges to the territorial integrity and ultimately the survival of their countries has made these leaders run for the protective cover of the Commonwealth of Independent States and its most powerful member, Russia. Post-independence euphoria (which was not as strong anyway in Central Asia as in Ukraine or the Baltic states) quickly wore off and left the leaders of Central Asia with the realization that Russia is the only realistic regional military power capable of preserving a degree of peace.

FIRST OF ALL,

Russia is already there as the leading military and political player in the CIS. It is also the historic homeland to an estimated 10 million ethnic Russians living in Central Asia, the biggest contributor to the CIS military budget, and the historic and intellectual homeland to tens of thousands of military personnel of Russian origin and their families deployed in Central Asia.

Second, the novelty and romance of political and cultural rapprochement with outside powers—most importantly Turkey, but also Saudi Arabia, Pakistan, and Iran—have been replaced by a more realistic assessment of such ties. While these Islamic contacts brought much-needed financial credits and added international recognition, not one of these countries could fill the void should Russia decide to withdraw its military, economic, and political presence.

Third, the price tag for regional and individual state security is too much for the straining economies of Central Asian countries. Having set forth initially ambitious plans for their own national security establishments, they quickly realized that such ambitions went beyond their means.

All Central Asian states with the exception of Tajikistan have signed bilateral security treaties with Russia which effectively provide for the stationing of Russian troops on their territories and Russian responsibility for the security of CIS external borders.

But no matter how much most Central Asian leaders strive to preserve Russia's stabilizing military presence in the region, the future of Moscow's involvement there remains in question. So far, Boris Yeltsin and his government have gone along with

requests for security assistance to Central Asia. But Russian foreign policy toward the countries of "near abroad," as the former Soviet republics have come to be somewhat condescendingly known, has yet to be fully formulated.

IN MOSCOW there

is now a new choir of "enlightened imperialists"—influential converts from the liberal-democratic camp, including state councillor Sergei Stankevich and chairman of the parliamentary foreign affairs committee Yevgeny Ambartsumov. In Ambartsumov's words:

"Russia is something more than the Russian Federation in its current borders. Therefore, its geopolitical interests must be considered much more broadly than what is currently defined on the maps. Based on that, we intend to build our relations with 'near abroad.' Its cornerstone [will be] the defense of interests of compatriots and maximum fulfillment of national-state interests."

However eager Central Asia's leaders may be for an external stabilizing presence, such statements by prominent Russian politicians stir indignation and renewed fears of Russian imperialism.

Dear as such declarations may be to the hearts of Russian nationalist patriots, there is little chance of their practical implementation. Far from being able to flex its military muscle in Central Asia in pursuit of some ill-defined "geopolitical interests," Russia's obligation to help maintain the status quo in the region constitutes a huge sacrifice, considering the current economic weakness. Yeltsin's Moscow is not able to take on an even bigger military burden.

Furthermore, aggressive pursuit of "geopolitical interests" in Central Asia, implied in Ambartsumov's statement, could lead to military confrontation once more with Afghanistan. Russia is still reeling from its "Afghan syndrome." Its public is not likely to be ready for another Afghanistan any time soon.

TO ERR on the side of cau-

tion, it is important to recognize the limits of Western, as well as Russian, involvement in Central Asian affairs. It is particularly important to acknowledge that traditional Western cure-alls—democratization and economic liberalization—may for a long time be counter-

productive in Central Asian countries. Attempting to impose alien concepts on traditional societies steeped in different values could undermine the already frail foundations of civil peace.

But this risk should not mean the *abandonment* of Western democratic and free-market ideals in pursuit of policies toward Central Asia. The key should be gradualism and long-term commitment.

This means:

• Active dialogue with Central Asian governments about strategies for economic and political development and security.

• Assistance programs with adequate financing and skilled professionals.

• Exchange programs for scholars, students, and cultural groups.

• Involvement of private-sector aid organizations in the dialogue.

• In sum, a long-term, nonoffensive "propaganda by example" approach intended to (1) increase Central Asian nations' involvement in the international community, (2) help them formulate plans for political and economic development, and (3) create popular constituencies for gradual change.

The dialogue should not be limited to dealings with Central Asian governments. Special efforts should be made to seek out nongovernment leaders with constructive alternative ideas for development of their nations. Western participants should be prepared to find few such groups, and may in effect have to build them through "propaganda by example" programs.

IN DESIGNING

economic assistance, priority should be given to alleviating widespread poverty rather than to abstract schemes for promoting private entrepreneurship.

Lessons learned from decades of success and failure in aiding third world nations will certainly apply in Central Asia. Its large but mostly unexplored mineral wealth, widespread poverty, and severe ecological needs present a promising opportunity for Western help. This is particularly true in regard to developing water resources, where strategically applied aid could produce disproportionately generous pay-offs that would be felt throughout Central Asian societies.

Governments and private international organizations should remind themselves that inaction is the worst kind of policy, and that nobody knows how long Central Asia's fragile peace will last.

Islam's Violent Improvisers

Without a formal structure, new religious radicals are hard to combat

Steve Coll and David Hoffman

Washington Post *Foreign Service*

On a dreary December dawn, four young Palestinians in an old sedan entered the streets of Lod, a mixed Arab-Jewish town in central Israel. They spotted Israeli border guard Nissim Toledano walking to work, ran him down, drove him back to their village just north of Jerusalem and dumped him in a cave. Two days later, frustrated that Israel had rebuffed their demands for a prisoner exchange, the men decided to kill Toledano. But since they did not know how to use a gun, they stabbed and strangled him.

Another morning, another city: In Cairo's timeworn Zeinhoum district last month, an Egyptian army officer was driving to work when automatic-weapons fire pierced the clamorous, crowded streets. The officer escaped, but a policeman and a bystander were killed, as were two attackers—members of Egypt's revolutionary Islamic Group. Estimated cost of the Islamic Group's poorly aimed but deadly ambush, including assault rifles, hand grenades and forged identity papers: about $7,700

These incidents and dozens like them reflect the new face of violent Islamic radicalism in Israel and Egypt and across the Middle East—a swelling wave of grass-roots movements that are improvised in their military operations, modest in budgetary requirements, diffuse in organization and committed to radical pan-Islamic ideology.

From Tel Aviv to Cairo to New York, a frustrated alliance of pro-Western governments is struggling to unravel the insurgents' intricate structures and their sources of financial and material support—all in the hope of containing the radicals' political and military power. But because the radicals are so loosely organized, the effort has proven immensely difficult.

"Radical Islam today is wheels within wheels within wheels," says Israeli scholar Ifrah Zilberman. "That's what makes it so frustrating for outside analysts and counter-terrorist efforts."

The movements arise from broadly based opposition politics in generally undemocratic countries. They seek to impose strict Islamic law on societies now mainly governed by an uneasy mix of modern politics and religious tradition. Frequently under intense pressure from their governments, these radical Islamic movements have given birth to extremist factions or groups that seek to achieve their goals through direct revolutionary violence.

The ascendant movements mark a basic change in the structure and character of Middle Eastern political violence. The tightly organized revolutionary organizations sponsored during the 1970s and 1980s by such governments as Syria, Iraq and Libya—including the Palestine Liberation Organization and the group headed by the Palestinian Sabri Banna, or Abu Nidal—are in decline. On the rise in the 1990s is a much more fluid trend—unorganized groups of angry young men involved in self-proclaimed religious war and broadly based protest politics.

The recent terrorism cases in New York can be seen as part of this broader picture, according to the evidence so far. More evidence may yet be mustered in court about links between the New York defendants and outside governments or other sponsors, but it seems clear that the sums of money required for their terrorist operations were small and that their support networks were organized largely around family, informal contacts and local institutions, such as neighborhood mosques.

Yet at the same time, some defendants have ties to international, charismatic personalities, such as radical Egyptian preacher Sheik Omar Abdel Rahman, as well as to transnational institutions like Brooklyn's Alkifah Refugee Center, which helped send Muslim volunteer fighters to Afghanistan and runs branch offices in Pakistan and Croatia.

Seeking to mollify their publics and to find sympathy in the United States, Egyptian and Israeli politicians sometimes blame Iran's revolutionary Islamic government in Tehran for funding and stoking these radical movements. After the killing of Toledano in December—an incident that triggered the expulsion from Israel of more than 400 suspected Islamic activists—Prime Minister Yitzhak Rabin pointed the finger at "radical-fanatic Muslim insanity," which he described as "a megalomaniac system headed by Iran."

"The Arab world—the world in general—will pay, if the cancer of the radical-fundamentalist Islam is not halted at the house of study of [ayatollah Ruhollah] Khomeini and his followers in Iran," Rabin declared. Egyptian President Hosni Mubarak has made similar accusations about Iran's role during the last six months.

But the Israeli and Egyptian charges are misleading in many ways, according to results of those countries' police investigations, as well as interviews with dozens of participants in the Islamic movements, officials and specialists. Iran provides funding to Islamic radicals abroad, including in Israel, they say. But these Islamic movements are in many ways home-grown. The outside support they receive comes more often from wealthy individuals in Saudi Arabia, other Persian Gulf countries and elsewhere than it does from Iran, say movement participants, Israeli and Egyptian officials and Western specialists.

Iran's strengths as it competes for influence with Islamic movements are the inspirational power of its original revolution and its willingness to defy the West and Israel. But Iran is hampered in its efforts to export revolution. Iran's Shiite Islamic faith is in the minority throughout the Arab world, and its strong ethnic Persian identity raises hackles with many Arabs, regardless of Islamic ideology.

The Islamic movements now so dynamic in Israel, Egypt and other countries arise from complex factors, including the failures of secular institutions, economic troubles, an absence of democracy, perceptions of injustice, the deep cultural roots of Islamic faith, the legacy of the war in Afghanistan and rapid social change in the Muslim world.

That outside support for these movements comes, to a large extent, from wealthy individuals in Saudi Arabia and other Persian Gulf countries reflects the diffuse, often informal character of the present Islamic revival.

Funding from abroad to Egypt's Islamic Group "either comes through individuals or bank transfers to individuals not known to security," says Egyptian Interior Minister Hassan Mohammed Alfi. "We do not know the exact amount" of money coming from gulf sources. "These operations took place secretly," he says. "It has to be large sums of money."

According to Palestinian and Israeli sources familiar with Hamas, the largest Islamic organization among the 1.8 million Palestinians in the Israeli-occupied West Bank and Gaza Strip, most outside support to the movement comes not from Iran but from private groups and individuals in Saudi Arabia and the Persian Gulf emirates and is often passed through Jordan.

Although the transfers are well hidden, it is known that some comes as charitable contributions for such institutions as schools, clinics and mosques, and some is cash for military operations smuggled by individuals across the Allenby Bridge into the West Bank.

All told, this outside support may amount to $20 million a year—just a fraction of the estimated $500 million a year that the secular Palestine Liberation Organization reaped until recently from the gulf states.

Neither are the movements' relatively small budgets coherently organized. The institutional and financial heart of the Muslim world's vibrant Islamic revival lies in the "*jamaa*," an Arabic word that means "group" or "society" and is chosen by modern Islamic radicals to connote loose structure but firm commitment to religious principles.

In dissecting the transnational finances of these organizations, it is difficult to draw a line between private, cross-border Islamic charitable contributions to legitimate institutions and patronage of violent Islamic revolutionaries. Some groups attract militant young radicals prone to violence. But most such organizations publicly forswear violence, promoting radical Islam through charity, education or unions.

Governments seeking to quell Islamic movements often have trouble distinguishing one sort of jamaa from another—indeed, the peaceful and violence-prone ones are sometimes interconnected, say participants, specialists and officials. In other cases, mosques or Islamic education societies originally funded from abroad for peaceful, evangelical purposes have more recently been taken over in such places as Upper Egypt and the Israeli-occupied West Bank by younger Islamic radicals committed to violent revolution, they say.

"Islamic movements must be understood on two levels—organizations and structures, and then secondly as fluid, multidimensional, interactive," says Khurshid Ahmed, a leading Pakistani Islamic activist and charity manager with wide contacts in the radical Arab world.

Typically, formal outside sponsorship is not central to an Islamic jamaa. Rather, the group depends on *zakaat*, the 2.5 percent annual contribution set down by Islamic law and demanded of wealthy Muslims who expect to reach heaven.

Zakaat "has nothing to do with the borders of countries," says Rachid Ghannouchi, exiled leader of Tunisia's radical Nahda, or Renaissance, movement. "The Islamic movement relies on this individual sharing, financial participation."

Pious Muslims with the most to give tend to live in Saudi Arabia and other oil-rich gulf states. Their contributions often involve cash or diversions through legitimate businesses or charities; the use of prolific modern technology—such as fax machines, computers and electronic banking—and informal, person-to-person cross-border contacts.

In Egypt's case, "there is a group of Islamic Group members working in Saudi Arabia," explains one of the radical movement's lawyers in Upper Egypt. "They are both Egyptians and Saudis, and they try to help people here financially."

The Egyptians involved are not from the Islamic Group's military or proselytizing wings, but are among the "affiliated but undeclared members" who clandestinely cooperate with the radical movement, the lawyer says.

"Likewise, there are Saudis who belong to the Islamic Group who are undeclared," he adds. "So they meet in various places far from the eyes of authority. For example, someone from here goes to Saudi as a doctor or engineer or lawyer, and he interacts with Saudis. . . . Both groups are looking for someone to convey the real *sharia*" or Islamic law, he says.

To understand what these splintered and voluntary Islamic movements look like on the ground and why they so vex the secular, pro-Western governments seeking to contain them, consider the developments underway today in Jenin, a dusty, violence-wracked city of 220,000 on the northern side of the Israeli-occupied West Bank. Jenin used to be a stronghold of the secular PLO, which stateless Palestinians looked on for decades as a surrogate state. Besides fighters, the PLO financed an array of institutions from schools to hospitals to newspapers, as well as payments to families whose sons and fathers were imprisoned or had been killed. But the PLO is running out of money, and its network is falling apart. The Islamic movement is filling the vacuum.

Like the PLO, the Islamic movement has many faces. In addition to its military wing, Hamas is a broadly based religious movement with a foundation in mosques and a political and social service movement that has drawn the Palestinian merchant and intellectual classes, as well as the poor.

One of the movement's landmarks in Jenin is a gleaming new Islamic medical center, topped by a mosque, on a ridge above the city center. The hospital has room for up to 100 patients—nearly double the capacity of Jenin's only other medical center, an aging facility run by the Israeli military administration. The hospital has modern technology; orthopedic, pediatric and emergency services; a pharmacy and a laboratory. Funding for the hospital, mosque and a kindergarten—about $3 million since the mid-1980s—came from individual benefactors in the Persian Gulf, says Sheik Zaid Mahmoud Zakarneh, head of the zakaat fund that raised the money. Fund leaders wrote letters and traveled from the West Bank to Saudi Arabia and other gulf countries to solicit money from individual donors. Eventually, they found an exiled palestinian businessman in Riyadh, a Saudi Arabian businessman in Jeddah, a government charity in Kuwait and a Palestinian charity in Canada that were willing to send significant sums, Zakarneh says.

"It depends on Islam . . . on the understanding that every Muslim should by faith give part of his income," Zakarneh says. Among wealthy Saudis, adds Zakarneh's colleague Fuaz Hamad, "it is also a matter of prestige. He [the donor] says, 'I donated for Palestine,' and they ask for a certificate and put it on the wall."

The beneficiaries are Jenin's impoverished Palestinians. Families pay less than 60 cents to visit the medical center,

and those who can afford more pay just a few dollars. In the dental clinic, a patient says he came because "they are a humane and charitable society" and because "they're cheaper than anyone else. Because of good services, they have a good reputation."

The picture is equally striking in the Gaza Strip. The Islamic Society in Gaza, which began as a small sports club in a mosque at the Beach Refugee Camp, today provides hundreds of youths with activities, including a computer camp, kindergartens and lectures. "The people are in need of any services, from any institution," says Saleh Berheet, a society manager.

The group's budget is supported by individual and charity donations from the gulf, society officials say. So is the budget of Gaza's Islamic University, long the center of Islamic radicalism in the territory. "They [Saudis] don't know what they are donating to, but they want to salvage their souls," says Mordechai Abir, a former policy planning chief in the Israeli Defense Ministry and the country's leading specialist on Saudi Arabia. "And let's be honest with ourselves—what is peanuts to them is real money in the West Bank or Gaza."

Does the efficient, proselytizing Islamic religiosity of these charities, hospitals and schools really make them, per se, a part of the infrastructure of the violent factions of the Islamic movement? Officials at the facilities say that is preposterous—they describe themselves as undertaking social work, not sowing violent revolution. But the Israeli government sees these institutions as the superstructure of a broad Islamic movement whose most militant wing is openly dedicated to violent religious struggle. Thus, Israel has lately sought to contain the activities of the movement's support institutions, despite their benign appearance.

In Jenin, records and computer disks at the Islamic hospital were confiscated by Israeli authorities. Several doctors and board members, charged with being members of Hamas, were deported to Lebanon in December. Israel has denied permission for the Jenin clinic to import new equipment and an ambulance, say hospital and Israeli officials.

Elsewhere in the occupied territories, Israel recently closed a dozen or so mosques thought to be centers of radicalism. Board members from other Islamic charities and institutions were deported in December. The Israelis have tried to stanch the flow of money from abroad, but they confess they cannot keep track of it.

Dissecting its own radical Islamic opposition, Egypt's government faces a similar quandary. U.S. academic researcher Dennis Sullivan estimates that 2,000 Islamic charitable societies are registered in Egypt. Many are associated with the Muslim Brotherhood, once a violent Islamic movement publicly dedicated for the last 20 years to a peaceful, evolutionary transition to an Islamic state in Egypt.

5. CONFLICT

Brotherhood members forced into exile in Saudi Arabia and Europe during the 1960s have built up over the years a rich network of Islamic banks, companies and other institutions, in and out of Egypt. Some Egyptian government officials contend these elderly Brotherhood members are using their resources to fund the younger generation of Egyptian Islamic radicals committed to street violence. But the government has never produced evidence of such funding, and the local Brotherhood chapter denies any link to the younger radicals.

Attempts by Egypt and Israel to trace the support networks of young Islamic activists who pull the triggers in acts of religious or insurgent violence have yielded similar portraits of complexity and diffusion. One example is the recent finding of Israeli police investigators in the Toledano killing, a turning point for Israel in that it prompted the largest deportation in the country's peace-time history. The four Palestinians accused of the killing, arrested after months on the run, turned out to be in some respects an amateurish gang with no connections to Hamas's military wing when they undertook their campaign of violence. They decided to kidnap Toledano with "bare hands," as an Israeli security official puts it, and they had no experience with weapons.

The network they constructed was informal, built on a single acquaintance. After killing Toledano, one gang member contacted Ibrahim Nawadeh, an alleged Hamas activist and preacher he had known at an Islamic college and who had become the Jordanian-salaried imam in a small Jenin mosque, investigators say. From Nawadeh the gang sought money and guns. He gave them an Israeli-made Uzi submachine gun, a pistol and 4,000 Jordanian dinars (about $6,000), investigators say. When the Uzi proved defective, the preacher replaced it with another and helped the gang buy a new car similar to the kind driven by Israeli police and army officers, so the activists could not be easily detected.

Nawadeh was a go-between, but the gang picked their own targets, the investigators say. The preacher obtained money from yet another Hamas figure. When dealing with the gang, he "didn't give them orders," and he "didn't give them instructions," one investigator says.

Nawadeh's father, a retired merchant, denies that his son was involved with Hamas and says the charges against him are "exaggerated." He describes Nawadeh as a product of religious schools and says he had long been the most fervently religious member of his family.

The gang Nawadeh allegedly funded was not typical of all Hamas military cells—they were at the same time more ambitious and less well-prepared than many. Yet their efforts underscore the often fractured structure of contemporary violent Islamic radicals. "It is organic—there's no need for a department of this or a department of that," says Israeli scholar Zilberman. "It's organized around charisma or religious scholarship. . . . The best way to destroy charisma is to become bureaucratic."

Fighting Off Doomsday

Whether the threat comes from North Korea or Ukraine, the world worries about more fingers on the nuclear trigger

By BRUCE W. NELAN

NORTH KOREA'S KIM JONG IL, 51, wears high-heeled shoes and a bouffant hairdo in an attempt to look taller. He is a poor speaker and worries whether he can match his father's commanding power. But even those who laugh loudest at his vanities take one of his indulgences quite seriously: Kim, who has taken over day-to-day dictatorial duties from his 81-year-old father, "Great Leader" Kim Il Sung, appears determined to build a secret arsenal of nuclear weapons. His government had threatened to quit the 150-nation Treaty on the Nonproliferation of Nuclear Weapons last Saturday; it had ordered all foreigners except diplomats to leave and barred international inspectors from the country. If the outside world resorted to military force, a senior official in Pyongyang had warned, it would mean "plunging the whole Korean peninsula into the flame of war."

But at the eleventh hour, North Korea agreed late on Friday to "suspend" its withdrawal from the pact, pulling Asia back from the start of a nuclear arms race. If Pyongyang will permanently rejoin the treaty and agree to inspections, the U.S. is ready to cancel its yearly military exercises with South Korea and make a "no first use" pledge not to initiate the use of nuclear weapons on the peninsula. While U.S. officials are still puzzled by North Korea's actions, they say they now realize how deeply inspections disturbed its closed society.

Even though the cold war is over, leaders like Kim are making the world a more, not less, dangerous place. The superpower standoff that exerted precarious control over the use and proliferation of weapons of mass destruction has vanished along with the Soviet empire. North Korea has not only embarked on the road to the bomb, but according to many analysts, it has actually arrived. It reportedly has enough plutonium for at least one nuclear bomb, and it has successfully test-fired a new missile, the 650-mile-range No-Dong I, that could reach beyond South Korea to Japan, China or eastern Russia. Kim's government is an eager peddler of missiles to other countries, and Western analysts fear that Pyongyang could assist other would-be nuclear powers like Iran.

"We are facing a sophisticated Hydra of suppliers," warns CIA Director James Woolsey. More than 25 countries have or may be developing weapons of mass destruction. More than two dozen conduct research in chemical weapons or already stockpile them. More than a dozen have ballistic missiles that could one day loft nuclear warheads far beyond their borders.

Ukraine, along with the former Soviet republics of Kazakhstan and Belarus, stumbled into the nuclear club when the empire crumbled. Although all three have promised to banish the weapons entirely, Ukraine has been wavering on its commitment. A growing number of its leaders regard their atomic arsenal as a bargaining chip to trade for Western aid and security guarantees—and increasingly as a safeguard against possible Russian aggression that they are loath to relinquish.

Once again, the post–cold war era is turning out to be more complicated than anyone expected as the West searches for ways to stop nuclear proliferation. There

is no obvious answer, and the Western dithering that has accompanied the rape of Bosnia does not inspire confidence that the international community will come up with a strong plan of action soon. The U.S. is juggling competing objectives that undercut its own commitment to nonproliferation—the desire to improve relations with China or to secure Syria's cooperation in the Mideast peace talks—and so far, Washington has not figured out how to galvanize its main allies around a tougher antiproliferation policy.

North Korea is currently the gravest concern. Pyongyang signed the nonproliferation treaty in 1985 but grudgingly agreed only last year to allow inspectors to examine what it insisted was its purely civilian nuclear-power industry. When the monitors showed up, they confirmed intelligence reports that the installation at Yongbyon, north of the capital, had been processing plutonium at least since 1987.

No U.S. blandishments will keep Pyongyang honest—even if it remains formally in the nonproliferation pact—if its real intent is to free itself from international oversight while it pursues its nuclear dream. North Korea may have temporized to forestall U.N. economic sanctions that loomed if it became the first member to quit the treaty. But most observers are pessimistic that Kim will really cave in to political or economic pressure. "We're not dealing with rational people but with an unreconstructedly Stalinist regime," says a top British diplomat. "They don't believe in compromise but in maximum advantage."

Though the Security Council could authorize military means to disarm or pun-

5. CONFLICT

ish Pyongyang, any attempt to use force would be extremely tricky. Bombing a functioning nuclear facility could produce an instant Chernobyl and, probably, retaliation. "We might try to take out their nuclear capability with a scalpel," says a Western analyst in Seoul, "but they would respond with a chain saw."

Doing nothing about the North Korean bomb is a bad option too. South Korea was well along in the development of nuclear weapons in the 1970s until the U.S. pressured Seoul to cancel its program. It could quickly and easily change course again. A nuclear arsenal in North Korea "could result in the dissemination of nuclear weapons throughout the region," says Christophe Carle, research fellow at the Institut Français des Relations Internationales in Paris. "I can't imagine Japan and South Korea and Taiwan refraining from doing so short of extraordinary U.S. assurances." An East Asia in which six powers have nuclear arms would be perilously unstable.

China is not only a member of the nuclear club but also one of the world's leading proliferators of weapons of mass destruction. The Chinese have been selling ballistic missiles and nuclear equipment to all comers in the Third World. Its missile technology has gone to Pakistan, Saudi Arabia and Iran. CIA Director Woolsey has told Congress that China is getting new missile technology from Russia and Ukraine. This is ominous, he said, not only because the transfers improve China's military capabilities, but also because China could pass this more advanced technology to other states. So far, the U.S. has been unable to persuade China to curtail its sales.

The U.S. is struggling to find a lever to persuade Ukraine to give up the nuclear stockpile it inherited. A growing number of parliamentary deputies argue that Kiev should retain at least some of the 176 strategic missiles, 30 nuclear bombers and more than 1,600 warheads as a deterrent to any ultranationalist Russian government that might try to reimpose its rule on Ukraine. A more urgent fear is that Ukraine is close—12 to 18 months away—to cracking the Russian computer codes that prevent Kiev from retargeting or firing the nuclear missiles itself. If the Ukrainians succeed, they will gain operational control of the world's third largest stockpile of nuclear weapons. Moscow has not explicitly told the U.S. that it might attack Ukraine to prevent Kiev from obtaining control, but they have hinted at very high levels that this could happen. U.S. officials take these hints seriously.

Last week Defense Secretary Les Aspin proposed removing the nuclear warheads from the Ukraine missiles and placing them under international control; later they would be taken to Russia and

DECLARED NUCLEAR-WEAPON STATES	Ballistic missiles (longest known range in miles)	Chemical or biological
Britain*	2,900	
China*	9,300	☠
France*	3,100	☠
Russia*	8,100	☠
Belarus†	6,500	
Kazakhstan†	6,800	
Ukraine†	6,200	
U.S.*	9,200	☠
UNDECLARED NUCLEAR-WEAPON STATES		
India	1,550	☠
Israel*	930	☠
Pakistan	190	☠
WORKING ON OBTAINING NUCLEAR WEAPONS		
Algeria	40	
Iran	300	☠
Iraq	190	☠
Libya	190	☠
North Korea	300	
Syria	300	☠
CEASED DEVELOPING NUCLEAR WEAPONS		
Argentina	60	☠
Brazil	190	
South Africa	930	☠
South Korea	160	☠
Taiwan	60	☠

KEY: 100 miles or more / Less than 100 miles Yes ☠ Probably ☠

*Capable of delivering nuclear weapons †Committed to becoming nonnuclear states but currently possessing nuclear weapons under Russian control stationed in their territory. TIME Graphic by Steve Hart

dismantled, and Washington would purchase the fissile material inside. The U.S. Department of Energy has agreed to buy between $8 billion and $13 billion worth of the highly enriched uranium, which could net Ukraine a share reaching $2 billion. That might prove a powerful incentive for the cash-strapped country.

The West has even less leverage to prevent the further breakdown of administration all across the former Soviet Union that could lead to smuggling and illegal sales of some of the 27,000 nuclear warheads now under guard by various military units. "I do not believe the reports that one or more may have been sold already," says Harald Müller of the Hesse Institute for the Study of Peace and Conflict in Frankfurt. "But as discipline deteriorates we have to be afraid that the custodians will become ineffective."

Western officials have been worrying about nuclear proliferation for decades, but it took the Gulf War to focus everyone's attention. It startled the West to learn just how close Saddam Hussein had come to secretly acquiring an atomic arsenal. That made everyone realize the slow and massive military buildup to Operation Desert Storm would probably have been impossible if Iraq had had nuclear weapons, even mounted on inaccurate Scuds. And the high-tech efficiency of the victorious American forces telegraphed to all Third World countries that they should forget about tangling with the U.S. unless they had acquired nuclear weapons.

The problem, though, extends beyond nuclear to chemical and biological bombs and the means to deliver them to far-off targets. Ballistic missiles, with flight times of only a few minutes and an ability to penetrate most defenses, are the most psychologically destabilizing. High-performance jet aircraft can easily deliver nuclear, chemical or biological warheads. "Most countries have not yet equipped their delivery systems to carry weapons of mass destruction," said Robert Gates, former Director of Central Intelligence. But he warned that over the next decade many of them will do so if international controls fail.

THE SAD TRUTH IS THAT "PROLIFERation cannot be stopped," says Götz Neuneck, a physicist at the Institute for Peace Research and Security Policy in Hamburg. "If a country wants to develop these weapons, it can do it." Even slowing the spread is difficult. The nuclear nonproliferation treaty bars development by or transfer of the weapons to non-nuclear states. It has done some good, but it has not prevented additional states from acquiring the bomb. Several, including India, Pakistan and Israel, simply refused to sign. Iraq, on the other hand, signed the treaty but cheated. Iran and North Korea signed and have gone ahead with development.

Treaties also ban chemical and biological weapons but at least 18 countries stockpile either or both. An agreement among major supplying countries, most of them Western, limits the sale of ballistic missile systems. There are no enforcement provisions and North Korea pays no attention to it, while China promised Washington to obey the rules but continues to break them.

A major obstacle to controlling the spread of these weapons is that even medium-size countries can build them using domestic industries and imported "dual-use" equipment—high-tech items that have civilian as well as military applications. Last year, says Kenneth Timmerman, a specialist in Middle Eastern security issues, Germany sold a total of $5 billion worth of goods to Iran. Japan sold Tehran nearly $3 billion worth and the U.S. shipped almost $1 billion. Much of the trade involved "dual use" items.

In September 1991 the CIA established a center to keep track of weapons of mass destruction and stop the flow of dangerous technology to the Third World. To watch about 24 countries and more than 75 weapons programs, the center collects information from spies on the ground, satellite photos and electronic intercepts, which is used to apply pressure on importing and exporting nations. In some instances Washington quietly asks a friendly capital to stop certain exports because they are being diverted to a weapons program. In other cases the U.S. and its allies sometimes use covert action to halt the shipments.

President George Bush signed an intelligence finding authorizing covert CIA ac-

tion to disrupt the supply of dangerous weapons or components. How that authority has been used is secret, but an official in Washington confirms that "it has been used. Things have been prevented from getting from one place to another." Even so, says another official, controls over exports "cannot prevent but can only make it more difficult to produce nuclear weapons."

The Clinton Administration says it is determined to strengthen international controls. But it has yet to settle on a plan of action, much less begin to persuade friends and foes to go along. In the end, to head off nuclear arms races in various regions of the world the U.S. might have to offer security guarantees to worried governments and threaten to intervene, if necessary, to keep the peace. But that would require an overhaul of its alliance system and a major expansion of its overseas commitments.

However firm its stance, the U.S. cannot entirely eliminate the ambitions and fears that prod nations to acquire weapons of mass destruction. Washington could not, even if it wanted to, guarantee Arab states against Israel, India against China, Pakistan against India or Iran against Iraq. Some of them have the bomb now, and the others will get it. In the years to come, the U.S. will have to choose very carefully where to engage its interests and its military forces. It may have its hands full just protecting itself.

—Reported by James Carney/ Moscow, Richard Hornik/Seoul, Jay Peterzell and Elaine Shannon/Washington with other bureaus

CONTEST OVER ASIA
Search for Security
In the Pacific

Clayton Jones

Staff writer of The Christian Science
Monitor

SINGAPORE

Despite the diplomatic smiles at an unprecedented summit of Asia-Pacific leaders
this month, an uneasy, cold peace hangs
over the most economically dynamic
area of the world.

From boardrooms to warrooms, the region is probing for a new stability after
the cold war's demise, communism's decline, and the closing out of Western
colonialism in Asia.

The once-menacing ships of the Soviet
Pacific Fleet now rust in port. The 1991
retreat of the United States from its huge
Subic Bay naval base in the Philippines
has left a security vacuum. China's rush
to riches has allowed it to flex new military muscle, and Japan's economic dominance has led it to search for a role as
guardian of regional peace.

No longer convinced they can rely on
Western partners, Asians are being
forced to identify potential threats. Old
suspicions of one another are reviving;
large and small nations are stockpiling
arms.

Why, its neighbors ask, did China test a
nuclear bomb last month and why is it
building a military airstrip on an island in
the South China Sea? Why is Japan
building a fast warship that could be
converted to an aircraft carrier?

Smaller powers, too, from Thailand to
North Korea, are adding formidable
weapons to their arsenals. In 1991, Asia
surpassed the Middle East as the top
buyer of conventional arms, according to
the Stockholm International Peace Research Institute. "There is a strategic
contest for leadership in the Asia-Pa-

cific," says Derek da Cunha, a Singaporean military analyst. "So far, [it's] a
friendly arms race."

By 1999, Asia will have shaken off the
last vestige of Western colonialism when
tiny Portuguese-owned Macao reverts
back to China, almost 500 years after
Portuguese ships landed at Malacca port
on the Malaysian peninsula in search of
spices, converts, and gold, becoming the
first Westerners to plant a flag on Asian
soil. Their arrival inaugurated centuries of
colonialism in Asia, with European powers
carving up much of the region for economic gain.

But even with the departure of the
outsiders, ideological differences persist.
Four of the world's five remaining Com-
munist-run nations are in Asia. "Asia is
caught in a time warp," says Winston
Lord, US assistant secretary of state for
East Asian and Pacific affairs.

A number of latent issues and disputes
could escalate into war in the absence of a
security framework, concludes the London-
based International Institute for Strategic
Studies. Power is being redistributed between China, Japan, and the US, as well
as between the medium-sized powers of
Indonesia, Korea, and India, says Bilahari Kausikan, head of the East Asia and
Pacific bureau in Singapore's Foreign
Ministry.

You have all these adjustments
going on. A lot of them can't be
predicted," he says. "The uncertainties are high even though military
conflict is at its lowest. We have no pre-
cedents, no landmarks. Everyone is
groping."

To cope with the new anxieties, many
Asian nations are using preventive diplomacy, forming institutions for cooperation
and "confidence-building" that, at the

very least, keep historic and potential
adversaries talking to each other.

One such group is called the Asia Pacific Economic Cooperation forum, or
APEC, created just two years ago in an
attempt to liberalize trade and investment. The group has shown only a little
cohesion leading up to its Nov. 17–21
meeting in Seattle. Its formation has
been sluggish because of political maneuvering among the region's leading
nations. China, for example, had to be
cajoled into accepting Taiwan and Hong
Kong as APEC members.

Nonetheless, the region has "a much
greater sense of community," than it once
did, Mr. Lord says. "The outlines of a
Pacific community are taking shape."
President Clinton's request that a summit
meeting be held was itself a bold move to
re-exert US leadership in Asia.

A summit handshake between Mr. Clinton and Chinese President Jiang Zemin,
coming four years after the Tiananmen
massacre, could be regarded as either
the start of a new US–China partnership
or the onset of a post–cold-war contest
for influence.

"The US sees the importance of its
role in Asia, especially while China's intentions are still not clear and because
millions of US jobs depend on maintaining stability [in Asia]," says a US diplomat
in Singapore. "We are still worried about
the disparity between what China says
and what it is doing."

China's plans to build a far-reaching,
"blue water" navy, its recent nuclear test,
its forceful seizure of islands from Vietnam in 1988, and its reluctance to rule
out a violent takeover of Taiwan have kept
its neighbors on guard.

Few analysts say China is a threat now,
as it races toward market wealth and
appears to prefer regional stability. "After
the cold war, the main issue in Asia is the

absence of an overriding threat," says Zakaria Haji Ahmad, a security expert at the University of Malaya in Kuala Lumpur.

China's neighbors worry that it may want to reassert its historic role as the center of Asia, winning back what it thinks it has lost in wealth, territory, or influence.

Should China be estranged or engaged? The US is shifting toward engagement, while some nations, such as Malaysia, are not sure. "If you accept China as a military power, then you don't confront it," Dr. Ahmad says.

After the Tiananmen massacre, China looked for friends in Asia to side with it against the West. It found some backing in the Association of Southeast Asian Nations (ASEAN), a noncommunist group that includes Singapore, Malaysia, Thailand, Indonesia, Brunei, and the Philippines.

"We don't feel there is a threat from China—for many years," says Tommy Koh, a former Singaporean ambassador to the US. "But memories of China [under Mao Zedong] using the Chinese in Southeast Asia are still alive."

'There is a strategic contest for leadership in the Asia-Pacific. . . . So far, [it's] a friendly arms race.'

—Singaporean military analyst

Since 1977, ASEAN has debated how to rid Southeast Asia of any big-power influence by creating a "zone of peace, freedom, and neutrality." But it now realizes that the idea was a pipe dream. Sitting at the crossroads of two oceans, the region's geography is its destiny.

"We tried to deny that there would be a power vacuum if the US withdrew," says Kusuma Snitwongse, director of the Institute for Security and International Studies in Bangkok. "While it's old thinking to suggest that we should hang on to a US [military presence], in this uncertain period there's an ambivalence. If the US leaves, will Japan and China be more aggressive in the region?"

At present, Japan is seen as a very theoretical threat. Its military is constrained by a war-renouncing constitution and a dependence on US forces under a security treaty. The Japanese Army has

only 180,000 soldiers, and that number is shrinking. Japan's new prime minister, Morihiro Hosokawa, wants his country to lead the world in disarmament.

But what worries its neighbors is that Japan could turn its technological prowess into deadly weapons overnight or leave the American security umbrella. Some Japanese officials warn privately that Japan might build a nuclear bomb if North Korea does.

And a widespread feeling exists in the region that Japan has failed to learn from its occupation of Asia before and during World War II. "For Japan not to tell its children what happened in the war—it causes a lot of worry," Mr. Koh says.

Hoping to change that image, Japan made its first postwar overseas deployment of troops in 1992 by sending 600 soldiers to Cambodia to aid United Nations peacekeeping. But, Mr. Kusuma says, the deployment "didn't change perceptions of Japan. In fact, it reinforces the fear of Japan, because Southeast Asia insisted that Japan remain only under UN command."

Likewise, the threat of Russia's Pacific Fleet, while diminished, has not evaporated in the eyes of many Asians, especially since Moscow seeks to maintain some of its access to the warm-water port in Vietnam's Cam Ranh Bay.

Unlike Europe, where communism has gone to ashes, Asia still has remnants of the cold war, such as the standoff between North and South Korea, that make forming a security framework difficult.

In 1992, ASEAN decided to build on its 25-year success as a friendly regional group and invited Japan, China, Russia, as well as South Korea, Vietnam, Laos, Papua New Guinea, and Western nations to start a new group devoted to tackling security issues.

"The problem is not how to exclude anybody, but how to keep this happy state of affairs," Mr. Kausikan says. "It's a matter of a balance of big powers, not the vacuum of power."

The new group, known enigmatically as the ASEAN Regional Forum (ARF), met for a Sunday dinner last July in Singapore. Substantive talks are slated for next summer in Bangkok.

ARF has had a rough start. Japan did not want Russia and China to join. The US did not want Vietnam. "We have to go slowly," Kusuma says. "It's a meeting of the not-like-minded."

But, Koh says, "the takeoff of ARF has really surprised us. At a minimum, you

keep all the countries talking. The ASEAN way of doing things is very gradualist."

ARF's progress may be measured in inches. The first hurdle is how to convince each state to be more open about its military situation, especially arms purchases.

"We need to develop patterns of behavior that would lead people to resolve problems peacefully," the US diplomat says.

Even ASEAN, despite its members' successful track record of working together since 1967 on various issues, has failed to form its own security forum—until now.

For the first time, defense officials from all six ASEAN states will meet in coming months as a prelude to the ARF meeting. One of the first steps may be for each nation to issue a "white paper" describing military strategy and weapons.

"ASEAN is not and will not become a military pact," says Singaporean Prime Minister Goh Chok Tong. "But consultations among defense and military officials will help build an environment of confidence."

The move is risky. ASEAN does not want to appear to be an anti-China bloc. Vietnam, a historic enemy of China, wants to join the group, but ASEAN is wary.

"Once you form an ASEAN security forum, you have to ask, 'Who is the enemy?' " says Lee Tai To of the National University of Singapore. "ASEAN has already been a sort of secret security group—containing conflict with each other."

Indonesia's recent purchase of three former East German submarines has helped fuel concerns of an ASEAN arms race. So has Malaysia's plan to buy 18 Russian-built MIG-29 jet fighters and 8 US-made F-18 Hornets. Thailand plans to buy a Spanish-made helicopter carrier.

This nascent arms race in Asia must be kept in context, says Dr. da Cunha, a fellow at Singapore's Institute for Southeast Asian Studies. "Each nation buys weapons for a number of reasons, usually just for a matter of national pride. One of the lesser motives these days is to keep pace with potential adversaries."

Until now ASEAN nations have had only a spiderweb of bilateral military ties with each other, usually to conduct joint exercises. Singapore keeps a battalion in Brunei, primarily to

5. CONFLICT

help guard it against Malaysia. "They all still don't trust each other," Da Cunha says.

The US remains the glue among AS-EAN militaries. Since the Philippines closed the US bases on its soil in 1991, the US has had ready access to commercial ship-repair yards in Indonesia, Malaysia, and Singapore. Malaysia, despite its anti-US rhetoric, holds the most bilateral military exercises with the US.

"The withdrawal from the Philippines has allowed closer ties for the US with several Southeast Asian militaries," the US diplomat says. Singapore is now home to more than 100 US military personnel. Logistics and training exercises for the US Navy's 7th Fleet are managed here, and jets of the US Air Force 497th fighter squadron practice in Singapore at least six times a year.

The US presence, although small, serves as a "trip-wire," Da Cunha says. "No country wants to cross swords with America on day one of a conflict. The security of the US and Singapore are now one."

One US Navy commander in Singapore admits the US is here mainly for political reasons. "We could provide these services anyplace. But it allows Singapore to be a player in Southeast Asia, and it keeps the US more involved in the region."

"This is the most benign presence," the officer adds. "We have no combat capability. But we're right on the highway between two oceans."

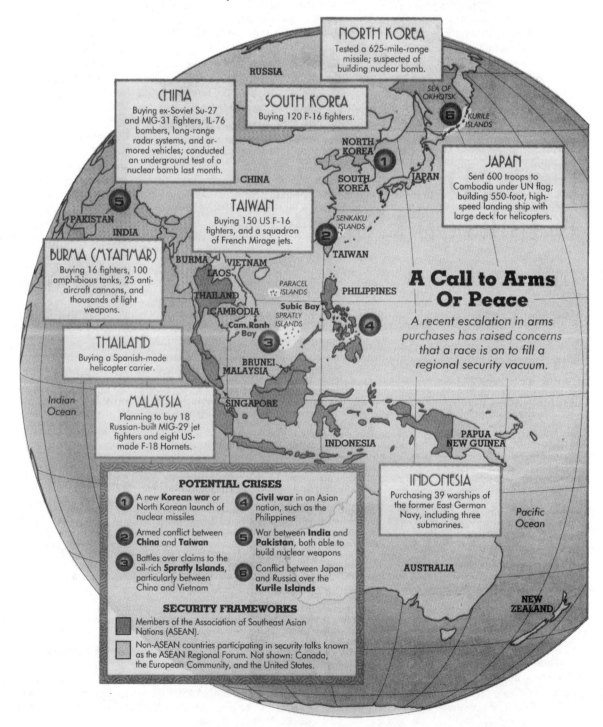

NORTH KOREA
Tested a 625-mile-range missile; suspected of building nuclear bomb.

CHINA
Buying ex-Soviet Su-27 and MIG-31 fighters, IL-76 bombers, long-range radar systems, and armored vehicles; conducted an underground test of a nuclear bomb last month.

SOUTH KOREA
Buying 120 F-16 fighters.

JAPAN
Sent 600 troops to Cambodia under UN flag; building 550-foot, high-speed landing ship with large deck for helicopters.

TAIWAN
Buying 150 US F-16 fighters, and a squadron of French Mirage jets.

BURMA (MYANMAR)
Buying 16 fighters, 100 amphibious tanks, 25 anti-aircraft cannons, and thousands of light weapons.

THAILAND
Buying a Spanish-made helicopter carrier.

MALAYSIA
Planning to buy 18 Russian-built MIG-29 jet fighters and eight US-made F-18 Hornets.

INDONESIA
Purchasing 39 warships of the former East German Navy, including three submarines.

A Call to Arms Or Peace

A recent escalation in arms purchases has raised concerns that a race is on to fill a regional security vacuum.

POTENTIAL CRISES

1. A new **Korean war** or North Korean launch of nuclear missiles
2. Armed conflict between **China** and **Taiwan**
3. Battles over claims to the oil-rich **Spratly Islands**, particularly between China and Vietnam
4. **Civil war** in an Asian nation, such as the Philippines
5. War between **India** and **Pakistan**, both able to build nuclear weapons
6. Conflict between Japan and Russia over the **Kurile Islands**

SECURITY FRAMEWORKS

Members of the Association of Southeast Asian Nations (ASEAN).

Non-ASEAN countries participating in security talks known as the ASEAN Regional Forum. Not shown: Canada, the European Community, and the United States.

DISMANTLING THE ARSENALS
Arms Control and the New World Agenda

Jack Mendelsohn

Jack Mendelsohn, a former State Department official, was a member of the U.S. SALT II and START delegations and served at the U.S. Mission to NATO. He is currently Deputy Director of the Arms Control Association in Washington, D.C.

The collapse of communism and the promise of a more cooperative East-West relationship have transformed the world of arms control. Goals that were once unthinkable—making enormous cuts in strategic forces or actually destroying nuclear warheads—are now at the top of the agenda. Developments that were always dangerous but of only secondary concern because of the primary East-West confrontation—the widespread deployment of short-range nuclear weapons or the spread of conventional weapons to the developing world—have now become urgent issues. And verification measures, originally born of deep distrust between East and West and intended to inform adversaries about each other's military programs, are now available to help monitor agreements, build trust, and reduce tensions.

Nuclear Weapons

Understandably, the most immediate concern of both the United States and Europe is the future of nuclear weapons in a disintegrating Soviet empire. For now, at least, the goals of the United States and Russia seem to be congruent: to ensure the centralized command and control of the nuclear forces of the newly formed Commonwealth of Independent States (CIS), to encourage the safe and secure withdrawal of tactical (and, eventually, strategic) nuclear weapons from the outlying republics to Russia, and to prevent the spread of nuclear hardware and brainpower to third countries. Programs to address these problems are already under way or under consideration, although concern about their continued successful implementation will certainly persist.

In the longer term a different set of nuclear arms control issues will challenge policymakers. The end of the Cold War offers a unique opportunity to push the size of U.S. and Russian strategic nuclear forces down to considerably lower levels. As Soviet President Gorbachev suggested last October, and as President Bush proposed in his State of the Union speech in January, the United States and Russia could readily cut in half the number of strategic weapons permitted under the Strategic Arms Reduction Treaty (START).

How low strategic forces can ultimately be taken will depend on the actual role assigned to nuclear weapons. Most analysts agree that the United States can maintain its present "warfighting" strategy with as few as 3,000–4,000 nuclear weapons (see table 1). If, on the other hand, the United States were prepared to abandon its current warfighting strategy, which targets thousands of military, political, and economic sites, in favor of a purely deterrent one involving a very limited set of military-industrial targets, it would facilitate even steeper reductions in strategic warheads. This is apparently the strategy that underlies Russian President Boris Yeltsin's recent offer to reduce strategic arsenals to 2,000–2,500 warheads.

An essentially deterrent strategy would be based on the premise that relatively few warheads are required to dissuade an adversary from launching a deliberate nuclear attack. According to former Secretary of Defense Robert McNamara, during the 1962 Cuban missile crisis, when the United States had approximately 5,000 strategic warheads to the Soviet Union's 300, "President Kennedy and I were deterred from even considering a nuclear attack on the USSR by the knowledge that, although such a strike would destroy the Soviet Union, *tens* of their weapons would survive to be launched against the United States" (emphasis added). Nothing in the past 30 years has invalidated that conclusion or diminished the deterrent value of even a few nuclear weapons.

From *The Brookings Review*, Spring 1992, pp. 34-39. © 1992 by The Brookings Institute. Reprinted by permission.

5. CONFLICT

Preventing Inadvertent Conflict

With the end of the adversarial relationship between the United States and Russia and the prospect of large-scale reductions in existing nuclear arsenals, longstanding fears of deliberate attack have yielded to a new concern about inadvertent conflict. To respond to this concern, the two nations will need to make it as difficult as possible to launch their nuclear weapons. They will have to ensure that all nuclear weapons are subject to both physical safeguards and chain-of-command arrangements that cannot be defeated or circumvented. To this end, all deployed and nondeployed nuclear weapons should have the latest technology electronic locks to prevent unauthorized use. Both arming and release codes for all nuclear weapons should be held by the national command authority (on-board commanders have access to the codes for U.S. ballistic missile submarines).

Another way to reduce the risk of inadvertent war is to increase the overall confidence of both sides in the survivability of their nuclear forces. This can be done by some relatively simple measures. For example, the president has proposed that land-based ballistic missile systems be limited by agreement to one warhead. That is one way to eliminate the concern that a small number of land-based multiple-warhead missiles on one side could be used early in a crisis and, in theory at least, destroy large numbers of similar systems on the other side. Alternatively, land-based systems could be made mobile or dispersed among multiple protective shelters. Finally, overall warhead reductions, on the scale discussed above, would by themselves decrease the number of multiple warhead systems and increase survivability by making it difficult, if not impossible, to undertake a disarming strike against the nuclear forces of the other side.

As one confidence-building measure, warheads could be removed from a portion of the land-based missile force and the systems taken off high state of alert. Ballistic missile submarines could patrol out of range of their targets, and aggressive anti-submarine warfare training activities could be strictly limited. Strategic bombers should remain off alert and their weapons stored away from operational bases. The sides could also limit the size and frequency of large-scale exercises and enhance confidence by exchanging data and giving advance notice of strategic force tests or practice alerts.

Finally, the United States, Russia, and the relevant CIS countries should agree to destroy the existing stockpile of retired and surplus nuclear weapons, perhaps 15,000 to 18,000 warheads on each side. As the two sides reduce their tactical and strategic arsenals, the number of warheads in storage will increase dramatically—as will concern over their possible theft, sale, misappropriation, or rapid redeployment. The destruction of redundant warheads should be coupled with a ban on the further production of fissile material for weapons purposes, a monitored limit on the production of new warheads to replace existing systems, and the storage, under international safeguards, of fissile material withdrawn from retired weapons.

Table 1. Selected Proposals for Strategic Arms Reductions below Warhead Levels in START

NUMBER OF WARHEADS	PROPOSAL
600	Andrei Kokoshin, *Bulletin of the Atomic Scientists*, September 1988
1,000	Carl Kaysen, Robert S. McNamara, and George W. Rathjens, *Foreign Affairs*, Fall 1991
1,000–2,000	Committee on International Security and Arms Control, National Academy of Science, 1991 (second-stage cuts)
1,000–2,000	Jonathan Dean and Kurt Gottfried, Union of Concerned Scientists, 1991
Below 2,000	Harold A. Feiveson and Frank N. von Hippel, *International Security*, Summer 1990
2,000–2,500	Boris Yeltsin, United Nations, 1992
Below 3,000	Harold Brown, *Arms Control Today*, May 1990
3,000	John D. Steinbruner, Michael M. May, and George F. Bing, *International Security*, Summer 1988*
3,000–4,000	Committee on International Security and Arms Control, National Academy of Science, 1991 (first-stage cuts)
4,700	George Bush, State of the Union Speech, 1992
4,000–6,000	Reed Report, Strategic Air Command, 1991
6,000	START Treaty, 1991**

*Most proposals consider 3,000 warheads to be the level beneath which current targeting strategy must be revised and 2,000 to be the level beneath which third-country forces (United Kingdom, France, China) must become involved in negotiations.

**START permits 6,000 "accountable" strategic warheads on each side. Because of lenient counting rules on air-launched weapons, each side may in reality deploy several thousand additional warheads.

Strategic Defenses

Closely related to the question of nuclear force reductions and to the shift from preparing for deliberate war to preventing inadvertent war is the issue of preserving the Anti-Ballistic Missile (ABM) Treaty's strict limits on strategic defensive systems. Despite the boost given anti-missile systems by the Scud-Patriot encounters during the Gulf war, the United States will have to tread carefully in its approach to tactical and strategic ballistic missile defenses. Strategic defenses, by their nature, undercut confidence in the retaliatory capability of strategic offensive forces and could therefore lessen the willingness of one side or another to make big cuts in strategic offensive forces. In some cases, such as those involving the relatively small national deterrent forces of France and Britain, deploying even a low level of strategic defenses may actually stimulate an increase in arsenals in order to overcome these anti-missile systems.

Thus the Bush administration's interest in rewriting the ABM Treaty to permit large-scale deployment of its newest version of Star Wars, known as Global

Protection against Limited Strikes (GPALS), runs contrary to a fundamental U.S. interest: to reduce nuclear arsenals in the CIS to as low a level as possible. Moreover, the goal cited by the administration in support of GPALS—to protect the United States against threats from third world "nondeterrables"—is questionable. CIA Director Robert Gates has predicted that it will be at least a decade before any country other than China or the CIS could strike the United States with long-range ballistic missiles. And most observers believe that long-range ballistic missiles would not be the delivery system of choice for any third world nation attempting to threaten the United States.

Although Yeltsin proposed a joint SDI program, it is unlikely, given the economic situation in the CIS, that in the long run Russia will really pursue such a costly defensive project. The same should be true for the United States. If the United States nonetheless persists in its efforts to deploy defenses, and if the Russians acquiesce to a similar program, then it will be critically important that any eventual strategic defensive deployments be limited to very few fixed land-based interceptors only. Anti–tactical ballistic missile systems, which are likely to be of interest to both sides and which are not prohibited by the ABM Treaty, should be designed so that neither their capability nor their widespread deployment will erode confidence in either side's strategic offensive retaliatory capabilities.

Conventional Weapons

In the short term, U.S., European, and CIS arms control goals regarding conventional weapons are likely to be similar: to encourage the prompt adherence to, and implementation of, past and pending arms control obligations, especially the recently concluded Conventional Armed Forces in Europe (CFE) agreement, and to complete the Open Skies and CFE follow-on talks (the former to create an aerial inspection regime and the latter to establish politically binding limits on troop levels). A third goal, to ensure the orderly transfer of conventional military forces from Union control to the newly formed states, is certainly shared by the West and Russia. But tensions among the states of the new CIS may make it difficult, or even impossible, to distribute conventional forces quickly or smoothly (see table 2).

In the longer term, now that the fear of a massive land war in Europe has become, in the words of the CIA director, "virtually nonexistent," the conventional weapons arms control agenda is likely to be occupied with four principal issues. The first is greater openness, or transparency, in military programs and activities. After several decades of relying primarily on satellites and sensors to monitor military activities, and as the infatuation with on-site inspection fades, we are just now beginning to recognize and exploit the potential of relatively straightforward cooperative measures to provide intelligence. Through extensive and intensive multilateral exchange, nations can increase

Table 2. CFE-Limited Conventional Weapons in the States of the Former Soviet Union (February 1991)

REPUBLIC	TANKS	ARMORED COMBAT VEHICLES	ARTILLERY	HELI-COPTERS	AIRCRAFT
Armenia	258	641	357	7	0
Azerbaijan	391	1,285	463	24	124
Belarus	2,263	2,776	1,384	82	650
Estonia	184	201	29	10	153
Georgia	850	1,054	363	48	245
Latvia	138	100	81	23	183
Lithuania	184	1,591	253	0	46
Moldova	155	402	248	0	0
Russia	5,017	6,279	3,480	570	2,750
Ukraine	6,204	6,394	3,052	285	1,431
TOTAL	15,644	20,723	9,710	1,049	5,582
Soviet forces in Germany*	5,081	9,167	4,228	432	1,029
TOTAL**	20,725	29,890	13,938	1,481	6,611
TOTAL PERMITTED UNDER CFE	13,150	20,000	13,175	1,500	5,150

Source: Arms Control Association.

* All Soviet forces in Germany are scheduled to be withdrawn by 1994.

** Under CFE, the states of the former Soviet Union west of the Urals (with the exception of Estonia, Latvia, and Lithuania) must agree to allocate among themselves the total equipment permitted the former Soviet Union. Surplus equipment must be destroyed.

the information available on budgets, force size, production levels, research, development and modernization programs, deployment plans, arms transfers, and operational practices. As such openness improves our ability to predict the evolution of the overall security environment, it will enhance stability and reduce the risk of overreaction.

A second objective regarding conventional arms is to defuse the dangers of localized or ethnic strife in Europe. While the threat of a general war in Europe is minimal, numerous potential regional flash points, such as Croatia-Serbia or Armenia-Azerbaijan, still exist. Even if the CFE treaty enters into force, a concentrated effort will still have to be made to deal with these problem areas by subregional arms control. Subregional constraints might involve lowering force levels in geographically restricted areas (force allotments in Hungary and Romania, for example, could be 25 percent beneath CFE levels); establishing disengagement zones (Hungary and Romania could both agree

5. CONFLICT

not to deploy military forces within 50 kilometers of their common border); or instituting special monitoring measures such as intensive aerial overflights or third-party inspections.

A third issue, how to integrate large numbers of demobilized soldiers into civilian life and forestall a "black market" in conventional military hardware, will be one of the most challenging, albeit nontraditional, new arms control tasks. But it may also be the one most amenable to direct economic intervention. The United States has already offered the CIS $400 million to help dismantle its nuclear and chemical warheads. The United States and its European allies may wish to consider establishing a similar Conference on Security and Cooperation in Europe (CSCE) fund to help destroy, securely store, or ultimately buy up surplus war material from Eastern Europe and the CIS states to keep it from leaking into the black market (as apparently happened during the Croatian-Serbian conflict).

We may also wish to use an international fund to help train, house, employ, or provide severance pay to demobilized CIS soldiers to keep them from becoming a disruptive social or political force. Germany did as much to speed the evacuation of Soviet soldiers from its territory, and the current Russian military budget has designated all its capital investment for housing. We may also wish to institute programs to train soldiers who remain in uniform to work on disaster relief, environmental clean-up, and other civil support missions.

Finally, with or without U.S. participation, the European states will need to work toward creating European-based peacekeeping, peacemaking (that is, interventionary), and conflict-resolution institutions to deal with continent-wide security issues. The U.S. government does not now favor such institutions because it fears that they would undercut U.S. influence in European security issues. But, at some point, the tensions created by Yugoslavian-type crises, where the United States adopted a hands-off policy and Europe had very limited tools to manage the conflict, will force the empowerment of one or another of the Euro-based organizations (the Conference on Security and Cooperation in Europe, the Western European Union, or the North Atlantic Cooperation Council), the United Nations, or another specially created body to deal directly and forcefully with subregional challenges to European security. Once some international institution is designated as the executive forum, it will have to earmark multinational forces for the peacekeeping task, and the member states will have to devise a decisionmaking process that keeps the parties to the problem from blocking action.

Stemming the Spread of Weapons

As the enormous changes in Europe have eased concerns about East-West conflict, the United States and other developed nations have turned their attention to the challenges to international security posed by the spread of weapons in the developing world. Ironically,

Table 3. U.S. Arms Transfers to the Middle East since the Iraqi Invasion of Kuwait

MILLIONS OF DOLLARS

COUNTRY	VALUE	EQUIPMENT
Bahrain	$ 37	Tanks
Egypt	2,170	Aircraft, munitions
Israel	467	Patriot, aircraft, helicopters
Kuwait	350	Air base upgrades
Morocco	250	Aircraft
Oman	150	Armored personnel carriers
Saudi Arabia	14,800	Aircraft, tanks, helicopters
United Arab Emirates	737	Helicopters
TOTAL	**$ 18,961**	

Source: Arms Control Association. The table lists transfers of major conventional weapons notified to Congress between August 2, 1990, and January 1, 1992.

the problem is largely the result of the developed world's own policies during the Cold War, when arming the enemy of one's enemy was considered to be the height of sophisticated geopolitics. Meeting the proliferation challenge will require of the developed world a full and rare measure of political will and self-restraint.

To be sure, regimes to control several types of proliferation already exist or are under negotiation. The nuclear Non-Proliferation Treaty, with some 140 members, has been a highly successful example of international cooperation and common perspective for a quarter of a century. Negotiations on a Chemical Weapons Convention are far advanced and likely to be concluded in the not-too-distant future. And major supplier groups (to control nuclear technology, chemical and biological weapons, missile technology, and conventional arms transfers to the Middle East) have already been established and are expanding their scope.

Building on the existing nonproliferation structures, arms control can make several useful contributions. The first is to encourage stronger supplier restraint. Supplier states first must resist domestic political or economic pressures to sell arms, and then they will have to demonstrate a high level of political skill to balance the concerns of the developed world with objections from less advanced countries that nonproliferation regimes will spark. The nuclear supplier group clearly increased the time and cost of Iraq's nuclear weapons program. Nonetheless, the extent of Iraq's program surprised almost everyone, a fact that underscores the need to strengthen and expand nuclear export guidelines to include limits on "dual use" items—an effort already under way.

The United States and the other major arms exporters will also have to make more explicit efforts to limit sales of conventional weapons to areas of tension. For example, in conjunction with a supplier regime, "caps" might be placed on the value of arms exports approved by the supplier group to any one country in any one year (see table 3). That would require an international register of arms transfer and agreement among at least the "big five" exporters (the United States, the United Kingdom, France, the former Soviet Union, and China, which accounted for nearly 90 percent of the arms trade in 1990) to declare transfers and respect the cap. Pressure could also be applied to potential arms recipients by linking, directly or informally, U.S. aid, as well as aid from international lending institutions, to military spending levels.

As important as supplier restraint may be, regional arms control will undoubtedly remain the best long-term way to slow proliferation. Models already exist: the Treaty of Tlatelolco (establishing a nuclear-free zone in Latin America) and the Conventional Forces in Europe treaty are examples. Rallying the political will and muscle to apply these models to regions of the world where the underlying tension has not been directly eased by the new cooperative spirit in Europe will be a challenge. But easing these regional concerns is the key to taking the pressure off the "demand" side of proliferation. In fact, supplier restraint should only be a tool to buy time for regional efforts to work.

Regional arms control in areas such as the Middle East, South Asia, and Korea will have to involve major outside players. The United States, Russia, France, or Britain, depending on the region involved, will have to take an active interest and leading role in bringing about even a modest reconciliation. This reconciliation process would involve, first, political dialogue (as between the two Koreas and at the Middle East peace talks), then transparency (as in the Sinai and on the Golan Heights), supplier restraint, confidence-building measures, and, eventually, explicit arms control measures to limit forces and disengage (or separate) threatening forces.

Improved verification and monitoring would also strengthen nonproliferation efforts. Confidence in arms control regimes and regional security arrangements can, in general, be buttressed by increased transparency and predictability. In the proliferation arena, where one is dealing, almost by definition, with countries trying to acquire military capabilities by clandestine means, comprehensive intelligence, monitoring, and verification regimes are critical. First, as the Iraq experience has demonstrated, all agreements dealing with weapons of mass destruction must permit the right to challenge inspections of suspect sites. Second, nations with sophisticated intelligence capabilities, the United States in particular, will have to begin to share intelligence more widely. Making information more generally accessible will increase the stake of other participating states in the nonproliferation regime, enhance their confidence in its viability, and strengthen any eventual case against violators.

Finally, arms control by example is an important adjunct to specific nonproliferation treaties and cooperative measures. Although it cannot by itself stop states or leaders determined to violate an international agreement or tacit understanding, it can enhance the moral authority of the major powers. Evidence of serious intent to implement supplier restraint, to pursue deeper nuclear force reductions, to destroy conventional weapons and nuclear warheads, to stop fissionable materials production, and to cease nuclear testing would bolster the case for "demand" reduction in the proliferation arena. It would also strengthen the hand of the major powers in making the case for taking collective action—whether export controls, political and economic sanctions, or military measures—against any state that violates international agreements or standards.

Cooperation

An individual in just about any location on Earth can write a letter to another person just about anywhere else, and if it is properly addressed, the sender can be relatively certain that the letter will be delivered. This is true even though the sender pays for postage only in the country of origin and not in the country where it is delivered. A similar pattern of international cooperation is true when an individual boards an airplane in one country and never gives the issues of potential language and technical barriers another thought, even though the flight's destination is halfway around the world.

Many of the most basic activities of our lives are the result of international cooperation. The creation of international organizational structures to monitor public health on a global scale or scientifically evaluate changing weather conditions are additional examples where governments have recognized that their self-interest directly benefits from cooperation (i.e., the creation of international governmental organizations or IGOs).

These transnational activities, furthermore, are not limited to the governmental level. There are now literally tens of thousands of international nongovernmental organizations (INGOs). These organizations stage the Olympic Games or actively discourage the hunting of whales and seals, to illustrate just two of the diverse activities of INGOs. The number and influence of these international organizations, it is important to note, have grown tremendously in the past 40 years.

In the same time period in which we have witnessed the growth in importance of IGOs and INGOs, there has been a parallel expansion of corporate activity across international borders. Most consumers are as familiar with products with a Japanese brand name as they are with products made in the United States, Germany, or elsewhere. The multinational corporation (MNC) is an important nonstate actor in the world today. The value of goods and services produced by the biggest MNCs is far greater than the Gross National Product (GNP) of many countries. The international structures that make it possible to buy an Italian automobile in Sacramento or a Swiss watch in Singapore have been developed over many years. They are the result of governments negotiating treaties and creating IGOs to implement these agreements. The manufacturers engaged in these activities have created complex networks of sales, distribution, and service that grow more complex with each passing day.

These trends at a variety of levels indicate to many observers that the era of the nation-state as the dominant player in international politics is passing. Others have observed these trends and have concluded that the state system has a monopoly of power and the diverse variety of transnational organizations depend on the state system and in many ways perpetuate it.

In many of the articles that appear elsewhere in this book, the authors have concluded by calling for greater international cooperation to solve our world's most pressing problems. The articles in this section show examples of successful cooperation. In the midst of a lot of bad news in the world, it is easy to overlook the fact that we are surrounded by international cooperation and that basic aspects of our lives are often the result of it.

Looking Ahead: Challenge Questions

What products do you own that were manufactured in another country?

What contacts have you had with people from another country? How was it possible for you to have these contacts?

How can the conflict and rivalry between the United States and Russia be transformed into meaningful cooperation?

What are the prospects for international governance? Would a trend in this direction enhance or threaten American values and constitutional rights?

Unit 6

THEY SHALL BEAT THEIR SWORDS INTO PLOWSHARES, AND THEIR SPEARS INTO PRUNING HOOKS. NATION SHALL NOT LIFT UP SWORD AGAINST NATION. NEITHER SHALL THEY LEARN WAR ANY MORE

CAN THE U.N. STRETCH TO FIT ITS FUTURE?

Who gets the seats? Who keeps the peace?
What about human rights, and for that matter,
what about the planet?

TAD DALEY

Tad Daley is a fellow of the RAND Graduate School of Policy Studies in Santa Monica, California, and a fellow of the RAND/UCLA Center for Soviet Studies.

S hortly before the first-ever United Nations Security Council summit convened in New York on January 31, a reporter asked British Prime Minister John Major whether he would recommend changing the composition of the council. The best response Major could muster was: "Why break up a winning team?" Following the summit, a reporter asked Russian President Boris Yeltsin whether he would propose permanent Security Council membership for Germany and Japan. "I think you're confusing me with someone else," he said.

Questions about the composition of the Security Council are often side-stepped these days. There is no good answer to them. The idea that the five great powers of the world of 1945 should forever retain the leading role in the maintenance of international peace and security simply doesn't play well anymore with the rest of the planet.

In a declaration issued at the summit, the Security Council invited Boutros Ghali, the new secretary-general, to recommend by July 1 steps the United Nations might take to strengthen its capacity for "preventive diplomacy, peacemaking, and peacekeeping."

Ghali may well produce some bold initiatives—all of which, as the declaration stipulated, will fall "within the framework and provisions of the Charter." But pressures to open the U.N. Charter have been building for many years, and they are likely to increase. The weakness of the arguments for indefinitely retaining the San Francisco Charter will likely soon produce other initiatives that go far beyond those that Ghali is likely to suggest in July.

A peace army

Because the U.N. Secretariat must now improvise each new operation from scratch, support is growing for ideas such as a standing system of logistical and financial support for peacekeeping efforts, a military staff college for training peacekeeping officers, and even a standing rapid deployment force for peacekeeping actions. French President François Mitterrand proposed such a force in his summit speech, pledging French willingness to commit 1,000 troops within 48 hours in a crisis.

Mitterrand did not specify whether the troops for this U.N. force would remain with their respective national military establishments until mobilized by the United Nations, or instead form a standing U.N. army. He was also unclear whether the authority to dispatch such a force would lay with the Security Council or the secretary-general. Mitterrand did suggest, however, that the rapid deployment force could operate under the command of the U.N. Military Staff Committee, which consists of the chiefs of staff of the "Perm Five" states. The Military Staff Committee has never commanded a force in the U.N.'s 47-year history, and the

From *The Bulletin of the Atomic Scientists,* April 1992, pp. 38-42. © 1992 by The Educational Foundation for Nuclear Science, 6042 South Kimbark, Chicago, IL 60637. A one-year subscription to *The Bulletin* is $30. Reprinted by permission.

Charter provides no guidelines for how the Perm Five might reach consensus decisions. Boris Yeltsin of Russia generally endorsed Mitterrand's proposal in his own summit speech, although he added that the "expeditious activation" of such a force should occur "upon the decision of the Security Council."

An effective U.N. rapid deployment force would possess several key elements: The United Nations must be able to discern that an outbreak of violence is imminent, either through its own intelligence sources or "borrowed" intelligence information from member nations. There must be authority to dispatch such a force, as Austrian Chancellor Franz Vranitzky's summit statement suggested, *before* a conflict ignites, and without necessarily obtaining the consent of all the parties to the potential conflict. Most important, the secretary-general must have the blanket authority to dispatch the force on his own initiative, without Security Council authorization. Such authority is essential to avoid "telegraphing the punch," even if that might sometimes act as a deterrent. Other mechanisms exist for such public deterrent efforts. While a July 1990 Security Council debate might have deterred Saddam Hussein's invasion of Kuwait, it might also have moved him to invade earlier.

Deployment of a U.N. force could be followed by compulsory U.N. mediation or by a hearing before the World Court. If a U.N. rapid deployment force had existed in the summer of 1990, and if the World Court had been prepared to hear the kinds of disputes (slant drilling, maritime access, and the like) that Iraq had with Kuwait, and if the world community had previously displayed a consistent commitment to the enforcement of international law, Iraq might never have invaded at all.

The summit declaration also noted with approval that the General Assembly had recently created a global arms registry for tracking transfers of conventional weapons (see March 1992 *Bulletin*). The British and the Japanese have gone further by pushing for a registry that would track both transactions and national inventories in conventional, nuclear, biological, and chemical weapons. Such an all-embracing register could deter both recipient and supplier, as in the famous phrase underlying American securities-disclo-

sure laws: "Sunlight is the best of disinfectants." With the Perm Five countries accounting for nearly 90 percent of arms sales around the world, exposing the full range of arms trafficking ought to be a natural role for tomorrow's United Nations.

Beyond peacekeeping

The U.N. role is likely to continue to expand beyond international security concerns into areas such as temporary governmental administration (now under way in Cambodia), election monitoring, humanitarian assistance, and disaster relief. The British have been pressing for the establishment of a new high-level U.N. position—a permanent undersecretary-general for disaster relief. The aid provided to victims of the May 1991 Bangladesh cyclone by American marines, who happened to be on their way home from the Persian Gulf, only underscored the inadequacy of the present system.

The maintenance of a healthy and sustainable biosphere may be the most important policy imperative facing the human community. Global environmental changes have made absolute national sovereignty over territories of importance to all of humankind—such as the Amazon rainforests—increasingly anachronistic. The U.N. Conference on Environment and Development, which convenes in June in Brazil, may go a long way toward creating an unprecedented body of global environmental law, as well as the enforcement mechanisms that global environmental protection will probably require.

Other problems, including drug trafficking, terrorism, AIDS, and sundry financial flim-flams—such as those perpetrated by the Bank of Credit and Commerce International—increasingly transcend national boundaries, and demand U.N. attention. But some attention must also be focused on the nearly universal Third World fears that the U.N.'s renaissance will be dominated by a First World perspective. The concerns of developing countries—such as debt, low prices for raw materials, and economic development—cannot be brushed aside. At the summit, several leaders of developing nations spoke passionately of the vast waste of human capital engendered by perpetual poverty.

In the broadest sense, the coming

decades will demand larger roles for international institutions in the *management* of environmental degradation, population growth, energy exhaustion, and the global movements of capital, goods, services, information, and people. Will the scale of management of human affairs keep up with the continuously increasing degree of global interdependence? The international community must address that question today, not tomorrow.

Fading sovereignty

Article 2, Paragraph 7 of the U.N. Charter prohibits U.N. intervention "in matters essentially within the domestic jurisdiction of any state." Nevertheless, we may be seeing the creeping emergence of a doctrine of humanitarian intervention in the internal affairs of sovereign states. An important theme in the speeches of the fifteen leaders gathered for the summit was the need to protect human rights everywhere. While most of the leaders spoke favorably of human rights as a common global value, some suggested even more directly that this value could be superior to national sovereignty.

Russia's Yeltsin, for instance, said that human rights "are not an internal matter of states, but rather obligations under the U.N. Charter," and maintained that the Security Council had a "collective responsibility for the protection of human rights and freedoms." And Secretary-General Ghali, echoing his predecessor, Javier Perez de Cuellar, said that "the misuse of state sovereignty may jeopardize a peaceful global life. Civil wars are no longer civil, and the carnage they inflict will not let the world remain indifferent."

Although Germany was not represented at the summit, Foreign Minister Hans-Dietrich Genscher had gone even further last fall in a speech to the General Assembly: "Today sovereignty must meet its limits in the responsibility of states for mankind as a whole.... When human rights are trampled underfoot, the family of nations is not confined to the role of spectator.... It must intervene."

The most notable event to date on the sovereignty front has been the haven for Kurds carved out of northern Iraq. Although the sponsors of U.N. Resolution 688 in April 1991 argued that the situation with Kurdish refugees threatened international stability, in reality external military intervention was used inside Iraq to prevent the Iraqi government from committing acts of aggression against its own people on its own territory.

Saddam Hussein's behavior also revived the idea of establishing an international criminal court that could not only try violators of international conventions regarding such matters as terrorism and drug trafficking, but also heads of state who violate international law through acts of international or internal aggression. Security Council Resolution 731, issued in January, also stepped into this territory. The resolution demands that Libya surrender the two intelligence agents accused of the bombing of Pan Am Flight 103. Not only does the resolution call upon Libya to subordinate its own procedures regarding extradition, but it implies, perhaps for the first time, that the writ of the Security Council extends not just to states, but to individuals anywhere in the world.

But the use of economic sanctions as a mechanism to pressure states to mend their ways may soon come up for reexamination. Economic sanctions are generally thought to be a lesser form of coercion than direct military action. Yet, as British journalist Edward Pearce has pointed out, although the international community condemns biological warfare, the economic sanctions preventing the repair of damaged Iraqi power plants and sewage treatment facilities have resulted in epidemic levels of cholera in Iraq. "That is different from deliberately seeding and spreading the cholera virus," says Pearce, "in the same way that manslaughter is different from murder."

The economic embargoes against Iraq—and now Haiti—are aimed directly at the removal of their governing regimes. But it is unclear how these sanctions can accomplish their desired ends. If Iraqi opposition forces could not overthrow Saddam Hussein at his weakest moment in the spring of 1991, sanctions that harm rulers less than the ruled seem hardly likely to increase the opposition's prospects.

In Haiti, where the economic embargo is hitting the general population far harder than the rich and well connected, the policy, rather than giving Haitians the incentive and the where-

"Continuing" the Soviet seat

As a matter of international law, it was not clear that Russia could automatically inherit the Soviet Union's seat on the Security Council after the Soviet Union disintegrated. Article 23 of the U.N. Charter names "the U.S.S.R." as one of the five permanent members of the council. Given that, it might have been argued that a charter amendment would have been required for Russia to take over the seat. On December 16, shortly after the birth of the Commonwealth of Independent States, Russian President Boris Yeltsin said Russia intended to "continue" to hold the Security Council seat. Washington, London, and Paris quickly supported Yeltsin's position. The speed of the Soviet Union's demise had taken everyone by surprise, and to maintain that a charter amendment was required for Russia to take over the Soviet seat might have paralyzed the United Nations. As one American official said quietly in late December, "the less said the better."

— T.D.

withal to overthrow the military regime, has instead resulted in a massive refugee crisis off the coast of the United States. Something has gone awry in the international system when we impose harsh and effective economic sanctions on a country, and then repatriate the consequent refugees because their motives are economic rather than political.

If it has become legitimate for the international community to endeavor to remove a governing regime, direct international removal efforts may be undertaken in the not-too-distant future. It may soon become widely accepted that world standards and laws apply to every individual on the planet, and that the international community will intervene to enforce those standards and laws. Whether this process continues in an evolutionary or revolutionary fashion, we may be witnessing the beginnings of a sea change in human history.

Taxation without representation

As the U.N.'s role in world affairs continues to expand, so too will pressure increase to bring the composition of the Security Council in line with the contemporary realities of international power. The framers of the Charter envisioned a dynamic institution that would evolve over time. Article 109 provides for the convening of a "General Charter Review Conference" upon

the approval of the two-thirds of the member states, including any nine members of the Security Council. And Article 108 allows Charter amendment upon the approval of two-thirds of the member states, including all five permanent members of the Security Council.

Japan and Germany, the second and third largest financial contributors to U.N. activities, are the two states most commonly cited as deserving permanent membership on the Security Council. Indeed, Japan contributes more to the United Nations than Britain and France combined, and thus already has considerable clout. The new secretary-general's first high-level appointment was Japan's Yasushi Akashi, who was named special representative to oversee the multibillion dollar U.N. peacekeeping operation in Cambodia. Tokyo's U.N. ambassador, Yoshio Hatano, reportedly reminded Ghali beforehand that Japan had pledged to pick up fully half the tab for the massive operation.

But Japan is not satisfied with only this intangible influence in U.N. decision making. Although the possibility of a Security Council membership for Japan has been long discussed, Japanese Prime Minister Kiichi Miyazawa was particularly direct at the summit, saying that membership on the council must be "more reflective of the realities of the new era." In case anyone failed to get the message, his press secretary, Masamichi Hanabusa, later said Tokyo expected a Security

Council seat by 1995, the U.N.'s fiftieth anniversary. Otherwise, he added, Japan would increasingly resent "taxation without representation."

Germany's approach is more low-key. In the short term, Germany seems to hope that Britain and France will informally "Europeanize" their seats as the European Community draws closer together. (Bonn, however, was reportedly miffed that it had not been consulted by London or Paris in preparation for the summit.) In the long term, German Chancellor Helmut Kohl said shortly before the summit that he was "strictly opposed" to Germany itself putting the Security Council issue on the table, but that he could imagine the European Community acquiring a permanent seat at some point.

Merging British, French, and German interests into a single European Community seat would require amending both Article 23 (which names the permanent members of the Security Council) and Article 4 (which limits U.N. membership to "states"). Once that Pandora's box is opened, all sorts of issues emerge. What about developing nations of increasing weight—such as India, Brazil, Nigeria, Egypt, and Indonesia? Indian Prime Minister P.V. Narasimha Rao made a strong case at the summit for expanding the Security Council's representation if it hopes to maintain political and moral effectiveness. And shortly after the summit, Nigerian President Ibrahim Babangida said that "to retain the structure of the Security Council in its present form is to run the risk of perpetuating what is at best a feudal anachronism."

What exactly are the criteria for selection as permanent members of the Security Council? Political power? Economic power? Military power? (The Perm Five happen to be the five major nuclear-weapon states.) Regional representation? Perhaps most important, if the Security Council expands its permanent membership, how can it retain the ability to act decisively?

Decisiveness or democracy?

Italian Foreign Minister Gianni de Michelis called for major Charter revisions in a speech to the General Assembly in September 1991. He proposed expanding the number of both permanent and rotating members of the Security Council, but not necessarily extending the right of veto to the new permanent members. He also suggested "a system of weighted voting in both the General Assembly and the Security Council."

Over the years, many weighted voting schemes have been discussed. Some would give added weight to the population of a member state, or to its financial contribution. Some would award a degree of representation to stateless ethnic groups—Kurds and Sikhs, for example. Others envision a bicameral system much like the U.S. Congress, with citizens all over the world electing local representatives to a "U.N. House" and national representatives to a "U.N. Senate."

Many U.N. watchers argue that any conceivable recomposition of the Security Council would tremendously complicate the process of reaching consensus, and might paralyze the United Nations again, just when it is beginning to fulfill its post–Cold War potential. Although the veto has become a rarity in recent years, it is not difficult to imagine circumstances in which it could again be regularly employed. In November 1990, the "Soyuz" group of deputies in the Supreme Soviet stated plainly that they would have vetoed Resolution 678 on the use of force against Iraq. Conservative Soviet commentator B. Zanegin said after the war that "the U.N. Security Council can serve as an instrument for legalizing unilateral decisions by the U.S. and imposing them on the world community." The new world order, he added, basically amounts to a "U.S. dictatorship or hegemony" that is exercised through the Security Council.

But if a more conservative leadership should again come to power in Moscow, it is not clear that they would fail to cooperate in the Security Council. A conservative Russia would still be a nation in decline. Even a single Security Council veto might lead Western states to reconsider the large-scale aid programs now under way. And a return to a "Mr. Nyet" approach could simply cause the United States and the West to again pursue their interests outside the U.N. framework, leaving Russia with virtually no voice in global political affairs.

Nevertheless, objective perceptions of national interest are seldom the sole determinants of a state's foreign poli-cies. A central objective of a right-wing Russian leadership, however harmful to Russian interests, might be simply to reverse the national humiliation stemming from the recent Russian subservience to the United States in the international arena. Future Russian Security Council vetoes, exercised as a means of demonstrating national pride and independence, are far from inconceivable.

In addition, Chinese Prime Minister Li Peng struck a discordant note at the summit when he insisted that China would consistently oppose all external interventions in the internal affairs of sovereign states "using human rights as an excuse." The stridency of Li's speech suggests that we could see the emergence of the Chinese veto as well. Many Third World nations are deeply disturbed by the sovereignty issue. China may see an opportunity to stand at the head of the developing world as the great defender of sovereignty, opposing and vetoing all proposed U.N. interventions in "domestic affairs."

The various democratic decision-making structures around the world today are rarely paralyzed into complete inaction. Though often contentious in their procedures, they usually manage to produce some kind of public policy, however imperfect. Is there something fundamentally different about a global decision-making structure? If "decisive action" were the sole U.S. value, the president would be allowed to act, in all cases, without congressional authorization. "Democratization, at the national level," said Ghali in his summit statement, "dictates a corresponding process at the global level."

If not now, when?

The post–Cold War world will require global institutions with the power and authority to address the increasingly global issues of the new millennium. That is why, shortly after the Gulf War ended, the Stockholm Initiative on Global Security and Governance received the endorsement of international luminaries including Benazir Bhutto, Willy Brandt, Jimmy Carter, Vaclev Havel, Robert McNamara, Julius Nyerere, and Eduard Shevardnadze. The initiative proposes measures such as "the elaboration of a global law enforcement mechanism," "the levying of fees on the emission of pollutants affecting the global environment," "a review of both the composition of the Security Council and the use of the veto," and the convening of "a World Summit on Global Governance, similar to the meetings in San Francisco and Bretton Woods in the 1940s."

Any new world order centered around the San Francisco Charter stands hostage to the prevailing political winds in Moscow and Beijing. Any opening of the Charter must endeavor to at least limit the Security Council veto so that some types of collective U.N. action can be undertaken even in the face of disagreement among the great powers. The protracted conflict between the United States and the Soviet Union was, after all, why the United Nations was essentially irrelevant for its first four decades.

The international community can pretend that the potential for paralysis-by-veto no longer exists, and it can keep bringing more and more issues to the Security Council in the hope that all will go well. Or it can begin seriously laying the groundwork, perhaps to coincide with the U.N.'s fiftieth anniversary in 1995, for an Article 109 Charter Review Conference.

"I am not an advocate for frequent changes in laws and constitutions," said Thomas Jefferson, in words inscribed on the Jefferson Memorial. "[But] as circumstances change, institutions must also advance to keep pace with the times. We might as well require a man still to wear the coat which fitted him when a boy, as require civilized society to remain ever under the regimen of their barbarous ancestors."

The San Francisco coat of the 1940s no longer fits the world of the 1990s. There are few worse things we could do to the legacy of Roosevelt, Churchill, and the U.N.'s other founders than to cast in stone the global structures they created for the world of their day. Politics, as every undergraduate knows, is the art of the possible. A great deal more is possible today, as we emerge from the Cold War era, than was possible when we entered it a half century ago.

Can it really be peace?

Only if those who want it strive harder than those who don't

THE unlocking of the gateway to a Middle Eastern peace gave the ceremony on the White House lawn on September 13th exceptional importance. Old combatants, let alone those who still fight on, may choose not to walk through. But until now they did not have the choice; however well-intentioned, peace-seekers hit an impenetrable obstacle. Now that a start has been made on dividing a small patch of land between the peoples who separately claim it, the way is open. The aim must now be to prevent it, once again, from being closed.

Egypt was ahead of the game 15 years ago, when its decision to seek a separate peace with Israel changed history by eliminating the possibility of a fourth full-scale Arab-Israeli war: Egypt was the only Arab country with the strength, and the natural leadership, to pursue such a vendetta. But the bilateral peace did not discourage smaller wars, and it created no wider stability. On the contrary: the region was torn by political and ideological dissent; Israel felt empowered to invade Lebanon in 1982 and never to leave it altogether; Anwar Sadat was assassinated in 1981 and Egypt now hovers on the verge of turmoil; from 1987 the territories occupied by Israel in 1967 were shaken by the stones, and latterly the bullets, of the Palestinian *intifada*.

Scholars looking back at the Middle East's tortuous road to peace will, with luck and hard work, conclude that the 1993 Rabin-Arafat handshake set off far more lasting change than did the 1979 Israeli-Egyptian treaty. The luck could well turn sour; the hard work could falter. Yet with the Palestinians explicitly, and the Israelis tacitly, acknowledging each other's rights, there is a feeling abroad that the region may indeed be able, within a few years, to rid itself of the Arab-Israeli cancer at its centre. If Palestinians and Israelis find a way to live side by side—and eventually decide on sharing or dividing their capital city—the whole wretched business could be history.

It is a big "if". At best, the working out of an Israeli-Palestinian peace will be painful; at worst, a half-dozen, not improbable, things could cripple the process. If the arrangement crashes, the road would again be blocked.

Here is but a sample of the things that could go wrong. The Israelis, perhaps under a change of government, could narrow their horizons so that the symbolic deal becomes a be-all and end-all in itself. This would confirm the Palestinians' fear that they are being ensnared in a "Gaza and Jericho first . . . and last" trap. Palestinians, whose hunger for the best makes them the enemy of the good, may confirm Israeli fears that they are not to be trusted. Palestinians and their fellow-Arabs could be engulfed by the religious wave sweeping the Muslim world; practical efforts to move forward, step by sensible step, would then be overwhelmed by a new unleashing of old passions. Atrocities of one kind or another could destroy confidence; Yasser Arafat is one obvious target for assassination.

Plainly, it would be silly to be starry-eyed. The Middle East is at a turning point, but a long way from being safely turned. The excitement is that, for the first time in five decades, the turning is there to take. The question is whether Arabs and Israelis, with the outside world looking on, have the courage of their half-convictions.

Let the Palestinians build

Half a century ago, when Britain retreated from its Palestinian mandate, leaving the key under the mat for the most aggressive to snatch, the Israelis were not only better fighters than the Arabs but were also smart enough to recognise the advantages that accrue from saying "yes". Zionist policy was to agree to every offer, however inadequate—such as the United Nations 1947 partition plan, which allotted Israelis a non-viable slice of Palestine—and then to build on

From *The Economist,* September 18, 1993, pp. 23-25. © 1993 by The Economist, Ltd. Distributed by The New York Times Special Features. Reprinted by permission.

it, by force and by guile. The Arabs, who believed justice and numbers to be on their side, said "no" to compromise, went to war—and suffered.

Here lies a lesson for today's "rejectionist" Palestinians and their allies, not all of whom are either radical or fundamentalist. Many Palestinians, particularly among the hundreds of thousands who still live as refugees outside the old mandate, have their minds set on getting back the homes in Jaffa or Haifa that their families were driven from in the late 1940s; they refuse to accept the Jewish state and all that has happened since. More to the point are those who have long since come to recognise the reality of an Israeli state and the need for a truncated Palestinian one beside it, but are not prepared to accept the compromise now on offer; they stand out for a clear route to independence in all the territory seized by Israel in 1967, including East Jerusalem.

Instead, as they see it, they are expected to be satisfied with an unhappy little strip of territory (Gaza), so turbulent that it managed to defeat Israel's harshest efforts at control, plus a dusty outpost (Jericho) that nobody is much interested in. In addition, they will get a degree of autonomy so modest that they have been turning it down for years. And although they are being prom-

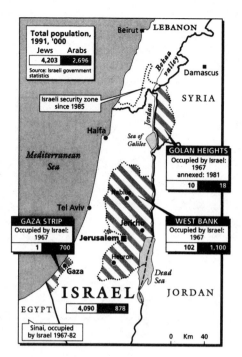

Where they are now
Worldwide distribution of Palestinians
% of total, 1991

Total 5.8m

Rest of world 7.8
Israel 12.6
Gaza 10.8
West Bank including East Jerusalem 18.6
Jordan 31.6
Lebanon 5.7
Syria 5.2
Other Arab countries 7.7

Source: Centre for Policy Analysis on Palestine

ised that, after a two-year period of proving themselves, they will be empowered to negotiate a permanent solution, the promise contains no commitment whatsoever on what this final settlement will be.

Is the deal as unattractive as that? Yes, in a way. Gaza is a horror that from December, when the Israeli soldiers start to withdraw, will be the responsibility of the PLO's own policemen, drawn from its militia. The autonomy offered in the West Bank is small compensation. Control over education, health and welfare, which will come into effect next month, has long been on offer and regularly rejected. Full control over the dot that is Jericho sounds an absurdity.

But, if the Palestinians keep their heads and the Israelis their courage, it will not be like this at all. The Palestinians can build on

an inauspicious beginning no less surely, and a lot faster, than the Israelis built on their toehold in the British mandate. When Mr Arafat, with his PLO ministers, army chiefs and officials, set themselves up in Jericho, their presence could be the basis for genuine self-government.

How, in practice, can Mr Arafat and his men be confined to one West Bank town, travelling by a set route to Gaza? Boundaries within the West Bank are imaginary; the roads are open to cars and buses. The PLO will roam from city to city, town to town, taking care of its constituents. It will neither look nor feel like municipal government. By July 1994, when the Palestinians will have elected their new council, the Israelis will have withdrawn from the towns, and the military government will no longer be operative. What then will be the difference between Hebron or Nablus and Jericho?

The PLO accepted the deal it once scorned because it was running out of options and money, and had the hot breath of Hamas (the Islamic Resistance Movement) on its neck. But Yitzhak Rabin's recognition gives it the chance to turn what was originally designed as no more than a cautious twist in a long process into an imaginative leap. The chance will depend on restraint and confidence. Mr Arafat's decision to call a conference of all Palestinian groups is a wise start. But peace will work only if the Israelis are reassured that the PLO's horns and cloven feet are vanished for good.

Let Israel be bold

The Israeli government, no less than the PLO, lacked a workable alternative: it had to reach an accommodation with the enemy. Under the former Likud government, Israel's policy towards the Palestinians was set on a road to nightmare: oppression fol-

lowed by revolt followed by oppression stretched aridly ahead. When the Labour government took over last year, its policies were as harsh as Likud's but, unlike the Likud, it saw these policies as finite. The *intifada* was gathering a psychological toll from Israelis who recoiled from their fate as child-killers. The PLO's terrorist face faded as Hamas's grew ever more threatening. The principle of land for peace, buried since it was first propounded by the United Nations in 1967, was discovered alive and well.

Yet the speed with which the secret diplomacy unfolded caught the Israelis, like others, off-balance—with the nay-sayers recovering the quickest, and the most vociferously. Now the positive-minded are taking over; a poll shows the proportion of Israelis supporting the deal rising from 52% last week to 62% this week. But, not unreasonably, Israelis are clamouring for a say as history flashes past them. Many are demanding a new election or a referendum; Mr Rabin has no intention of going to the country until he is forced to do so, but he might favour a referendum if he fails to get parliamentary backing for the deal.

The prime minister's decision to return from Washington by way of a call on King Hassan of Morocco was a deft domestic manoeuvre—quite apart from "the domino effect" that the Israelis are happily chattering about. "Secret" talks with the Moroccan government are a permanent Israeli fixture. But the 200,000 or so Israelis of Moroccan descent—who unlike Iraqi Jews retain bonds of affection for the old country—tend to vote for the Likud. If Labour can woo them in the name of the king, the opposition's support will be eroded; already there is a temporary crumbling.

Israel's counterparts to the rejectionist Hamas are the militant ultra-religious movements that sponsor settlement in the lands of the Bible. Israeli soldiers will protect Israeli settlers, in Gaza as in the West Bank, and there has been no whisper of an intent to winkle them out. Indeed, the families that are there from religious conviction will be immovable, to the last moment and even beyond. The others, who traipsed into

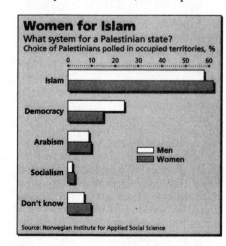

Women for Islam
What system for a Palestinian state?
Choice of Palestinians polled in occupied territories, %

Islam
Democracy
Arabism
Socialism
Don't know

☐ Men
■ Women

Source: Norwegian Institute for Applied Social Science

occupied territory in search of space, clean air and cheap housing, are expected to follow the pattern in Sinai where, after the peace agreement, Israeli settlers held out grimly but only for as golden a handshake as they could get.

Mr Rabin has to have his people with him. Having recognised the PLO and accepted the outline of the deal, he, like Mr Arafat, can now either make or break a precarious peace. But while the Palestinians need to do something stupid to bring the process to grief, the Israelis can probably accomplish the same result by default.

If Israel is mean with the economic cooperation (read economic help) that the deal calls for, the Palestinians will never get going. Over the past quarter-century the occupied territories have been pulled and pushed into near-total dependency on Israel; no public-works programme in Gaza can begin to soak up a labour force which for years has worked in Israel or not at all. There is now talk of Israel allowing 100,000 Gazans back into Israel to work: this is about as many as worked there until the *intifada* first stopped the traffic altogether, and then halved it.

Political generosity is no less important. Peace depends on the confidence that the two sides can mutually create; at present there is none. Ever since the Labour government took power last year, the Palestinians have looked in vain for a sign, in particular the token release of a few of the 13,000 Palestinians in prison. Now, at last, there are reports that some of the internees will be freed, in batches.

Jordanian growls

Israel needs peace with the Palestinians for its own sake and, even more, for the sake of a wider reconciliation with the Arab world. Most Arab governments would be relieved to settle; the lack of a stable peace has done them no good and, to some of them, much harm. But, for all, there are gains and losses in recognising the Jewish state.

The initial reaction of Israel's Arab neighbours to the Oslo breakthrough was consternation. They were miffed at being bypassed and none more so than Jordan, which shared a delegation with the Palestinians but, like almost everybody else, was kept in the dark. Last week Shimon Peres, Israel's foreign minister, was talking of a double-coup, with Jordan as well as with the Palestinians. But the Jordanians dampened his enthusiasm, agreeing only to a low-key affair on September 14th at which Jordan's ambassador to Washington and the chief Israeli negotiator initialled an agenda of the items on which Israel and Jordan now agree. The aim is a peace treaty but this, the Jordanians said, was some years off.

Yet peace with Jordan is easier for Israel than with either Syria or Lebanon. The only bit of Jordan that Israel is sitting on consists

of two small unoccupied strips that Israel has already said it is willing to give back. Harder to resolve are questions on water resources. And harder yet is the question of the possible return of Palestinian refugees living in Jordan, and enjoying Jordanian citizenship, most of whose families fled from the West Bank in 1967.

Jordan, which seized and ruled the West Bank and East Jerusalem between the 1948 and 1967 wars, grumbles that it has been getting the rough edge of the bargain ever since. Politically it is caught between two immense difficulties: more than half its population is Palestinian, which leaves it vulnerable to a takeover from an independent Palestinian state; its dominant political faction is the Muslim Brothers and their allies, which makes it cautious in moving towards an accommodation with Israel. The country's health depends on the health of its monarch, King Hussein, and that is precarious. Small wonder that Jordan steps back from risk-taking, over the Gulf war or over Israel.

But the country's rulers are now mildly outraged that Jordan could become the losing partner in what economists are beginning to see as an Israeli-Palestinian-Jordanian triangle. It suspects the Israelis of harbouring greedy plans to profit from the economic development help that may soon descend like manna on the West Bank and Gaza. Jordan, which has supported the Palestinians when it is not oppressing them—its latest gesture was to take in the 300,000 who were expelled from Kuwait after the Gulf war—is being elbowed aside. One source of Jordanian dismay is the suggested ceiling of $15m for annual exports to the West Bank; twice that amount is imported from the West Bank each year. Another is the exclusion of Jordan from the proposed new Palestinian police force.

Non-Jordanians tend to take Jordan's name in vain: the advantages and disadvantages of a Palestinian-Jordanian federation are discussed without much reference to its possibly disastrous effect on Jordan's own political balance. Crown Prince Hassan, King Hussein's outspoken brother, thinks it is time for Jordan to put itself first: as he told the London *Observer*: "The world is going to turn around and say 'bugger you' unless you get your act together."

Spoilers in waiting

The peace that Israel most craves is with Syria, which though it no longer has any desire to confront Israel head-on, does from time to time enjoy causing it intense grief. In theory this peace should not be hard: the basics have been in the open for months and both sides want it.

Israel would acknowledge Syria's sovereignty over the Golan Heights (somehow getting round the awkwardness caused by its foolish annexation in 1981) and start a

phased withdrawal from all of it, except perhaps for one or two small salients directly overlooking Galilee settlements. The place would be demilitarised and monitored by outsiders; the United States this week repeated its offer to take part in this operation. The Jewish settlers in the Golan are Labour supporters who would leave, however reluctantly, under orders. It may be harder to re-educate an Israeli public which has been taught for so long, by Mr Rabin in particular, that Israel's occupation of the plateau is essential for its own security.

Yet the Israelis, expecting fresh miracles after the Palestinian breakthrough, wondered for a time whether Mr Rabin would go for broke, recognising the PLO and promising withdrawal from Golan in a single swoop. The prime minister's caution prevailed as he decided that Israel could absorb only one momentous event at a time. As a result, Syria's Hafez Assad was cool towards the Palestinian deal, reserving his right to allow the radical Palestinian groups based in Damascus to oppose it. Mr Assad, as a spoiler of plans he does not care for, is to be greatly feared. The counter to this is that he may well be held in check by his desire to get on with the Americans—and by his determination to get back the Golan.

It may be trickier for Israel to negotiate successfully with Lebanon which in effect, since Beirut is still not in control of its own destiny, means negotiating at one remove with Syria. Israel occupies a strip of southern Lebanon—its self-styled security zone—which it will leave only when it decides that northern Israel is safe from attack by Islamic guerrillas led by Hizbullah. Control of the Hizbullah could, in theory, be part of a several-sided deal with Syria: the Golan Heights, the Bekaa valley and southern Lebanon make up a single troubled area waiting to be pacified.

The trouble is that though Syria has a degree of physical control over the Hizbullah, the guerrillas' ideological loyalty is to Iran. And Iran, unlike Syria, is a wrecker unrestrained. Fundamental Islamists—in Iran, Lebanon, Egypt, Jordan and the occupied territories themselves—cannot be placated with handshakes, better terms or economic aid. The anti-Israel battle-cry has been useful in their long-term war with secularism, providing them with a popular cause and recruits. They are not yet ready to give it up.

So, in a sense, battle-lines are joined. On one side is the Israeli government, a handful of Arab governments, the PLO and a majority of the Palestinians in the West Bank and Gaza: they all have, or should have, an overwhelming interest in making the peace work. Ranged against them are the cynical, the unhappy and the greedy backed by militant fundamentalists, some Jewish and many Muslim, who do not want any deal, good or bad. It is quite unclear at this stage which group will emerge the strongest.

GATT'S AFTERMATH

What's Next for World Trade?

Howard LaFranchi

Staff writer of The Christian Science Monitor

Trade negotiators who were jubilant at the successful conclusion of the seven-year-old Uruguay Round sounded like the winners in an American presidential campaign: It was worth the fight, many said.

But most participants of the General Agreement on Tariffs and Trade (GATT) agree that the likes of this round, which took up everything from agriculture to services and future technologies, will not be seen again. At the same time, calls for international negotiations on issues ranging from trade and the environment to workers' rights, probably mean new talks are not far off.

One of the Uruguay Round's problems was that "new" issues arose that in 1986 were not commonly linked to trade negotiations. One example is the environment: Now many see the link between trade and dwindling natural resources—for instance, between log exports and deforestation.

United States chief trade negotiator Mickey Kantor says environmental issues must be taken up in international trade talks soon after ratification of the Uruguay Round—expected by January 1995. Sooner still, a work program on the environment is to be presented for approval when trade ministers meet in Marrakesh, Morocco, next April to sign the accord.

But for "green" groups that may not be substantial enough. If the work program does not promote action, groups like Greenpeace and the World Wildlife Fund say they will oppose national ratifications.

Other areas which might be taken up by the future World Trade Organization—GATT's successor—include competition policy, workers' rights, investment rules, and developing-world issues, such as commodities trade (coffee and tin, for example) and migrant workers.

The European Union (EU) is keen to address competition. With the growing importance of multinational corporations, questions of industrial subsidies, mergers, and monopoly will become more vital. The US has pressed for talks on international standards for workers' rights—a move generally opposed by developing nations who fear it would be a cover for shackling countries with low labor costs.

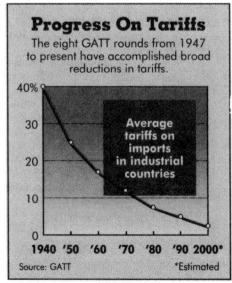

Progress On Tariffs

The eight GATT rounds from 1947 to present have accomplished broad reductions in tariffs.

Average tariffs on imports in industrial countries

Source: GATT   *Estimated

DAVE HERRING – STAFF

Global Economic Gains by 2002

These figures were based on a projected 30 percent worldwide tariff reduction. In fact, GATT negotiations did slightly better, coming up with $230 billion in annual gains by the year 2005.

Annual gains from trade liberalization in billions of 1992 dollars		Sub total
China	$37.0	
Low income Asia	1.8	
India	4.6	**43.4**
Indonesia	–1.9	
Upper income Asia	20.6	**18.7**
South Africa	–0.4	
Other Africa	–0.6	
Nigeria	–1.0	
Maghreb nations	–0.6	**–2.6**
Mediterranean	–1.6	
Gulf Region	3.1	**1.5**
Brazil	3.4	
Mexico	0.3	
Other Latin America	4.4	**8.1**
US	18.8	
Canada	2.5	
Australia/New Zealand	1.1	
Japan	25.9	
EU	80.7	
EFTA	12.8	**141.8**
Eastern Europe	1.4	
Former Soviet Union	0.8	**2.2**
TOTAL		**$213.1**

Source: OECD, May 1993

DAVE HERRING – STAFF

Looking Back: Accomplishments of the Uruguay Round

Despite farmers' protests in Paris, Tokyo, and Seoul, the disappointments of Hollywood on one hand and the grandiose predictions of a multitrillion-dollar boost to the global economy on another, the world continued to turn as usual following conclusion Dec. 15 of the Uruguay Round of trade liberalization negotiations.

But the accord reached by 117 countries after seven years of talks under the auspices of the General Agreement on Tariffs and Trade (GATT), will change the world as it takes effect in January 1995. It will accelerate globalization of the world economy and will bring more countries and regions into a more open trading system.

Following are some of the key areas:

Industrial markets

The Uruguay Round's goal of cutting tariffs on industrial products by one-third was surpassed. Average tariff levels will fall from nearly 7 percent to about 4 percent. Principal industrialized traders will drop duties altogether on more than a third of their imports, including construction, farm and medical equipment, furniture, wood, and paper. For the first time many developing countries made tariff commitments on industrial products. The agreement should boost markets for everything from cars to computers—improving job prospects in those sectors—and reduce prices.

Services

Results in the services sector—banking and other financial services, insurance, telecommunications, tourism, air and maritime transport, the entertainment industry, accounting, construction—were less ambitious than originally foreseen, with telecommunications dropping out altogether. But the big step was putting services under international agreement for the first time.

The United States and the European Union failed to resolve their differences on entertainment products, which means a continued battle over television, films, music, video and satellite sales. In the short term the US will limit access to its banking and financial markets to countries that make equivalent market-openings. Negotiations in 1995 will reveal whether Japan is ready to open its lucrative financial services market.

Nevertheless, services, which already account for a fifth of the world economy, should feel a boost.

Intellectual property

The accord includes the strongest and most comprehensive rules ever for protecting patents, copyright, trade marks, recording artists, microchip and other industrial designs, and trade secrets. Included are protection standards plus enforcement requirements.

The accord is a boon to IBM, which says it alone loses $1 billion in annual sales to product pirates.

Industries should feel freer to invest in developing countries, although some critics say it will also mean higher prices for poor countries.

Agriculture

The accord brings trade in farm products under the GATT for the first time. The world's most efficient producers, and consumers in protected markets, should benefit by the turn of the century. The high farm subsidizers—chief among them the EU and the US—must chop subsidized exports by 36 percent in value over six years. Japan and South Korea will gradually open their closed rice markets a little—Japan to 8 percent by 2007.

The deal translates into 50 million tons less subsidized wheat on the world market by 2000, which means non- or low-subsidizing countries like Australia, Canada, and Argentina will have better access. Consumers in Japan—where rice prices are five times world market levels—will see price drops. Subsidy reductions, however, will increase world food prices and hit developing countries dependent on food imports.

Textiles and clothing

The accord puts the textiles sector back under multilateral trade rules, after a 20-year hiatus during which bilateral accords reigned under the Multi-Fiber Agreement regime. Most tariffs and quotas in developed countries will be eliminated over the decade. Developing countries will take a growing share of textiles and clothing trade, worth $250 billion in 1992.

Consumers should enjoy lower prices, while developed-world manufacturers will continue to feel the heat.

Tougher, broader trade rules

Observers say an agreement on stronger, clearer, and less arbitrary trading rules may do more to boost world trade than the accord's other sections combined. Among other provisions, the accord includes new rules for settling dumping disputes. The new rules should reduce arbitrary anti-dumping decisions that protect inefficient domestic industries.

Finally, the host of new trade regulations will be administered and adjudicated not by GATT—which since its creation in 1947 has been a provisional body to oversee successive trade accords—but by the newly created World Trade Organization.

—**Howard LaFranchi**

Many business leaders warn, however, against increased regulation.

"We want to watch now for moves that would replace tariff measures with bureaucratic impediments to trade," says Caroline Walcot, assistant secretary general of the European Roundtable of Industrialists.

Trade officials from developed countries will also be keeping an eye on China's accession to GATT and the conditions for admission.

China's bid to rejoin GATT after a 43-year absence has been stalled by the US and the EU, who want special measures to guarantee against floods of Chinese products. Growing impatient, Chinese officials this week said they might forgo membership if China is not readmitted by 1995.

But other countries are concerned about how the coming economic giant might skew world markets. "It's not a question of China acceding to GATT," quipped one GATT official recently, "but of GATT acceding to China."

Hunting for Africa's Wildlife Poachers

Help for efforts in Tanzania is international, while pragmatism still allows a lucrative game business

W. Sean Roberts

Special to The Christian Science Monitor

DAR ES SALAAM, TANZANIA For three hours under a glaring African sun, the anti-poaching patrol struggled through the dense Tanzania woodland, at times waist deep in flooded thickets, often forced to steer clear of the volatile Cape buffalo, and constantly at odds with the tsetse fly. Suddenly one scout gave a whistle, calling the six other men and one woman.

Pressed into a muddy highway of buffalo tracks were several sets of human footprints and a blood trail—tell-tale signs of poachers pursuing a wounded animal. After another 20 minutes, the game scouts were directly below a cloud of vultures and had run head on into a band of eight villagers hauling out their kill. The scouts gave chase, firing wildly over the poachers' heads as the melee stretched deeper into the bush.

Emerging without a single *jangili* (Swahili for poacher), these scouts patrolling Tanzania's sprawling 33,000 square-mile Selous Game Reserve will have ample opportunity to set the score straight in the days and weeks to come. With an estimated 700,000 animals illegally hunted in Tanzania per year, they have their hands full—but not their pockets.

As the prime protector of Tanzania's high-profile animals, such as the wild dog, cheetah, African elephant, and black rhinoceros, all of which have been drastically reduced in numbers during the last decade, a game scout averages about 39 cents a day or $12 per month—

not enough to make ends meet even in one of the world's least developed countries.

As low on morale as they are on funds, game scouts are often forced to poach wildlife to supplement their diets or to sell to villagers for cash. Many lack the motivation to apprehend poachers who may be relatives or friends. Logistical support is another problem, almost nonexistent in some cases. And those who persist in carrying out their duties despite the odds may find themselves fleeing from the very criminals they were hired to apprehend. Game-scout weaponry is archaic at best, while poachers may sport modern automatic weapons.

Riding to the scout's rescue, however, are a plethora of organizations intent on helping Tanzania preserve its natural environment. The Frankfurt Zoological Society, World Wildlife Fund for Nature, Friends of Conservation, and the Deutshe Gesellschaft für Technische Zusammenarbeit (GTZ), the German government's official aid organization, to name a few, have contributed to the cause.

POPULATION GROWTH A THREAT

As a cofounder and the principal benefactor of the Selous Conservation Programme (SCP), GTZ has contributed well over $3 million during a five-year effort to insure the integrity of Africa's largest protected habitat.

One of the main tasks of the SCP has been to provide scouts with logistical support.

"The game scout is basically the pillar on whom the whole system in the bush rests," says Dr. Rolf Baldus, project coordinator for the SCP. "You have to get involved with management at higher levels, policy dialogue with the government, ecological monitoring and all that. But for me the first person to look at is always the game scout."

The battle to save Tanzania's ecosystems extends well beyond the scouts or even their government's capabilities. After 30 years of Marxism, which has kept the country's economy in the same primeval state as its natural habitats, poaching, runaway population growth, and development now threaten such showcase lands as the Serengeti, Kilimanjaro and Ngorongoro Crater wilderness areas with modern environmental problems.

As a result of its poor economic showing, Tanzania has sought to guarantee the sanctity of its protected areas by relying on international assistance in the form of aid, expertise, and mandates, as well as using the ability of wildlife to "pay for itself" through a lucrative tourist and sport hunting market.

One measure that continues to be of great assistance to the Tanzanian wildlife authorities in preserving the elephant is the 1990 international ban on ivory. By shutting down markets for ivory, the ban put an abrupt end to the blitzkrieg of poaching that slashed the African elephant population from 1.3 million to just over 600,000 animals during the 1980s alone.

Some southern African countries are currently crying out for a lifting of the ban, citing ivory as an important source of revenue. They claim that elephant herds have grown so large that they threaten the balance of the ecosystems. But if the ban were to go down, so too would the elephant, at least in Tanzania.

Edward Kishe, principal park warden in charge of law enforcement for Tanzania's national parks, doubts that his country could manage a responsible harvesting of ivory.

"I don't advocate that at all," Mr. Kishe says of a lifting of the ban. "We don't have the means to properly oversee this. Immediately if we started this ivory trade again, some people would poach and we could not stop all of them," he adds.

Agreeing with Kishe on the importance of the ivory ban is the Frankfurt Zoological Society's Representative for East Africa, Marjus Borner.

"I was against the ban on ivory in the beginning," Dr. Borner says, "because it didn't really make sense to me then. But looking at the results it has made a [great] difference. . . . I've been counting elephants here for the last 15 years and everywhere I went it was always down, down, down. It is in the last two or three years that there has been the same amount [of elephants] and at least in the Serengeti we have the first increase of any kind of elephant population anywhere."

HUNTING BRINGS INCOME

Another effective tactic that has greatly reduced poaching on otherwise unprotected lands, brought in much needed hard currency to conservation efforts, and is changing the way locals view wildlife is Tanzania's hunting enterprises.

Although the European and North American public, who have funded so much of the conservation effort in Tanzania today, may wince at the thought of the great white hunter on the savannas of the dark continent, Africa is a place that demands pragmatism.

Operating on "blocks" of land allotted to them by the government, professional hunting companies routinely and aggressively patrol their areas for poachers. Villages neighboring hunting blocks have been shown the value of preserving wildlife by companies donating meat or funding village projects, such as building schoolrooms or drilling wells in return for their support.

And with a 10-day safari averaging around $15,000 per client, hunting is a big business that few conservationists in Tanzania want to see nullified as long as

it continues to act as a benefit instead of a plague. It provides employment for local villagers and brings in much needed currency through licensing and other fees, which are pumped back into conservation.

"I do not hunt and I don't understand why people do," Borner says. "But you can't keep areas which are 10,000 square kilometers larger than Switzerland without any revenue coming out of them. Tanzania can't afford it. There are some protected areas that are completely dependent on hunting for revenue, and that is why they are still there. I think [hunting] is a very important contribution to conservation in this country."

But Tanzania's soaring population has long gone unaddressed by its government or aid organizations and may soon prove to be the most dire hazard to its natural habitats. With some villages near parks and reserves growing 10 percent a year, competition with wildlife has increased. And in a country that has traditionally viewed a large population as a benefit to its labor force, family planning has been slow in coming.

Although conservation organizations realize the threat Tanzania's population boom poses to wildlife, they have done very little in the way of addressing the problem.

Values and Visions

The final unit of this book considers how humanity's view of itself is changing. Values, like all other elements discussed in this anthology, are dynamic. Visionary people with new ideas can have a profound impact on how a society deals with problems and adapts to changing circumstances. Therefore, to understand the forces at work in the world today, values, visions, and new ideas must be examined.

Novelist Herman Wouk, in his book *War and Remembrance*, notes that there have been many institutions so embedded in the social fabric that the people of the time assumed they were part of human nature. Slavery and human sacrifice are two examples. However, forward-thinking people opposed these institutions. Many knew they would never see the abolition of these systems within their own lifetimes, but they pressed on in the hope that someday these institutions would be eliminated. Wouk believes the same is true for warfare. He states, "Either we are finished with war or war will finish us." Aspects of society such as warfare, slavery, racism, and the secondary status of women are creations of the human mind; history suggests that they can be changed by the human spirit.

The articles of this unit have been selected with the previous six units in mind. Each explores some aspect of world affairs from the perspective of values and alternative visions of the future. Changes in information technology, for example, redefine the role of the citizen. How must values about technological innovation change to protect individual rights? New ideas are critical to meeting these challenges. The examination of well-known issues from new perspectives also can yield new solutions to old problems.

It was feminist Susan B. Anthony who once remarked that "social change is never made by the masses, only by educated minorities." The redefinition of human values (which, by necessity, will accompany the successful confrontation of other global issues) is a task that few people take on willingly. Nevertheless, in order to deal with the dangers of nuclear war, overpopulation, and environmental degradation, educated people must take a broad view of history. This is going to require considerable effort and much personal sacrifice.

When people first begin to consider the challenges of contemporary global problems, they often become disheartened and depressed. They might ask: What can I do? What does it matter? Who cares? There are no easy answers to these questions, but people need only look around to see good news as well as bad. How individuals react to the world in which they live is not a function of that world but a reflection of themselves. Different people react differently to the same world. The study of global issues, therefore, is the study of people, and the study of people is the study of values. Ideally, people's reactions to these issues (and many others) will help provide them with some insight into themselves as well as the world at large.

Looking Ahead: Challenge Questions

Is it naive to speak of international politics and economics in terms of ethics? What role can governments, international organizations, and even the individual play in making the world a more moral place in which to live?

Are the values of democracy easily transferred to new settings such as Russia?

How does modern information technology threaten the traditional values of a democracy? Conversely, how does it support these values?

In addition to some of the ideas presented here, what other new ideas are being expressed and how likely are they to be widely accepted?

How do the contemporary arts reflect changes in how humanity views itself?

How will the world be different in the year 2030? What factors will contribute to these changes? What does your analysis reveal about your own value system?

50 Trends Shaping the World

The nuclear threat that kept antagonists at bay for the last four decades has largely been removed. While much turmoil has resulted, trends toward new alliances and cooperation to solve global problems bode well for sustaining peace.

Marvin Cetron and Owen Davies

About the Authors

Marvin Cetron is president of Forecasting International, Ltd., 1001 North Highland Street, Arlington, Virginia 22210. He is co-author (with Owen Davies) of *American Renaissance: Our Life at the Turn of the 21st Century* (St. Martin's Press, 1989) and co-author (with Margaret Gayle) of *Educational Renaissance: Our Schools at the Turn of the Twenty-First Century* (St. Martin's Press, 1991).

Owen Davies is co-author of *American Renaissance* and former senior editor of *Omni* magazine. His address is P.O. Box 355, Hancock, New Hampshire 03449.

This article is adapted from their book, *Crystal Globe: The Haves and Have-Nots of the New World Order* (St. Martin's Press, 1991).

The world will be a more peaceful and prosperous place in the 1990s than it has been in the decades since World War II, because the premise by which it operates has changed. In the coming years, it will no longer be influenced by the needs of ideological and military competition, but instead by the need to promote international trade and the well-being of the trading nations. Major military conflicts will be all but unthinkable, because they are contrary to the mutual interests of nations that are interdependent in the global economy. Wars will not suddenly disappear, but they will be primarily small and regional in nature. These conflicts will stem from local antagonisms and the ambitions of Third World rulers, and peace will be restored by the joint effort of the entire world community.

This fundamental change will be the guiding theme of the 1990s.

Politically, this will be an interesting era. Nations will increasingly band together, however briefly, with traditional enemies to further their short-term interests.

No single nation will have the power to dominate in this new global order. World leaders will be military powers as well as leaders from the three powerful regional economic blocs now coming to dominate international commerce: the European Community, the Pacific Rim, and the North American alliance. Each group will be heavily influenced by its largest members but will act primarily by consensus in all matters of common interest.

Vast regions of the world will be left out of this interlocking arrangement, save on the occasions when they can serve the interests of the major powers. The Middle East will retain much of its wealth and influence, thanks to the continued importance of oil. Africa, the Indian subcontinent, and Southeast Asia will remain much as they are now, doomed to poverty largely by their own leaders and used by the industrialized nations as little more than stockpiles of raw material.

Yet, even these nations should benefit from the new global structure. In a more peaceful and prosperous world, the developed nations will have a better opportunity to help their less-fortunate neighbors deal with economic and social problems, to whatever extent local politics allow it. Progress will come slowly in the Third World, but it will move more quickly under the new commercial priorities than it did under ideological and military domination.

In the pages that follow, we will outline many of the trends that are emerging from today's ferment to form tomorrow's new world order.

Population

1. In the industrialized countries, the "birth dearth" has cut growth almost to nothing, while in the developing world, the population bomb is still exploding.

• The rich get richer, the poor have children: Throughout the industrialized world, workers can look forward to national retirement programs or social security. In the developing lands, those too old for labor rely on their children to support them — so they have as many as they can.

• Thanks to better health care, children have a greater chance to survive into adulthood and produce children of their own. This will tend to accelerate population growth, but contraceptive use is increasing, with an opposite effect on growth.

• In the developed world, the vast Baby Boom generation is approaching middle age, threatening to overwhelm both medical and social-

 From *The Futurist*, September/October 1991, pp. 11-21. Adapted from *Crystal Global: The Haves and Have-Nots of the New World Order.* © 1991 by Marvin J. Cetron and Owen Davies (St. Martin's Press) and reprinted with permission by the World Future Society.

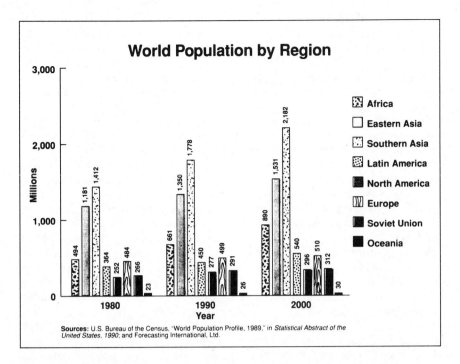

World Population by Region

	Africa
	Eastern Asia
	Southern Asia
	Latin America
	North America
	Europe
	Soviet Union
	Oceania

1980: 494, 1,181, 1,412, 364, 252, 484, 266, 23
1990: 661, 1,350, 1,778, 450, 277, 499, 291, 26
2000: 890, 1,531, 2,182, 540, 296, 510, 312, 30

Sources: U.S. Bureau of the Census, "World Population Profile, 1989," in *Statistical Abstract of the United States, 1990;* and Forecasting International, Ltd.

security programs. These costs will consume an increasing portion of national budgets until about 2020.

2. The AIDS epidemic will slaughter millions of people worldwide, especially in Africa.

• According to the World Health Organization, the AIDS-causing human immunodeficiency virus will have infected up to 40 million people by 2000.

• By 1990, some 5 million people in sub-Saharan Africa already carried the disease — twice as many as just three years earlier. In some cities, as much as 40% of the population may be infected.

3. A host of new medical technologies will make life longer and more comfortable in the industrialized world. It will be many years before these advances spread to the developing countries.

4. As the West grows ever more concerned with physical culture and personal health, developing countries are adopting the unhealthy practices that wealthier nations are trying to cast off: smoking, high-fat diets, and sedentary lifestyles. To those emerging from poverty, these deadly luxuries are symbols of success.

• In the United States, smokers are kicking the habit. Only 35% of American men smoke, down from 52% twenty years ago; 29% of women smoke, down from a peak of 34%.

• However, the developing world continues to smoke more each year. Even Europe shows little sign of solving this problem.

5. Better nutrition and the "wellness" movement will raise life expectancies.

• In developed countries, children born in the 1980s will live to an average age of 70 for males, 77 for females. In developing countries, the average life expectancies will remain stalled at 59 years for males and 61 for females.

Food

6. Farmers will continue to harvest more food than the world really needs, but inefficient delivery systems will prevent it from reaching the hungry.

• According to the World Bank, some 800 million people are chronically malnourished by U.N. standards. As the world population grows, that number will rise.

7. The size and number of farms are changing.

• In the United States, the family farm is quickly disappearing. Yet, giant agribusinesses reap vast profits, while small, part-time "hobby" farms also survive. This trend will begin to affect other developed nations during the 1990s and will even-

tually spread to the rest of the world.

• Former Iron Curtain countries will find it difficult to turn their huge, inefficient collective farms back to private owners; progress in this effort will be uneven.

• Land reform in the Philippines and Latin America will move at a glacial pace, showing progress only when revolution threatens. Most of the vast holdings now owned by the rich and worked by the poor will survive well into the twenty-first century.

8. Science is increasing the world's supply of food.

• According to the U.S. Office of Technology Assessment, biotechnology and other yield-increasing developments will account for five-sixths of the growth in world harvests by 2000; the rest will come from newly cultivated croplands.

• Biotechnology is bringing new protein to developing countries. Bovine growth hormone can produce 20% more milk per pound of cattle feed, while genetic engineering is creating fish that grow faster in aquafarms.

9. Food supplies will become healthier and more wholesome.

• Most nations will adopt higher and more-uniform standards of hygiene and quality, the better to market their food products internationally. Consumers the world over will benefit.

10. Water will be plentiful in most regions. Total use of water worldwide by 2000 will be less than half of the stable renewable supply. Yet, some parched, populous areas will run short.

• The amount of water needed in western Asia will double between 1980 and 2000. The Middle East and the American West are in for dry times by the turn of the century. Two decades later, as many as 25 African nations may face serious water shortages.

• We already know how to cut water use and waste-water flows by up to 90%. In the next decade, the industrialized countries will finally adopt many of these water-saving techniques. Developing countries reuse little of their waste water, because they lack the sewage systems required to collect it. By 2000, building this needed infrastructure will become a high priority in many parched lands.

• Cheaper, more-effective desalination methods are on the horizon. In the next 20 years, they will make it easier to live in many desert areas.

Energy

11. Despite all the calls to develop alternative sources of energy, oil will provide more of the world's power in 2000 than it did in 1990.

• OPEC will supply most of the oil used in the 1990s. Demand for OPEC oil grew from 15 million barrels a day in 1986 to over 20 million just three years later. By 2000, it will easily top 25 million barrels daily.

12. Oil prices are not likely to rise; instead, by 2000 they will plummet to between $7 and $9 a barrel. A number of factors will undermine oil prices within the next 10 years:

• Oil is inherently cheap. It costs only $1.38 per barrel to lift Saudi oil out of the ground. Even Prudhoe Bay and North Sea oil cost only $5 per barrel.

• The 20 most-industrialized countries all have three-month supplies of oil in tankers and storage tanks. Most have another three months' worth in "strategic reserves." If OPEC raises its prices too high, their

customers can afford to stop buying until the costs come down. This was not the case during the 1970s oil shocks.

• OPEC just is not very good at throttling back production to keep prices up when their market is glutted. They will not get any better at doing so in the 1990s.

13. Growing competition from other energy sources will also help to hold down the price of oil:

• Natural gas burns cleanly, and there is enough of it available to supply the world's entire energy need for the next 200 years.

• Solar, geothermal, wind-generated, and wave-generated energy sources will contribute where geographically and economically feasible, but their total contribution will be small.

• Nuclear plants will supply 12% of the energy in Eastern Europe and the Soviet Union by the end of the century.

Environment

14. Air pollution and other atmospheric issues will dominate eco-policy discussions for years to come.

• Soot and other particulates will be more carefully scrutinized in the near future. Recent evidence shows

that they are far more dangerous than sulfur dioxide and other gaseous pollutants formerly believed to present major health risks. In the United States alone, medical researchers estimate that as many as 60,000 people may die each year as a direct result of breathing particulates. Most are elderly and already suffering from respiratory illness.

• By 1985, the concentration of carbon dioxide in the atmosphere had increased 25 times since preindustrial days. By 2050, the concentration is likely to increase 40% over today's levels if energy use continues to grow at its current pace. Burning fossil fuel will spew about 7 billion tons of carbon into the air each year by 2000, 10–14 billion in 2030, and 13–23 billion in 2050.

• Blame global warming for at least some of the spread of Africa's deserts. Before the process runs its course, two-fifths of Africa's remaining fertile land could become arid wasteland. Up to one-third of Asia's non-desert land and one-fifth of Latin America's may follow. Global warming will not only hurt agriculture, but will also raise sea levels, with consequent impacts on habitation patterns and industries.

• Brazil and other nations will soon halt the irrevocable destruction of the earth's rain forests for very temporary economic gain. Those countries will need economic help to make the transition. The World Bank and the International Monetary Fund (IMF) will help underwrite alternatives to rain-forest destruction.

• Acid rain such as that afflicting the United States and Canada will appear whenever designers of new power plants and factories neglect emission-control equipment. Watch for it in most developing countries.

15. Disposal of mankind's trash is a growing problem, especially in developed nations. Within the next decade, most of the industrialized world will all but run out of convenient space in its landfills.

• The U.S. Environmental Protection Agency estimates that existing technologies could reduce the total amount of hazardous waste generated in the United States by 15%–30% by 2000.

• For now, recycling is a necessary nuisance. By 2000, recyclables will

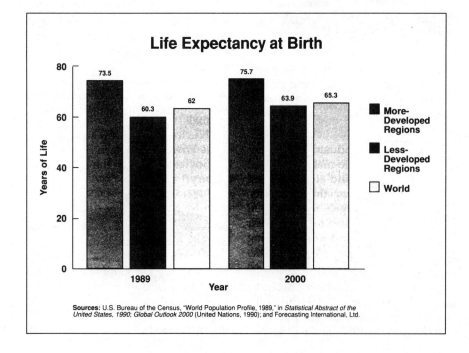

Life Expectancy at Birth

	1989			2000	
More-Developed Regions	73.5			75.7	
Less-Developed Regions	60.3			63.9	
World		62			65.3

Years of Life

Year

Sources: U.S. Bureau of the Census, "World Population Profile, 1989," in *Statistical Abstract of the United States, 1990*; *Global Outlook 2000* (United Nations, 1990); and Forecasting International, Ltd.

become valuable resources, as research finds profitable new uses for materials currently being discarded. Recycling will save energy as well: Remanufacturing requires less energy than does the full iron-ore-to-Cadillac production process.

Science and Technology

16. High technological turnover rates are accelerating.

• All the technological knowledge we work with today will represent only 1% of the knowledge that will be available in 2050.

17. Technology has come to dominate the economy and society in the developed world. Its central role can only grow.

• For some economists, the numbers of cars, computers, telephones, facsimile machines, and copiers in a nation define how "developed" the country is.

• Personal robots will appear in homes in the developed world by 2000. Robots will perform mundane commercial and service jobs and environmentally dangerous jobs, such as repairing space-station components in orbit.

18. The technology gap between developed and developing countries will continue to widen.

• Developed countries have 10 times as many scientists and engineers per capita as the developing world. The gap between their spending on research and development grew threefold from 1970 to 1980.

• Technologically underdeveloped countries face antiquated or nonexistent production facilities, a dearth of useful knowledge, ineffective organization and management, and a lack of technical abilities and skills. Under these conditions, underdevelopment is often self-perpetuating, which weakens the country's ability to compete in international markets.

• The widening technology gap will aggravate the disparity in North–South trade, with the developed nations of the Northern Hemisphere supplying more and more high-tech goods. The less-developed countries of the South will be restricted to exporting natural resources and relatively unprofitable low-tech manufactured products.

19. Nations will exchange scientific information more freely, but will continue to hold back technological data.

• Basic research is done principally in universities, which have a tradition of communicating their findings.

• Fifty-three percent of Ph.D. candidates in U.S. science and engineering programs are from other countries. Anything they learn will return to their homelands when they do.

• The space-faring nations — soon to include Japan — will share their findings more freely.

• Technological discoveries, in contrast, often spring from corporate laboratories, whose sponsors have a keen interest in keeping them proprietary. More than half of the technology transferred between countries will move between giant corporations and their overseas branches or as part of joint ventures by multinationals and foreign partners.

20. Research and development (R&D) will play an ever-greater role in the world economy.

• R&D outlays in the United States have varied narrowly (between 2.1% and 2.8% of the GNP) since 1960 and have been rising generally since 1978.

• R&D spending is growing most rapidly in the electronics, aerospace, pharmaceuticals, and chemical industries.

Communications

21. Communications and information are the lifeblood of a world economy. Thus, the world's communications networks will grow ever more rapidly in the next decade.

• A constellation of satellites providing position fixing and two-way communication on Earth, 24 hours a day, will be established in the 1990s. A person equipped with a minitransceiver will be able to send a message anywhere in the world.

22. The growing power and versatility of computers will continue to change the way individuals, companies, and nations do their business.

• Processing power and operating speeds for computers are still increasing. By 2000, the average personal computer will have at least 50 times the power of the first IBM PCs and 100 or more times the power of the original Apple II.

• Computers and communications are quickly finding their way into information synthesis and decision making. "Automatic typewriters" will soon be able to transcribe dictation through voice recognition. Computers will also translate documents into various languages. Today's best translation programs can already handle a 30,000-word vocabulary in nine languages.

• The revolution in computers and communications technologies offers hope that developing countries can catch up with the developed world. However, few have yet been able to profit from the new age of information. In 1985, developing countries owned only 5.7% of the total number of computers in the world; most of these computers are used mainly for accounting, payroll processing, and similar low-payoff operations.

Labor

23. The world's labor force will grow by only 1.5% per year during the 1990s — much slower than in recent decades, but fast enough to provide most countries with the workers they need. In contrast, the United States faces shortages of labor in general, and especially of low-wage-rate workers.

• Multinational companies may find their operations handicapped by loss of employees and potential workers to the worldwide epidemic of AIDS, especially in Africa, since many firms rely on indigenous workers.

24. The shrinking supply of young workers in many countries means that the overall labor force is aging rapidly.

• Persons aged 25 to 59 accounted for 65% of the world labor force in 1985; almost all growth of the labor force over the next decade will occur in this age group.

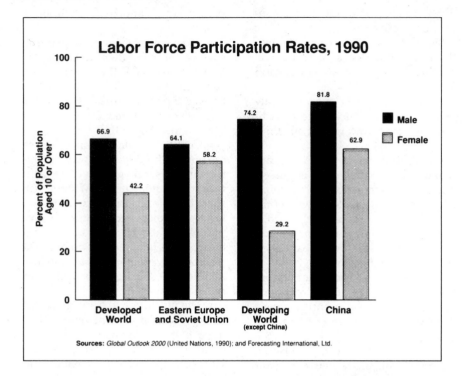

Labor Force Participation Rates, 1990

Percent of Population Aged 10 or Over

■ Male
▨ Female

	Male	Female
Developed World	66.9	42.2
Eastern Europe and Soviet Union	64.1	58.2
Developing World (except China)	74.2	29.2
China	81.8	62.9

Sources: *Global Outlook 2000* (United Nations, 1990); and Forecasting International, Ltd.

25. Unions will continue to lose their hold on labor.

• Union membership is declining steadily in the United States. It reached 17.5% in 1986. According to the United Auto Workers, it will fall to 12% by 1995 and to less than 10% by 2000.

• Unionization in Latin America will be about the same as in the 1980s; unionization in the Pacific Rim will remain low; unionization in the developing world as a whole will remain extremely low.

• Increased use of robots, CAD/CAM, and flexible manufacturing complexes can cut a company's work force by up to one-third.

• Growing use of artificial intelligence, which improves productivity and quality, will make the companies adopting it more competitive, but will reduce the need for workers in the highly unionized manufacturing industries.

26. People will change residences, jobs, and even occupations more frequently, especially in industrialized countries.

• High-speed MAGLEV trains will allow daily commutes of up to 500 miles.

• The number of people who retrain for new careers, one measure of occupational mobility, has been increasing steadily.

• The new information-based organizational management methods — nonhierarchical, organic systems that can respond quickly to environmental changes — foster greater occupational flexibility and autonomy.

27. The wave of new entrepreneurs that appeared in the United States during the 1970s and 1980s is just the leading edge of a much broader trend.

• In 1986, the number of new businesses started in the United States hit a record 700,000. In 1950, there were fewer than 100,000 new business incorporations. A similar trend has appeared in Western Europe, where would-be entrepreneurs were until recently viewed with suspicion. And a new generation of entrepreneurs is growing throughout Eastern Europe and even in Japan.

• From 1970 to 1980, small businesses started by entrepreneurs accounted for most of the 20 million new jobs created in America. In 1987, small businesses accounted for 1 million new jobs, compared with 97,000 in larger companies.

28. More women will continue to enter the labor force.

• In both developed and developing regions, the percentage of working women has increased since 1950. Women represented 36.5% of the world's labor force in 1985. This growth is expected to continue at a moderate rate, with developed nations showing the fastest increases.

Industry

29. Multinational and international corporations will continue to grow, and many new ones will appear.

• Companies will expand their operations beyond national borders. For example, Marconi Space Systems (a British General Electric company) and Matra Espace (of France) got together to form Matra Marconi Space, "the first international space company."

• Many other companies will go international by locating new facilities in countries that provide a labor force and benefits such as preferential tax treatment, but that do not otherwise participate in the operation. Ireland pioneered this practice with U.S. companies in the insurance, electronics, and automobile industries. It found that when companies leave, for whatever reason, the country loses revenue and gains an unemployed labor force.

30. Demands will grow for industries to increase their social responsibility.

• A wide variety of environmental disasters and public-health issues (e.g., the *Exxon Valdez* oil spill and Union Carbide's accident at Bhopal, India) have drawn public attention to the effects of corporate negligence and to situations in which business can help solve public problems not necessarily of their own making.

• In the future, companies will increasingly be judged on how they treat the environment — and will be forced to clean up any damage resulting from their activities.

• Deregulation will be a thing of the past. There will be increased government intervention: Airlines will be compelled to provide greater safety and services; the financial-service industry will be regulated to reduce economic instability and costs; electric utilities will be held responsible for nuclear problems; and chemical manufacturers will have to cope with their own toxic wastes.

31. The 1990s will be the decade

of microsegmentation, as more and more highly specialized businesses and entrepreneurs search for narrower niches.

Education and Training

32. Literacy will become a fundamental goal in developing societies, and the developed world will take steps to guard against backsliding toward illiteracy. Throughout the world, education (especially primary school for literacy) remains a major goal for development as well as a means for meeting goals for health, higher labor productivity, stronger economic growth, and social integration. Countries with a high proportion of illiterates will not be able to cope with modern technology or use advanced agricultural techniques.

• Most developed countries have literacy rates of more than 95%. The increasing levels of technological "savvy" demanded by modern life, however, often are more than people are prepared to meet, even in the most modern societies.

• The proportion of illiterates among the world's adult population has steadily decreased, although the absolute number has grown. In developing countries, the proportion of illiterates will drop from 39% in 1985 to 28% by 2000, while the number of illiterate adults will have climbed by 10 million.

• Worldwide, the proportion of children not enrolled in school will fall from 26% in 1985 to 18% by 2000. Primary-education enrollment has risen dramatically in most of the developing world except for Africa. In 31 sub-Saharan countries reporting their enrollment rates, the rates had fallen for boys in 13 countries and for girls in 15.

• Useful, job-oriented knowledge is becoming increasingly perishable. The half-life of an engineer's professional information today is five years.

33. Educational *perestroika* is changing American schools. In the long run, this will repair the nation's competitive position in the world economy.

• The information economy's need for skilled workers requires educational reform.

• Science and engineering schools will be actively recruiting more students.

• Foreign-exchange programs will grow markedly in an attempt to bolster the competence of American students in international affairs.

34. Higher education is changing as quickly as primary and secondary schools.

• The soaring cost of higher education may force program cuts. If so, developing countries face an ultimate loss of foreign exchange, as their industries fall further behind those of cheaper, more-efficient competitors.

• There are too few jobs for liberal arts college graduates in many developing countries. For instance, Egypt cannot keep its promise to give a job to every graduate; the civil service is grossly overstaffed already.

• The concept of "university" is changing. Increasingly, major corporations are collaborating with universities to establish degree-granting corporate schools and programs. Examples include the General Motors Institute, Pennsylvania State University's affiliation with a major electronics company, and Rutgers University's affiliation with a major pharmaceutical house.

• More private companies will market large electronic databases, eventually replacing university libraries.

World Economy

35. The world economy will grow at a rapid rate for the foreseeable future, but the gap between rich and poor countries will widen.

• World trade will grow at a brisk 4.5% annually in the next decade. As one result, international competition will continue to cost jobs and income in the developed market economies.

• The gross domestic products (GDPs) of the developed market economies will grow at 3.1% on average in the 1990s as investment demand increases and the economic integration in Europe introduces capital efficiency.

• The economies of Eastern Europe and the Soviet Union may recover with a GDP growth rate of 3.6%.

• The developing economies will fall further and further behind the industrialized nations, largely because their populations will continue to rise faster than their incomes. GDPs in the developing economies will grow by 4.3% a year (well below the 5.1% rate they enjoyed in the 1970s). In the 1970s, their per capita GDP was one-tenth that of the developed countries. By 1985, it had fallen to one-twelfth. By 2000, it will be one-thirteenth.

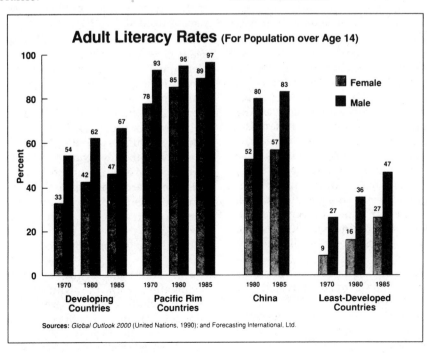

Adult Literacy Rates (For Population over Age 14)

Sources: *Global Outlook 2000* (United Nations, 1990); and Forecasting International, Ltd.

7. VALUES AND VISIONS

• By reducing military budgets, the fabled "new world order" will make more money available for business.

36. The world economy will become increasingly integrated.

• There is a "ripple effect" among closely linked national stock exchanges. The impact of a major event on one exchange perturbs all the others. Stock markets will become more fully connected and integrated.

• By 2000 or so, all national currencies will be convertible, following a model similar to the European Community's Exchange Rate Mechanism.

• It will become increasingly difficult to label a product by nation (e.g., "Japanese cars") since parts often come from several countries to be assembled in others and sold in yet others. Protective tariffs will become obsolete — for the good of the worldwide economy.

37. The world is quickly dividing itself into three major blocs: the European Community, the North American free-trade zone, and Japan's informal but very real Pacific development area. Other regions will ally themselves with these giants: Eastern Europe with the EC, Mexico with the United States and Canada. The nations of Latin America will slowly build ties with their neighbors to the North. The Australia–New Zealand bloc is still trying to make up its mind which of these units to join — the Pacific Rim, where its nearest markets are, or Europe and North America, where its emotional bonds are strongest.

• The economic structure of all these regions is changing rapidly. All but the least-developed nations are moving out of agriculture. Service sectors are growing rapidly in the mature economies, while manufacturing is being transferred to the world's developing economies.

• Within the new economic blocs, multinational corporations will *not* replace the nation-state, but they will become far more powerful, especially as governments relinquish aspects of social responsibility to employers.

38. The European Community will become a major player in the world economy.

• By 1992, the EC will represent a population of 325 million people with a $4-trillion GDP.

• By 1996, the European Free Trade Association countries will join with the EC to create a market of 400 million people with a $5-trillion GDP. Sweden, Norway, Finland, Austria, and Switzerland will join the founding 12.

• By 2000, most of the former East Bloc countries will be associate members of the EC.

39. The 25 most-industrialized countries will devote between 2% and 3% of their GDP to help their poorer neighbors.

• Much aid to poorer countries will be money that formerly would have gone to pay military budgets.

• The World Bank and IMF will help distribute funds.

• Loans and grants may require developing nations to set up population-control programs.

40. Western bankers will at last accept the obvious truth: Many Third World debtors have no hope of ever paying back overdue loans. Creditors will thus forgive one-third of these debts. This will save some of the developing nations from bankruptcy and probable dictatorship.

41. Developing nations once nationalized plants and industries when they became desperate to pay their debts. In the future, the World Bank and the IMF will refuse to lend to nations that take this easy way out. (Debtors, such as Peru, are eager to make amends to these organizations.) Instead, indebted nations will promote private industry in the hope of raising needed income.

42. Washington, D.C., will supplant New York as the world financial capital. The stock exchanges and other financial institutions, especially those involved with international transactions, will move south to be near Congress, the World Bank, and key regulatory bodies.

• Among the key economic players already in Washington: the Federal Reserve Board, the embassies and commercial/cultural attachés of nearly every country in the world, and the headquarters of many multinational and international corporations.

• In addition, several agencies cooperating with the United Nations, including the International Monetary Fund and the General Agreement on Tariffs and Trade, have their headquarters or routinely conduct much of their business in Washington.

Warfare

43. The world has been made "safer" for local or regional conflicts. During the Cold War, the superpowers could restrain their aggressive junior allies from attacking their neighbors. With the nuclear threat effectively gone, would-be antagonists feel less inhibited. Iraqi President Saddam Hussein was only the first of many small despots who will try to win by conquest what cannot be achieved by negotiation.

• The United States and the Soviet Union will sign a long procession of arms treaties in the next decade. The two countries will make a virtue of necessity, but both will act primarily to cut expensive military programs from their budgets.

• The Warsaw Pact has already disintegrated. NATO, seeking a new purpose, will eventually become an emergency strike force for the United Nations. The number of guns, tanks, and military planes in Europe will fall to little more than half their peak levels.

• Terrorist states will continue to harbor chemical and biological weapons until the international community finally takes a firm stand.

44. Brushfire wars will grow more frequent and bloody. Among the most likely are:

• Israel vs. the Arab countries. We foresee one last conflict in this region before the peace that now seems near actuality becomes a reality. Israel will win this one, too.

• India vs. Pakistan. The two have feuded with each other since the British left in 1947; religious differences, separatism in Kashmir, and small stocks of nuclear weapons make this a hot spot to watch carefully.

• Northern Ireland vs. itself. This perpetually troubled land will remain its own worst enemy. In trying to keep Ireland under control, the British face an increasingly unpleasant task.

45. Tactical alliances formed by common interests to meet immediate

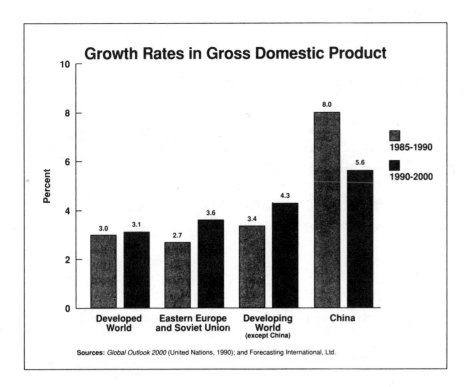

Growth Rates in Gross Domestic Product

■ 1985-1990
■ 1990-2000

	1985-1990	1990-2000
Developed World	3.0	3.1
Eastern Europe and Soviet Union	2.7	3.6
Developing World (except China)	3.4	4.3
China	8.0	5.6

Sources: *Global Outlook 2000* (United Nations, 1990); and Forecasting International, Ltd.

needs will replace long-term commitments among nations.

• In the Middle East, "the enemy of your enemy is your friend." Iran and Iraq will tolerate each other in their stronger hatred for the West. The United States and Syria will never be friends, but both dislike Iraq.

• Turkey and Greece will be hard-pressed to overlook their differences about Cyprus, but may do so in an effort to counter terrorism.

International Alignments

46. The Information Revolution has enabled many people formerly insulated from outside influences to compare their lives with those of people in other countries. This knowledge has often raised their expectations, and citizens in many undeveloped and repressed lands have begun to demand change. This trend can only spread as world telecommunications networks become ever more tightly linked.

• East Germans learned of reforms elsewhere in Eastern Europe via West German television; Romanians learned through Hungarian media.

• International broadcasting entities such as Voice of America, the British Broadcasting Corporation, and Cable News Network disseminate information around the world, sometimes influencing and inspiring global events even as they report on them.

47. Politically, the world's most important trend is for nations to form loose confederations, either by breaking up the most-centralized nations along ethnic and religious lines or by uniting independent countries in international alliances.

• Yugoslavia will soon split into a loose confederation based on the region's three dominant religions: Greek Orthodoxy, Roman Catholicism, and Islam. Czechoslovakia is already loosening the ties between its Czech and Slovak regions. And, following a brief, unsuccessful attempt at new repression by the right wing of the Communist Party, the Soviet Union will reorganize itself as a confederation of 15 largely independent states.

• Quebec will secede from Canada, probably in 1996. The four eastern Canadian provinces will be absorbed into the United States by 2004, and the other Canadian provinces will follow suit by 2010.

• Hong Kong and Macao will rejoin China, through previously made

agreements, by 1997. Taiwan will seek to join Mainland China shortly thereafter. The two Koreas will reunite before 2000.

48. The role of major international organizations will become extremely important in the new world order.

• The United Nations will finally be able to carry out its mission. The World Court will enjoy increased prestige. UNESCO's food, literacy, and children's health funds will be bolstered. The World Health Organization will make progress in disease eradication and in training programs. The Food and Agriculture Organization will receive more funding for starvation relief and programs to help teach farming methods.

• More countries will be willing to reform internally to meet requirements for International Monetary Fund loans and World Bank programs that provide development and education funds and grants.

• More medical aid from developed countries will be provided, frequently under the auspices or coordination of the United Nations or Red Cross/Red Crescent, to countries devastated by plagues, famine, or other natural disasters. Red Cross and Red Crescent will step up activities in such areas as natural-disaster relief and blood programs.

• Cooperation will develop among intelligence agencies from different countries (e.g., Interpol, the CIA, and the KGB) in order to monitor terrorism and control antiterrorism programs and to coordinate crime fighting worldwide.

49. International bodies will take over much of the peacekeeping role now being abandoned by the superpowers. The Conference on Security and Cooperation in Europe (CSCE) — a group of 35 nations (including the United States and the Soviet Union) — will pick up where NATO and the Warsaw Pact left off by creating a pan-European security structure.

• CSCE will transform the diplomatic process into an institution.

• The methods of operation for voting on CSCE matters will likely be revised (currently, each of the member nations holds veto power).

50. The field of public diplomacy will grow, spurred by advances in communication and by the increased importance and power of international organizations.

Take a Trip into the Future on the

ELECTRONIC SUPERHIGHWAY

A new world of video entertainment and interactive services is coming to your home—sooner than you think

Philip Elmer-Dewitt

Everybody knows what the telephone is for. It rings. You pick it up. A voice travels down a wire and gets routed and switched right to your ear.

Everybody knows what to do with the television. You turn it on, choose a channel and let advertising, news and entertainment flow into your home.

Now imagine a medium that combines the switching and routing capabilities of phones with the video and information offerings of the most advanced cable systems and data banks. Instead of settling for whatever happens to be on at a particular time, you could select any item from an encyclopedic menu of offerings and have it routed directly to your television set or computer screen. A movie? Airline listings? Tomorrow's newspaper or yesterday's episode of *Northern Exposure?* How about a new magazine or book? A stroll through the L. L. Bean catalog? A teleconference with your boss? A video phone call with your lover? Just punch up what you want, and it appears just when you want it.

Welcome to the information highway. It's not here yet, but it's arriving sooner than you might think. Already the major cable operators and telephone companies are competing—and collaborating—to bring this communicopia to your neighborhood, while the Clinton Administration is scrambling to see how the government can join in the fun.

Driving this explosive merger of video, telephones and computers are some rather simple technological advances:
► The ability to translate all audio and video communications into digital information
► New methods of storing this digitized data and compressing them so they can travel through existing phone and cable lines.
► Fiber-optic wiring that provides a virtually limitless transmission pipeline.
► New switching techniques and other breakthroughs that make it possible to bring all this to neighborhoods without necessarily rewiring every home.

Suddenly the brave new world of video phones and smart TVs that futurists have been predicting for decades is not years away but months. The final bottleneck—the "last mile" of wiring that takes information from the digital highway to the home—has been broken, and a blue-chip corporate lineup has launched pilot projects that could be rolled out to most of the country within the next six or seven years. Now the only questions are whether the public wants it and how much it is willing to pay.

We won't have to wait long to find out. By this time next year, vast new video services will be available, at a price, to millions of Americans in all 50 states. Next spring Hughes Communications will introduce DirecTv, a satellite system that delivers 150 channels of television through a $700 rooftop dish the size of a large pizza pie. At about the same time, Tele-Communications, Inc. (TCI), the world's biggest cable-TV operator, will begin marketing a new cable decoder that can deliver as many as 540 channels; next week it will announce plans to provide this service to 100 cities within the first year. Time Warner (the parent company of this magazine) is up and running with a 150-channel system in Queens, New York, and early next year will launch an interactive service that will provide video and information on demand to 4,000 subscribers in Orlando, Florida.

The prospect of multiplying today's TV listings has launched a furious debate over what a fragmented and TV-anesthetized society will do with 100—or 500—offerings. Will scores of narrowcast channels devoted to arcana like needlepointing or fly fishing fracture whatever remains of a mass culture, leaving Americans with little common ground for discourse? Or will the slots be given over to endless rebroadcasts of a handful of hit movies and TV shows—raising the nightmarish specter of

the Terminator saying "I'll be back" every few minutes, day in and day out?

But to focus on the number of channels in a TV system is to miss the point of where the revolution is headed. When the information highway comes to town, channels and nightly schedules will begin to fade away and could eventually disappear. In this postchannel world, more and more of what one wants to see will be delivered on demand by a local supplier (either a cable system, a phone company or a joint venture) from giant computer disks called file servers. These might store hundreds of movies, the current week's broadcast programming and all manner of video publications, catalogs, data files and interactive entertainment. Remote facilities, located in Burbank, California, or Hollywood or Atlanta or anywhere, will hold additional offerings from HBO and Showtime, as well as archived hits from the past: *I Love Lucy, Star Trek, The Brady Bunch.* Click an item on the menu, and it will appear instantly on the screen.

This is the type of system that most of the top cable companies—including TCI, Time Warner, Viacom and Cablevision—hope to build within the next year or two, at least on a demonstration basis. Many of the regional Bell operating companies (the so-called Baby Bells) are trying to create their own interactive networks, either by themselves or in partnership with cable companies. Bell Atlantic is scheduled to begin offering video on demand to 300 homes in northern Virginia this summer. U.S. West has announced plans to deploy enough fiber-optic lines and coaxial cable (the pencil-thick wire used by cable systems) across 14 states to deliver "video dial tones" to 13 million households starting next year.

Once the storage and switching systems are in place, all sorts of interactive services become possible. The same switches used to send a TV show to your home can also be used to send a video from your home to any other—paving the way for video phones that will be as ubiquitous and easy to use as TV. The same system will allow anybody with a camcorder to distribute videos to the world—a development that could open the floodgates to a wave of new filmmaking talent or a deluge of truly awful home movies.

TODAY'S HOME SHOPPING NETworks could blossom into video malls stocked with the latest from Victoria's Secret, Toys "R" Us and the Gap. Armchair shoppers could browse with their remote controls, see video displays of the products that interest them, and charge these items on their credit cards with the press of a button—a convenience that will empower some folks and surely bankrupt others.

In the era of interactive TV, the lines between advertisements, entertainment and services may grow fuzzy. A slick demonstration put together by programmers at Microsoft shows how that might be so. The presentation opens with a Seattle Mariners baseball game. By clicking a button on a mouse or remote control, a viewer can bring up a menu of options (displayed as buttons on the screen). Click on one, and the image of the batter at the plate shrinks to make room for the score and the player's stats—RBIs, home runs and batting average—updated with every pitch. Click again, and you see the Mariners' home schedule. Click yet again, and a diagram of the Kingdome pops up, showing available seats and pricing. Click one more time, and you have ordered a pair of field box seats on the first-base side (and reduced your credit-card balance by about $25).

This is the vision that has the best minds from Madison Avenue to Silicon Valley scrambling for position at the starting gate. The telephone companies, with their switching networks already in place, want to build the superhighway and control what travels over it. The cable-TV companies, with their coaxial systems, think they should own the right-of-way. Computer companies such as IBM, Hewlett-Packard and Sun want to build the huge file servers that will act as video and information libraries. Such software companies as Microsoft and Apple want to build the operating systems that will serve as the data highway's traffic cops, controlling the flow of information to and from each viewer's screen. Meanwhile, *TV Guide* is racing against InSight, TV Answer and Discovery Communications to design electronic navigators that will tell viewers what's on TV and where to find it.

"Make no mistake about it," says Vice President Al Gore, who was talking about information highways long before they were fashionable. "This is by all odds the most

important and lucrative marketplace of the 21st century." If Gore is right, the new technology will force the merger of television, telecommunications, computers, consumer electronics, publishing and information services into a single interactive information industry. Apple Computer chairman John Sculley estimates that the revenue generated by this megaindustry could reach $3.5 trillion worldwide by the year 2001. (The entire U.S. gross national product today is about $5.9 trillion.)

During the 1992 presidential campaign, Clinton and Gore made building a "data superhighway" a centerpiece of their program to revitalize the U.S. economy, comparing it with the government's role in creating the interstate highway system in the 1950s. The budget proposal the Administration submitted in February includes nearly $5 billion over the next four years to develop new software and equipment for the information highway.

Private industry, fearful of government involvement and eager to lay claim to pieces of the game, has been moving quickly in the past few months to seize the initiative. GTE, the largest independent telephone company, has already built a system in Cerritos, California, that lets customers pay bills, play games, read children's stories and make airline reservations through the same wire that brings them basic cable television and 30 pay-per-view channels. Three hundred fifty miles north, in Castro Valley, Viacom, the purveyor of MTV and Nickelodeon, is building a similar system to test consumer reaction to the new services.

Some of the projects *seem* more impressive than they are. TCI customers in the suburbs of Denver already have what looks like true video on demand. By pointing a remote control at the TV set, they can select from among 2,000 offerings (from *Hook* to old Marx Brothers movies to last night's MacNeil Lehrer NewsHour) and have their choices appear on screen whenever they want them, any time, day or night. But behind the high-tech service is an almost laughably low-tech delivery system. When a customer presses the Enter button, a bell goes off in a three-story building a few miles away, alerting a TCI attendant that he has five minutes to run to the video library, grab the proper tape and slot it into one of a bank of VCRs.

TCI's Denver setup reveals the weakness behind a lot of the information-super-highway hype: for all their posturing, neither the phone companies nor the cable-TV operators are quite ready to build a fully interactive and automated data highway that stretches from coast to coast. But thanks to a number of technical innovations, they are getting awfully close.

The key to the entire enterprise is fiber. Fiber-optic cable, made up of hair-thin strands of glass so pure you could see

through a window of it that was 70 miles thick, is the most perfect transmitter of information ever invented. A single strand of fiber could, in theory, carry the entire nation's radio and telephone traffic and still have room for more. As it is deployed today, fiber uses less than 1% of its theoretical capacity, or bandwidth, as it's called in the trade. Even so, it can carry 250,000 times as much data as a standard copper telephone wire—or, to put it another way, it can transmit the contents of the entire *Encyclopedia Britannica* every second.

In the mid-1980s, AT&T, MCI and Sprint installed fiber-optic cable between major U.S. cities to increase the capacity of their long-distance telephone lines. At about the same time, the Federal Government, spurred by Gore, leased some of these lines to give scientists a high-speed data link to supercomputers funded by the National Science Foundation. These two networks, private and public, carry the bulk of the country's telephone and data traffic. In the superhighway system of the future, they are the interstate turnpikes.

The problem comes when you get off the turnpike onto the roadways owned by local phone companies and cable-TV operators. Some of these are being converted to high-bandwidth fiber optic. But at the end of almost every local system—the "last mile" that goes from the local-service provider to the house—you run into the electronic equivalent of a bumpy country road. In the phone system, the bottleneck is that last bit of copper wiring, which seems far too narrow to admit the profusion of TV signals poised to flow through it. In cable TV, the roadblocks are the long cascades of amplifiers that run from the company's transmission headquarters to the home, boosting the signal every quarter-mile or so. These amplifiers are notoriously unreliable and generate so much electronic noise that two-way traffic in a cable-TV system is all but impossible.

It has long been assumed that nothing was going to change much in telecommunications or television until fiber was brought all the way to the home, a Herculean task that was expected to cost $200 billion to $400 billion and take more than 20 years to complete. The breakthrough that is bringing the info highway home much sooner than expected is the discovery, by both the phone companies and the cable industry, that it is possible to get around the bottlenecks in their respective last miles without replacing the entire system.

For the cable-TV companies, the key insight came in the fall of 1987, when cable engineers demonstrated that coaxial wire could carry information quite effectively over short distances; in fact, for a quarter-mile or so, it has almost as much bandwidth as fiber. They pointed out that by using fiber to bring the signal to within a few blocks of each home and coaxial cable to carry it the rest of the way, the cable companies could get a "twofer": they could throw away those cranky amplifiers (giving them a system that has more capacity and is easier to maintain) and get two-way interactivity almost cost-free.

For the phone companies, the breakthrough came three years ago when scientists at Bellcore, the research arm of the Baby Bells, found a way to do what everybody had assumed was impossible: squeeze a video signal through a telephone wire. The technology, known as asymmetric digital subscriber line, has some drawbacks. It cannot handle live transmissions, and the picture it produces is not as clear as that provided by a well-tuned cable hookup—never mind the high-definition TV signals expected to come on line before the end of the decade. Bellcore researchers say they have already improved the quality of the picture and that with further compression they may be able to accommodate several channels of live video.

THE GOVERNMENT IS THE DARK horse in the race to the information highway. It got into the business almost by accident: thanks to Gore's lobbying during the 1980s, it funded the fiber-optic links that form the backbone of Internet, the sprawling computer grid that is for students, scientists and the Pentagon what Prodigy and CompuServe are for ordinary computer users. Today Internet has grown into the world's largest computer bulletin board and data bank, home to 10 million to 15 million networkers who use it for many of the purposes the information highway might serve: sending and receiving mail, sharing gossip and research results, searching for information in hard-to-reach libraries, playing games with opponents in other cities, even exchanging digitized sounds, photographs and movie clips.

During the 1992 campaign, Clinton and Gore repeated the information-highway metaphor so often that many voters—and industry leaders—were left with the impression that the government actually planned to build it, to use taxpayer dollars to construct a data freeway that anybody could ride. But the spending proposals released after the election make it clear that the Administration's goals are more modest. Of the $5 billion requested for the next four years, nearly $3 billion would be spent building supercomputers. Most of the rest would be set aside for developing techniques for transmitting different kinds of data over the networks—such as CAT scans and engineering blueprints—

and on pilot projects to give schools, hospitals, libraries and other nonprofit institutions access to Internet.

The government is more likely to play a critical role in cutting through the thicket of state and federal regulations that have grown up over the years to keep the local telephone and cable-TV monopolies out of each other's business. White House officials say they want to give the private sector incentives to invest in the data highways. At the same time, however, they insist on preserving features of the current system that voters value, such as universal access to affordable phone and television service and protection against price gouging.

In a speech in New York City two weeks ago, acting Federal Communications Commission Chairman James Quello cautioned industry executives against making all television pay per view. Free TV, he warned, "is essential to a well-informed citizenry and electorate in a democracy." As if to punctuate his remarks, the FCC last week voted to cut the cost of most cable-TV services 10% and to make it harder for operators to raise rates in the future. The commission also issued a ruling in an ongoing dispute between the TV networks and the Hollywood studios, relaxing restrictions that have prevented the networks from owning shows and sharing in the lucrative rerun market. As new ways of packaging and delivering these shows emerge, skirmishes over copyrights and program ownership are likely to become increasily bitter and complex.

What shape the highway takes will depend to some extent on who ends up building it. The cable companies tend to think in terms of entertaining mass audiences. Their emphasis is on expanded channels, video on demand and video-shopping networks. They admit the possibility of more special-interest programming—such as MTV, the Discovery Channel and Black Entertainment Television—but only if they can be convinced that the demographics are sufficiently attractive.

The phone companies, with their background in point-to-point switching, tend to focus on connectivity and anything that will rack up message units. They emphasize services that will generate a lot of two-way traffic, such as video phones, video conferencing and long-distance access to libraries.

The computer users, and some enthusiasts within the Clinton Administration, tend to see the information highway as a glorified extension of computer bulletin boards. Vice President Gore talks about making it possible for a schoolchild in Arkansas to have access to a book stored on a computer in the Library of Congress or

take a course at a distant college. Mitch Kapor, co-founder of a computer watchdog group called the Electronic Frontier Foundation, wants the superhighway to do for video what computer bulletin boards did for print—make it easy for everyone to publish ideas to an audience eager to respond in kind. He envisions a nation of leisure-time video broadcasters, each posting his creations on a huge nationwide video bulletin board.

The technology makes all these things possible. It's easy to imagine families exchanging video Christmas cards. Or high school students shopping for a college by exploring each campus interactive video. Or elementary schools making videos of the school play available to every parent who missed it.

It's even easier to picture the information highway being exploited to make a lot of money. The powers that be in entertainment and programming have their eyes on the $4 billion spent each year on video games, the $12 billion on video rentals, the $65 billion on residential telephone service, the $70 billion on catalog shopping. They are eager to find out how much customers will shell out to see last night's *Seinfeld* or the latest Spielberg. They are exploring the market for addictive video games and trying to figure out how much they can charge for each minute of play. It won't be long before someone begins using video phones for the multimedia equivalent of "dial-a-porn" telephone-sex lines. All these services can be delivered easily and efficiently by the information highway, and they can be backed up by a threat with real teeth. As TCI chairman John Malone puts it, "If you don't pay your bill, we'll turn off your television."

In the end, how the highway develops and what sort of traffic it bears will depend to a large extent on consumers. As the system unfolds, the companies supplying hardware and programming will be watching to see which services early users favor. If they watch a lot of news, documentaries and special-interest programming, those offerings will expand. If video on demand is a huge money-maker, that is what will grow. If video bulletin boards—or teleconferencing, or interactive Yellow Pages, or electronic town meetings—are hot, those services too will thrive and spread.

We will in effect be voting with our remote controls. If we don't like what we see—or if the tolls are too high—the electronic superhighway could lead to a dead end. Or it could offer us more—much more—of what we already have. Just as likely, it could veer off in surprising directions and take us places we've never imagined.   —*With reporting by*
David S. Jackson/Denver

THE WORLD'S
Throw-away
CHILDREN

Germaine W. Shames

• *Germaine W. Shames, a free-lance writer based in Newton, New Jersey, U.S.A., has traveled extensively and reported on a variety of subjects.*

It is personally unacceptable, ethically unthinkable, that on the eve of the 21st century, children and youth by the tens of millions should have to call the streets their homes."

—JAMES GRANT
Executive Director,
UNICEF

You see them in nearly every major city, shining shoes, selling chewing gum, minding parked cars, begging, picking through the garbage . . . surviving. Powerless to demand their rights though they number in the tens of millions, easy prey to drug dealers and pimps, gang leaders and child molesters, they live by their wits, gradually becoming as hardened as the streets from which they take their name.

Street children. Children forced by hunger, neglect, abuse, or orphaning to live and work on city streets.

Nazir, 14, lives at the railway station in New Delhi, his "home" since age five. He earns ten rupees a day by carrying suitcases. Fleeing famine in Nepal, Nazir's father brought him by train to India—then abandoned him.

Mario, 13 and small for his age, cleans windshields on a busy street corner in Tegucigalpa, Honduras. On a good day he pockets 10 to 12 lempiras, half of which he turns over to a gang leader. With the rest he buys soda and a small hit of Resistol (glue), which he inhales, he says, because it helps him forget how hungry he is.

Kham Suk, a delicate girl with fathomless eyes, hovers in the doorway of a Bangkok brothel in Thailand. Three months ago, on her 12th birthday, her mother walked her across the border from Myanmar (Burma), and sold her to a pimp for 2,000 baht.

"Everywhere, from the slums of São Paulo to the squats of Moscow, the

This homeless boy in Brazil uses all his wiles to survive on the streets. Many become prostitutes and drug addicts.

stories of street children are strikingly similar," says Marilyn Rocky, North American director of Childhope, an international organization dedicated to helping these children. "The reasons they're on the street are the same, the conditions under which they live are the same—and so are the dead-end futures they face if they don't receive help."

Childhope estimates that the number of street children worldwide exceeds 100 million. The largest numbers are found in Latin America, Asia, and Africa. But they are increasingly present in industrialized countries, gravitating to such cities as New York, Toronto, Paris, Berlin, Barcelona, London, Rome, Moscow, Bucharest . . . anywhere "socioeconomic conditions fail to guarantee basic rights," asserts the Save the Children Alliance.

Street children are the mute testimony of economic recession, increasing poverty, the break-up of traditional life, family disruption, and the inability—or unwillingness—of governments to respond. Because street children exist in greatest numbers in the most troubled societies, their needs often go unattended.

A Moscow policeman expressed their plight graphically: "The presence of thousands of children on the streets is like a cut finger in a country whose guts are spilling out."

7. VALUES AND VISIONS

Unfed and unprotected, denied access to education and health care, such children are virtual slaves to survival, and are easily exploited.

During a recent visit to Rio de Janeiro, Brazil, James Grant, executive director of the United Nations Children's Fund (UNICEF), stopped to talk with a group of children who were sleeping on the street. They confided to him their fears of being robbed, beaten, sexually abused, picked up by police, and killed. Sadly, their fears are well founded.

Grant says, "Street youth's situation at the margins of society effectively strips them of the rights most children are able to enjoy. They face multiple risks and dangers inherent to being on the streets at such vulnerable ages, risks that come with being poorly fed and poorly educated."

The threats are ubiquitous. In parts of Asia, perfectly healthy children are maimed and sent out to beg, revealed *The Christian Science Monitor* in its chilling report on "Children in Darkness." More recently, the *Sunday Times* of India brought to light the ordeal of children used to push drugs, "with even infants being operated on and inserted with heroin packets."

Child traffickers lure many children into prostitution and pornography, often with the complicity of parents and other adult family members. There are an estimated one half million prostitutes under the age of 20 in Brazil, 75,000 in the Philippines, and 200,000 in the United States. Sex tourism continues to thrive in Asia, despite the threat of AIDS.

Predictably, the incidence of HIV and AIDS is on the rise among street children. Although data is limited, studies in São Paulo and Rio de Janeiro, Brazil; Khartoum, Sudan; and New York City, U.S.A., show HIV positive rates of between two and 10 percent for street youth.

One Guatemalan street youth spoke for many when he said, "Why should I care about AIDS? If I get infected today, I may die in seven years. So what? I could die tomorrow just from being on the street."

Drug dealers tempt young survivors with an escape from the grim realities of their lives, only to entangle them in the even grimmer

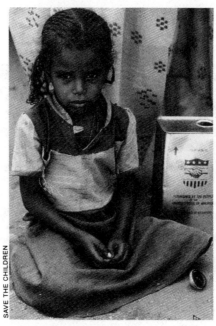

In Africa, an increasing number of children are becoming orphans as their parents die from AIDS.

web of addiction. The majority of street children in developing countries use inhalants, including industrial glue, paint thinners, and other solvents. (A week's supply of glue costs 75 cents in Honduras, far less than the cost of maintaining a regular diet.) Regular users pay dearly for this fleeting euphoria: Medical consequences include irreversible damage to the brain and kidneys.

Moreover, drug use by street children exposes them to a "drug culture" rife with violence. "The drug traffickers made their own private armies out of the youth of this city, teaching them how to steal, kidnap, and murder," says Omar Flórez Vélez, mayor of Medellín, Colombia.

What Vélez fails to mention is the corresponding surge of violence by police and vigilante squads, of which street children have been a primary target. In February 1991, Childhope issued a report claiming "in Guatemala and Brazil there is mounting evidence that police and private security forces—including death squads—are executing street children and other youth from low-income neighborhoods in the name of crime prevention."

In November 1991, *Omni* magazine reported, "Eyewitnesses confirm that

Guatemala's *niños de la calle* (children of the street) are being subjected to a spree of tortures matched only by the Holy Inquisition."

The stigma of drug abuse and delinquency has complicated efforts to win public support for policies and programs aimed at alleviating the plight of working children. In the minds of many, these children have become "the problem."

"They are seen as trash, to be swept up and thrown away," says Thereza Mauro, a social worker in Rio.

The problem of homeless children is also becoming increasingly common in the former Soviet Union, as people scramble to fend for themselves in a society in disarray.

There are an estimated 15,000 children on the streets of Moscow and another 10,000 in St. Petersburg. Casualties of the upheaval in Soviet society, they have no clear value system, and no object in life other than survival.

"With foreigners pouring into the cities, the streets are filled with children begging or hawking," says Marilyn Rocky of Childhope, recently back from a fact-finding mission to the region. Because the phenomenon of children living on the streets is so recent here, government officials, social scientists, and child-welfare workers find themselves without a conceptual framework with which to discuss the problem—let alone resolve it.

Childhope suggests the term "disconnected children" to describe their alienation and aimlessness. Yet there is no consensus on how best to reconnect them, or how to solve such a complex problem.

In the meantime, authorities continue to treat street youth as runaways, delinquents, or—worse—mentally handicapped.

The founder of one of St. Petersburg's refuges, himself a former street child, laments, "The militia mentally crushes the children like a tank."

Such disparagement by the rest of society contributes to the low self-esteem of street children, despite their considerable achievements in surmounting difficulties that even most adults would find daunting.

"Street children try to survive with intelligence and skill in very difficult circumstances," says Stefan Vanisten-

230

Homeless children in Guatemala seek refuge in crowded, unsanitary shanty villages.

Many homeless children, like these in Brazil, sniff glue to deaden their pain.

dael, a child advocate on the board of Childhope who has worked with street children for more than a decade. "Some people may find them a nuisance, but street children may find adults a nuisance."

Despite the immensity of the problem, many people at the national and local level are trying to help. In addition, private voluntary organizations (including Rotary) are reaching out to street youth, quelling their hunger pangs, offering a respite from the struggle for survival, and daring them to imagine a brighter future.

Rotarians have taken an active interest in the welfare of street children. Clubs in the U.S., Japan, and Germany were among the charter donors to the Russian Children's Fund, one of the first nongovernment charities in the former Soviet Union. Rotary contributions enable the fund to provide medical assistance to severely ill and disfigured orphans and street children.

The Rotary clubs of Tempe, Arizona, U.S.A., and Cuernavaca, Mexico, joined efforts to establish a local orphanage. A Health, Hunger, and Humanity (3-H) Grant from The Rotary Foundation of R.I. provided equipment for the orphanage's vocational workshops and established a loan program, making it possible for hundreds of disadvantaged youth to learn a trade and manage their own small businesses.

Children of the Americas, an organization serving the "gamines" (homeless children) of Colombia and Santo Domingo, Dominican Republic, found itself at a critical juncture when local authorities shut down its medical clinic. The Rotary Club of Santo Domingo provided a new Land Rover, which was converted into a mobile medical facility. This clinic-on-wheels provides care to the San Salvador Orphanage, another Rotary project.

In Thailand, Rotarians in the resort city of Pattaya support an orphanage run by a Chicago priest, Father Ray Brennan (a former Rotarian). He had intended to stay only a few years in Thailand, but he couldn't walk away from the children who needed him so badly. Today, "his children"—once beggars, prostitutes, or disabled outcasts—receive vocational training, medical care, and love. Most of them are eventually adopted by families.

Another priest, father William Wasson—or Padre Bill, as his children call him—is the founder of *Nuestros Pequeños Hermanos*, a growing network of homes for orphaned boys and girls in Mexico, Honduras, and Haiti. His mission started inadvertently when he was asked to testify against a Mexican street child who had robbed the church poor box in order to eat. The priest requested and received custody of the boy. A week later he adopted eight more homeless boys and, by the end of the first year, was "father" to 32. Within a decade his family had grown to 400, and in two decades to over 1,000. To date, the homes have taken in 10,000 children.

In the slum areas of Nairobi, Kenya, the Undugu Society offers street children shelter, health education, and the opportunity to learn a trade alongside local artisans. Save The Children Federation funds a street project in Addis Ababa, Ethiopia, which prepares children for vocational training and oversees a credit union for those who wish to start small businesses.

In Colombia, the Bosconia program in Bogotá gives street youth an even start in life through education, community activism, and in cooperation with the American Field Service (AFS) student exchange. At the Nukkad Center (*nukkad* means "street corner" in Hindi) above New Delhi's railway station, children meditate, study, and manage their first savings accounts.

Every night on the darkest and most dangerous streets of major cities across the United States, Covenant House outreach counselors comfort young people with food and shelter; once the children's immediate needs are provided for, ongoing programs offer them a second chance in life through counseling, mentoring, and vocational training.

Unfortunately these organizations, for all their good intentions and hard-won support, cannot reach out to all street children. For every child who is helped, a hundred are left, hungry and vulnerable, to their own devices.

How can an individual fail to be moved by the sight of 10-and 12-year-olds begging on street corners, sleeping in subways? Yet so enormous is the problem, so daunting, even the most charitable person may be tempted to take the path of inaction.

Father Wasson, founder of Nuestros Pequeños Hermanos, recalls passing by a badly disfigured boy on a hot, dusty street of San Pedro Sula in Honduras.

"I hated to look at him at first, so grotesque did he look because of his eyes, which had been badly damaged and scarred when another boy wrapped barbed wire around his head."

The priest looked away and kept walking. He had gone a block before he was seized by regret and realized

How you can help

You can contact the following organizations for information on how to help street children in various regions:

Save The Children
54 Wilton Road
Westport, CT 06881 USA
Works with communities in Africa, Asia, Latin America, the Middle East, and the United States to make lasting, positive changes in the lives of disadvantaged children.

Nuestros Pequeños Hermanos
Apartado Postal 30-500
México 4, D.F.
Mexico 06470
Homes for orphaned boys and girls in Mexico, Honduras, and Haiti.

Foundation for Children
1492/3 Banglumpoo Lang
Careon-Nakorn Road
Klongsarn
Bangkok, Thailand 10600
Protects childrens' rights.

Childhope
333 East 38th Street
New York, NY 10016 USA
International movement on behalf of street children.

UNICEF
(United Nations Children's Fund)
UNICEF House
3 UN Plaza
New York, NY 10017
UN agency with key role in safeguarding the world's children through advocacy and education.

Save The Children Federation's Street Children Project
P.O. Box 387
Addis Ababa, Ethiopia
Offers comprehensive health, educational, and vocational services to street children to help them attain self-sufficiency.

Children of the Americas
Apartado Postal 2466
Santo Domingo,
Dominican Republic
Offers medical assistance, health talks, and hope to the "gamines" of Bogotá and Santo Domingo.

Covenant House
346 W. 17th St.
New York, NY 10011
Serves needy children in the U.S. and Central America through outreach, crisis intervention, vocational guidance, and aftercare.

World Learning, Inc.
Kipling Road
P.O. Box 676
Brattleboro, VT 05302
Through its Projects in International Training and Development office, sponsors various programs that benefit street children, with particular attention to child prostitutes and AIDS orphans.

he could not turn his back on the child.

"I had been walking past things all my life," he said. "I had to go back."

All it takes is one person to go back—to care enough to save the life of a child.

WOMEN'S ROLE IN POST-INDUSTRIAL DEMOCRACY

Eleanora Masini Barbieri

Italian sociologist, is the Director of the Executive Board of the World Futures Studies Federation and holds the Chair of Social Forecasting at the Gregorian University in Rome. Among her works published in English is Visions of Desirable Societies *(1983).*

ACCORDING to the American sociologist Elise Boulding, there are three areas in which the work of women has built what she calls a "civic society" based on mutual respect. The first is related to children and teaching. In almost all societies, women are responsible for the education of children up to their seventh year. Psychologists agree that these are the years in which the child's world-vision is formed.

The second is related to women's hidden economic role. Its arena may be the kitchen or the garden, the small production unit which played a crucial role in agricultural societies and has also often been, though less visibly, the salvation of the highly-industrialized societies of our time.

The third area has also been largely unnoticed. Women are and have been what Elise Boulding calls the "cement of society". They have fulfilled this role in private, in family life, and even in dynastic alliances between villages or towns over the centuries.

Boulding has described these areas, which belong to the "underside of history", as "society's green space, its visioning space, its bonding space. It is a space where minds can learn to grapple with complexities that are destroying the overside."

Women's efforts to build a viable society of respect and understanding also contribute to the creation of a democratic culture. Children learn respect, tolerance, and other principles of democratic behaviour at a very early stage, in their relations with other members of the family and the community. In this context, it is interesting to observe and compare the attitudes of families in different parts of the world: the strong community sense of the hierarchically organized extended family in Africa, the profound respect with which the elder members of the Chinese family are regarded, and the focus on younger family members in modern Western society. Women play a central role in the shaping of these attitudes through the way they behave and the example they set. It is because their public role has been invisible that they have learned respect for others—a respect that encourages democratic behaviour rather than the dominating behaviour often expected of men. Respect does not, however, mean accepting domination by others; it is coupled with the demand that women be respected in their turn.

Many examples could be cited of women's civic spirit. Polish women contributed to the rebuilding of Warsaw's schools after the Second World War; Japanese women organized support systems after Hiroshima, as did the women of Mexico after the 1984 earthquake.

The concept of the democratic society developed in the industrial era. Today, industrial society appears to have reached its limits. The natural environment has been exploited, especially by the rich countries, in a way that certainly cannot be called democratic. Nor have people found happiness in material wealth, as is clearly evident among the young people of the wealthier countries of North America and Europe. We have reached both external and internal limits, to use a phrase coined by Aurelio Peccei, the founder of the Club of Rome. Our inner selves require answers that are far more profound than those industrial society has provided. In post-industrial society, whatever form it takes, a new mentality will be essential. We must use the many capacities of people, and especially the specific capacities of women, that are now untapped.

WOMEN CITIZENS OF TOMORROW

Post-industrial society will be a complex, uncertain society, in which such tools and methods of industrial society as specialization, separation of tasks, hierarchical structures, and mass production will no longer be relevant. Notable among its features will be decentralized networks of small units, diversified activities peformed by the same person or unit, and rapidity of action.

The society of the future will require people to be flexible. They will have to perform several tasks at the same time. They will need to possess a new sense of time. Production will be "personalized" rather than "standardized". As technology develops, people will have to learn new tasks and skills during their working lives, and in many cases to change jobs to keep pace with technological change.

In this society women are bound to play an increasingly important role, if only because in almost every country they have a higher life expectancy than men and head one-third of the world's households. The future of many major technological innovations, especially in biotechnology, will depend on whether women accept or reject them.

Women possess many of the capacities that will be needed in post-industrial society. Research in various countries has shown that

they are particularly flexible and adaptable. Since their life-cycle forces them to stop and start work, often changing jobs, they are used to change. They have to be versatile. In addition to cooking, looking after the children, ironing and doing other household tasks, they may also have a job to do at home—sewing, perhaps, in developing countries, computer work in the industrialized world.

Women also tend to have a temporal rhythm which is closer to real time than to what Lewis Mumford called "clock time". This capacity too will be increasingly important in an overcrowded, unsynchronized society. Women find it difficult to standardize their production. In the society of the future, non-standardized production will become increasingly sought-after.

UNTAPPED POTENTIAL

In social life too, women seem to have capacities which will be important for the future—the capacity to create solidarity, to establish priorities, and to reject hierarchies.

Traditionally women have sought group solidarity. They exchange information about their children, their old people, matters of health and so on, as they collect water from the village well and as they meet in the supermarket. Whatever changes technology may bring, women will be unlikely to give up this exchange with each other. At moments of great distress—in time of war, revolution, natural catastrophe, during refugee movements—this capacity has been vital. The capacity of women to create solidarities and to understand and live with people from different cultures and backgrounds can make an enormous contribution to the building of a democratic culture.

Women have a strong sense of priorities. In times of need or stress, they make choices relating to their children and their future well-being, rather than to short-term benefits. In China, Canada, and in other countries with a large migrant population, research has shown that mothers faced with a range of choices put their children's education first. In developing countries, women's first priority might be water or food for their children rather than other economic benefits. There is also evidence that women are less inclined to accept hierarchical structures than men. This is important if, as the American futurologist Alvin Toffler believes, we are moving towards an increasingly egalitarian society.

Solidarity, the capacity to put first things first, and the rejection of hierarchies are traits that, if fostered rather than suppressed, may lead to a more democratic society, one that emerges from the behaviour of its citizens rather than from structures and laws.

If one accepts that the building of a democratic society depends more on citizens than on laws, institutions and structures, then women will have an essential contribution to make. And full use has not yet been made of their capacities.

We should be seeking to create democratic citizens, with the school working hand in hand with the family to foster democratic education. Although much has been accomplished already, much still remains to be done. The education system has undoubtedly changed for the better since the late 1960s, but in some countries there is plenty of room for improvement.

A democratic culture emerges from the sharing of values, however differently expressed, and from behaviour related to shared values. Only thus can a culture be built. There can be no democratic society without democratic citizens to construct it. Citizens rather than ideas, structures or institutions must be the starting-point.

The Post-Communist Nightmare

Václav Havel

President Havel gave the following speech on April 22, at George Washington University in Washington, DC, at a convocation honoring him with a presidential medal.

I remember a time when some of my friends and acquaintances used to go out of their way to avoid meeting me in the street. Though I certainly didn't intend it to be so, they saw me, in a way, as a voice of their conscience. They knew that if they stopped and talked with me, they would feel compelled to apologize for not openly defying the regime too, or to explain to me why they couldn't do it, or to defend themselves by claiming that dissent was pointless anyway. Conversations like this were usually quite an ordeal for both sides, and thus it was better to stay away from them altogether.

Another reason for their behavior was the fear that the police were following me, and that just talking to me would cause them complications. It was easier not to go near me. Thus they would avoid both an unpleasant conversation and the potential persecution that could follow. In short, I was, for those friends, an inconvenience, and inconveniences are best avoided.

For long decades, the chief nightmare of the democratic world was communism. Today—three years after it began to collapse like an avalanche—it would seem as though another nightmare has replaced it: postcommunism. There were many, not just in the West, but in the East as well, who had been looking forward for years to the fall of communism, and who had hoped that its collapse would mean that history had at last come to its senses. Today, these same people are seriously worried about the consequences of that fall. Some of

them may even feel a little nostalgic for a world that was, after all, slightly more transparent and understandable than the present one.

I do not share sentiments of that kind. I think we must not understand postcommunism merely as something that makes life difficult for the rest of the world. I certainly didn't understand communism that way. I saw it chiefly as a challenge, a challenge to thought and to action. To an even greater extent, postcommunism represents precisely that kind of challenge.

Anyone who understands a given historical phenomenon merely as an inconvenience will ultimately see many other things that way too: the warnings of ecologists, public opinion, the vagaries of voters, public morality. It is an easy, and therefore seductive, way of seeing the world and history. But it is extremely dangerous because we tend to remain aloof from things that inconvenience us and get in our way, just as some of my acquaintances avoided me during the Communist era. Any position based on the feeling that the world, or history, is merely an accumulation of inconveniences inevitably leads to a turning away from reality, and ultimately, to resigning oneself to it. It leads to appeasement, even to collaboration. The consequences of such a position may even be suicidal.

What in fact do we mean by postcommunism? Essentially it is a term for the state of affairs in all the countries that have rid themselves of communism. But it is a dangerous simplification to put all these countries in one basket. While it is true that they are all faced with essentially the same task—that is, to rid themselves of the disastrous legacy of communism, to

repair the damage it caused, and to create, or renew, democracy—at the same time, and for many reasons, there are great differences between them.

I will not go into all the problems encountered by post-Communist countries; experts are no doubt already writing books on the subject. I will mention only some of the root causes of the phenomena that are arousing the greatest concern in the democratic West, phenomena such as nationalism, xenophobia, and the poor moral and intellectual climate which—to a greater or lesser extent—go along with the creation of the new political and economic system.

The first of these causes I see in the fact that communism was far from being simply the dictatorship of one group of people over another. It was a genuinely totalitarian system, that is, it permeated every aspect of life and deformed everything it touched, including all the natural ways people had evolved of living together. It profoundly affected all forms of human behavior. For years, a specific structure of values and models of behavior was deliberately created in the consciousness of society. It was a perverted structure, one that went against all the natural tendencies of life, but society nevertheless internalized it, or rather was forced to internalize it.

When Communist power and its ideology collapsed, this structure collapsed along with it. But people couldn't simply absorb and internalize a new structure immediately, one that would correspond to the elementary principles of civic society and democracy. The human mind and human habits cannot be transformed overnight; to build a new system of living values and to identify with them takes time.

Address by President Václav Havel at George Washington University, April 22, 1993. Published in *The New York Review of Books* as "The Post-Communist Nightmare," May 27, 1993, pp. 8, 10. Reprinted by permission of Aurapont Literary Agency.

In a situation where one system has collapsed and a new one does not yet exist, many people feel empty and frustrated. This condition is fertile ground for radicalism of all kinds, for the hunt for scapegoats, and for the need to hide behind the anonymity of a group, be it socially or ethnically based. It encourages hatred of the world, self-affirmation at all costs, the feeling that everything is now permitted and the unparalleled flourishing of selfishness that goes along with it. It gives rise to the search for a common and easily identifiable enemy, to political extremism, to the most primitive cult of consumerism, to a carpetbagging morality, stimulated by the historically unprecedented restructuring of property relations, and so on and so on. Thanks to its former democratic traditions and to its unique intellectual and spiritual climate, the Czech Republic, the westernmost of the post-Communist countries, is relatively well off in this regard, compared with some of the other countries in the region. Nevertheless we too are going through the same great transformation that all the post-Communist countries are and we can therefore talk about it with the authority of insiders.

Another factor that must be considered in any analysis of post-Communist phenomena is the intrinsic tendency of communism to make everything the same. The greatest enemy of communism was always individuality, variety, difference—in a word, freedom. From Berlin to Vladivostok, the streets and buildings were decorated with the same red stars. Everywhere the same kind of celebratory parades were staged. Analogical state administrations were set up, along with the whole system of central direction for social and economic life. This vast shroud of uniformity, stifling all national, intellectual, spiritual, social, cultural, and religious variety, covered over any differences and created the monstrous illusion that we were all the same. The fall of communism destroyed this shroud of sameness, and the world was caught napping by an outburst of the many unanticipated differences concealed beneath it, each of which—after such a long time in the shadows—felt a natural need to draw attention to itself, to emphasize its uniqueness and its

difference from others. This is the reason for the eruption of so many different kinds of old-fashioned patriotism, revivalist messianism, conservatism, and expressions of hatred toward all those who appeared to be betraying their roots or identifying with different ones.

The desire to renew and emphasize one's identity, one's uniqueness, is also behind the emergence of many new countries. Nations that have never had states of their own feel an understandable need to experience independence. It is no fault of theirs that the opportunity has come up decades or even centuries after it came to other nations.

This is related to yet another matter: for a long time, communism brought history, and with it all natural development, to a halt. While the Western democracies have had decades to create a civil society, to build internationally integrated structures, and to learn the arts of peaceful international coexistence and cooperation, the countries ruled by communism could not go through this creative process. National and cultural differences were driven into the subterranean areas of social life, where they were kept on ice and thus prevented from developing freely, from taking on modern forms in the fresh air, from creating, over time, the free space of unity in variety.

At the same time many of the nations suppressed by communism had never enjoyed freedom, not even before communism's advent, and thus had not a chance to resolve many of the basic questions of their existence as countries. Consequently thousands of unsolved problems have now suddenly burst forth into the light of day, problems left unsolved by history, problems we had wrongly supposed were long forgotten. It is truly astonishing to discover how, after decades of falsified history and ideological manipulation, nothing has been forgotten. Nations are now remembering their ancient achievements and their ancient suffering, their ancient suppressors and their allies, their ancient statehood and their former borders, their traditional animosities and affinities—in short, they are suddenly recalling a history that, until recently, had been carefully concealed or misrepresented.

Thus in many parts of the so-called post-Communist world, it is not just

the regional order (sometimes referred to as the Yalta order) that is being corrected. There are also attempts to correct certain shortcomings in the Versailles order, and even to go farther back into history and exploit the greatest freedom some of them have ever had to make farther amends. It is an impossible desire, of course, but understandable all the same.

If we wish to understand the problems of the post-Communist world, or some of them at least, then we must continually remind ourselves of something else. It is easy to deny the latent problems, ambitions, and particularities of nations. It is easy to make everything the same by force, to destroy the complex and fragile social, cultural, and economic relationships and institutions built up over centuries, and to enforce a single, primitive model of central control in the spirit of a proud utopianism. It is as easy to do that as it is to smash a piece of antique, inlaid furniture with a single blow from a hammer. But it is infinitely more difficult to restore it all, or to create it directly.

The fall of the Communist empire is an event on the same scale of historical importance as the fall of the Roman empire. And it is having similar consequences, both good and extremely disturbing. It means a significant change in the countenance of today's world. The change is painful and will take a long time. To build a new world on the ruins of communism might be as extended and complex a process as the creation of a Christian Europe—after the great migrations—once was.

What are we to do if we don't wish to understand postcommunism simply as a new inconvenience that would be better avoided by sticking our heads in the sand and minding our own business?

I think the most important thing is not just to take account of external and more or less measurable phenomena like the gross national product, the progress of privatization, the stability of the political system, and the measurable degree to which human rights are observed. All of these things are important, of course, but something more is necessary. There must be an effort to understand the profound events taking place in the womb of post-Communist societies, to take note of their historical meaning and think about their global implications. The temptation must be resisted to adopt a disparaging and slightly astonished attitude, one based on a subconscious feeling of superiority on the part of observers who are better off. Just as Czechs should not sneer at the problems of Tadzhikistan, so no one should sneer at the problems of the Czech Republic. It is only against this background of understanding that meaningful ways of assistance can be sought.

It seems to me that the challenge offered by the post-Communist world is merely the current form of a broader and more profound challenge to discover a new type of self-understanding for man, and a new type of politics that should flow from that understanding. As we all know, today's planetary civilization is in serious danger. We are rationally capable of describing, in vivid detail, all the dangers that threaten the world: the deepening gulf between the rich and the poor parts of the world, the population explosion, the potential for dramatic confrontations between different racial and cultural groups, the arming of whom no one seems able to stop, the nuclear threat, the plundering of natural resources, the destruction of the natural variety of species, the creation of holes in the ozone layer, and the unstoppable global warming. What is unsettling is that the more we know about such dangers, the less able we seem to deal with them.

I see only one way out of this crisis: man must come to a new understanding of himself, of his limitations and his place in the world. He should grasp his responsibility in a new way, and reestablish a relationship with the things that transcend him. We must rehabilitate our sense of ourselves as active human subjects, and liberate ourselves from the captivity of a purely national perception of the world. Through this "subjecthood" and the individual conscience that goes with it, we must discover a new relationship to our neighbors, and to the universe and its metaphysical order, which is the source of the moral order.

We live in a world in which our destinies are tied to each other more closely than they ever have been before. It is a world with a single plane-

tary civilization, yet it contains many cultures that, with increasing vigor and singlemindedness resist cultural unification, reject mutual understanding, and exist in what amounts to latent confrontation. It is a deeply dangerous state of affairs and it must be changed. The first step in this direction can be nothing less than a broad-based attempt by people from these cultures to understand one another, and to understand each other's right to existence. Only then can a kind of worldwide, pluralistic metaculture...evolve. It is only in the context of such a metaculture that a new sense of political responsibility—global responsibility—can come into being. And it is only with this newly born sense of responsibility that the instruments can be created that will enable humanity to confront all the dangers it has created for itself.

The new political self-understanding I am talking about means a clear departure from the understanding of the world that considers history, foreign cultures, foreign nations, and ultimately all those warnings about our future, as a mere agglomeration of annoying inconveniences that disturb our tranquility. A quiet life on the peak of a volcano is just as illusory as the notion I talked about at the beginning: that by avoiding an encounter with a dissident in the street, we can avoid the problem of communism and the question of how to deal with it.

Ultimately, I understand postcommunism as one of many challenges to contemporary man—regardless of what part of the world he lives in—to awaken to his global responsibilities, and to awaken to them before it is too late.

This morning I had the honor of taking part in the opening of the Holocaust Memorial Museum.

On this occasion, as I have so often before, I asked myself how could this have happened? How could people in the twentieth century, aware of the theory of relativity, of quantum mechanics, who have penetrated to the heart of the atom and are exploring the reaches of outer space, have committed acts of horror so awful that to call them bestial would be to do an incredible disservice to all those creatures who happen not

to be human. How could they have permitted it to happen?

In the context of what I have been talking about here, one aspect of a possible answer occurs to me. It was a failure of democracy, in which the politics of appeasement gave way to evil: what in my country we call the spirit of Munich. The inability of Europe and the world to recognize the emerging evil in time and stop it from growing to monstrous proportions is merely another form of what I have called here an understanding of the world as an agglomeration of inconveniences. The issue here is the absence of a wider sense of responsibility for the world.

Czechs remember well a remark made by a democratic statesman shortly before he signed the Munich agreement, the real beginning of all the horrors of the Second World War. He was appalled, he said then, that his country was digging trenches and trying on gas masks "because of a quarrel in a faraway country between people of whom we know nothing." It is a classic example of how suicidal it is to try to avoid inconveniences. This politician regarded Nazism as a problem that would go away if he stuck his head in the sand, or as it were crossed over to the other side of the street.

And so the chosen people were chosen by history to bear the brunt for all of us. The meaning of their sacrifice is to warn us against indifference to things we foolishly believe do not concern us.

In today's world, everything concerns everyone. Communism also concerned everyone. And it is also a matter of concern to everyone whether or not, and in what way, we manage to build a new zone of democracy, freedom, and prosperity on its ruins. Every intellectual and material investment in the post-Communist world that is not haphazard, but based on a deep understanding of what is happening there, will repay the whole world many times over.

And not only that: it will also be one more step on the thorny pilgrimage of the human race toward a new understanding of its responsibility for its destiny.

—translated from the Czech
by Paul Wilson

The Global Village Finally Arrives

Pico Iyer

This is the typical day of a relatively typical soul in today's diversified world. I wake up to the sound of my Japanese clock radio, put on a T shirt sent me by an uncle in Nigeria and walk out into the street, past German cars, to my office. Around me are English-language students from Korea, Switzerland and Argentina—all on this Spanish-named road in this Mediterranean-style town. On TV, I find, the news is in Mandarin; today's baseball game is being broadcast in Korean. For lunch I can walk to a sushi bar, a tandoori palace, a Thai café or the newest burrito joint (run by an old Japanese lady). Who am I, I sometimes wonder, the son of Indian parents and a British citizen who spends much of his time in Japan (and is therefore—what else?—an American permanent resident)? And where am I?

I am, as it happens, in Southern California, in a quiet, relatively uninternational town, but I could as easily be in Vancouver or Sydney or London or Hong Kong. All the world's a rainbow coalition, more and more; the whole planet, you might say, is going global. When I fly to Toronto, or Paris, or Singapore, I disembark in a world as hyphenated as the one I left. More and more of the globe looks like America, but an America that is itself looking more and more like the rest of the globe. Los Angeles famously teaches 82 different languages in its schools. In this respect, the city seems only to bear out the old adage that what is in California today is in America tomorrow, and next week around the globe.

In ways that were hardly conceivable even a generation ago, the new world order is a version of the New World writ large: a wide-open frontier of polyglot terms and postnational trends. A common multiculturalism links us all—call it

Planet Hollywood, Planet Reebok or the United Colors of Benetton. *Taxi* and *hotel* and *disco* are universal terms now, but so too are *karaoke* and *yoga* and *pizza*. For the gourmet alone, there is *tiramisù* at the Burger King in Kyoto, echt angel-hair pasta in Saigon and enchiladas on every menu in Nepal.

But deeper than mere goods, it is souls that are mingling. In Brussels, a center of the new "unified Europe," 1 new baby in every 4 is Arab. Whole parts of the Paraguayan capital of Asunción are largely Korean. And when the prostitutes of Melbourne distributed some pro-condom pamphlets, one of the languages they used was Macedonian. Even Japan, which prides itself on its centuries-old socially engineered uniculture, swarms with Iranian illegals, Western executives, Pakistani laborers and Filipina hostesses.

The New World Order is a version of the New World writ large: a wide-open frontier of polyglot terms and post national trends

---

The global village is defined, as we know, by an international youth culture that takes its cues from American pop culture. Kids in Perth and Prague and New Delhi are all tuning in to *Santa Barbara* on TV, and wriggling into 501 jeans, while singing along to Madonna's latest in English. CNN (which has grown 70-fold in 13 years) now reaches more than 140 countries; an American football championship pits London against Barcelona. As fast as the world comes to America, America goes round the world—but it is an America that is itself multi-tongued and many hued, an America of

Amy Tan and Janet Jackson and movies with dialogue in Lakota.

For far more than goods and artifacts, the one great influence being broadcast around the world in greater numbers and at greater speed than ever before is people. What were once clear divisions are now tangles of crossed lines: there are 40,000 "Canadians" resident in Hong Kong, many of whose first language is Cantonese. And with people come customs: while new immigrants from Taiwan and Vietnam and India—some of the so-called Asian Calvinists—import all-American values of hard work and family closeness and entrepreneurial energy to America, America is sending its values of upward mobility and individualism and melting-pot hopefulness to Taipei and Saigon and Bombay.

Values, in fact, travel at the speed of fax; by now, almost half the world's Mormons live outside the U.S. A diversity of one culture quickly becomes a diversity of many: the "typical American" who goes to Japan today may be a third-generation Japanese American, or the son of a Japanese woman married to a California serviceman, or the offspring of a Salvadoran father and an Italian mother from San Francisco. When he goes out with a Japanese woman, more than two cultures are brought into play.

None of this, of course, is new: Chinese silks were all the rage in Rome centuries ago, and Alexandria before the time of Christ was a paradigm of the modern universal city. Not even American eclecticism is new: many a small town has long known Chinese restaurants, Indian doctors and Lebanese grocers. But now all these cultures are crossing at the speed of light. And the rising diversity of the planet is something more than mere cosmopolitanism: it is a fundamental recoloring of the very complexion of societies. Cities like Paris, or Hong Kong, have always had a soigné, international air and served as magnets for exiles and émigrés, but now smaller places are multinational too. Marseilles speaks French with a distinctly North African twang. Islamic fundamentalism has one of its strongholds in Bradford, England. It is the sleepy coastal towns of Queensland, Australia, that print their menus in Japanese.

The dangers this internationalism presents are evident: not for nothing did the Tower of Babel collapse. As national borders fall, tribal alliances, and new manmade divisions, rise up, and the world learns every day terrible new meanings of the word Balkanization. And while some places are wired for international transmission, others (think of Iran or North Korea or Burma) remain as isolated as ever, widening the gap between the haves and the have-nots, or what Alvin Toffler has called the "fast" and the "slow" worlds. Tokyo has more telephones than the whole continent of Africa.

Nonetheless, whether we like it or not, the "transnational" future is upon us: as Kenichi Ohmae, the international economist, suggests with his talk of a "borderless economy," capitalism's allegiances are to products, not places. "Capital is now global," Robert Reich, the Secretary of Labor, has said, pointing out that when an Iowan buys a Pontiac from General Motors, 60% of his money goes to South Korea, Japan, West Germany, Taiwan, Singapore, Britain and Barbados. Culturally we are being reformed daily by the cadences of world music and world fiction: where the great Canadian writers of an older generation had names like Frye and Davies and Laurence, now they are called Ondaatje and Mistry and Skvorecky.

As space shrinks, moreover, time accelerates. This hip-hop mishmash is spreading overnight. When my parents were in college, there were all of seven foreigners living in Tibet, a country the size of Western Europe, and in its entire history the country had seen fewer than 2,000 Westerners. Now a Danish student in Lhasa is scarcely more surprising than a Tibetan in Copenhagen. Already a city like Miami is beyond the wildest dreams of 1968; how much more so will its face in 2018 defy our predictions of today?

It would be easier, seeing all this, to say that the world is moving toward the *Raza Cósmica* (Cosmic Race), predicted by the Mexican thinker José Vasconcelos in the '20s—a glorious blend of mongrels and mestizos. It may be more relevant to suppose that more and more of the world may come to resemble Hong Kong, a stateless special economic zone full of expats and exiles linked by the lingua franca of English and the global marketplace. Some urbanists already see the world as a grid of 30 or so highly advanced city-regions, or technopoles, all plugged into the same international circuit.

The world will not become America. Anyone who has been to a baseball game in Osaka, or a Pizza Hut in Moscow, knows instantly that she is not in Kansas. But America may still, if only symbolically, be a model for the world. *E Pluribus Unum,* after all, is on the dollar bill. As Federico Mayor Zaragoza, the director-general of UNESCO, has said, "America's main role in the new world order is not as a military superpower, but as a multicultural superpower."

The traditional metaphor for this is that of a mosaic. But Richard Rodriguez, the Mexican-American essayist who is a psalmist for our new hybrid forms, points out that the interaction is more fluid than that, more human, subject to daily revision. "I am Chinese," he says, "because I live in San Francisco, a Chinese city. I became Irish in America. I became Portuguese in America." And even as he announces this new truth, Portuguese women are becoming American, and Irishmen are becoming Portuguese, and Sydney (or is it Toronto?) is thinking to compare itself with the "Chinese city" we know as San Francisco.

Credits/ Acknowledgments

Cover design by Charles Vitelli

1. A Clash of Views
Facing overview—United Nations photo by John Isaac.

2. Population
Facing overview—United Nations photo by Maggie Steber.

3. Natural Resources
Facing overview—United Nations photo by Jeffrey Foxx.

4. Development
Facing overview—United Nations photo by A. Jongen.

5. Conflict
Facing overview—U.S. Navy photo. 196—Map by Dave Herring/The Christian Science Monitor.

6. Cooperation
Facing overview—United Nations photo.

7. Values and Visions
Facing overview—IBM Corporation.

ANNUAL EDITIONS ARTICLE REVIEW FORM

■ NAME: _____ DATE: _____

■ TITLE AND NUMBER OF ARTICLE: _____

■ BRIEFLY STATE THE MAIN IDEA OF THIS ARTICLE: _____

_____

_____

_____

_____

■ LIST THREE IMPORTANT FACTS THAT THE AUTHOR USES TO SUPPORT THE MAIN IDEA:

_____

_____

_____

_____

_____

■ WHAT INFORMATION OR IDEAS DISCUSSED IN THIS ARTICLE ARE ALSO DISCUSSED IN YOUR TEXTBOOK OR OTHER READING YOU HAVE DONE? LIST THE TEXTBOOK CHAPTERS AND PAGE NUMBERS:

_____

_____

_____

_____

_____

■ LIST ANY EXAMPLES OF BIAS OR FAULTY REASONING THAT YOU FOUND IN THE ARTICLE:

_____

_____

_____

_____

■ LIST ANY NEW TERMS/CONCEPTS THAT WERE DISCUSSED IN THE ARTICLE AND WRITE A SHORT DEFINITION:

_____

_____

_____

_____

We Want Your Advice

ANNUAL EDITIONS: GLOBAL ISSUES 94/95
Article Rating Form

Here is an opportunity for you to have direct input into the next revision of this volume. We would like you to rate each of the 50 articles listed below, using the following scale:

1. **Excellent: should definitely be retained**
2. **Above average: should probably be retained**
3. **Below average: should probably be deleted**
4. **Poor: should definitely be deleted**

Your ratings will play a vital part in the next revision. So please mail this prepaid form to us just as soon as you complete it.
Thanks for your help!

Annual Editions revisions depend on two major opinion sources: one is our Advisory Board, listed in the front of this volume, which works with us in scanning the thousands of articles published in the public press each year; the other is you—the person actually using the book. Please help us and the users of the next edition by completing the prepaid article rating form on this page and returning it to us. Thank you.

Rating	Article	Rating	Article
	1. Preparing for the 21st Century: Winners and Losers		25. Africa in the Balance
	2. Jihad vs. McWorld		26. The Burden of Womanhood
	3. Economic Time Zones: Fast Versus Slow		27. Third-World Debt: The Disaster That Didn't Happen
	4. Global Unemployment at 700 Million		28. Toward a New World Economic Order
	5. Megacities		29. Global Village or Global Pillage?
	6. The Numbers Game		30. Push Comes to Shove: Western Europe Is Ailing, Angry, and Afraid of the Future
	7. Sixty Million on the Move		31. Number One Again
	8. The War on Aliens: The Right Calls the Shots		32. Japan's Non-Revolution
	9. Hobson's Choice for Indigenous Peoples		33. Privatization in the Former Soviet Empire
	10. The AIDS Pandemic in Africa		34. The New Challenges to Global Security
	11. The Greenhouse Effect: Apocalypse Now or Chicken Little?		35. Why Yugoslavia Fell Apart
	12. Can We Save Our Seas?		36. Who'll Stop the Next 'Yugoslavia'?
	13. Sacrificed to the Superpower		37. Islam's Violent Improvisers
	14. Green Justice: The Facts		38. Fighting Off Doomsday
	15. A Planet in Jeopardy		39. Contest over Asia: Search for Security in the Pacific
	16. Facing a Future of Water Scarcity		40. Dismantling the Arsenals: Arms Control and the New World Agenda
	17. The Landscape of Hunger		41. Can the U.N. Stretch to Fit Its Future?
	18. A New Strategy for Feeding a Crowded Planet		42. Can It Really Be Peace?
	19. Oil: The Strategic Prize		43. What's Next for World Trade?
	20. Paradise Islands or an Asian Powder Keg?		44. Hunting for Africa's Wildlife Poachers
	21. Canada Is Ready to Exploit Huge Oil Reserves Locked in Sands		45. 50 Trends Shaping the World
	22. A New Energy Path for the Third World		46. Electronic Superhighway
	23. China Sees 'Market-Leninism' as Way to Future		47. The World's *Throw-Away* Children
	24. New Tally of World's Economies Catapults China into Third Place		48. Women's Role in Post-Industrial Democracy
			49. The Post-Communist Nightmare
			50. The Global Village Finally Arrives

(Continued on next page)

ABOUT YOU

Name_____ Date_____

Are you a teacher? ☐   Or student? ☐

Your School Name _____

Department _____

Address _____

City _____ State _____ Zip _____

School Telephone # _____

YOUR COMMENTS ARE IMPORTANT TO US!

Please fill in the following information:

For which course did you use this book? _____

Did you use a text with this Annual Edition?   ☐ yes   ☐ no

The title of the text? _____

What are your general reactions to the Annual Editions concept?

Have you read any particular articles recently that you think should be included in the next edition?

Are there any articles you feel should be replaced in the next edition? Why?

Are there other areas that you feel would utilize an Annual Edition?

May we contact you for editorial input?

May we quote you from above?

ANNUAL EDITIONS: GLOBAL ISSUES 94/95

BUSINESS REPLY MAIL

| First Class | Permit No. 84 | Guilford, CT |

Postage will be paid by addressee

The Dushkin Publishing Group, Inc.
Sluice Dock
DPG **Guilford, Connecticut 06437**